Lecture Notes in Computer Science

Lecture Notes in Artificial Intelligence 16302

Founding Editor

Jörg Siekmann

Series Editors

Randy Goebel, *University of Alberta, Edmonton, Canada*
Wolfgang Wahlster, *DFKI, Berlin, Germany*
Zhi-Hua Zhou, *Nanjing University, Nanjing, China*

The series Lecture Notes in Artificial Intelligence (LNAI) was established in 1988 as a topical subseries of LNCS devoted to artificial intelligence.

The series publishes state-of-the-art research results at a high level. As with the LNCS mother series, the mission of the series is to serve the international R & D community by providing an invaluable service, mainly focused on the publication of conference and workshop proceedings and postproceedings.

Max Bramer · Frederic Stahl

Editors

Artificial Intelligence XLII

45th SGAI International Conference
on Artificial Intelligence, AI 2025
Cambridge, UK, December 16–18, 2025
Proceedings, Part II

 Springer

Editors
Max Bramer
University of Portsmouth
Portsmouth, UK

Frederic Stahl
DFKI
Oldenburg, Germany

ISSN 0302-9743 ISSN 1611-3349 (electronic)
Lecture Notes in Artificial Intelligence
ISBN 978-3-032-11441-9 ISBN 978-3-032-11442-6 (eBook)
https://doi.org/10.1007/978-3-032-11442-6

LNCS Sublibrary: SL7 – Artificial Intelligence

This Springer imprint is published by the registered company Springer Nature Switzerland AG
The registered company address is: Gewerbestrasse 11, 6330 Cham, Switzerland

If disposing of this product, please recycle the paper.

Preface

Artificial Intelligence XLII comprises the refereed papers presented at the forty-fifth SGAI International Conference on Innovative Techniques and Applications of Artificial Intelligence, held in December 2025. It is published as two volumes: containing papers for the technical stream and the application stream, respectively. The conference was organised by SGAI, the British Computer Society Specialist Group on Artificial Intelligence. This year 93 papers were submitted and all were single-blind peer reviewed by either 2 or 3 reviewers plus the expert members of the Executive Program Committee for each stream of the conference. Forty-seven full papers and 20 short papers were accepted.

This year's Donald Michie Memorial Award for the best refereed technical paper was won by a paper entitled 'DESS: Dimensional-PDFs for Embedding Space Sampling' by Jakob Voigt, Morten Grundetjern, Per-Arne Andersen and Morten Goodwin (University of Agder, Norway).

This year's Rob Milne Memorial Award for the best refereed application paper was won by a paper entitled 'Detect, Decide, Explain: An Intelligent Framework for Zero-Day Network Attack Detection' by Saif Alzubi (University of Exeter, UK), Frederic Stahl (German Research Center for Artificial Intelligence, Germany), and Mohammed Al-Khafajiy (University of Lincoln, UK).

The other technical stream full papers included are divided into sections on Deep Learning, Large Language Models, Machine Learning, Neural Networks, and Techniques of AI. The other application stream full papers are divided into sections on Evolutionary Algorithms, Machine Learning, Neural Networks, Medical Computing and Health Informatics, Large Language Models, Natural Language Processing and Machine Vision, and Applications of Artificial Intelligence. Both volumes also include the text of short papers presented as posters at the conference.

On behalf of the conference Organising Committee, we would like to thank all those who contributed to the organisation of this year's programme, in particular the Program Committee members, the Executive Program Committees and our administrators Kerry Wear and Bryony Bramer.

September 2025

Max Bramer
Frederic Stahl

Organization

Conference Committee

Conference Chair

Max Bramer

University of Portsmouth, UK

Technical Program Chair

Max Bramer

University of Portsmouth, UK

Application Program Chair

Frederic Stahl

DFKIGerman Research Center for Artificial
Intelligence, Germany

Workshop Organizer

Adrian Hopgood

University of Portsmouth, UK

Treasurer

Rosemary Gilligan

SGAI, UK

Poster Session Organizer

Juan Augusto

Middlesex University London, UK

FAIRS Organizer

Giovanna Martinez

University of Nottingham, UK

Conference Administrator

Kerry Wear

BCS, UK

Paper Administrator

Bryony Bramer   SGAI, UK

Technical Executive Program Committee

Max Bramer (Chair)   University of Portsmouth, UK
Frans Coenen   University of Liverpool, UK
Adrian Hopgood   University of Portsmouth, UK
John Kingston   Nottingham Trent University, UK

Application Executive Program Committee

Frederic Stahl (Chair)   DFKIGerman Research Center for Artificial
                                  Intelligence, Germany
Richard Ellis   RKE Consulting, UK
Rosemary Gilligan   SGAI, UK
Lars Nolle   Jade University of Applied Sciences, Germany
Richard Wheeler   Iceland Scientific, Iceland

Technical Program Committee

Mercedes Arguello Casteleiro   BCS-SGAI, UK
Matt Armstrong-Barnes   Servita, UK
Juan Augusto   Middlesex University London, UK
Tiwonge Banda   Robert Gordon University, UK
Raed Sabri Hameed Batbooti   Southern Technical University/Basra Engineering
                                  Technical College, Iraq
Soufiane Boulehouache   University of 20 Août 1955-Skikda, Algeria
Max Bramer   University of Portsmouth, UK
Henrik Brådland   University of Agder, Norway
Marcos Bueno   Radboud University, The Netherlands
Zuzana Cernekova   Comenius University Bratislava, Slovakia
Darren Chitty   University of Exeter, UK
Frans Coenen   University of Liverpool, UK
Nicolas Durand   Aix-Marseille University, France
Frank Eichinger   DATEV eG, Germany
Martin Fyvie   Robert Gordon University, UK
Adrian Hopgood   University of Portsmouth, UK

Chris Huyck	Middlesex University London, UK
Mohamed Ihmeida	Birmingham City University, UK
Stelios Kapetanakis	Distributed Analytics, UK
Mathias Kern	BT, UK
Ivan Koychev	Sofia University "St. Kliment Ohridski", Bulgaria
Andrew Langworthy	BT, UK
Nicole Lee	University of Hong Kong, China
Mirko Lenz	German Research Center for Artificial Intelligence (DFKI), Germany
Haiming Liu	University of Southampton, UK
Jixin Ma	University of Greenwich, UK
Giovanna Martinez-Arellano	University of Nottingham, UK
Ken McGarry	University of Sunderland, UK
Silja Meyer-Nieberg	Universität der Bundeswehr München, Germany
Ciprian Daniel Neagu	University of Bradford, UK
Lars Nolle	Jade University of Applied Sciences; Germany
Joanna Isabelle Olszewska	University of the West of Scotland, UK
Daniel O'Leary	University of Southern California, USA
Fernando Sáenz-Pérez	Universidad Complutense de Madrid, Spain
Pradeep Kumar Saraswathi	Salesforce, USA
Muhammad Shahzad	University of Reading, UK
Xinming Shi	Queen's University Belfast, UK
Simon Thompson	GFT Technology, UK

Application Program Committee

Nadia Abouayoub	BCS-SGAI, UK
Hatem Ahriz	Robert Gordon University, UK
Manal Almutairi	University of Reading, UK
Saif Alzubi	University of Exeter, UK
Vasileios Argyriou	Kingston University, UK
Juan Carlos Augusto	Middlesex University London, UK
Lakshmi Babu Saheer	Anglia Ruskin University, UK
Felix Becker	German Research Center for Artificial Intelligence GmbH (DFKI), Germany
Elmar Berghöfer	German Research Center for Artificial Intelligence GmbH (DFKI), Germany
Nikolay Burlutskiy	ContextVision AB, Sweden
Xiaochun Cheng	Swansea University, UK
Sarah Jane Delany	Technological University Dublin, Ireland

Tarek El-Mihoub	German Research Center for Artificial Intelligence GmbH (DFKI), Germany
Richard Ellis	RKE Consulting, UK
Ahmed Elsayed	German Research Center for Artificial Intelligence GmbH (DFKI), Germany
Xiaohong Gao	Middlesex University London, UK
Rosemary Gilligan	University of Hertfordshire, UK
John Gordon	AKRI Ltd., UK
Holmer Hemsen	German Research Center for Artificial Intelligence GmbH (DFKI), Germany
Martin Holen	University of Agder, Norway
Chris Huyck	Middlesex University London, UK
Lars Erik Olof Jacobson	E.O.J. Group, UK
Colin Johnson	University of Nottingham, UK
Stelios Kapetanakis	Distributed Analytics Solutions, UK
Mathias Kern	BT, UK
Martin Kumm	Jade University of Applied Sciences, Germany
Daniel Lukats	German Research Center for Artificial Intelligence GmbH (DFKI), Germany
Christoph Manß	German Research Center for Artificial Intelligence GmbH (DFKI), Germany
Ammar Memari	Jade University of Applied Sciences, Germany
Andre Miedtank	German Research Center for Artificial Intelligence GmbH (DFKI), Germany
Lars Nolle	Jade University of Applied Sciences, Germany
Silvia Podestà	IBM, Denmark
Jing Qi	University of Essex, UK
Juan Antonio Recio Garcia	Complutense University of Madrid, Spain
Robert Rettig	German Research Center for Artificial Intelligence GmbH (DFKI), Germany
Sam Richardson	AstraZeneca, UK
Eike Rodenbäck	German Research Center for Artificial Intelligence GmbH (DFKI), Germany
Miguel A. Salido	Universitat Politècnica de València, Spain
Georgios Samakovitis	University of Greenwich, UK
Janina Schneider	German Research Center for Artificial Intelligence GmbH (DFKI), Germany
Frederic Stahl	German Research Center for Artificial Intelligence GmbH (DFKI), Germany
Daphne Theodorakopoulos	Leibniz University Hanover, Germany
Christoph Tholen	German Research Center for Artificial Intelligence GmbH (DFKI), Germany
Wamberto Vasconcelos	University of Aberdeen, UK

Frank Wallhoff   Jade University of Applied Sciences, Germany
Richard Wheeler   Iceland Scientific, Iceland

Contents – Part II

Large Language Models

Natural Language Processing and Machine Vision

Applications of Artificial Intelligence

Short Application Papers

Contents – Part I

Techniques of AI

Short Technical Papers

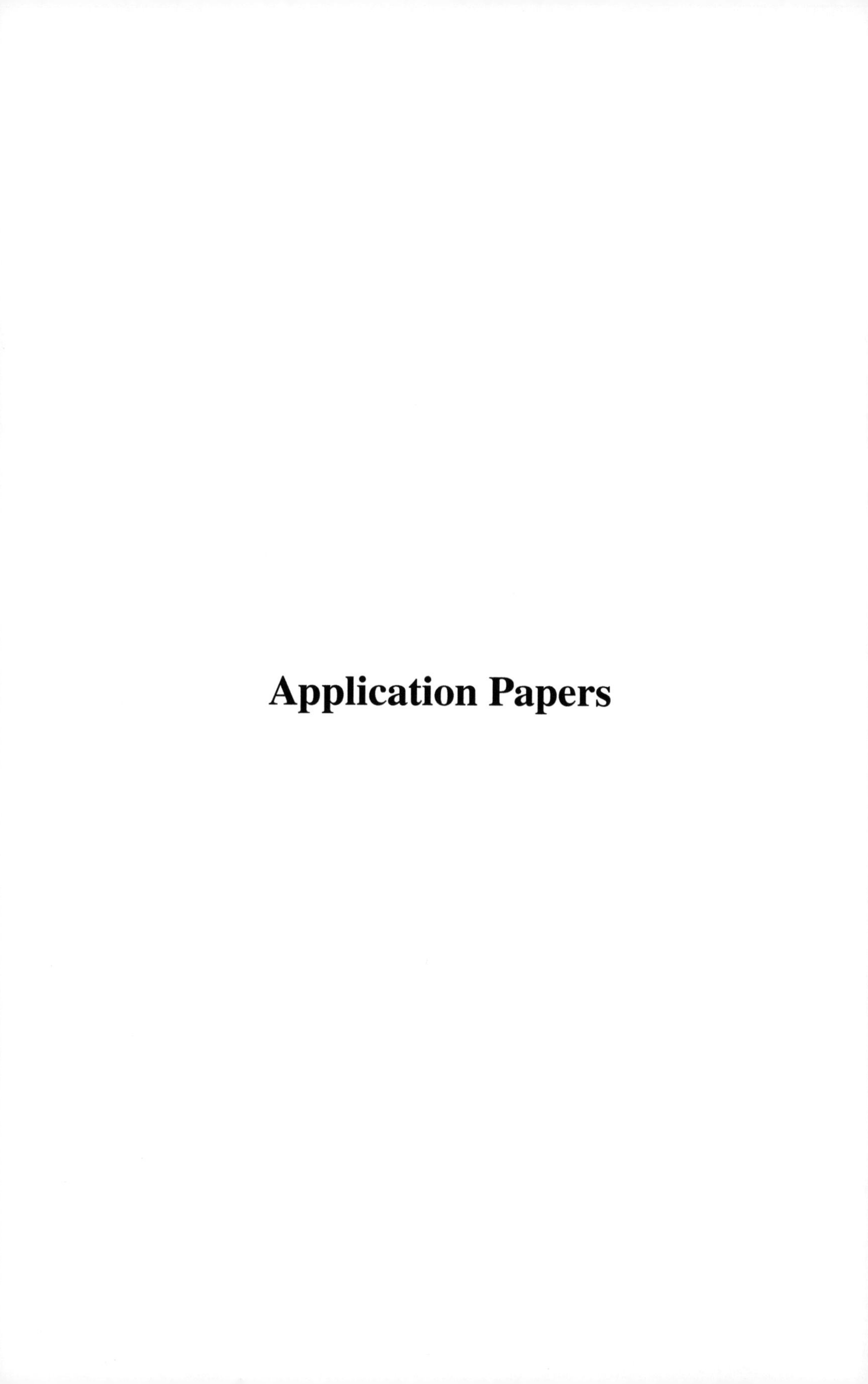

Application Papers

Detect, Decide, Explain: An Intelligent Framework for Zero-Day Network Attack Detection

Saif Alzubi[1]([✉]), Frederic Stahl[2], and Mohammed Al-Khafajiy[3]

[1] Department of Computer Science, University of Exeter, Exeter EX4 4QE, UK
s.m.y.alzubi@exeter.ac.uk
[2] Marine Perception, German Research Center for Artificial Intelligence GmbH
(DFKI), Marie-Curie-Straße 1, 26129 Oldenburg, Germany
Frederic_Theodor.Stahl@dfki.de
[3] School of Engineering and Physical Sciences, University of Lincoln, Lincoln, UK
MAlKhafajiy@lincoln.ac.uk

Abstract. The growing complexity and diversity of network traffic have made the detection of previously unseen cyberattacks a critical challenge. While supervised learning models perform well on known threats, they often fail to generalise to novel attack types. In earlier work, we introduced the Unknown Network Attack Detector (UNAD), an unsupervised ensemble-based framework trained exclusively on benign traffic to detect anomalies. This paper presents an enhanced version of UNAD, referred to as UNAD+, which incorporates three key improvements. First, a Weighted Majority Voting (WMV) mechanism replaces majority voting to prioritise stronger detectors and eliminate ambiguous predictions. Second, a supervised refinement stage is introduced, where pseudo-labelled anomalies are used to train a secondary classifier that improves detection accuracy and reduces false positives. Third, a post-hoc explainability layer is added, combining LIME and surrogate tree modelling to provide both local and global interpretability of the system's decisions. Evaluations on CICIDS2017 and NSL-KDD show that UNAD+ substantially improves detection performance compared with the original UNAD baseline, achieving an F1-score of up to 98.25% and reducing false positives by over 98%, while enhancing transparency and operational suitability through integrated explainability.

Keywords: Network Intrusion Detection · Anomaly Detection · Unsupervised algorithms

1 Introduction

The increasing frequency and sophistication of network-based attacks pose significant challenges to modern cybersecurity infrastructures. Intrusion Detection Systems (IDSs) continue to serve as a core defensive mechanism by monitoring and analysing network traffic to identify potentially malicious activity [1]. Many of these systems are based on supervised learning [2], but their effectiveness is

The original version of the chapter has been revised. A correction to this chapter can be found at https://doi.org/10.1007/978-3-032-11442-6_40

limited to previously seen attack types, as they must be trained on labelled data that explicitly includes these attacks.

In contrast, unsupervised learning methods attempt to detect anomalous activity without relying on labelled attack data [3], making them well-suited for identifying previously unknown or zero-day attacks (i.e., attacks not previously seen by the system). However, they often suffer from high false positive rates (FPR) [4], which hinders their practical applicability.

To overcome these limitations, this paper introduces a novel IDS framework that combines the strengths of both unsupervised and supervised approaches. In the first stage, an ensemble of unsupervised anomaly detection models is employed to identify unknown (zero-day) attacks in the traffic stream. Detections from the ensemble are treated as pseudo-labels to iteratively train a supervised classifier, which learns to refine and validate the attack predictions with greater precision. This two-stage system not only facilitates adaptive learning from evolving threats but also reduces reliance on large volumes of labelled data. Hybrid machine learning systems show promise in enhancing detection performance; however, a lack of transparency often hinders their adoption in operational environments [5].

Although some classifiers used in hybrid IDSs are inherently explainable, the interaction between models can result in black-box behaviour at the system level, limiting transparency and interpretability. This opacity not only undermines analyst trust but also complicates root-cause analysis, incident triage, and compliance in regulated sectors such as finance and healthcare [6]. Therefore, this paper integrates explainable artificial intelligence (XAI) methods into the IDS pipeline. By applying local and global explanation models, the system provides interpretable justifications for its decisions, thereby enhancing usability, auditability, and trustworthiness [7]. To address these challenges, this paper extends the previously proposed UNAD [8] framework with three enhancements: (i) Weighted Majority Voting for improved ensemble integration, (ii) supervised refinement to reduce false positives, and (iii) explainable AI to enhance interpretability. These improvements balance detection performance and transparency, validated on two benchmark datasets.

The paper is organised as follows: Sect. 2 reviews related work on ensemble-based intrusion detection, hybrid supervised-unsupervised approaches, and explainability techniques. Section 3 introduces the enhanced UNAD+ framework, detailing its weighted ensemble voting, supervised refinement using pseudo-labels, and post-hoc explainability components. Section 4 presents the experimental evaluation. Section 5 outlines future research directions, followed by conclusions in Sect. 6.

2   Related Work

Machine learning plays a central role in IDS, with many relying on supervised models [9]. However, these approaches depend on labelled datasets [10], which are often incomplete or biased toward known attacks, limiting their ability to detect zero-day threats. Unsupervised anomaly detection identifies deviations from normal behaviour without labelled attack data [11], making it well-suited for unknown threats. Yet, such models often suffer from high false positive rates [12], especially in dynamic environments where legitimate traffic patterns evolve. Techniques like clustering, autoencoders, and density-based methods (e.g., Isolation Forest and Local Outlier Factor) have been applied, but their performance varies across datasets and network conditions.

Ensemble approaches improve stability and accuracy by aggregating outputs from diverse base detectors [13]. Most ensemble-based IDSs use simple majority voting, assuming equal model reliability, an assumption that is often invalid. Some studies explore weighting classifiers based on performance or confidence scores [14,15], improving detection for ambiguous cases, though these remain underexplored in IDS.

Hybrid frameworks that combine unsupervised detection with supervised refinement show promise. Zoppi and Ceccarelli [16] proposed a stacking framework where anomaly scores are refined by a supervised meta-classifier. Similarly, Kale et al. [17] combined clustering, semi-supervised learning, and supervised classification. However, many hybrid IDSs lack incremental learning or structured use of pseudo-labels for refinement.

Explainability remains a key challenge as IDS complexity grows. Explainable AI (XAI) tools like Local Interpretable Model-Agnostic Explanations (LIME) [18] and SHapley Additive exPlanations (SHAP) [19] provide local explanations, but many works applying XAI to security [20,21] remain disconnected from detection pipelines and rarely integrate with ensemble or hybrid systems. Benchmarking IDS frameworks is also difficult due to dataset diversity. CICIDS2017 [22] and NSL-KDD [23] are widely used datasets; however, they differ in attack types and complexity. Although many systems report strong performance on these datasets [4,24], few provide transparent decision-making or structured refinement mechanisms.

Overall, prior work has advanced ensemble modelling, hybrid detection, and explainability; however, fully integrated systems that dynamically detect unknown threats, refine predictions through supervised feedback, and provide transparent reasoning remain limited. In response to this gap, this motivates the UNAD+ framework proposed in this paper.

3   UNAD+: An Enhanced Framework for Unknown Attack Detection

This section outlines the original UNAD framework and presents the key enhancements introduced in UNAD+, including weighted voting, supervised refinement, and explainability.

3.1   Previous Work: UNAD

The UNAD [8] is an unsupervised, ensemble-based intrusion detection framework designed to identify previously unseen attacks. Unlike signature-based or supervised IDSs, UNAD is trained exclusively on benign traffic, enabling it to detect anomalies without prior knowledge of attack signatures or labelled malicious data.

UNAD employs a heterogeneous ensemble of 100 base learners combining Local Outlier Factor (LOF) [25] and Isolation Forest (iForest) [26], with 50 learners of each type. Each base learner is trained on a bootstrapped subset of benign data using bagging to promote diversity and reduce overfitting. Predictions from all learners are aggregated using simple majority voting, where each model casts a vote for either "benign" or "attack", and the majority class determines the final output. However, this original design presented several limitations. The equal-weight voting scheme failed to account for variability in base model performance, while tie cases (equal benign and attack votes) required human analyst intervention, slowing automated decision-making. Furthermore, UNAD lacked any form of model interpretability, limiting its suitability for real-world, regulated environments where transparency and analyst trust are essential.

3.2   UNAD+: Enhanced Architecture Overview

To overcome the limitations of UNAD, we propose UNAD+, which preserves the benign-only unsupervised detection capability of UNAD and introduces three additional components: (1) Weighted Majority Voting, (2) a supervised refinement stage, and (3) a post-hoc explainability layer.

Figure 1 presents a high-level overview of the proposed framework, illustrating the interaction between its three components (components C1-C3). This modular design enhances detection accuracy, transparency, and reliability.

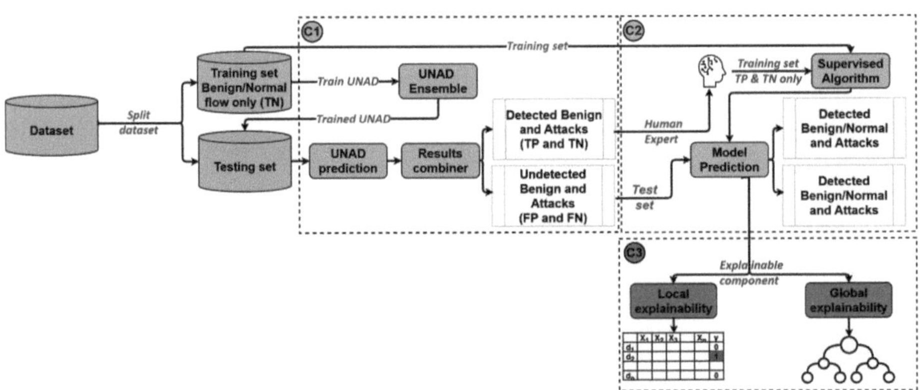

Fig. 1. Architecture of UNAD+: (1) unsupervised ensemble trained on benign data; (2) supervised refinement using pseudo-labels; (3) post-hoc explainability for local and global interpretation.

To further strengthen operational robustness, a human-in-the-loop checkpoint is introduced between the unsupervised ensemble and the supervised refinement stage (components C1 and C2). It allows analysts to review or override low-confidence pseudo-labels before supervised training. This prevents error propagation and supports adaptation to evolving threats.

3.3   Ensemble Composition and Bagging Strategy

Figure 2 shows the UNAD+ workflow, including pre-processing pipeline and ensemble construction. Input traffic undergoes Min-Max scaling and dimensionality reduction via Principal Component Analysis (PCA), with the number of retained components selected per dataset (e.g., 7 for CICIDS2017 and 16 for NSL-KDD). The transformed data feeds two parallel streams of 50 LOF and 50 iForest learners, each trained on distinct bootstrapped benign subsets. This architecture extends the original design, improving generalisability and resilience through bagging. The modular structure allows for future integration of other unsupervised algorithms for various network environments.

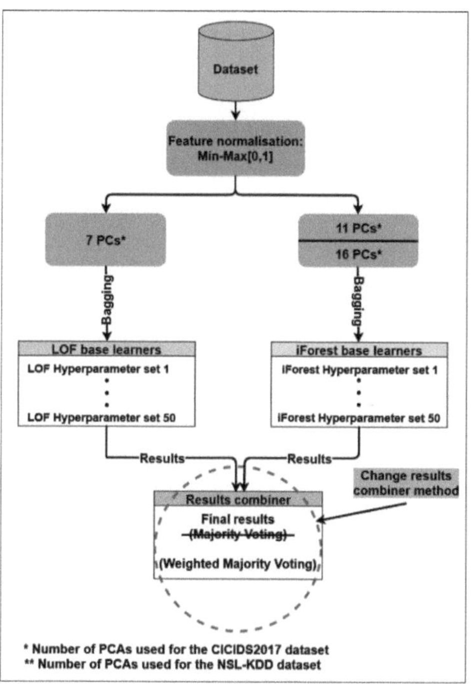

Fig. 2. UNAD+ workflow.

Unlike the original equal voting, UNAD+ uses (WMV), assigning weights proportional to each model's F1-score on a validation set.

3.4   Voting Strategy: Weighted Majority Voting (WMV)

A critical limitation of the original UNAD framework was its reliance on simple majority voting, giving equal weight to all models, regardless of performance. This approach ignored ensemble heterogeneity and allowed underperforming models to reduce accuracy.

To address this, UNAD+ replaces simple majority voting with a Weighted Majority Voting (WMV) scheme. During validation, each base learner gets a weight based on its F1-score. At inference, predictions (0 for benign, 1 for attack) mask their weights. Scores for each class are summed, and the higher score becomes the ensemble output.

This approach gives stronger detectors more influence in the final decision, reduces the impact of noisy models, and eliminates tie cases. Since weighted scores are continuous, exact ties are highly unlikely, allowing the system to operate autonomously without fallback logic. The full voting procedure is outlined in Algorithm 1.

Algorithm 1. Weighted Majority Voting in UNAD+

1: **Input:**
     Predictions $P = [p_1, p_2, \ldots, p_n]$, where $p_i \in \{\text{benign}, \text{attack}\}$
     F1-scores $F = [f_1, f_2, \ldots, f_n]$ for each base learner
2: **Output:** Final class label for the instance
3:
4: **Initialize:** $Score_{benign} \leftarrow 0$, $Score_{attack} \leftarrow 0$
5: **for** $i = 1$ to n **do**
6:     **if** $p_i = \text{benign}$ **then**
7:         $Score_{benign} \leftarrow Score_{benign} + f_i$
8:     **else**
9:         $Score_{attack} \leftarrow Score_{attack} + f_i$
10:     **end if**
11: **end for**
12: **if** $Score_{attack} > Score_{benign}$ **then**
13:     **return** attack
14: **else**
15:     **return** benign
16: **end if**

3.5   Supervised Refinement Stage

To further reduce false positives, UNAD+ incorporates a supervised refinement stage following weighted ensemble voting. This stage validates and improves the ensemble's preliminary decisions by training a supervised model on pseudo-labelled data.

The correctly detected outputs of the WMV ensemble serve as pseudo-labels, assigning each instance as either "benign" or "attack." These pseudo-labelled instances are merged with the original benign training data, forming a composite training set that better reflects real-world traffic patterns. This allows the supervised model to better distinguish complex attack behaviours and filter out false positives.

Multiple classifiers were evaluated, including AdaBoost, Naive Bayes, K-Nearest Neighbours, and Random Forest. For all classifiers, feature selection was performed using Information Gain (IG), evaluating top-ranked features incrementally in sets ranging from 5 to 30. Hyperparameters were then optimised using 10-fold cross-validation with Grid Search, using F1-score as the selection criterion.

To address class imbalance in the combined training set, the Synthetic Minority Oversampling Technique (SMOTE) [27] was applied to achieve a balanced 1:1 attack-to-benign ratio. In order to ensure adaptability over time, the supervised model can be periodically retrained with updated pseudo-labelled data, allowing it to adapt to evolving traffic patterns and emerging attacks.

For evaluation, each candidate classifier was tested on a dedicated hold-out set comprising benign flows and attack instances that were undetected by the WMV ensemble (false positives and false negatives). This evaluation setup was applied to both CICIDS2017 and NSL-KDD, enabling the model to enhance overall detection and address the ensemble's residual weaknesses.

Based on the results, Random Forest consistently outperformed the other classifiers in terms of the selection criterion (F1-score) and overall detection performance. Based on this superior performance, Random Forest was selected as the refinement classifier. In addition to its strong performance, Random Forest is robust to overfitting and supports post-hoc interpretability through feature importance analysis and surrogate models [28,29].

3.6 Explainability Layer

The original UNAD lacked interpretability mechanisms. This limited its practicality for security-critical environments, where human oversight, auditability, and regulatory compliance are essential. To address this, the enhanced framework introduces a post-hoc explainability layer for local and global interpretability, enabling analysts to understand, validate, and trust the system's decisions.

At the local level, LIME [18] was applied to Random Forest. LIME perturbs input features and observes prediction changes to identify the most influential features. LIME was chosen for its model-agnostic design, ease of integration, and minimal tuning when models are updated. It supports tabular network traffic features and enables analysts to interpret predictions without accessing model internals [18]. Compared to alternatives such as SHAP, which provides theoretically consistent Shapley value explanations, SHAP suffers from substantial computational complexity, particularly under feature dependencies [30]. In contrast, LIME offers approximate local explanations at lower computational cost [18], making it well-suited for real-time intrusion detection.

For global interpretability, a Decision Tree surrogate model approximates the Random Forest's decision logic by mapping input samples to predictions and extracting a simplified tree structure. Although the surrogate is simpler than the original model, it still provides a high-fidelity overview of key decision boundaries and feature interactions [31]. As a result, security analysts can inspect and audit these decision rules for transparency and accountability.

4   Experimental Evaluation

This section presents the evaluation of UNAD+ on the CICIDS2017 and NSL-KDD datasets. We assess detection performance, robustness, and the effects of weighted voting, supervised refinement, and explainability, comparing UNAD+ to its original version and baseline classifiers. To conduct these evaluations, all experiments were implemented in Python 3.9 using Google Colaboratory.

4.1   Datasets and Hyperparameter Settings

CICIDS2017 represents modern attack scenarios in a realistic network setting. After pre-processing, it included 2,827,672 flows (2,271,117 benign and 556,555 attacks (e.g., Brute Force, DDoS, Heartbleed). Benign traffic from Monday (529,445 flows) was used for training, while the rest was split evenly into validation (1,149,111) and test (1,149,116) sets, each containing 76% benign and 24% attack samples. Pre-processing steps included the removal of duplicate and missing value records, dropping of basic features (e.g., IDs, IP addresses, and ports), and min-max scaling, resulting in 76 final features.

NSL-KDD improves KDD'99 by reducing redundancy and addressing class imbalance. It comprises 148,517 records with 43 features across four attack categories (DoS, U2R, R2L and Probe). The WMV ensemble was trained on a 60% benign subset of KDDTrain+ (40,405 records). The remaining 40% of KDDTrain+ (which includes attack instances), along with KDDTest+, was combined and split into validation (37,791) and test (35,140) sets, each containing a balanced mix of benign and attack samples. Pre-processing steps were similar to CICIDS2017, with the addition of one-hot encoding (expanding to 122 features).

For hyperparameter tuning, LOF and iForest were optimised separately using grid search, and the best configurations were selected based on F1-score. CICIDS2017 used LOF (contamination 0.07, 30 neighbours) and iForest (contamination 0.24, 400 estimators, 25% samples). NSL-KDD used LOF (0.14 contamination, 5 neighbours) and iForest (0.10 contamination, 100 estimators, 100% samples). For supervised refinement, the best Random Forest configuration included 100 estimators, depth 10, and min samples split 8 (CICIDS2017), and 300 estimators, depth 15, and min samples split 4 (NSL-KDD).

4.2   Evaluation Metrics

Evaluation employed standard classification metrics: Precision, Recall, F1-score, ROC-AUC, and FPR, using a binary scheme where all attack types were labelled anomalous and all normal flows as benign. These metrics jointly assess detection capability and reliability, both critical in IDSs where missed threats or false positives pose operational risks.

Precision reflects the proportion of correctly identified attacks among flagged instances, while Recall measures the model's ability to detect true attacks. F1-score, as their harmonic mean, balances precision and recall. ROC-AUC quantifies the model's discrimination across varying thresholds, and FPR indicates the proportion of benign traffic incorrectly flagged as attacks.

4.3   Performance on CICIDS2017 and NSL-KDD

Detection performance was evaluated for the original UNAD (simple majority voting), the Weighted Majority Voting (UNAD WMV), the supervised refinement classifier, and the full combined UNAD+ framework. Tables 1 and 2 report the results on CICIDS2017 and NSL-KDD across standard metrics.

Table 1. CICIDS2017 Results (%).

Model	Accuracy	Precision	Recall	F1-score	ROC-AUC
Original UNAD	87.23	70.99	79.92	75.19	84.74
UNAD WMV	86.84	69.57	81.14	74.91	84.90
Second Component Classifier	93.86	96.69	85.22	90.59	91.83
Final Combined Results	**99.19**	**99.44**	**99.21**	**98.31**	**98.52**

Table 2. NSL-KDD Results (%).

Model	Accuracy	Precision	Recall	F1-score	ROC-AUC
Original UNAD	93.45	93.90	92.86	93.38	93.44
UNAD WMV	93.22	93.52	92.80	93.16	93.22
Second Component Classifier	74.02	69.76	89.67	78.47	73.10
Final Combined Results	**98.24**	**97.26**	**99.26**	**98.25**	**98.24**

The original UNAD with simple majority voting achieved good performance, especially on NSL-KDD (F1-score 93.38%), but lacked model weighting, refinement, and suffered frequent tie cases. WMV reduced ties to 0% and improved ensemble stability. The supervised refinement stage further enhanced performance by learning from pseudo-labelled data. On CICIDS2017, F1-score increased from 75.19% (Original UNAD) to 98.31% (UNAD+), with precision rising from 70.99% to 99.44%. NSL-KDD saw F1-score improve from 93.38% to 98.25%. These results confirm that combining weighted ensembles with supervised refinement substantially improves detection, particularly under complex traffic conditions.

4.4   Impact of Supervised Refinement

An ablation study was conducted to assess the contribution of the supervised refinement stage compared with the base ensemble using only WMV. The key objective was to evaluate its effect on false positive reduction.

Figure 3 shows that on CICIDS2017, the FPR decreased from 11.34% in the WMV ensemble to 0.18% after refinement, a reduction exceeding 98%. On NSL-KDD, FPR dropped from 6.37% to 2.77%, a decrease of more than half.

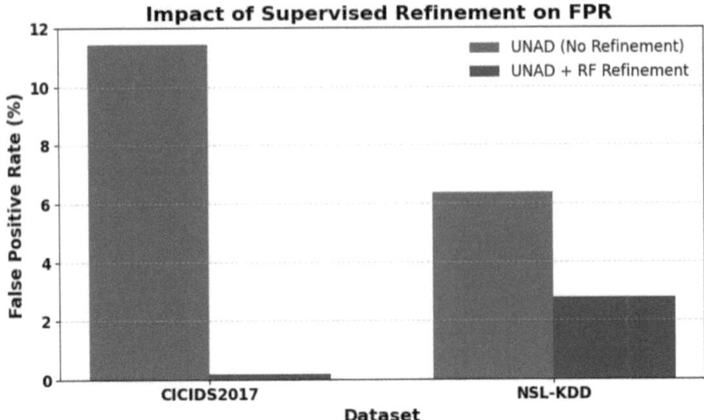

Fig. 3. Impact of Supervised Refinement on False Positive Rate (FPR) for CICIDS2017 and NSL-KDD datasets.

These substantial improvements confirm that the refinement stage effectively suppresses spurious alerts, especially in complex environments where benign and malicious behaviours can overlap. In such cases, the supervised stage learns more precise boundaries by incorporating pseudo-labelled benign and attack samples.

The supervised refinement classifier was evaluated on dedicated test sets comprising flows previously misclassified by the ensemble, specifically, false positives and false negatives. This included 151,245 instances for CICIDS2017 (65% benign, 35% attack) and 2,383 instances for NSL-KDD (47% benign, 53% attack). These results quantify the refinement model's contribution to correcting ensemble misclassifications and improving overall detection performance.

4.5   Effect of Ensemble Voting Strategy

To evaluate the impact of WMV, we compared it to the original majority voting on CICIDS2017 and NSL-KDD. The majority voting approach produced tie occurrences in 15.1% of predictions on CICIDS2017 and 2.5% on NSL-KDD, indicating frequent indecision when models were treated equally. As shown in Fig. 4, WMV reduced ties entirely to 0% by weighting votes according to each base learner's F1-score, prioritising stronger detectors and yielding more decisive outputs. The effect was most pronounced on CICIDS2017, where diverse traffic types often create voting ambiguity. By resolving ties automatically, WMV enhances system robustness and operational reliability without requiring manual intervention.

4.6   Attack-Level Detection Analysis

The second refinement stage contributed substantially to detecting high-variance attack types. On CICIDS2017, detection of SSH-Patator rose from 43.42% to

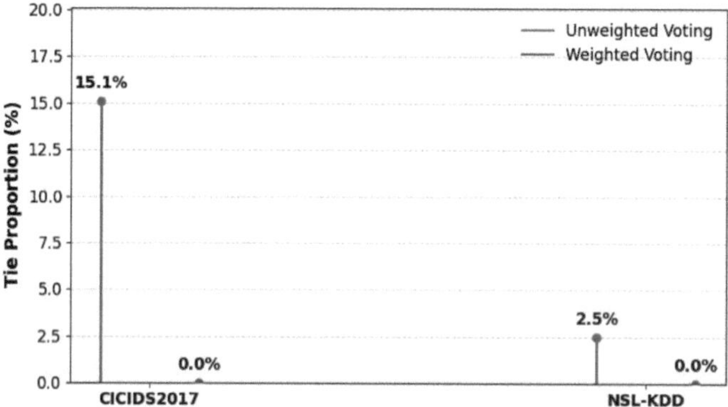

Fig. 4. Comparison of the proportion of tie cases between majority voting and weighted majority voting on CICIDS2017 and NSL-KDD.

98.03%, and DoS Slowhttptest improved from 53.58% to 97.71%. Similar gains were observed for DoS Hulk, Slowloris, and FTP-Patator. However, attacks such as XSS, SQL Injection, and Infiltration remained undetected due to insufficient training instances reaching the supervised stage.

NSL-KDD showed a similar trend. R2L and U2R attacks, which are rare and complex, saw detection rates improve from 51.55% to 92.33% and 77.72% to 94.06%, respectively. These results highlight the hybrid system's ability to improve coverage for rare but critical attack classes.

4.7   Explainability Evaluation

To evaluate the effectiveness of the post-hoc explainability layer, LIME [18] was applied to randomly sampled predictions generated by the supervised refinement classifier. For CICIDS2017, explanations were extracted from correctly classified instances of representative attacks, including SSH-Patator and DoS Slowhttptest. LIME consistently highlighted features such as Init Win Bytes Backward, Subflow Bwd Packets, Fwd Packet Length Max, and Packet Length Variance, attributes that, in our experiments, appeared strongly associated with abnormal flow behaviour. This suggests that the model's reasoning aligns with established threat signatures. Moreover, LIME's ability to attribute importance to semantically meaningful features improves analyst trust and supports root-cause analysis during forensic investigations.

On NSL-KDD, LIME explanations for DoS and R2L instances frequently emphasised features such as dst bytes, flag, and service, which in our evaluations were consistently associated with patterns of suspicious or anomalous activity. The explanations were stable across repeated runs and resilient to small input perturbations, supporting their robustness in security auditing workflows.

For global interpretability, a Decision Tree surrogate model was trained to approximate Random Forest predictions [31]. The surrogate achieved 99%

fidelity on test instances, capturing dominant decision rules and feature splits. Analysts can inspect this global structure to understand the broader decision logic of the system, making it easier to identify systemic biases or operational blind spots. Hence, the dual-layered interpretability approach, combining local explanations using LIME and global understanding through a surrogate model, offers a coherent explanation strategy that enhances transparency, facilitates model debugging, and supports compliance in regulated domains such as finance and healthcare [6].

Overall, the results discussed in this section (Sect. 4) confirm that UNAD+ achieves strong detection performance with significantly reduced false positives. The weighted ensemble and supervised refinement improve both precision and rare attack detection, while the explainability layer offers interpretable, analyst-accessible insights.

5   Future Work

Future work aims to enhance UNAD+ for real-world deployment. Reducing false positives in encrypted traffic remains a priority due to limited feature visibility. Another key direction involves integrating online learning for both unsupervised and supervised stages, allowing incremental adaptation without full retraining. Lightweight online variants of Isolation Forests and decision trees are being evaluated for continuous updates. Further, the ensemble voting mechanism will be extended with dynamic weighting based on recent detection performance, improving adaptability to evolving conditions. Finally, temporal modelling using Recurrent Neural Networks (RNNs), Long Short-Term Memory (LSTM) networks, and Temporal Convolutional Networks (TCNs) will be explored to better capture evolving temporal dependencies and detect stealthy, long-term attacks.

6   Conclusions

This paper presented UNAD+, an enhanced intrusion detection framework designed to overcome key limitations of the original UNAD, namely, reliance on simple majority voting, lack of refinement, and absence of interpretability. By introducing a performance-weighted ensemble mechanism, a supervised refinement stage with pseudo-labelled data, and a post-hoc explainability layer, UNAD+ significantly improves detection accuracy and substantially reduces false positives, thereby addressing critical challenges faced by existing IDS approaches.

Comprehensive experiments on CICIDS2017 and NSL-KDD demonstrated strong gains across all key performance metrics, including precision, recall, and F1-score, confirming the effectiveness and robustness of the proposed enhancements. In addition to these quantitative improvements, the integration of interpretability components and human-in-the-loop feedback supports greater transparency and operational trust, which are essential for adoption in critical sectors such as healthcare and finance.

Overall, UNAD+ offers a modular and extensible architecture capable of adapting to evolving and increasingly sophisticated threats, representing a promising step toward more resilient and explainable intrusion detection. Future directions include incorporating online learning, temporal models, and dynamic ensemble strategies to further enhance robustness and scalability.

References

1. Chawla, A., Lee, B., Fallon, S., Jacob, P.: Host based intrusion detection system with combined CNN/RNN model. In: Alzate, C., et al. (eds.) ECML PKDD 2018. LNCS (LNAI), vol. 11329, pp. 149–158. Springer, Cham (2019). https://doi.org/10.1007/978-3-030-13453-2_12
2. Pinto, A., Herrera, L.-C., Donoso, Y., Gutierrez, J.A.: Survey on intrusion detection systems based on machine learning techniques for the protection of critical infrastructure. Sensors **23**(5), 2415 (2023)
3. Tong, J., Zhang, Y.: A real-time label-free self-supervised deep learning intrusion detection for handling new type and few-shot attacks in IoT networks. IEEE Internet Things J. (2024)
4. de Araujo-Filho, P.F., Naili, M., Kaddoum, G., Fapi, E.T., Zhu, Z.: Unsupervised GAN-based intrusion detection system using temporal convolutional networks and self-attention. IEEE Trans. Netw. Serv. Manag. **20**(4), 4951–4963 (2023)
5. Nolle, L., Stahl, F., El-Mihoub, T.: On explanations for hybrid artificial intelligence. In: Bramer, M., Stahl, F. (eds.) SGAI 2023. LNCS, vol. 14381, pp. 3–15. Springer, Cham (2023). https://doi.org/10.1007/978-3-031-47994-6_1
6. Hassija, V., et al.: Interpreting black-box models: a review on explainable artificial intelligence. Cogn. Comput. **16**(1), 45–74 (2024)
7. Gunning, D., Aha, D.W.: Darpa's explainable artificial intelligence (XAI) program. AI Mag. **40**(2), 44–58 (2019)
8. Alzubi, S., Stahl, F., Gaber, M.M.: Towards intrusion detection of previously unknown network attacks. In: Al-Begain, K., Iacono, M., Campanile, L., Bargiela, A. (eds.) Proceedings of the 35th International ECMS International Conference on Modelling and Simulation, ECMS 2021, Virtual Event, UK, 31 May–2 June 2021, pp. 35–41. European Council for Modeling and Simulation (2021)
9. Parhizkari, S.: Anomaly detection in intrusion detection systems. In: Anomaly Detection-Recent Advances, AI and ML Perspectives and Applications. IntechOpen (2023)
10. Hou, Y., Teo, S.G., Chen, Z., Wu, M., Kwoh, C.-K., Truong-Huu, T.: Handling labeled data insufficiency: semi-supervised learning with self-training mixup decision tree for classification of network attacking traffic. IEEE Trans. Depend. Secure Comput. (2022)
11. Nisioti, A., Mylonas, A., Yoo, P.D., Katos, V.: From intrusion detection to attacker attribution: a comprehensive survey of unsupervised methods. IEEE Commun. Surv. Tutor. **20**(4), 3369–3388 (2018)
12. Qiu, J., Shi, H., Yuhen, H., Zujun, Yu.: Unraveling false positives in unsupervised defect detection models: a study on anomaly-free training datasets. Sensors **23**(23), 9360 (2023)
13. Ibomoiye Domor Mienye and Yanxia Sun: A survey of ensemble learning: concepts, algorithms, applications, and prospects. IEEE Access **10**, 99129–99149 (2022)

14. Awad, Z., Zakaria, M., Hassan, R.: An enhanced ensemble defense framework for boosting adversarial robustness of intrusion detection systems. Sci. Rep. **15**(1), 14177 (2025)
15. Alhowaide, A., Alsmadi, I., Tang, J.: Ensemble detection model for IoT ids. Internet Things **16**, 100435 (2021)
16. Zoppi, T., Ceccarelli, A.: Prepare for trouble and make it double! supervised-unsupervised stacking for anomaly-based intrusion detection. J. Netw. Comput. Appl. **189**, 103106 (2021)
17. Kale, R., Lu, Z., Fok, K.W., Thing, V.L.L.: A hybrid deep learning anomaly detection framework for intrusion detection. In: 2022 IEEE 8th International Conference on Big Data Security on Cloud (BigDataSecurity), IEEE International Conference on High Performance and Smart Computing,(HPSC) and IEEE International Conference on Intelligent Data and Security (IDS), pp. 137–142. IEEE (2022)
18. Ribeiro, M.T., Singh, S., Guestrin, C.: "why should i trust you?" Explaining the predictions of any classifier. In: Proceedings of the 22nd ACM SIGKDD International Conference on Knowledge Discovery and Data Mining, pp. 1135–1144 (2016)
19. Lundberg, S.M., Lee, S.-I.: A unified approach to interpreting model predictions. In: Guyon, I., et al. (eds.) Advances in Neural Information Processing Systems 30: Annual Conference on Neural Information Processing Systems 2017, 4–9 December 2017, Long Beach, CA, USA, pp. 4765–4774 (2017)
20. Zhang, Z., Al Hamadi, H., Damiani, E., Yeun, C.Y., Taher, F.: Explainable artificial intelligence applications in cyber security: state-of-the-art in research. IEEE Access **10**, 93104–93139 (2022)
21. Neupane, S., et al.: Explainable intrusion detection systems (x-ids): a survey of current methods, challenges, and opportunities. IEEE Access **10**, 112392–112415 (2022)
22. Sharafaldin, I., Lashkari, A.H., Ghorbani, A.A.: Toward generating a new intrusion detection dataset and intrusion traffic characterization. In: Mori, P., Furnell, S., Camp, O. (eds.) Proceedings of the 4th International Conference on Information Systems Security and Privacy. ICISSP 2018, Funchal, Madeira - Portugal, 22–24 January 2018, pp. 108–116. SciTePress (2018)
23. Tavallaee, M., Bagheri, E., Lu, W., Ghorbani, A.A.: A detailed analysis of the kdd cup 99 data set. In: 2009 IEEE Symposium on Computational Intelligence for Security and Defense Applications, pp. 1–6. IEEE (2009)
24. Hnamte, V., Nhung-Nguyen, H., Hussain, J., Hwa-Kim, Y.: A novel two-stage deep learning model for network intrusion detection: LSTM-AE. IEEE Access **11**, 37131–37148 (2023)
25. Breunig, M.M., Kriegel, H.P., Ng, R.T., Sander, J.: LoF: identifying density-based local outliers. In: Proceedings of the 2000 ACM SIGMOD International Conference on Management of Data, pp. 93–104 (2000)
26. Liu, F.T., Ting, K.M., Zhou, Z.-H.: Isolation-based anomaly detection. ACM Trans. Knowl. Discov. Data **6**(1), 3:1–3:39 (2012)
27. Chawla, N.V., Bowyer, K.W., Hall, L.O., Kegelmeyer, W.P.: SMOTE: synthetic minority over-sampling technique. J. Artif. Intell. Res. **16**, 321–357 (2002)
28. Halabaku, E., Bytyçi, E.: Overfitting in machine learning: a comparative analysis of decision trees and random forests. Intell. Autom. Soft Comput. **39**(6) (2024)
29. Aria, M., Cuccurullo, C., Gnasso, A.: A comparison among interpretative proposals for random forests. Mach. Learn. Appl. **6**, 100094 (2021

30. Aas, K., Jullum, M., Løland, A.: Explaining individual predictions when features are dependent: more accurate approximations to Shapley values. Artif. Intell. **298**, 103502 (2021)
31. Herbinger, J., Dandl, S., Ewald, F.K., Loibl, S., Casalicchio, G.: Leveraging model-based trees as interpretable surrogate models for model distillation. In: Nowaczyk, S., et al. (eds.) ECAI 2023. CCIS, vol. 1947, pp. 232–249. Springer, Cham (2023). https://doi.org/10.1007/978-3-031-50396-2_13

Evolutionary Algorithms

Evolutionary Optimization of Autonomous Agents for Decreasing Resource Intensity on Geographically Located Interdependent Task Sets

Martin Fyvie[1]([✉]) [iD], John A.W. McCall[1,2] [iD],
and Alexandru-Ciprian Zăvoianu[1] [iD]

[1] The Robert Gordon University, Garthdee Road, Aberdeen, UK
{m.fyvie,j.mccall,c.zavoianu}@rgu.ac.uk
[2] PlanSea Solutions, Edinburgh, UK
john@plansea.co.uk

Abstract. Autonomous agents offer a promising approach to managing complex, resource-intensive operations such as vehicle routing, scheduling, and offshore decommissioning, where fleets must coordinate interdependent tasks across geographical locations under environmental and logistical constraints. This paper presents a simulationoptimization framework in which autonomous agents make local task selections using meta-heuristic-weighted decision criteria. These criteria, along with schedules and task queue sizes, are co-evolved by a Genetic Algorithm to minimize KPIs. We applied our approach to a North Sea decommissioning case study involving pipeline and structure removal, achieving up to 36% CO_2 and fuel usage reduction when compared to a single-vessel baseline. Results show fixed-policy scenarios performed worse, while dynamic configurations enabled more adaptive and efficient scheduling. These findings demonstrate the potential of agent-based optimization to support low-emission campaign planning, aligning with North Sea Transition Authority 50% emission reduction targets for decommissioning activities.

Keywords: Evolutionary Algorithms · Simulation ·
Decommissioning · Carbon Emissions · Optimization · Artificial
Intelligence · Autonomous Agents

1 Introduction

Agentic systems, multi-agent frameworks with individual decision heuristics, have been applied to complex, dynamic planning problems for some time. In logistics and scheduling [1] they were used for task allocation for vehicle routing and more recently in resource allocation for smart grids [2].

Multi-objective evolutionary optimization was shown to effectively tune both agent behaviours and global coordination in emergency response simulations [3],

M. Bramer and F. Stahl (Eds.): SGAI-AI 2025, LNAI 16302, pp. 21–34, 2026.
https://doi.org/10.1007/978-3-032-11442-6_2

leading to agentic decision heuristic systems co-evolved via evolutionary computation. Similarly, a combination of integer-linear programming with heuristic search, termed "matheuristic", was used to optimize vessel scheduling in offshore wind farm decommissioning [4].

Early AI applications in the decommissioning area targeted strategic option selection. Dimensionalityreduction and supervisedlearning techniques [5] have been shown capable of classifying decommissioning options for a small set of UK projects with high accuracy, reducing reliance on time-consuming stakeholder scoring matrices. This has been expanded to a database of 120 projects [6], showing that an XGBoost classifier retained predictive power even when several criteria were omitted. At the task scale, pipeline and umbilical removal have been cast as precedence constrained routing problems. Using genetic algorithms (GAs), the results show that they out-performed manual plans by up to 18% in predicted vessel days for a Gulf of Mexico case [7].

Industry cost-breakdown data for the United Kingdom Continental Shelf (UKCS) show that wells account for approximately 50% of total decommissioning spend, while the vessel-intensive topside and substructure removal phases represent approximately 2530%. Within those removal phases, heavy-lift and support spreads (all the vessels working or deployed on a specific field) account for as much as half of the budget and a significant proportion of the emissions [8].

The method proposed in this paper aims to address such NSTA targets by simulating the decommissioning activities using a combination of semi autonomous vessel models and a decision-support evolutionary algorithm. Our method generates task allocations for a decommissioning fleet at the campaign-level by having each vessel run a local task-selection heuristic with priority weights that are co-evolved by a global GA. The remainder of this paper is structured as follows: Section 2 outlines our proposed framework using a Genetic Algorithm (GA) to co-evolve Agentic decision making criteria. Section 3 introduces a case study for which our approach is applied to. Section 4 contains the analysis of the resulting simulation runs. Lastly, in Section 5 we discuss our conclusions drawn from the application of our approach to the case study and future plans.

2   Proposed Approach

The framework outlined in this paper is designed to simulate the activities of a fleet of semi-autonomous agents (operating with tactical but not strategic autonomy) as they complete a given list of tasks. The tasks are assigned a priority score, in simulation, by the agent which then decide the order in which tasks are to be completed, given a set of strategic decision-weightings from a Genetic Algorithm (GA) derived solution. As seen in [3], the use of this combination of evolutionary algorithm and simulator is not unique however the framework outlined in this paper is designed to be applicable to a range of problems in which task dependencies are vital.

A simulation of the fleet is then run for each set of GA-derived weightings with the aim of finding higher quality solutions as the optimization run continues. In our approach we use a Discrete Event Simulation (DES) system in which the fleet performs their selected tasks.

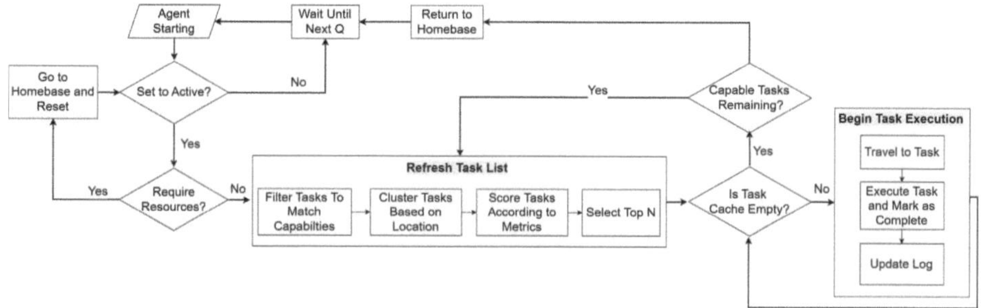

Fig. 1. Agent Decision Workflow

Each agent in the fleet follows a set of decision criteria as illustrated in Fig. 1. This workflow demonstrates how each agent decides which task to complete by scoring tasks according to Eq. 4, ranking them using GA-supplied weightings, then executing tasks until cache depletion. As this framework is designed to be applicable to a range of location-based, interdependent tasks we identified four key parameters that encompass the main requirements for discovering high-quality solutions: **Distance**, **Quantity**, **Continuity**, and **Equipment**.

We employ a GA in our framework due to their ability to explore vast solution spaces without guaranteeing optimality but efficiently finding near-optimal solutions. In smaller problems options such as Linear programming and other optimization techniques could be used however this becomes computationally infeasible as the problem size grows. In the case study shown later in this paper, a problem size of 139! or 10^{238} possible routes exist, lending itself well to meta-heuristic search.

2.1 Discreet Event Simulation

Discrete-event simulation models system evolution as an ordered sequence of instantaneous, time-stamped events responsible for discontinuous state changes. Between events, the system remains in a state of inactivity while the simulation clock advances directly to the next scheduled event [9]. This next-event time progression provides substantial computational advantages over fixed-step methods for systems with sparse state changes, distinguishing it from continuous simulation where differential equations drive updates across all time intervals [10,11]. The DES engine maintains a global clock and future-event list (typically a priority queue), repeatedly dequeuing imminent events, executing their logic, updating system state, and scheduling secondary events [12]. During execution, event routines interact with three principal components: a state vector capturing system variables, an event routine library embodying domain rules, and statistical accumulators collecting performance metrics. This process is illustrated in Fig. 2.

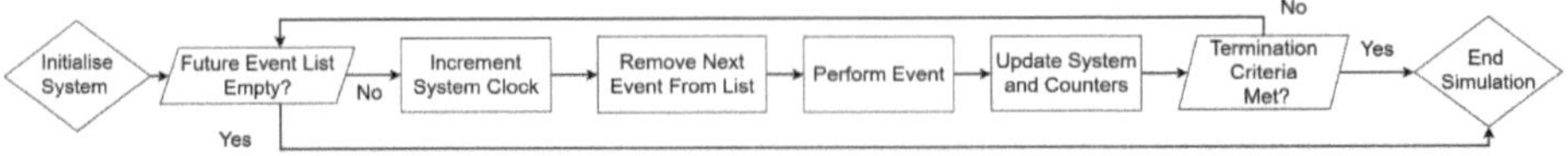

Fig. 2. Discreet Event Simulation Steps

2.2   Genetic Algorithm

This paper implements a $(\mu + \lambda)$ Genetic Algorithm for the metaheuristic element of our approach, where μ represents the initial population and λ the offspring population. Each generation applies Selection, Crossover, and Mutation operations to parent solutions. Two parent solutions are randomly selected via tournament selection. Crossover employs simulated binary crossover (SBX) [13], while mutation uses a polynomial function [13,14]. The eta parameter, which controls the exponential distribution in SBX and mutation intensity, was set to 3.0. Higher values produce less mutated offspring.

For this mixed-variable problem with three variable sets having different bounds, initial sampling constrains values within upper and lower limits as shown in Eq. 3. Rounding repair ensures variables exceeding bounds are set to the nearest valid value.

2.3   Solution Representation

We define a GA solution, X, as a 36-bit integer string representing four *quarter* blocks ($Q1$ to $Q4$) shown in Eq. 1, each quarter representing one fourth of the total simulation length. Each quarter contains (i) an integer cache-size parameter $\mathbf{c_i}$, defining the maximum agent task list size, (ii) a 4-dimensional weight vector $\mathbf{w}^{(i)}$ and (iii) a 4-dimensional agent-active switch $\mathbf{v}^{(i)}$. Formally:

$$X = \begin{cases} c_1, \ldots, c_4, & \rightarrow \text{ Q1-Q4 Cache Parameters} \\ w_1, \ldots, w_4, & \rightarrow \text{ Q1-Q4 Weight Parameters} \\ v_1, \ldots, v_4 & \rightarrow \text{ Q1-Q4 Agent Parameters} \end{cases} \tag{1}$$

where:

$$\mathbf{w}^{(i)} = (w_1^{(i)}, \ldots, w_4^{(i)}), \ \mathbf{v}^{(i)} = (v_1^{(i)}, \ldots, v_4^{(i)}) \tag{2}$$

$$c_i \in \{5, \ldots, 100\}, \ w_j^{(i)} \in \{-20, \ldots, 20\}, \ v_k^{(i)} \in \{0, 1\} \tag{3}$$

Each c_i sets the *cache size* used during quarter i. Quarter i's parameters are the 4-dimensional weight vector $\mathbf{w}^{(i)} = (w_1^{(i)}, w_2^{(i)}, w_3^{(i)}, w_4^{(i)})$ and the 4-dimensional binary agent-switch vector $\mathbf{v}^{(i)} = (v_1^{(i)}, v_2^{(i)}, v_3^{(i)}, v_4^{(i)})$. We therefore have one set $(\mathbf{c_i}, \mathbf{w}^{(i)}, \mathbf{v}^{(i)})$ for each of the four quarters.

We split the optimization period to quarters to allow for the periodic re-evaluation of operational weightings given to the fleet including the cache-size parameters.

This allows the algorithm to adapt to changing task priorities, agent or vehicle status, workload, and any operationally required resource. A smaller cache prompts more frequent priority updates, mirroring how coordinators might release tasks as the campaign advances. To keep the focus on routing and assignment, every task is assumed to take a uniform one hour however, as noted in the conclusions, future work will look to improve upon this should the data be available in specific applications of our approach.

2.4   Task Priority Calculation

Shown in Eq. 4 is how each agent scores a provided task from the global list of unassigned work. Each agent, when their cache is empty, will score all outstanding tasks according to this equation. Once ranked, the highest valued set of tasks, up to the size of the current cache size limit c_i, are assigned exclusively.

$$PS = w_1^{(i)} \left(1 - \frac{d}{md} \right) + w_2^{(i)} \left(1 - \frac{c}{q} \right) + w_3^{(i)} B - w_4^{(i)} E \left(\frac{dh}{md} \right) \tag{4}$$

Here PS is the task Priority Score. Shown in Table 1 are the parameter descriptions, where: $w_1^{(i)}$ is the **Distance** weighting, $w_2^{(i)}$ is the **Quantity** weighting, $w_3^{(i)}$ is the **Continuity** weighting, and $w_4^{(i)}$ is the **Equipment** penalty weighting from quarter i in solution X.

Table 1. Notation used in the optimization model

Symbol	Meaning
d	Distance from the agent to the task
md	Maximum distance between any two points in the problem domain
dh	Distance from the agent to its home base
c	Collected quantity at the task location
q	Required quantity at the task location ($\mathbf{q} > 0$)
B	Continuity bonus indicator (1 if current task is adjacent to previous, 0 otherwise)
E	Equipment mismatch indicator (1 if required equipment is unavailable, 0 otherwise)

Distance $\mathbf{d}$ is a measure from an agent to any task location. The distance term $(1 - \frac{d}{md})$ is normalized to $[0, 1]$, where closer tasks (smaller d) yield higher values. When $w_1^{(i)} > 0$, agents prefer nearby tasks; when $w_1^{(i)} < 0$, agents prefer distant tasks. The quantity term $(1-\frac{c}{q})$ represents the fraction of work remaining at a task location, ranging from 0 (completed) to 1 (untouched). Positive $w_2^{(i)}$ values encourage task completion, while negative values favour starting new tasks. Continuity $w_3^{(i)} \cdot B$ provides a bonus when the current task is adjacent to the previous one in the sequence when $w_3^{(i)} > 0$. The equipment penalty term $w_4^{(i)} E\left(\frac{dh}{md}\right)$ is subtracted when equipment mismatch occurs ($E = 1$), with the penalty magnitude proportional to the normalized distance to a home base. Higher $w_4^{(i)}$ values increase the penalty for equipment changes when far from that base.

3   Case Study - North Sea Janice Gas Export Flowline

Offshore oil and gas decommissioning, particularly in mature basins like the North Sea, is rapidly increasing. Global expenditure is projected to exceed £300 billion by 2050 [15], with the UK Continental Shelf alone facing £24 billion between 2023–2032 [16] and a £40 billion whole-life cost. The North Sea Transition Authority (NSTA) now mandates up to 50% emissions reduction for decommissioning plans [17], promoting data-driven scheduling and shared-vessel campaigns. In 2023A NSTA pipeline removal study [18] demonstrated 30% savings in cost, fuel, and CO_2 through smarter tooling, highlighting the impact that incremental changes and innovations can make in overall CO_2 figures during long campaigns.

The case study used in this paper and associated datasets were provided by PlanSea Solutions, who are interested in low-carbon decommissioning campaigns in the North sea. We aimed to investigate the Janice Gas Export Flowlines by utilizing our framework to find lower emission task assignments across a 12 week period. The dataset provided includes a decommissioning scenario with interdependent tasks, locations, and pre-calculated pipeline removal quantities. The study's objective was to identify fuel-efficient task allocations for a simulated decommissioning vessel fleet operating between ports Aberdeen (A) and Blyth (B) in the North Sea. The Janice Gas Export Flowlines are approximately 280 km east of the British coast, located in UKCS Blocks 30/ $(7, 12, 13, 17, 18)$ as shown in Fig. 3.

The dataset contained details on pipeline paths, types, diameters and current status. For subsea structures, similar features were made available for those that lie along or are connected to these pipelines. The two main pipelines in this location are **PL1631 - Janice Oil Export Flowline** and **PL1632 - Janice Gas Export Flowline**. In this application, distance is evaluated using the `geopy.distance.geodesic` routine [19], which implements the VincentyKarney [20] solution on the WGS-84 reference ellipsoid, a standard used in the UKCS.

The pipeline length to be removed in the case-study was 49.53 km - the maximum distance found, as required in Eq. 4, is 297 km between Blyth port and the most northern pipeline termination show in Fig. 3.

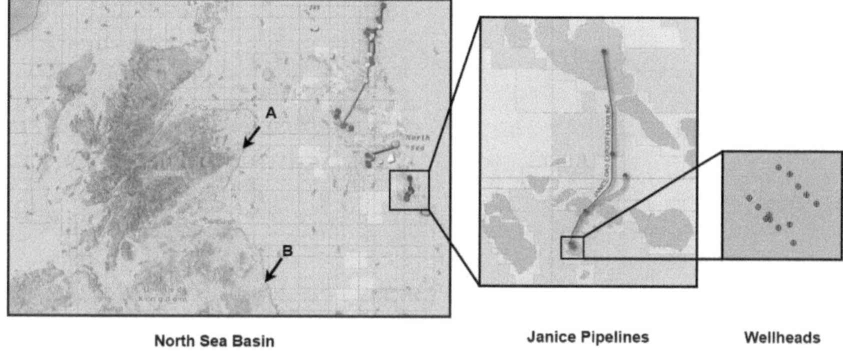

Fig. 3. Janice Pipeline and Port Locations

3.1 Subsea Infrastructure and Fleet Configuration

The simulation models 31 pipeline locations (49.53 km total) and 13 wellheads, resulting in 132 tasks: 93 pipeline tasks following the sequence *Cleaning* → *Cutting* → *Removal*, and 39 structure tasks requiring *Surveying* → *Disconnect* → *Removal*. Each pipeline location is divided into sections where cleaning and cutting must occur before removal. If a vessel reaches capacity mid-location, it returns to base to offload and refuel before resuming work.

Both pipelines are approximately 350 mm in diameter. Using reference data from a UK Government pipelines comparative assessment report [21] and those provided by PlanSea, a mean weight of 2.58 tonnes per 24 m pipeline section was calculated - an upper limit of pipeline segment length used in decommissioning. This value determines vessel storage capacity in terms of sections before requiring return to port for offloading in our simulations.

A fleet of 4 decommissioning vessels was created due to the expensive nature of their operation and limited availability. All vessels have identical specifications: $3000\,\text{m}^3$ fuel capacity, $3\,\text{m}^3/\text{h}$ consumption during travel, and $0.6\,\text{m}^3/\text{h}$ when using dynamic positioning systems (dps) while stationary at a task site. These values are based on large pipe-lay vessel data [22]. Sailing speed is 15 km/h for all vessels.

Cargo capacity provides 2800t port side storage, translating to 1000 segments of 24 m per vessel when using the value 2.58t per segment. Structure capacity is limited to 3 units due to their substantial size. Non-depleting activities (Cleaning, Cutting, Surveying, and Disconnecting) have unlimited capacity since fuel, crew, and maintenance are the primary operational constraints rather than cargo capacity.

The fleet contains one pipeline-dedicated vessel (V1) capable of performing all required pipeline tasks. Vessels V2 and V3 are ROV support vessels, capable of completing pipeline activities once cleaning is done as well as surveying subsea structures. Vessel V4 is a structure removal vessel capable of removing up to three wellheads per trip as seen in Table 2.

Table 2. Fleet vessel configurations and capabilities

Vessel	Port	Clean	Cut	Pipe	Surv	Disc	Struc	Fuel (m^3/h)
V1	A	✓	✓	1000	-			3.0
V2	A		✓	1000	✓	-	-	3.0
V3	A	-	✓	1000	✓	-	-	3.0
V4	B				✓	✓	3	3.0

The ports used were specified in the decommissioning scenario as representative maritime hubs with required infrastructure where decommissioning activities are already conducted. Port A is Aberdeen, Scotland and Port B is Blyth, England, both marked on Fig. 3 for reference.

To generate a baseline campaign, we ran the simulation with one idealised vessel capable of performing all possible tasks but with realistic capacities in terms of fuel, pipe capacity and structure removal capacity. This resulted in a fuel usage of 2409.54 m^3 and a campaign length of 953 h. We use these results as a baseline, comparing the results of using a larger fleet with vessel-specific capabilities that are more realistic.

3.2   Optimization Goal

All parameters in solution X are evolved via the genetic algorithm to minimize the total *fuel consumption* across all vessels. Fuel usage strongly correlates with the sum of travelled distances needed to complete all tasks. Hence, the GA attempts to reduce the fleet's overall fuel consumption (and thereby emissions) while still covering every task's requirements by finding a set of decision weightings that results in the shortest overall travel time. This goal is shown in the optimization function in Eq. 5. Here, $\mathcal{V}$ is the set of all vessels used in the simulation.

$$\min_{X} \sum_{v, \in, \mathcal{V}} \left[f_{\text{travel}} \frac{D_{\text{total}}(v, X)}{s} + f_{\text{dps}} T_{\text{work}}(v, X) \right] + P \tag{5}$$

The variables in Eq. 5 area as follows: f_{travel} and f_{dps} denote fuel consumption rates during transit and dynamic positioning while working respectively; $D_{\text{total}}(v, X)$ is the total distance travelled by vessel v under solution X; s is the sailing speed (km/h); $T_{\text{work}}(v, X)$ represents the vessel's working time; and P is a penalty applied if any task remains incomplete in solution X.

3.3   Experimental Setup

Three system configurations were tested in this study. The first configuration, FullGA, gave the system full control: selecting vessel usage or standby status per quarter, varying task cache sizes quarterly, and generating fleet-wide weightings for task priority criteria. The second scenario (AV) maintained these capabilities but enforced all vessels were used in all quarters. The third configuration (VC) enforced all vessels were used and used static cache sizes of 10, 50, and 100 across all quarters, leaving only the decision weightings to the GA to determine as shown in Table 3.

Table 3. Scenario Run Settings

Scenario	Cache	Vessel Sel	Runs	N	g	P
Full GA (GA)	GA	GA	50	50	50	5000
All Vessels (AV)	GA	All	50	50	50	5000
All Vessels, Fixed Cache (VC)	10/50/100	All	50	50	50	5000

Here the penalty, P, is set to 5000. This penalty is added to give the GA a strong signal to prioritize task completion. This value as used as it is higher than the baseline minimum ensuring that solutions with fewer completed tasks are avoided. Each scenario was run 50 times with a population size (N) of 50 and termination after 50 generations (g). All simulations had a 2000 simulated hour time limit (approximately 12 weeks) for vessels to complete the decommissioning campaign - the set of all required tasks. Solutions failing to complete all 132 required tasks within this timeframe were penalized.

4   Results

Figures 4a and 4b present the mean fitness per generation and the distribution of cache sizes for the FullGA and AV scenarios. As shown in Fig. 4a, fixed-cache scenarios VC10, VC50 and VC100 show rapid convergence, indicating a restricted search space where fixed cache sizes limited the GA's exploration. VC50 and VC100 consistently performed above the baseline (2409.54 m^3 shown in red dashes), suggesting that inflexible, large cache configurations did not yield superior or lower-emission solutions compared to an unconstrained single-vessel scenario.

FullGA and AV scenarios exhibited decreasing fitness (lower fuel/emissions) as optimization progressed, both achieving values below or near the baseline. This highlights that greater flexibility of FullGA's full algorithmic control and AV's partial autonomy enabled the GA to identify more resource-efficient allocations. FullGA notably found significantly lower fitness solutions after generation 5, broadly converging by generation 25 to a mean of 1538.42 m^3 as shown in Fig. 4a and Table 4.

Figure 4b plots the distribution of cache sizes generated by the GA for the FullGA and AV configurations. The FullGA scenario, with full algorithmic control over parameters, cache size, and vessel selection, showed significant variability and generally higher median cache allocations. This suggests dynamic resource allocation enabling broader exploration of task assignments.

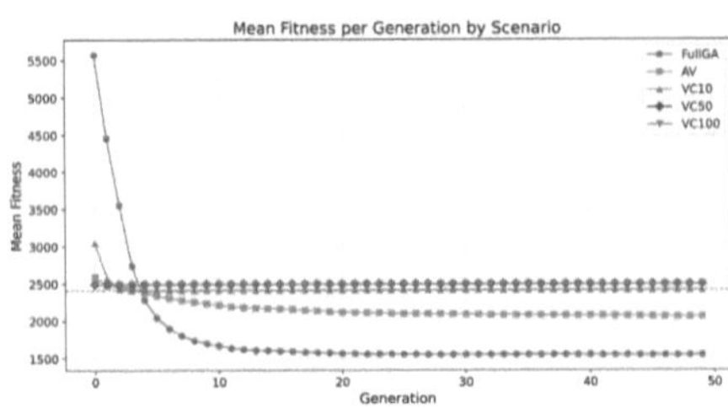
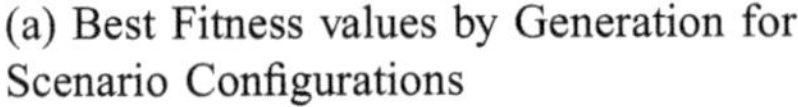

(a) Best Fitness values by Generation for Scenario Configurations

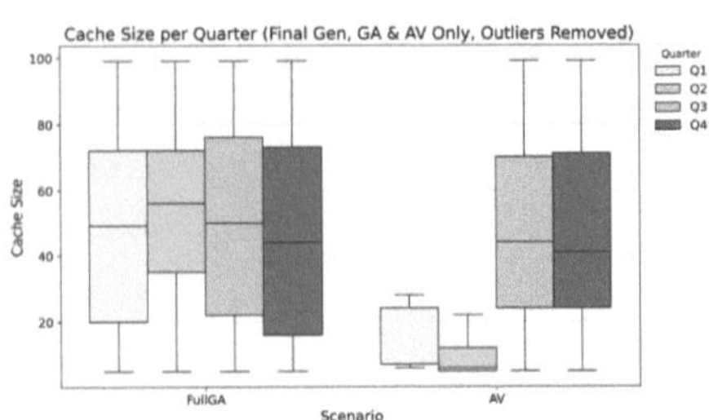

(b) Cache size per quarter distributions (outliers removed)

Fig. 4. Scenario Fuel Usage and Cache Size Results

Table 4. Final Generation Scenario Results

Scenario	Mean F (m^3)	Std Dev	Min	Max
FullGA	1538.42	139.09	1370.69	1815.58
AV	2054.83	139.27	1826.17	2373.54
VC10	2408.17	0.00	2408.17	2408.17
VC50	2488.78	0.00	2488.78	2488.78
VC100	2488.78	0.00	2488.78	2488.78

In contrast, the AV scenario, which was enforced full vessel usage, shows a distinct cache profile. While some variability occurred between Q3 and Q4 when comparing scenarios, cache sizes for Q1 and Q2 were noticeably lower and less varied than FullGA. This implies that AV's vessel usage restrictions led to reduced cache sizes, consequently increasing task scoring and allocation frequency. As indicated in Fig. 5b the significantly shorter campaign lengths of AV compared to FullGA suggest most tasks were completed by Q3, emphasizing the initial two quarters.

Figure 5a shows the final generation fitness value distributions for different GA configurations with the baseline figure of $2409.54m^3$ shown in red dashes. Figure 5b presents the corresponding distribution of campaign lengths generated by the end of each optimization run. Shown in red dashes in this figure is baseline length of 953 h.

The fixed-cache configurations of VC10, VC50 and VC100 consistently led to higher fuel usage results. As Fig. 5a and Table 4 detail, their mean fitness values ($2408.17\,m^3$, $2488.78\,m^3$, $2488.78\,m^3$ respectively) remained above baseline. Figure 5a's tight distributions for those three scenarios confirm that fixed cache sizes severely restricted the GA's optimization for lower fuel consumption. The FullGA and AV scenarios demonstrated considerably better quality final solutions. FullGA achieved the lowest fitness (mean $1538.42\,m^3$), significantly below baseline, while AV also performed well (mean $2054.83\,m^3$).

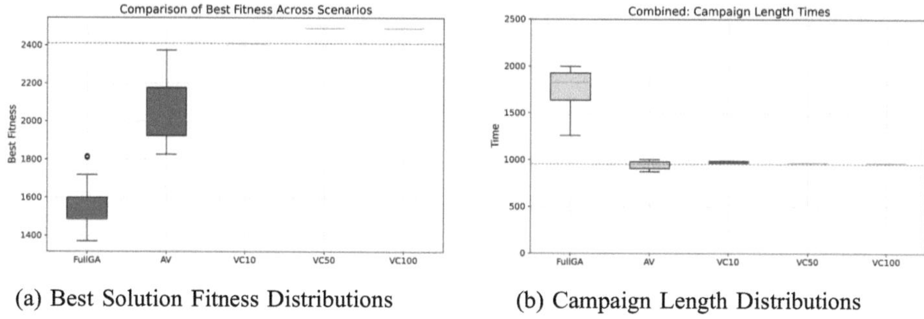

(a) Best Solution Fitness Distributions   (b) Campaign Length Distributions

Fig. 5. Scenario Final Solution Campaign Lengths and Fuel Usage Distributions

When considering the campaign lengths shown in Fig. 5b, FullGA consistently resulted in significantly longer campaigns, extending to the 2000-hour simulation limit, indicating a clear trade-off between fuel efficiency and operational time. The AV, VC10, VC50, and VC100 scenarios maintained campaign lengths very close to or slightly above the baseline, showing consistent convergence for these configurations. An example of this can be seen in Fig. 6 which shows a comparison between two campaigns, the best found solution from the FullGA and from AV. Here, we can clearly see that the FullGA schedule is significantly longer than the AV derived solution at the cost of a lower overall fuel usage ($1370.69\,\text{m}^3$ vs $1826.17\,\text{m}^3$ respectively), where the FullGA has reduced the number of used vessels to 3.

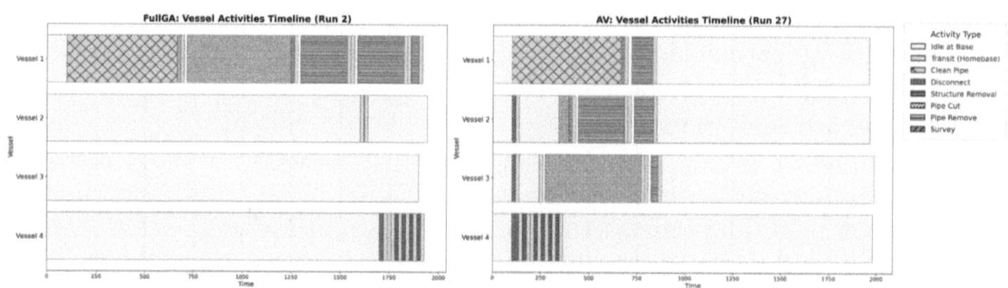

Fig. 6. Campaign Comparison

Figure 7 shows the decision weights derived by the GA for the four key features: Distance, Quantity, Continuity, and Equipment, broken down by quarters for each scenario. These weightings reflect the GA's implicit strategy in allocating resources. Across all experiments, Distance weightings remain largely centred around zero, with consistent interquartile ranges around $[-10, 10]$. This may suggest a moderate, consistent emphasis on minimizing travel, irrespective of cache strategy. FullGA and AV results show slightly tighter distributions in Q1 and Q2, indicating early convergence on balanced routing.

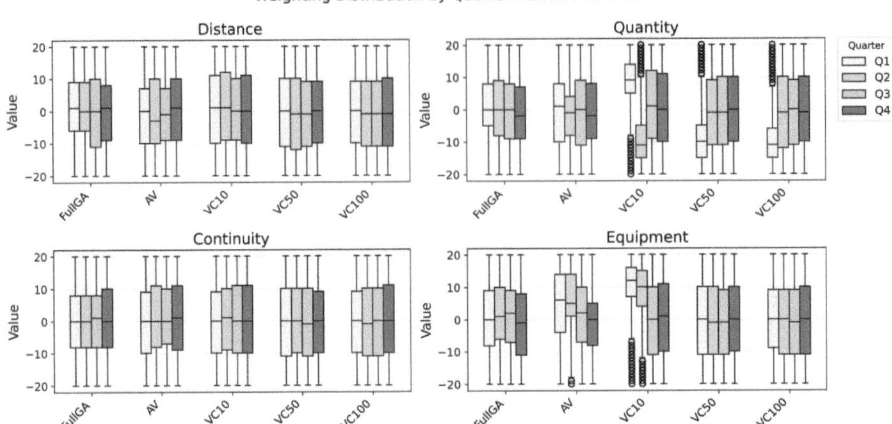

Fig. 7. Weighting Distribution by Scenario

Quantity distributions exhibit more pronounced variation. Notably, VC10 displays a strong positive weighting in Q1 with a mean value of 9.01, followed by a sharp drop in Q2 to -10.17. This sharp swing implies that VC10's shorter cache size encourages early maximization of task quantity, followed by a corrective reweighting in Q2, likely as many tasks are already underway and cannot be allocated to another vessel. VC50 (mean -10.11) and VC100 (mean -10.38) begin with a significantly negative mean in Q1, indicating a slower ramp-up in prioritizing task volume as a comparison.

Continuity weightings across all scenarios are relatively stable, centred near zero and symmetric across all quarters. This may reflect a consistent preference for task sequence smoothness, regardless of scenario conditions.

For Equipment, VC10 demonstrates a distinct strategic bias, with a positively skewed distribution and a mean value of 11.34 in Q1, continuing into Q2 with a mean of 9.70. This indicates an early and sustained prioritization of equipment changes. AV also shows higher mean values in Q1 (4.76) and Q2 (5.25), then trends downwards as the simulation continues; however, as most tasks are complete by this point, the overall impact would be reduced.

5   Conclusions and Future Work

This paper introduces a simulation-optimization framework for reducing resource intensity of semi-autonomous vessel agents working on geographically located interdependent task sets interdependent via evolutionary methods.

Discrete-event simulation is combined with a genetic algorithm that co-evolves agent priority weightings, cache sizes, and vehicle utilization to generate resource-efficient task allocations that respect vehicle capabilities and inter-task dependencies. Applied to a North Sea pipeline decommissioning case study, the system achieved up to 36% fuel savings compared to a single-vessel baseline. Scenarios with fixed cache sizes constrained performance, whereas dynamic cache adjustment and selective vessel deployment led to substantially better outcomes. These results highlight the importance of flexible task allocation and priority weightings in reducing emissions through adaptive, context-aware scheduling.

Among configurations tested, the FullGA scenario produced the lowest emission campaigns but at the cost of longer durations–indicating a clear trade-off between fuel efficiency and campaign time, especially since campaign length was not explicitly penalized. Conversely, the AV configuration yielded faster schedules with modest fuel savings, making it a strong candidate for time-critical operations. Analysis of the evolved task-weight vectors revealed interesting behavioural differences across scenarios. Distance and continuity weights remained centred near zero, while quantity and equipment weights shifted significantly depending on cache strategy. This suggests that cache capacity influences both allocation frequency and the strategic balancing of resource consumption versus routing efficiency. Future work will integrate realistic task durations and tooling constraints to better reflect operational conditions and evaluate novel technologies. We will also explore "hot-start" scenarios–vessels entering mid-campaign–and investigate joint optimization of fleet composition and vessel load-outs to minimize asset requirements. Finally, introducing campaign length as an explicit objective in a multi-objective GA could yield Pareto-optimal trade-offs between emissions and time.

References

1. Gorodetski, V., Karsaev, O., Konushy, V.: Multi-agent system for resource allocation and scheduling. In: Multi-Agent Systems and Applications III, Lecture Notes in Computer Science, vol. 2691, pp. 236–246. Springer (2003)
2. Nair, A.S., et al.: Multi-agent systems for resource allocation and scheduling in a smart grid. Technol. Econ. Smart Grids Sustain. Energy **3**(1), 15 (2018)
3. Narzisi, G., Mysore, V., Mishra, B.: Multi-Objective Evolutionary Optimization of Agent-Based Models: An Application to Emergency Response Planning, pp. 228–232 (01 2006)
4. Irawan, C.A., Wall, G., Jones, D.: An optimisation model for scheduling the decommissioning of an offshore wind farm. OR Spectr. **41**(2), 513–548 (2019)
5. Martins, I.D., Bahiense, L., Infante, C.E.D., de Arruda, E.F.: Dimensionality reduction for multi-criteria problems: an application to the decommissioning of oil and gas installations. Expert Syst. Appl. **148**, 113236 (2020)
6. Vuttipittayamongkol, P., Coates, G.: A data-driven decision support tool for offshore oil and gas decommissioning. IEEE Access **9**, 137063–137080 (2021)
7. da Silva Bressan, R., Artigas, D.: Task scheduling for subsea flexible pipes decommissioning. In: Proceedings of the Offshore Technology Conference (OTC-31066-MS) (2021)
8. Sottilotta, S.: North sea decommissioning costs estimated as double those in Southeast Asia. J. Petrol. Technol. (2020). https://jpt.spe.org/north-sea-decommissioning-costs-estimated-double-those-se-asia
9. Law, A.M.: Simulation Modeling and Analysis, 5th edn. McGraw-Hill Education, New York (2015)

10. Banks, J., Carson, J.S., Nelson, B.L., Nicol, D.M.: Discrete-Event System Simulation, 5th edn. Pearson, Boston (2014)
11. April, J., Glover, F., Kelly, J.P., Laguna, M.: Practical introduction to simulation optimization. In: Proceedings of the 2003 Winter Simulation Conference, pp. 71–78. IEEE, New Orleans, LA, USA (2003)
12. Leemis, L.M., Park, S.K.: Discrete-Event Simulation: A First Course. Pearson Prentice Hall, Upper Saddle River (2006)
13. Deb, K., Sindhya, K., Okabe, T.: Self-adaptive simulated binary crossover for real-parameter optimization. In: Proceedings of the 9th Annual Conference on Genetic and Evolutionary Computation. GECCO '07, pp. 1187–1194. Association for Computing Machinery, New York, NY, USA (2007)
14. Deb, K., Deb, D.: Analysing mutation schemes for real-parameter genetic algorithms. Int. J. Artif. Intell. Soft Comput. 4, 1–28 (2014)
15. Wood Mackenzie: Global Decommissioning Anxiety Rises - Report Summary (2021). https://www.woodmac.com/reports/upstream-oil-and-gas-global-decommissioning-anxiety-rises-507552
16. North Sea Transition Authority: UKCS Decommissioning Cost and Performance Update 2024 (2024). https://www.nstauthority.co.uk/media/ppvlelgd/ukcs-decom-cost-and-performance-update-01.pdf
17. UK Government: North Sea Transition Deal (2021). https://www.gov.uk/government/publications/north-sea-transition-deal. Accessed 26 June 2025
18. North Sea Transition Authority: UKCS Decommissioning Cost and Performance Report 2023 (2023). https://www.nstauthority.co.uk/media/lnmhqq2l/decom-cost-report-2023-final-accessible-1.pdf. Accessed 01 July 2025
19. Contributors, G.: Geopy: Geocoding library for Python (2024). Version 2.4.1. https://github.com/geopy/geopy. Accessed 26 June 2025
20. Karney, C.F.F.: Algorithms for geodesics. J. Geodesy 87(1), 43–55 (2013). https://link.springer.com/article/10.1007/s00190-012-0578-z
21. UK Government: Subsea Cumulative Assessment (2022). https://assets.publishing.service.gov.uk/media/6374c6808fa8f5771d20d3e5/Subsea_CA.pdf. Accessed 26 June 2025
22. Subsea7: Seven Borealis: Pipelay & Heavy Lift Vessel Datasheet (2023). https://www.subsea7.com/en/media/datasheets.html

Explaining Recommender Systems' Performance via User Behaviour Patterns

GianCarlo A. P. I. Catalano[1]([⊠]) , Klaudia Dynak[2] , Alexander E. I. Brownlee[1] , and Piotr Lipinski[2]

[1] Computing Science and Mathematics, University of Stirling, Stirling, UK
`{g.a.catalano,alexander.brownlee}@stir.ac.uk`
[2] Computational Intelligence Research Group, University of Wrocław, Wrocław, Poland
`{klaudia.dynak,piotr.lipinski}@cs.uni.wroc.pl`

Abstract. Recommender systems are widely adopted in digital retail platforms, and stakeholders increasingly demand transparency in how and when they perform reliably. We introduce **PS4XRS** (Partial Solutions for Explainable Recommender Systems), as a novel XAI tool.

Methodology: Using a dataset of user interactions and model performance, we can generate explanations in the form *"When the user interacts with at least 3 of these groups of items, we expect the model performance to be ..."*.

These explanations are obtained via a **multi-objective evolutionary algorithm**, with objectives based on interpretability, performance and the knowledge from latent item representations derived from the deep recommender system.

We performed **experiments** to determine the most effective parameters for the evolutionary process, and evaluate the trade-offs between explanation complexity and stakeholder usability. Source code for our work can be found athttps://github.com/Giancarlo-Catalano/PSSearch.

Keywords: Partial Solutions · Recommender Systems · eXplainable Artificial Intelligence · Genetic Algorithms

1 Introduction

Recommender Systems are AI tools that allow for personalized content retrieval. They are used in various domains, such as e-commerce, e-learning, multimedia, social media, and news.

With the complexity of the models and the competition in serving content (e.g., on banner ads), there is a need to understand the inner workings of the model, in particular to understand when and how the use of RS translates into business value.

Unfortunately, modern recommender systems such as self-attention or Graph Neural Networks (GNN) lack **transparency**: they are black boxes which provide little insight [8].

M. Bramer and F. Stahl (Eds.): SGAI-AI 2025, LNAI 16302, pp. 35–47, 2026.
https://doi.org/10.1007/978-3-032-11442-6_3

In this work, we use the concept of **P**artial **S**olutions (PS) [3] to find patterns in user behaviour that are associated with high model performance. PSs were originally developed to explain combinatorial optimisation, and in our work they find a novel use.

A real example of the explanations produced by our system is presented in Fig. 1, which can be used by the stakeholders to determine relevant elements to model performance and inform business decisions.

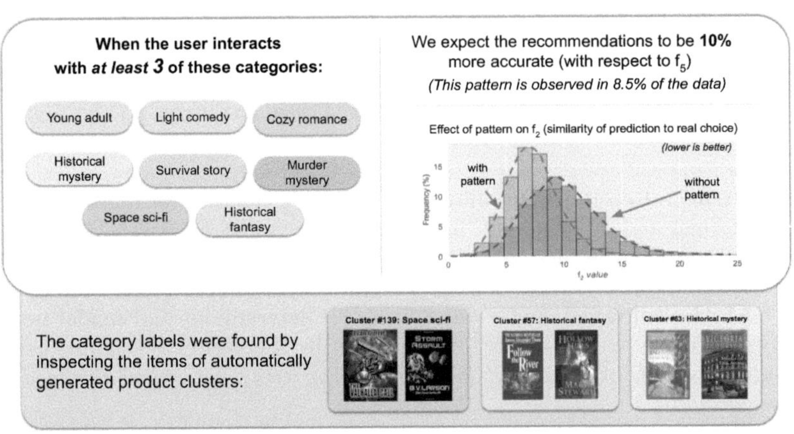

Fig. 1. A real example of an explanation produced by our system. The entire set of books is clustered in categories, and the explanation relates to users that have interacted with at least 3 from a specific subset. This user behaviour is observed 8.5% of the time, and leads to better model performance with respect to multiple metrics (described in Sect. 4.3).

The contributions of this work are as follows:

- **A novel explainability method for RS to describe scenarios with high model performance.**
- **An application of PSs to ML with new objectives and operators.**
- **A novel application of Evolutionary Algorithms to XAI.**
- **Experiments to compare the outcomes of different parameters.**

The paper structure is as follows: Sect. 2 introduces recommender systems and the data available, Sect. 3 discusses XAI and evolutionary methods, Sect. 4 introduces our methodology to generate explanations, Sect. 5 contains formal evaluation and finally Sect. 6 contains our final remarks.

2   Recommender Systems

A **Recommender System** (RS) enables automatic content serving based on a given user's and other users' previous activities. In this work, we focus on Collaborative Filtering (CF), where the model is trained using historical interactions of all users rather than item metadata.

In this section, we provide a formal task statement for RS and describe LightGCN [6], the model which we further used in our experiments.

2.1   Task Statement

Formally, we consider a set of N retail items $\mathcal{I} = \{i_1, i_2, \ldots, i_N\}$ and a set of M users $\mathcal{U} = \{u_1, u_2, \ldots, u_M\}$. Historical data consist of user-item pairs for which an interaction has been made (an interaction is any click, purchase or review):

$$\mathcal{D} = \{(u, i) \in \mathcal{U} \times \mathcal{I} : \text{user } u \text{ has interacted with item } i\}.$$

Using this dataset, the model should determine for each user K items that they might be interested in. This is achieved in CF RSs by representing each product and each user's interest as **embedded vectors**, which are learned from historical data. The compatibility between a user and a product is scalar product between their embeddings.

2.2   LightGCN

The explainability method presented in this paper is model agnostic, but it is necessary to discuss the model used in the experiments in this paper, a simplified Graph Convolutional Network (GCN) called LightGCN [6].

In the RS context, there is a **bipartite user-item graph**, where nodes represent users and items, and edges represent interactions. A GCN aims to learn embedded vectors for nodes by aggregating information from neighbouring nodes and non-linear transformations. LightGCN is a simple GCN architecture that only uses the aggregation step: at iteration $l + 1$, the embeddings for items $e_i^{(l+1)}$ and users $e_u^{(l+1)}$ are a weighed sum of their neighbours $\mathcal{N}$.

$$e_u^{(l+1)} = \sum_{i \in \mathcal{N}_u} \frac{1}{\sqrt{|\mathcal{N}_u|}\sqrt{|\mathcal{N}_i|}} e_i^{(l)}, \quad e_i^{(l+1)} = \sum_{u \in \mathcal{N}_i} \frac{1}{\sqrt{|\mathcal{N}_i|}\sqrt{|\mathcal{N}_u|}} e_u^{(l)}, \qquad (1)$$

Early iterations express local context, whereas later iterations are more global. To capture both aspects, the final embedded vectors are a sum over the embeddings at different stages:

$$e_u = \frac{1}{L + 1} \sum_{l=0}^{L} e_u^{(l)}, \quad e_i = \frac{1}{L + 1} \sum_{l=0}^{L} e_i^{(l)}. \qquad (2)$$

The model is trained with the BPR [10] loss function and the K item recommendations for user u are those that yield the highest dot-product. Although the architecture of the model is quite simple, the model remains a **black-box**, as we do not know what information is represented by the embeddings.

3 Black Box Systems, Explainability and Evolutionary Algorithms

Machine learning models and many algorithms, including RS, are **black boxes**: human users cannot understand the relationship between inputs and outputs. This lack of **interpretability** leads to a lack of trust, and thus it negatively affects the adoption of new methodologies [9]. Additionally, debugging and improvement of existing black box systems is significantly impeded by their un-interpretability [1]. In response to this, the topic of **eXplainable AI** (XAI) has developed various techniques to make these methods more compatible with human understanding. The advantages of XAI can be summarised as: **explain to discover**, **explain to justify**, **explain to control** (ability to detect and debug system faults) and **explain to improve** [5].

In the context of Evolutionary Algorithms, the explainability method of Partial Solutions was developed for these purposes, which we briefly summarise.

3.1 Combinatorial Optimisation and Evolutionary Algorithms

A combinatorial optimisation problem is a task where the aim is to find the vector of discrete values (generally boolean, called the **solution**) which maximises a **fitness function** F. While in some cases it is possible to use exact mathematical methods, it is often necessary to use stochastic search methods, namely **Evolutionary Algorithms** (**EAs**).

These methods are widely used in many fields, including medicine and engineering [11,12], but they are **black boxes** and it might not be clear why a solution would have high fitness [1]. This issue is similar to what is encountered in RSs: what makes a model perform more accurately for certain users compared to others?

3.2 Partial Solutions

Partial Solutions. (PS) have been proposed to explain the solutions produced by EAs for combinatorial optimisation problems [2,3]. The main advantage of PSs is that they are flexible: they are found from a static dataset and their quality metrics can be easily customised. These properties allow for the methodology to be applicable to RS, resulting in the new variant of Partial Solutions for Explainable Recommender Systems (**PS4XRS**).

A PS is a recurring sub-pattern found in high-fitness solutions. For binary problems, PSs are represented by 0, 1, and * (wildcard). For example, the PS [1 * 0 *] matches chromosomes such as [1 0 0 0], [1 1 0 1], and others. The core idea is that large, complex solution can be understood in terms of the PSs they contain. These PSs serve as interpretable indicators of solution quality.

PSs are found through a **multi-objective optimisation** process, where each candidate PS is evaluated on the following objectives:

- **Simplicity**: Favour patterns with more wildcards (*), indicating generality.

- **Mean Fitness**: PSs should occur in solutions with high average fitness.
- **Atomicity**: The non-* variables in the pattern are linked in some way.

Let S be the set of all solutions and s^ψ a candidate PS. A solution $s \in S$ contains s^ψ if it matches all non-* symbols:

$$\text{contains}(s, s^\psi) \iff s_i = s_i^\psi \; \forall \; i \in [1..D] \text{ where } s_i^\psi \neq * \tag{3}$$

We then use $S_{\text{match}} = \{s \in S \mid \text{contains}(s, s^\psi)\}$ to indicate all the matching solutions in the dataset. The three objectives are then computed as:

$$\text{simplicity}(s^\psi) = \left| \{i \in [1..D] \mid s_i^\psi = *\} \right| \tag{4}$$

$$\text{mean\_fitness}(s^\psi) = \sum\nolimits_{s \in S_{\text{match}}} F(s) \, / \, |S_{\text{match}}| \tag{5}$$

$$\text{atomicity}(s^\psi) = \text{avg}\{ \text{MI}(i,j) \mid i < j, \;\; s_i^\psi \neq *, \; s_j^\psi \neq * \} \tag{6}$$

For an optimisation problem, we measure how "linked" variables are by measuring their mutual information (MI in n Eq. (6)). This is discussed in more detail in [2], but in this work it is implemented by measuring the cosine similarity between embedded vectors, as described in Sect. 2.

To discover high-quality PSs, a multi-objective solver is used. Following recommendations from prior work [2], NSGA-II is used [4], which produces a diverse Pareto front of patterns representing different trade-offs between simplicity, fitness, and atomicity.

4   Partial Solutions for Explaining Recommender Systems (PS4XRS)

It is possible to adapt the methodology of PSs to work on the data available in an RS context, with some modifications: pre-processing the RS data, and modifying PSs to suit the RS domain.

4.1   PS4XRS Methodology Summary

The methodology used to produce the explanatory patterns is summarised as follows. A **multi-objective evolutionary algorithm** (NSGA-II) is used to generate patterns that maximise 4 objectives: simplicity, **user count**, mean fitness and (similarity-based) atomicity. The patterns to be evolved are essentially **sets of integers**, where every integer is a **cluster of products**. These **clusters** are obtained by using the cosine similarity as a distance metric, with random item embeddings as cluster centroids.

The patterns are "matched" against user interaction sets relating to the RS data, and the matches are based on a **threshold** t, which can be fixed or part of the "genome" of the patterns (and additionally it can be turned off, so that the entire pattern needs to match). The search operators (sampling, mutation, crossover) can be customised to this task as well, mainly by using the similarities between the clusters of products.

A multi-objective search is executed with a population size of 100 and an evaluation budget of 10000, which was found to be sufficient but will be explored in future research. The end result is a collection of patterns which can then be used as explanations. A summary of the methodology is shown in Fig. 2.

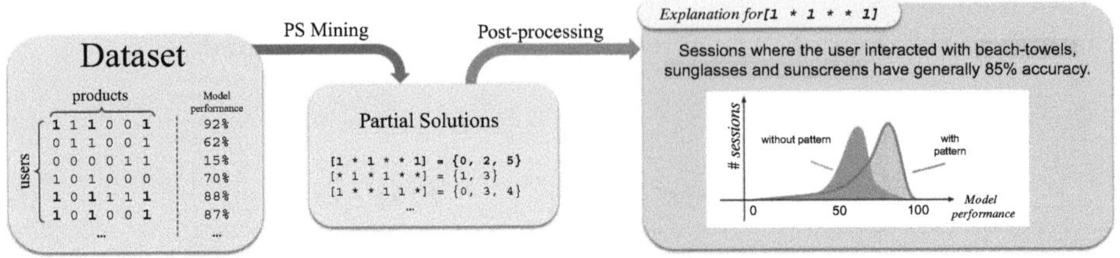

Fig. 2. The dataset of user interactions is mined for PSs, and each PS can be used as an explanation.

4.2   Explanations Produced and Their Utility

It is useful to discuss briefly the explanations produced by our methodology. The **investors** in the RS are interested in knowing when the recommendations are going to be accurate; in other words when the model performs well.

Our system produces explanations in the form: *"When the user interacts with at least n item groups out of this list {A, B, C,...}, then the model accuracy is on average avg% with standard deviation std%. This pattern matches the behaviour of count% users"*.

Provided with this information, the stakeholder can infer:

– What products they should focus on;
– When the model performs well, and if it is worth going into an online bid;
– How well the model is expected to perform.

4.3   Obtaining and Preprocessing the Dataset

We used the **Amazon Book** data set with standard pre-processing and a train-test split. Using train data, we trained a **LightGCN** recommender. We calculated the recommendations on the test data, which was then assessed with several quality measures (further used as *fitness* values) for each user:

– probability (soft-max normalised dot-product) of the target item $[f_1]$,
– dot-product between predicted user interest and closest target item $[f_2]$,
– cosine similarity between predicted user interest and closest target item $[f_3]$,
– hit-rate (for K = 20, 100) $[f_4$ and f_5, respectively],
– recall (for K = 20, 100) $[f_6$ and f_7, respectively].

Clustering. Challenges like extreme sparsity and long-tailed frequency distribution remain open in the field of RS. The users interact only with a few items, several of them seem to be very similar, and many have been interacted with only a few times. To address those challenges in the context of explanations, we use **product clusters** instead of considering each item separately. N centroids for the clusters are picked at random to match the unevenness of the embedding distribution, and the distance of products is based on the cosine similarity of their embeddings. This results in N clusters, each being a set $C_j = j$th cluster $= \{i_{(0)}, i_{(1)}, ...\}$, where $i_{(.)} \in \mathcal{I}$ is an item.

A higher quantity of clusters leads to better granularity in product categories and high (undesirable) sparsity (see Table 1), while less clusters lead to more broad categories of products. Here we opted for a higher quantity of clusters, meaning that the sparsity of the data will need to be taken into consideration.

Determining the Dataset to be Explained. There are various possible datasets that can be generated from the RS, using on different clustering methods and model quality metrics. To determine which one is the best suited for explanations, we based our judgement on the idea that explanations are essentially a prediction model, therefore explanations can only make sense on data where other models have some prediction accuracy.

Therefore we applied some simple models (Linear, Decision Trees, Multi-Layer Perceptrons) to determine which combination works best, and the results are in Table 2. This preliminary analysis showed that the best fitness to use is f_2, and that N $\geq$ 250 is sufficient. We opted to choose N $= 250$, since the results should also be representative of other cluster quantities.

User Interaction History. Having produced N clusters of products, it is now possible to represent the interaction history of each user concisely with N booleans. For each user we find userVector$(u_x) = [v_0...v_{N-1}]$, where $v_j = 1$ if the user u_x interacted with a product from cluster C_j, otherwise $v_j = 0$. For each user there is a **fitness** representing the model's performance for their interaction history (f_2 as defined in Sect. 4.3).

Importantly, this data (vectors and fitness values) is similar to what would be observed in a binary combinatorial optimisation problem: sequences of binary values associated with a fitness. In order to make PSs fully compatible with the RS data, a few adaptations are required first.

Negative Interactions. A traditional PS consists of 0, 1, and * symbols, and in our case a 0 would represent a non-interaction. These are not of interest to the stakeholders (too common, not very informative), so they can be avoided to make only positive interactions appear in explanations. This is implemented by representing PSs as **set of cluster indices** of interactions, such as $\{6, 12, 144\}$ representing *"a user who interacted with product clusters 6, 12 and 144"*.

Table 1. Data sparsity for different quantity of clusters. For every cluster of products, there is a certain probability that a given user has interacted with it.

#Clusters	Probability of interaction
20	47%
50	25%
75	19%
100	16%
125	13%
250	7.7%
500	4.4%
1000	2.4%

Table 2. Top 10 dataset-fitness combinations passed to different models (entries sorted by R^2). LR = Linear Regression, MLP = Multi-Layer-Perceptron, DT = Decision Tree. It shows that f_2 is the best fitness for explanations mining.

Model	Cluster quantity	Fitness	R^2
LR	1000	f_2	0.336
LR	500	f_2	0.33
LR	250	f_2	0.326
LR	100	f_2	0.282
MLP	20	f_2	0.244
LR	50	f_2	0.234
MLP	50	f_2	0.222
LR	20	f_2	0.187
MLP	100	f_2	0.086
LR	250	f_3	0.084

Addition of a Threshold t. The sparsity of the data causes most patterns to be incredibly rare and unusable for a stakeholder. Instead, we can say that a pattern is matched if at least t item categories were interacted with. For example, an explanation of the kind *"At least 3 categories out of this list of 10"* is expected to be applicable 15% of the time.

Formally, this is implemented by modifying the definition of Equation (3):

$$\text{contains}(s, s^\psi) = \sum_{i \in s^\psi} (s_i) \geq t$$

Sensible parameters for t range between 1 and 5, since most user sessions involve less than 5 user interactions (in our dataset). Additionally, $t \leq 2$ is too trivial and is thus not desirable for explanations. In the testing section, we investigate whether it is better to not use the threshold ($t = $ off), to have if fixed during evolution ($t = 3, 4, 5$), or to evolve t for every single pattern ($t = $ auto).

Adding a User Count Objective. While the use of the threshold allows for patterns that are less rare, this does not mean that the evolution process will find commonly occurring patterns, especially since the original methodology for PSs does not prioritise this aspect. To remedy this, we include a new objective which we call **User Count**, that counts how many user sessions are matched by the pattern, defined as $\text{UserCount}(s^\psi) = |S_{\text{match}}|$.

Modifying the Atomicity Metric. The atomicity metric originally used for PSs is not entirely appropriate for this task. It determines how well connected the variables are in the pattern, and while in combinatorial problems this can be statistical linkage, in our context it can be defined in terms of **cosine similarity** between clusters. More specifically, every variable corresponds to a cluster with a centroid, and the similarity of variables (linkage in Eq. 6) is the cosine similarity of the corresponding cluster centroids. Using this metric, the process that generates PSs is incentivised to produce **patterns with similar item clusters**, for interpretability.

4.4   Customising Search Operators for Pattern Evolution

The search operators used to evolve patterns – sampling, mutation, and crossover – can be customised to improve their ability to discover useful patterns. A "traditional" set of operators is defined in [3], and we adapt each of them to better suit our setting.

Algorithm 1. Traditional Sampling

   function SAMPLE
      $s^\psi \leftarrow \emptyset$
      while random() < 0.8 **do**
         $s^\psi \leftarrow s^\psi \cup \{\mathrm{randint}(1, N)\}$
      return s^ψ

Algorithm 2. RS-Sampling

   function SAMPLE
      $s^\psi \leftarrow \emptyset$
      for $i \leftarrow 0$ **to** $N - 1$ **do**
         if random() $< p_i$ **then**
            $s^\psi \leftarrow s^\psi \cup \{i\}$
      return s^ψ

In traditional sampling a pattern is initially "empty", and following a geometric distribution they are filled with random indices (Algorithm 1). **RS-sampling** will use the probability of each cluster being interacted with (here it will be p_i) to determine how often each item appears in PSs initially (Algorithm 2)

Custom Mutation and Crossover via Markov Similarities. To guide modifications based on semantic similarity, we use a Markov-like transition model, where the transition probability between clusters i and j is based on the cosine similarity of their embedded centroids, and constitutes element M_{ij} of a matrix M. We then rescale (to have values between 0 and 1, M_s) and normalise (sum of each row is 1) to construct a Markov transition matrix M_n:

$$M_s = \frac{M - \min(M)}{\max(M) - \min(M)}, \quad M_n[i, :] = \frac{M_s[i, :]}{\sum_j M_s[i, j]}$$

Let $r \in [0, 1]^N$ be the binary vector where $r_i = 1$ for items in s^ψ, 0 otherwise.

Then $r' = r M_n$ gives a similarity-weighted probability that each item should appear in the next version of the pattern. We can then "quantise" r' into a new pattern (i.e., converting from probabilities to a PS): Quantise(r') = $\{i \mid \mathrm{random}() < r_i'\}$.

However, it is hard to control the size of the patterns produced by quantising r'. The average quantity of "successes" from the quantisation is actually the sum of probabilities in r' [7], and we can easily rescale r' to have a desired expected average size. Let this be a, then $r'' = r' \cdot \frac{a}{\sum r'}$.

RS Mutation makes use of these ideas directly, where a mutation is an iteration through the Markov process Algorithm 4 (where $a = \text{len}(s^\psi)$), whereas **Traditional Mutation** performs single-point mutation.

Algorithm 3. Traditional Mutation

> **function** MUTATE(s^ψ)
>> **for** $i \leftarrow 0$ **to** $N - 1$ **do**
>>> **if** random() $< 1/N$ **then**
>>>> **if** $i \in s^\psi$ **then**
>>>>> remove i from s^ψ
>>>>
>>>> **else**
>>>>> add i to s^ψ
>>
>> **return** s^ψ

Algorithm 4. RS-Mutation

> **function** MUTATE(s^ψ)
>> $r \leftarrow$ as_vector(s^ψ)
>> $r' \leftarrow r \cdot M_n$
>> $r'' \leftarrow r' \cdot \frac{\text{len}(s^\psi)}{\sum r'}$
>> **return** Quantise(r'')

Traditional Crossover performs uniform crossover (Algorithm 5). In **RS Crossover** the parents are merged and then split via similarity-based transition, keeping expected size equal to the average parent size (Algorithm 6). To note is that shared elements of the parents are present in both children, and the union of the children will be the same as the union of the parents.

Algorithm 5. Traditional Crossover

> **function** CROSSOVER(a^ψ, b^ψ)
>> **for** $i \leftarrow 0$ **to** $N - 1$ **do**
>>> **if** $(i \in a^\psi) \neq (i \in b^\psi)$ **then**
>>>> **if** random() $< 1/N$ **then**
>>>>> **if** $i \in a^\psi$ **then**
>>>>>> move i from a^ψ to b^ψ
>>>>>
>>>>> **else**
>>>>>> move i from b^ψ to a^ψ
>>
>> **return** a^ψ, b^ψ

Algorithm 6. RS-Crossover

> **function** CROSSOVER(a^ψ, b^ψ)
>> $merged \leftarrow a^\psi \cup b^\psi$
>> $r \leftarrow$ as_vector($merged$)
>> $r' \leftarrow r \cdot M_n$
>> $\ell \leftarrow \frac{|a^\psi| + |b^\psi|}{2}$
>> $r'' \leftarrow r' \cdot \frac{\ell}{\sum r'}$
>> $s^\psi \leftarrow$ Quantise(r'')
>> $t^\psi \leftarrow ((a^\psi \cup b^\psi) \setminus s^\psi) \cup (a^\psi \cap b^\psi)$
>> **return** $son1, son2$

---

5 Evaluation

To validate our approach and present its properties under different settings, we run a number of experiments. We aim to answer the following research questions:

- **RQ1**: Do the PSs generalise on test data?
- **RQ2**: Do the custom operators provide improvement?
- **RQ3**: How do different objectives and thresholds impact the PSs?
- **RQ4**: Are the PSs sufficiently diverse?

5.1 Evaluation Methodology

To access the quality of the obtained PS, we used the following metrics:

- quantity of patterns (prefer higher): the method should produce enough patterns to give a good selection to the stakeholders;
- pattern size (prefer lower, but higher than 2): the patterns should be small enough (in quantity of variables) to be understood. Patterns of 0, 1 or 2 variables are too "trivial" and not very useful;
- coverage (prefer high SD): the proportion of the dataset covered by a PS;
- HR 20, 100 (prefer higher): the averagequality of the sessions matched by the pattern based on the Hit Rate (f_4 and f_5).

Certain metrics should have high SD so that the stakeholder has more choice in which explanations they prefer best (e.g., high coverage lower HR vs low coverage high HR), when picking from the Pareto front of PSs.

For each combination of parameters, the dataset is split into train-test data (80% vs 20%) and the PSs are produced from the training data. Then they are evaluated on the test data using the metrics above. The results are produced by doing 100 runs per parameter combination to ensure statistical significance. The tested combinations are used to show what elements are necessary to obtain satisfactory results.

5.2   Results

Detailed results can be found in the Table 3. The results of the experiments are summarised as follows:

1. The PSs have **consistent results between train and test data**, meaning that they are generalising and are applicable to unseen data;
2. **RS-Mutation is an improvement over the original operator**, but Sampling and Crossover are less impactful;
3. The four objectives and the threshold are essential to get a range of PSs with sufficient coverage and sizes (both in mean and SD);
4. The SD of the pattern size and coverage indicate that there is a wide range of PSs.

Using the 4 objectives, with a threshold and using the new operators is the best approach. The threshold itself can be fixed to a certain value or be evolved, and these yield slightly different results which are generally satisfactory.

Comparing the performance of the algorithm when the **4 objectives** against when one is missing reveals how essential each of them is. For example, [SCMA, $t = 3$, custom operators] results in patterns with 20% coverage on average, whereas the same method but without the user session count objective yields $3\% \pm 1\%$. When the **threshold** is not used ($t = $ off), only patterns of 1 or 2 variables can be found (see the average pattern size) which have coverage between 3 and 15%. When it is enabled, the pattern sizes are on average 20 (although with large SD) and they can be much more general.

Another necessary element is the use of the **specialised mutation operator**, since its removal results in much smaller patterns (average size is 5.62) which have less coverage (average is 9%). The sampling and crossover operators are less impactful, since swapping them for the more "traditional" alternative appears to have no effect.

Table 3. Statistics for different ways of obtaining the PSs for $N = 250$. Here, we test different objectives, match thresholds and search operators. In the objectives, S = Simplicity (pattern size), U = User Count, M = Mean Fitness, A = Atomicity. In threshold, $t =$ auto means that t was evolved, and $t =$ off means that the entire pattern had to match. In the search operators, TS = Traditional Sampling, TM = Traditional Mutation, TC = Traditional Crossover. RS, RM and RC are the customised counterparts. The metrics reported are quantity of patterns per run, pattern size, proportion of sessions matched (coverage), Hit Rate (HR). Means and SD are reported, since having a good spread is in some cases more important that the average itself.

objectives	threshold	Search operators	average #patterns	pattern size mean ± SD	metrics on test			metrics on train		
					coverage mean ± SD	HR 20 mean ± SD	HR 100 mean ± SD	coverage mean ± SD	HR 20 mean ± SD	HR 100 mean ± SD
SUMA	$t = 3$	RS, RM, RC	64.55	20.84 ± 18.64	20% ± 22%	29% ± 4%	61% ± 5%	20% ± 22%	29% ± 3%	61% ± 5%
	$t = 4$		63.62	24.80 ± 17.97	16% ± 17%	30% ± 4%	63% ± 5%	16% ± 17%	30% ± 4%	63% ± 5%
	$t = 5$		66.14	29.56 ± 18.80	13% ± 14%	31% ± 4%	64% ± 5%	13% ± 14%	31% ± 4%	64% ± 5%
	$t =$ auto		72.93	26.69 ± 30.95	53% ± 33%	26% ± 2%	56% ± 3%	53% ± 33%	26% ± 2%	56% ± 3%
UMA	$t = 3$	RS, RM, RC	72.91	124.14 ± 61.17	86% ± 17%	24% ± 1%	55% ± 1%	86% ± 17%	24% ± 1%	55% ± 1%
SMA			23.39	6.30 ± 1.99	3% ± 1%	34% ± 5%	67% ± 6%	3% ± 1%	34% ± 4%	67% ± 5%
SUA			78.09	63.62 ± 46.33	60% ± 33%	26% ± 3%	57% ± 4%	60% ± 33%	26% ± 2%	57% ± 4%
SUM			74.44	43.69 ± 33.00	44% ± 31%	27% ± 3%	58% ± 5%	44% ± 31%	27% ± 3%	58% ± 5%
SUMA		TS, RM, RC	60.63	21.18 ± 20.14	20% ± 23%	29% ± 4%	61% ± 5%	20% ± 23%	29% ± 3%	61% ± 5%
		RS, TM, RC	73.49	5.62 ± 2.37	9% ± 5%	32% ± 3%	65% ± 4%	9% ± 5%	32% ± 3%	65% ± 4%
		RS, RM, TC	62.40	20.45 ± 18.47	20% ± 21%	29% ± 4%	61% ± 5%	20% ± 21%	29% ± 3%	61% ± 5%
SUMA	$t =$ off	RS, RM, RC	51.00	1.70 ± 0.50	10% ± 13%	30% ± 4%	63% ± 6%	10% ± 13%	30% ± 4%	63% ± 5%
UMA			43.43	1.79 ± 0.46	10% ± 14%	30% ± 4%	63% ± 5%	10% ± 14%	30% ± 4%	63% ± 5%
SMA			8.18	1.92 ± 0.41	3% ± 1%	32% ± 7%	64% ± 8%	3% ± 1%	32% ± 6%	64% ± 8%
SUA			8.97	1.89 ± 0.32	15% ± 22%	28% ± 5%	60% ± 7%	15% ± 22%	28% ± 4%	60% ± 6%
SUM			28.32	1.44 ± 0.54	14% ± 16%	31% ± 4%	63% ± 5%	14% ± 16%	31% ± 4%	64% ± 4%
SUMA		TS, RM, RC	49.88	1.68 ± 0.48	10% ± 13%	30% ± 5%	63% ± 6%	10% ± 13%	30% ± 4%	63% ± 5%
		RS, TM, RC	68.96	2.37 ± 0.79	8% ± 10%	32% ± 4%	66% ± 5%	8% ± 10%	32% ± 4%	66% ± 5%
		RS, RM, TC	50.03	1.69 ± 0.50	10% ± 13%	30% ± 4%	63% ± 6%	10% ± 13%	31% ± 4%	63% ± 5%
SMA	$t =$ off	TS, TM, TC	10.43	2.23% ± 0.7%	3% ± 1%	32% ± 5%	65% ± 7%	3% ± 1%	32% ± 5%	65% ± 7%

6   Conclusions

The proposed methodology can generate explanations for an RS dataset which give insight that is useful to stakeholders when adopting the system. The explanations cover a wide range, with a clear trade-off between their generality and model prediction improvement, thanks to the use of **multi-objective search**.

Using the knowledge from the deep learning model encoded in the embedded space allowed us to develop meaningful clustering, evolutionary operators and suitable objectives, and it is likely to be useful for future developments.

Future Research will investigate the relationship between interpretability and predictive power of our system, and investigate methods of generating more sophisticated explanations.

Acknowledgement. This work was supported by the Polish National Science Centre (NCN) under grant OPUS-18 no. 2019/35/B/ST6/04379.

References

1. Bacardit, J., Brownlee, A.E.I., Cagnoni, S., Iacca, G., McCall, J., Walker, D.: The intersection of evolutionary computation and explainable AI. In: Proceedings of GECCO '22'. GECCO '22, pp. 1757–1762. ACM, New York, NY, USA (2022). https://doi.org/10.1145/3520304.3533974
2. Catalano, G.A.P.I., Brownlee, A.E.I., Cairns, D., McCall, J.A.W., Fyvie, M., Ainslie, R.: Explaining a staff rostering problem using partial solutions. In: Bramer, M., Stahl, F. (eds.) SGAI 2024. LNCS, vol. 15447, pp. 179–193. Springer, Cham (2025). https://doi.org/10.1007/978-3-031-77918-3_13
3. Catalano, G.A., Brownlee, A.E.I., Cairns, D., Mccall, J., Ainslie, R.: Mining potentially explanatory patterns via partial solutions. In: Proceedings of GECCO '24. GECCO '24, pp. 567–570. Companion, ACM, New York, NY, USA (2024). https://doi.org/10.1145/3638530.3654318
4. Deb, K., Pratap, A., Agarwal, S., Meyarivan, T.: A fast and elitist multiobjective genetic algorithm: NSGA-II. IEEE Trans. Evol. Comput. **6**(2), 182–197 (2002). https://doi.org/10.1109/4235.996017
5. Ding, W., Abdel-Basset, M., Hawash, H., Ali, A.M.: Explainability of artificial intelligence methods, applications and challenges: a comprehensive survey. Inf. Sci. **615**, 238–292 (2022). https://doi.org/10.1016/j.ins.2022.10.013, https://www.sciencedirect.com/science/article/pii/S002002552201132X
6. He, X., Deng, K., Wang, X., Li, Y., Zhang, Y., Wang, M.: LightGCN: simplifying and powering graph convolution network for recommendation. In: Proceedings of the 43rd International ACM SIGIR Conference on Research and Development in Information Retrieval. SIGIR '20, pp. 639–648. ACM, New York, NY, USA (2020). https://doi.org/10.1145/3397271.3401063
7. Papoulis, A.: Probability, Random Variables, and Stochastic Processes, 2nd edn. McGraw-Hill, New York (1984)
8. Peake, G., Wang, J.: Explanation mining: post hoc interpretability of latent factor models for recommendation systems. In: Proceedings of the 24th ACM SIGKDD International Conference on Knowledge Discovery and Data Mining. KDD '18, pp. 2060–2069. Association for Computing Machinery, New York, NY, USA (2018). https://doi.org/10.1145/3219819.3220072
9. Phillips, P.J., et al.: Four principles of explainable artificial intelligence (2021-09-29 04:09:00 2021). https://doi.org/10.6028/NIST.IR.8312
10. Rendle, S., Freudenthaler, C., Gantner, Z., Schmidt-Thieme, L.: BPR: Bayesian personalized ranking from implicit feedback. In: Proceedings of the Twenty-Fifth Conference on Uncertainty in Artificial Intelligence. UAI '09, pp. 452–461. AUAI Press, Arlington, Virginia, USA (2009)
11. Roeva, O.: Real-World Applications of Genetic Algorithms. Books on Demand, NY (2012)
12. Slowik, A., Kwasnicka, H.: Evolutionary algorithms and their applications to engineering problems. Neural Comput. Appl. **32**(16), 12363–12379 (2020). https://doi.org/10.1007/s00521-020-04832-8

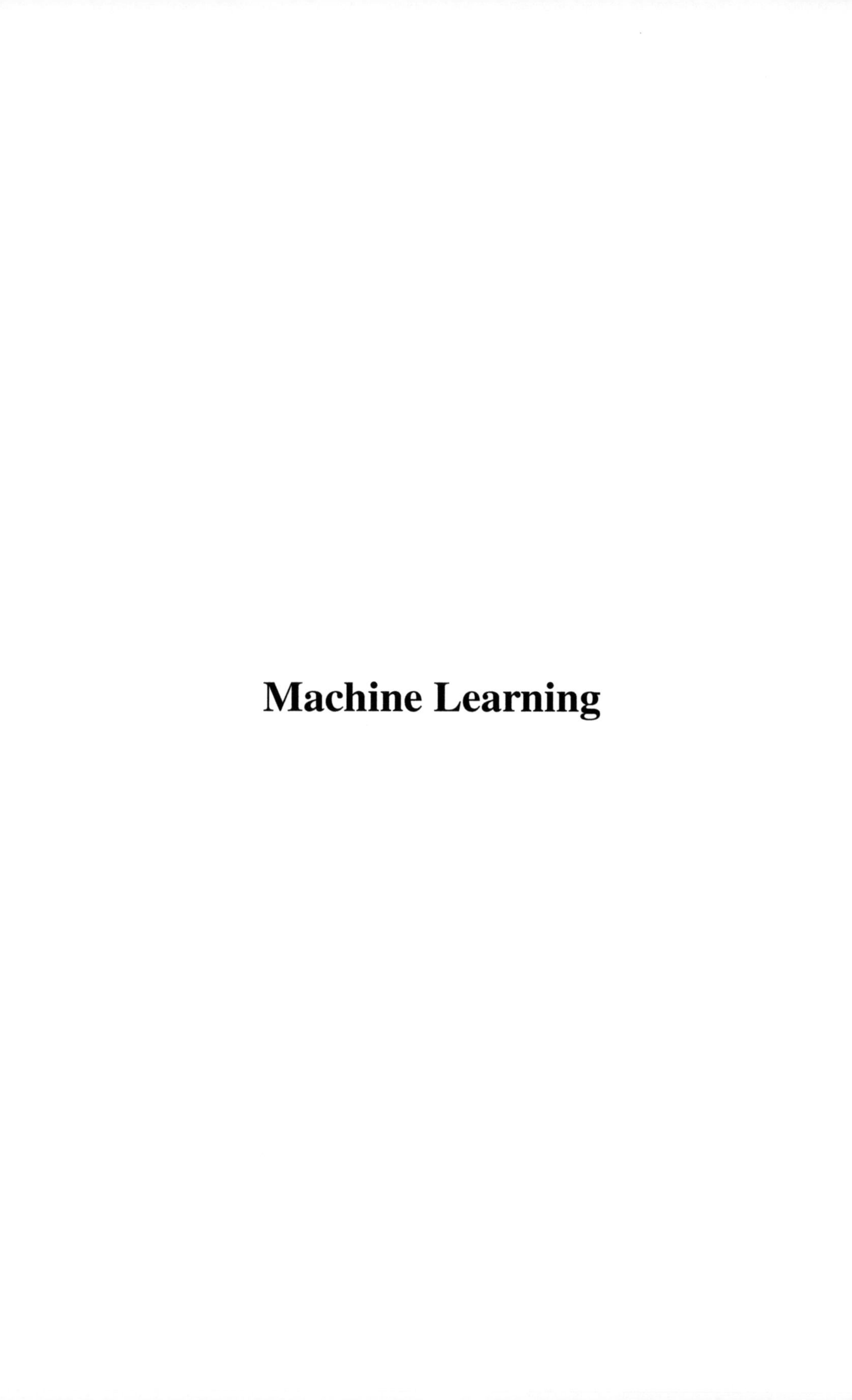

Machine Learning

Soft Actor-Critic Reinforcement Learning for Reactive Current Injection Protocols

Mohana Fathollahi[1,2]([✉])(iD), Antonio Camacho[2](iD), Cecilio Angulo[1,2](iD), and Jerrad Hampton[3](iD)

[1] Intelligent Data Science and Artificial Intelligence Research Centre (IDEAI),
Universitat Politècnica de Catalunya, Barcelona, Spain
`{mohana.fathollahi,cecilio.angulo}@upc.edu`
[2] Automatic Control Department, Universitat Politècnica de Catalunya,
Barcelona, Spain
`antonio.camacho.santiago@upc.edu`
[3] Siemens Energy AG, Barcelona, Spain
`https://ideai.upc.edu/en`, `https://esaii.upc.edu/en`,
`https://www.siemens-energy.com/global/en`

Abstract. Modern power grids are increasingly challenged by the growing reliance on renewable energy sources. Due to their inherent intermittency, these sources can cause voltage fluctuations and phase imbalances, particularly during grid disturbances. Among these perturbations, voltage sags are the most critical ones, occurring within seconds or even milliseconds. A required mitigation strategy involves injecting reactive current into the phase experiencing low voltage. Traditional approaches for determining the appropriate amount of reactive current rely on grid codes, which define the minimum value based on measured voltages; therefore, there is no optimization, nor adaptability to better attend to the grid's needs. In this study, we propose an alternative solution based on Soft Actor-Critic (SAC), a model-free and off-policy reinforcement learning (RL) algorithm which addresses the weaknesses of previous approaches. Simulation results during the inference phase demonstrate that the SAC-based method closely matches the performance of optimization-based approaches, while offering better generalization to unseen data within a fast response time in milliseconds.

Keywords: Reinforcement Learning · Soft Actor-Critic · Low-Voltage Ride-Through · Power Grid · Voltage Sag

1 Introduction

Growing integration of decentralized renewable energy sources, such as solar and wind, into electricity generation, a shift intended to reduce CO_2 emissions, leads to changes in the operation of the electrical grid. Due to their intermittent nature, these sources can give rise to voltage fluctuations and imbalances,

M. Bramer and F. Stahl (Eds.): SGAI-AI 2025, LNAI 16302, pp. 51–65, 2026.
https://doi.org/10.1007/978-3-032-11442-6_4

particularly during grid disturbances [27]. Hence, new challenges emerge to maintaining grid stability and reliability. A notable example occurred on April 28, 2025, when a widespread power outage affected Spain, Portugal, and southern France, which severely disrupted critical infrastructure. At the time, both Spain and Portugal were sourcing approximately 80% of their electricity from solar and wind power [14]. In such low-inertia systems, imbalances must be corrected more rapidly to prevent outages and ensure the continued stability of the grid [9]. Therefore, new approaches should be proposed to make the power grid stable even during disturbances.

Among power system disturbances, voltage sags are the most significant ones, typically lasting from a few milliseconds to a few seconds. They are often caused by short circuits in the power grid, leading to a sudden drop in voltage levels [13]. The ideal system should be able to show Low-Voltage Ride-through (LVRT) capability, that is to remain connected to the power grid during low voltage periods [19]. Therefore, instead of disconnecting during faults, LVRT-capable devices stay online and help to have a stable grid. This method, which is mostly based on the reactive current injection (RCI) protocol [33], not only prevents cascading failures and ensures continuous power system operation during disturbances, but also is a cost-effective solution. RCI is a technology that has been used in electrical power systems to enhance voltage stability and improve power quality by injecting or absorbing reactive power into the grid.

Optimization-based approaches [16] can maintain grid stability during disturbances by determining the appropriate amount of reactive current to inject into the phase experiencing a voltage sag. However, they face several challenges: Firstly, real-time optimization requires significant computational resources, making it impractical for voltage sag, which needs a fast response. Moreover, when optimization is performed offline for various scenarios and stored in a lookup table, it provides limited accuracy for input scenarios not covered in the lookup table. Furthermore, this approach lacks flexibility in adapting to changes in the input space: additional variables, data, or network modifications lead to an entirely new optimization process.

A potential solution is the transition from traditional rule-based methods to data-driven and Artificial Intelligence (AI)-based approaches. The potential of AI methods in overcoming optimization challenges has been demonstrated. AI-based model address the challenge of real-time optimization by replacing costly online computations with fast, low-latency inference models. In addition, the AI-based approach learns the underlying structure or patterns in the data, rather than simply mapping inputs to outputs as a lookup table does. This means that if the AI model successfully captures this structure, it can generalize to unseen data [29], which addresses a key limitation of offline optimization methods. This approach is also more flexible in handling changes in input variables.

A key capability desired in AI-based approaches is effective sequential decision-making in dynamic environments. Reinforcement Learning (RL) provides a powerful framework for this purpose [28], where an agent continuously learns an optimal policy through interaction with the environment by taking actions and receiving feedback in the form of rewards [2]. This inherent adaptability makes it well-suited for managing uncertain conditions in power systems. Furthermore, RL agents can inject reactive current with remarkable speed, outperforming real-time optimization. Our objective is to demonstrate RL's potential, in particular the Soft Actor-Critic (SAC) algorithm, as a strong approach for resolving the limitations found in traditional techniques in RCI protocols.

This article is organized as follows: first, related work in the area is provided; next, a formal problem formulation is set along with the RL environmental setup, especially for the SAC algorithm; implementation and simulation results are then provided showing the performance of our approach; the manuscript concludes with the conclusions.

2 Related Work

Reinforcement Learning (RL) has been applied in different sectors of the power grid, such as energy management, energy routing, demand response, electricity market, operational control, system optimization [36]. Since the primary focus of this study is on voltage control, a summary of relevant studies in this area is provided in this section.

Challenges in operational control for power systems are becoming more complex with the growing integration of renewable energy sources. This is the case in voltage regulation, one of the key areas of operational control, the focus of this study. The literature suggests that RL offers a promising framework by enabling real-time learning and decision-making, even in large-scale systems with limited information [10].

An optimal reactive power support strategy is implemented in [35] to minimize long-term voltage deviations by configuring capacitors. Deep Q-Networks (DQN) are used to determine the optimal configuration of capacitors required to reduce voltage fluctuations. The effectiveness of this approach is demonstrated on a real-world 47-bus[1] distribution network and the IEEE 123-bus test feeder. Similarly, DQN is applied in [6] for voltage control. The agent takes actions based on generator voltage set point adjustment which will affect the system conditions, including active and reactive power flows on transmission lines and transformers, as well as bus voltage magnitudes and phase angles.

In [30], focus is put on minimizing network losses and enhancing voltage quality in power systems with renewable energy integration. It employs the Deep Deterministic Policy Gradient (DDPG) algorithm for reactive power and voltage control. Compared to the traditional Particle Swarm Optimization (PSO) method for voltage and reactive power control, the proposed approach demonstrates slightly better performance and greater efficiency. The approach is tested on different levels of renewable energy penetration and its effectiveness is validated on a 33-bus system.

---

[1] A bus in a power grid represents a central node where different electrical elements such as generators, transformers, and transmission lines-are interconnected, acting as a hub for directing power flow.

Work in [6] is extended in [34] from a single-agent centralized to a multi-agent decentralized control system. A system comprising 200 buses is analyzed and partitioned into six zones, assigned to 3 different agents, using a heuristic method. The multi-agent deep deterministic policy gradient (MADDPG) algorithm is adapted to learn an effective centralized policy from operating data.

The MADDPG algorithm is significantly improved in [4] by incorporating an attention model, allowing it to selectively focus on the most relevant information, which improves scalability and helps to address the challenges of managing multiple agents in complex environments. In this study, each state includes the active load demand, reactive load demand, and active power injection from PV systems. Additionally, the action taken corresponds to the reactive power of a corresponding PV inverter.

Focus in [5] is on reducing voltage deviation while minimizing the active power curtailment of photovoltaic (PV) systems through the application of a multi-agent soft actor-critic (MASAC) approach. Its performance has been compared with other methods on the IEEE 123-node and 342-node systems. The results indicate that MASAC achieves superior voltage regulation with minimal PV curtailment.

In a recent study in this field [7], we presented preliminary work on applying Proximal Policy Optimization (PPO) algorithms to enhance voltage ride-through operations when voltage sag happened. In that study, reference power was not considered, and only the voltage of a single phase was analyzed rather than all three phases. Since a three-phase[2] power system is the backbone of modern power grids, it is critical to consider all three phases.

While injecting the maximum reactive current is an effective strategy for handling voltage drops, it isn't always the optimal solution, especially when considering other factors like reference power. In this study, by leveraging RL techniques, RCI is optimized in conjunction with voltage support and active power maximization during grid faults, aiming to reduce the risk of cascade disconnection yielding to a blackout.

3   Problem Formulation

In this part, the power plant under consideration, the RL environment setup, and the soft actor-critic model are described in detail.

3.1   Power Plant Structure

Main components of a modern power system include power generation units such as traditional power plants and renewable energy sources, inverters, points of common coupling (PCC), and the grid. The single line diagram of the power

---

[2] It delivers power through three alternating currents (AC) that are synchronized and offset by 120°. This configuration provides a more constant and efficient power supply compared to single-phase systems and is ideal for heavy industrial loads due to its inherent efficiency and reliability.

plant is depicted in Fig. 1. In distributed generation systems, inverters export active power from the power source into the grid. In between, a dc-link capacitor helps to balance the power flows. The inverter output is then filtered with an LCL-type filter to remove high-frequency components before connecting to the PCC. Finally, the scheme shows the grid source and an equivalent impedance with resistance R and inductance L.

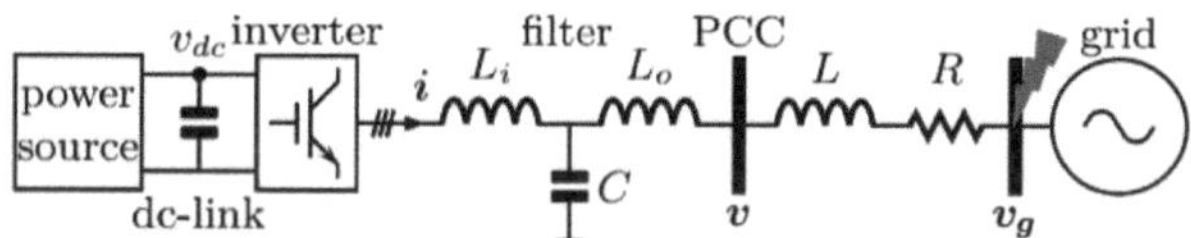

Fig. 1. The single-line diagram of the power plant model [16]. v_{dc}: dc voltage to balance power production in the dc-link capacitor, i: inverter current, L_i and L_o: filter inductors of the inverter, C: capacitor filter, v: voltage at Point of Common Coupling (PCC), L: grid inductance, R: grid resistance, v_g: grid voltage at a distant location.

A key operational challenge arises from faults in the grid. If a fault occurs too close to the power plant or is not quickly cleared by circuit breakers, the plant may need to disconnect to protect its components. However, if the fault is farther away and cleared promptly, the system is expected to remain connected and support grid stability [33]. Huge photovoltaic farms and wind parks are in charge of this service by adding this functionality to the controller of the power converter. In this context, the inverter plays a crucial role to stabilize voltage levels and maintain grid integrity by injecting reactive current during grid faults, a requirement known as fault ride-through (FRT) capability. Once the fault is cleared, the inverter resumes supplying active power. In the following, the RL approach to determine the optimal strategy for RCI is described.

3.2 RL Environment Setup

In a power system experiencing severe voltage disturbance, varying amounts of reactive current are injected into the voltage phases to enhance the voltage support and enable more effective control. To allow RL algorithms to effectively manage this process, the dynamical system is represented by a Markov Decision Process [31] formally defined by the tuple $M = (S, A, p, r)$. Hence, we consider a fully observable environment with continuous state space S and action space A. The state transition probability, $p : S \times A \times S \rightarrow [0, \infty)$, defines the probability of moving to the next state $s_{t+1} \in S$ given the current state $s_t \in S$ and action $a_t \in A$. At each transition, the environment provides an instantaneous reward $r : S \times A \rightarrow [r_{min}, r_{max}]$ related with the goal [24].

The environment, a single-line diagram depicted in Fig. 1, is implemented in MATLAB. Scripts are converted to C++ codes to speed up the process and improve the efficiency of the RL training, developed in Python. The Nanobind library [18] is used to call C++ codes from Python.

A custom Gymnasium environment [3] is designed in Python, so the agent produces actions and receives feedback to improve actions. The most important aspects of this customization include the initialization of the action space, the state space, and the reward structure. During training, each episode begins with a specific generated state. The agent dynamically takes actions to maximize the cumulative reward and the episode ends when the stopping criterion of 2000 timesteps is reached.

The state space comprises the three-phase voltages and the reference power in time t,

$$s_t := (V_{a,t}, V_{b,t}, V_{c,t}, P_{r,t}) \tag{1}$$

where $V_{x,t}$ refers to voltage in phase x and time t, $x = a, b, c$ and $P_{r,t}$ refers to reference power in time t. The original ranges for the three-phase voltages and reference power are $[44, 93]$ volts and $[100, 1400]$ watts, respectively. However, to ensure consistency and improve training stability and efficiency [17], the continuous state space is normalized within the range $[0, 1]$. Specifically, each voltage value is scaled by the nominal voltage of $110V$, and the reference power is normalized by dividing to the maximum reference power, which is $2000W$.

To compensate low voltages in each phase, reactive current is injected as an action,

$$a_t := (I_{qa,t}, I_{qb,t}, I_{qc,t}) \tag{2}$$

for the phases a, b and c in time t. In general, action values range from 0 to 10, where 0 corresponds to no injection of reactive current, and 10 represents the maximum rated current of the inverter. As mentioned in [25], normalizing the action space has a considerable effect on improving the performance of off-policy models. Therefore, the action space has been normalized and first restricted to the interval $[0, 1]$.

To further improve learning efficiency and guide the agent toward feasible and effective solutions, it is important to precisely define the lower bound of the action space with respect to the problem conditions. In Fig. 2, the MRC line represents the Minimum Reactive Current (MRC), which sets the lower bound for I_q. Additionally, the feasible range for the reactive current is shown by the hatched area, indicating that I_q must remain between the MRC and I_{rated}. The usual MRC values for different voltage ranges are,

$$\text{MRC} := \begin{cases} I_q^{\max}, & V < V_{\text{sat}} \\ I_q^{\max} + (V - V_{\text{sat}}) \dfrac{I_q^{\min} - I_q^{\max}}{V_{\text{db}} - V_{\text{sat}}}, & V_{\text{sat}} < V < V_{\text{db}} \\ 0, & V > V_{\text{db}} \end{cases} \tag{3}$$

and the corresponding parameter; saturated voltage v_{sat}, dead band voltage v_{db}, minimum and maximum reactive currents I_q^{min}, I_q^{max} and rated inverted current I_{rated} which all expressed in per unit (p.u.) or normalized form are listed in Table 1.

The agent is addressed to produce actions that make the system near optimal performance, through a reward function. Optimal performance is defined by two

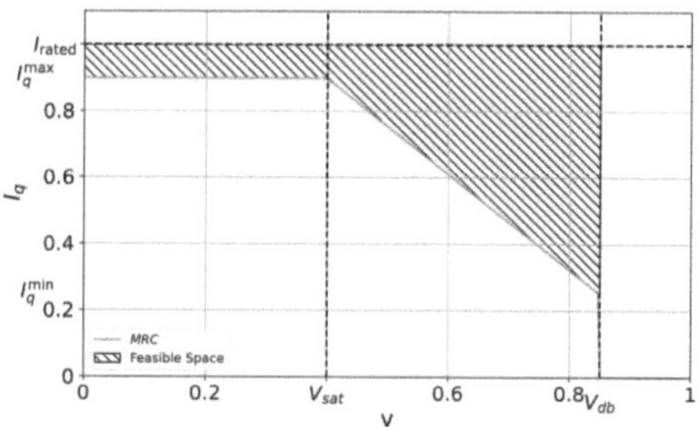

Fig. 2. RCI protocol in grid codes. The orange line represents the Minimum Reactive Current, the hashed area marks the feasible solution space [16] (Color figure online).

Table 1. Nominal parameter values corresponding to the RCI protocol based on p.u. illustrated in Fig. 2.

Quantity	Symbol	Nominal value
low saturation voltage	V_{sat}	0.4 p.u.
low dead band voltage	V_{db}	0.85 p.u.
minimum reactive current	I_q^{min}	0.25 p.u.
maximum reactive current	I_q^{max}	0.90 p.u.
rated inverter current	I_{rated}	1 p.u.

balanced goals to be achieved: (i) inject reactive current to increase the voltage in each phase to a value near to nominal level, and (ii) inject the maximum possible active power p into the grid by tracking the constant reference power P_r, which is generated from sun, while minimizing curtailment during voltage sags. As injecting more power reduces the capability to improve the voltage, and vice versa, a trade-off among goals exists. Moreover, inverters are physically limited in the maximum current injected into the system; hence, both objectives compete for the room to allocate the active and the reactive currents. However, by employing smart strategies, both injected power to the grid and reactive current injection can be precisely allocated to better support the grid during the perturbation.

Therefore, the weighted reward function is composed of several terms,

$$r_t := -\alpha \left((v'_{a,t} - 1)^2 + (v'_{b,t} - 1)^2 + (v'_{c,t} - 1)^2 \right)$$
$$- \beta \left((p_t - P_{r,t})^2 - p_t^2 \right) \tag{4}$$
$$+ \sum_{i \in \{a,b,c\}} \text{penalty}_{i,t}$$

The first three terms, negatively weighted, align with the primary objective of maintaining the voltage in each phase close to the nominal value. After injecting the reactive current, the voltage in phase i is updated to normalized voltage v'_i. To evaluate the quality of the voltage support, the deviation of v'_i from 1 is considered.

The second term is addressing the second goal, which is maximizing the injected active power and minimizing the active power curtailment. Finally, penalties are added for the three phases, which are only applied when the generated reactive current falls below the established threshold or MRC in Fig. 2,

$$\text{penalty}_{i \in \{a,b,c\}, t} := \begin{cases} \gamma(I_{qi,t} - MRC_i), & I_{qi,t} < MRC_i \\ 0, & I_{qi,t} \geq MRC_i \end{cases} \tag{5}$$

Unlike the β parameter, considered constant for all the cases, the parameters α and γ have been fine-tuned for each specific case of training.

3.3 Soft Actor-Critic Algorithm

RL algorithms come in various types, including model-free [7,35,37] and model-based approaches [15,22], as well as off-policy [6,35] and on-policy [1,7,23] methods. Since modeling the environment's dynamics is complex and efficient use of data is important, a model-free, off-policy approach is well suited for this problem. One of these approaches recently highlighted in power systems is the Soft Actor-Critic (SAC) algorithm. During the training phase, two key components are considered: the actor and the critic. The actor receives the system state at time t, denoted as s_t, and selects an action according to a policy $\pi(a_t|s_t)$. Meanwhile, the critic evaluates the quality of the actor's decision by taking the state-action pair, (s_t, a_t) as input and estimating its reward. This value serves as feedback to guide the actor's learning process [21].

The core contribution of the SAC algorithm is the incorporation of entropy regularization into the reward function [11], encouraging broader exploration of the policy space and reducing the risk of premature convergence to suboptimal policies [32]. Hence, the objective function to be maximized is,

$$J(\pi) := \mathbb{E}_{(s_t,a_t) \sim \rho_\pi} \left[r(s_t, a_t) + \alpha \mathcal{H}(\pi(\cdot|s_t)) \right] \tag{6}$$

with

$$\mathcal{H}(\pi(\cdot \mid s)) = \mathbb{E}_{a \sim \pi(\cdot|s)} \left[-\log \pi(a|s) \right] \tag{7}$$

where $r(s_t, a_t)$, represents the reward obtained by taking action a_t in state s_t at time t and $\mathcal{H}(\pi(\cdot \mid s_t))$, denotes the entropy of the policy π, encouraging stochasticity in action selection. The parameter α is a temperature coefficient that controls the trade-off between reward maximization and entropy regularization [12]. Additionally, the SAC algorithm uses replay buffer, which improves sample efficiency and enhances its ability to generalize across different scenarios, which helps to prevent overfitting [8].

Once the training phase is completed and the actor network has learned an effective policy, the model transitions to the inference phase for real-time decision-making. During the inference phase of the SAC model, only the actor network is required to generate actions based on the observed states, simplifying the runtime architecture and reducing computational time during execution. As depicted in the diagram in Fig. 3, the actor network is held simple, a feed-forward

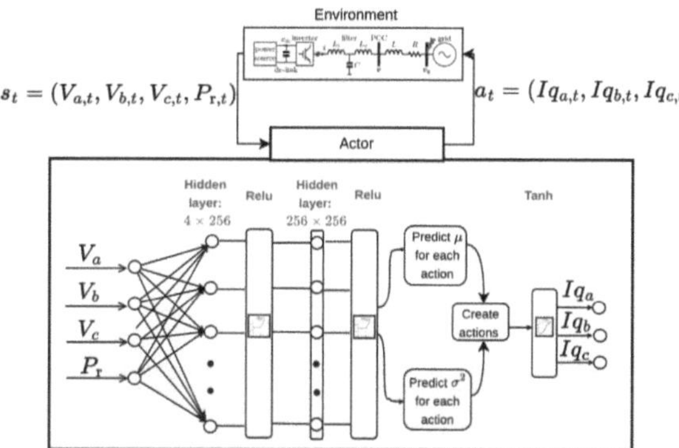

Fig. 3. Schematic diagram of the actor model in prediction of actions or reactive currents based on a feedforward network and the state of environment, power grid, at time t as its input.

neural network with 2 hidden layers, 256 neurons each, and ReLU activation functions. The action is generated based on the Gaussian distribution, $\mathcal{N}(\mu, \sigma^2)$. Finally, a *tanh* activation function is applied in the last layer to normalize the output within a bounded range.

4   Implementation and Results

In this section, the different training and testing implemented experiments are described along with the obtained results.

4.1   Training

As previously discussed, the voltage range varies between 44 and 93, while P_r ranges from 100 to 1400. Effective policy learning is sensitive to the scale of the reward signal, making it essential to characterize how rewards for optimal actions vary across different voltage levels and values of P_r. Our analysis showed that reward values associated with optimal actions depend on specific combinations of voltage and P_r. To improve model convergence, we grouped voltage and P_r pairs with similar reward ranges [20], and used these groupings to define specialized configurations for the custom Gymnasium environment, resulting in multiple (five) tailored scenarios summarized in Table 2.

P_r range was divided into two intervals: $[100, 650]$ and $[700, 1400]$. For the first interval, voltage was split into two segments; for the second, into three. As shown, the optimal reward is negative when the voltage lies within the range $[44, 60]$, and it gradually becomes positive for voltages greater than 60. In the last column, the normalized action range for each scenario has been determined by evaluating Eq. 3 for the upper bound of the voltage range in each scenario.

Table 2. Configuration of each environment based on voltage range, P_r range, reward range and normalized action range.

Environment Id	Voltage range	P_r range	Reward range	Normalized action range
Env1	[44, 60]	[100, 650]	[−1.5, 1.5]	[0.69, 1]
Env2	[60, 93]	[100, 650]	[0, 3.5]	[0.26, 1]
Env3	[44, 60]	[700, 1400]	[−8, 0]	[0.69, 1]
Env4	[60, 76]	[700, 1400]	[1.5, 5.5]	[0.48, 1]
Env5	[76, 93]	[700, 1400]	[2.5, 11]	[0.26, 1]

It ensures that most feasible solutions are captured, while a penalty is applied to discourage actions that fall below the threshold.

The SAC model has been trained on these five environments by employing the Stable-Baselines3 library [26], a set of reliable implementations of RL algorithms in PyTorch, with default hyperparameters. Multiple agents have been independently trained for around 1.2 million time steps in these five gym environments. Hyperparameters for the reward function, α and γ, are tuned for each scenario. After evaluating, non-exhaustively, multiple hyperparameter configurations, the following combinations have yielded the highest reward: env1 ($\alpha = 1.5, \gamma = 1.5$), env2 ($\alpha = 1, \gamma = 0.1$), and env3, env4, and env5, sharing a common set of values, ($\alpha = 1, \gamma = 1.5$). In all cases, β was fixed at 0.1.

The evolution of the cumulative reward for all scenarios is provided in Fig. 4. As observed, the reward values on y-axis differ between environments, reflecting the varying reward range for each environment based on Table 2. Despite fluctuations, the agent's training mostly exhibits upward trend in cumulative rewards, demonstrating effective learning and policy improvement. In addition, the inclusion of the entropy term improves both the stability of exploration and the convergence to high-reward values. Training lasts approximately one day, performed in parallel using five NVIDIA GeForce RTX 3090 GPUs, each equipped with 24,576 MiB of memory and Python's multiprocessing library. In contrast, brute-force optimization may require several days to find optimal values.

4.2   Testing

The performance of the trained models is compared with the optimization-based method or ground truth introduced in [16]. In addition, the execution time of the RL inference model is also presented.

Performance. The RL model was evaluated against the ground truth using a test set comprising 25% of the environment's data, excluded from training. To ensure fair comparison, its output was scaled to the reactive current range from 0 to 10 A. The evaluation metric employed is the mean absolute error (MAE), and the comparison between the two approaches is carried out in two aspects of predicting reactive currents across the three phases: (i) MAE (%) relative to

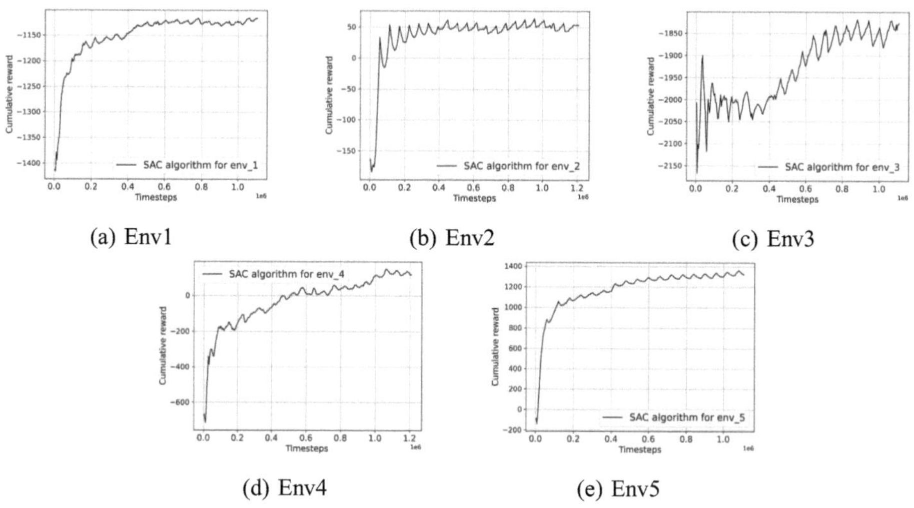

(a) Env1   (b) Env2   (c) Env3

(d) Env4   (e) Env5

Fig. 4. Evolution of cumulative reward over timesteps for different environments, RL agent converges after approximately 1.2 million timesteps.

the reference active power, as presented in Table 3, and (ii) MAE (%) under different environments, as presented in Table 4. According to Table 3, the RL model exhibited the largest deviation from the ground truth, approximately

Table 3. MAE (%) comparison between the optimization and RL approaches with respect to varying P_r values for phases a, b, and c.

$P_r(w)$	$MAE : I_{qa}$	$MAE : I_{qb}$	$MAE : I_{qc}$
100	2.6	2.1	4.2
200	0.6	0.8	2.9
300	0.6	0.2	0.2
400	1.9	1.2	1.3
500	1.7	0.7	0.9
600	2.0	0.5	1.2
700	9.7	3.2	6.8
800	6.3	3.4	5.2
900	5.5	4.9	5.0
1000	3.1	4.4	3.0
1100	0.3	1.8	0.7
1200	0.3	0.3	0.2
1300	0.7	1.0	1.3
1400	1.1	1.0	1.6

Table 4. MAE (%) comparison between the optimization and RL approaches with respect to environment for phases a, b, and c.

Env Id	$MAE : I_{qa}$	$MAE : I_{qb}$	$MAE : I_{qc}$
Env1	1.28	0.87	2.68
Env2	1.68	1.02	1.17
Env3	4.33	4.80	3.98
Env4	2.21	2.69	2.56
Env5	3.69	0.28	2.57

9.7%, at $P_\mathrm{r} = 700$ in phase a. From Table 4, it can be observed that Env2 yields the lowest error, while Env3 results in the highest error. Although the observed errors are not critical and the system demonstrates improved baseline performance, future work will focus on further reducing these errors.

Execution Time. The execution time for the RL inference model was measured in MATLAB R2023b on a system equipped with an Intel® Core™ i7-1355U CPU and 16 GB of RAM. The execution time includes the following steps: normalizing the input state, selecting the appropriate inference model based on the current state, predicting the unscaled action for each voltage phase, and scaling the predicted actions to fit within the valid action space. The execution time of the RL inference model, measured over 20 samples, had an average, maximum, and standard deviation of 0.089, 0.099, and 0.0063 s, respectively, with no significant variation observed across different environments. Having in mind that the shortest voltage sags have a duration of 0.2 s, this is a valid value for real-time response.

5   Conclusion

Recently, the vulnerability of power grids has increased, particularly due to the growing penetration of renewable energy sources in electricity supply. A notable example of this vulnerability is the power outage that affected Spain and Portugal for several hours in April 2025 and impacted critical infrastructure. This paper proposes an RL-based approach to take smart action and to mitigate the effects of voltage sags occurring within fractions of a second. We benchmarked the proposed method against a traditional optimization-based voltage control strategy, which served as the ground truth in this study [16]. The results showed that the RL agent achieved comparable voltage regulation performance while significantly outperforming the online optimization approach in terms of response time. Compared to the offline optimization method, the RL agent also demonstrated stronger generalization capabilities, particularly when exposed to unseen scenarios. In addition, the RL-based approach is more flexible and adaptive to dynamic changes in the system's state.

As future work, the proposed approach can be improved in two lines. First, improving model performance in predicting reactive currents. Moreover, the prediction or execution time can be reduced by converting five inference models to one model and further tuning hyperparameters to reduce the MAE error.

Acknowledgments. This work is supported by Siemens Energy and the Universitat Politècnica de Catalunya under the agreement TSI-100930-2023-5, but "Siemens Energy AI Chair. Energy sustainability for a decarbonized Society 5.0" and by I+D+i PID2021-122835OB-C21 research project through MCIN/AEI/ 10.13039/501000011033 and FEDER "Una manera de hacer Europa".

References

1. Murugesan, A., Durgadevi, K., Contractor, D., Rathod, Y.: Machine learning-driven intelligent voltage control in renewable-rich grids. J. Renew. Energy Syst. (2025). Graph-based MARL likely uses on-policy PG methods like PPO. https://www.sciencedirect.com/science/article/abs/pii/S0378779625004602
2. Barto, A.G., Sutton, R.S., Watkins, C.: Learning and Sequential Decision Making, vol. 89. University of Massachusetts Amherst, MA (1989)
3. Brockman, G., et al.: OpenAI Gym. arXiv preprint arXiv:1606.01540 (2016)
4. Cao, D., Hu, W., Zhao, J., Huang, Q., Chen, Z., Blaabjerg, F.: A multi-agent deep reinforcement learning based voltage regulation using coordinated PV inverters. IEEE Trans. Power Syst. **35**(5), 4120–4123 (2020)
5. Cao, D., et al.: Data-driven multi-agent deep reinforcement learning for distribution system decentralized voltage control with high penetration of PVs. IEEE Trans. Smart Grid **12**(5), 4137–4150 (2021)
6. Diao, R., Wang, Z., Shi, D., Chang, Q., Duan, J., Zhang, X.: Autonomous voltage control for grid operation using deep reinforcement learning. In: 2019 IEEE Power & Energy Society General Meeting (PESGM), pp. 1–5. IEEE (2019)
7. Fathollahi, M., Camacho Santiago, A., Velasco, M., Martí, P., Angulo Bahon, C., Hampton, J.D.: Improving voltage ride-through procedures in distributed generation systems by reinforcement learning. In: Tallón-Ballesteros, A. (ed.) Frontiers in Artificial Intelligence and Applications, pp. 274 – 277. IOS Press (2024). https://doi.org/10.3233/FAIA240448
8. Fedus, W., et al.: Revisiting fundamentals of experience replay. In: International Conference on Machine Learning, pp. 3061–3071. PMLR (2020)
9. Fernández-Guillamón, A., Gómez-Lázaro, E., Muljadi, E., Molina-García, Á.: Power systems with high renewable energy sources: a review of inertia and frequency control strategies over time. Renew. Sustain. Energy Rev. **115**, 109369 (2019)
10. Glavic, M., Fonteneau, R., Ernst, D.: Reinforcement learning for electric power system decision and control: past considerations and perspectives. IFAC-PapersOnLine **50**(1), 6918–6927 (2017)
11. Haarnoja, T., Tang, H., Abbeel, P., Levine, S.: Reinforcement learning with deep energy-based policies. In: International Conference on Machine Learning, pp. 1352–1361. PMLR (2017)
12. Haarnoja, T., et al.: Soft actor-critic algorithms and applications. arXiv preprint arXiv:1812.05905 (2018)
13. Heine, P., Pohjanheimo, P., Lehtonen, M., Lakervi, E.: A method for estimating the frequency and cost of voltage sags. IEEE Trans. Power Syst. **17**(2), 290–296 (2002)
14. Horton, H.: What caused the blackout in Spain and Portugal and did renewable energy play a part? (2025). http://bit.ly/4ew5oFW
15. Hossain, R.R., et al.: Efficient learning of voltage control strategies via model-based deep reinforcement learning (2022). https://arxiv.org/abs/2212.02715
16. Iñiguez, J.I., Duarte, J.N., Camacho, A., Miret, J., Castilla, M.: Voltage support provided by three-phase three-wire inverters with independent reactive phase-current injection. IEEE Trans. Industr. Electron. **71**(10), 11806–11816 (2024)

17. Ioffe, S., Szegedy, C.: Batch normalization: accelerating deep network training by reducing internal covariate shift. In: International Conference on Machine Learning, pp. 448–456. PMLR (2015)
18. Jakob, W.: nanobind: tiny and efficient C++/Python bindings (2022). https://github.com/wjakob/nanobind
19. Joshi, J., Swami, A.K., Jately, V., Azzopardi, B.: A comprehensive review of control strategies to overcome challenges during LVRT in PV systems. IEEE Access **9**, 121804–121834 (2021)
20. Li, L., Walsh, T.J., Littman, M.L.: Towards a unified theory of state abstraction for MDPs. AI&M **1**(2), 3 (2006)
21. Lowe, R., Wu, Y.I., Tamar, A., Harb, J., Pieter Abbeel, O., Mordatch, I.: Multi-agent actor-critic for mixed cooperative-competitive environments. Adv. Neural Inf. Process. Syst. **30** (2017)
22. Oldeen, J., Sharma, V.: Reinforcement learning for grid voltage stability with FACTS. Master's thesis, University of Uppsala (2020). https://uu.diva-portal.org/smash/get/diva2:1447070/FULLTEXT01.pdf
23. Petrusev, A., Putratama, M.A., Rigo-Mariani, R., Debusschere, V., Reignier, P., Hadjsaid, N.: Reinforcement learning for robust voltage control in distribution grid under uncertainties (2023, unpublished manuscript). Uses two-stage RL with PPO (on-policy) and TD3PG. https://www.researchgate.net/publication/365485928_Reinforcement_learning_for_robust_voltage_control_in_distribution_grids_under_uncertainties
24. Puterman, M.L.: Markov decision processes. In: Handbook of Markov Decision Processes, vol. 2, pp. 331–434 (1990)
25. Raffin, A.: Getting SAC to work on a massive parallel simulator: an RL journey with off-policy algorithms. araffin.github.io, February 2025. https://araffin.github.io/post/sac-massive-sim/
26. Raffin, A., Hill, A., Gleave, A., Kanervisto, A., Ernestus, M., Dormann, N.: Stable-baselines3: reliable reinforcement learning implementations. J. Mach. Learn. Res. **22**(268), 1–8 (2021)
27. Schmietendorf, K., Peinke, J., Kamps, O.: On the stability and quality of power grids subjected to intermittent feed-in. arXiv preprint arXiv:1611.08235 (2016)
28. Silver, D., Singh, S., Precup, D., Sutton, R.S.: Reward is enough. Artif. Intell. **299**, 103535 (2021)
29. Soldati, P., Ghadimi, E., Demirel, B., Wang, Y., Gaigalas, R., Sintorn, M.: Design principles for model generalization and scalable AI integration in radio access networks. IEEE Commun. Mag. (2024)
30. Sun, Y., et al.: Optimization methods for optimal power flow problems in distribution networks: a brief review. In: 2023 8th Asia Conference on Power and Electrical Engineering (ACPEE), pp. 1400–1406. IEEE (2023)
31. Sutton, R.S., Barto, A.G.: Reinforcement Learning: An Introduction, 2nd edn. The MIT Press (2018). http://incompleteideas.net/book/the-book-2nd.html
32. Sutton, R.S., Barto, A.G., et al.: Reinforcement Learning: An Introduction, 2nd edn., vol. 1, no. 2, p. 25. MIT Press Cambridge (2018)
33. Tsili, M., Papathanassiou, S.: A review of grid code technical requirements for wind farms. IET Renew. Power Gener. **3**(3), 308–332 (2009)
34. Wang, S., et al.: A data-driven multi-agent autonomous voltage control framework using deep reinforcement learning. IEEE Trans. Power Syst. **35**(6), 4644–4654 (2020)

35. Yang, Q., Wang, G., Sadeghi, A., Giannakis, G.B., Sun, J.: Two-timescale voltage control in distribution grids using deep reinforcement learning. IEEE Trans. Smart Grid **11**(3), 2313–2323 (2019)
36. Zhang, Z., Zhang, D., Qiu, R.C.: Deep reinforcement learning for power system applications: an overview. CSEE J. Power Energy Syst. **6**(1), 213–225 (2019)
37. Zhou, Y., Zhou, L., Shi, D., Zhao, X.: Coordinated frequency control through safe reinforcement learning (2022). https://arxiv.org/abs/2202.00530

Car Drag Coefficient Prediction from 3D Point Clouds Using a Slice-Based Surrogate Model

Utkarsh Singh[1]([envelope]) [ID], Absaar Ali[1] [ID], and Adarsh Roy[2] [ID]

[1] Delhi Technological University, Shahbad Daulatpur, Delhi 110042, India
{utkarshsingh_me21b16_52,absaarali_co20b2_24}@dtu.ac.in
[2] Indian Institute of Technology, Hauz Khas, Delhi 110016, India
adarsh.roy@iitdalumni.com

Abstract. The automotive industry's pursuit of enhanced fuel economy and performance necessitates efficient aerodynamic design. However, traditional evaluation methods such as computational fluid dynamics (CFD) and wind tunnel testing are resource intensive, hindering rapid iteration in the early design stages. Machine learning-based surrogate models offer a promising alternative, yet many existing approaches suffer from high computational complexity, limited interpretability, or insufficient accuracy for detailed geometric inputs. This paper introduces a novel lightweight surrogate model for the prediction of the aerodynamic drag coefficient (C_d) based on a sequential slice-wise processing of the geometry of the 3D vehicle. Inspired by medical imaging, 3D point clouds of vehicles are decomposed into an ordered sequence of 2D cross-sectional slices along the stream-wise axis. Each slice is encoded by a lightweight PointNet2D module, and the sequence of slice embeddings is processed by a bidirectional LSTM to capture longitudinal geometric evolution. The model, trained and evaluated on the DrivAerNet++ dataset, achieves a high coefficient of determination ($R^2 > 0.9528$) and a low mean absolute error ($MAE \approx 6.046 \times 10^{-3}$) in C_d prediction. With an inference time of approximately $0.025\,\mathrm{s}$ per sample on a consumer-grade GPU, our approach provides fast, accurate, and interpretable aerodynamic feedback, facilitating more agile and informed automotive design exploration.

Keywords: Drag Coefficient Prediction · Automotive Aerodynamics · Surrogate Modeling · Slice-Based Model · Point Clouds · Deep Learning

1 Introduction

Aerodynamic efficiency is paramount in the automotive industry, directly impacting fuel economy, emissions, vehicle stability, and the range of electric vehicles. Reducing aerodynamic drag, quantified by the drag coefficient (C_d), is a primary design goal. However, conventional evaluation methods, namely Computational Fluid Dynamics (CFD) and wind tunnel testing, present significant

M. Bramer and F. Stahl (Eds.): SGAI-AI 2025, LNAI 16302, pp. 66–79, 2026.
https://doi.org/10.1007/978-3-032-11442-6_5

bottlenecks. CFD simulations, while detailed, are computationally expensive and time consuming, with typical runs taking hours to days and requiring substantial high-performance computing (HPC) resources [6,16]. Wind tunnel tests, though crucial for validation, involve costly facility operation and lengthy model fabrication times [7], limiting their use in the early iterative design phases. These constraints are a hindrance to rapid exploration of the design space.

To overcome these limitations, few machine learning surrogate models have emerged as a promising alternative for rapid aerodynamic prediction [1]. These models learn a complex mapping from vehicle geometry to aerodynamic properties from data generated by high-fidelity simulations. Once trained, they can predict C_d in seconds or milliseconds. However, existing ML surrogates face several challenges. Voxel-based methods, using 3D Convolutional Neural Networks (CNNs), suffer from resolution bottlenecks and can lose fine geometric details [10]. Projection-based methods, which convert 3D shapes into 2D images for 2D CNNs [14], can suffer from information loss due to occlusions or choice of viewpoints and may lack physical interpretability. Point cloud-based methods, such as PointNet [12] and its variants [2,13], operate directly on 3D surface points but often treat points permutation-invariantly, potentially missing crucial directional cues inherent in aerodynamic flow. More recent graph neural networks [4] and transformer-based architectures [8,9,15], while powerful, can be computationally intensive and complex. For instance, TripNet [2] uses triplane representations and achieves high accuracy, but still involves sophisticated geometric processing. Many of these models, particularly complex deep learning architectures, act as "black boxes," offering limited insight into how specific geometric features influence aerodynamic performance.

This paper proposes a novel lightweight, sequential and interpretable approach for C_d prediction. Our core idea is to represent the 3D vehicle geometry as an **ordered** sequence of 2D cross-sectional slices along the primary (streamwise) direction of airflow, analogous to how MRI or CT scans represent 3D anatomical structures. This structured representation explicitly captures the front-to-rear evolution of the vehicle's shape, which is fundamental to its aerodynamic behavior. Each 2D slice, represented as a set of points, is processed by our lightweight **PointNet2D** module (our 2D adaptation of PointNet [12]) to extract local geometric features. The sequence of these per-slice feature embeddings is then fed into a **Bidirectional Long Short-Term Memory (LSTM)** network, which models the dependencies and progression of shape features along the vehicle's length. Finally, a Multi-Layer Perceptron (MLP) regresses the C_d from the LSTM's aggregated representation. This approach offers several advantages:

- **Efficiency:** By processing 2D slices, it avoids the high computational cost of full 3D convolutions or global attention mechanisms on large point clouds.
- **Interpretability:** The model directly captures the flow-aware, front-to-rear progression of the vehicle's shape. This intuitive approach provides a basis for attributing drag contributions to specific longitudinal sections of the vehicle.

We validate our model using the large-scale DrivAerNet++ dataset [5], which provides high-fidelity CFD-computed C_d values for thousands of parametric car models. Our initial results demonstrate competitive accuracy with state-of-the-art methods, but with significantly reduced computational complexity and enhanced interpretability.

The remainder of this paper is organized as follows: Sect. 2 details the dataset, data pre-processing techniques, and, the proposed model architecture. Section 3 presents the experimental results, including performance comparisons and training dynamics. Section 4 discusses the implications of these results, limitations, and comparisons. Finally, Sect. 5 concludes the paper and outlines future research directions.

2   Methods

This section details the dataset, pre-processing steps, the architecture of our proposed slice-based sequential model, and the training procedure.

2.1   Dataset

We utilize the DrivAerNet++ dataset [5], a large-scale multi-modal car aerodynamics dataset. It contains over 8,000 parametric car models, spanning various body styles (fastback, notchback, estateback, SUV) and configurations (e.g., with/without detailed underbodies, rotating wheels). For each model, the dataset provides a 3D mesh, a point cloud representation, and the ground truth drag coefficient (C_d) computed using Reynolds-Averaged Navier-Stokes (RANS) $k-\omega$ SST CFD simulations. We use the point cloud representation provided via the PaddleScience platform [11]. After filtering for complete data, our working dataset comprises 7,713 unique car geometries. We adopt the following split: 5398 samples for training, 1115 for validation, and 1200 for testing. This choice ensures a fair comparison with prior studies, which also evaluated on a 1200-sample test set. The point clouds are consistently oriented with the X-axis along the streamwise direction, Y-axis laterally, and Z-axis vertically.

2.2   Data Pre-processing

The core of our pre-processing pipeline is the conversion of each 3D car point cloud into an ordered sequence of 2D cross-sectional slices.

Cross-Sectional Slicing. Each 3D point cloud (typically $\sim$100,000 points) is sliced along the primary flow direction (X-axis).

1. **Number of Slices (S):** We chose $S = 80$ slices. This value was empirically found to provide a good balance between capturing sufficient geometric detail along the car's length and maintaining a manageable sequence length for the LSTM. Too few slices would blur important local features, while too many would increase computational cost and redundancy.

2. **Binning:** For each car, the range of x coordinates (x_{min}, x_{max}) is determined. This range is then divided into S equal bins. The width of each bin w is $(x_{max} - x_{min})/S$.
3. **Projection to YZ-Plane:** All points within the i-th bin (that is, $x \in [x_{min}+ (i-1)w, x_{min} + iw))$ are projected onto the YZ-plane by discarding their x coordinate. This results in a set of 2D representing the cross-sectional profile of the car at that longitudinal station.

This process yields a sequence of $S = 80$ slices, each represented by a variable number of 2D points (y, z). The overall slicing strategy is conceptually depicted in Fig. 1, while Fig. 2 visualizes the sequence for a sample vehicle, showcasing the detailed evolution of its cross-sectional shape from front to rear.

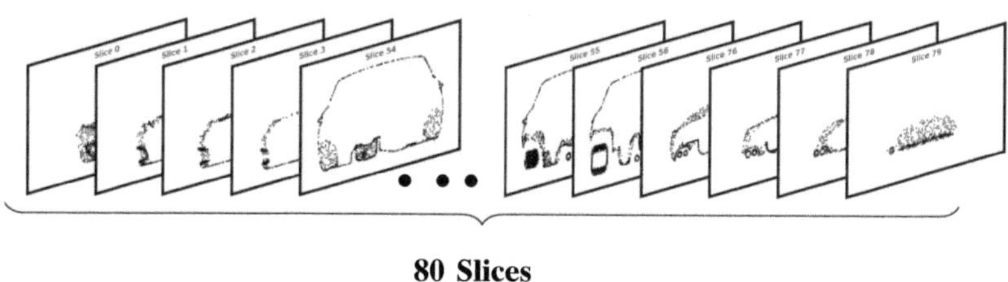

80 Slices

Fig. 1. Illustration of 80 streamwise (x-axis) slices extracted from a car's point cloud. This isometric side view demonstrates how dense slicing captures detailed shape variation from front to back.

Padding and Masking. The number of points in each 2D slice varies. To create fixed-size tensors for batch processing, we pad each slice.

- We determined the maximum number of points observed in any single slice in the entire dataset, M_{max} (found to be 6,500).
- Each 2D slice is zero-padded to have M_{max} points. Thus, each slice becomes a tensor of shape $(M_{max}, 2)$.
- A binary mask tensor of shape (S, M_{max}) is created to identify real points and ignore padded entries. Although the mask is available, PointNet2D's global max-pooling is generally robust to zero-padded points, provided features are non-negative.

The final input representation for each car is a tensor of shape $(S, M_{max}, 2)$, i.e., $(80, 6500, 2)$.

2.3   Model Architecture

Our proposed model consists of three main components: a slice-level feature extractor (PointNet2D), a sequence model (Bi-LSTM), and a regression head (MLP). The complete model architecture is depicted in Fig. 3.

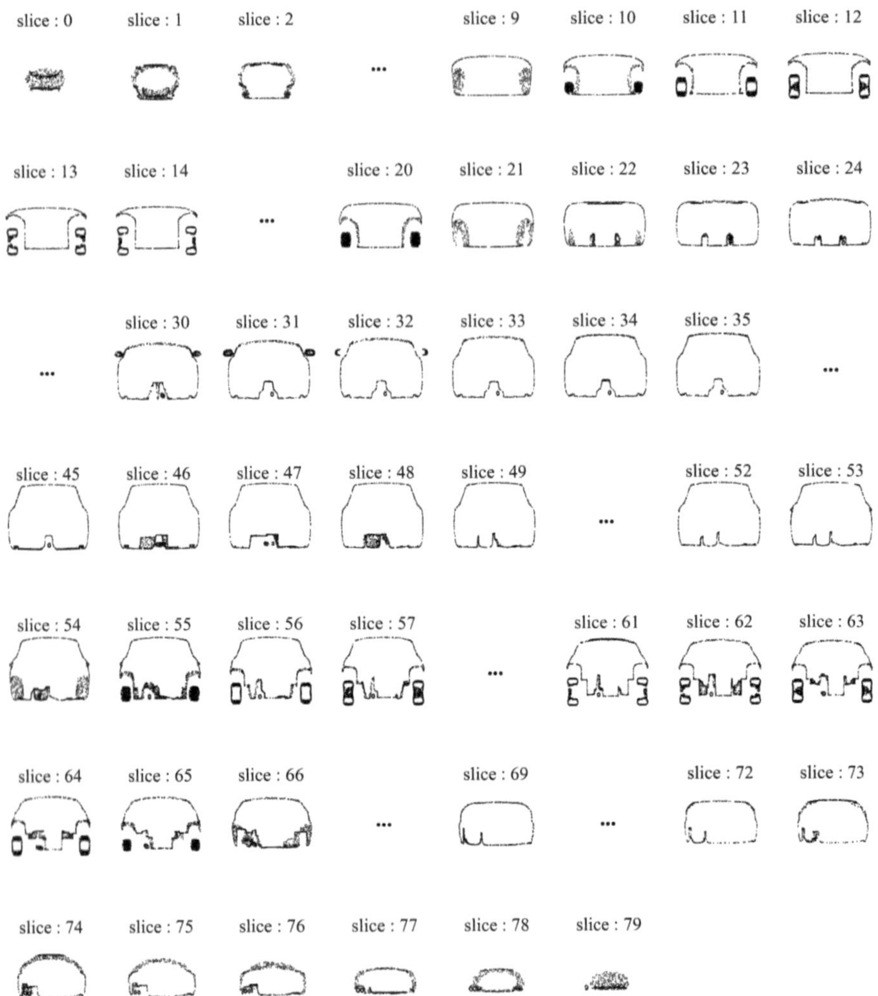

Fig. 2. Visualization of 80 streamwise (X-axis) cross-sectional slices extracted from a vehicle's point cloud. This grid displays the individual 2D point sets, sequentially arranged to highlight the progression of the vehicle's contour from front to back, as used for feature extraction.

Slice-Level Feature Extraction: PointNet2D. Each 2D slice (a set of M_{max} points in $\mathbb{R}^2$) is processed independently by our PointNet2D module. This module is a simplified adaptation of the original PointNet [12] tailored for 2D point sets and designed to be lightweight. As shown in Fig. 3, the PointNet2D module consists of a series of shared 1D convolutional layers (effectively acting as MLPs applied to each point) followed by a global max-pooling operation.

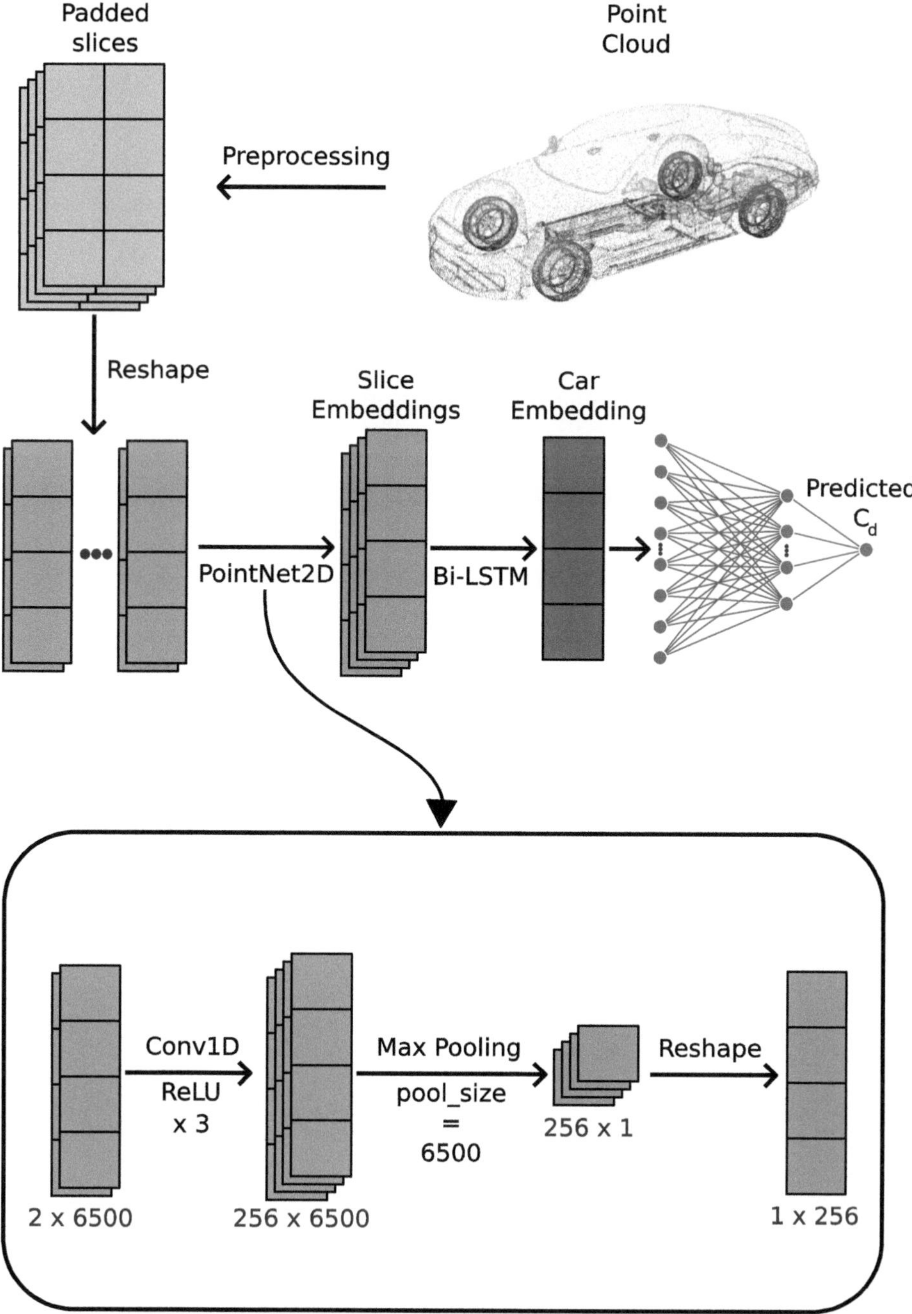

Fig. 3. Complete model architecture of the proposed sequential slice-based drag prediction model. 3D point clouds are sliced. Each slice is encoded by PointNet2D. The sequence of embeddings is processed by a Bi-LSTM and an MLP regresses C_d.

- Input: A slice of shape $(M_{max}, 2)$.
- Layers: Three 1D convolutional layers with kernel size 1. Channel sizes are $2 \to 32 \to 64 \to d_e = 256$. Each convolution is followed by a ReLU activation function.
- Max-Pooling: A global max-pooling operation is applied across the M_{max} points dimension to obtain a single feature vector of dimension $d_e = 256$ for each slice. This ensures permutation invariance for points within a slice.

The output for each car, after this stage, is a sequence of 80 embeddings, resulting in a tensor of shape $(80, 256)$.

Sequence Modeling: Bi-Directional LSTM. The sequence of $S = 80$ slice embeddings (each of dimension $d_e = 256$) is processed by a Bidirectional Long Short-Term Memory (Bi-LSTM) network. The Bi-LSTM captures dependencies and contextual information from both forward (front-to-rear) and backward (rear-to-front) directions of the slice sequence.

- Layers: 2 Bi-LSTM layers.
- Hidden Dimension: Each LSTM direction has a hidden state dimension of 256.
- Output: The final hidden states from the forward and backward passes of the last Bi-LSTM layer are concatenated to form a single feature vector representing the entire vehicle. For a hidden dimension of h=256, this process creates a 512-dimensional car-level embedding.

Regression Head: MLP. The 512-dimensional car embedding from the Bi-LSTM is fed into a Multi-Layer Perceptron (MLP) to regress the scalar C_d value.

- Layers: The MLP consists of three fully connected layers: $512 \to 256 \to 64 \to 1$.
- Activations: ReLU activations are used after the first two layers. A dropout layer with a rate of 0.3 is applied after the first ReLU for regularization.
- Output: A single scalar value representing the predicted C_d.

The total number of trainable parameters in the model is approximately 2.79 million. A summary of the model's component-wise structure, derived directly from its PyTorch implementation, is as follows:

```
CdPredictor(
  (pointnet): PointNet2D(
    (slice_encoder): Sequential(
      (0): Conv1d(2, 32, kernel_size=(1,), stride=(1,))
      (1): ReLU(inplace=True)
      (2): Conv1d(32, 64, kernel_size=(1,), stride=(1,))
      (3): ReLU(inplace=True)
      (4): Conv1d(64, 256, kernel_size=(1,), stride=(1,))
```

```
      (5): ReLU(inplace=True)
    )
  )
  (sequential_encoder): LSTMSliceEncoder(
    (lstm): LSTM(256, 256, num_layers=2, batch_first=True,
                dropout=0.2, bidirectional=True)
  )
  (regressor): CdRegressor(
    (net): Sequential(
      (0): Linear(in_features=512, out_features=256, bias=True)
      (1): ReLU()
      (2): Dropout(p=0.3, inplace=False)
      (3): Linear(in_features=256, out_features=64, bias=True)
      (4): ReLU()
      (5): Linear(in_features=64, out_features=1, bias=True)
    )
  )
)
```

2.4   Training Details

- **Loss Function:** We use the Smooth L1 Loss (Huber Loss), as defined in Eq. 1, which is less sensitive to outliers than Mean Squared Error and provides smooth gradients.

$$\mathcal{L}(y, \hat{y}) = \begin{cases} 0.5(y - \hat{y})^2, & \text{if } |y - \hat{y}| < \beta \\ \beta(|y - \hat{y}| - 0.5\beta), & \text{otherwise} \end{cases} \tag{1}$$

We use $\beta = 1.0$.
- **Optimizer:** Adam optimizer with an initial learning rate of 1×10^{-4}.
- **Batch Size:** A batch size of 4 was used due to GPU memory constraints with the large M_{max}.
- **Epochs:** The model was trained for 100 epochs, and the best model was selected based on the highest R^2 score on the validation set.
- **Hardware:** A single NVIDIA RTX 4060 Laptop GPU.

3   Results

This section presents the performance of our proposed slice-based sequential model. We first define the evaluation metrics, then provide quantitative comparisons with state-of-the-art methods, discuss computational efficiency, and finally analyze training dynamics and error distributions.

3.1   Evaluation Metrics

We use standard regression metrics to evaluate model performance:

- **Mean Squared Error (MSE):** $\frac{1}{N}\sum_{i=1}^{N}(\hat{y}_i - y_i)^2$.
  Measures the average squared difference between predicted and true values.
- **Mean Absolute Error (MAE):** $\frac{1}{N}\sum_{i=1}^{N}|\hat{y}_i - y_i|$.
  Measures the average absolute difference, less sensitive to outliers than MSE.
- **Coefficient of Determination (R^2):** $1 - \frac{\sum_{i=1}^{N}(\hat{y}_i-y_i)^2}{\sum_{i=1}^{N}(y_i-\bar{y})^2}$.
  Represents the proportion of variance in the dependent variable that is predictable from the independent variables. An R^2 of 1 indicates perfect prediction.
- **Maximum Absolute Error (MaxAE):** $\max_i |\hat{y}_i - y_i|$. Indicates the worst-case prediction error.

For these metrics, y_i is the true C_d, $\hat{y}_i$ is the predicted C_d, $\bar{y}$ is the mean of true C_d values, and N is the number of samples.

3.2   Quantitative Performance

We compare our model's performance on the DrivAerNet++ test set (1200 samples) against several published surrogate models. Table 1 summarizes these results. Our PointNet2D + BiLSTM model achieves an R^2 of 0.9528 and an MAE of 6.046×10^{-3}.

Table 1. Quantitative comparison of drag–prediction models on the DrivAerNet++ test set.

Model	Dataset subset	MSE (10^{-5})	MAE (10^{-3})	MaxAE (10^{-2})	R^2
PointNet2D+BiLSTM (Ours)	DrivAerNet++ (1200)	**6.50**	**6.046**	**4.50**	0.9528
TripNet [2]	DrivAerNet++ (1200)	9.10	7.17	7.70	**0.957**
RegDGCNN [4][a]	DrivAerNet++ (1200)	14.20	9.31	12.79	0.641
PointNct [12][a]	DrivAcrNct｜｜ (1200)	14.90	9.60	12.45	0.643

[a] Reported in [5].

Our model demonstrates performance comparable to the state-of-the-art TripNet on DrivAerNet++ in terms of R^2, while significantly outperforming earlier methods like RegDGCNN and PointNet. The low MAE indicates that, on average, our predictions are very close to the true C_d values.

3.3   Computational Efficiency

Our model is lightweight, with 2.79 million parameters, and achieves the average inference time of 0.025 s per sample on an NVIDIA GeForce RTX 4060 Laptop GPU demonstrating the model's suitability for real-time feedback on consumer-grade hardware.

3.4   Training Dynamics and Error Analysis

The model was trained for 100 epochs in a single, end-to-end process. Figure 4a shows the Smooth L1 training loss curve, indicating steady convergence. Figure 4b displays the validation R^2 score per epoch, with the best performance achieved at epoch 68, which was selected as the final model.

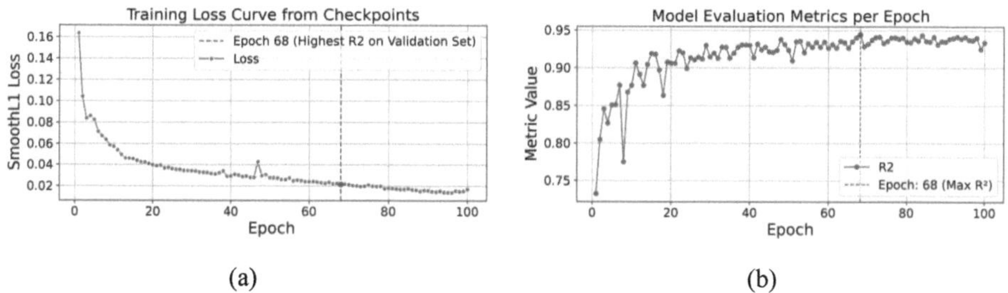

(a)   (b)

Fig. 4. Training dynamics: (a) Training loss curve. (b) Validation R^2 score over epochs. Best validation R^2 was achieved at epoch 68.

To analyze the prediction quality on the test set, Fig. 5 presents a scatter plot of predicted versus true C_d values and a histogram of prediction errors.

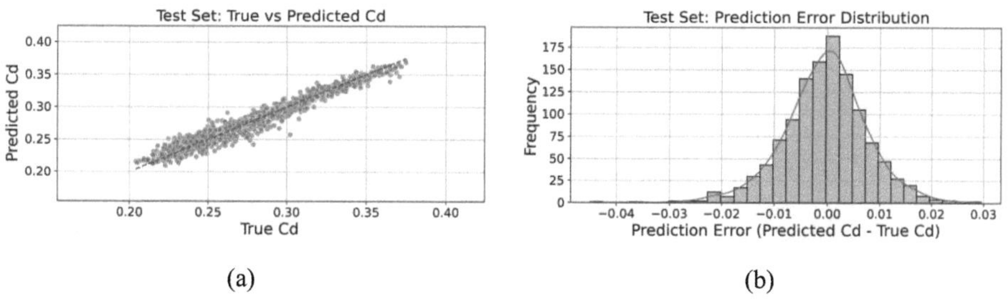

(a)   (b)

Fig. 5. Test set performance analysis: (a) Scatter plot showing strong correlation between predicted and true C_d values. (b) Histogram of prediction errors, centered near zero with small spread.

The scatter plot (Fig. 5a) shows a tight clustering of points around the $y = x$ line, indicating high agreement between the predictions and the ground truth. The error histogram (Fig. 5b) is unimodal and centered close to zero, with the majority of errors falling within a narrow range (e.g., $\pm 0.015 C_d$). This demonstrates that the model generalizes well to unseen data and does not exhibit significant systemic bias. The MaxAE of 0.045 indicates that even the largest errors are within a reasonable range for early-stage design guidance.

4   Discussion

The results presented in Sect. 3 demonstrate that our proposed sequential slice-based model achieves high accuracy and efficiency for aerodynamic drag prediction. The R^2 value of 0.9528 on the DrivAerNet++ test set signifies that the model captures over 95% of the variance in drag coefficients, performing comparably to more complex state-of-the-art methods such as TripNet [2], while using a simpler architecture and fewer parameters. The low MAE of approximately 6.046×10^{-3} indicates that the average prediction error is very small, making it a reliable tool for shortlisting design candidates.

The effectiveness of the slice-based approach can be attributed to its ability to explicitly model the geometric evolution of the vehicle's shape along the **streamwise axis**, a progression that is critical to drag formation. Aerodynamic drag is highly sensitive to how the cross-sectional area and shape change from the front of the vehicle to the rear. By processing an ordered sequence of 2D slices in this direction, the PointNet2D module learns salient features from each local cross-section, and the Bi-LSTM integrates this information to learn the impact of these **progressive changes**. This sequential analysis is key; slicing in other directions, such as at right angles to the flow, would fail to capture this **crucial front-to-back narrative**, as each slice would contain parts of the vehicle's front, middle, and rear, thereby losing the causal geometric information beneficial for drag prediction. This limitation is also found in methods that treat the point cloud as an unordered set.

A key advantage of our model is its computational efficiency. With an inference time of ∼0.025 s per sample on a consumer-grade GPU, it is substantially faster than traditional CFD and many complex deep learning surrogates (e.g., those based on 3D convolutions or full transformers on point clouds). This speed is critical for early-stage design, enabling engineers to rapidly evaluate numerous design variations, perform sensitivity analyses, and conduct shape optimization interactively. Furthermore, the relatively low parameter count contributes to faster training times and reduced risk of overfitting, especially when datasets might be limited for very specific vehicle types not yet covered by large public benchmarks.

Compared to other approaches, our method strikes a balance between performance and interpretability. While global 3D methods like PointNet or DGCNNs can be powerful, their permutation-invariant nature or complex graph structures can make it difficult to understand which parts of the geometry contribute most to the prediction. Our slice-based sequence allows, at least conceptually, for an investigation into how individual slices or segments of slices influence the final C_d prediction through analysis of LSTM activations or attention mechanisms if a transformer were used for sequence modeling. This potential for enhanced interpretability, by linking drag to longitudinal sections, can provide designers with more actionable feedback.

Despite its strengths, the proposed method has limitations.

1. **Inter-slice Information Loss:** While 80 slices provide good resolution, some fine 3D geometric details that do not significantly alter the 2D pro-

file of any single slice but exist between slice planes or are inherently 3D in nature (e.g., complex underbody channels, small winglets with specific orientations not aligned with slices) might not be fully captured. The projection onto the YZ plane also means that 3D curvature within a slice's thickness is lost.

2. **Surface-only Scalar Prediction:** The current model predicts only the scalar C_d value and does not provide information about pressure or velocity fields on the vehicle surface or in the surrounding flow. Such field predictions are valuable for detailed aerodynamic analysis and are offered by some more complex surrogate models [2,3].

3. **Absence of Explicit Physics Priors:** The model is purely data-driven. It does not inherently enforce physical laws like conservation of mass or momentum. This could lead to less robust predictions for out-of-distribution shapes not well-represented in the training data.

4. **Fixed Number of Slices:** The choice of $S = 80$ slices was based on empirical observation. An adaptive slicing strategy, allocating more slices to regions with higher geometric variation, could improve performance or efficiency but would also introduce additional complexity.

The broader impact of such a fast and accurate surrogate model is the potential to democratize aerodynamic analysis in the early stages of automotive design. It allows for more extensive design space exploration, leading to potentially more aerodynamically efficient vehicles developed in shorter timeframes and at lower costs.

5   Conclusion

This paper introduced a lightweight and efficient neural network architecture for predicting automotive aerodynamic drag coefficients (C_d) from 3D vehicle point clouds. Our novel approach transforms the 3D geometry into an ordered sequence of 2D cross-sectional slices along the streamwise axis. These slices are individually encoded using a PointNet2D module, and their sequential geometric evolution is captured by a bi-directional LSTM, with a final MLP regressing the C_d.

Trained and evaluated on the large-scale DrivAerNet++ dataset, our model achieved a coefficient of determination (R^2) of 0.9528 and a mean absolute error (MAE) of 6.046×10^{-3}. These results are competitive with more complex state-of-the-art surrogate models, demonstrating the efficacy of the slice-based sequential representation. A key advantage of our method is its computational efficiency, with an inference time of approximately 0.025 s per vehicle on a consumer-grade hardware and a modest parameter count of 2.79 million. This enables rapid aerodynamic feedback, facilitating extensive design iteration and optimization in the early conceptual phases of vehicle development. The inherent structure of the model, focusing on longitudinal geometric progression, also offers potential for enhanced interpretability compared to global "black-box" 3D models.

Future work will focus on several avenues. Enhancing slice encoding with more sophisticated 2D shape descriptors or exploring advanced sequence models like transformers could further improve accuracy. Extending the model to predict surface pressure distributions or even simplified flow fields would provide richer aerodynamic insights. Investigating adaptive slicing techniques and incorporating physics-informed neural network principles could enhance robustness and accuracy, particularly for out-of-distribution geometries. Ultimately, integrating such fast and interpretable surrogate models into interactive CAD tools holds the promise of significantly accelerating and improving aerodynamic design in the automotive industry.

Disclosure of Interests. The authors have no competing interests to declare that are relevant to the content of this article.

References

1. Akasaka, K., Chen, F., Teraguchi, T.: Surrogate model development for prediction of car aerodynamics using machine learning. Nissan Tech. Rev. **89**, 79–84 (2022). https://www.nissan-global.com/EN/TECHNICALREVIEW/PDF/NISSAN_TECHINICAL_REVIEW_89_En_ALL.pdf. Accessed 08 Sept 2025
2. Chen, Q., Elrefaie, M., Dai, A., Ahmed, F.: TripNet: learning large-scale high-fidelity 3D car aerodynamics with triplane networks. arXiv preprint (2025). https://doi.org/10.48550/arXiv.2503.17400
3. Choy, C., Kamenev, A., Kossaifi, J., et al.: Factorized implicit global convolution for automotive computational fluid dynamics prediction. arXiv preprint (2025). https://doi.org/10.48550/arXiv.2502.04317
4. Elrefaie, M., Ahmed, F., Dai, A.: DrivAerNet: a parametric car dataset for data-driven aerodynamic design and graph-based drag prediction. In: ASME 2024 International Design Engineering Technical Conferences and Computers and Information in Engineering Conference, November 2024. https://doi.org/10.1115/DETC2024-143593
5. Elrefaie, M., Morar, F., Dai, A., Ahmed, F.: DrivAerNet++: a large-scale multimodal car dataset with computational fluid dynamics simulations and deep learning benchmarks. In: Thirty-Eighth Conference on Neural Information Processing Systems Datasets and Benchmarks Track (2024). https://doi.org/10.48550/arXiv.2406.09624
6. Ferrari, S., Pipolo, D., Fontanesi, S.: An automated computational fluid dynamics workflow for simulating the internal flow of race car radiators. Fluids **8**(7), 202 (2023). https://doi.org/10.3390/fluids8070202
7. Ford Motor Company: Ford invests $200M in new wind tunnel facility. Press Release (2017). https://www.motorauthority.com/news/1108886_ford-invests-200m-in-new-wind-tunnel-facility. Accessed 08 Sept 2025
8. He, J., Luo, X., Wang, Y.: DrivAer transformer: a high-precision and fast prediction method for vehicle aerodynamic drag coefficient based on the DrivAerNet++ dataset (2025). https://doi.org/10.48550/arXiv.2504.08217
9. Jiang, J., Li, G., Jiang, Y., Zhang, L., et al.: TransCFD: a transformer-based decoder for flow field prediction. Eng. Appl. Artif. Intell. **123**, 106340 (2023). https://doi.org/10.1016/j.engappai.2023.106340

10. Liu, Z., Tang, H., Lin, Y., Han, S.: Point-voxel CNN for efficient 3D deep learning. In: Advances in Neural Information Processing Systems, vol. 32 (2019). https://doi.org/10.48550/arXiv.1907.03739
11. PaddleScience Contributors: DrivAerNet++ PaddleScience documentation (2025). https://paddlescience-docs.readthedocs.io/zh-cn/latest/zh/examples/drivaernetplusplus/#drivaernet. Accessed 12 May 2025
12. Qi, C.R., Su, H., Mo, K., Guibas, L.J.: PointNet: deep learning on point sets for 3D classification and segmentation. In: Proceedings of the IEEE Conference on Computer Vision and Pattern Recognition (CVPR), pp. 652–660 (2017). https://doi.org/10.1109/CVPR.2017.16
13. Qi, C.R., Yi, L., Su, H., Guibas, L.J.: PointNet++: deep hierarchical feature learning on point sets in a metric space. In: Advances in Neural Information Processing Systems, vol. 30, pp. 5099–5108 (2017). https://proceedings.neurips.cc/paper/7095-pointnet-deep-hierarchical-feature-learning-on-point-sets-in-a-metric-space.pdf
14. Song, J., et al.: Data-driven car drag prediction with depth and normal renderings. J. Mech. Des. **146**(5), 051714 (2024). https://doi.org/10.1115/1.4068104
15. Xiang, H., Ma, Y., Dai, Z., Wang, C., Zhang, B.: AeroDiT: diffusion transformers for Reynolds-Averaged Navier-Stokes simulations of airfoil flows. arXiv preprint (2024). https://doi.org/10.48550/arXiv.2412.17394
16. Zacks Equity Research: ANSS sets CFD simulation record using AMD GPUs. Online Article (2025). https://www.nasdaq.com/articles/anss-sets-cfd-simulation-record-using-amd-gpus-frontier-supercomputer. Accessed 08 Sept 2025

A Reinforcement Learning Environment for Job Shop Scheduling with Tool Management

Reshma Maharjan[✉], Per-Arne Andersen, and Lei Jiao

Department of ICT, University of Agder, Kristiansand, Norway
{reshma.maharjan,per.andersen,lei.jiao}@uia.no

Abstract. The Job Shop Scheduling Problem (JSSP) is a well-known challenge in operations research and computer science, widely applied in manufacturing. However, classic formulations often neglect practical tool management aspects such as tool compatibility, changeover time, and slot limitations. This paper introduces an extended formulation, namely JSSP with tool management (JSSP-TM), which explicitly incorporates these tool-related constraints. We model the problem as a Markov Decision Process (MDP) and develop a simulation environment to enable Reinforcement Learning (RL) solutions. Several RL-based methods are explored, including Q-learning with a custom reward function, Stable-Baselines3 algorithms such as Proximal Policy Optimization (PPO), Deep Q-Network (DQN), and Advantage Actor-Critic (A2C), together with traditional heuristic-based solutions. Experimental results show that PPO achieves the best results in terms of makespan and average machine utilization in the test case, demonstrating its potential in solving complex, tool-aware scheduling problems.

Keywords: Job Shop Scheduling · Reinforcement Learning · Q-Learning · Tool Management · Scheduling Optimization

1 Introduction

The Job Shop Scheduling Problem (JSSP) is a classic NP-hard optimization challenge in operations research and computer science, attracting continued interest due to its complexity and real-world relevance [6]. In a typical job shop environment, a set of jobs must be processed on a set of machines, where each job comprises a sequence of operations, each with specific machine requirements and processing times. The main objective of the classic JSSP is to identify the most efficient sequence of operations for each machine, with the goal of minimizing key performance metrics, particularly total completion time (makespan).

To study JSSP, it is essential to formulate the JSSP mathematically, which enables a systematic representation of the problem's constraints, objectives, and decision variables, providing a solid foundation to analyze the problem and identify high-quality solutions. Foundational studies such as [1,4,11] modeled the

M. Bramer and F. Stahl (Eds.): SGAI-AI 2025, LNAI 16302, pp. 80–93, 2026.
https://doi.org/10.1007/978-3-032-11442-6_6

scheduling problems as all-integer programs, which utilized binary variables to capture item-machine assignments, integer variables for time tracking, and linear constraints to handle complex temporal relationships and resource limitations. Formulating the problems deepens the understanding of the problem structure and supports the development of effective solutions [10].

Recent studies have also explored using mathematical formulations as a foundation for machine learning-based approaches, particularly those involving neural networks (NN) and reinforcement learning (RL). In these frameworks, the problem is first structured using classical scheduling constraints and objectives and then addressed by learning models. For RL, it often involves reformulating the problem into a format suitable for learning, such as a sequential decision-making process within the mathematical framework of Markov Decision Processes (MDP). For the JSSP, which is typically modeled using conventional constraints, a solution method has been proposed that integrates Artificial Neural Networks (ANN) with Genetic Algorithms (GA) to solve the JSSP [13]. Similarly, a neural network scheduler has been developed that is trained on optimal solutions generated from a mathematical formulation solved via GA [12]. These approaches preserve the structure and logic of classical formulations while harnessing the generalization power of neural models, effectively bridging the gap between exact modeling and data-driven optimization.

Despite these advances, an important practical aspect remains underexplored in JSSP: tool management. In machining environments, tools must be mounted on machines before operations can begin. Each tool has specific compatibility requirements, and tool changes introduce time overheads that impact overall efficiency. Moreover, the limited number of tool slots on machines necessitates frequent unloading and replacement, adding layers of complexity that are typically ignored in conventional JSSP models. As a result, many classical problem formulations and the corresponding solutions may fall short when applied in realistic production settings.

To address this gap, we extend the traditional JSSP to incorporate tool-related constraints, defining the JSSP with Tool Management (JSSP-TM). This formulation captures machine-tool compatibility, limited tool slot capacity, and tool switching times. Building on this extended formulation, we implemented a simulation environment suitable for testing RL algorithms. This contributes not only to more realistic modeling but also to the advancement of intelligent, adaptive scheduling strategies. The main contributions of this work include:

1. A formal definition of JSSP-TM, incorporating tool compatibility constraints and tool switching durations.
2. A simulation environment of the JSSP-TM, enabling the application of RL algorithms.
3. A comparison of various RL solutions within the environment, which validates its functionality and highlights the efficiency of the algorithms.

Notation: A set is denoted as $\mathcal{X}$. Bold uppercase letters denote matrices, bold lowercase letters represent column vectors, and non-bold lowercase letters denote scalars. $[\boldsymbol{x}]_i$ is the i-th entry of vector $\boldsymbol{x}$, and $[\boldsymbol{X}]_{i,j}$ is the (i, j)-th entry of matrix $\boldsymbol{X}$.

2 Problem Formulation

This section formally defines the JSSP-TM by introducing the sets, parameters, decision variables, and constraints used in the mathematical model. The goal is to optimize scheduling decisions while considering machine capabilities, tool constraints, and precedence relationships.

The JSSP-TM extends the classic JSSP with additional tool-related components and constraints. Let $\mathcal{J} = \{J_1, J_2, \ldots, J_I\}$ represents a set of jobs, where each job $J_i \in \mathcal{J}$, for $i = 1, 2, \ldots, I$, consists of a sequence of operations $O_{i,1} \to O_{i,2} \to \ldots \to O_{i,h_i}$ that must be executed in order. Here h_i is the total number of operations for the i-th job.

Each job operation is defined within the set $\mathcal{O} = \{O_{i,j} \mid i \in \{1, 2, \ldots, I\}, j \in \{1, 2, \ldots, h_i\}\}$, where $O_{i,j}$ denotes the j-th operation of job J_i. A set of machines is denoted by $\mathcal{M} = \{M_1, M_2, \ldots, M_K\}$, where each machine $M_k \in \mathcal{M}$, for $k = 1, 2, \ldots, K$, can process operations with machine-dependent processing times.

In traditional JSSP, each machine is equipped with a single tool and is capable of performing only a specific task. However, in modern industrial settings, machines are often designed with multiple tool slots, allowing them to carry and utilize various tools to perform a broader range of operations. In this work, we extend the conventional JSSP to include machines with multiple tool slots, as detailed in the following paragraphs. Let $b_k \in \mathbb{N}$ represent the maximum number of tool slots on machine M_k. Furthermore, each machine is assumed to be equipped with a dedicated tool station.

Each operation requires a machine from the set $\mathcal{M}$ and may also require one or more tools from the toolset to be executed. The processing time of an operation $O_{i,j}$ on machine M_k is denoted by $p_{i,j,k} \in \mathbb{R}_+$. Moreover, each (i,j)-th operation is associated with a set of eligible machines, denoted by $\bar{\mathcal{M}}_{i,j} \subseteq \mathcal{M}$. If $\bar{\mathcal{M}}_{i,j} = \{M_k\}$, then the operation can only be processed on machine M_k.

Let $\mathcal{L} = \{L_1, L_2, \ldots, L_N\}$ denote the set of all available tools that can be used by machines to perform operations. For each machine $M_k \in \mathcal{M}$, the subset $\mathcal{L}_{M_k} \subset \mathcal{L}$ denotes the tools that are compatible with the k-th machine, while $\mathcal{L}_{O_{i,j}, M_k} \subseteq \mathcal{L}_{M_k}$ represents the tools required to perform a specific operation $O_{i,j}$ on the k-th machine. In practical scenarios, it is obvious that it requires a certain time to change the tools equipped in a machine with the other one. To address this, the machine M_k is also associated with a tool change time matrix $\boldsymbol{\Psi}_k \in \mathbb{R}^{(N+1) \times (N+1)}$, where $[\boldsymbol{\Psi}_k]_{i,0}$ represents the time to remove tool L_i from the machine, $[\boldsymbol{\Psi}_k]_{0,j}$ denotes the time to add tool L_j to the machine, and $[\boldsymbol{\Psi}_k]_{i,j}$ denotes the time required to replace tool L_i with tool L_j.

In practical manufacturing environments, certain jobs cannot start until others are completed due to shared resources, assembly sequences, or other constraints. To accurately model such real-world scenarios, job-level precedence constraints are incorporated. These dependencies ensure that scheduling decisions respect the logical and technical order of job execution, thereby improving the feasibility and applicability of the generated schedules. To this end, let $\mathcal{D}^{\mathcal{J}} \subseteq \mathcal{J} \times \mathcal{J}$ (the Cartesian product of $\mathcal{J}$ with itself) be the set of job dependencies, where $(J_i, J_{i'}) \in \mathcal{D}^{\mathcal{J}}$ for $i \neq i'$ indicates that job J_i can only start after the completion of job $J_{i'}$. Similarly, $\mathcal{D}^{\mathcal{O}} \subseteq \mathcal{O} \times \mathcal{O}$ (the Cartesian product of $\mathcal{O}$ with itself) denotes the set of operation dependencies, where $(O_{i,j}, O_{i',j'}) \in \mathcal{D}^{\mathcal{O}}$ for $i \neq i', j \neq j'$ implies that operation $O_{i,j}$ can only start after the completion of operation $O_{i',j'}$.

2.1   Variables and Objective Function

For our mathematical formulation, we define the decision variables summarized in Table 1.

Table 1. Decision variables used in the model.

Variable	Description
$x_{i,j,k} \in \{0,1\}$	Equals 1 if operation $O_{i,j}$ is assigned to machine M_k, 0 otherwise.
$\tau_{i,j} \in \mathbb{R}_+$	Start time of operation $O_{i,j}$ in seconds.
$c_{i,j} \in \mathbb{R}_+$	Completion time of operation $O_{i,j}$ in seconds.
$\bar{\tau}_{i,j,k} \in \mathbb{R}_+$	Tool change time for operation $O_{i,j}$ on machine M_k in seconds.
$z_{i,j,k,l} \in \{0,1\}$	Equals 1 if tool L_l is mounted on machine M_k for operation $O_{i,j}$, 0 otherwise. (Mount means the tool is available on the machine during the operation.)
$\delta_{i,j,k,l} \in \{0,1\}$	Equals 1 if tool L_l is added to machine M_k for operation $O_{i,j}$, 0 otherwise.
$\omega_{i,j,k,l} \in \{0,1\}$	Equals 1 if tool L_l is removed from machine M_k for operation $O_{i,j}$, 0 otherwise.

The primary objective here is to minimize the makespan, defined as the completion time of the last operation of all jobs:

$$\min_{x,\ c,\ \tau,\ \bar{\tau},\ z,\ \delta,\ \omega} \left\{ \max_{i \in \{1,2,\ldots,I\}} c_{i,h_i} \right\}, \tag{1}$$

subjected to constraints which are detailed in Sect. 2.2. The completion time of each operation is calculated based on its start time, processing time, and any tool change time needed before the operation begins:

$$c_{i,j} = \tau_{i,j} + \sum_{k=1}^{K} x_{i,j,k}(p_{i,j,k} + \bar{\tau}_{i,j,k}), \quad \forall i,j. \tag{2}$$

This problem is usually NP-hard [3]. Therefore, heuristic or learning-based methods such as RL are often used, aiming for near-optimal solutions.

2.2 Constraints

The constraints ensure that all scheduling and tool management rules are respected. They guarantee feasibility by enforcing assignment correctness, operation ordering, machine capacity limits, correct tool availability, and accurate computation of operation times. Equation (1) is subject to multiple constraints, which are detailed in the following.

Assignment Constraints: These constraints ensure that each operation is assigned to exactly one eligible machine. They also prevent operations from being assigned to machines that cannot process them according to the eligibility rules. Specifically, each operation must be assigned to exactly one machine such that $\sum_{k=1}^{K} x_{i,j,k} = 1$ for all $i \in \{1, 2, \ldots, I\}$ and $j \in \{1, 2, \ldots, h_i\}$, and operations can only be assigned to eligible machines requiring that $x_{i,j,k} = 0$ for all i, j, k such that $M_k \notin \bar{\mathcal{M}}_{i,j}$.

Precedence Constraints: Precedence constraints enforce the required order of operations both within a single job (sequential operations) and between jobs (inter-job dependencies), ensuring the logical execution flow of the schedule. Operations within a job must be processed in order, requiring that $\tau_{i,j} \geq c_{i,j-1}$ for all $i \in \{1, 2, \ldots, I\}$ and $j \in \{2, 3, \ldots, h_i\}$. Operation dependencies across jobs mandate that $\tau_{i,j} \geq c_{i',j'}$ for all $(O_{i,j}, O_{i',j'}) \in \mathcal{D}^{\mathcal{O}}$. Job dependencies ensure that $\tau_{i,1} \geq c_{i',h_{i'}}$ for all $(J_i, J_{i'}) \in \mathcal{D}^{\mathcal{J}}$, where $\tau_{i,1}$ is the start time of the first operation of job J_i and $c_{i',h_{i'}}$ is the completion time of the last operation of job $J_{i'}$.

Machine Capacity Constraints: These constraints ensure that operations are processed sequentially on each machine without overlap, following the order in which they are scheduled. Each machine can process only one operation at a time. When operation $O_{i,j}$ is assigned to machine M_k, the machine becomes unavailable until the operation completes. The machine availability is updated such that $[m_{t+1}]_k = c_{i,j}$ when operation $O_{i,j}$ is scheduled on M_k. The start time of any operation must respect machine availability, requiring that $\tau_{i,j} \geq [m_t]_k$ when operation $O_{i,j}$ is assigned to M_k. For operations scheduled sequentially on the same machine, the scheduling order inherently ensures that $\tau_{i,j} \geq c_{i',j'}$ when $O_{i',j'}$ precedes $O_{i,j}$ on M_k.

Tool Management Constraints: Tool management constraints guarantee that all tools required by an operation are properly mounted on the machine during processing. They also model tool loading and unloading events as part of the scheduling process. Required tools must be mounted during an operation. Formally, $z_{i,j,k,l} = 1$ if operation $O_{i,j}$ is assigned to machine M_k (i.e., $x_{i,j,k} = 1$) and tool L_l is required for that operation ($L_l \in \mathcal{L}_{O_{i,j},M_k}$). Tool capacity constraints ensure that the total number of tools mounted on a machine during an operation does not exceed the machine's tool slot capacity, which is expressed as $\sum_{l=1}^{N} z_{i,j,k,l} \leq b_k$ for all operations $O_{i,j}$ assigned to machine M_k, meaning when $x_{i,j,k} = 1$. Similarly, tool compatibility constraints ensure that only compatible tools can be mounted on a machine, which is enforced by setting $z_{i,j,k,l} = 0$ for any tool L_l not belonging to the compatible tool set $\mathcal{L}_{M_k}$.

2.3   Tool Management Extension

The tool management extension adds complexity to the classic JSSP by incorporating tool-related decisions. We focus on two key aspects:

Tool Selection and Change Tracking: When a machine has limited tool slots, tool selection and changes are tracked as operations are processed sequentially using:

$$\delta_{i,j,k,l} \geq z_{i,j,k,l} - z_{i',j',k,l}, \quad \forall i,j,i',j',k,l, \tag{3}$$

$$\omega_{i,j,k,l} \geq z_{i',j',k,l} - z_{i,j,k,l}, \quad \forall i,j,i',j',k,l, \tag{4}$$

where operation $O_{i',j'}$ precedes $O_{i,j}$ on machine M_k. The tool change variables δ and ω capture additions and removals by comparing the tool state before and after an operation.

Tool Change Duration Calculation: The time required to change tools for the j-th operation of the i-th job on the k-th machine is calculated using the following equation, which accounts for both tool additions and removals.

Let $[\boldsymbol{\Psi}_k]_{i,j}$ denote the (i,j)-th element of the tool change time matrix $\boldsymbol{\Psi}_k$ for machine M_k, where $[\boldsymbol{\Psi}_k]_{0,l}$ represents the time required to add (load) tool L_l to machine M_k, $[\boldsymbol{\Psi}_k]_{l,0}$ represents the time required to remove (unload) tool L_l from machine M_k, and $[\boldsymbol{\Psi}_k]_{l_1,l_2}$ represents the time required to directly replace tool L_{l_1} with tool L_{l_2} on machine M_k (for $l_1, l_2 \neq 0$). The total tool change time is calculated as the sum of all individual tool addition and removal operations:

$$\bar{\tau}_{i,j,k} = \sum_{l=1}^{N} \delta_{i,j,k,l}[\boldsymbol{\Psi}_k]_{0,l} + \sum_{l=1}^{N} \omega_{i,j,k,l}[\boldsymbol{\Psi}_k]_{l,0}, \tag{5}$$

for all i,j,k where $x_{i,j,k} = 1$.

Note that the matrix uses a special indexing convention where index 0 represents the absence of a tool (empty slot), while indices $1, 2, \ldots, N$ correspond to tools $L_1, L_2, \ldots, L_N$ respectively. This formulation assumes that tool changes are performed sequentially (first all removals, then all additions) rather than using direct tool-to-tool replacements.

3   Reinforcement Learning Environment Design

In this section, we model the above JSSP-TM as a MDP, detailing the state and action spaces, transition dynamics, and reward structure, preparing for RL-based solutions, particularly, for Q-learning-based solutions.

3.1   Markov Decision Process Formulation

An MDP is defined by the tuple $(\mathcal{S}, \mathcal{A}, P, r, \gamma)$, where $\mathcal{S}$ is the state space, $\mathcal{A}$ is the action space, P represents the transition probabilities, r is the immediate reward, and γ is the discount factor.

3.2   State Space

The state $s \in \mathcal{S}$ at time t is defined as: $s_t = (\boldsymbol{\Gamma}_t, \boldsymbol{m}_t, \boldsymbol{\nu}_t, \boldsymbol{g}_t, \boldsymbol{\Omega}_t)$, where $\boldsymbol{\Gamma}_t \in \mathbb{R}_+^{I \times H}$ is the job progress matrix, where $[\boldsymbol{\Gamma}_t]_{i,j}$ stores the scheduled completion time of operation $O_{i,j}$ once the operation has been scheduled, and 0 if the operation has not yet been scheduled. Here, $H = \max_{i \in \{1,2,\dots,I\}} h_i$ represents the maximum number of operations across all jobs. Additionally, $\boldsymbol{m}_t \in \mathbb{R}_+^K$ is the machine availability vector, with $[\boldsymbol{m}]_k$ representing the time machine M_k becomes available. Furthermore, $\boldsymbol{\nu}_t \in \mathbb{Z}_+^I$ is the next operation vector, with $[\boldsymbol{\nu}_t]_i$ representing the index of the next operation to be scheduled for job J_i. Moreover, $\boldsymbol{g}_t \in \{0,1\}^I$ is the job completion vector, with $[\boldsymbol{g}_t]_i = 1$ if job J_i is completed. Finally, $\boldsymbol{\Omega}_t \in \{0,1\}^{K \times N}$ is the tool state matrix, with $[\boldsymbol{\Omega}_t]_{k,l} = 1$ if tool L_l is mounted on machine M_k. The state representation captures the current status of all jobs, machines, and tools, making the environment fully observable.

3.3   Action Space

An action $a \in \mathcal{A}$ at time t is defined as: $a_t = (i_t, j_t, k_t)$, where i_t is the job index, j_t is the operation index, k_t is the machine index. The action represents scheduling operation O_{i_t, j_t} on machine M_{k_t}. At each decision point, only a subset of actions is valid, determined by inter-job dependencies, operation dependencies, machine eligibility, and tool compatibility.

3.4   Transition Function

The transition function $P(s_t, a_t, s_{t+1})$ describes how the state evolves after taking action a_t in state s_t. The environment supports parallel processing, allowing multiple machines to operate simultaneously on different operations from the same job or different jobs, provided all precedence and dependency constraints are satisfied. The transition proceeds as follows:

1. Calculate Operation Start Time: The start time for operation O_{i_t,j_t} is determined by:

$$\tau_{i_t,j_t} = \max \left\{ [\boldsymbol{m}_t]_{k_t}, [\boldsymbol{\Gamma}_t]_{i_t,j_t-1}, \max_{(O_{i_t,j_t},O_{i'_t,j'_t})\in\mathcal{DO}} [\boldsymbol{\Gamma}_t]_{i'_t,j'_t}, \max_{(J_{i_t},J_{i'_t})\in\mathcal{DJ}} [\boldsymbol{\Gamma}_t]_{i'_t,h_{i'_t}} \right\}.$$

The four elements inside the maximum function represent different timing constraints that must all be satisfied. The first element, $[\boldsymbol{m}_t]_{k_t}$, represents the machine availability constraint, which is the earliest time when the assigned machine becomes free. The second element, $[\boldsymbol{\Gamma}_t]_{i_t,j_t-1}$, captures the intra-job precedence constraint, specifically the completion time of the immediately preceding operation within the same job. The third element, $\max_{(O_{i_t,j_t},O_{i'_t,j'_t})\in\mathcal{DO}} [\boldsymbol{\Gamma}_t]_{i'_t,j'_t}$, enforces the operation dependency constraint by considering the latest completion time among all prerequisite operations from other jobs. Finally, the fourth element, $\max_{(J_{i_t},J_{i'_t})\in\mathcal{DJ}} [\boldsymbol{\Gamma}_t]_{i'_t,h_{i'_t}}$, addresses the job dependency constraint through the completion time of all prerequisite jobs. Taking the maximum ensures that the operation starts only after all constraints are satisfied.

2. Calculate Tool Changes: The tool change time for operation O_{i_t,j_t} on machine k_t is calculated using Eq. (5), which sums the time required to add all new tools and remove all unnecessary tools based on the current machine configuration.

3. Update Job Progress Matrix: The completion time of the scheduled operation is recorded in the job progress matrix. This completion time is calculated as the sum of three components as:

$$[\boldsymbol{\Gamma}_{t+1}]_{i_t,j_t} = \tau_{i_t,j_t} + p_{i_t,j_t,k_t} + \bar{\tau}_{i_t,j_t,k_t} \tag{6}$$

where τ_{i_t,j_t} is the start time of operation O_{i_t,j_t} determined by machine availability and precedence constraints, p_{i_t,j_t,k_t} is the actual processing time required to execute the operation on machine M_{k_t}, and $\bar{\tau}_{i_t,j_t,k_t}$ is the time required for tool changes before the operation begins, as calculated in Eq. (5). This total completion time represents when the operation (including all tool changes and processing) will be finished, and is used to update machine availability and enforce future precedence constraints.

4. Update Machine Availability: The availability time of the used machine is updated as $[\boldsymbol{m}_{t+1}]_{k_t} = [\boldsymbol{\Gamma}_{t+1}]_{i_t,j_t}$.

5. Update Next Operation Index: The index of the next operation for the scheduled job is incremented as $[\boldsymbol{\nu}_{t+1}]_{i_t} = [\boldsymbol{\nu}_t]_{i_t} + 1$.

6. Update Job Completion Status: The completion status of the scheduled job is updated:

$$[\boldsymbol{g}_{t+1}]_{i_t} = \begin{cases} 1, \text{ if } [\boldsymbol{\nu}_{t+1}]_{i_t} > h_{i_t}, \\ 0, \text{ otherwise.} \end{cases} \tag{7}$$

7. Update Tool Configuration: The tool configuration of the used machine is updated as

$$[\mathbf{\Omega}_{t+1}]_{k_t,l} = \begin{cases} 1, & \text{if } L_l \in \mathcal{L}_{O_{i,j},M_k} \text{ or } ([\mathbf{\Omega}_t]_{k_t,l} = 1 \text{ and } L_l \text{ not removed,}) \\ 0, & \text{otherwise.} \end{cases}$$

$$(8)$$

The transition function is deterministic because given a current state and an action, the next state is uniquely determined with probability 1. For any current state s_t and action a_t, there exists exactly one next state s_{t+1} such that $P(s_t, a_t, s_{t+1}) = 1$, and for all other possible next states $s'_{t+1} \neq s_{t+1}$, $P(s_t, a_t, s'_{t+1}) = 0$.

3.5   Reward Function

The reward function is a critical component of the RL approach to JSSP-TM. It shapes the agent's behavior by providing feedback on the quality of scheduling decisions. The reward function $r(s_t, a_t, s_{t+1})$ balances multiple objectives through a weighted combination of components:

$$r(s_t, a_t, s_{t+1}) = r_{process} - r_{tool} - r_{duration} - r_{makespan}, \qquad (9)$$

where $r_{process} = \eta_1$ is a constant positive reward encouraging the completion of operations, $r_{tool} = \eta_2 \cdot \bar{\tau}_{i_t,j_t,k_t}$ is a penalty proportional to the time spent changing tools on machines, $r_{duration} = \eta_3 \cdot p_{i_t,j_t,k_t}$ is a penalty proportional to the processing time of operations, and $r_{makespan} = \eta_4 \cdot \max_{i \in \{1,2,...,I\}} [\mathbf{\Gamma}_{t+1}]_{i,h_i}$ if all jobs are completed, 0 otherwise, is a terminal penalty based on the schedule's makespan, applied only when all jobs are completed. Here, $[\mathbf{\Gamma}_{t+1}]_{i,h_i}$ represents the completion time of the final operation of job J_i, and the makespan is the maximum among all jobs' completion times. Parameters $\eta_1, \eta_2, \eta_3, \eta_4 \in \mathbb{R}$ are the scaling factors that needs to be chosen experimentally.

3.6   Q-Learning Approach

To solve JSSP-TM formulated as an MDP, we employ Q-learning as an example, which is a model-free RL algorithm that learns an action value function $Q(s_t, a_t)$ representing the expected long-term reward of taking action a_t in state s_t. The Q-learning update rule [8] is:

$$Q(s_t, a_t) \leftarrow Q(s_t, a_t) + \alpha \left[r + \gamma \max_a Q(s_{t+1}, a_{t+1}) - Q(s_t, a_t) \right], \qquad (10)$$

where α is the learning rate, r is the immediate reward, γ is the discount factor, s_{t+1} is the next state, $\max_a Q(s_{t+1}, a_{t+1})$ is the maximum Q-value in the next state.

Action Selection Strategy: We employ an ϵ-greedy exploration strategy [5], where with probability ϵ, a random action is selected, and with probability $1-\epsilon$, the action with the highest Q-value is chosen:

$$a_t = \begin{cases} \text{random action from valid actions,} & \text{with probability } \epsilon, \\ \arg\max_{a \in \text{available}(s_t)} Q(s_t, a_t), & \text{with probability } 1 - \epsilon. \end{cases} \tag{11}$$

The value of ϵ decreases over time according to a multiplicative decay schedule:

$$\epsilon_{t+1} = \max(\epsilon_{\min}, \epsilon_t \cdot \epsilon_{\text{decay}}), \tag{12}$$

where $\epsilon_{\min}$ is the minimum exploration rate, ϵ_0 is the initial exploration rate, and ϵ_{decay} controls the decay rate.

Q-Learning Configuration: In our experiments, the Q-learning algorithm was configured with specific parameters to facilitate the learning process for the JSSP-TM. The learning rate α was set to 0.1, which controls the step size for updating the Q-values. The exploration strategy was initialised with an exploration rate ϵ_0 of 0.3, gradually decaying over time with an exploration decay rate ϵ_{decay} of 0.999 down to a minimum exploration rate ϵ_{min} of 0.01. This decaying ϵ-greedy approach balances the exploration of new actions with the exploitation of learned optimal actions. The discount factor γ was set to 0.9, determining the importance of future rewards in the current decision-making process. The values of scaling factors described in Eq. (9) are set to be $\eta_1 = 20$, $\eta_2 = 2$, $\eta_3 = 1$, and $\eta_4 = 0.1$. These parameter settings were crucial for the Q-learning agent to effectively learn a policy that minimises the makespan while considering tool management overheads and are chosen experimentally.

4   Experimental Analysis

This section illustrate the performance of Q-learning, heuristic methods, and other stable baseline approaches on the studied JSSP-TM problem. We constructed a concrete test instance that captures the essential characteristics of real-world manufacturing tasks involving both machine and tool constraints.

4.1   Test Instance

The test instance consists of 4 jobs ($I = 4$) with varying numbers of operations ($h_1 = 3, h_2 = 3, h_3 = 2$, and $h_4 = 4$ operations respectively), resulting in a total of 12 operations. The shop floor includes 3 machines ($K = 3$) with different tool slot capacities: Machine M_1 has 4 slots, i.e., $b_1 = 4$, Machine M_2 has $b_2 = 2$, and Machine M_3 has $b_3 = 3$. A pool of 6 distinct tools ($N = 6$) is available, with machine-specific tool compatibility constraints. Machine M_1 can use all 6 tools, i.e., $\mathcal{L}_{M_1} = \{1, 2, 3, 4, 5, 6\}$. Machine M_2 can only use tools $\mathcal{L}_{M_2} = \{2, 3, 4\}$, while machine M_3 can use tools $\mathcal{L}_{M_3} = \{1, 3, 4, 5\}$. Each operation requires exactly 2 tools from the machine's compatible tool set. The tool change time matrices $\boldsymbol{\Psi}_k$ for each machine are as follows:

$$\boldsymbol{\Psi}_1 = \begin{bmatrix} 0 & 8 & 10 & 12 & 15 & 18 & 20 \\ 6 & 0 & 5 & 8 & 10 & 12 & 15 \\ 8 & 5 & 0 & 6 & 8 & 10 & 12 \\ 10 & 8 & 6 & 0 & 5 & 8 & 10 \\ 12 & 10 & 8 & 5 & 0 & 6 & 8 \\ 15 & 12 & 10 & 8 & 6 & 0 & 5 \\ 18 & 15 & 12 & 10 & 8 & 5 & 0 \end{bmatrix}, \boldsymbol{\Psi}_2 = \begin{bmatrix} 0 & 0 & 15 & 18 & 20 & 0 & 0 \\ 0 & 0 & 0 & 0 & 0 & 0 & 0 \\ 12 & 0 & 0 & 10 & 12 & 0 & 0 \\ 15 & 0 & 10 & 0 & 8 & 0 & 0 \\ 18 & 0 & 12 & 8 & 0 & 0 & 0 \\ 0 & 0 & 0 & 0 & 0 & 0 & 0 \\ 0 & 0 & 0 & 0 & 0 & 0 & 0 \end{bmatrix}, \boldsymbol{\Psi}_3 = \begin{bmatrix} 0 & 10 & 0 & 12 & 15 & 18 & 0 \\ 8 & 0 & 0 & 10 & 12 & 15 & 0 \\ 0 & 0 & 0 & 0 & 0 & 0 & 0 \\ 10 & 8 & 0 & 0 & 8 & 10 & 0 \\ 12 & 10 & 0 & 8 & 0 & 8 & 0 \\ 15 & 12 & 0 & 10 & 8 & 0 & 0 \\ 0 & 0 & 0 & 0 & 0 & 0 & 0 \end{bmatrix}.$$

The matrices $\boldsymbol{\Psi}_1$, $\boldsymbol{\Psi}_2$, and $\boldsymbol{\Psi}_3$ are for M_1, M_2, and M_3 machines respectively, with vertical separators between them. In these matrices, rows and columns represent tools (including the 0-th index for no tool), and each entry $[\boldsymbol{\Psi}_k]_{i,j}$ represents the time required to change from tool i to tool j on machine k. Zero values indicate either no change time (diagonal) or incompatible tool changes.

Processing times $p_{i,j,k}$ for each operation are specifically defined as follows:

- Job 1 (J_1): operations with durations $p_{1,1,1} = 4$, $p_{1,2,1} = 3$, and $p_{1,3,1} = 5$ time units on machines M_1, M_2, and M_3 respectively.
- Job 2 (J_2): operations with durations $p_{2,1,2} = 3$, $p_{2,2,1} = 6$, and $p_{2,3,3} = 4$ time units on machines M_2, M_1, and M_3 respectively.
- Job 3 (J_3): operations with durations $p_{3,1,3} = 2$, and $p_{3,2,1} = 3$, time units on machines M_3 and M_1 respectively.
- Job 4 (J_4): operations with durations $p_{4,1,1} = 5$, $p_{4,2,2} = 4$, $p_{4,3,3} = 3$, and $p_{4,4,1} = 4$ time units on machines M_1, M_2, M_3, and M_1 respectively

Each operation is assigned to exactly one machine. The test instance incorporates precedence constraints as described in Sect. 2.2. Specifically, in addition to the sequential operations within a job, we added two types of dependencies: operation-level dependencies between different jobs and job-level dependencies. For operation-level dependencies: Operation $O_{3,2}$ can only start after the completion of operation $O_{1,2}$, and Operation $O_{4,3}$ can only start after the completion of operation $O_{2,2}$. For job-level dependencies: J_3 can only start after the completion of J_1, and J_4 can only start after the completion of J_2.

These dependencies create a complex precedence network that challenges scheduling algorithms to find efficient execution sequences while respecting all constraints. This test instance balances complexity and clarity, enabling meaningful evaluation of the learning-based and heuristic scheduling strategies while maintaining a manageable problem size for experimental analysis.

4.2   Baseline

In addition to the Q-learning, the RL baselines consist of three policy-gradient-based algorithms, namely, Deep Q-Network (DQN), Proximal Policy Optimization (PPO), and Advantage Actor-Critic (A2C), implemented using the Stable-Baselines3 [7] framework, which offers reliable and well maintained RL implementations. These algorithms were selected to represent both value-based and policy-based RL methods. In addition, three heuristic scheduling rules, FIFO [2], MWKR, and SPT, were used as non-learning baselines due to their widespread use, simplicity, and interpretability in JSSP.

4.3   Performance Metrics

The performance of JSSP-TM algorithms is evaluated using two key metrics: makespan and average machine utilization. Makespan represents the total time required to complete all jobs, with a lower makespan indicating more efficient scheduling. Average machine utilization reflects the percentage of time machines are actively processing jobs, indicating resource efficiency. An effective scheduling algorithm aims to minimize makespan while maximizing machine utilization.

4.4   Results

Table 2 presents the performance comparison of various scheduling approaches on a benchmark test case, evaluated using two key metrics. Among the RL methods, PPO achieved the best results, with the lowest makespan of 148 and the highest average machine utilization of 56.97%. This indicates that PPO effectively identified efficient scheduling sequences that minimize total completion time while maximizing resource utilization. A2C followed closely, with a makespan of 151 and utilization of 55.83%, also showing strong performance. In contrast, Q-learning and DQN yielded higher makespans of 206 and 211, respectively, with lower machine utilization rates, suggesting that these value-based methods may be less effective in handling the complexities of JSS compared to policy-gradient approaches.

Table 2. The comparision on test case with different benchmarks.

	RL Algorithms				Heuristic		
	Q-Learning	DQN	PPO	A2C	FIFO	MWKR	SPT
Makespan	206	211	148	151	210	209	211
Avg. Mach. Util. (%)	41.57	38.9	56.97	55.83	38.4	41	38.9

The heuristic methods, FIFO, MWKR, and SPT, produced makespans between 209 and 211 and machine utilization in the range of 38.4% to 41%. While these rule-based strategies are straightforward and interpretable, their performance remains limited due to their lack of adaptability to dynamic scheduling scenarios. In general, the results highlight the effectiveness of the RL policies in progress algorithms, particularly PPO and A2C, in optimizing both the completion time and machine utilization in JSSP.

Figure 1 illustrates the Gantt chart representation of the job schedule generated by the PPO approach for the JSSP-TM problem. The chart displays the

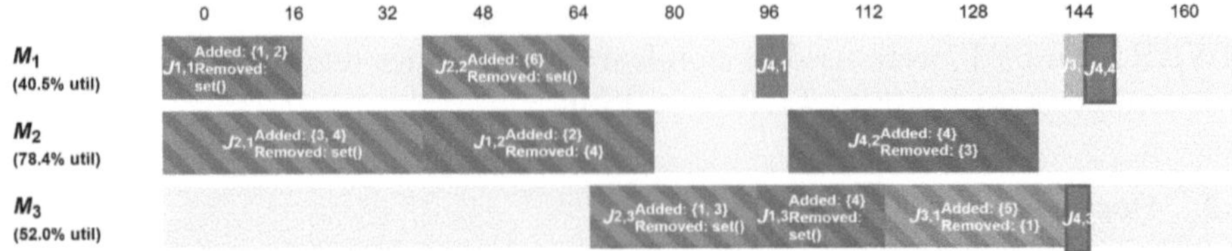

Fig. 1. Gantt chart visualization of job sequencing using PPO. Horizontal bars represent scheduled operations ($O_{i,j}$) assigned to machines. The label format $J_{i,j}$, denotes the job J_i, and the operation $O_{i,j}$ within that job, consistent with the definition $O_{i,j}$ in Sect. 2. Solid colors indicate operations without tool changes, while striped patterns represent operations requiring tool changes.

time evolution of operations scheduled across three machines, each capable of executing different operations with tool-related constraints and dependencies. The PPO method is selected for visualization due to its superior performance in minimizing the makespan among all tested approaches.

Each operation cell displays "Added" and "Removed" information, indicating the tools that were added to or removed from the machine's magazine when the operation was processed. For instance, on machine M_1, operation $J_{1,1}$ shows "Added: $\{1, 2\}$" and "Removed: set()", meaning tools 1 and 2 were added to the machine magazine and no tools were removed. Later, operation $J_{2,2}$ on the same machine shows "Added: $\{6\}$" with no removals, demonstrating how the algorithm effectively utilizes available magazine capacity while preserving previously loaded tools for subsequent operations. Notably, operations $J_{4,1}$, $J_{3,2}$, and $J_{4,4}$ executed on M_1 execute without any tool changes, highlighting the intelligent sequencing that maximizes tool reuse across dependent jobs. Similarly, on machines, M_2 and M_3, the PPO algorithm demonstrates efficient tool management by strategically adding and removing tools based on operation requirements and magazine capacity constraints.

The Gantt chart reveals that M_2 has the highest utilization (78.4%), while M_1 has the lowest (40.5%), likely due to fewer eligible operations or tool change delays. Operations follow job precedence constraints and inter-job dependencies as specified in the test instance. The chart's length represents the makespan, illustrating how the RL-based policy dynamically assigns operations to machines and manages tool allocations to minimize overall completion time.

5   Conclusion

In this paper, we present a novel and comprehensive formulation of the JSSP-TM, incorporating tool-related constraints and costs. Our approach extends the classic JSSP by considering tool compatibility, tool change durations, and tool slot limitations, providing a more practical framework for real-world manufacturing environments. To address this complex problem, we model it as an MDP, develop a simulation environment, and implement various RL solutions. Experimental results demonstrate the significant impact of integrated tool management on schedule quality. While Q-learning with shaped rewards balanced processing efficiency and tool change minimization, policy-gradient methods, particularly PPO, outperformed all others. PPO achieved the lowest makespan and highest machine utilization, outperforming DQN, A2C, and heuristic rules such as FIFO, MWKR, and SPT. We acknowledge that this initial evaluation was performed on a single representative test instance. Future work will further assess generalizability and scalability.

Acknowledgement. This research is part of the RHINOCEROS project [9]. Funded by the European Union under Grant Agreement No 101069685. Views and opinions expressed are however those of the author(s) only and do not necessarily reflect those of the European Union or the European Climate, Infrastructure and Environment Executive Agency (CINEA). Neither the European Union nor the granting authority can be held responsible for them.

References

1. Bowman, E.H.: The schedule-sequencing problem. Oper. Res. **7**(5), 621–624 (1959)
2. Eilon, S., Chowdhury, I.: Due dates in job shop scheduling. Int. J. Prod. Res. **14**(2), 223–237 (1976)
3. Garey, M.R., Johnson, D.S., Sethi, R.: The complexity of flowshop and jobshop scheduling. Math. Oper. Res. **1**(2), 117–129 (1976)
4. Manne, A.S.: On the job-shop scheduling problem. Oper. Res. **8**(2), 219–223 (1960)
5. Mnih, V., et al.: Playing Atari with deep reinforcement learning. arXiv preprint arXiv:1312.5602 (2013)
6. Ngwu, C., Liu, Y., Wu, R.: Reinforcement learning in dynamic job shop scheduling: a comprehensive review of AI-driven approaches in modern manufacturing. J. Intell. Manuf., 1–16 (2025)
7. Raffin, A., Hill, A., Gleave, A., Kanervisto, A., Ernestus, M., Dormann, N.: Stable-Baselines3: reliable reinforcement learning implementations. JMLR **22**(268), 1–8 (2021)
8. Sutton, R.S., Barto, A.G.: Reinforcement Learning: An Introduction. MIT Press (2018)
9. Union, E.: Rhinoceros (2022). Online. https://www.rhinoceros-project.eu/. Accessed 15 May 2024
10. Unlu, Y., Mason, S.J.: Evaluation of mixed integer programming formulations for non-preemptive parallel machine scheduling problems. Comput. Ind. Eng. **58**(4), 785–800 (2010)
11. Wagner, H.M.: An integer linear-programming model for machine scheduling. Nav. Res. Logist. Q. **6**(2), 131–140 (1959)
12. Weckman, G.R., Ganduri, C.V., Koonce, D.A.: A neural network job-shop scheduler. J. Intell. Manuf. **19**, 191–201 (2008)
13. Zhao, F., Hong, Y., Yu, D., Chen, X., Yang, Y.: Integration of artificial neural networks and genetic algorithm for job-shop scheduling problem. In: International Symposium on Neural Networks, pp. 770–775. Springer (2005)

HAD-QC: A Hybrid AI Approach for Automated Quality Control of Argo Float Data

Shivshankar Aiwale[1], Frederic Stahl[2]([✉]), and Lily Sun[1]

[1] Department of Computer Science, University of Reading, Whiteknights, 225, Reading RG6 6AY, UK
`s.r.aiwale@pgr.reading.ac.uk, lily.sun@reading.ac.uk`
[2] German Research Center for Artificial Intelligence GmbH (DFKI), Marine Perception, Marie-Curie-Straße 1, 26129 Oldenburg, Germany
`Frederic_Theodor.Stahl@dfki.de`

Abstract. The Argo programme has transformed ocean monitoring, deploying over 4,000 floats for climate modelling and ocean forecasting. However, quality control remains a significant challenge as Real-Time Quality Control often misses subtle issues, and Delayed-Mode Quality Control is time-consuming, delaying validated datasets by over a year. Erroneous profiles can distort climate analyses. This paper introduces Hybrid Anomaly Detection - Quality Control (HAD-QC), a novel framework combining machine learning with existing Argo QC rules to enhance accuracy and scalability. HAD-QC integrates an autoencoder for unsupervised anomaly detection, a supervised ensemble classifier and 18 traditional Argo QC tests, with outputs fused via a weighting scheme. Tested on 3,200 Argo float profiles across different ocean basins, HAD-QC substantially improves anomaly finding, outperforming Real-Time Quality Control significantly. It achieved an F1-score of 90.4%, an 87% anomaly detection rate and 93% overall accuracy, overall a better performance compared with current approach to Real-Time Quality Control. HAD-QC is designed for compatibility with Argo Data Assembly Center pipelines, offering interpretability and traceability of Quality Control decisions, and is extensible to emerging Deep and Biogeochemical Argo missions.

Keywords: Argo Profiling Floats · Hybrid Anomaly Detection - Quality Control (HAD-QC) · Ocean Data Anomaly Detection · AI-Based Environmental Monitoring · Autoencoder for Oceanographic QC · Machine Learning in Geosciences · Rule-Based and AI QC Fusion · Real-Time Ocean Observation · Explainable Artificial Intelligence (XAI) · Robust QC for Biogeochemical Data · Operational Oceanography · Intelligent Data Preprocessing · Ensemble Learning Models · Environmental Data Integrity · Scalable Ocean Data QC Framework · Deep Learning

1   Introduction

The Argo program has revolutionised global ocean monitoring over the past two decades by deploying over 4,000 autonomous profiling floats that gather near real-time measurements of temperature, salinity and pressure from the upper 2,000 m of the ocean[1]. The resulting dataset serves as the foundation for critical applications in climate modelling, ocean forecasting, and marine ecosystem research [8,14,15]. As of 2023, Argo floats generate more than 12,000 profiles per month, constituting the largest oceanographic data collection ever assembled.

However, quality control of this data remains a major challenge. Argo employs a two-step process: Real-Time Quality Control applies automated checks soon after profile transmission, but often misses subtle issues, while Delayed-Mode Quality Control involves detailed human review and validation, thus this approach is time-consuming and frequently delays validated datasets often by over a year [2,4,18]. These limitations carry real consequences. Erroneous Argo profiles that evade detection could distort climate analyses, skew ocean models, and degrade seasonal predictions and carbon estimates. Moreover, as Argo expands into biogeochemical observation and deep-ocean exploration, the volume and intricacy of readings will vastly exceed what people can manually validate, necessitating scalable automated solutions [9]. In response, we present Hybrid Anomaly Detection - Quality Control (HAD-QC), a novel framework merging machine learning with existing Argo Quality Control (QC) rules to strengthen accuracy and scalability in quality control.

HAD-QC combines autoencoder anomaly detection trained on validated profiles, a supervised classifier ensemble trained on human labels, and complete execution of 18 QC tests whose outputs integrate with model results via a weighting scheme. These simple QC rules establish threshold checks for global ranges, spikes, gradient consistency and more. They help flagging profiles with physically dubious or suspicious measurements. Testing on over 2000 profiles across various regions and platforms demonstrated that HAD-QC substantially improves anomaly finding—including better detection and fewer missed issues, compared with rule-based control alone. As an accurate and transparent tool, HAD-QC offers a practical means of integrating into real-time and delayed Argo data management. While prior work has explored machine learning for Argo anomaly detection [12,21], most approaches lack a hybrid fusion of unsupervised, supervised and rule-based components, or do not have evaluated models at an operational scale. HAD-QC addresses this gap with a deployable, adaptable system grounded in Argo's functional needs. Through a fusion of these hybrid methods, the system can identify intricate, non-obvious anomalies while still maintaining traceability to transgressed rules, thereby achieving both higher accuracy and interpretability.

The paper is structured as follows, Sect. 2 provides related work, Sect. 3 introduces the HAD-QC Methodology followed by an evaluation of the system in Sect. 4. Section 5 discusses HAD-QC's future application prespective followed by concluding remarks in Sect. 6.

---

[1] https://argo.ucsd.edu.

2   Related Work

Recent years have seen growing interest in applying machine learning techniques to tackle the pressing challenge of ocean data quality control within programs like Argo [6,14,19].

As the volume and complexity of float data proliferate, with additional insights from biogeochemical sensors, deeper deployments, and real-time operational needs, conventional rule-based methods have proven too rigid for anomaly identification of subtle, context-dependent, or complex anomalies in Argo float data, not only gross outliers, but structures that may depend on depth, or region, or season, or sensor drift, or on sensor- specific behaviors [9].

The Argo data quality control (QC) system is divided into two steps: the real-time QC (RTQC) and the delayed mode QC (DMQC). Automated RTQC is performed on a time scale of hours and is driven by a fixed set of rule-based quality checks (e.g., range, spike, and gradient tests) to identify physically unrealistic values [15]. These rules are effective for gross errors, but they have no context and often are insensitive to more subtle anomalies, especially when there are some complex or noisy measurement scenarios [1]. DMQC is more extensive and more accurate, however, it could take 12 to 24 months for peer-reviewed corrections, hampering its operational applicability.

Various research has introduced automated anomaly detection methods based on statistical or machine learning. For instance, the authors of [20] also used autoencoders to model normal float behaviour and raised warning when new behaviours deviated significantly. The authors of [13] tested various classifiers including random forests and Support Vector Machines in supervised QC error detection of Argo profiles. Similarly, [24] proposed semi-supervised ensemble learning to identify outliers without total dependence on labeled data.

While demonstrating promise, these studies are limited in critical ways.

- Many models function as *black boxes* with limited interpretability, a major barrier to operational adoption by Argo Data Assembly Centers (DACs) and scientific users.
- Few integrate the existing QC rules into the decision logic, restricting compatibility with Argo protocols.
- Most systems are tested on restricted or narrow subsets of the expansive Argo dataset, leaving scalability and generalisability uncertain.

The authors of [7] highlight the opportunity to develop data mining models that are adaptive and able to run over streaming data in real time. This is parallel to the Argo QC problem where floats output data regularly and auto-systems have to cope in near real-time without spoiling the precision or the reliability.

Furthermore, the combination of unsupervised anomaly detection, supervised classification, and domain specific rule-based logic has not been widely studied under a single framework. HAD-QC, uses the best of both worlds: autoencoders for finding nonlinear data patterns to score an anomaly, and ensemble classifiers to take advantage of the known (labeled) training set, and Argo specific rules to provide domain-aligned QC flags. While the authors of [23], highlight the requirement for interpretable AI in oceanography, they do not extend to the operational integration of these approaches. Many QC systems based on machine learning incorporate complex models that do not provide clear explanations of the reasons behind their decisions, a problem that is referred to in the literature as the "black-box" problem. But in oceanographic quality control, such traceability and interpretability are crucial. As Rudin argues, policy-relevant scientific decisions need to be based on interpretable models [16]. HAD-QC bridges these gaps and provides an interpretable and traceable hybrid quality control solution adapted to the context and constraints of the Argo data system.

The work presented in this paper addresses this gap. HAD-QC is specially designed to satisfy the operational needs of Argo QC while incorporating the flexibility and learning capabilities of Artificial Intelligence (AI). By merging data-driven models with domain-specific rules, HAD-QC balances performance with traceability and interpretability of decisions, permitting real-time deployment without sacrificing reliability of the quality control process, which is vital for subsequent oceanographic research and applications downstream.

3   Hybrid Anomaly Detection Quality Control (HAD-QC)

3.1   Argo Datasets

This study relies on a quality-controlled data set of Argo float profiles that were measured between January 2020 and April 2025 and were extracted through the Argo Global Data Assembly Centres[2] using the Ifremer FTP server[3] and the US Argo DAC[4]. The profiles are written in NetCDF (Network Common Data Form) format following the Argo Data Management Version 3.1 format, including Real-Time (RT) and Delayed-Mode (DM) quality control flags [4]. The following fundamental oceanographic parameters and associated quality control flags were extracted from each profile:

1. Temperature (TEMP): uncorrected and corrected (TEMP_ADJUSTED)
2. Salinity (PSAL): primary and adjusted value (PSAL_ADJUSTED)
3. Pressure (PRES): corresponding raw and adjusted values
   (PRES_ADJUSTED)
4. Associated quality control flags for each variable: QC, ADJUSTED_QC e.g. TEMP (Temperature) is Oceanographic, but TEMP_QC Not oceanographic (it's meta-data about QC status)
5. Positional or temporal metadata such as latitude, longitude, JULD (Julian date), cycle number(float profile iteration index)

The selection of these features was based on their direct applicability to Argo's physical consistency checks, and their impact on measurement anomalies detection. All analyses were based on 3,200 profiles. Of these:

---

1. For training, we used 2,400 profiles, as only high quality profiles (QC flag = 1) in delayed mode were used as input to learn normal procedures.
2. 800 profiles were reserved and used for testing, consisted of 80%-"good" and 20%-"bad" profiles to assess performance of HAD-QC on real-world anomalies.

We adopted a stratified random sampling without replacement strategy for constructing the training and testing datasets to achieve a stable generalisation across different float types, ocean basins, and sensor behaviors.

In order to avoid overfitting to any specific float type or location, the dataset was initially binned by float type and ocean basin. For each of these two groups, profiles were randomly divided into 80% training and 20% test datasets with a balanced split according to float models and geographic regions. This stratification guaranteed that no float profile occurred in both sets, and that both sets continued to reflect the full heterogeneity present in the source data. All the anomaly labels utilised for supervised training were based on delayed-mode QC flags or manually reviewed annotations.

Here, this type of sampling increases the ecological value of the assessment, in that it could provide a measure of what the HAD-QC model might achieve in operational conditions of new floats and new regions.

The dataset is composed of various float types and ocean basins, which includes Apex, Navis, and PROVOR models; an additional 15 different float types are deployed in the Atlantic, Pacific, and Indian oceans[5,6]. This diversity provides strong variety in sensor performance, calibration strategies and regional oceanographic environments. All the normalised profiles were first cleaned in a systematic procedure to deal with missing values. In particular, profiles with 10% or more pairs of missing data for any of the 3 critical attributes (TEMP, PRES or PSAL) were removed from training and validation. For the remaining profiles, some isolated missing entries were estimated through linear interpolation on the vertical pressure axis. In addition, to make the profiles comparable across floats, the profiles were pressure-aligned through linear interpolations to a standard depth level. Such heterogeneity is crucial for strong generalisation and to avoid overfitting to certain float configurations[7].

3.2   HAD-QC Method and Implementation

The proposed HAD-QC method is described in this section, it aims to compensate the limitations of traditional QC in oceanographic data management. This core idea of the HAD-QC pipeline, which is a modularisable pipeline where different pieces can be replaced to yield ensemble models, rule-based decision logic, and unsupervised learning that scales to perform QC decisions on profiles of Argo floats, while being interpretable and accurate. The framework includes four primary parts: data preprocessing, autoencoder-based anomaly detection,

---

[5] https://www.argodatamgt.org/Documentation/Metadata.
[6] https://argo.ucsd.edu/data/float-types.
[7] https://doi.org/10.5670/oceanog.2009.36.

ensemble classification, and hybrid QC decision fusion. The overall workflow is illustrated in Fig. 1.

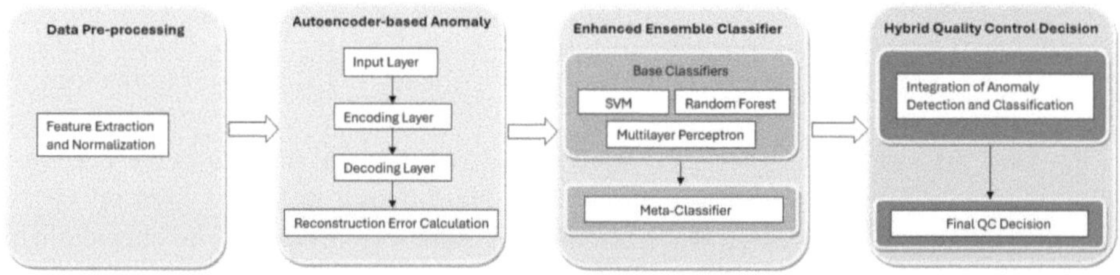

Fig. 1. Overview of the four-stage HAD-QC architecture combining machine learning and rule-based components.

3.3   Data Pre-processing

The data pre-processing prepares the original Argo NetCDF profiles for machine learning anomaly detection/classification. The pre-processing stage consists of three main procedures

1. **Feature extraction:** Essential physical and geographic variables are extracted from each NetCDF Argo data file: PRES, TEMP and PSAL (pressure, temperature and salinity respectively) alongside adjusted values and real-time QC flags. Metadata, such as latitude, longitude, Julian date (JULD), and profile direction (DIRECTION), is also kept in order to maintain the contextual continuity in space and in time.
2. **Normalisation and Scaling:** Continuous variables are standardised with z-score normalisation to have consistent treatment for numbers across features. This transformation improves the convergence properties of neural models by aligning the feature distributions and variances [24].
3. **Outlier and Missing Value Treatment:** For data control, obvious outliers (e.g. physically infeasible pressures or salinities less than zero) are captured by means of the QC rules (e.g., range test, spike test) and excluded. Missing values are imputed by linear interpolation. Empty values in vertical profiles are handled by depth-wise interpolation for input to the neural model such that matrices are compatible [18].

These procedures result in a clean and uniform dataset that can be robustly fed into the downstreams of HAD-QC models, and, hence, enhance the generalisability of models and the sensitivity of anomaly detection.

3.4   Anomaly Detection with Autoencoder

In the second stage, a deep autoencoder is used in HAD-QC, which is an unsupervised neural network, which learns a compact representation of input data. It is based on symmetric encoder and decoder layers, optimised by mean squared error (MSE) between input and reconstruction.

Only of those high-quality profiles (the ones with QC Flag $= 1$ in the core variables) are considered for training. It is to ensure that model could detect the normal oceanographic state in the latent space, and would be sensitive to abnormalities that could be instrument failure, calibration drifts, or environmental anomalies.

During inference the autoencoder computes a reconstruction error for every data point—how much the input is close to the normal patterns learned by the model. The anomaly score is taken as the reconstruction error. The thresholding value is determined empirically, by examining the Receiver Operating Characteristic (ROC) curve which graphs the true positive rate versus false positive rate. All data points with anomaly scores that exceeds the threshold are labeled as potential anomalies.

Autoencoders can be an effective choice for high-dimensional, structured, and temporal data such as Argo profiles. Their architecture is capable of capturing the nonlinear relationships among variables such as temperature, salinity, and pressure and learning compact representations of "regular" oceanographic behavior. This lends itself well to anomaly detection, where deviations with these learned representations suggest potential data quality problems.

Although classical techniques like Isolation Forests and k-Nearest Neighbors have been employed to perform unsupervised detection of anomalies, they work on shallow representations and perform poorly in the presence of multivariate temporal patterns or sensor noise [3,11]. Recent comparisons of deep learning models with traditional methods for ocean data domains reveal that the performance of autoencoders is generally superior to that of Isolation Forest, in terms of precision and recall [13,22]. Additionally, Isolation Forests do not have the reconstruction property, so they are not easily interpreted and are difficult to incorporate in a hybrid QC framework for which the reconstruction error can be utilised to measure the severity of the anomalies.

3.5 Enhanced Ensemble Classifier

To complement the anomalous pattern detection using label-based verification, HAD-QC involves a supervised ensemble classifier by employing a set of base learners:

1. **Random Forest:** Works well with feature noise and correlation.
2. **Support Vector Machine:** Provides largest margin separation in the feature space of high dimensionality.
3. **Multilayer Perceptron:** Models complex nonlinear relationships among vertical profile data.

A **meta-classifier** (logistic regression) is then trained on the base classifiers' prediction features in order to extract a final decision. Profiles in the training set are labeled with delayed-mode QC flags (*_ADJUSTED_QC), the highest-quality annotations in the Argo system [4]. We perform experiments on each classifier using stratified cross-validation and record the accuracy, precision, recall and F1 score as the key performance metrics for the benchmark. The system uniformly improves on individual models by decreasing both Type I (false positive) and Type II (false negative) errors.

Ensemble learning improves generalisation and robustness, especially if the classifiers are irregularly distributed over profile patterns [5]. This is crucial for oceanographic data sets in which anomalies can be local, transitory, and/or multivariate.

3.6   The Hybrid Quality Control Decision Fusion

The last step of HAD-QC combines the outputs of the autoencoder and the ensemble classifier with conventional rule-based RTQC tests. Each profile is analysed by applying the following logic:

- That is, if a profile violates any of the Argo critical rules (e.g., density inversion, impossible date/location), it is automatically flagged.

- If both the anomaly detector and ensemble model output a "bad" classification, the profile is flagged with high confidence.

- In the case of disagreement, profile scores are weighted and profiles are flagged for manual review depending on the severity of the autoencoder score and rules.

This combination provides the capacity for context-aware quality control decisions by capitalising on the generalisation properties of machine learning to discover relationships across a rich set of oceanographic conditions, but also the application of domain-specific rule logic to express specific anomalies and the enforcement of expert-validated thresholds. In this way, the decision-making scheme is adaptive to novel samples and rooted in known scientific theory.

Rule-based systems are interpretable but inflexible; ML models are flexible but opaque. Combining the two, HAD-QC attains the properties of traceability, automation, and resilience.

4   Evaluation

The effectiveness of the developed HAD-QC was validated in terms of accuracy, robustness, and generalisation to detect oceanographic anomalies in Argo float data. This section also provides a detailed comparison of HAD-QC against the current RTQC, including what improvements are gained by combining the AI approach into the system.

4.1   Comparative Performance: HAD-QC Versus RTQC

Table 1. Performance Comparison of HAD-QC versus RTQC.

Metric	RTQC (Baseline)	HAD-QC (Proposed)	Improvement
Precision	78.4%	**91.3%**	**+16.4%**
Recall	66.2%	**89.5%**	**+23.3%**
F1-Score	71.7%	**90.4%**	**+18.7%**
Anomaly Detection Rate	61%	**87%**	**+26%**
Overall Accuracy	75%	**93%**	**+18%**

HAD-QC outperforms RTQC in terms of all the performance measures. It obtains higher precision (91.3% vs 78.4%), better recall (89.5% vs 66.2%) and much stronger F1-score (90.4% vs 71.7%), demonstrating better detection of anomaly in both precision and recall. Moreover, the accuracy of anomaly detection increased by 26% and likewise the overall accuracy rose from 75% to 93%. These enhancements demonstrated the strong ability of HAD-QC to detect anomalies, reducing the number of false detections, and render it thus more robust and scalable in the context of Argo data quality control.

4.2   ROC Curve and Confusion Matrix

To test how well the proposed HAD-QC system detects and classifies anomalies, we used standard performance metrics, including the ROC curve and a confusion matrix that provides a deeper look into the model's discrimination and error types. Figure 2 shows the ROC curve obtained with the test set. The ROC curve is based on the True Positive Rate which is the ratio of actual anomalies correctly identified to the False Positive Rate, which is the ratio false alarms, where normal profiles (non-anomalous) are identified as anomalies. Here, a false positive is classified as an Argo float observation marked as anomalous by HAD-QC, but validated as the correct observation in the delayed-mode expert QC dataset. On the contrary, false negatives would be explained as undetected anomalies that were accepted by the HAD-QC filter and later identified by the manual QC procedures.

One important metric of this is the Area Under the Curve (AUC) which reflects how well the model can rank positive instances higher than negative ones overall. An AUC of 0.94 means that there is a 94% likelihood that the HAD-QC system will rank a true anomaly higher (with respect to an anomaly score) than to a valid profile. This high performance also demonstrates good discriminative power and validates the robustness of HAD-QC over different operating points.

In addition, the Confusion Matrix (see Fig. 3 provides a summarised version of real versus predicted classification results. Of the dataset, the model successfully detected 806 anomalies (true positive) and 857 good profiles (true negative). There were 42 false negatives and 51 false positives (valid profiles that

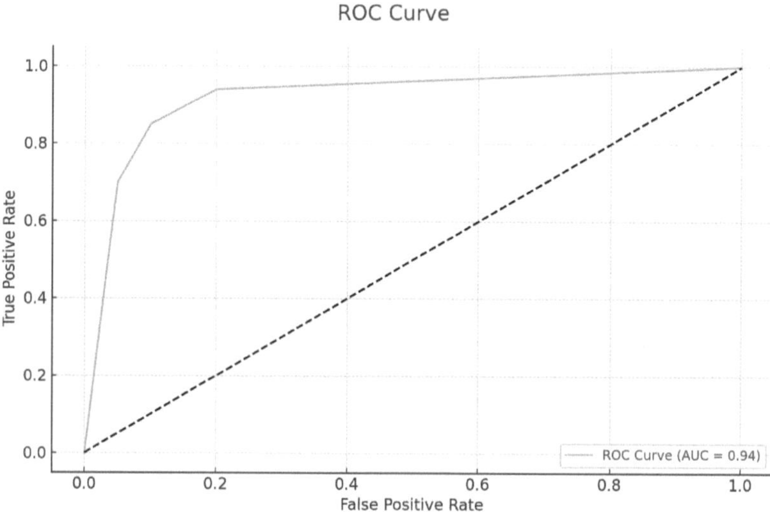

Fig. 2. ROC Curve showing the trade-off between True Positive Rate and False Positive Rate.

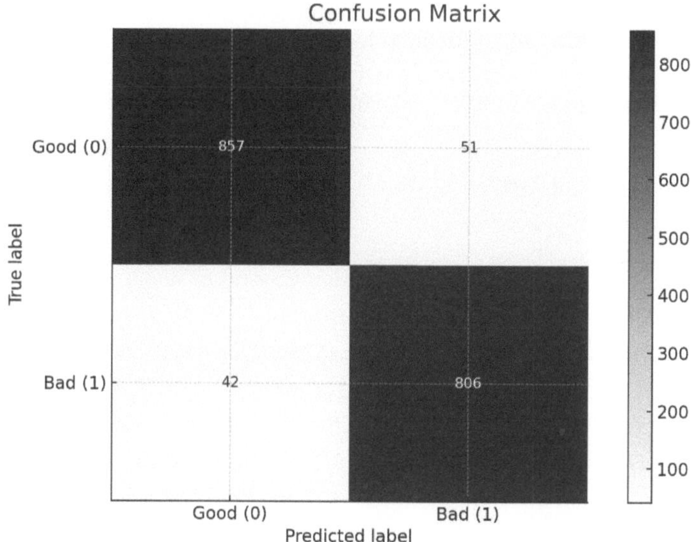

Fig. 3. Confusion Matrix for HAD-QC classification.

were erroneously identified as bad). The confusion matrix offers a more detailed insight into how a model is behaving. The low false positive and false negative rates demonstrate that HAD-QC is not only sensitive for detecting anomalies, but also accurate without raising too many false alarms. These results contribute to the strong performance metrics (F1-Score: 90.4%, Precision: 91.3%, Recall: 89.5%) given in Table 1. Overall, the ROC curve and confusion matrix confirm that HAD-QC is highly reliable with low false positive and false negative rates, rendering it valid for applying on real-time and delayed-mode QC procedures in Argo data.

4.3   Generalisation Across Floats and Ocean Basins

The robustness of the generalisation performance of the HAD-QC algorithm over different float types and ocean basins is also illustrated. As shown in Table 2, the F1-scores are all high for the APEX, SOLO-II and NAVIS floats, with a global average higher than 89%. Of interest is that the highest worldwide F1-score 90.3% did belong to the NAVIS floats, which implies a good match with this type of hardware. Performance remains high throughout regional basins, although slightly less for SOLO-II, possibly due to its more complex environment and a lower float density in the training set. This small degradation in performance of the SOLO-II floats (Global Avg F1: 89.4%) when compared to APEX or NAVIS could be caused by their deployment in regions with more complex oceanographic dynamics, in terms of higher levels of mesoscale variability or mixed-layer turbulence. These factors in the environment can result in harder data conditions and subtle anomalies that make anomaly detection and classification more difficult. This also highlights the flexibility and scalability of HAD-QC with respect to various float types and deployment conditions, and its potential for widespread operational deployment.

Table 2. F1-Score Comparison by Float Type and Ocean Basin (HAD-QC versus RTQC)

Float Type	Atlantic	Pacific	Indian	Southern	Global Avg	Improvement
APEX (RTQC)	73.2%	71.0%	72.6%	69.4%	71.5%	–
APEX (HAD-QC)	**91.2%**	**89.9%**	**90.4%**	**88.1%**	**89.9%**	**+18.4%**
SOLO-II (RTQC)	72.4%	73.3%	70.2%	68.1%	71.0%	–
SOLO-II (HAD-QC)	**90.3%**	**91.5%**	**88.8%**	**86.9%**	**89.4%**	**+18.4%**
NAVIS (RTQC)	74.0%	72.6%	73.5%	69.0%	72.3%	–
NAVIS (HAD-QC)	**92.1%**	**90.8%**	**91.0%**	**87.3%**	**90.3%**	**+18.0%**

5   Future Work

Looking forward, we note that HAD-QC provides a number of compelling ways for further development and practical use. One key focus of the ongoing work is to improve the support for both real-time and delayed-mode Argo operations by incorporating HAD-QC at a plugin module level within existing Data Assembly

Centre pipelines. This would allow the operational Argo community to take more advantage of it.

Additionally, effort is in progress to generalise the HAD-QC approach to biogeochemical (BGC) quantities such as oxygen, nitrate, and chlorophyll which will necessitate further tuning of domain adaptatiaon and anomaly detection, due to the even greater variance and sensor-specific properties of BGC data.

The authors of [10,17] have shown here that machine learning models can predict Photosynthetically Available Radiation from such floats or float like devices. This is evidence that ML methods are also well-suited for upscaling more complex ecologically relevant Argo-derived variables.

An alternative direction for future work would be to commission a user-facing dashboard (ideally web-based) that would display the QC decisions, anomaly scores and rule-based attributions to help illuminate and provide transparency toward a user's requirements both for scientists and data operators.

To promote reproducibility and community development, we are planning to release the project open-source with documentation.

6   Conclusions

This paper introduces HAD-QC, a new hybrid system that represents a substantial improvement of the quality control of Argo float data by combining rule-based, supervised and unsupervised methods in a single framework. Conventional RTQC techniques, while rapid and operationally mature, incorporate static thresholds and fixed logic, and are thus susceptible to overlooking subtle, context-dependent anomalies. Whereas HAD-QC uses autoencoder-based anomaly detection to learn normal oceanographic profiles and anomalies, disregarding human-defined criteria, then uses an ensemble classifier to improve the robustness of classification by voting from multiple algorithms (Random Forest, Support Vector Machine, Multilayer Perceptron). Finally, we fuse these with traditional Argo QC rules to improve both accuracy and interpretability. It was also demonstrated that, based on an extensive validation using over 3,200 Argo float profiles from various float types and from all-ocean basins, HAD-QC achieved an F1-score 90.4%, which surpassed RTQC by approximately 19%, and increased the anomaly detecting rates by approximately 26%. It had high precision and recall, with low false positives and negatives, which made it particularly well suited for operational deployment. Crucially, HAD-QC's final decisions are entirely traceable, such that oceanographers can audit model-driven predictions, comparing model-derived values against QC flags and rule output. Thanks to its modular architecture and the possibility to ingest potentials based on NetCDF, HAD-QC will, in future work, be directly integrated within an Argo Data Assembly Center processing pipeline. The ability to scale up automated QC to all BGC Argo floats, which measure variables such as nitrate, oxygen, and pH, can follow naturally. Such capability is essential for the exploration of deeper oceans and biogeochemical domains as the Argo program grows.

Acknowledgments. This work was partially funded by Zukunft. Niedersachsen (ZN4365).

References

1. Barker, P., Wong, A., Johnson, K.S.: Limitations of Argo RTQC: anomaly assessment and delayed mode improvements. Ocean Science (2022)
2. Barker, P.M., Dunn, J.R., Church, J.A.: Improving quality assurance of ocean data: a review of Argo delayed-mode QC. Front. Mar. Sci. **9**, 838479 (2022). https://doi.org/10.3389/fmars.2022.838479
3. Breunig, M.M., Kriegel, H.P., Ng, R.T., Sander, J.: LoF: identifying density-based local outliers. ACM SIGMOD Rec. **29**(2), 93–104 (2000)
4. Carval, T., Bittig, H.C., Argo Data Management Team: Argo User's Manual V3.4. Argo Data Management (2021). Version 3.4. https://doi.org/10.13155/29825
5. Dietterich, T.G.: Ensemble methods in machine learning. In: International Workshop on Multiple Classifier Systems, pp. 1–15. Springer (2000)
6. Griffiths, G., Bittig, H.C., Johnson, K.S., Carval, T., Wong, A.P.S.: Ai4argo: advancing automated quality control of Argo ocean profiles using machine learning. Fronti. Marine Sci. **9**, 862134 (2022). https://doi.org/10.3389/fmars.2022.862134
7. Idrees, M.M., Stahl, F., Badii, A.: Adaptive learning with extreme verification latency in non-stationary environments. IEEE Access **10**, 127345–127364 (2022). https://doi.org/10.1109/ACCESS.2022.3225225
8. Jayne, S.R., Roemmich, D., Zilberman, N., et al.: The Argo program: present and future. Oceanography **30**(2), 18–28 (2017). https://doi.org/10.5670/oceanog.2017.213
9. Johnson, K.S., Claustre, H., Takeshita, Y.: Observing biogeochemical cycles at global scales with profiling floats and gliders. Ann. Rev. Marine Sci. **13**, 23–43 (2021). https://doi.org/10.1146/annurev-marine-121219-081559
10. Kumm, M.M., Nolle, L., Stahl, F., Jemai, A., Zielinski, O.: On an artificial neural network approach for predicting photosynthetically active radiation in the water column. In: Bramer, M., Stahl, F. (eds.) Artificial Intelligence XXXIX, pp. 112–123. Springer, Cham (2022). https://doi.org/10.1007/978-3-031-21441-7_8
11. Liu, F.T., Ting, K.M., Zhou, Z.H.: Isolation forest. In: 2008 Eighth IEEE International Conference on Data Mining, pp. 413–422. IEEE (2008)
12. Lopez, C., Yang, F., Singh, R.: Machine learning methods for Argo Float QC: a comparative analysis. J. Atmos. Oceanic Tech. **39**(9), 1451–1467 (2022)
13. López, A.M., Gonzalez, P., Shen, X.: Deep anomaly detection for Argo profile data. In: IEEE OCEANS Conference (2022)
14. Roemmich, D., Gilson, J., Davis, R., et al.: The Argo program: observing the global ocean with profiling floats. Oceanography **22**(2), 34–43 (2009). https://doi.org/10.5670/oceanog.2009.36
15. Roemmich, D., Johnson, G.C., Riser, S., et al.: The global Argo program: a decade of progress. Oceanography **36**(1), 22–33 (2023). https://doi.org/10.5670/oceanog.2023.110
16. Rudin, C.: Stop explaining black box machine learning models for high stakes decisions and use interpretable models instead. Nat. Mach. Intell. **1**(5), 206–215 (2019)

17. Stahl, F.T., Nolle, L., Jemai, A., Zielinski, O.: A model for predicting the amount of photosynthetically available radiation from BGC-ARGO float observations in the water column. In: Proceedings of the ECMS, pp. 174–180 (2022)
18. Wong, A.P.S., Keeley, R., Carval, T., Argo Data Management Team: Argo quality control manual for CTD and trajectory data (2020). https://doi.org/10.13155/33951, version 3.4
19. Wong, A.P., Wijffels, S., Riser, S.C.: Argo data 1999–2019: two million temperature-salinity profiles and subsurface velocity observations from a global array of profiling floats. Front. Marine Sci. **7** (2020). https://doi.org/10.3389/fmars.2020.00700
20. Xie, J., Zhang, R., Wang, H.: Unsupervised anomaly detection in Argo float data using isolation forest. Remote Sens. Lett. **11**(4), 365–372 (2020)
21. Xie, J., Li, Z., Zhao, Z.: Detecting Argo profile anomalies with autoencoders. Remote Sens. **12**(5), 817 (2020). https://doi.org/10.3390/rs12050817
22. Xie, W., Li, X., Du, J.: Anomaly detection for oceanographic profiles using autoencoder neural networks. IEEE Access **8**, 119660–119670 (2020)
23. Yigit, A., Klein, M., Douglass, E.: Interpretable AI for environmental monitoring: a review. Environ. Model. Softw. **139**, 105031 (2021)
24. Zhang, K., Zhong, Z., Wang, Y.: Data standardization for deep learning: a survey. Neural Process. Lett. (2019)

Multi-Agent Reinforcement Learning Framework for Modelling Astrocyte-Neuron Interactions in Neural Microenvironments

Zhen Chen[1] and Shufan Yang[2(✉)]

[1] School of Cyber Science and Technology, University of Science and Technology of China, Hefei, China
[2] Institute of Medical and Biological Engineering, University of Leeds, Leeds, UK
`s.f.yang@leeds.ac.uk`

Abstract. Astrocytes represent a major glial cell population that regulates synaptic transmission, neural plasticity, and homeostasis through complex spatiotemporal interactions with neuronal networks. This paper presents a novel Multi-Agent Reinforcement Learning (MARL) framework for modelling astrocytic behaviour within neural microenvironments. In this simulation, individual astrocytes are modeled as autonomous learning agents that independently regulate glutamate dynamics while coordinating with neighbouring astrocytic domains. The model is evaluated by comparing glutamate release rates against standard reinforcement learning approaches. including independent proximal policy optimisation (IPPO), QMIX, and Value Decomposition Networks(VDN). Experimental results indicated that the adaptive IPPO based method achieves around 1% deviation from reported values. The proposed computational model addresses the dual role of astrocytes in maintaining glutamate homeostasis under physiological conditions while potentially contributing to neuronal damage in disease conditions. This study demonstrates the potential of the framework for applications in organ-on-chip platforms and therapeutic intervention research.

1 Introduction

Astrocytes constitute approximately 50% of brain cells and play critical roles in neural function through their interactions with synaptic structures and extracellular environments [10]. These glial cells form interconnected networks that regulate synaptic transmission, maintain ionic homeostasis, and modulate neural plasticity [4]. Under normal physiological conditions, astrocytes function as neuroprotective agents by buffering extracellular glutamate concentrations and preventing excitotoxicity, which damages neurons [3]. It is crucial to understand how astrocytes can paradoxically contribute to neuronal damage through excessive glutamate release while under normal conditions they balance glutamate

M. Bramer and F. Stahl (Eds.): SGAI-AI 2025, LNAI 16302, pp. 108–119, 2026.
https://doi.org/10.1007/978-3-032-11442-6_8

concentration levels. These emergent collective behaviours of astrocytic populations motivate a computational framework based on Multi-Agent Reinforcement Learning (MARL) [1,10]. Traditional linear models inadequately capture the complex dynamics of astrocyte-neuron interactions due to their distributed decision-making processes and emergent collective behaviors. This limitation motivates the development of computational frameworks capable of representing the autonomous nature of individual astrocytes while accounting for their collective dynamics within neural microenvironments.

While MARL methodologies have predominantly focused on artificial agents, simulations explicitly incorporating astrocytic dynamics remain scarce. Recent projects, such as AstroError [6] and advances in neuron-astrocyte network modelling [10], illustrate the promise of MARL-based astrocytic simulations as an emerging research avenue. Our research represents the first dedicated effort to construct an in silico simulation that captures the competitive and conflicting behaviours of astrocytes in maintaining neuron-astrocyte interactions. In this proposed framework, individual astrocytes operate as autonomous learning agents, capable of independent decision-making within a shared neural microenvironment encompassing neuronal populations, synaptic connections, and extracellular glutamate dynamics. Our contributions facilitate reproducible and collaborative simulation approaches essential for developing in vitro organ-on-chip systems. Such systems enable precise predictions of baseline glutamate concentrations, real-time monitoring of astrocyte-neuron interactions, and provide critical decision-making inputs for optimising in-vitro workflows.

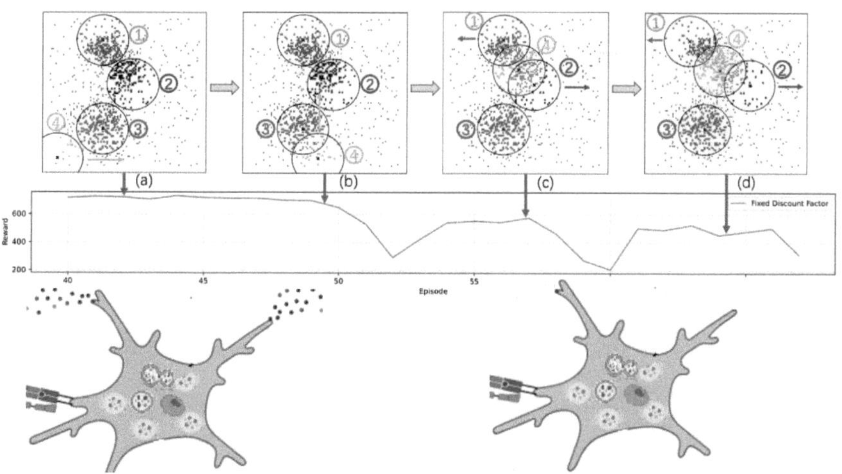

Fig. 1. Glutomate Release States with two Astrocyte Conditions

2   Preliminary

2.1   Multi-agent Systems in Neuroscience

Multi-Agent Reinforcement Learning has emerged as a promising approach for modeling complex biological systems with distributed control mechanisms [2]. A Markov decision process (MDP) with a 5-tuple $(\mathcal{S}, \mathcal{A}, \mathcal{P}, \mathcal{R}, \gamma)$ is used to model the astrocyte-neuron interactions where:

- State space $\mathcal{S}$: is a set of states.

$$\text{Extracellular glutamate concentrations:} \quad [\text{Glu}]_{\text{ext}}(t)$$
$$\text{Neuronal firing patterns:} \quad F_{\text{neuron}}(t)$$
$$\text{Intracellular astrocytic calcium dynamics:} \quad [\text{Ca}^{2+}]_{\text{astro}}(t)$$

- Action space $\mathcal{A}$: is a finite and discrete set of actions through their environment through glutamate uptake rate modulation; glutamate release regulation; synaptic efficacy modification via bidirectional plasticity mechanisms.
- Transition probability $\mathcal{P}$: is the probability that action a_t in state s_t at time t will lead to state s_{t+1} at time t+1.
- Reward $\mathcal{R}$: is the immediate reward received after the transition from state s_t to state s_{t+1}, due to action a. The negative reward will be given if optimal glutamate concentration not observed.
- Discount factor γ: Discount factor $\gamma \in [0, 1]$ quantifies how much to prioritise immediate homeostatic needs versus future outcomes. Since astrocytes operate across multiple timescales-from millisecond glutamate update to minutes-long calcium waves, those bioloigcal reality require dynamic approach to temporal weighting, as different astrocytic functions occur on vastly different time horizons.

In an MDP $(\mathcal{S}, \mathcal{A}, \mathcal{P}, \mathcal{R}, \gamma)$, the expected return $V^{\pi}(s) : \mathcal{S} \rightarrow \mathbb{R}(\pi \in \Pi, e.g., \mathcal{S} \rightarrow \mathcal{A})$ is defined such that

$$V^{\pi}(s) = \mathbb{E}\left[\sum_{t=0}^{\infty} \gamma^t R_t | s_0 = s, \pi\right] \tag{1}$$

the agent's goal is to find the optimal policy which can be defined as

$$\pi^*(s) = \underset{\pi \in \Pi}{argmax}\, V^{\pi}(s) \tag{2}$$

2.2   Astrocytes Behaviours Modelling

The MARL framework successfully reproduces astrocytic homeostatic behaviour under physiological conditions, with agents coordinating to maintain glutamate concentrations within normal ranges. Inter-agent communication emerges through local calcium signalling dynamics, facilitating distributed regulatory responses. Inspired by the work [8], we adopt independent policy proxima-tion modeling (IPPO) with adaptive discounting method to model astro-cytes behaviour. The architecture of Independent Proximal Policy Optimization (IPPO) aligns closely with the biological characteristics of astrocytes for the following reasons: (1) each agent, representing an individual astrocyte, maintains an independent policy, allowing for decentralized decision-making; (2) agents operate without the need for centralized coordination; and (3) this decentralized autonomy reflects the intrinsic nature of astrocytes, which function as spatially distributed, self-regulating cells within neural networks. The mathematics formation of the IPPO follows with a single-agent Proximal Policy Optimisation Modelling (PPO), but each agent maintains its own independent policy. **PPO Objective:**

The central PPO objective for a single agent is defined as:

$$L^{CLIP}(\theta) = \mathbb{E}_{s,a \sim \pi_{\theta_{old}}} \left[\min \left(r_t(\theta) A_t, \ \text{clip} \left(r_t(\theta), 1 - \epsilon, 1 + \epsilon \right) A_t \right) \right]$$

where:

- θ represents the current policy parameters.
- θ_{old} represents the parameters of the policy used to sample experiences.
- A_t is the advantage function, indicating how much better taking action a in state s is compared to an average action:

$$A_t = Q(s, a) - V(s_t)$$

As shown in Fig. 1, the goal of the agents is to maintain the glutamate concentration within physiological range. Agent 1: Maintains consistent high-density glutamate uptake throughout the sequence; Agent 2: Shows moderate activity with spatial expansion over time; Agent 3: Exhibits intense localized activity, likely responding to excitonic stress; Agent 4: Demonstrates adaptive territorial expansion and contraction. Figure 1(a)–(b) shows initial stable configuration with defined territorial boundaries. Figure 1(b)–(c) shows Agent 4 expands territory while Agent 2 begins coordinated response (purple arrows). The reward curve illustrates the collective performance of the system over time. During episodes 40 to 45, a high reward of approximately 600 indicates optimal homeostatic coordination among agents. This is followed by a sharp decline in episodes 45 to 50, suggesting the onset of excitotoxic conditions. Between episodes 50 and 55, a partial recovery is observed as the agents begin to adapt their strategies. Finally, episodes 55 to 60 show stabilization at a lower reward level, reflecting a persistent state of stress in the system.

In this environment, two agents must collaborate to release glutamate to all of the neurons in the environment. In addition, these agents are punished when their released gltomate higher than the neibougr agents. Reinforcement learning (RL) fundamentally relies on the discount factor γ to determine the value of future rewards [5]. Traditionally, γ is set to a fix value to emphasise the significance of long-term gains. However, the biological system has able to manage to find the balance for optimal gain. In this work, we proposed noisy biological environments, where extracellular glutamate concentrations fluctuate rapidly," astrocytes need dynamic temporal weighting mechanisms rather than static optimization strategies. This mirrors how real astrocytes adaptively respond to changing neural conditions.

3   Method

3.1   Motivation for Adaptive Discount Factor

Biological systems demonstrate remarkable capacity to achieve optimal homeostatic balance despite conflicting regulatory demands. Traditional reinforcement learning approaches use fixed discount factors (*gamma*) that maintain constant temporal weighting throughout training. However, astrocytes in neural microenvironments must dynamically balance immediate glutamate buffering needs against long-term homeostatic maintenance across multiple timescales— from millisecond glutamate uptake to minutes-long calcium waves. This biological reality motivates our adaptive discount factor method, which dynamically adjusts temporal weighting parameters to emulate how astrocytic agents effectively resolve functional conflicts in environments characterized by sparse or delayed reward signals.

The adaptive discount factor mechanism effectively captures several key biological phenomena relevant to astrocytic function. First, it enables dynamic prioritization, allowing astrocytes to shift between immediate glutamate buffering and long-term homeostatic maintenance in response to changing neural conditions. Second, it supports multi-timescale integration, reflecting the diverse temporal dynamics of astrocytic processes—from rapid glutamate uptake to slower calcium signaling pathways. Additionally, the mechanism facilitates homeostatic adaptation, as the balance between exploration and exploitation mirrors the ability of biological systems to maintain stability while responding to environmental fluctuations. Finally, through performance-based adjustment, the model replicates the way astrocytes resolve competing regulatory demands, effectively simulating conflict resolution in real neural microenvironments.

3.2   Adaptive Discount Factor Algorithm

The main loop of the algorithm (as shown in Fig. 2) operates in two distinct phases: exploratory Phase and exploitation phase. The exploratory phase is actively searches for optimal discount factor values and exploitation Phase is to uses current optimal values with occasional exploration. The parameters in this algorithm are below:

γ_0: Initial base discount factor value.

γ: Current adaptive discount factor.

g_{vf}: Gamma variance factor (adjustment rate), initially set to 0.1.

MaxR: Maximum average reward achieved across all previous episodes.
AveR: Average reward of the current episode.
exploration: Boolean control variable for adjustment mode.
ϵ: Probability threshold for exploration in non-exploratory mode.

In the **exploratory mode** (where exploration $=$ true), the agent continuously compares the average reward of the current episode (AveR) with the historical maximum reward (MaxR) to assess performance. Based on this comparison, the discount factor γ is dynamically adjusted. Specifically, if the current performance exceeds the historical maximum (i.e., AveR $>$ MaxR), γ is reduced by a predefined value g_{vf}, such that $\gamma = \gamma - g_{vf}$, to encourage further optimization. This is based on the rationale that improved performance suggests the current direction of adjustment is beneficial. Conversely, if performance does not improve (i.e., MaxR $\geq$ AveR), γ is reset to its previous value, and g_{vf} is increased, reflecting the assumption that the adjustment direction may be suboptimal. This process continues until changes in γ no longer yield improvements in reward, at which point the system transitions to **exploitation mode** (exploration $=$ false). During exploitation, the agent maintains the current optimal γ value to ensure stable performance. To avoid premature convergence to local optima and to adapt to dynamic environments, the system occasionally re-enters exploratory mode with a small probability ϵ, enabling *stochastic re-exploration* when needed.

Algorithm CC-MARL

Require: $MaxR \leftarrow$ the maximum average reward in all episodes, $AveR \leftarrow$ the average reward in the current episode, $\gamma \leftarrow$ current discount factor, $\hat{\gamma} \leftarrow$ discount factor for maximum average reward, $Exploration \leftarrow$ decide whether to continue exploring discount factor, $gvf \leftarrow \gamma$ variance factor

1: Initialize discount factor $\gamma \leftarrow \gamma_0$
2: Initialize $Exploration \leftarrow 1$
3: Initialize $gvf \leftarrow 0.1$
4: **for** $episode = 1 \rightarrow n$ **do**
5:     **if** $Exploration$ **then**
6:         **if** $MaxR < AveR$ **then**
7:             $\hat{\gamma} \leftarrow \gamma$
8:             $\gamma \leftarrow \hat{\gamma} - gvf$
9:         **else**
10:            $\gamma \leftarrow \hat{\gamma}$
11:            $gvf \leftarrow f_{gvf}(\gamma, \hat{\gamma})$
12:            $Exploration \leftarrow 0$
13:        **end if**
14:    **else**
15:        With probability ϵ do
16:            $\gamma \leftarrow \hat{\gamma} - gvf$
17:            $Exploration \leftarrow 1$
18:        Otherwise $\gamma \leftarrow \hat{\gamma}$
19:    **end if**
20:    **return** γ
21: **end for**

Fig. 2. Adaptive Discount Factor Algorithm

3.3 Gamma Variance Factor (gvf) Adaptation

The gvf parameter controls the granularity of discount factor adjustments using a precision-based scaling mechanism Eq. 3:

$$
f_{gvf}(\gamma, \hat{\gamma}) = \begin{cases} gvf + SCU(gvf), & \gamma > \lfloor \hat{\gamma} \rfloor \\ SCU(gvf)/10, & \text{otherwise} \end{cases} \tag{3}
$$

Where, $\lfloor \gamma_{\text{optimal}} \rfloor$ represents the floor value of the optimal discount factor. For example, $\lfloor 0.9 \rfloor = 0$ and $\lfloor 0.27 \rfloor = 0.2$.

$SCU(g_{vf})$ denotes the *Smallest Counting Unit* of g_{vf}. This scaling mechanism ensures that the system performs coarse adjustments when it is far from the optimal values, gradually transitions to fine-tuning as it approaches the optimal region, and achieves high precision during final convergence, thereby avoiding suboptimal plateaus at coarse values such as 0.5 or 0.6.

4   Experiment

In this study, we used Independent Proximal Policy Optimisation(IPPO), Monotonic Value Function Factorisation (QMIX) [7] and Value Decomposition Network(VDN) [9] as baselines. All baselines used a fixed discount factor value of 0.99, which encourages long-term homeostatic strategies. The accumulated reward is the normalised activities of transport of astrocytes to release glutamate rates are normalised. **Results:** Figure 3 demonstrates that our method finds the appropriate discount factor to meet the agreement find in the experiment [4].

Results: Figure 4 depicts IPPO, QMIX, VDN with adaptive discount factor adjustment. The trend is less uniform, but the reward remains relatively stable across discount factors for QMIX and VDN, with a slight decrease as the discount factor increases. IPPO shows more volatility. The dotted line indicates the performance of our method added to the baseline, which consistently outperforms the baseline algorithms across the range of discount factors, indicating the robustness and effectiveness of our method.

4.1 Visualisation of Policies and Value Functions

Explainable the decision-making process of each agent in deep reinforcement learning process can be achieved through visualise a combination of policy map, value function and reward decomposition to compare with observation in in-vivo organ-in-chip.

Test Setting: We visualise the agent decision making process for our adaptive discounting IPPO method for explain how agent make autonomous decision. We choose the rewards, actual rewards, variance of rewards, collision frequencies, and Q-values among different agents in the neural microenvironment as a indication for visualisation. Here, the actual reward refers to the maximum theoretical number of users that an agent can connect.

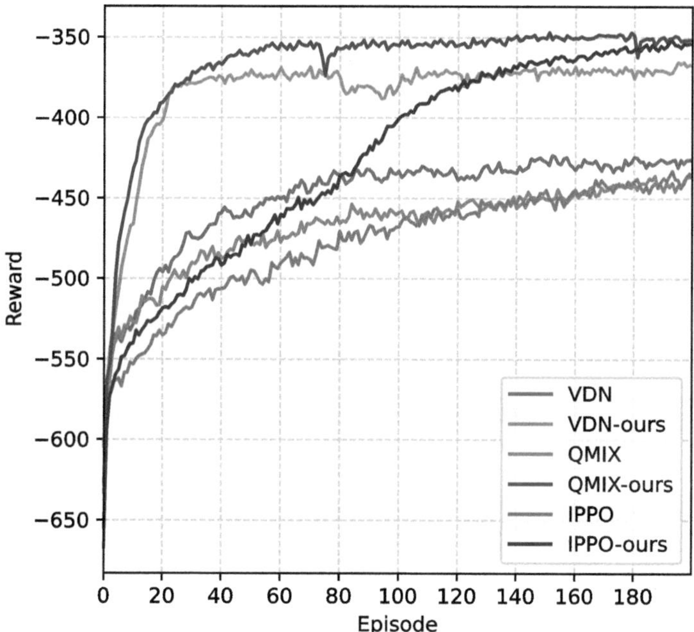

(a) Release rates of Glutomate.

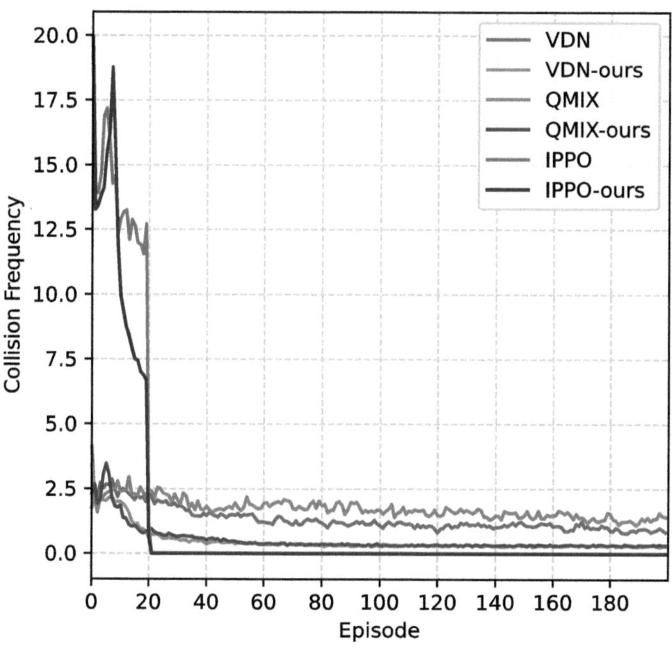

(b) Conflict in multi.

Fig. 3. Comparative results with baselines algorithms

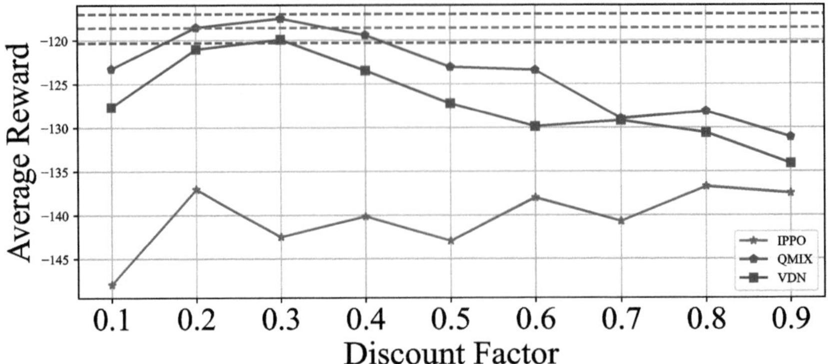

Fig. 4. Performance in various discount factor

Results: Each astrocyte-based agent exhibits a distinct performance profile, reflecting the underlying biological heterogeneity of astrocytic subtypes and their functional specialization within neural microenvironments.

We use the "collision" metric to serve as a proxy for an astrocyte's ability to resolve competing objectives, such as immediate glutamate buffering versus long-term homeostatic regulation, mimicking real-world biochemical trade-offs. The observed stabilisation in reward variance under adaptive discounting supports the notion that dynamic temporal weighting mechanisms are critical in noisy biological environments, where extracellular glutamate concentrations fluctuate rapidly. As shown in Fig. 5, each radar chart in the study illustrates six core performance metrics used to evaluate agent behaviour: actual reward to representing the direct environmental feedback; Q-value for the estimated state-action value; Reward is represent the immediate reward signal; Var-reward is used to indicating the variance and stability of the reward signal; Collision is measured for reflecting conflict resolution capacity. Agent-specific performance analysis is shown in Fig. 5(a)–(d), capturing distinct behavioural patterns: Agent 1 demonstrates balanced performance under the adaptive discounting scheme (blue), with particularly strong collision avoidance. In contrast, using a fixed discount factor (*gamma* = 0.5) results in reduced Q-value estimation and has low conflict resolution capability. This highlights the agent's significant reliance on adaptive temporal weighting for efficient decision-making in high-conflict scenarios. Agent 2 maintains a high actual reward and moderate Q-value performance under the adaptive approach. While the fixed *gamma* = 0.5 strategy yields a qualitatively similar trend, it consistently show variations. This suggests that Agent 2 also benefits from adaptive discounting, though to a slightly lesser degree than Agent 1. Agent 3 exhibits excellent performance in terms of actual reward and Q-value under adaptive discounting. However, fixed discounting leads to a marked degradation in both collision avoidance and reward stability which is not observed in experiment from literature review [4]. These results imply that Agent 3 is particularly sensitive to temporal dynamics and that adaptive strategies are essential to handle its complex local interactions. Agent 4 achieves balanced outcomes with strong conflict resolution under adaptive discounting. The fixed *gamma* = 0.5 condition produces a pronounced decline across all metrics, especially in Q-value estimation and collision handling. This suggests that Agent 4 requires adaptive mechanisms to simulate astrocyte-neuron interaction in homoeostatic. Across all agents, adaptive discounting consistently outperforms fixed strategies. This provides computational validation for its biological plausibility, suggesting that astrocytes may leverage dynamic decision frameworks rather than static optimisation when navigating complex neural dynamics.

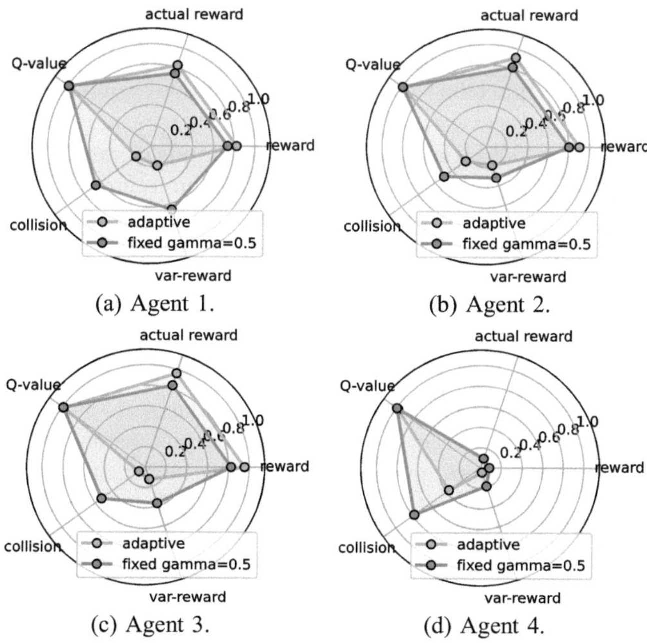

Fig. 5. Individual astrocytic agents balance multiple competing objectives using adaptive versus fixed discount factors

5   Conclusion and Future Work

This study presents a novel Multi-Agent Reinforcement Learning framework that successfully models astrocyte-neuron interactions in neural microenvironments through autonomous learning agents. The proposed adaptive discount factor IPPO modelling addresses the fundamental challenge of temporal decision-making in biological systems, where astrocytes must balance immediate gluta-mate buffering requirements against long-term homeostatic maintenance. The research demonstrates three primary contributions to computational neuroscience. First, the Independent Proximal Policy Optimisation (IPPO) implementation with adaptive discount factor adjustment achieves remarkable accuracy, with glutamate release rates showing only 1% deviation from experimental literature values. This validation establishes the framework's biological plausibility and computational precision. Second, the adaptive discount factor methodology significantly outperforms fixed-parameter approaches across multiple performance metrics, including buffering glutamete to avoid collision. Third, the framework successfully captures the dual nature of astrocytic function, modeling both neuroprotective glutamate buffering and pathological excitotoxic contributions within a unified computational paradigm.

The heterogeneous performance profiles observed across individual astrocytic agents reflect the underlying biological diversity of astrocytic subtypes and their specialised functions within neural microenvironments. The superior performance of adaptive versus fixed discount factors across all agents provides computational validation for dynamic temporal weighting mechanisms in biological systems. While the current validation relies primarily on qualitative agreement with experimental observations due to limited quantitative data availability, the framework establishes a foundation for future empirical validation through organ-on-chip systems and in vitro experimental collaborations. The modular design facilitates reproducible research and collaborative development, essential for advancing computational astrocyte modelling. Future research directions include extending the framework to larger-scale neural network simulations and investigating micro-level neurovascular coupling scenarios that model dynamic interactions between neurons, astrocytes, and vascular cells as autonomous decision-making entities. The integration of additional cellular populations, such as endothelial cells and smooth muscle cells, will provide more comprehensive modelling of neural microenvironments and their regulatory mechanisms.

References

1. Araque, A., Carmignoto, G., Haydon, P.G., Oliet, S.H., Robitaille, R., Volterra, A.: Gliotransmitters travel in time and space. Neuron **81**(4), 728–739 (2014). https://doi.org/10.1016/j.neuron.2014.02.007
2. Jiang, H.J., et al.: Modeling neuron-astrocyte interactions in neural networks using distributed simulation. bioRxiv, p. 2024-11 (2024)
3. Kazemipour, A., Novak, O., Flickinger, D., et al.: Kilohertz frame-rate two-photon tomography. Nat. Meth. **16**, 778–786 (2019)
4. Li, J., Tang, J., Ma, J., et al.: Dynamic transition of neuronal firing induced by abnormal astrocytic glutamate oscillation. Sci. Rep. **6**, 32343 (2016). https://doi.org/10.1038/srep32343
5. Naik, A., Shariff, R., Yasui, N., Yao, H., Sutton, R.S.: Discounted reinforcement learning is not an optimization problem. arXiv preprint arXiv:1910.02140 (2019)
6. Publications Office of the European Union: Computational approaches to reveal the role of norepinephrine-astrocyte signaling in reinforcement learning. Publications Office of the European Union (2025)

7. Rashid, T., Samvelyan, M., De Witt, C.S., Farquhar, G., Foerster, J., Whiteson, S.: Monotonic value function factorisation for deep multi-agent reinforcement learning. J. Mach. Learn. Res. **21**(1), 7234–7284 (2020)
8. Schulman, J., Wolski, F., Dhariwal, P., Radford, A., Klimov, O.: Proximal policy optimization algorithms. arXiv preprint arXiv:1707.06347 (2017)
9. Sunehag, P., et al.: Value-decomposition networks for cooperative multi-agent learning. arXiv preprint arXiv:1706.05296 (2017)
10. Volterra, A., Meldolesi, J.: Astrocytes, from brain glue to communication elements: the revolution continues. Nat. Rev. Neurosci. **6**(8), 626–640 (2005). https://doi.org/10.1038/nrn1722

Transformer-Based and Generative Classifiers for Mining Imbalanced Datasets

Piotr Jedrzejowicz$^{(\boxtimes)}$ and Izabela Wierzbowska

Gdynia Maritime University, Gdynia, Poland
{p.jedrzejowicz,i.wierzbowska}@wi.umg.edu.pl

Abstract. The paper focuses on the possibility of using transformer-based and generative models for mining imbalanced datasets. We briefly review recent developments in constructing transformers and generative models and their application in machine learning. Next, we explain how to use public domain libraries to build a local transformer-based classifier, that can be used solo or in conjunction with a combined transformer-based and VAE model for generating synthetic minority data or generative model for synthetic minority data generation. The approach is validated in the computational experiment showing that transformer-based classifiers perform well and can be an interesting alternative to classic methods of mining imbalanced datasets.

Keywords: Artificial intelligence · Imbalanced datasets mining · Generative model · Transformer-based classifier

1 Introduction

Recent years have brought spectacular advances in Transformer-based and Generative Models. Transformers, initially designed for natural language processing (NLP), have become a dominant force across various domains. The core strength of transformers lies in their attention mechanism, which allows the model to weigh the importance of different parts of the input data, enabling them to capture long-range dependencies effectively. Among breakthrough transformers, one should mention:

- Vision Transformers (ViT) [7].
- Long-Sequence Transformers that handle very long sequences using techniques such as sparse attention [24] and linear attention mechanisms.
- Multimodal Transformers.

1.1 Generative Models

Generative models learn the underlying distribution of data and can then generate new samples that resemble the training data. Advanced generative models include:

M. Bramer and F. Stahl (Eds.): SGAI-AI 2025, LNAI 16302, pp. 120–133, 2026.
https://doi.org/10.1007/978-3-032-11442-6_9

- Diffusion models that have emerged as a powerful alternative to GANs (Generative Adversarial Networks) for image generation. Models like DALL-E 2 [15] and Imagen [16] use a diffusion process to gradually add noise to an image and then learn to reverse this process, generating high-quality images from noise.
- Large Language Models (LLMs) as Generators. LLMs like GPT family [2] have demonstrated remarkable capabilities in generating realistic and coherent text.
- Neural Radiance Fields (NeRFs). NeRFs [14] are a type of generative model that can create novel views of a 3D scene from a set of 2D images.

The primary goal of generative models is learning the underlying probability distribution of a dataset and generating new data samples that resemble the training data. In essence, they aim to create new content. Their core mechanism varies depending on the type of generative model. GANs (Generative Adversarial Networks) use a generator network to create samples and a discriminator network to distinguish between real and generated samples. They're trained in an adversarial manner. VAEs (Variational Autoencoders) learn a latent space representation of the data and then generate new samples by sampling from this latent space and decoding it. Diffusion Models gradually add noise to data and then learn to reverse the noise process to generate new samples.

Transformer-based architectures have been originally designed for sequence-to-sequence tasks, especially in NLP. Their primary goal is understanding relationships within sequential data and mapping input sequences to output sequences. While they can be used for generative tasks, that's not their sole purpose. They're also used for tasks like classification, regression, and understanding/reasoning. Transformers' core mechanism is the "attention mechanism," which allows the model to weigh the importance of different parts of the input data when processing it. This is particularly effective for capturing long-range dependencies in sequences.

Generative models are used for data generation, while transformer-based architectures are used for sequence modeling (but can be used for generation). The typical output of generative models is new data samples, while the typical output of transformer-based models is mappings between sequences, classifications, etc. It should be noted that transformers can be used as part of generative models.

In this study, we attempt to show how generative and transformer-based models for mining imbalanced datasets can be constructed locally using available open libraries. Real-world datasets often have skewed class distributions. For example, fraud cases are far rarer than legitimate transactions. In response, the last five years has seen substantial progress in imbalanced learning [11].

Data-level techniques modify the training data to balance classes. Common strategies include oversampling the minority class and undersampling the majority class. For example, the SMOTE algorithm [3] synthetically generates new minority examples by interpolating between nearest neighbors. Many SMOTE variants have been proposed - e.g., Borderline-SMOTE, ADASYN, Safe-Level

SMOTE - to focus synthesis near decision boundaries or account for density [4]. More recently, mixup-based methods (Remix, Balanced-MixUp, etc.) create synthetic points by blending features and labels from different classes [11]. Likewise, deep generative models (VAEs and GANs) have been used to model the minority distribution and sample new examples [8,21]. These approaches can produce more diverse, realistic minority data. Each sampling method has trade-offs: oversampling increases minority representation but can overfit or introduce noise [4] while undersampling may lose valuable information.

Algorithm-level methods adjust the learning model itself to account for class imbalance. The most used strategy is cost-sensitive learning: assigning higher weights or costs to minority-class errors. In effect, the classifier's objective is altered so that mistakes on rare classes carry more penalties [4]. A simple implementation is to scale the cross-entropy loss by the inverse class frequency or effective sample count [5]. Other algorithmic methods include threshold adjustment (moving the decision threshold to favor the minority) and specialized cost matrices. Ensembling multiple classifiers is another major strategy for mining imbalanced datasets [23].

In this study, we would follow three different paths shown in Fig. 1. The first one assumes that both – synthetic generation of the minority class examples and the classification model are based on transformers. In the second path, synthetic examples are produced by a generative model, and a classifier is identical to the first path. The third path assumes that a transformer-based classifier is used for mining and that no oversampling or undersampling is needed. The study focuses on transformer-based classifiers since classifiers based on the generative paradigm have been already in use for several years and are well-known. Examples include the Naive Bayes Classifier [9], Gaussian Mixture Models, and Variational Autoencoders (VAEs) for Anomaly Detection [12].

We believe that transformer-based models, which excel in capturing complex patterns through attention mechanisms, can be effectively used to address imbalanced datasets by emphasizing relevant features and context.

The rest of the paper is constructed as follows. Section 2 gives details of the transformer-based classifier used. Section 3 describes a transformer-based model for generating synthetic minority examples. Section 4 describes the generative model producing synthetic minority examples. Section 5 provides a description of the computational experiment carried out covering each path, and comparisons of the obtained results. Final Sect. 6 contains conclusions and suggestions for future research.

2   Transformer-Based Classifier

One of the most important innovations in Artificial Intelligence is the emergence of the transformer architecture. Transformer architecture was introduced by Vaswani and co-authors [20] in the seminal paper "Attention is All You Need". This paper suggested replacing recurrence-based models like Long Short-Term Memory networks (LSTMs) and Gated Recurrent Units (GRUs) used in natural

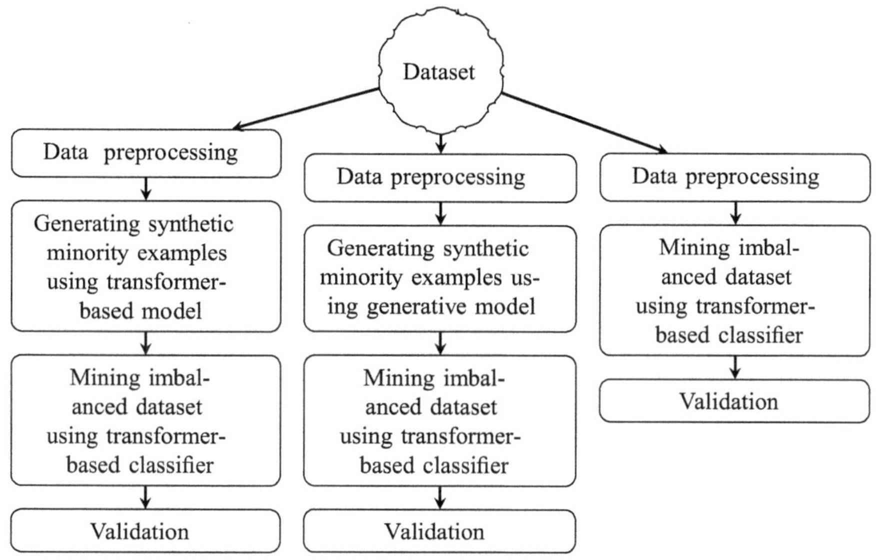

Fig. 1. Different paths for mining imbalanced datasets using generative and transformer-based models.

language processing, speech recognition, and other sequence modeling tasks, with self-attention mechanisms, significantly improving parallelization and efficiency in sequence modeling. In 2018 the Bidirectional Encoder Representations from Transformers (BERT) was introduced in [6]. BERT used a bidirectional transformer encoder, pre-trained with the Masked Language Model (MLM) and Next Sentence Prediction (NSP) tasks, setting new state-of-the-art results on NLP benchmarks. Since 2021 various advancements in transformer model variants have been proposed. Among them Vision Transformers adopted for computer vision tasks [7], and Efficient Transformers such as Linformer, Performer, and Longformer introducing optimizations to handle longer sequences with reduced computational complexity [19].

For this study, we use publicly available software libraries to construct a local transformer-based binary classifier. For its integration, we use components and functions from PyTorch. Its main features and functionalities include:

- Tensor Operations.
- Automatic Differentiation.
- Neural Network Library (torch.nn).
- GPU Acceleration.

More information on PyTorch and its usage can be found in [18], and [10].

From earlier models, for example, BioBERT for biomedical text classification [13], FinBERT for sentiment analysis on financial texts [1], or "A Transformer-Based Framework for Payload Malware Detection and Classification" [17] it appears that a transformer-based classifier should be constructed from the following components and functionalities:

- Input Sequence & Linear Projection.
- Positional Encoding.
- Transformer Encoder.
- Mean Pooling Layer.
- Fully Connected Output Layer.

Input Sequence & Linear Projection Transforms the input into a higher-dimensional space (`d_model`) using `nn.Linear(input_dim, d_model)` to map features to the predefined number of dimensions. Value `d_model` defines the size of feature embeddings used in the Transformer and determines the number of neurons in self-attention and feedforward layers. `nn.Linear` is a fully connected (dense) layer in PyTorch's `torch.nn` module. It applies a linear transformation to the input data using learnable weights and biases.

Positional Encoding is needed since transformers do not have an inherent sequence order. Its role is to ensure the model understands sequence structure. To model dependencies between input features self-attention mechanism is used. It captures important interactions between different parts of the sequence.

The mean pooling layer takes the average across the sequence dimension and converts variable-length sequences into fixed-size embeddings summarizing the output from the Transformer.

Finally, the Fully Connected Output Layer maps the final transformer output to a single value in the range between 0 and 1 (label prediction) using a fully connected (dense) layer.

In Fig. 2 the diagram displaying action flows of the discussed transformer-based classifier is shown.

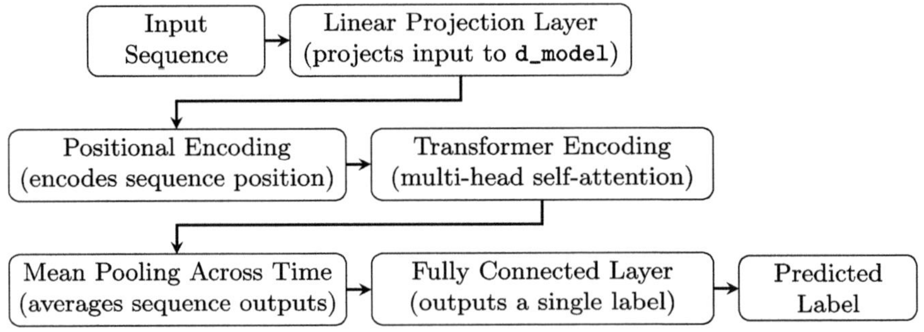

Fig. 2. Action flows of the transformer-based classifier used.

When training a Transformer-based classifier, several hyperparameters impact model performance, training stability, and generalization. Most important, from the classifier performance point of view include:

- Number of Epochs (`epochs`).
- Model Dimension (`d_model`).
- Number of Transformer Layers (`num_layers`).
- Batch Size (`batch_size`).
- Loss Function/Criterion (`criterion`).
- Learning Rate (`learning_rate`).
- Dropout Rate (`dropout`).

The number of epochs define how many times the model sees the entire dataset during training. Too few epochs result in underfitting (the model hasn't learned enough). Too many epochs result in overfitting (model memorizes instead of generalizing).

Model Dimension defines the size of feature embeddings used in the Transformer. It determines the number of neurons in self-attention and feed-forward layers. Smaller dimensions result in faster training and less expressive models larger assure better feature representation but require more data and memory.

A number of transformer layers defines how deep the model is (stacked Transformer Encoder layers). Each layer learns more complex patterns in the data. More layers assure better performance for complex data at the cost of slower training.

Batch Size defines how many samples the model processes before updating weights. Smaller batch assures better generalization and slower training. Larger batch offers faster training but may generalize worse.

The loss function (or criterion) measures how far predictions are from actual labels. For example, nn.MSELoss() is typically used with linear and sigmoid layers, while nn.BCEWithLogitsLoss(), recommended for binary classification, is used with a linear output layer, as it internally applies the sigmoid activation.

The Learning Rate Controls how much the model updates its weights after each batch. If the Rate is too high model may never converge (jumps around). A low Learning Rate results in slow learning.

Finally, the Dropout Rate prevents overfitting by deactivating at random a specified percentage of neurons within a layer during learning.

Hyperparameter tuning is essential for maximizing model performance and avoiding overfitting or underfitting. Tuning can be based on exhaustive search (for simple and small problems), on random search (trials-and-errors), or on Bayesian Optimization.

3   Combined Transformer-Based and VAE Model for Generating Synthetic Minority Data

For generating synthetic minority data we use an architecture consisting of the Transformer combined with a Variational Autoencoder (VAE). The VAE encodes input data into a latent space. This involves mapping the input to a mean and a variance, which define a Gaussian distribution in the latent space. From this distribution, the VAE samples latent variables, ensuring that similar inputs have similar representations. This sampling mechanism introduces a degree of variability in the generated outputs. The latent variables are then passed to the decoder, which attempts to reconstruct the original input data. When combined with a Transformer, the architecture can generate sequential data.

The Transformer model, using self-attention mechanisms, captures long-range dependencies in sequences. It is used in conjunction with a VAE to model sequences in a more coherent and contextually aware manner. The Transformer in our case serves as the decoder in the VAE framework. When used as the decoder, the Transformer interprets the latent variables generated by the VAE and converts them into coherent sequences, leveraging its self-attention layers to maintain consistency and context. The VAE ensures that the latent representations are smooth and meaningful, while the Transformer enhances the quality and coherence of generated sequences.

Using a Transformer combined with a Variational Autoencoder (VAE) to generate synthetic minority examples is an innovative approach to address class imbalance in datasets. In Fig. 3 the diagram displaying action flows of the discussed combined transformer-based and VAE model is shown.

After preprocessing and cleaning examples from the minority class are gathered for training. Next, the VAE Encoder encodes the features of the minority class examples into latent space. Latent space is sampled to obtain new points, possibly with slight perturbations to encourage diversity.

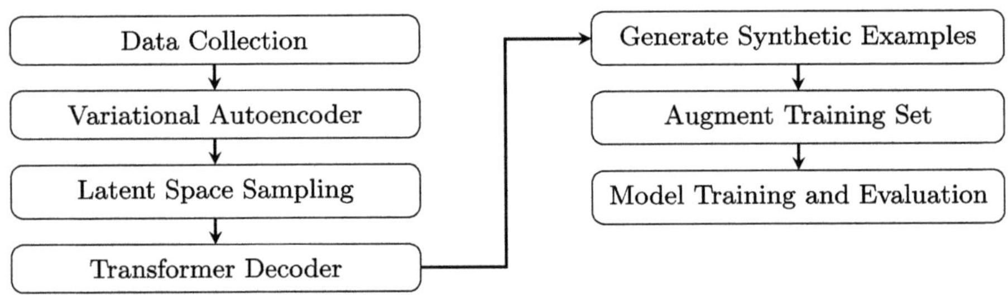

Fig. 3. Action flows of the combined transformer-based and VAE model.

The Transformer model serves to decode sampled latent variables into realistic data points. Context and coherence are ensured through self-attention. Following the decoding, synthetic examples that augment the original minority class dataset are produced to augment the original training set. Finally, a classifier is trained on the augmented dataset and its performance can be evaluated.

For a combined Transformer+VAE model used to generate synthetic minority examples, the main hyperparameters can be grouped into two categories: those specific to the VAE and those specific to the Transformer, along with some that govern their integration.

4   Generative Model for Synthetic Minority Data Generation

To generate synthetic minority class examples we have decided to use the CTGAN (Conditional Generative Adversarial Network for Tabular Data) which is suitable for tabular data. CTGAN is based on the generative adversarial network (GAN) framework, but with adaptations for handling tabular data [22]. Its architecture includes a Generator, Discriminator, and Conditioning Mechanism. The generator produces synthetic samples that resemble real data. It takes random noise and conditional information (related to feature values and class labels) as input. The discriminator attempts to distinguish between real and synthetic samples. It takes both real and generated data along with their conditional inputs. The conditioning mechanism handles discrete and continuous variables, making it suitable for generating tabular data with various data types.

The implementation discussed in this study is based on the publicly available CTGAN framework. A general workflow sequence for the implemented generative model with minority class examples as the outcome, is shown in Fig. 4.

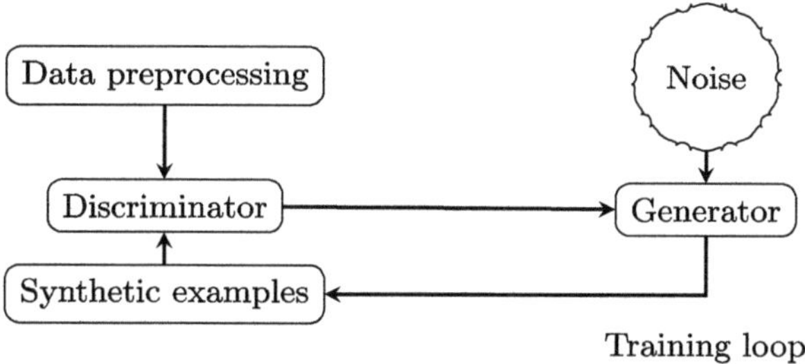

Fig. 4. Workflow sequence of the generative model for producing minority class examples.

A Generator Network is a neural network with an input layer that accepts random noise and a condition input that, in our case, is the minority class label. The network maps this input to a potential data example.

A Discriminator Network is a neural network that distinguishes between real and generated data. It should also receive conditions as input to ensure that decisions are made in the context of the specified class or feature condition.

Training Loop involves the conditional sampling. For each batch, conditions that reflect the preferred characteristics of the minority class are defined. This directs the generator to focus on producing examples within this specific context. When training the discriminator, a batch of real data and synthetic data generated based on the chosen conditions is sampled. The discriminator is trained to classify real data as real and synthetic data as fake, computing the loss based on classification accuracy. Next, the generator produces a new batch of synthetic data under the same conditions. The generator is trained with the goal of deceiving the discriminator, computing the loss based on how well the synthetic data is mistaken for real data. Iterating the training loop gradually improves both networks' abilities. The generator gets better at producing realistic data, while the discriminator becomes more proficient at identifying the fake data.

Once the training is complete, a collection of synthetic samples for the minority class is generated. Synthetic samples need to be evaluated concerning their quality. This requires confirmation that these synthetic samples realistically reflect the characteristics of the minority class without sacrificing variability. Synthetic examples can be combined with the original dataset, bolstering the minority class. The class distribution is thus rebalanced to improve the dataset utility for subsequent training of predictive models.

Key hyperparameters of the model include:

- Batch Size.
- Learning Rate.
- Generator and Discriminator Architecture.
- Training Epochs.
- Noise Dimension.
- Conditional Training Parameters.
- Packing (PAC) parameter.
- Regularization Parameters.
- Loss Function Weights.

5   Computational Experiment

5.1   Experiment Plan and Assumptions

To validate the described approach we carried out a computational experiment. Its goal was to evaluate the quality and potential of the transformer-based architecture for mining imbalanced datasets. In the experiment, we used 20 datasets randomly selected from the Keel Imbalanced Dataset Repository. Their main characteristics including name, number of instances, number of examples, and imbalanced ratio (IR) are shown in Table 1.

To evaluate the performance of different model configurations studied, we used three metrics: accuracy, area under the curve (AUC), and F1 score. All results reported in the study have been obtained using a 10-fold cross-validation scheme and next averaged over all folds and two runs of the scheme.

The experiment involved the following models:

- Transformer-based classifier, denoted **T**.
- Transformer-based and VAE models for generating minority class examples, denoted **TVAE**.
- A generative model for producing minority class examples, denoted **G**.
- SMOTE [3], denoted **S**.
- CART classifier from scikit-learn library in Python, denoted **CART**.

The above models were used in the following configurations: TVAE+T, G+T, T, S+TVAE, and S+CART. All experiments have been carried out on the CPU, on server equipped with 4 Intel Xeon E7-4860 CPUx, each featuring 10 cores.

Table 1. Characteristics of datasets used in the experiment.

#	Dataset	# Examples	# Attributes	IR
1	abalone-3-vs-11	502	8	32,47
2	dermatology-6	358	34	16,9
3	ecoli-0-1-vs-5	240	6	11
4	ecoli-0-4-6-vs-5	203	6	9,15
5	ecoli1	336	7	3,36
6	page-blocks-1-3-vs-4	472	10	15,86
7	segment0	2308	19	6,02
8	shuttle-2-vs-5	3316	9	66,67
9	vehicle0	846	18	3,25
10	vowel0	988	13	9,98
11	wisconsin	683	9	1,86
12	kddcup-land-vs-portsweep	1061	41	49,52
13	kddcup-land-vs-satan	1061	41	75,67
14	segment0	2308	19	6,02
15	yeast-0-2-5-7-9-vs-3-6-8	1004	8	9,14
16	yeast5	1484	8	32,73
17	ecoli2	336	7	5,46
18	ecoli3	336	7	8,6
19	yeast1	1484	8	2,46
20	cleveland-0-vs-4	280	6	12,63

Source: Keel-Dataset Repository, https://sci2s.ugr.es/keel/imbalanced.php

5.2 Computational Experiment Results

The first part of the experiment involved a comparison of results obtained using the above model configurations. For models generating synthetic minority examples, the balancing was continued until the IR reached the value of 2. For datasets with IR < 2, no balancing was performed. The main hyperparameter values used for each model and other than default are shown in Table 2. Guidelines as to setting their values have been provided by Open AI GPT-4o, and Gemini, followed by trial-and-error procedure.

In Table 3, experiment results averaged over all considered datasets, all runs of the 10-CV scheme, and all repetitions of this scheme are shown. In configurations with oversampling, the dataset balancing was based on the following rule: If dataset IR<2 then no balancing is carried out. Otherwise, generated synthetic minority class examples are sequentially added to the original dataset until the IR=2 is reached.

To compare the groups of results shown in Table 3, we applied the Friedman non-parametric test. The null hypothesis is that there are no significant

Table 2. Parameter values set in the experiment.

Model	Parameter values
T	epochs = 20 or 50, d_model = 16, n_head = 4, num_layers = 2, batch_size = 8, learning_rate = 0.0001
TVAE	latent_dim = 8, feature_dim = 3 or 4, lr = 0.001 reconstruction loss weight = 1 KL divergence weight = 1 loss function = sum of mean squared errors + KL divergence
CTGAN in G	epochs = 10 or 20 activation_functions = ReLU and Sigmoid criterion = adversarial loss/feature matching loss
S	all default
CART	criterion = "entropy"

Table 3. Experiment results for different model configurations.

Measure	TVAE+T	G+T	T	S+T	S+CART
Acc.	0,960	0,951	0,965	0,960	0,951
AUC	0,923	0,908	0,911	0,928	0,898
F1	0,867	0,820	0,844	0,850	0,801

differences between the groups being compared. The alternative hypothesis is that there are significant differences between at least two of the groups. All following conclusions have been drawn at the significance level of 0.05:

- For the Accuracy measure the null hypothesis holds.
- For the AUC measure the null hypothesis has to be rejected and the alternative hypothesis holds.
- For the F1 measure the null hypothesis has to be rejected and the alternative hypothesis holds.

Considering the above findings, one can observe that for each, AUC and F1 measure, there is a significant difference between at least two of the considered groups, and at least one group comes from a different distribution than the others. The experiment does not allow drawing any general conclusions as to the ranking of model configurations except that the classic approach (S+CART) is outperformed by configurations using transformer-based models as learners.

Applying the Friedman non-parametric test to groups consisting of results produced by three model configurations (TVAE+T, T, S+T) shows that for all performance measures and balancing up to IR = 2, the null hypothesis holds. This fact implies that such oversampling does not bring any significant improvement in classification performance in the case where a transformer-based classifier is used. This finding is further supported by the fact that increasing the balancing level up to IR=1 does not improve classification performance for each model configuration used, as supported by data shown in Table 4. From this table, it is also clear that oversampling to reach a full balance between minority and majority examples may not be optimal for AUC and F1 measures.

Table 4. Experiment results for 2 balancing strategies.

Measure	Balancing up to IR $= 2$		Balancing up to IR $= 1$	
	TVAE+T	G+T	TVAE+T	G+T
Acc.	0,960	0,951	0,953	0,947
AUC	0,923	0,908	0,898	0,903
F1	0,867	0,820	0,816	0,806

In terms of the computational resource requirements, an important and costly hyperparameter is the number of epochs set for transformer-based and generative models. In general, increasing the number of epochs should improve a model's performance at a risk of overfitting. It also increases substantially the computation time. In reality, while computation time grows with increasing the number of epochs, performance measures do not necessarily behave similarly. This is demonstrated in Table 5, where results obtained for the subset of datasets numbered 1–10 plus dataset 20, are shown.

Table 5. Experiment results for 50 and 20 epochs.

Config.	50 epochs						20 epochs					
	IR = 1			IR = 2			IR = 1			IR = 2		
	Acc.	AUC	F1	Acc.	AUC	F1	Acc.	AUC	F1	Acc.	AUC	F1
TVAE+T	0,975	0,927	0,858	0,976	0,934	0,878	0,975	0,965	0,930	0,974	0,925	0,852
G+T	0,969	0,942	0,870	0,973	0,940	0,870	0,971	0,940	0,868	0,976	0,942	0,874
S+T	0,972	0,932	0,855	0,973	0,933	0,864	0,972	0,932	0,855	0,977	0,955	0,891

Another question that has to be answered before applying the proposed models is which path from the available ones as depicted in Fig. 1 should be selected to obtain satisfactory results for a classification problem at hand. Our experiment has not provided a clear answer. However, the performance of transformer-based classifier suggests that perhaps oversampling would not be always needed for mining effectively imbalanced datasets using transformer-based models.

6   Conclusions

It is difficult to definitively state whether transformer-based learners and synthetic data generation models are equally effective as using generative models for all scenarios. Transformers excel at capturing complex relationships in data, especially in sequences like text or time series. Pre-trained transformers can be fine-tuned on specific tasks, reducing the need for large labeled datasets. Their strength came from the attention mechanisms making them prioritize relevant features, which can be beneficial in imbalanced scenarios by focusing on minority class characteristics. They, however, require substantial data for effective training, which can be problematic with scarce minority class samples. Another drawback are high resource requirements for training and inference. Transformer-based models are not inherently designed for class imbalance, hence may still be biased toward majority classes and may require class weighting or sampling.

Generative models like GANs and VAE can synthesize new minority class examples to mitigate imbalance, improving classifier performance. They are able to generate realistic samples that can help provide more balanced datasets and thus improve classification accuracy.

Classic approaches include resampling, cost-sensitive learning, and traditional classifiers. They are easy to implement and interpret and are less computationally intensive. Classic approaches are well-understood with established methodologies like SMOTE, undersampling, or cost-sensitive algorithms. On the other hand, their effectiveness is limited by the lack of mechanisms for capturing complex relationships in data.

Combining the above approaches (e.g., using generative models or classic approaches like SMOTE for data augmentation with transformers for classification) could be a promising path in future research on imbalanced data tasks.

Acknowledgments. This research was funded from Gdynia Maritime University research project number WI/2025/PZ/03.

Disclosure of Interests. The authors have no competing interests to declare that are relevant to the content of this article.

References

1. Araci, D.: FinBERT: financial sentiment analysis with pre-trained language models (2019). https://arxiv.org/abs/1908.10063
2. Brown, T.B., et al.: Language models are few-shot learners (2020). https://arxiv.org/abs/2005.14165
3. Chawla, N.V., Bowyer, K.W., Hall, L.O., Kegelmeyer, W.P.: SMOTE: synthetic minority over-sampling technique. J. Artif. Intell. Res. **16**, 321–357 (2002). https://doi.org/10.1613/jair.953
4. Chen, W., Yang, K., Yu, Z., Shi, Y., Chen, C.L.P.: A survey on imbalanced learning: latest research, applications and future directions. Artif. Intell. Rev. **57**(6), 137 (2024). https://doi.org/10.1007/s10462-024-10759-6

5. Cui, Y., Jia, M., Lin, T.Y., Song, Y., Belongie, S.: Class-balanced loss based on effective number of samples (2019). https://arxiv.org/abs/1901.05555
6. Devlin, J., Chang, M.W., Lee, K., Toutanova, K.: BERT: pre-training of deep bidirectional transformers for language understanding (2019). https://doi.org/10.48550/arXiv.1810.04805
7. Dosovitskiy, A., et al.: An image is worth 16x16 words: transformers for image recognition at scale (2021). https://arxiv.org/abs/2010.11929
8. Douzas, G., Bacao, F., Last, F.: Improving imbalanced learning through a heuristic oversampling method based on k-means and SMOTE. Inf. Sci. **465**, 1–20 (2018). https://doi.org/10.1016/j.ins.2018.06.056
9. Duda, R., Hart, P., G.Stork, D.: Pattern Classification. Wiley, January 2001
10. Foster, D.: Generative Deep Learning: Teaching Machines to Paint, Write, Compose and Play. O'Reilly Media (2019)
11. Gao, X., et al.: A comprehensive survey on imbalanced data learning (2025). https://arxiv.org/abs/2502.08960
12. Kingma, D.P., Welling, M.: Auto-encoding variational Bayes (2022). https://arxiv.org/abs/1312.6114
13. Lee, J., et al.: BioBERT: a pre-trained biomedical language representation model for biomedical text mining. Bioinformatics **36**(4), 1234–1240 (2019). https://doi.org/10.1093/bioinformatics/btz682
14. Mildenhall, B., Srinivasan, P.P., Tancik, M., Barron, J.T., Ramamoorthi, R., Ng, R.: NeRF: representing scenes as neural radiance fields for view synthesis (2020). https://arxiv.org/abs/2003.08934
15. Ramesh, A., Dhariwal, P., Nichol, A., Chu, C., Chen, M.: Hierarchical text-conditional image generation with CLIP Latents (2022). https://arxiv.org/abs/2204.06125
16. Saharia, C., et al.: Photorealistic text-to-image diffusion models with deep language understanding (2022). https://arxiv.org/abs/2205.11487
17. Stein, K., Mahyari, A., Francia III, G., El-Sheikh, E.: A transformer-based framework for payload malware detection and classification (2024). https://arxiv.org/abs/2403.18223
18. Stevens, E., Antiga, L.P., Viehmann, T.: Deep Learning with PyTorch: build, train, and tune neural networks using Python tools. Manning (2020)
19. Tay, Y., et al.: Transformer memory as a differentiable search index (2022). https://arxiv.org/abs/2202.06991
20. Vaswani, A., et al.: Attention is all you need (2023). https://arxiv.org/abs/1706.03762
21. Wan, Z., Zhang, Y., He, H.: Variational autoencoder based synthetic data generation for imbalanced learning. In: 2017 IEEE Symposium Series on Computational Intelligence (SSCI), pp. 1–7 (2017). https://doi.org/10.1109/SSCI.2017.8285168
22. Xu, L., Skoularidou, M., Cuesta-Infante, A., Veeramachaneni, K.: Modeling tabular data using conditional GAN (2019). https://arxiv.org/abs/1907.00503
23. Yang, Y., Lv, H., Chen, N.: A survey on ensemble learning under the era of deep learning. Artif. Intell. Rev. **56**(6), 5545–5589 (2022). https://doi.org/10.1007/s10462-022-10283-5
24. Zaheer, M., et al.: Big bird: transformers for longer sequences (2021). https://arxiv.org/abs/2007.14062

DeLSTM-AE: A Decomposition-Driven Framework for Univariate Time Series Anomaly Detection

Mustafa Albalushi[(✉)] and Saif Alzubi

Department of Computer Science, University of Exeter, Exeter EX4 4QE, UK
{ma889,s.m.y.alzubi}@exeter.ac.uk

Abstract. The reliability of modern applications increasingly depends on the stability of underlying distributed web services. Monitoring these services through time series analysis is essential for detecting performance degradations and security anomalies. However, many existing anomaly detection models struggle to adapt to the dynamic nature of cloud-based environments, particularly when dealing with evolving service patterns or system reconfigurations. To help address these challenges, this paper proposes DeLSTM-AE, a novel framework that integrates time series decomposition with a Long Short-Term Memory (LSTM) and an Autoencoder (AE) to improve the detection of anomalies in univariate time series data. By separating seasonal, trend, and residual components prior to training, our model enables more targeted learning of distinct temporal structures, thereby improving its ability to capture subtle anomalies. We evaluate the proposed framework on the benchmark AIOps Challenge 2018 dataset, which includes real-time Key Performance Indicator (KPI) logs from major cloud service providers such as eBay, Sogou, and Tencent. DeLSTM-AE achieves superior performance compared to existing state-of-the-art methods, with a Precision of 99%, Recall of 94%, F1 score of 96%, and Accuracy of 94% across multiple KPI test sets. The results demonstrate that decomposition-based preprocessing substantially enhances both anomaly detection accuracy and model generalisation, offering a scalable and effective solution for real-world monitoring systems.

Keywords: Time Series Anomaly Detection · KPI Monitoring · LSTM Autoencoder

1 Introduction

In today's digital landscape, many modern applications, such as social networks, search engines, and online shopping platforms, rely heavily on distributed web services [1]. These services generate vast volumes of log data, which are commonly transformed into Key Performance Indicators (KPI) [2]. KPIs serve as critical metrics for evaluating the performance, stability, and security of these

M. Bramer and F. Stahl (Eds.): SGAI-AI 2025, LNAI 16302, pp. 134–148, 2026.
https://doi.org/10.1007/978-3-032-11442-6_10

services [3]. Represented as time series data, they are essential within complex environments shaped by evolving software architectures, APIs, and DevOps practices.

Anomaly detection in KPI time series involves identifying unusual patterns or deviations from normal system behaviour over time [4]. This task can be applied to univariate time series, which monitor a single KPI over time, or multivariate time series, which track multiple KPIs simultaneously. While multivariate analysis provides richer context, it introduces significant computational and interpretability challenges [5]. In contrast, univariate anomaly detection is simpler, less resource-intensive, and particularly useful during the early stages of system deployment when minimal data is available [6].

Recent advances in hybrid deep learning models, such as LSTM-TF, CNN-LSTM, and LSTM-AE, have shown promise in overcoming the limitations of traditional machine learning approaches. In particular, LSTM-AE combine the temporal modelling capabilities of Long Short-Term Memory (LSTM) networks with the reconstruction-based strengths of autoencoders, making them well-suited for time series anomaly detection [7].

However, due to the increasing complexity and seasonality of real-world KPIs, even LSTM-AE models may struggle to isolate complex anomalies. To address this, decomposition-based approaches can be used to separate a time series into trend, seasonal, and residual components, offering clearer insights into time-varying patterns [8].

In this paper, we propose a novel hybrid model called DeLSTM-AE, which integrates time series decomposition with an LSTM-AE framework. Our approach decomposes KPI time series prior to modelling, allowing the system to better capture seasonal trends and residual anomalies. This improves detection accuracy and strengthens the model's robustness to diverse anomaly patterns.

The main contributions of this work are as follows: First, we propose DeLSTM-AE, a novel reconstruction-based deep learning model that combines LSTM-AE with time series decomposition, specifically designed to handle long and complex univariate KPI time series. Second, by integrating a decomposition module into the anomaly detection pipeline, our approach isolates seasonal components and residual fluctuations, thereby enhancing the model's sensitivity to complex anomalies. Finally, we demonstrate that DeLSTM-AE improves the performance monitoring and stability of web services by enabling more accurate detection of anomalous behaviour in univariate time series data.

2   Background and Related Work

This section reviews existing methods relevant to univariate time series anomaly detection and decomposition.

2.1   Anomaly Detection on Univariate Time Series

Univariate time series anomaly detection focuses on identifying irregularities using a single metric, such as the KPI value in this study. Unlike multivariate models that analyse interdependent features, univariate approaches concentrate on modelling the temporal dynamics of individual KPIs [9].

Several recent works have explored univariate anomaly detection. For instance, GGIAnomaly [10] employs a four-stage pipeline involving preprocessing, intermetric dependency analysis, temporal modelling, and anomaly detection. Although operating on univariate inputs, it still extracts dependencies across different KPI sequences.

Other approaches have used frequency-domain analysis. The Spectral Residual (SR) method [11], for instance, detects anomalies by analysing spectral features in static data. However, SR does not model temporal dependencies and thus falls short for time series analysis.

Recent advances focus on deep generative models. Xu et al. [12] introduced a Variational Autoencoder (VAE)-based unsupervised model tailored for seasonal KPIs in web services. Similarly, Chen et al. [13] extended this with a Conditional VAE (CVAE) framework applied to real-world datasets from large-scale internet platforms, incorporating both temporal and contextual information to improve detection accuracy.

2.2 Time Series Decomposition

Time series decomposition is a widely used technique for separating a time-dependent signal into distinct components, typically including trend, seasonality, and residual [14]. Standard decomposition methods include additive and multiplicative models, as well as more advanced techniques such as X-12-ARIMA and Seasonal-Trend decomposition using Loess (STL) [15]. Among these, STL is particularly favoured for its robustness and flexibility in handling irregular seasonal patterns, especially in the presence of anomalies [16].

As time series data become longer and more complex, detecting anomalies across the whole sequence becomes increasingly challenging. Decomposition helps address this by isolating stable components, trend and seasonality, from the residual, which often contains noise and potential anomalies. This separation improves both the interpretability and effectiveness of downstream anomaly detection algorithms [17].

Several studies have incorporated decomposition techniques into anomaly detection frameworks. For example, Deshcherevskii and Sidorin [18] applied signal decomposition to extract seasonal, trend, and residual components, subsequently optimising the residuals for improved feature representation. Similarly, Liu et al. [19] employed STL decomposition to enhance residual peak detection, utilising an autoencoder model to learn compact data representations and facilitate dimensionality reduction.

Decomposition enhances feature quality by isolating structured components such as trend and seasonality [20]. However, the effectiveness of anomaly detection ultimately depends on the modelling approach used [21].

2.3   Time Series Anomaly Detection Methods

Time series anomaly detection methods are broadly categorised into traditional statistical models and modern deep learning-based approaches. Traditional methods, such as Autoregressive Integrated Moving Average (ARIMA) [22], rely on historical data and forecast errors to detect deviations. ARIMA models are well-suited for stationary time series and integrate autoregressive (AR), integrated (I), and moving average (MA) components to model underlying temporal structures. However, these models are often limited in their ability to handle non-linear or non-stationary time series, which are common in real-world applications.

Recent advances in deep learning have led to the development of more robust models for capturing complex dependencies in time series data. For example, the Long Short Term Memory anomaly detection model (LSTM-AD) for time series, introduced in [23] outperformed RNN-based alternatives by effectively modelling both short- and long-term dependencies in normal behaviour sequences. This highlights the strength of LSTM architectures in learning temporal patterns from noisy or irregular data.

Furthermore, hybrid architectures that combine convolutional neural networks (CNNs) with recurrent networks have gained attention for their ability to extract both spatial and temporal features. As Xue et al. [24] demonstrated CNN-RNN models enable more comprehensive analysis of time-varying signals, leading to improved anomaly detection accuracy in high-dimensional or noisy datasets.

3   Motivation

This paper aims to enhance anomaly detection in complex univariate time series by employing a reconstruction-based hybrid model that combines LSTM networks and autoencoders. The proposed model, DeLSTM-AE, is specifically designed to detect anomalies in long and complex sequences by learning typical temporal patterns and highlighting deviations from these patterns.

To improve detection sensitivity and robustness, the model incorporates time series decomposition using STL. This enables a more focused analysis of constituent signal patterns, trend, seasonality, and residual, rather than treating the time series as a single undifferentiated signal. The decomposition step allows the model to isolate different types of anomalous behaviours that may only be detectable within specific components (e.g., short spikes in residuals or slow drifts in trends).

Given the critical importance of early anomaly detection in performance monitoring and failure prevention, particularly in large-scale internet services and cloud platforms, an effective solution must be both generalisable across diverse signals and capable of capturing subtle deviations in behaviour. This motivates the development of DeLSTM-AE as a model that fuses sequence modelling with decomposition-aware learning.

4   Overview of the Framework

This section provides an overview of the proposed DeLSTM-AE framework. The architecture consists of three core components: an *encoder*, a *latent space*, and a *decoder*, as illustrated in Fig. 1. These elements collectively enable the model to differentiate between normal and anomalous data points by learning and reconstructing normal temporal patterns from decomposed univariate time series.

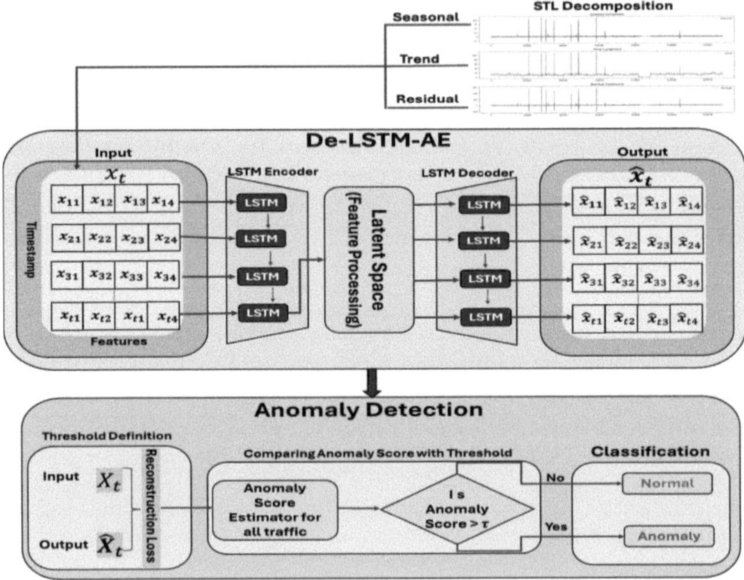

Fig. 1. Framework Overview (DeLSTM-AE processing pipeline).

As shown in Fig. 1, the system processes input time series data decomposed into seasonal, trend, and residual components, which are then reshaped into a three-dimensional tensor with the format [batch size, time steps, features]. This design ensures compatibility with the LSTM-based model while enabling it to capture distinct anomaly characteristics that might be obscured in the raw combined series. Analysing each component separately allows the model to detect different types of anomalies more effectively: the trend component captures long-term gradual shifts indicative of performance degradation, the seasonal component highlights cyclic pattern irregularities and timing inconsistencies, and the residual component isolates short-term spikes and noise often linked to transient failures or point anomalies.

The encoder compresses the input sequences into a fixed-length representation that captures temporal dependencies and structural information. This representation is passed to the latent space, where essential features are retained and refined. The latent space serves as a compact representation of the input time series, capturing essential temporal dynamics while filtering out irrelevant fluctuations. By summarising patterns across the seasonal, trend, and residual components, the latent space facilitates the separation of typical behaviours from rare deviations. Anomalous sequences, which deviate from learned temporal dependencies, result in higher reconstruction errors during decoding, thereby enabling effective anomaly detection. The decoder then reconstructs the original time series from the latent representation.

The model outputs a reconstructed version of the input sequence, which is compared to the original input to compute the reconstruction error. This error, or loss, serves as the primary anomaly score. The complete DeLSTM-AE workflow is summarised in Algorithm 1.

Algorithm 1. DeLSTM-AE

1: **Input:** Time series sequences
2: **Decomposition:**
3:    $(Seasonal, Trend, Residual) \leftarrow \text{STL}(sequences, period = 24)$
4: **Prepare Data:**
5:    $combined\_data \leftarrow \text{concatenate } (Seasonal, Trend, Residual)$
6:    $sequences\_3d \leftarrow \text{reshape } combined\_data \text{ to shape } [-1, time\_steps, 3]$
7: **Encoder:**
8:    $h_n \leftarrow Encoder(sequences\_3d)$
9: **Latent Representation:**
10:    $latent \leftarrow Linear(h_n)$
11: **Decoder:**
12:    $output \leftarrow Decoder(latent)$
13: **Loss Function:**
14:    $MSELoss \leftarrow \frac{1}{N} \sum (output - target)^2$
15: **Threshold for Anomaly Detection:**
16:    $threshold \leftarrow Quantile(reconstruction\_errors, 0.93)$
17: **Classify:**
18:    **if** reconstruction_error > threshold **then** mark as anomalous

---

As described in Algorithm 1, the reconstruction error is used to compute the anomaly score and set the classification threshold. The threshold is determined as the 93rd percentile of the reconstruction error distribution observed during training, capturing the top 7% of sequences most likely to reflect deviations from normal behaviour. This value was selected based on empirical tuning on the validation set to balance between precision and recall, maintaining sensitivity to complex anomalies, while reducing the false positive rate. Any data point whose reconstruction error exceeds the threshold is classified as anomalous; otherwise, it is considered normal.

5 Experimental Setup

5.1 Dataset and Preprocessing

This study uses the publicly available AIOps 2018 dataset [25], published as part of the AIOps Anomaly Detection Challenge by Tsinghua University in collaboration with major internet service providers in China. The dataset contains 26 univariate KPI time series from companies such as Sogou, Tencent, and eBay, representing web service performance metrics including stability, utilisation, and response time.

Four KPIs were selected for evaluation, labelled as KPI_TR, KPI1, KPI2, and KPI3. Each record in the KPIs includes four features: timestamp (5-min intervals), value (monitored value), KPI ID, and label (normal or anomalous).

Figure 2 shows the distribution of KPI_TR, revealing both sharp spikes and gradual fluctuations. Anomalies often occur in periodic clusters, indicating system failures or traffic surges.

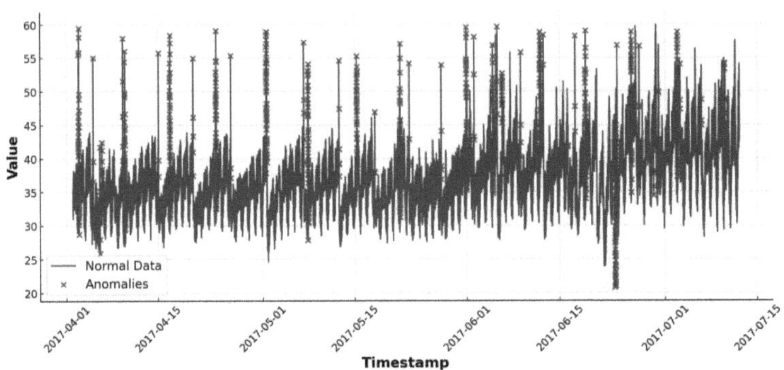

Fig. 2. Distribution of data points in KPI_TR. Red points indicate anomalies, while the blue line represents the normal KPI trend over time. (Color figure online)

Correlation analysis was conducted between the training KPI (KPI_TR) and the test KPIs (KPI1, KPI2, KPI3) using the Pearson correlation coefficient, yielding low values of $r = 0.18$, $r = 0.02$, and $r = 0.25$, respectively, indicating minimal linear dependence. This supports the evaluation of generalisation across diverse anomaly patterns.

Preprocessing included data cleaning (to handle missing values and correct inconsistencies in timestamps and KPI values), normalisation, and label encoding. These steps ensured accurate anomaly timing and reliable value measurements, providing a fair basis for comparison with existing methods without introducing data-related biases. Each time series was then decomposed using STL, producing seasonal, trend, and residual components. These were reshaped into three-dimensional tensors for input into the DeLSTM-AE model.

The AIOps 2018 dataset is imbalanced, with anomalies being relatively rare. To mitigate this, evaluation metrics that are robust to class imbalance (precision, recall, F1-score, and AUC-ROC) were employed, and the anomaly detection threshold was automatically tuned on the validation set to balance sensitivity and specificity.

5.2   Experimental Environment

Experiments were performed on a machine with an 8th Generation Intel Core i7 vPro processor and 16 GB of RAM. The operating system used was Windows 10 Enterprise. All model development and experimentation were implemented in Python 3.8. The key libraries used included PyTorch2.3 for model construction and training, and Scikit-learn [26] for evaluation metrics and preprocessing utilities.

5.3   Experimental Parameter Setting

To ensure optimal model performance, a grid search was used to tune the hyperparameters of the DeLSTM-AE model. These included the learning rate, dropout rate, batch size, number of training epochs, and the threshold quantile used for anomaly classification. The evaluated values for each hyperparameter are listed in Table 1. The grid search was applied consistently to both the encoder and decoder components of the model.

The best-performing hyperparameter combination, which achieved the highest generalisation performance across all four KPI datasets, was as follows: dropout = 0.7, learning rate = 0.0001, batch size = 32, and threshold sensitivity = 0.93. The final model was trained and tested using these parameters for 50 epochs.

Table 1. Hyperparameters used in the grid search and their descriptions.

Hyperparameter	Values	Description
Learning Rate	0.01, 0.001, 0.0001	Controls the step size during gradient descent
Dropout	0.5, 0.7	Fraction of input units randomly set to zero
Batch Size	32, 64	Number of sequences passed per training step
Epochs	50, 100	Number of complete passes through the dataset
Threshold Sensitivity	Quantile = 0.93, 0.95	Defines the boundary between normal and anomalous data

5.4   Training and Testing Procedure

Model training and evaluation were conducted using the four selected KPI time series. KPI_TR served as the training and validation set, with an 80%âĂŞ20% split. Hyperparameter tuning was performed using grid search as detailed in (Table 1), with the selected values applied consistently to both encoder and decoder components. Early stopping based on validation loss was used to prevent overfitting and ensure model generalisation.

Each decomposed sequence, comprising seasonal, trend, and residual signals, was reshaped into a [batch size, time steps, features] format suitable for LSTM-based processing. The encoder compressed these inputs into latent representations, which were decoded to reconstruct the input sequence. The reconstruction error, calculated as the difference between the original and reconstructed inputs, served as the anomaly score.

For testing, the final 20% of KPI1, KPI2, and KPI3 were used, preserving temporal consistency with the validation split. These subsets contain labelled anomalies for performance evaluation. Reconstruction errors on the test data were compared against a threshold, set at the 0.93 quantile of the training reconstruction error distribution, to classify each point as normal or anomalous.

6   Results and Evaluations

6.1   Results

The model's performance was evaluated across the selected KPIs. The loss curves (Fig. 3) illustrate progressive reduction in reconstruction error across training, and validation, demonstrating effective learning of temporal patterns and stable convergence without overfitting.

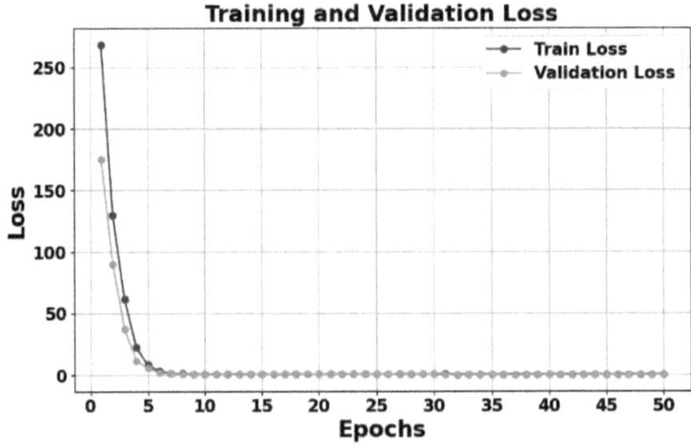

Fig. 3. Loss curves for training, and validation phases across epochs.

To further assess classification performance, confusion matrices were generated for the test sets. Across the three test KPIs, the model consistently maintained a high true positive rate, with the highest number of correctly identified anomalies reaching 23,637, and a moderate number of false positives, with a maximum of 638, highlighting its consistent ability to distinguish normal from anomalous behaviour.

Evaluation using AUC-ROC analysis (Fig. 4) further demonstrates the model's effectiveness on the test datasets. The AUC values reached 92.1% for KPI1, 87% for KPI2, and 84% for KPI3. Each curve rose sharply toward the upper-left corner, indicating a high true positive rate and a low false positive rate, a crucial trait for reliable anomaly detection in real-world scenarios.

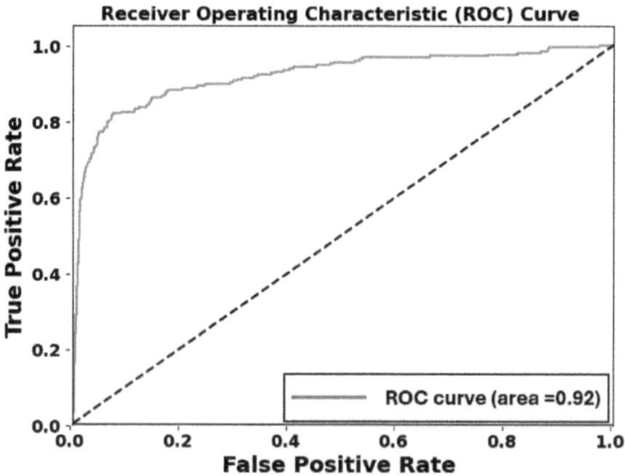

Fig. 4. KPI1 AUC-ROC

6.2   Evaluation

The model's classification performance was assessed using precision, recall, F1-score, accuracy, and AUC-ROC.

Table 2 summarises the final evaluation results across the three test KPI sets (KPI1, KPI2, and KPI3). All three test sets exhibit consistently high precision (99%) and F1-scores (96%), indicating that the model reliably detects anomalies while minimising false positives. Recall values range from 93% to 94%, demonstrating strong sensitivity to true anomalies across diverse time series patterns.

Table 2. Evaluation results for each test KPI (%)

KPI Set	Precision	Recall	F1	AUC	Accuracy	FPR
KPI1	99.1	94.0	96.0	92.1	94.0	6.4
KPI2	99.1	93.2	96.0	87.0	93.2	6.6
KPI3	98.7	93.2	95.6	84.0	93.2	6.5

In addition to standard classification metrics, we report the False Positive Rate (FPR), which is particularly important in real-world anomaly detection scenarios. The FPRs for KPI1, KPI2, and KPI3 were 6.4%, 6.6%, and 6.5%, respectively, demonstrating the model's ability to minimise false alarms while preserving detection sensitivity. These FPR values demonstrate that the model maintains reasonable specificity and high sensitivity, despite the inherent class imbalance.

Among the test sets, KPI1 achieved the highest accuracy (94%) and AUC-ROC (92.1%), reflecting strong generalisation and discriminative performance.

KPI2 and KPI3 yielded comparable results, each attaining an accuracy of 93.2% and AUC-ROC scores of 87% and 84%, respectively, suggesting stable and effective performance across heterogeneous data sources. Despite the inherent imbalance, the DeLSTM-AE model maintains a robust balance between sensitivity and specificity, achieving reliable anomaly detection across all test datasets.

7 Comparison with State-of-the-Art Methods

To evaluate the performance of the proposed DeLSTM-AE model, we compared it with several state-of-the-art approaches designed explicitly for anomaly detection in time series data.

7.1 Overview of Baseline Models

Niu et al. [27] proposed a hybrid model integrating LSTM networks, VAE, and Generative Adversarial Networks (GAN) using the AIOps 2018 dataset [25]. The model leveraged the temporal learning capacity of LSTMs, the generative capability of VAEs, and the discriminative power of GANs to improve anomaly detection performance. This approach yielded promising results across various evaluation metrics, demonstrating the effectiveness of combining generative and discriminative techniques.

Qi et al. [28] introduced KPI-TSAD, a supervised deep learning model tailored for detecting anomalies in time series data, especially within cloud-based KPIs. The model employed a combination of CNN, LSTM units, and a VAE-based oversampling technique to mitigate class imbalance. The model evaluation conducted on the Yahoo Webscope S5 and AIOps datasets, demonstrated the model's strong detection capability in real-time monitoring scenarios.

Garg et al. [29] proposed PROFCAD, a three-stage supervised anomaly detection framework based on forecasting, feature engineering, and classification. Designed for monitoring KPI data in cloud environments, PROFCAD constructed detailed behavioural profiles of KPIs to identify deviations indicative of anomalies. The results highlighted the effectiveness of combining profiling techniques with traditional machine learning classifiers.

7.2 Quantitative Evaluation and Discussion

To evaluate the performance of the proposed DeLSTM-AE model, we performed a comparative analysis with the baseline models described in Sect. 7.1, using their reported evaluation metrics on the AIOps 2018 dataset. The results are summarised in Table 3, presenting key evaluation metrics: precision, recall, F1 score, AUC, and accuracy.

DeLSTM-AE consistently outperforms existing approaches across all metrics and test KPIs. It achieves an F1-score of 96% and AUC values between 84% and 92.1%, demonstrating excellent classification performance. High precision

Table 3. Performance comparison with state-of-the-art models (%)

Model	Precision	Recall	F1	AUC	Accuracy
DeLSTM-AE (KPI1)	**99.1**	**94.0**	**96.0**	**92.1**	**94.0**
DeLSTM-AE (KPI2)	**99.1**	**93.0**	**96.0**	**87.0**	**93.0**
DeLSTM-AE (KPI3)	**98.7**	**93.2**	**95.6**	**84.0**	**93.2**
LSTM-VAE-GAN [27]	95.0	50.0	65.5	70.0	70.0
KPI-TSAD [28]	80.0	91.0	72.0	90.0	83.0
PROFCAD [29]	82.6	92.9	85.8	92.9	89.0

(99.1%) reflects a low false positive rate, while strong recall (93.2%âĂŞ94%) indicates its capacity to detect a substantial proportion of true anomalies.

In comparison, the LSTM-based VAE-GAN [8] suffers from low recall (50%) and F1 (65.5%), while KPI-TSAD [28] exhibits high recall (91%) but lower precision (80%), indicating a higher false positive rate. PROFCAD [29] remains competitive but it falls slightly behind DeLSTM-AE in both F1 and accuracy across all test sets.

The superior performance is attributed to DeLSTM-AE's decomposition-based design, which isolates trend and seasonal components, allowing the model to focus on residual deviations where anomalies manifest. This design yields robust representations and enhanced sensitivity to complex temporal irregularities.

Moreover, DeLSTM-AE demonstrates strong generalisation across diverse KPIs, which is evident in its consistent performance despite the low inter-KPI correlation. This robustness is crucial for real-world deployments, where anomaly patterns vary significantly across services or systems.

In summary, DeLSTM-AE advances prior models by leveraging decomposition-based learning to achieve high classification accuracy while maintaining a strong balance between precision and recall. These capabilities make it well-suited for practical anomaly detection in operational monitoring environments.

7.3   Ablation Study: Impact of Decomposition

An ablation study was conducted to isolate the specific contribution of STL decomposition. As shown in Table 4, the inclusion of decomposition leads to consistently improved anomaly detection performance across all test KPIs.

Models trained without decomposition exhibit notably lower recall and AUC scores, indicating diminished sensitivity to true anomalies and reduced discriminative capability. By isolating trend and seasonal patterns prior to training, decomposition allows the model to better focus on residual deviations where anomalies are typically most evident. These results empirically validate that decomposition is a critical component contributing to the improved robustness and accuracy of the DeLSTM-AE framework.

Table 4. Performance with and without decomposition across test KPIs (%)

KPI Set	Method	Precision	Recall	F1	AUC	Accuracy
KPI1	**With Decomposition**	**99.1**	**94.0**	**96.0**	**92.1**	**94.0**
KPI1	Without Decomposition	98.6	89.8	93.9	60.2	89.8
KPI2	**With Decomposition**	**99.1**	**93.2**	**96.0**	**87.0**	**93.2**
KPI2	Without Decomposition	99.0	90.1	94.2	78.6	90.1
KPI3	**With Decomposition**	**98.7**	**93.2**	**95.6**	**84.0**	**93.2**
KPI3	Without Decomposition	98.7	90.3	94.1	80.1	90.3

8 Conclusion

This study proposed DeLSTM-AE, a framework for univariate time series anomaly detection that integrates time series decomposition with LSTM-AE. By decomposing the KPI time series into seasonal, trend, and residual components before modeling, the framework enables more precise learning of temporal patterns and improves anomaly detection sensitivity.

Evaluated on the AIOps 2018 dataset, DeLSTM-AE demonstrated consistently high precision, recall, and accuracy, highlighting its robustness in detecting anomalies across diverse KPI sequences. Decomposition played a crucial role in isolating complex temporal dynamics, allowing the model to identify complex deviations often obscured by dominant trends or recurring patterns.

The model also exhibits strong generalisation across heterogeneous KPIs and remains effective under noisy or imbalanced data. Its efficient architecture facilitates timely anomaly detection, supporting operational monitoring needs where early intervention can prevent failures and reduce downtime.

In summary, DeLSTM-AE offers a robust and scalable solution for univariate time series anomaly detection, leveraging decomposition and LSTM-based reconstruction to enhance detection accuracy across diverse data conditions. Future work will explore extending this research to multivariate time series anomaly detection and further addressing deployment challenges, such as evolving sequence patterns, adaptive system optimisation, and reconfigurations, to ensure stability and availability.

References

1. Golightly, L., Modesti, P., Garcia, R., Chang, V.: Securing distributed systems: a survey on access control techniques for cloud, blockchain, IoT and SDN. Cyber Secur. Appl. **1**, 100015 (2023)
2. Jena, B., Mishra, D., Mishra, S.: Building an effective KPI monitoring system for an OTT platform. In: 2024 International Conference on Emerging Systems and Intelligent Computing (ESIC), pp. 225–230. IEEE (2024)
3. Nadeem, F.: A unified framework for user-preferred multi-level ranking of cloud computing services based on usability and quality of service evaluation. IEEE Access **8**, 180054–180066 (2020)

4. Shumway, R.H., Stoffer, D.S., Stoffer, D.S.: Time Series Analysis and Its Applications, vol. 3. Springer, Davis (2000)

5. Zhang, S., et al.: Efficient KPI anomaly detection through transfer learning for large-scale web services. IEEE J. Sel. Areas Commun. **40**(8), 2440–2455 (2022)

6. Sun, W., Li, H., Liang, Q., Zou, X., Chen, M., Wang, Y.: On data efficiency of univariate time series anomaly detection models. J. Big Data **11**(1), 83 (2024)

7. Minaee, S., Kalchbrenner, N., Cambria, E., Nikzad, N., Chenaghlu, M., Gao, J.: Deep learning-based text classification: a comprehensive review. ACM Comput. Surv. (CSUR) **54**(3), 1–40 (2021)

8. Darban, Z.Z., Webb, G.I., Pan, S., Aggarwal, C.C., Salehi, M.: Deep learning for time series anomaly detection: a survey (2022). arXiv preprint arXiv:2211.05244

9. Braei, M., Wagner, S.: Anomaly detection in univariate time-series: a survey on the state-of-the-art. arXiv preprint arXiv:2004.00433 (2020)

10. Shu, Y., Gao, T., Zhang, Z., Zhang, J.: A general KPI anomaly detection using attention models. In: 2022 IEEE International Conference on Services Computing (SCC), pp. 114–119. IEEE (2022)

11. Ren, H., et al.: Time-series anomaly detection service at Microsoft. In: Proceedings of the 25th ACM SIGKDD International Conference on Knowledge Discovery & Data Mining, pp. 3009–3017 (2019)

12. Xu, H., et al.: Unsupervised anomaly detection via variational auto-encoder for seasonal KPIS in web applications. In: Proceedings of the 2018 World Wide Web Conference, pp. 187–196 (2018)

13. Li, Z., Chen, W., Pei, D.: Robust and unsupervised KPI anomaly detection based on conditional variational autoencoder. In: 2018 IEEE 37th International Performance Computing and Communications Conference (IPCCC), pp. 1–9. IEEE (2018)

14. Bo, W., Fang, C., Yao, Z., Yanhui, T., Chen, Y.: Decompose auto-transformer time series anomaly detection for network management. Electronics **12**(2), 354 (2023)

15. Vallis, O., Hochenbaum, J., Kejariwal, A.: A novel technique for {Long-Term} anomaly detection in the cloud. In: 6th USENIX Workshop on Hot Topics in Cloud Computing (HotCloud 14) (2014)

16. Wen, Q., Gao, J., Song, X., Sun, L., Huan, X., Zhu, S.: RobustSTL: a robust seasonal-trend decomposition algorithm for long time series. In: Proceedings of the AAAI Conference on Artificial Intelligence vol. 33, pp. 5409–5416 (2019)

17. Dudek, G.: STD: a seasonal-trend-dispersion decomposition of time series. IEEE Trans. Knowl. Data Eng. **35**(10), 10339–10350 (2023)

18. Deshcherevskii, A.V., Sidorin, A.Ya.: Iterative algorithm for time series decomposition into trend and seasonality: Testing using the example of co2 concentrations in the atmosphere. Izv. Atmos. Ocean. Phys. **57**(8), 813–836 (2021)

19. Liu, S., et al.: Time series anomaly detection with adversarial reconstruction networks. IEEE Trans. Knowl. Data Eng. **35**(4), 4293–4306 (2022)

20. Qin, Y., Zhao, C.: Comprehensive process decomposition for closed-loop process monitoring with quality-relevant slow feature analysis. J. Process Control **77**, 141–154 (2019)

21. Backhus, J., Rao, A.R., Venkatraman, C., Gupta, C.: Time series anomaly detection using signal processing and deep learning. Appl. Sci. (2076-3417), **15**(11) (2025)

22. Box, G.E.P., Pierce, D.A.: Distribution of residual autocorrelations in autoregressive-integrated moving average time series models. J. Am. Stat. Assoc. **65**(332), 1509–1526 (1970)

23. Malhotra, P., Vig, L., Shroff, G., Agarwal, P., et al.: Long short term memory networks for anomaly detection in time series. In: Proceedings, vol. 89, p. 94 (2015)
24. Xue, N., Triguero, I., Figueredo, G.P., Landa-Silva, D.: Evolving deep CNN-LSTMs for inventory time series prediction. In: 2019 IEEE Congress on Evolutionary Computation (CEC), pp. 1517–1524. IEEE (2019)
25. NetManAIOps. KPI-anomaly-detection: 2018aiops (2018). https://github.com/netmanaiops/kpi-anomaly-detection
26. Pedregosa, F., et al.: Scikit-learn: machine learning in python. J. Mach. Learn. Res. **12**, 2825–2830 (2011)
27. Niu, Z., Ke, Yu., Xiaofei, W.: LSTM-based VAE-GAN for time-series anomaly detection. Sensors **20**(13), 3738 (2020)
28. Qiu, J., Qingfeng, D., Qian, C.: KPI-TSAD: a time-series anomaly detector for KPI monitoring in cloud applications. Symmetry **11**(11), 1350 (2019)
29. Garg, R., Ambekar, C.K., Saha, K., Girish Rao Salanke, N.S.: PROFCAD: an algorithm to detect anomalies in cloud applications for KPI monitoring systems. In: 2021 IEEE International Conference on Computation System and Information Technology for Sustainable Solutions (CSITSS), pp. 1–7. IEEE (2021)

Forecasting Uranium Prices Using LSTM and VMD-Based Ensemble Models

Sasheendran Gopalakrishnakone$^{(\boxtimes)}$ (iD)

Department of Computing University of London, London, UK
`sgopa001@gold.ac.uk`

Abstract. Uranium is critical in the production of nuclear power and formulation of a clean energy policy. Our research objective is to apply deep learning models to predict uranium prices with higher precision. We benchmark a range of Long Short-Term Memory (LSTM) models to forecast uranium price returns over a 360-month period. Applying LSTM models, we consider 3 types of optimisers, 8 optimiser layer configurations, up to 3 steps ahead training and benchmark against 6 types of ARIMA models and 6 exponential smoothing models. Compared to price data, returns are noisy which accounts for the superior performance of LSTM models. ARIMA models perform well, but LSTM tops the forecast benchmarks on all 3 optimisers achieving on average RMSE of 0.07. To outperform the best ARIMA and LSTM forecast models, we introduce a novel ensemble Variational Mode Decomposition technique. VMD-LSTM model leads to an average RMSE of 0.034404, MAE of 0.027578 and MAPE of 1.1698. This is a significant forecast improvement of 54.39%, 53.35% and 53.47% over the leading ADAM, SGDM and RMSPROP optimiser-based LSTM models respectively.

Keywords: LSTM · uranium · Variational Mode Decomposition

1 Introduction

Nuclear power is a reliable source of long-term electricity production. In 2017, nuclear power plants operated at 92% capacity compared to coal (54%), natural gas (55%), wind (37%) and solar (27%) [1]. Modern economies seeking to diversify from oil and gas, can contemplate the benefits of investing in nuclear reactors by observing their contribution to powering growth in states with existing nuclear infrastructure. Factories and data centres relying on nuclear power are effectively hedged against oil price volatility and geopolitics associated with petroleum supply chains. With regards to electricity generation, nuclear power is demonstrably more stable than wind, solar and gas power plants even during inclement weather conditions. Access to cheaper uranium could be a path to accelerating divestment from crude oil extraction and mitigating atmospheric pollution. Energy density of nuclear material make it cost-effective in comparison with solar, wind and geothermal energy. Single 1" uranium pellet produces

M. Bramer and F. Stahl (Eds.): SGAI-AI 2025, LNAI 16302, pp. 149–162, 2026.
https://doi.org/10.1007/978-3-032-11442-6_11

the equivalent of approximately 1 tonne of coal, 120 gallons of oil or 17,000 cubic feet of natural gas or 17 million British Thermal Units of energy [1].

Nuclear power firms rely on futures contracts to secure the best price for importing uranium. In this paper, we examine predictability of uranium prices under conditions of limited data. In contrast with other commodities, uranium futures present an interesting test of neural network predictive performance as trading is infrequent and restricted. We conjecture that deep learning models can bridge this gap in predicting uranium price trajectory and even produce more precise short-term forecasts than current models. This has useful policy implications in terms of long-term energy supply infrastructure, production and civilian energy planning during times of energy market volatility.

Uranium is the main element in nuclear power production. Its energy density and reliability make it an important consideration powering infrastructure with high energy demands. Price discovery for uranium is challenging however, as it is less frequently traded compared to other commodities. Demand for nuclear power generation has decreased noticeably in Japan and Germany, but predicted to increase in China with ongoing plans to construct approximately 100 on the east coast. Light water reactors in particular are predicted to be the predominant source of future nuclear power generation [2]. Forecasting uranium prices is therefore critical in early-stage planning phase for this capital-intensive infrastructure development. Nuclear power plants take significantly longer time to complete than other power sources. Hedging against future price volatility however, underscores the importance of price prediction for energy security.

Using time series data available for academic research, deep learning models provide a framework for understanding historical and future price trajectory. [3] finds that uranium prices correlate closely with competing fossil fuels and uranium supply significantly dependent on gold prices. Electricity prices are also found to be important driver of uranium demand after 1990. Given the capital-intensive nature of nuclear power installations in the short term, minimising overpayment for uranium is necessary in saving taxpayers from higher electricity bills in future. Cost and risk mitigation strategy is therefore attained by making precise forecasts of uranium prices to secure an optimal futures contract.

2   Literature Review

Uranium accounts for a significant allocation of the nuclear fuel cycle cost calculation [4] and it is imperative to produce a more reliable price prediction model. Nuclear engineering cost calculation method uses the base price point and factors in an escalation rate to predict future price of uranium [5]. Premise of this method however has raises questions given the divergence from actual historical price. [7] demonstrates a high degree of divergence between the actual and forecast uranium price using base year of 2013 and the escalation rate model is clearly inadequate in predicting monthly prices with a high degree of accuracy. Escalation rate model continues to be applied in the nuclear industry as it gives a prompt estimation [6] of uranium prices. Escalation rate method is formulated by: $UP_t = UP_b((1+e))^{(t-b)}$ where UP_t uranium price at year t, UP_b uranium price at base year b and e refers to escalation rate which usually refers to US Consumer Price Index or Gross Domestic Price Inflators (in US dollar priced contracts). Argument for its continued application is that the escalation rate model provides a quicker estimation [6] a point echoed by [8] in which sophisticated models are unlikely to lead to improvement in forecast accuracy. Furthermore, uranium market experiences much lower frequency price changes than oil and gas, during periods of geopolitical uncertainty. This is due to a low trading volume market structure compared to other commodities. Consequently, there is scarcity of usable data. This makes near-term price prediction an interesting research challenge. Neural network models are considered an improvement over the current escalation rate formula in modelling uranium price dynamics.

[7] address this by testing 10 different permutations of ARIMA models to forecast uranium prices, finding ARIMA(1,0,0) and ARIMA(2,1,2) statistically viable. The research however uses quarterly data and error metrics in forecast prices from 2016Q1 to 2018Q4 are omitted. Only 2015 price forecast shows 5.4% margin of error. Using actual data available currently, we find both ARIMA models overestimate future uranium prices during out-of-sample forecast period while still being a significant improvement over the escalation rate model. [9] find the ARIMA(2,1,0) applied to monthly uranium price data from January 2000 to June 2017 within 7% margin of error. Their research uses a comprehensive model selection of up to 4 AR and MA orders to find the configuration with least Bayesian Information Criterion (BIC).

2.1   Brief Overview of Benchmark Models

Autoregressive (AR) models are time series models in which current value is driven by immediate prior values and time series is autocorrelated. AR(2) model is driven by previous 2 values. Moving Average (MA) models are driven by prior error terms and time series has seasonality. MA(1) would thus be driven by preceding value's error term only. Consequently, ARMA models are driven by both terms. ARIMA models are stationary compared to nonstationary ARMA models. Stationarity is induced by first differencing the time series. ARIMA(2,1,2) is thus driven by 2 previous values, 2 prior error terms and integrated to the first order making it stationary series.

Smoothing models are represented by: $y_t = \mu_t + \beta_t t + s(t) + a_t$ where μ_t is time-varying mean, β_t is time-varying gradient, $s(t)$ is one of the s time-varying seasonal terms and a_t refers to innovations. We benchmark against seasonal exponential smoothing, linear(Holt) exponential smoothing, double(Brown) exponential smoothing and Winters additive method.

[10] examines the economic constraints in the nuclear power market by arguing that the correlation of exploration expenditure with price in addition to the demand forecasts should factor into a model of long-term uranium price dynamics. [8] tests a range of models including Random walk, ARIMA, Exponential smoothing, Unobserved Components (UC), theta method which won M3 competition and Artificial Neural Networks (ANN) consisting of Multilayer Perceptron

(MLP) and Extreme Learning Machines (ELM). Applying Box-Cox transformations, they benchmark 9 different models up to 12 months horizon and find the UC model produced forecast improvement of between 4.5–8.2% over the naive forecast. Default value of lambda $= 0$ for the Box-Cox transformation is demonstrated to be ineffective for uranium prices. Furthermore, both MLP and ELM neural network models underperform compared to the naive model. They argue that neural network shortcomings may be attributed to the fewer datapoints.

[11] uses an ensemble method on monthly data from 1982–2012. Their method comprises of Empirical Mode Decomposition (EMD), Phase Space Reconstruction (PSR) and Extreme Learning Machine (ELM) and finds that it outperforms Radial Basis Function Neural Networks (RBFNN) at RMSE, MAE and Directional prediction Statistics (DS) forecast metrics. RMSE for EMD-PSR-ELM model comes in at 0.8246 compared to 3.4425 for the RBFNN model. [12] using monthly uranium prices from 1989 to 2018, applies Bayesian regularisation of the multilayer feed-forward neural network to address the specific issue of overfitting during training. The proposed neural networks use a single hidden layer with 50 neurons and 252 out of 360 datapoints are used for training over 1000 epochs. Average Mean Relative Error (AMRE) using Bayesian Regularisation is 0.0559 compared to 0.0663 using Levenberg-Marquardt (LM).

Neural networks such as the deep learning models however take significantly longer time to train and calculate in comparison to the escalation rate model used in practice. Precision of LSTM models is improved with hyperparameter tuning leading to more robust forecasting models. In this paper we benchmark deep learning models to compare the forecasting performance for ADAM (Adaptive Moment estimation), Root Mean Square Propagation (RMSPROP) and Stochastic Gradient Descent with Momentum (SGDM) optimisation algorithms each with 4 separate pairs of LSTM optimiser layers on monthly uranium monthly prices. While the naïve or random walk model may be reliable over the medium and long-term, LSTM models can be instrumental in predicting short-term variation in the time series even for a relatively low frequency dataset which address some of the challenges in [8].

3   Data

UxC Uranium U3O8 Swap Futures End of Day Settlement Price time series of 361 monthly datapoints of uranium prices from October 1993 to September 2023 is extracted from https://www.indexmundi.com/commodities/? commodity=uranium. Dataset has also been verified for accuracy with FRED database for global uranium price (code: PURANUSDM). Figure 1 shows the series, returns and realised volatility of uranium prices. Around May to August 2007 saw a sharp increase in uranium prices with the chart shows prices peaking to about $136.22 in June. Prices however remained relatively stable even through the recent pandemic and conflict in Eastern Europe despite increase in realised volatility.

4   LSTM Network Architecture

Long Short-Term Memory (LSTM) models are a class of recurrent neural network models formulated by [13]. LSTM can learn from several prior time steps making it the ideal deep learning model for time series for processing low and high frequency components of a time series. We use monthly uranium price returns time series and partition our dataset into 70% training and 30% test allocations.

We test LSTM network architecture consisting of a 5-layer sequence with an optimiser layer set to test 4 pairs of configurations. BiLSTM layer learns bidirectional long-term dependencies between time steps that allows the network to learn the entire time series at each subsequent monthly data point from start to finish and vice-versa. It therefore applies a forward and backward hidden layer to learn long-range information from the time series. Gated Recurrent Unit (GRU) layer consists of a reset gate, update gate and a candidate state. Hidden state of GRU layer at time step t contains output of the layer for that time step and at each time step, GRU adds or removes information from the state using these 3 gates. Number of hidden units is the quantity of information remembered between time steps. Hidden state at any point in time can thus contain all previous information despite the number of time steps, which is an advantage over the escalation rate model. We test 64 and 128 hidden units for LSTM, BiLSTM and GRU layers. In addition, we test an LSTM-projected layer that also learns long term dependencies between time series datapoints using projected learnable weights while retaining 64 and 128 hidden units for comparison.

Using a larger value for hidden state can lead to potential overfitting risks and this is addressed by adding a dropout layer to the LSTM architecture. While rule of thumb for this dropout layer is 20% we opt to use 0.5 or discard 50% of the information between iterations. Such mitigation measures for overfitting risks lead to a more reliable out-of-sample forecast. We compare forecasting metrics of ADAM (Adaptive Moment Estimation), Stochastic Gradient Descent with Momentum (SGDM) and Root Mean Square Propagation (RMSPROP) optimisation algorithms using similar training options. For each algorithm, initial learn rate is set to 0.01, mini batch size at 128, L2 regularisation at 0.0001 and max epochs training time is fixed at 100.

5   Prediction Model Performance and Benchmark

We include up to 3 steps ahead training of LSTM models. In line with [7] and [9], we benchmark ARIMA models together with a set of smoothing models. Damped-Trend Linear Exponential Smoothing, Simple Exponential Smoothing, Winters Method (Additive), Seasonal Exponential Smoothing, Linear (Holt) Exponential Smoothing and Double (Brown) Exponential Smoothing are included to compare the RMSE, MSE, MAE and MAPE of LSTM models. For ADAM, SGDM and RMSPROP optimisers, forecast metrics are summarised in Table 1, Table 2 and Table 3 respectively.

Figure 2 provides a clear benchmark summary of all forecasting models of uranium price returns ordered by ascending RMSE. Top prediction model is lstm-layer(64) 1 step ahead forecast with the lowest RMSE of 0.075425. ARIMA group of models generally predict better than LSTM models on all 4 metrics. Exponential smoothing models appear to be the least accurate with double (brown) exponential smoothing model with RMSE of 0.101691 and a large MAPE of 691.8247. Winters, linear and seasonal exponential smoothing models are also among worst performers with excessive MAPE over 400.

SGDM optimiser, the BiLSTMlayer models with 1 step ahead training surpassing the ARIMA models with the lowest RMSE OF 0.073743 and MAPE of 91.23377. ARMA(1,1) attains RMSE of 0.076063 and MAPE of 117.3201. Similar to using the ADAM optimiser, the exponential smoothing models are the least accurate models.

RMSPROP optimiser brings a distinct improvement in model prediction with LSTM models in the top 5 rankings. BiLSTMlayer(64) with 3 step ahead training achieving lowest RMSE of 0.073935 and MAPE of 96.18178. AR(1) is the best prediction among group of ARIMA models with RMSE OF 0.07603 and MAPE of 117.6809.

In summary, deep learning models demonstrate outperformance in forecasting uranium price returns with a surpassing ARIMA models. RMSPROP optimiser provides better forecasting precision for LSTM models than ADAM and SGDM optimisers. Compared to forecasting prices, forecasting returns presents a unique challenge as the time series is extremely noisy and LSTM models tend to project through the mean instead of fluctuating over time. We address overfitting concerns by limiting training time to 100 epochs and with a 0.5 dropout layer.

6   Ensemble VMD-LSTM Prediction Model

Compared to price index, returns index is considerably noisier as seen in Fig. 1 which explains the superior performance of LSTM compared to exponential smoothing models. Fluctuations in the returns index can be better processed by using a method that addresses the issue of high-frequency noisy data overlapping low-frequency trends. Variational Mode Decomposition (VMD) is a data-adaptive multiresolution analysis method introduced by [14] designed to improve on the accuracy of Empirical Mode Decomposition (EMD) methods. VMD technique filters oscillating components according to Intrinsic Mode Functions or IMFs. VMD avoids the use of fixed functions (wavelets) for extraction and this in turn precludes the need for searching for the optimal wavelet basis function. IMFs (IMF1...IMF10) are produced from concurrent extraction of modes on identifying signal peaks in frequency domain and are instrumental in finding narrow band oscillatory components than trend. Figure 3 gives an overview of the VMD decomposition of the price returns series into 10 IMF components each series being time-aligned which is an advantage of Fourier transform.

In the context of uranium price returns, we introduce an ensemble model that leverages deep learning capabilities of LSTM models for each of the IMF modes. Through decomposition into 10 modes, we allocate 70% to training and 30% to test sets. Open loop forecast shown in Fig. 4 then predicts the subsequent step ahead in the training or input set and updates the model accordingly. 30% set is then forecast for each of the IMFs and mean of all forecast RMSE metrics gives the overall forecast which is tabulated in Table 4.

7   Discussion and Policy Implications

Uranium market is illiquid compared to other financial assets as the commodity is traded in restricted markets, limiting price discovery and challenging assumptions of future price trajectory. Compared to escalation rate, the industry practice of pricing uranium, our novel ensemble VMD-LSTM methodology using deep learning models offers a route to forecasting low frequency monthly data with a higher degree of accuracy. This allows policy makers to reliably plan for nuclear fuel cycle costing even on a monthly basis.

8   Concluding Remarks

We approached uranium price returns forecasting with a limited dataset using LSTM models with 3 types of optimisers, 8 optimiser layer configurations, up to 3 steps ahead training and benchmarked against 6 types of ARIMA models and 6 exponential smoothing models. LSTM tops the ranking in terms of RMSE metric on all 3 optimiser types achieving on average RMSE of 0.07. To improve forecast precision further, we used an ensemble VMD-LSTM model to attain an improvement in RMSE to 0.034. To exceed the best ARIMA and LSTM forecast models we introduced an ensemble VMD-LSTM model that achieved on average RMSE of 0.034404, MAE of 0.027578 and MAPE of 1.1698. This is a significant forecast improvement of 54.39%, 53.35% and 53.47% over the best ADAM, SGDM and RMSPROP optimiser-based LSTM models respectively.

Acknowledgments. The authors have no competing interests to declare that are relevant to the content of this article. No funding was received for this research.

A   Appendix

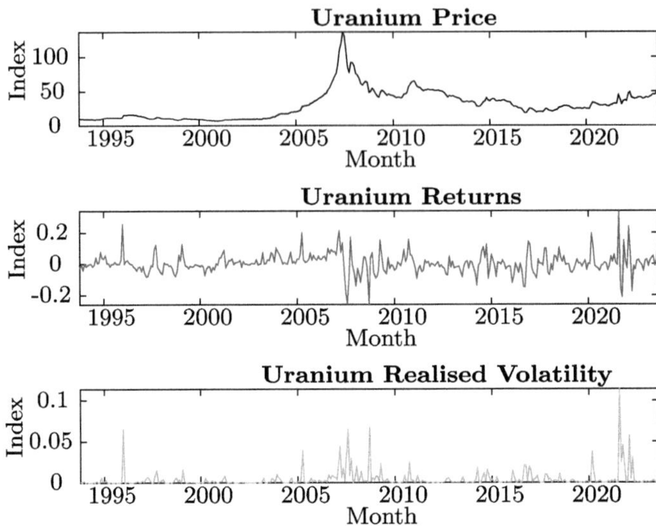

Fig. 1. Dataset comprises of UxC Uranium U3O8 Swap Futures End of Day Settlement Price time series of 361 monthly datapoints of uranium prices from October 1993 to September 2023. Uranium price (black), returns (red) and realised volatility (yellow) over 361 monthly time steps which is the maximum number of datapoints available at the time of research. Returns and realised volatility consist of 360 datapoints. (Color figure online)

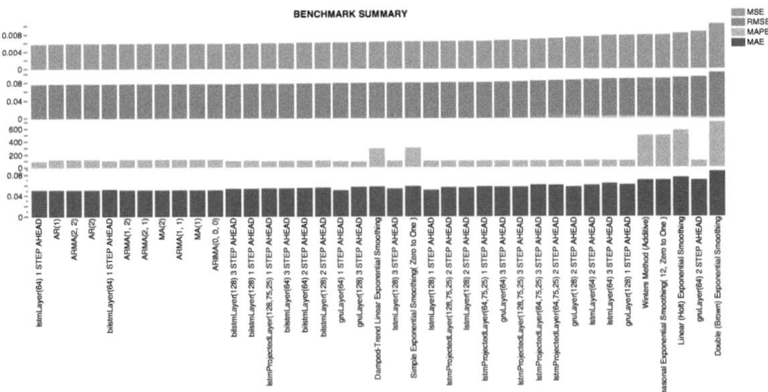

Fig. 2. ADAM optimiser LSTM models benchmarked against other prediction models and ranked according to ascending RMSE (second row/red). MSE, MAE and MAPE metrics are included for comparison. (Color figure online)

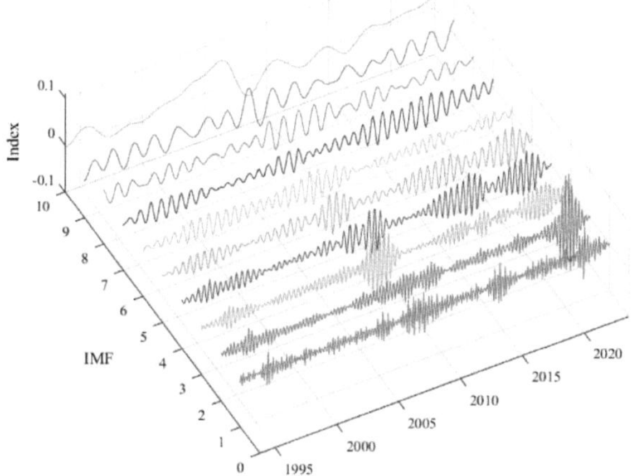

Fig. 3. VMD decomposition of monthly uranium price returns into 10 Intrinsic Mode Functions (IMFs) with the highest frequency at IMF 1 to the lowest at IMF 10. Returns are stationary and are calculated by taking the first difference on prices. Advantage of VMD over EMD and Wavelet multiresolution analysis is its capacity to extract closely spaced high frequency oscillations.

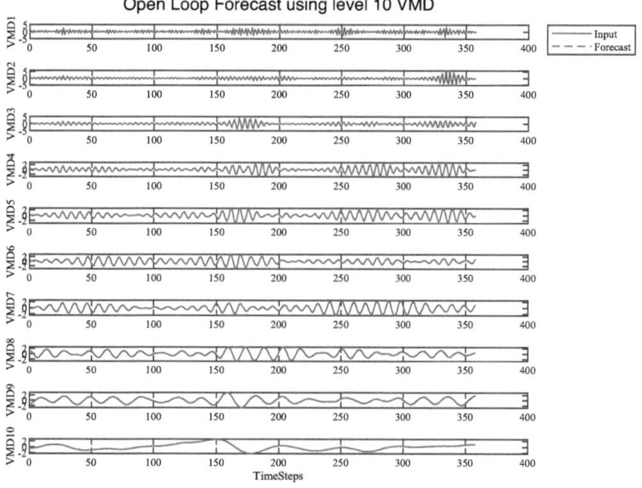

Fig. 4. Open loop forecast of each of the 10 VMD modes concurrently with the training and test allocation identical to the those used in the previous benchmarks. Input (blue) training data 70% and remaining 30% is used in the test sample to forecast. Forecasts for each IMF and mean RMSE of all 10 IMFs are given in Table 4. (Color figure online)

Table 1. ADAM optimiser LSTM model benchmarked against ARIMA and smoothing models. Prediction models are ranked by RMSE in ascending order. ADAM refers to the solver name for the LSTM model and lstmlayer(64) refers to the optimiser layer with 64 hidden nodes.

Prediction model	RMSE	MSE	MAPE	MAE
lstmLayer(64) 1 STEP AHEAD	0.075425	0.005689	87.80258	0.049958
AR(1)	0.07603	0.005781	117.6809	0.050078
ARMA(2, 2)	0.076046	0.005783	117.1679	0.050059
AR(2)	0.076052	0.005784	117.2201	0.050069
bilstmLayer(64) 1 STEP AHEAD	0.076054	0.005784	98.77164	0.051096
ARMA(1, 2)	0.076054	0.005784	117.2393	0.050072
ARMA(2, 1)	0.076057	0.005785	117.2497	0.050075
MA(2)	0.076058	0.005785	117.1825	0.05007
ARMA(1, 1)	0.076063	0.005786	117.3201	0.050084
MA(1)	0.076122	0.005795	117.2098	0.050113
ARIMA(0, 0, 0)	0.076156	0.0058	117.6176	0.050143
bilstmLayer(128) 3 STEP AHEAD	0.076282	0.005819	97.57022	0.052428
bilstmLayer(128) 1 STEP AHEAD	0.076545	0.005859	99.01065	0.052116
lstmProjectedLayer(128,75,25) 1 STEP AHEAD	0.076686	0.005881	91.21886	0.052766
bilstmLayer(64) 3 STEP AHEAD	0.076806	0.005899	97.68978	0.053309
bilstmLayer(64) 2 STEP AHEAD	0.077559	0.006015	99.44667	0.053531
bilstmLayer(128) 2 STEP AHEAD	0.077906	0.006069	98.60281	0.054627
gruLayer(64) 1 STEP AHEAD	0.078051	0.006092	91.70444	0.049453
gruLayer(128) 3 STEP AHEAD	0.078183	0.006113	85.86734	0.055384
Damped-Trend Linear Exponential Smoothing	0.079002	0.006241	286.0684	0.056286
lstmLayer(128) 3 STEP AHEAD	0.079272	0.006284	95.9069	0.052493
Simple Exponential Smoothing (Zero to One)	0.079281	0.006285	295.5566	0.056744
lstmLayer(128) 1 STEP AHEAD	0.079401	0.006305	93.85944	0.049569
lstmProjectedLayer(128,75,25) 2 STEP AHEAD	0.079553	0.006329	93.43355	0.054707
lstmLayer(128) 2 STEP AHEAD	0.079743	0.006359	93.801	0.05414
lstmProjectedLayer(64,75,25) 1 STEP AHEAD	0.079899	0.006384	93.74366	0.056107
gruLayer(64) 3 STEP AHEAD	0.080943	0.006552	96.86141	0.055548
lstmProjectedLayer(128,75,25) 3 STEP AHEAD	0.08109	0.006576	92.54271	0.0557
lstmProjectedLayer(64,75,25) 3 STEP AHEAD	0.082759	0.006849	93.69792	0.059257
lstmProjectedLayer(64,75,25) 2 STEP AHEAD	0.083514	0.006975	99.3597	0.05877
gruLayer(128) 2 STEP AHEAD	0.084725	0.007178	93.84594	0.055683
lstmLayer(64) 2 STEP AHEAD	0.085892	0.007377	100.0983	0.058674
lstmLayer(64) 3 STEP AHEAD	0.087547	0.007664	100.3629	0.06173
gruLayer(128) 1 STEP AHEAD	0.087816	0.007712	94.45524	0.059593
Winters Method (Additive)	0.088122	0.007765	485.8927	0.068435
Seasonal Exponential Smoothing (12, Zero to One)	0.088122	0.007765	485.893	0.068435
Linear (Holt) Exponential Smoothing	0.090457	0.008183	561.539	0.073429
gruLayer(64) 2 STEP AHEAD	0.092169	0.008495	95.94644	0.068588
Double (Brown) Exponential Smoothing	0.101691	0.010341	691.8247	0.085329

Table 2. SGDM optimiser benchmarked against ARIMA and smoothing models. Prediction models are ranked by RMSE in ascending order.

Prediction model	RMSE	MSE	MAPE	MAE
bilstmLayer(128) 1 STEP AHEAD	0.073743	0.005438	91.23377	0.04901
bilstmLayer(64) 1 STEP AHEAD	0.074505	0.005551	91.27723	0.048329
AR(1)	0.07603	0.005781	117.6809	0.050078
ARMA(2, 2)	0.076046	0.005783	117.1679	0.050059
AR(2)	0.076052	0.005784	117.2201	0.050069
ARMA(1, 2)	0.076054	0.005784	117.2393	0.050072
ARMA(2, 1)	0.076057	0.005785	117.2497	0.050075
MA(2)	0.076058	0.005785	117.1825	0.05007
ARMA(1, 1)	0.076063	0.005786	117.3201	0.050084
MA(1)	0.076122	0.005795	117.2098	0.050113
ARIMA(0, 0, 0)	0.076156	0.0058	117.6176	0.050143
bilstmLayer(64) 2 STEP AHEAD	0.076581	0.005865	98.1585	0.051881
bilstmLayer(128) 2 STEP AHEAD	0.077271	0.005971	99.26831	0.0525
gruLayer(64) 1 STEP AHEAD	0.077694	0.006036	90.7624	0.050361
gruLayer(128) 1 STEP AHEAD	0.078039	0.00609	90.6782	0.050066
lstmProjectedLayer(64,75,25) 1 STEP AHEAD	0.078774	0.006205	91.82789	0.052951
gruLayer(128) 3 STEP AHEAD	0.078814	0.006212	98.85963	0.053004
lstmProjectedLayer(128,75,25) 1 STEP AHEAD	0.078836	0.006215	91.30135	0.052864
Damped-Trend Linear Exponential Smoothing	0.079002	0.006241	286.0684	0.056286
Simple Exponential Smoothing (Zero to One)	0.079281	0.006285	295.5566	0.056744
gruLayer(128) 2 STEP AHEAD	0.07949	0.006319	96.8099	0.053722
lstmLayer(128) 1 STEP AHEAD	0.080215	0.006434	94.5658	0.0529
gruLayer(64) 2 STEP AHEAD	0.082036	0.00673	97.96693	0.056881
gruLayer(64) 3 STEP AHEAD	0.082983	0.006886	99.81176	0.058189
lstmLayer(64) 1 STEP AHEAD	0.084272	0.007102	96.46833	0.058528
bilstmLayer(128) 3 STEP AHEAD	0.084492	0.007139	101.3289	0.062719
lstmLayer(64) 3 STEP AHEAD	0.084528	0.007145	100.7423	0.059924
lstmProjectedLayer(128,75,25) 2 STEP AHEAD	0.084623	0.007161	99.77281	0.060166
bilstmLayer(64) 3 STEP AHEAD	0.084629	0.007162	100.8367	0.063258
lstmLayer(64) 2 STEP AHEAD	0.086382	0.007462	101.7213	0.062187
Winters Method (Additive)	0.088122	0.007765	485.8927	0.068435
Seasonal Exponential Smoothing(12, Zero to One)	0.088122	0.007765	485.893	0.068435
lstmProjectedLayer(128,75,25) 3 STEP AHEAD	0.088243	0.007787	100.2193	0.063671
lstmProjectedLayer(64,75,25) 2 STEP AHEAD	0.088736	0.007874	102.4722	0.064967
lstmLayer(128) 2 STEP AHEAD	0.089524	0.008015	102.0436	0.064939
Linear (Holt) Exponential Smoothing	0.090457	0.008183	561.539	0.073429
lstmProjectedLayer(64,75,25) 3 STEP AHEAD	0.09073	0.008232	102.5084	0.067349
lstmLayer(128) 3 STEP AHEAD	0.091796	0.008427	101.3858	0.066059
Double (Brown) Exponential Smoothing	0.101691	0.010341	691.8247	0.085329

Table 3. RMSPROP optimiser benchmarked against ARIMA and smoothing models. Prediction models are ranked by RMSE in ascending order.

Prediction model	RMSE	MSE	MAPE	MAE
bilstmLayer(64) 3 STEP AHEAD	0.073935	0.005466	96.18178	0.049367
gruLayer(64) 3 STEP AHEAD	0.074037	0.005481	89.88837	0.052101
lstmLayer(128) 2 STEP AHEAD	0.075361	0.005679	88.82032	0.050718
bilstmLayer(128) 1 STEP AHEAD	0.075772	0.005741	98.58433	0.050531
bilstmLayer(64) 1 STEP AHEAD	0.075925	0.005765	98.91061	0.050473
AR(1)	0.07603	0.005781	117.6809	0.050078
ARMA(2, 2)	0.076046	0.005783	117.1679	0.050059
AR(2)	0.076052	0.005784	117.2201	0.050069
ARMA(1, 2)	0.076054	0.005784	117.2393	0.050072
ARMA(2, 1)	0.076057	0.005785	117.2497	0.050075
MA(2)	0.076058	0.005785	117.1825	0.05007
ARMA(1, 1)	0.076063	0.005786	117.3201	0.050084
MA(1)	0.076122	0.005795	117.2098	0.050113
bilstmLayer(128) 3 STEP AHEAD	0.076156	0.0058	99.28978	0.050485
ARIMA(0, 0, 0)	0.076156	0.0058	117.6176	0.050143
bilstmLayer(64) 2 STEP AHEAD	0.076229	0.005811	99.04631	0.051289
lstmLayer(64) 2 STEP AHEAD	0.076742	0.005889	95.08838	0.050036
lstmLayer(64) 1 STEP AHEAD	0.076845	0.005905	90.57043	0.050059
bilstmLayer(128) 2 STEP AHEAD	0.076855	0.005907	99.37682	0.052169
lstmProjectedLayer(128,75,25) 3 STEP AHEAD	0.077005	0.00593	92.92267	0.053855
lstmProjectedLayer(128,75,25) 2 STEP AHEAD	0.077658	0.006031	94.7636	0.053334
lstmLayer(64) 3 STEP AHEAD	0.078433	0.006152	93.02289	0.052401
lstmProjectedLayer(64,75,25) 2 STEP AHEAD	0.078578	0.006174	91.37442	0.055517
Damped-Trend Linear Exponential Smoothing	0.079002	0.006241	286.0684	0.056286
Simple Exponential Smoothing (Zero to One)	0.079281	0.006285	295.5566	0.056744
gruLayer(128) 2 STEP AHEAD	0.079713	0.006354	91.97124	0.056073
gruLayer(128) 3 STEP AHEAD	0.080308	0.006449	94.82283	0.057377
lstmLayer(128) 1 STEP AHEAD	0.08148	0.006639	94.66896	0.054515
lstmLayer(128) 3 STEP AHEAD	0.081512	0.006644	97.21537	0.058756
gruLayer(64) 2 STEP AHEAD	0.083275	0.006935	89.27253	0.057306
lstmProjectedLayer(128,75,25) 1 STEP AHEAD	0.083513	0.006974	93.85382	0.056229
lstmProjectedLayer(64,75,25) 1 STEP AHEAD	0.084151	0.007081	91.28574	0.057696
lstmProjectedLayer(64,75,25) 3 STEP AHEAD	0.085236	0.007265	104.0446	0.057907
gruLayer(64) 1 STEP AHEAD	0.086504	0.007483	94.0405	0.055493
Winters Method (Additive)	0.088122	0.007765	485.8927	0.068435
Seasonal Exponential Smoothing (12, Zero to One)	0.088122	0.007765	485.893	0.068435
gruLayer(128) 1 STEP AHEAD	0.089413	0.007995	101.0733	0.061234
Linear (Holt) Exponential Smoothing	0.090457	0.008183	561.539	0.073429
Double (Brown) Exponential Smoothing	0.101691	0.010341	691.8247	0.085329

Table 4. Ensemble VMD-LSTM model forecast at each IMF mode with averages stated in column headings. 10 level VMD decomposition of the uranium price returns with the mean RMSE of 0.034404 which is the mean of all 10 mode forecasts stated in parentheses. Mean MAE and MAPE show significant performance improvement compared to the forecast metrics of LSTM and ARIMA models in Table 1, Table 2 and Table 3.

IMF	RMSE (Mean = 0.034404)	MAE (Mean = 0.027578)	MAPE (Mean = 1.1698)
1	0.05916454	0.048082902	11.85748004
2	0.052841309	0.043932896	5.185069832
3	0.032827348	0.025978068	0.712755371
4	0.043368716	0.034797206	−6.27916263
5	0.029573993	0.023383891	0.219705882
6	0.028450581	0.022471647	−4.995229219
7	0.025967862	0.021288262	−0.045956836
8	0.025905922	0.021269742	6.008504486
9	0.02273123	0.01698848	−7.276684085
10	0.023211251	0.017586016	6.311160572

References

1. U.S. Department of Energy, The Ultimate Fast Facts Guide to Nuclear Energy (2019)
2. Gabriel, S., et al.: Building future nuclear power fleets: the available uranium resources constraint. Resour. Policy **38**(4), 458–469 (2013). https://doi.org/10.1016/j.resourpol.2013.06.008
3. Kahouli, S.: Re-examining uranium supply and demand: new insights. Energy Policy **39**(1), 358–376 (2011). https://doi.org/10.1016/j.enpol.2010.10.007
4. Apostolakis, G.P., Hejzlar, P., Shwageraus, E.: The Future of the Nuclear Fuel Cycle: An MIT Interdisciplinary Study. Massachusetts Institute of Technology, Cambridge (MA) (2010)
5. Urso, M.-E., Lokhov, A., Cameron, R.: The economics of the back end of the nuclear fuel cycle. NEA News **31**(2), 15 (2013)
6. Shin, H.: Intermediate Accounting, pp. 439–445. Tamjin Press (2005)
7. Kim, S., et al.: Statistical model for forecasting uranium prices to estimate the nuclear fuel cycle cost. Nucl. Eng. Technol. **49**(5), 1063–1070 (2017). https://doi.org/10.1016/j.net.2017.05.007
8. Pedregal, D.J.: Forecasting uranium prices: some empirical results. Nucl. Eng. Technol. **52**(6), 1334–1339 (2020). https://doi.org/10.1016/j.net.2019.11.028
9. Amangeldi, M.: Estimation and application of best ARIMA model for forecasting the uranium price, pp. 1–8. Nazarbayev University School of Science and Technology (2018)
10. Monnet, A., Gabriel, S., Percebois, J.: Analysis of the long-term availability of uranium: the influence of dynamic constraints and market competition. Energy Policy **105**, 98–107 (2017). https://doi.org/10.1016/j.enpol.2017.02.010

11. Yan, Q., Wang, S., Li, B.: Forecasting uranium resource price prediction by extreme learning machine with empirical mode decomposition and phase space reconstruction. Discret. Dyn. Nat. Soc. **2014**(1), 390579 (2014). https://doi.org/10.1155/2014/390579
12. Moshkbar-Bakhshayesh, K.: Performance study of Bayesian regularization based multilayer feed-forward neural network for estimation of the uranium price in comparison with the different supervised learning algorithms. Prog. Nucl. Energy **127**, 103439 (2020). https://doi.org/10.1016/j.pnucene.2020.103439
13. Hochreiter, S., Schmidhuber, J.: Long short-term memory. Neural Comput. **9**(8), 1735–1780 (1997)
14. Dragomiretskiy, K., Zosso, D.: Variational mode decomposition. IEEE Trans. Signal Process. **62**(3), 531–544 (2014). https://doi.org/10.1109/TSP.2013.2288675

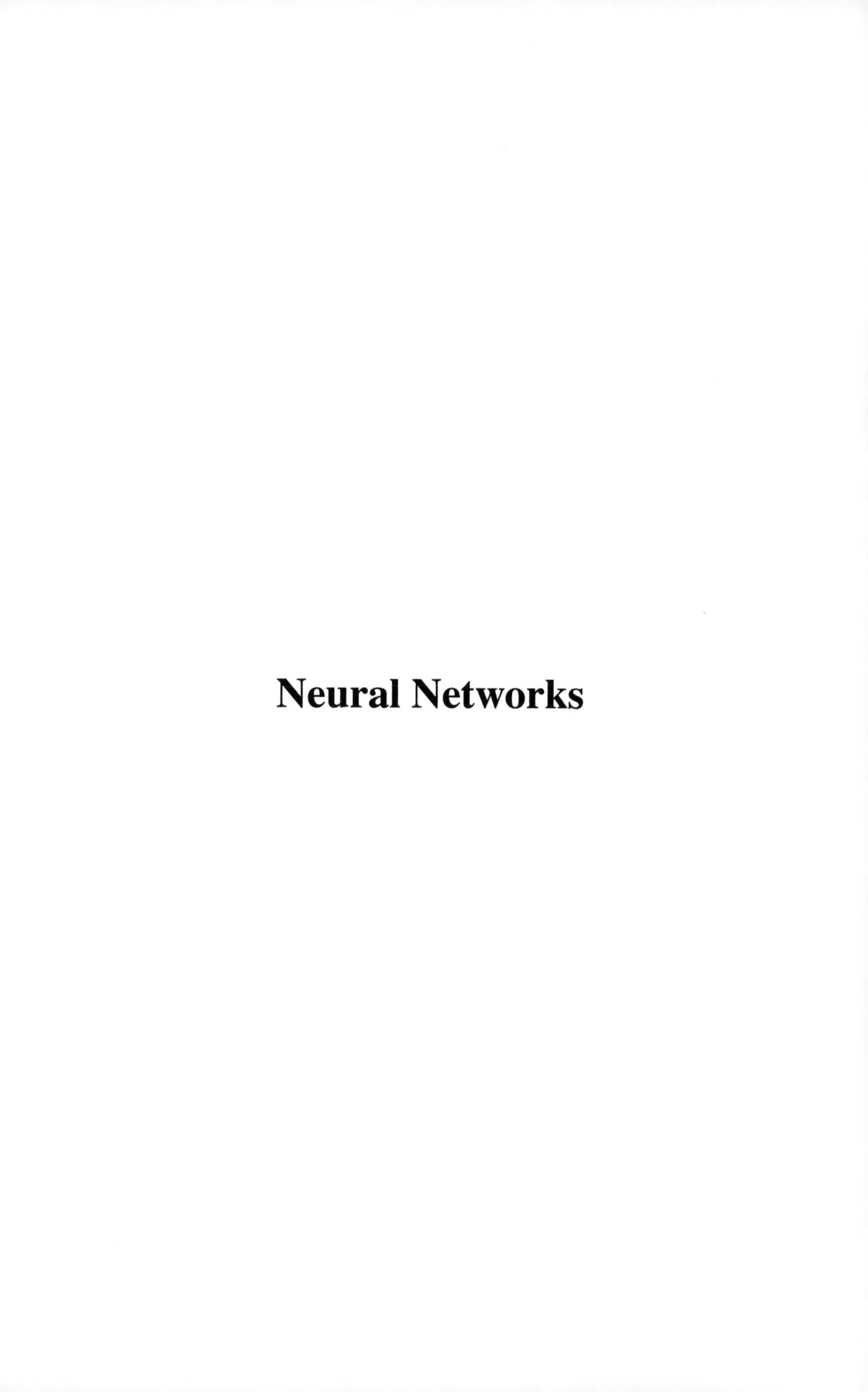

Neural Networks

Evaluation of Explanations for Object Detection Using Transformers with Sonar Data

Christoph Manss[(✉)][iD] and Tarek A. El-Mihoub[iD]

German Research Centre for Artificial Intelligence GmbH (DFKI),
Marie-Curie-Straße 1, Oldenburg 26129, Lower Saxony, Germany
christoph.manss@dfki.de

Abstract. For underwater object detection, sonar imagery generated from Forward Looking Sonar (FLS) and Side Scan Sonar (SSS) systems is usually inspected by experts while AI algorithms are currently under investigation. The transparency and reasoning of AI-based object detection models are crucial for users of these detectors. However, the black-box nature of AI-based detectors limits their interpretability. For a few years, transformer networks have been employed more extensively for object detection and are also used together with sonar data. This paper investigates transformer models for object detection on sonar data and evaluates explanations for the detected objects. We test multiple transformer object detectors, which are evaluated on two datasets. One dataset is a FLS dataset and one is a SSS dataset. After training the transformer models, attribution maps are generated and used for explainability. Here, two XAI methods are used for post-hoc explanations for object detection. The post-hoc explanations are evaluated based on eXplainable Artificial Intelligence (XAI) metrics considering faithfulness and localisation. It turns out that transformer networks with standard backbones provide reasonable accuracies, together with useful attribution maps if used for sonar data. However, multiple XAI methods have to be used to get good explanations.

Keywords: XAI · Saliency Maps · Attention · ODAM · D-RISE

1 Introduction

Nowadays, AI is widely applied in many applications. One of these applications is underwater object detection using sonar imagery, whereas multiple sensory devices can be differentiated for sonar. A Forward Looking Sonar (FLS) produces data that appears similar to an optical image, although the FLS image represents distances to the observed scene. On the other hand, Side Scan Sonar (SSS) records data in a push-broom scanner fashion, which must be aligned in post-processing. All of these sensory devices create images from reflected and scattered signals of sound waves. Due to their low resolution, only a small percentage of the image corresponds to a detectable object [30], and due to the

M. Bramer and F. Stahl (Eds.): SGAI-AI 2025, LNAI 16302, pp. 165–178, 2026.
https://doi.org/10.1007/978-3-032-11442-6_12

measurement method, objects often cast a shadow, which makes accurate detection challenging.

Nonetheless, deep neural networks have been used for detecting objects underwater for FLS data [7,8,13,15,22,25,33,34,36]. For example, in [15], the authors presented how to use a You Only Look Once (YOLO) model to do real-time object detection based on FLS data. YOLO models have also been applied in [4,7,22] for object detection on FLS images or for object detection on Multibeam Forward Looking Sonar (MFLS) images [36]. Yet other neural networks, such as the Mask Recurrent Convolutional Neural Network (RCNN), have been applied to detect objects in MFLS data [8]. In [13], the authors used techniques of Automated Machine Learning (AutoML) to find efficient network structures to detect objects in FLS sonar imagery. For SSS data, similar approaches have been chosen [16,31,39,40], where YOLO models are the dominant choice for object detection. However, custom models are developed as in [29].

All of the aforementioned methods for object detection use Convolutional Neural Network (CNNs) to extract the important features from the sonar imagery. Within recent years, transformer networks have been applied to object detection as well [14,26,28], and have yielded equal or better performance. In comparison to networks based solely on CNNs, transformer networks make use of a so-called attention mechanism, which correlates embeddings taken from the image with each other. Consequently, they are computationally more complex compared with networks based on CNNs. Moreover, because of the attention mechanism, transformer networks use up more memory during computation. Therefore, such models are currently not usable in resource-constrained systems. Despite this downside, it is reasonable to assume that soon, transformers will become more resource-efficient and that they will be applied more frequently in sonar imagery as well.

The authors in [7] trained an object detector based on transformer networks on sonar data. The authors exploited the attention mechanism of the transformer to justify the resulting detections of the transformer. However, the use of eXplainable Artificial Intelligence (XAI) methods on detections estimated with transformers in regard to sonar data has not been investigated. Yet, explanations for detected objects in sonar data might help users and further augment the detections.

Therefore, this paper looks at object detection transformers for detecting objects in underwater sonar imagery and analyses their interpretability and explainability. Because sonar data can be obtained from multiple measurement methodologies, we use SSS and FLS data. For this paper, the guiding question is: *To what extent can state-of-the-art XAI methodologies be used to provide explanations of detected objects in sonar data, if a transformer is used?* In particular, we use two XAI methods for object detection, Detector Randomized Input Sampling for Explanation (D-RISE) [24] and Object Detector Activation Maps (ODAM) [42] to produce attribution maps. These XAI methods are then evaluated by XAI metrics that focus on faithfulness and localisation. Moreover, this paper should also act as a starting point for developers of future transformer object detectors in the SONAR domain. Thus, we also aim to provide details on other datasets and other related work on this subject.

The rest of the paper is structured as follows. The next section introduces the datasets used. Section 3 presents the used transformer networks, followed by a section that introduces the considered XAI methods. Section 5, evaluates the accuracy of the transformer networks and how well the detected objects can be explained based on the presented XAI methods. Section 6 concludes this paper and presents an outlook on future work.

2   The Datasets

Although sonar is widely used in the maritime area, public datasets for training neural networks are still rare. This might also be the case due to the variety of sonar types and how they are used. One type is the SSS, where usually one or more transducers emit a sound signal, and the reflected/scattered signal is received at multiple receivers. In [3], the authors published a SSS dataset for wall detection, which is labelled for neural network applications. The authors in [37], used a combination of two SSS datasets – Sonar Common Target Detection (SCTD) [41] and SeabedObjects-KLSG [12] – for training neural networks. SeabedObjects-KLSG comprises 1190 sonar images and contains the classes: wrecks, aeroplanes, mines, drowned victims, and seafloor. The corresponding publication further presents a pipeline to generate more synthetic sonar images to enhance the dataset even further. This dataset was originally intended for classification tasks and was extended by box annotations in [37] into the VOC format. The SCTD dataset consists of 357 SSS sonar images with the classes aircraft, human, and ship for object detection tasks. In this paper, we refer to the combination of these datasets as D2MFNet, as in [37].

Another type of sonar is the FLS, which measures a 2-D sonar image. The sensor itself usually uses much higher frequencies for measuring and thus is mostly applied in short-distance measurements. In [38], the authors published the Underwater Acoustic Target Detection (UATD) dataset with box annotations and ten classes. The downside of this dataset is that the annotations are in pixel coordinates, and the image is in polar coordinates. Thus, if the image is rectified, the box annotations should be transformed as well, which might lead to distortions. Another dataset is presented in [34], where household debris is recorded with an FLS sonar for detection in shallow water. This dataset provides ten classes and a variety of annotation formats.

The current paper looks into both sonar applications and uses the combined dataset presented in [37] for SSS detection and the marine debris dataset [34] for object detection with FLS recorded data.

3   Object Detection with Transformer The Detection Transformer Family

Transformer networks have their origin in natural language processing for, e.g. translating texts. The key component of these networks is the attention mechanism [35]. Later, these networks have been utilised for image classification as well as for object detection [6,14,18,26,28,32]. Just recently, they have also been applied to sonar images [7].

Transformers can be categorised broadly into three categories: encoder-based transformer, decoder-based transformer, and encoder-decoder-based transformer. In this paper, we focus on an encoder-decoder-based transformer, which takes an image as input and predicts objects within the image with box annotations. In particular, we focus on the Detection Transformer (DETR) transformer [5] and other versions that emerged from it: conditional DETR, Detection Transformers with Assignment (DETA) [23], Real Time Detection Transformer (RT-DETR), and Real Time Detection Transformer v2 (RT-DETRv2). All models can be used through the Python `transformers` library of Huggingface[1]. The benefit of using these transformers is that they are open source, have a common API, and are well documented. DETR is a one-stage transformer for object detection that can be trained end-to-end. It consists of an encoder-decoder architecture, where the box predictions of the decoder are evaluated through a bipartite matching loss. The assignment of each detection with the ground truth for the bipartite matching loss is computed through the Hungarian algorithm. This algorithm finds the optimal one-to-one mapping between predicted and actual boxes based on a similarity metric, typically a negative Intersection-Over-Union (IOU) score. This procedure removes the necessity of a Non-Maximum Suppresion (NMS) to calculate the resulting object detections. To extract features, the encoder consists of a backbone, a position encoding, and a multi-head self-attention mechanism. The backbone can be CNN network, here a ResNet50 or ResNet101 [10]. The DETR transformer is particularly interpretable, because the embedding is created on each feature after the CNN backbone, such that each attention weight can be related to the input pixel.

Since its first publication, DETR has been improved through a variety of enhancements [28]. Yet, the computational demand of such algorithms remains a challenge, limiting their practical application and their ability to achieve real-time detection. While DETR simplifies the object detection process, its high computational requirements make real-time detection difficult to attain. Therefore, the authors in [43] present RT-DETR – a real-time version of DETR – and later improved on with RT-DETRv2 [20]. In the first version of RT-DETR, the authors improved the encoder significantly and neglected queries with a high uncertainty. RT-DETRv2 improves RT-DETR's accuracy by introducing a selective multi-scale feature extraction and a discrete sampling operator, besides a parameter optimisation for better training.

DETA is another version of DETR and is presented in [23]. It uses a two-stage approach together with NMS, because it substantially improves the mean Average Precision (mAP), as the authors claim. Thus, as a first stage, they use a similar encoder architecture as in DETR, but in a class-agnostic version, to yield box predictions. These are then filtered through NMS. The second stage

---

[1] The models are documented in https://huggingface.co/docs/transformers, accessed on the 7th of July, 2025.

uses the predicted boxes as initial boxes and is then trained with a different loss. A big change is the removal of the self-attention layer. Likewise to DETR, the backbone of DETA, as implemented on Huggingface, consists of either a ResNet50 backbone or a Shifting Window (SWin) transformer [19].

4 Methods for Explaining Object Detection

The explainability of object detections with neural networks is currently actively researched [2,9,17,21,27]. In the paper at hand, we focus on two XAI methods that are specifically designed for explaining object detections with saliency maps, but can be applied to a variety of models, i.e., D-RISE [24] and ODAM [42]. Those methods are chosen as a representative method of their kind - perturbation based methods and gradient based methods. The applied XAI methods are outlined in the following.

D-RISE as Perturbation Based Method: Generally, perturbation methods create variations of the input that are forwarded to a neural network to estimate the importance of the image parts. In D-RISE, the input image is divided into a coarse grid of active and inactive parts. This grid is then upsampled to the image size by means of a bilinear transformation, which leads to a mask with values between zero and one. The input image is then multiplied by this mask to reduce the influence of random parts of the image. Through many forward passes of various perturbed images, the influence of specific regions in the image is then estimated for each target detection separately. The benefit of such methods is that they are model agnostic. However, they often require many model evaluations, which is computationally expensive. Moreover, the way parts of the input images are *deactivated* can create a bias for the estimation; if a part of the image is set to black or blurred out, it does not necessarily *deactivate* this part of the image.

Table 1. |Training results from all used transformer models and for all datasets. The evaluation is adapted from the COCO evaluation. The highest mAP for each dataset is marked in bold.

Transformer	Backbone	Fixed	MarineDebris mAP@.5:.95	D2MFNet mAP@.5:.95
DETR	Res50	no	0.680	0.038
	Res50	yes	0.637	0.002
	Res101	no	0.648	0.021
	Res101	yes	0.600	0.002
DETA	Res50	no	0.639	0.180
	Res50	yes	0.675	0.163
RT-DETR	Res50	no	0.814	**0.669**
RT-DETRv2	Res50	no	**0.824**	0.591
Conditional DETR	Res50	no	0.754	0.432

ODAM as Gradient Based CAM Method: CAM-based explanations combine feature activation maps of an intermediate layer through a weighted sum. The weights can be computed in multiple ways, e.g. through the gradient that is computed using back propagation. ODAM is a version of the Grad-CAM method that utilises gradients as weights for the activation maps, but for object detection tasks. According to the original paper, ODAM creates a less cluttered visual explanation compared with D-RISE and can also be computed faster as it only requires a single forward pass.

5   Experimental Evaluation

The following section presents the empirical evaluations. First, the accuracies of the trained object detectors are presented. Then, the qualitative and quantitative results of the XAI methods are shown.

5.1   Evaluation of the Transformer Networks

For the implementation of the models, the Huggingface transformer API is used. Through this API, multiple transformer implementations with different backbones can be downloaded and tested. Here, we trained the selected transformer (see Tab. 1) with ResNet backbones on the two suggested datasets with a training-validation split of 80% and 20%, respectively. All models have been pretrained on the ImageNet dataset, as provided by Huggingface. For training, transfer learning is used with and without fixed backbones for the DETR and DETA models. This way, we want to test if the detected features of a model, pretrained in another data domain, help with the detection in the sonar domain or if the backbone has to be re-trained as well. For the other methods, we trained only the ResNet50 backbone without fixing the backbone of the model. As evaluation metric to asses the performance of each model, we used the mAP@.5:.95 of the COCO evaluator for multiple IOUs. The results of the training are presented in the Table 1.

An example detection of objects in the marineDebris dataset for the DETR transformer is presented in Fig. 1(a). It is worth noting that the attention can also be seen as an explanation for the detection. Thus, for one pixel (highlighted by a bright circle with an asterisk in it) in the image on the right, the self-attention map is presented. On the upper-left, the query-attention map is presented for a possible detection result—in this case, the drink-carton. These attention maps are based on the embeddings of the feature maps of the backbone. The query-attention maps appear to be highly localised; however, the self-attention maps are not that clear. The latter shows all correlating input tokens, i.e. pixels, of the input image. Input tokens with a high self-attention value might contribute more to the detection.

The DETR transformer trained on the D2MFNet dataset does not yield good accuracies. This is due to the noisy images and also due to the large shadows that are cast by the relatively large objects. This is exemplified in Fig. 1(b), which also presents the attention maps and an example detection for DETR and the D2MFNet dataset. For this dataset, the self-attention attributes more input tokens as relevant, and also the query map for the detection of the aircraft considers many distributed input tokens. Thus, the detection result becomes unclear and vague.

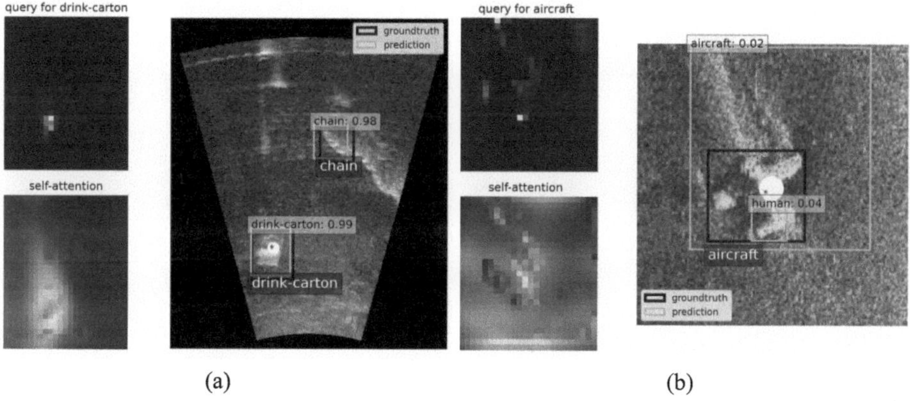

Fig. 1. Attention for the Detection Transformer (DETR) model (a) for the marineDebris dataset and (b) for the D2MFNet. For each image, the upper-left presents the decoder attention at a given query. The lower left displays the self-attention maps at the positions marked on the right.

5.2 Interpretability with Attribution Maps

After presenting the performances of the models and how the attention – at least for the DETR model– can be used for interpretation, the following presents the explainability with attribution maps. It should be mentioned that a poor-performing model, i.e. a low accuracy on the detection, can not generate meaningful attribution maps for explanations because the detection is going to be poor. Therefore, the DETR and DETA models are not evaluated further for the D2MFNet dataset as they have a very low mAP. Starting with the marineDebris dataset, Fig. 2 displays the attribution maps for the DETR transformer for both attribution methods. Here, two objects have been detected; thus, two attribution maps are calculated, one for each object. The D-RISE method (Fig. 2(a)) yields a blurry attribution map, while the ODAM method (Fig. 2(b)) yields a relatively clear attribution map, i.e. most attribution values appear inside the bounding boxes.

For the same dataset, Figs. 3(a) and 3(b) present the attribution maps the DETA model for D-RISE and ODAM, respectively. Here, the D-RISE method creates a blurry image as well, but also high attribution values appear outside of the bounding boxes. This could result from how D-RISE *deactivates* parts of the image: Here, image parts are deactivated by setting it to zero, which is a common approach. However, probably because for the marineDebris dataset, large parts of the image are zero, it could be difficult for D-RISE to create clear attribution maps. Another reason could be that these images are grayscale images of distances, and zeros have a physical meaning. Consequently, zero values inside the SONAR beam are as informative as outside. In the example presented for the DETR model, this effect is less, but still visible.

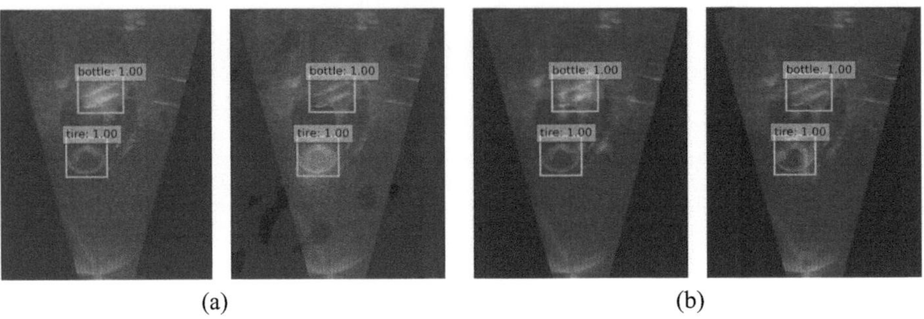

(a)   (b)

Fig. 2. Attribution maps for the DETR transformer on marineDebris data, generated with (a) D-RISE and (b) ODAM. Both XAI methods enable individual attribution maps per box.

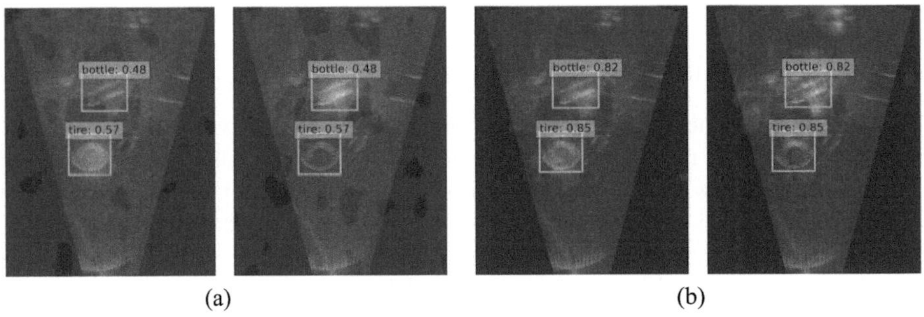

(a)   (b)

Fig. 3. Attribution maps for the DETA transformer with a Res50 backbone on marineDebris data, generated with (a) D-RISE and (b) ODAM. Both XAI methods enable individual attribution maps per box.

To get quantitative results, we evaluated the XAI methods through four evaluation metrics for XAI, where two can be accounted for *faithfulness* and the other two for *localisation*. This is calculated based on the 20% validation split of each dataset. For the localisation, we used the pointing game and the attribution localisation. The pointing game is a binary metric that checks if the highest attribution value is inside the bounding box. Attribution localisation, on the other hand, computes the ratio of the sum of attribution values inside the bounding box compared with the sum of all attribution values. A high value indicates, therefore, that most of the attributions are inside the bounding box. For both metrics, a high value indicates a better localisation property of the explanation. The results are presented in Table 2.

Table 2. The localisation metrics for different combinations of models, datasets, and XAI methods.

Model	Backbone	Dataset	XAI	Pointing Game	Attribution localization
DETR	Res50	marineDebris	ODAM	0.216	0.353
	Res50		D-RISE	0.231	0.029
DETA	Res50	marineDebris	ODAM	0.19	0.298
	Res50		D-RISE	0.255	0.031
RT-DETR	Res50	marineDebris	ODAM	0.204	0.325
			D-RISE	0.284	0.033
		D2MFNet	ODAM	0.422	0.636
			D-RISE	0.54	0.304
RT-DETRv2	Res50	marineDebris	ODAM	0.233	0.221
			D-RISE	0.22	0.033
		D2MFNet	ODAM	0.366	0.545
			D-RISE	0.634	0.285
Conditional DETR	Res50	marineDebris	ODAM	0.254	0.299
			D-RISE	0.3	0.029
		D2MFNet	ODAM	0.257	0.477
			D-RISE	0.298	0.246

For the pointing game, explanations of detections for models with a higher mAP tend to have high attribution values inside the bounding box. This is true across the XAI methods. The reason for this is that a model with a a high mAP is well trained on the dataset; important features in the image are assigned to the corresponding class and used to define the boundaries of the detected box. On the other hand, a low mAP yields from disturbances in the data that confuse the detection; features of other objects in the image interfere with each other. Thus, if a class is not well trained, a high attribution value might appear outside the detected box, while the majority of the attribution values are inside the bounding box, which yields a poor pointing game metric. When looking at the attribution localisation, ODAM yields higher metrics compared to D-RISE. This holds for all datasets, and can also be seen in the previously shown examples in Figs. 2 and 3, where the attribution maps of ODAM are much clearer. Moreover, the D-RISE methods seem to be inappropriate for creating clear results for the marineDebris dataset, as the attribution localisation metrics are always small.

On the other side, D-RISE seems to have the highest attribution value more often inside the bounding box compared to ODAM. The fact that these XAI methods yield different results for the same category of evaluation metrics might relate to a disagreement problem between the evaluation metrics themselves, as pointed out in [11].

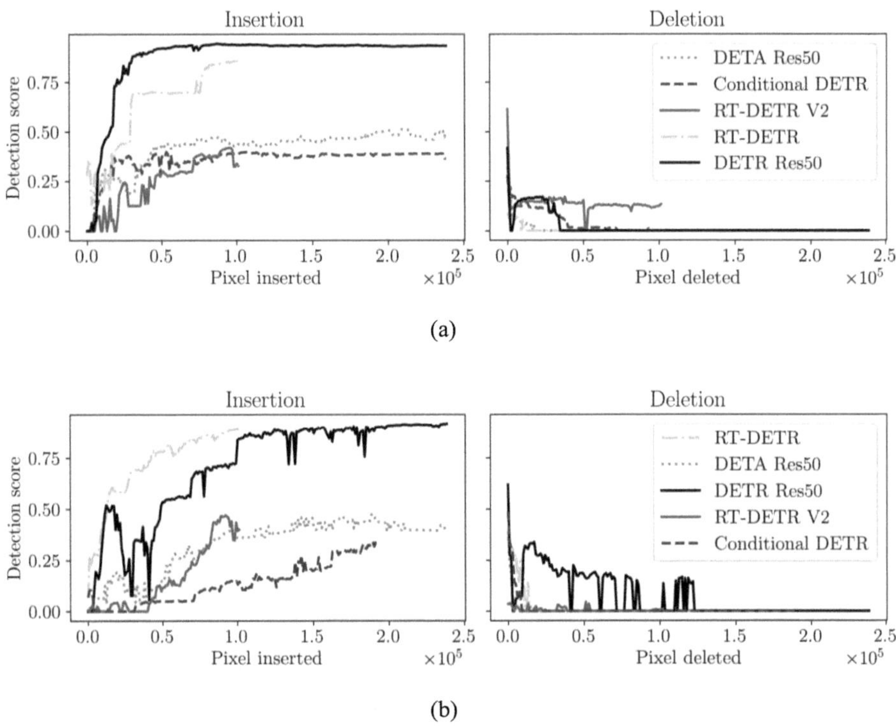

Fig. 4. Insertion and deletion for (a) D-RISE and (b) ODAM and the marineDebris dataset.

Faithfulness evaluates whether the generated attribution maps coincide with the box detection result. We evaluated this through the insertion and deletion metrics, which are presented for the marineDebris dataset in Fig. 4(a) for the D-RISE method and in Fig. 4(b) for the ODAM method. The deletion metric removes pixels from the input images in the order of their highest attribution value. Consequently, the detection result should degrade fast. The insertion metric inserts pixels in the order of their highest attribution values such that the detection result should increase as fast as possible. If pixels are removed, it is important to choose what to insert in their place. Likewise, it is important to choose the *empty* image to start from—similar to the perturbation in D-RISE. For the insertion metric, we used a blurred image and inserted the pixels into the blurred image to avoid alias effects on the image [24]. When pixels are removed, we replace them with zero values.

Although ODAM has a higher result in the attribution localisation compared with D-RISE, the faithfulness of ODAM is not as good as for D-RISE. This can be because the normalisation and attention layers break the gradient information, also known as the conservation property [1], or the gradients are small. Consequently, the attribution values might not reflect the actual detection score and become small. Yet, it can be accounted as a better explanation if the detection score reaches a plateau. According to Fig. 4(b), explanations created with the ODAM method for detections of the RT-DETR and DETR models seem to explain the actual detection of the model better compared with the other models. However, the deletion metric is worst for DETR, which could be due to the way pixels are *deactivated* (see above). On the other side, for Fig. 4(a), the explanations seem to be more faithful, as more curves stabilise.

6   Conclusion and Outlook

This paper investigates new transformer models for object detection on two different sonar datasets (marineDebris and D2MFNet) and evaluates their explainability qualitatively and quantitatively. For explainability, two XAI methods for object detection have been applied that yield attribution maps. The interpretation of these attribution maps helps future developers to understand transformer models for object detection in SONAR data.

Although good datasets for object detection in sonar are rare and small, transformer models with reasonable accuracies can be trained with them. The results of this paper indicate that a better mAP (yet minimal) for SONAR data can be yielded if the backbone is also retrained. For some transformer models, the attention mechanism can also be exploited to understand the detections of the transformer models. However, some models are more optimised to be fast and small, such that the attention can not always be utilised for explanation. Then, new XAI methods showed to be helpful. The results of the paper also indicate that multiple XAI methods must be used, depending on what should be explained. As the results show, it can also happen that XAI methods disagree for the same category of evaluation metrics due to, e.g. the dataset. Moreover, XAI methods should also be adjusted, if possible. For example, for the marineDebris dataset, which is recorded by an FLS, D-RISE could be adjusted to yield clearer attribution maps.

For future work, XAI methods for object detection for sonar data should be evaluated as they can help to highlight specific structures in the images that could be important for the user. Then, more metrics have to be tested to objectively evaluate the quality of the provided explanations. Also, more user-centric explanations could be helpful for sonar data, such as counterfactual and prototypical explanations.

Acknowledgments. The work presented in this paper is funded by the Federal Ministry of Education and Research, Germany, grant number 01IW23003.

References

1. Ali, A., Schnake, T., Eberle, O., Montavon, G., Müller, K.R., Wolf, L.: XAI for transformers: better explanations through conservative propagation. In: Proceedings of the 39th International Conference on Machine Learning, pp. 435–451. PMLR (2022)
2. Andres, A., Martinez-Seras, A., Laña, I., Del Ser, J.: On the black-box explainability of object detection models for safe and trustworthy industrial applications. Res. Eng. **24**, 103498 (2024). https://doi.org/10.1016/j.rineng.2024.103498
3. Aubard, M., Antal, L., Madureira, A., Ábrahám, E.: Knowledge distillation in YOLOX-ViT for side-scan sonar object detection (2024). https://doi.org/10.48550/arXiv.2403.09313
4. Cao, X., Ren, L., Sun, C.: Research on obstacle detection and avoidance of autonomous underwater vehicle based on forward-looking sonar. IEEE Trans. Neural Netw. Learn. Syst. **34**(11), 9198–9208 (2023). https://doi.org/10.1109/TNNLS.2022.3156907
5. Carion, N., Massa, F., Synnaeve, G., Usunier, N., Kirillov, A., Zagoruyko, S.: End-to-End Object Detection with Transformers (2020). https://doi.org/10.48550/arXiv.2005.12872
6. Dosovitskiy, A., et al.: An image is worth 16x16 words: transformers for image recognition at scale. arXiv:2010.11929 [cs] (2021)
7. El-Mihoub, T.A., Gadi, A.E., Nolle, L., Stahl, F.: On object detection and explainability with sonar imagery. In: IEEE 2nd International Maghreb Meeting of the Conference on Sciences and Techniques of Automatic Control and Computer Engineering (MI-STA) (2024)
8. Fan, Z., Xia, W., Liu, X., Li, H.: Detection and segmentation of underwater objects from forward-looking sonar based on a modified Mask RCNN. SIViP **15**(6), 1135–1143 (2021). https://doi.org/10.1007/s11760-020-01841-x
9. Fernandes, L., Fernandes, J.N.D., Calado, M., Pinto, J.R., Cerqueira, R., Cardoso, J.S.: Intrinsic explainability for end-to-end object detection. IEEE Access **12**, 2623–2634 (2024). https://doi.org/10.1109/ACCESS.2023.3347038
10. He, K., Zhang, X., Ren, S., Sun, J.: Deep Residual Learning for Image Recognition. arXiv:1512.03385 [cs] (2015)
11. Hedström, A., Bommer, P., Wickstrøm, K.K., Samek, W., Lapuschkin, S., Höhne, M.M.C.: the meta-evaluation problem in explainable ai: identifying reliable estimators with MetaQuantus (2023). https://doi.org/10.48550/arXiv.2302.07265
12. Huo, G., Wu, Z., Li, J.: Underwater object classification in sidescan sonar images using deep transfer learning and semisynthetic training data. IEEE Access **8**, 47407–47418 (2020). https://doi.org/10.1109/ACCESS.2020.2978880
13. Karimanzira, D., Renkewitz, H., Shea, D., Albiez, J.: Object detection in sonar images. Electronics **9**(7), 1180 (2020). https://doi.org/10.3390/electronics9071180
14. Khan, S., Naseer, M., Hayat, M., Zamir, S.W., Khan, F.S., Shah, M.: Transformers in vision: a survey. ACM Comput. Surv. **54**(10s), 1–41 (2022). https://doi.org/10.1145/3505244
15. Kim, J., Yu, S.C.: Convolutional neural network-based real-time ROV detection using forward-looking sonar image. In: 2016 IEEE/OES Autonomous Underwater Vehicles (AUV), pp. 396–400. IEEE (2016). https://doi.org/10.1109/AUV.2016.7778702
16. Kong, W., et al.: YOLOv3-DPFIN: a dual-path feature fusion neural network for robust real-time sonar target detection. IEEE Sens. J. **20**(7), 3745–3756 (2020). https://doi.org/10.1109/JSEN.2019.2960796

17. Kuroki, M., Yamasaki, T.: BSED: baseline shapley-based explainable detector. IEEE Access **12**, 57959–57973 (2024). https://doi.org/10.1109/ACCESS.2024.3391424
18. Lin, T., Wang, Y., Liu, X., Qiu, X.: A survey of transformers. AI Open **3**, 111–132 (2022). https://doi.org/10.1016/j.aiopen.2022.10.001
19. Liu, Z., et al.: Swin transformer: hierarchical vision transformer using shifted windows. arXiv:2103.14030 [cs] (2021)
20. Lv, W., Zhao, Y., Chang, Q., Huang, K., Wang, G., Liu, Y.: RT-DETRv2: Improved Baseline with Bag-of-Freebies for Real-Time Detection Transformer (2024). https://doi.org/10.48550/arXiv.2407.17140
21. Moradi, M., Yan, K., Colwell, D., Samwald, M., Asgari, R.: Model-agnostic explainable artificial intelligence for object detection in image data. Eng. Appl. Artif. Intell. **137**, 109183 (2024). https://doi.org/10.1016/j.engappai.2024.109183
22. Neves, G., Ruiz, M., Fontinele, J., Oliveira, L.: Rotated object detection with forward-looking sonar in underwater applications. Expert Syst. Appl. **140**, 112870 (2020). https://doi.org/10.1016/j.eswa.2019.112870
23. Ouyang-Zhang, J., Cho, J.H., Zhou, X., Krähenbühl, P.: NMS Strikes Back (2022)
24. Petsiuk, V., et al.: Black-box explanation of object detectors via saliency maps. In: Proceedings of the IEEE/CVF Conference on Computer Vision and Pattern Recognition, pp. 11443–11452 (2021)
25. Preciado-Grijalva, A., Wehbe, B., Firvida, M.B., Valdenegro-Toro, M.: Self-supervised learning for sonar image classification. In: 2022 IEEE/CVF Conference on Computer Vision and Pattern Recognition Workshops (CVPRW), pp. 1498–1507. IEEE (2022). https://doi.org/10.1109/CVPRW56347.2022.00156
26. Rekavandi, A.M., Rashidi, S., Boussaid, F., Hoefs, S., Akbas, E., bennamoun, M.: Transformers in small object detection: a benchmark and survey of state-of-the-art (2023). https://doi.org/10.48550/arXiv.2309.04902
27. Sahatova, K., Balabaeva, K.: An overview and comparison of XAI methods for object detection in computer tomography. Procedia Comput. Sci. **212**, 209–219 (2022). https://doi.org/10.1016/j.procs.2022.11.005
28. Shehzadi, T., Hashmi, K.A., Stricker, D., Afzal, M.Z.: Object Detection with Transformers: A Review (2023). https://doi.org/10.48550/arXiv.2306.04670
29. Shi, P., Sun, H., Xin, Y., He, Q., Wang, X.: SDNet: image-based sonar detection network for multi-scale objects. IET Image Proc. **17**(4), 1208–1223 (2023). https://doi.org/10.1049/ipr2.12707
30. Steiniger, Y., Kraus, D., Meisen, T.: Survey on deep learning based computer vision for sonar imagery. Eng. Appl. Artif. Intell. **114**, 105157 (2022). https://doi.org/10.1016/j.engappai.2022.105157
31. Le Thanh, H., Phung, S.L., Chapple, P.B., Bouzerdoum, A., Ritz, C.H., Tran, L.C.: Deep gabor neural network for automatic detection of mine-like objects in sonar imagery. IEEE Access **8**, 94126–94139 (2020). https://doi.org/10.1109/ACCESS.2020.2995390
32. Touvron, H., Cord, M., Douze, M., Massa, F., Sablayrolles, A., Jégou, H.: Training data-efficient image transformers & distillation through attention (2021). https://doi.org/10.48550/arXiv.2012.12877
33. Valdenegro-Toro, M.: Objectness scoring and detection proposals in forward-looking sonar images with convolutional neural networks. In: Schwenker, F., Abbas, H.M., El Gayar, N., Trentin, E. (eds.) ANNPR 2016. LNCS (LNAI), vol. 9896, pp. 209–219. Springer, Cham (2016). https://doi.org/10.1007/978-3-319-46182-3_18

34. Valdenegro-Toro, M.: Submerged marine debris detection with autonomous underwater vehicles. In: 2016 International Conference on Robotics and Automation for Humanitarian Applications (RAHA), pp. 1–7. IEEE, Amritapuri, Kollam (2016). https://doi.org/10.1109/RAHA.2016.7931907
35. Vaswani, A., et al.: Attention is all you need. arXiv:1706.03762 [cs] (2017)
36. Wang, J., Feng, C., Wang, L., Li, G., He, B.: Detection of weak and small targets in forward-looking sonar image using multi-branch shuttle neural network. IEEE Sens. J. **22**(7), 6772–6783 (2022). https://doi.org/10.1109/JSEN.2022.3147234
37. Wang, W., Zhang, Y., Li, H., Gong, X., Liu, L., Kang, Y.: D2MFNet: A Dual-Domain Multi-Frequency Network for Side-Scan Sonar Image Detection (2023). https://doi.org/10.20944/preprints202309.2024.v1
38. Xie, K., Yang, J., Qiu, K.: A dataset with multibeam forward-looking sonar for underwater object detection. Sci. Data **9**(1), 739 (2022). https://doi.org/10.1038/s41597-022-01854-w
39. Yu, Y., Zhao, J., Gong, Q., Huang, C., Zheng, G., Ma, J.: Real-time underwater maritime object detection in side-scan sonar images based on transformer-YOLOv5. Remote Sens. **13**(18), 3555 (2021). https://doi.org/10.3390/rs13183555
40. Yulin, T., Jin, S., Bian, G., Zhang, Y.: Shipwreck target recognition in side-scan sonar images by improved YOLOv3 model based on transfer learning. IEEE Access **8**, 173450–173460 (2020). https://doi.org/10.1109/ACCESS.2020.3024813
41. Zhang, P., Tang, J., Zhong, H., Ning, M., Liu, D., Wu, K.: Self-trained target detection of radar and sonar images using automatic deep learning. IEEE Trans. Geosci. Remote Sens. **60**, 1–14 (2022). https://doi.org/10.1109/TGRS.2021.3096011
42. Zhao, C., Chan, A.B.: ODAM: gradient-based instance-specific visual explanations for object detection. In: The Eleventh International Conference on Learning Representations (2022)
43. Zhao, Y., et al.: DETRs beat YOLOs on real-time object detection (2024). https://doi.org/10.48550/arXiv.2304.08069

Predicting London's Precipitation:
A Spatio-Temporal Neural Network Approach

Huma Zafar[1], Stelios Kapetanakis[1(⊠)], Giacomo Nalli[2], and Khuong Nguyen[3]

[1] Distributed Labs, 30 Churchill Pl, London 14 5RE, UK
{huma,stelios}@dstr.co.uk
[2] Middlesex University, The Burroughs, London NW4 4BT, UK
giacomo.nalli@mdx.ac.uk
[3] Royal Holloway University, Egham Hill, Egham TW20 0EX, UK
Khuong.Nguyen@rhul.ac.uk

Abstract. This study presents a data-driven approach to forecasting total precipitation in London using an Artificial Neural Network (ANN) within a spatio-temporal framework. Leveraging ERA5 data from 2010 to 2025, the methodology includes automated NetCDF extraction, feature engineering with lagged precipitation and cyclic time encodings, and dimensionality reduction via a trained Autoencoder. The ANN, designed in a GenCast-style architecture, was trained using the Adam optimiser over 50 epochs and achieved strong performance. SHAP analysis highlighted the importance of lag features and seasonal time variables, enhancing interpretability and supporting the model's application in urban flood risk management and climate resilience.

Keywords: Total precipitation forecasting · Artificial Neural Networks (ANN) · Spatio-temporal modelling

1 Introduction

Total precipitation significantly impacts urban infrastructure, water management, and socio-economic stability. Extreme or irregular rainfall can lead to flash floods, overwhelmed drainage systems, and disruptions in transport and agriculture [13].

Accurate forecasting of total precipitation is essential for urban mobility and strategic planning across agriculture and industry [2]. Traditional statistical models, which rely on linear associations with weather variables, often fall short due to the complexity of rainfall dynamics [1].

Nevertheless, precipitation forecasting remains challenging due to its spatial and temporal variability, especially in urban areas like London [5]. ANN effectiveness still depends heavily on data quality, model design, and the specific forecasting objective [1]. Luk et al. (2000) [8] paved the way for advancements in short-term rainfall forecasting within urban environments by proposing the use of ANNs. Their work was further complemented by Valverde Ramírez et al. (2005) [12] proposed an ANN-based method for Sao Paulo, Brazil. Their approach involved establishing a non-linear relationship

M. Bramer and F. Stahl (Eds.): SGAI-AI 2025, LNAI 16302, pp. 179–189, 2026.
https://doi.org/10.1007/978-3-032-11442-6_13

between regional ETA model output data and surface rainfall data. Bilgili and Sahin (2010) [3] successfully employed ANN architecture to model monthly rainfall and temperature in the context of Turkey. Suparta and Samah (2020) [11] built three different ANN models for rainfall forecasting, evaluating their respective performance and potential for further development. This suggests ANFIS could be a valuable tool for flood risk management.

This work focuses on London, a densely populated urban place, which faces significant challenges with total precipitation. This is due to a unique combination of its population density, aging drainage infrastructure, and increasing climate volatility. Erratic or extreme rainfall events have far-reaching consequences, leading to flash floods, overwhelmed drainage systems, and disruptions to both transportation and agriculture [6]. Precipitation patterns are also linked to increased air pollution episodes, adding another layer of environmental concern [4]. Ultimately, accurate forecasting of total precipitation is vital for London's urban planning, climate resilience, and early warning systems.

2 Background

2.1 Dataset Description

The data for this study is sourced from the Copernicus Climate Data Store (CDS), a leading provider of climate data. The data is in NetCDF format and has been preprocessed using xarray, an open-source library that helps managing numerical arrays, allowing for more concise and less error-prone user experience whilst efficiently handling multi-dimensional arrays. The temporal coverage spans from 2010 to 2025, focusing on total precipitation (tp) recorded at 00:00 UTC. To ensure relevance to the study area, the spatial resolution is clipped specifically to the London boroughs, using a coordinate system defined by Latitude, Longitude, sand Time.

2.2 Precipitation Patterns in London (2010–2025)

Analysis of total precipitation data over London for selected years (2010, 2015, 2020, 2025) reveals distinct spatio-temporal patterns. The provided precipitation maps, with London boroughs outlined, illustrate the distribution of precipitation in millimeters (mm) at 00:00 UTC for these years.

2010 (Fig. 1) In 2010, the total precipitation across London at 00:00 UTC varied, with some areas experiencing higher levels (darker shades, up to 22 mm) and others relatively lower (lighter shades, around 18 mm). The western and south-eastern parts of London appear to have received more precipitation compared to the central and eastern regions.

2015 (Fig. 2) By 2015, there was a noticeable increase in total precipitation values compared to 2010, with some regions reaching up to 30 mm. The overall precipitation levels seem higher across the city, indicating a potentially wetter period or a specific event captured at this time. The spatial variability remains, but the intensity has increased.

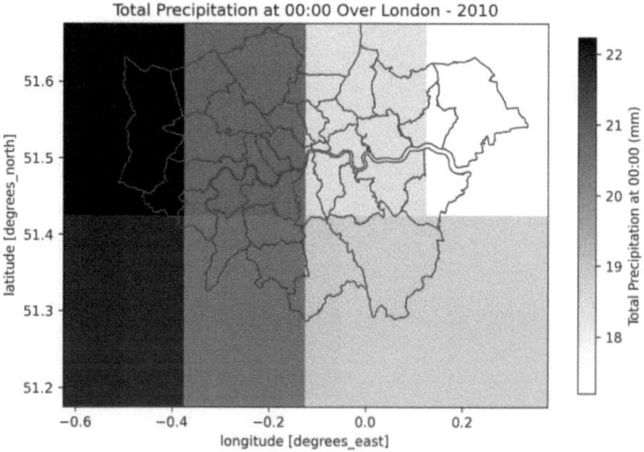

Fig. 1. 2010, Total Precipitation across London

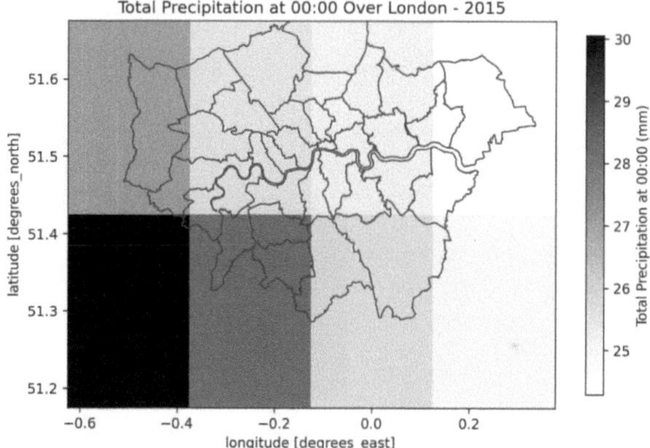

Fig. 2. 2015 - Total Precipitation across London

2020 (Fig. 3) The precipitation map for 2020 shows a shift in the distribution and intensity. While some areas still exhibit higher precipitation (up to 25 mm), there are also significant areas with lower values. Notably, the southern central area appears to have experienced particularly low precipitation at this specific time, highlighted by the darkest shades indicating values around 22 mm. This suggests localized variations in rainfall.

2025 (Fig. 4) The forecast for 2025 indicates a significant decrease in total precipitation compared to previous years, with values ranging from approximately 9 mm to 10.2 mm. This suggests a much drier outlook at 00:00 UTC for London. The shift towards lower precipitation levels across the entire city is quite pronounced, potentially implying a drier climate trend or a specific dry period.

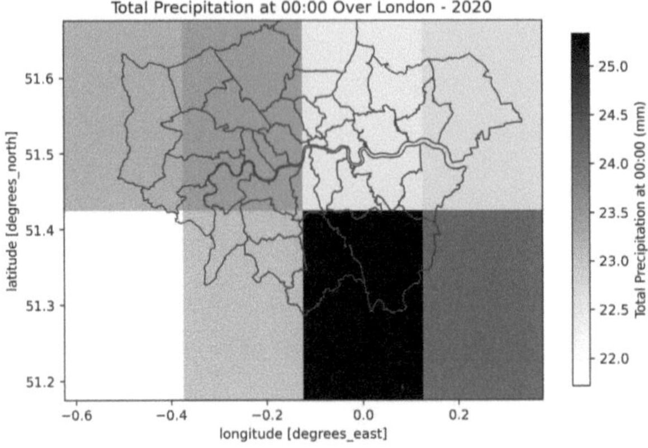

Fig. 3. 2020 - Total Precipitation across London

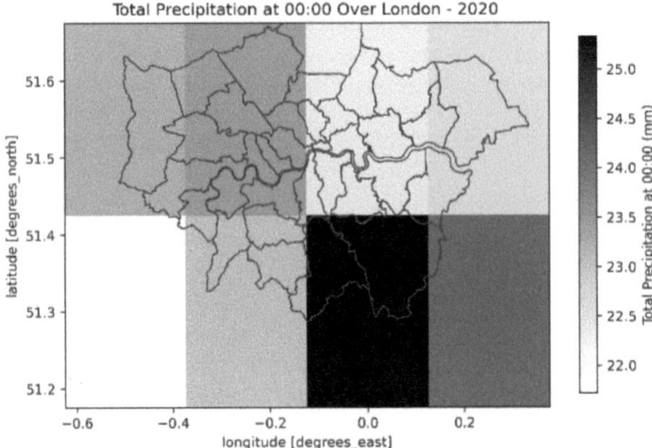

Fig. 4. 2025 - Total Precipitation across London

2.3 Monthly Mean Precipitation Analysis

A deeper insight into London's precipitation patterns can be gained by examining the monthly mean precipitation for the selected years (2010, 2015, 2020, 2025), as illustrated in the histogram (Fig. 5).

The histogram, "Monthly Mean Precipitation at 00:00 for Selected Years," provides a comparative view of average monthly rainfall across these four years.

First, there is considerable variability in monthly precipitation across the years. For example, January recorded relatively high rainfall in 2010 and 2025, while showing much lower values in 2015 and 2020. February displays similar fluctuations, with a notable peak in 2015. Second, seasonal peaks do not occur consistently in the same months each year, reflecting the non-stationary nature of precipitation patterns. July experienced a significant peak in 2010, whereas October showed an unusually high spike in 2020, indicating a particularly wet autumn. Third, some months appear consistently drier across

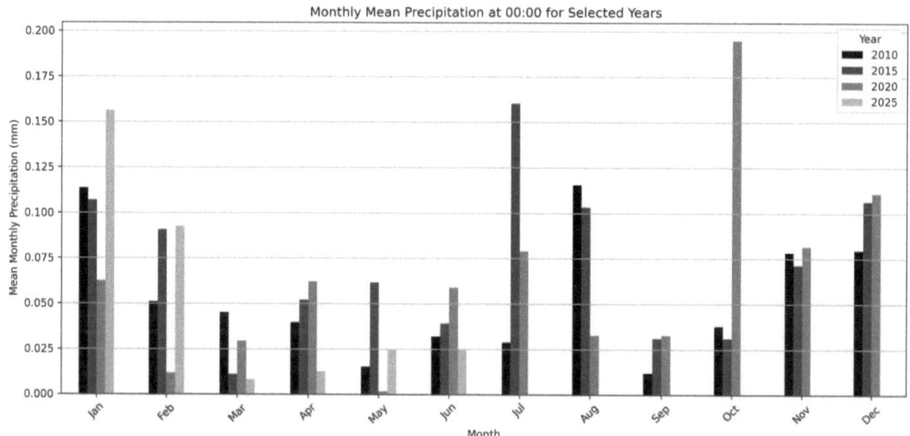

Fig. 5. Monthly Mean Precipitation at 00:00 for 2010–2025

all years; September, for instance, generally receives lower average precipitation, with May and June also tending to show reduced rainfall. Hence, the data reveals a high degree of year-to-year variability, with extreme differences such as the wet October of 2020 compared to much drier conditions in the same month during 2015 and 2025. Likewise, while July 2010 was markedly wet, July in both 2020 and 2025 was significantly drier. These patterns underscore the complexity of long-term precipitation forecasting and the importance of models capable of capturing such extremes.

Based on the analysis of precipitation maps and monthly mean histograms highlights the complex and dynamic nature of rainfall in London. High spatial and temporal variability, along with shifting climate patterns, makes accurate total precipitation forecasting both essential and challenging. Therefore, there is a clear need for advanced AI models that can learn from and adapt to these details, thereby supporting effective urban planning, climate resilience, and early warning systems.

Dataset Background

The dataset used in this study was sourced from the Copernicus Climate Data Store (CDS), a leading repository for climate information. Provided in NetCDF format, the data was preprocessed using the xarray library to efficiently handle its multi-dimensional structure. Covering the period from 2010 to 2025, it focuses on total precipitation (denoted as 'tp') recorded at 00:00 UTC. The spatial resolution was clipped to the boundaries of the London boroughs, using a coordinate system defined by latitude, longitude, and time to ensure geographic relevance.

The primary variable, 'tp', was structured along the dimensions of 'valid_time', 'latitude', and 'longitude', reflecting its spatio-temporal nature. Metadata revealed that the dataset originated from the European Centre for Medium-Range Weather Forecasts (ECMWF), and conformed to CF−1.7 climate data conventions. The history attribute indicated prior conversion from GRIB to NetCDF. In total, the dataset comprises 45,272 precipitation records, forming a robust foundation for analysis.

3 Methodology

3.1 Data Loading and Exploration

The NetCDF file was accessed programmatically from a compressed archive. Using xarray, the dataset was loaded and examined to understand its variables, coordinates, and attributes. Key dimensions included valid_time for temporal indexing, and latitude and longitude for spatial mapping. Additional metadata coordinates such as number and expver provided contextual details about data versions and origins.

3.2 Feature Engineering

To prepare the dataset for machine learning models, several features were engineered to capture complex temporal dynamics:

- **Lag Features:** Time-lagged precipitation values were generated (e.g., tp_lag_1, tp_lag_3, tp_lag_6, tp_lag_12) to allow the model to learn from past rainfall events.
- **Cyclical Time Encoding:** Sine and cosine transformations were applied to cyclic time variables such as month, day, and day of year (e.g., month_sin, dayofweek_cos) to retain their periodic nature while avoiding linear assumptions.
- **Autoencoder-Derived Features:** An Autoencoder trained on scaled precipitation data produced low-dimensional representations (3D and 7D), capturing latent, non-linear patterns. These were visualised using scatter plots and pairwise comparisons (Figs. 6 and 7), offering deeper insight into precipitation variability.

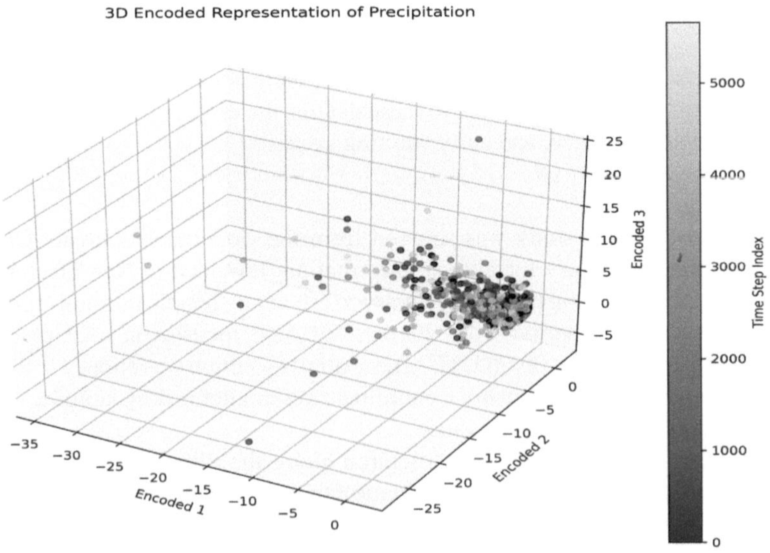

Fig. 6. Encoded Representation of Precipitation

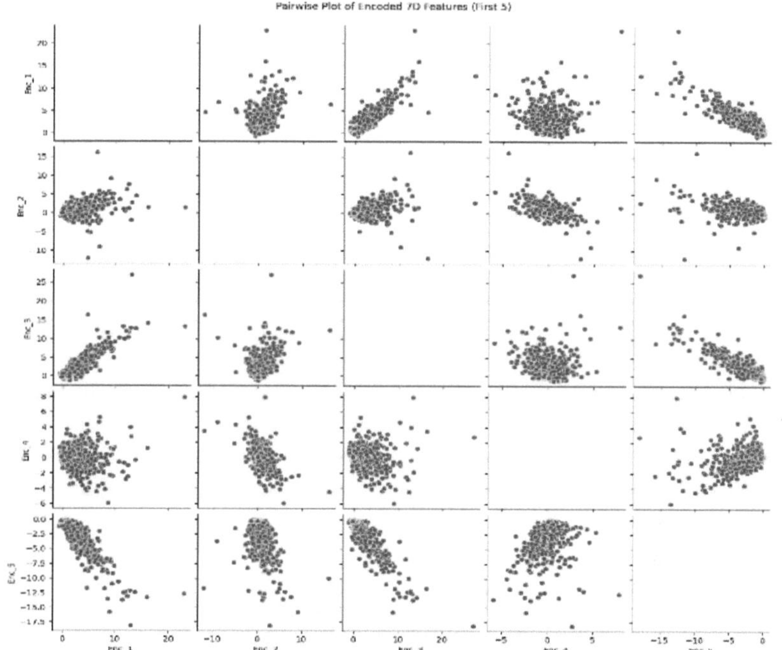

Fig. 7. Pairwise plot of encoded features

All target variables ('tp') were normalised using StandardScaler, ensuring consistent scale and stable convergence during model training.

3.3   Data Splitting and Preprocessing

The processed dataset was split into training (60%), validation (20%), and test (20%) sets using a two-step approach via train_test_split from scikit-learn. First, 60% of the data was allocated for training, with the remaining 40% split equally for validation and testing. This stratified partitioning ensured representativeness and prevented data leakage.

Following the split, input features and target variables in each subset were further scaled using StandardScaler to maintain consistent data distributions. This step is critical for neural network models, which perform optimally when inputs are normalised across features.

3.4   Model Training and Performance Evaluation

An Artificial Neural Network (ANN), based on a structure suited for spatio-temporal data (often referred to as a *GenCast-style* model), was developed to predict total precipitation ('tp'). This architecture was designed to leverage the engineered time series features, capturing complex temporal patterns.

The network consisted of:

- **Input layer**: Receiving all preprocessed features, with the number of neurons equal to the number of input variables.
- **Two hidden layers**: Fully connected layers using Rectified Linear Unit (ReLU) activations, which introduce non-linearity and allow the model to learn intricate precipitation dynamics that traditional linear models may miss.
- **Output layer**: A single neuron with a linear activation function, appropriate for continuous-value regression tasks.

The model was trained using the Adam optimiser, aiming to minimise the Mean Squared Error (MSE) loss function. Training occurred over 50 epochs with a batch size of 32, and incorporated a validation split to monitor generalisation performance across epochs. This validation process is crucial: while the model learns patterns in the training data, it must also avoid overfitting—performing well only on familiar data.

Post-training, model predictions and corresponding test labels were inverse-transformed to their original scales using the StandardScaler applied earlier. This enabled a direct and interpretable comparison between predicted and observed precipitation values.

Model performance was measured using three regression metrics: the R^2 score, which shows how much of the variation in the data the model can explain, with higher values meaning better predictions; the mean squared error (MSE), which calculates the average squared difference between predicted and actual values and, although it is sensitive to outliers, gives a good indication of overall accuracy; and the mean absolute error (MAE), which finds the average of the absolute differences, making it easier to understand and less affected by large errors.

4 Results

The ANN achieved an R^2 score of 0.7698, meaning it explained approximately 77% of the variance in total precipitation. While this does not represent perfect prediction, it demonstrates strong learning of underlying patterns in the data. On the other hand, both MSE and MAE were remarkably low, indicating minimal average errors between predictions and actual values. Though small errors may accumulate over longer forecasting horizons, the model's accuracy on test data remains robust.

To conclude, these results confirm that the ANN model is highly effective for short-to medium-term precipitation forecasting in complex urban environments.

4.1 SHAP Analysis of the ANN Model

To improve the interpretability of the Artificial Neural Network (ANN) and understand how features affect its predictions, SHAP (SHapley Additive exPlanations) analysis was performed on test data. SHAP values show each feature's contribution to predictions, indicating their importance and whether their impact is positive or negative.

The SHAP Summary Plot (Figure: SHAP Summary Plot – Feature Importance) displays the distribution of SHAP values for all features as we can see in Fig. 8. The x-axis shows the effect on predictions, and colours indicate feature values (darker = high, lighter = low). The spread of points reflects each feature's overall importance.

Top 5 Influential Features (ranked by mean absolute SHAP values):

1. tp_lag_1 (0.0104): Previous precipitation was the strongest predictor, showing a positive link with current precipitation, especially seasonally.
2. month_cos (0.0100): Captures seasonal cycles, showing significant variation in precipitation by time of year.
3. dayofweek_sin (0.0064): Suggests a mild weekly precipitation pattern, possibly linked to weather or human activity.
4. dayofweek_cos (0.0041): Complements the weekly pattern with variations across years.
5. day_sin (0.0037): Reflects finer monthly or yearly cycles influencing precipitation.

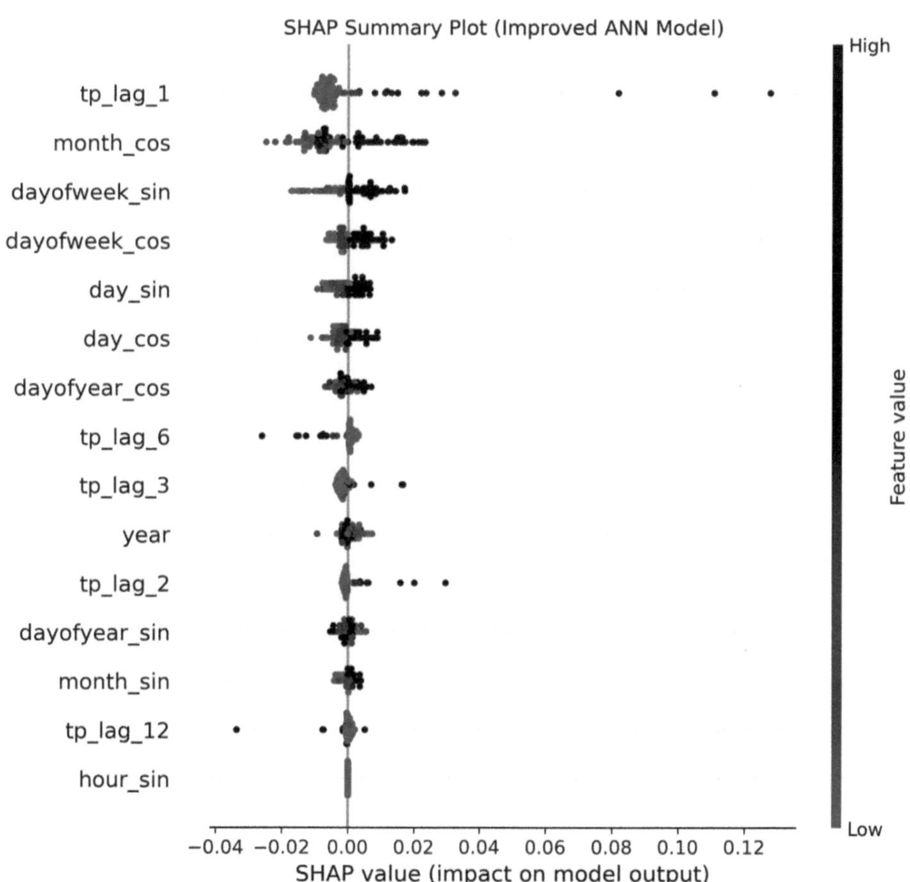

Fig. 8. SHAP Summary Plot

Although the ANN is inherently a black-box model, SHAP offers a robust framework for revealing its internal decision processes. In contrast, the analysis confirms that the model relies on features with strong meteorological grounding—particularly lagged precipitation and cyclic time components. Even so, certain features exert weaker influence, yet still contribute to nuanced predictions.

Conclusively, the SHAP analysis substantiates that the ANN model aligns closely with known physical drivers of precipitation. This added interpretability increases confidence in the model's outputs and confirms its practical value for urban forecasting, infrastructure planning, and climate risk mitigation. Specifically, the analysis shows that lagged precipitation values and cyclic temporal features (month, day of week, day) are the main factors influencing the model's predictions for total precipitation in London. Such interpretability is vital for validating the model's logic and reinforcing trust in its forecasts, as it corresponds with established meteorological knowledge.

Discussing the results in regard to recent advances in rainfall forecasting; the literature shows combined statistical models with machine-learning techniques. Traditional statistical approaches assess correlations between rainfall and atmospheric factors but are limited by the inherent non-linearity of precipitation and can be computationally demanding [10]. To address these challenges, Artificial Neural Networks (ANNs) have been widely adopted, as they effectively capture non-linearity and require minimal prior knowledge of variable relationships [7]. GenCast by DeepMind employs diffusion models and graph transformers to generate high-resolution probabilistic weather forecasts up to 15 days ahead, outperforming traditional ensemble systems [9]. Yet its reliance on large-scale models and high-performance hardware makes it costly and resource-intensive, so this study instead applies ANNs to predict precipitation at large scale as a more practical option.

5 Conclusion

Building on the success of this ANN-based forecasting approach, several promising avenues for future research emerge. Future research should first focus on improving computational efficiency to develop more practical and affordable models, as current advanced methods like GenCast demand high resources unsuitable for real-time use. Second, incorporating additional meteorological variables such as temperature, humidity, wind speed, and pressure could enhance forecast accuracy. Third, using higher spatial and temporal resolution data would improve localisation, crucial for urban rainfall prediction. Fourth, ensemble modelling that combines various ANN architectures and traditional methods can increase reliability by leveraging diverse strengths. Fifth, explicitly quantifying forecast uncertainty would help decision-makers better assess confidence and manage risks. Further areas include real-time deployment challenges and applying models to future climate scenarios to assess climate change impacts on London's precipitation.

References

1. AbuSaleh, M., Rasel, H.M., Ray, B.: A comprehensive review towards resilient rainfall forecasting models using artificial intelligence techniques. Green Technol. Sustain. **2**, 100–104 (2024)

2. Aguasca-Colomo, R., Castellanos-Nieves, D., Méndez, M.: Comparative analysis of rainfall prediction models using machine learning in Islands with complex orography: Tenerife Island. Appl. Sci. **9**(22), 4931 (2019). https://doi.org/10.3390/app9224931

3. Bilgili, M., Sahin, B.: Prediction of long-term monthly temperature and rainfall in Turkey. Energy Sources Part A: Recovery, Utilization, and Environmental Effects **32**(1), 60–71 (2010). https://doi.org/10.1080/15567030802467522

4. Czarnecka, M., Nidzgorska-Lencewicz, J.: Impact of weather conditions on winter and summer air quality. Int. Agrophysics. **25**(1), 7–12 (2011)

5. Dos Santos, R.S.: Estimating spatio-temporal air temperature in London (UK) using machine learning and earth observation satellite data. Int. J. Appl. Earth Obs. Geoinf. **88**, 102066 (2020). https://doi.org/10.1016/j.jag.2020.102066

6. Hanlon, H.M., Bernie, D., Carigi, G., et al.: Future changes to high impact weather in the UK. Clim. Change **166**, 50 (2021). https://doi.org/10.1007/s10584-021-03100-5

7. Liu, Q., Zou, Y., Liu, X., Linge, N.: A survey on rainfall forecasting using artificial neural network. Int. J. Embed. Syst. **11**(2), 240–249 (2019)

8. Luk, K.C., Ball, J.E., Sharma, A.: A study of optimal model lag and spatial inputs to artificial neural network for rainfall forecasting. J. Hydrol. **227**(1–4), 56–65 (2000). https://doi.org/10.1016/S0022-1694(99)00165-1

9. Price, I., et al.: Probabilistic weather forecasting with machine learning. Nature. **637**, 84–90 (2025). https://doi.org/10.1038/s41586-024-08252-9

10. Singh, P., Borah, B.: Indian summer monsoon rainfall prediction using artificial neural network. Stoch. Env. Res. Risk Assess. **27**(7), 1585–1599 (2013)

11. Suparta, W., Samah, A.A.: Rainfall prediction by using ANFIS times series technique in South Tangerang, Indonesia. Geodesy Geodyn. **11**(6), 411–417 (2020). https://doi.org/10.1016/j.geog.2020.08.001

12. Valverde Ramírez, M.C., de Campos Velho, H.F., Ferreira, N.J.: Artificial neural network technique for rainfall forecasting applied to the São Paulo region. J. Hydrol. **301**(1), 146–162 (2005). https://doi.org/10.1016/j.jhydrol.2004.06.028

13. Yao, R., Sun, P., Bian, Y., Yu, S., Sun, Z., Singh, V.P., Ge, C., Zhang, Q.: Responses of agricultural drought to meteorological drought under different climatic zones and vegetation types. J. Hydrol. **619**, 129305 (2023). https://doi.org/10.1016/j.jhydrol.2023.129305

Medical Computing and Health Informatics

Generation, Use and Effects of Synthetic Data to Train Medical AI's: Examined Using the Example of Knee Arthroplasty

Tobias Neiss-Theuerkauff[1,2,3(✉)] , Arne Schierbaum[1,3] ,
Yves Korte-Wagner[1,2], Thomas Luhmann[1,3] , Till Sieberth[1,3] ,
and Frank Wallhoff[1,2]

[1] Jade Hochschule, 26121 Oldenburg, Germany
{tobias.neiss-theuerkauff,arne.schierbaum,yves.korte-wagner,
thomas.luhmann,till.sieberth,frank.wallhoff}@jade-hs.de
[2] ITAS - Institute for Technical Assistance Systems, Karlsruhe, Germany
[3] IAPG - Institute for Applied Photogrammetry and Geoinformatics,
Oldenburg, Germany

Abstract. The use of computers and artificial intelligence (AI) has become firmly established in everyday human life. Computer-assisted surgery is already an integral part of many medical applications. AI is being used successfully to help with medical decision-making and to support various medical processes and interactions. To provide reliable assessments, AI systems must be trained on realistic and representative datasets. In sensitive domains such as medicine, there is often an insufficient amount of high-quality data available for effective AI training. Therefore, in this study, we model and prepare synthetic training data of a human knee for further use, aiming to eliminate the need for physically installed markers. We investigate the application of synthetic AI training data in the field of surgery, using total knee arthroplasty as a representative example.

Keywords: Artificial Intelligence · Synthetic Data · AI Training · AI in Surgery · Total Knee Arthroplasty · AI in Surgery · Segmentation · Annotation · Optical Measurement Photogrammetry

1 Introduction

1.1 Background

In medicine, AI is increasingly applied across various domains, including surgery [5,10]. AI is utilized in the planning and execution of surgical procedures [1], can be employed in primary care for the identification of diseases [19] and is increasingly integrated in medical training [12,18].

A surgical intervention is typically divided into three distinct phases [19]:

M. Bramer and F. Stahl (Eds.): SGAI-AI 2025, LNAI 16302, pp. 193–206, 2026.
https://doi.org/10.1007/978-3-032-11442-6_14

1. Preoperative phase
2. Intraoperative phase
3. Postoperative phase

In the preoperative phase, imaging data (such as MRI and CT scans) can be analyzed with the assistance of AI, supporting surgeons by generating 3D models of anatomical structures. These models can then be utilized during both the planning and operative phases [7].

During the intraoperative phase, AI can be employed to support collaborative surgery, monitor surgical procedures, or accelerate operative interventions. The implementation of AI can minimize the risks associated with surgical procedures and expedite the subsequent healing process [9,11,17].

Furthermore, AI can be used in the postoperative phase for monitoring and prognosis. Through the analysis of patient data and sensor based real-time-monitoring, postoperative complications can be predicted, and follow-up care can be adjusted and improved accordingly [5,16]

It is expected that the use of AI will continue to grow and gain further significance in the future [2,3,18,20].

1.2   Data Preparation for Total Knee Arthroplasty

During a surgical procedure aimed at resolving a primary condition, additional interventions are often required to enable computer-assisted surgery. In the case of total knee arthroplasty, optical markers are screwed into the femur and tibia to determine the patient's leg axis.

In [11,15], a concept is presented in which these physical markers, which are temporarily fixed during knee surgery, could be replaced in the future by non-contact, image-based methods. For this purpose, a trinocular camera system is intended to capture image sequences of the knee joint, which are then aligned using AI-based matching methods [4,14]. From these aligned images, a dense point cloud of the knee surface can be generated [15].

Accurate recognition of bone structures is crucial for 3D-reconstruction, since the knee joint is in motion during the acquisition process and image matching can only be performed reliably using the respective bones. The resulting 3D-model of the knee joint is used for orienting the joint along the mechanical leg axis. This axis, defined by the centers of the hip and ankle joints, serves as the basis for preoperative planning of the bone resection. Thus, the preoperative plan can be effectively transferred to the surgical setting.

1.3   Use of Synthetic Data

The use of real-world data for training AI models in the medical domain presents numerous challenges. Medical data is subject to strict data protection regulations and ethical guidelines. Additionally, the availability of suitable datasets is limited, particularly when data from surgical procedures is required. Another important factor is the time- and cost-intensive preprocessing of data for AI training. All imaging data must be manually segmented and annotated, which demands significant human and computational resources.

In contrast, synthetic data can be generated, segmented, and annotated with considerably less effort. This allows for the creation of substantially larger datasets for training, which can also represent a virtually unlimited range of variability and complexity within AI models. However, there are some challenges related to the complexity of real surgical scenarios that need to be examined more closely. In particular, the obscuring of bones by tissue and fluids must be taken into account in the future.

The goal is to simulate all conceivable data and scenarios necessary for training an AI model that is ultimately capable of processing real-world data.

In this work, synthetic data is incrementally extended with new elements to closely approximate the real surgical scenario. With the step-by-step approach, the influence of the individual aspects on AI training can be examined.

2   General Concept

To enable the use of synthetic data for AI training, a basic 3D dataset must first be created, which can be visualized and modified within a 3D environment. For this purpose, the open-source software *Blender*[1] is used. Subsequently, the Blender plugin *vision_blender*[2] is employed to compute ground truth data for individual objects. The ground truth data is used to generate segmented training data by annotating labeled regions in the rendered image. These data serve as the basis for training the AI model. For each rendered 2D image, a corresponding ground truth dataset is generated, containing the polygonal outlines of the relevant bones (femur and tibia).

2.1   Virtual Scene

To construct the virtual environment, artificial bone models of the femur and tibia were scanned using a 3D scanner and integrated into the visualization. Both bones can be independently transformed and rotated to simulate various knee joint angles. A surgical drape was added as a background to replicate the operating room environment. To represent only the visible areas of the bones during surgery, a simplified human leg skin model was designed and incorporated into the scene. This skin model is flexible and adjusts to the specific knee joint angles. Light sources are configured to simulate the lighting conditions of a real operating environment. Because the brightness in the operating room varies, the scene is illuminated with different brightness levels (Fig. 1).

Several virtual cameras are placed within the scene to support image rendering. Since the final data acquisition will be performed using a multi-camera system, this system was virtually reconstructed. It consists of three industrial

---

[1] version 4.30, Blender Foundation, Amsterdam, Netherlands.
[2] vision_blender, version 1.0, https://github.com/Cartucho/vision_blender.

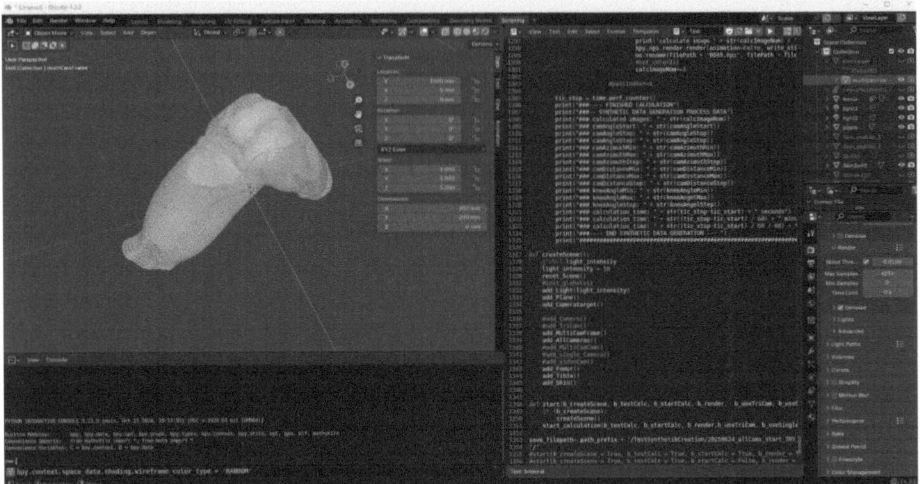

Fig. 1. Visualization in Blender – Wired skin with femur and tibia, Python script and scene content.

cameras arranged in a triangular configuration [15]. The intrinsic and extrinsic camera parameters were replicated in the virtual environment. Additionally, two more cameras were implemented: one more industrial *Basler* camera with given parameters, and a generic of the shelf camera with default parameters.

The entire visualization is controlled in real-time via a Python script, allowing for the automated rendering of a large number of images from various camera positions, lighting conditions, knee angles, and other additional parameters.

Further elements can be dynamically added to the scene in the future as the visualization has a modular structure.

2.2 Image Rendering

In the default settings of the implemented rendering process, various parameters are dynamically adjusted during runtime. The camera is rotated around the knee in 20-degree increments, completing a full 360° rotation. After each pass, the camera's elevation angle is increased in 20° steps, ranging from 30° to 90°. This procedure is iterated with different camera-to-object distances (from 500 mm to 800 mm in 100 mm increments) and three knee joint positions (flexed: 90°, extended: 180°, and intermediate: 120°). A single rendering pass under these base conditions results in 864 images.

During rendering, ground truth data of the labeling for the relevant structures (femur and tibia) are simultaneously generated. These data are stored in separate files for each image and consist of closed polygons with X-Y point coordinates and corresponding object labels (Fig. 2).

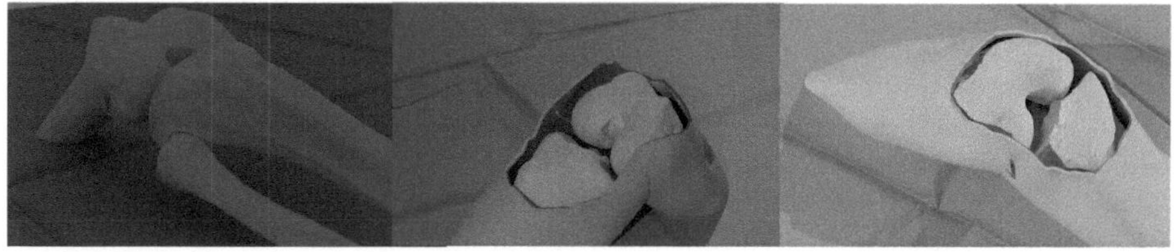

Fig. 2. Rendered images with different models, camera positions, and lighting conditions.

2.3   The AI Training Approach

The synthetic image data is subsequently used for training the AI models. By combining various image datasets, multiple training models can be developed. The detailed training procedure is described in Sect. 3. These trained models are later deployed to analyze the images captured by the cameras during surgical procedures. The objective is to enable the AI system to reliably detect and segment the femur and tibia, so that only the relevant image regions are considered in subsequent processing.

2.4   Further Process

In the further processing stage, the segmented image regions are masked. Using the resulting images, a 3D model of the knee joint is constructed via photogrammetric techniques [15]. To ensure sufficient surface coverage, the knee must be flexed and extended during the data acquisition process. The 3D reconstruction is achieved by aligning individual images through feature matching algorithms. Since the motion of the knee prevents the entire joint from being reconstructed as a single object, precise masking is essential to reconstruct and align the femur and tibia individually [11,15]. The final 3D models of the femur and tibia are then used to determine the orientation of the knee joint along the mechanical axis of the leg. For this purpose, we aim to register the reconstructed models with preoperative CT data to transfer the mechanical axis into the intraoperative environment.

3   AI Training Framework

3.1   AI Framework

For training the AI models, the open-source framework *Detectron2*, developed by *Facebook AI Research (Meta)*[3], was utilized. This framework enables model development in two fundamental ways: either by using pretrained models based on the COCO dataset [8], or by training models from scratch. Various pretrained models are available, each using the same training data but different underlying algorithms.

---

[3] Detectron2 (Meta), Version v0.6, Facebook AI Research (Meta).

3.2   Evaluation Factors in AI-Training

Various parameters can be analyzed for the evaluation of AI training methods. In this work the differently trained models are compared to each other with the values described below.

1. Accuracy-Value: Indicates how good the predictions are during training (the higher, the better)
2. Total-Loss-Value: Indicates how large the error is during training (the lower, the better)
3. Validation-Value: Indicates how well the model works on **unknown** data (the higher, the better)

3.3   Basic Definitions of AI-Training

In this study pretrained models and models trained exclusively on custom datasets were evaluated. Furthermore, three different AI training algorithms were compared with each other. For all training runs the same training settings, size of training-, validation- and test-datasets, number of iterations, evaluation steps were used in order to ensure comparability.

The Total-Loss-Value (see Subsect. 3.2) during AI training was used as the first comparative index in order to obtain an assessment of whether the use of pre-trained models makes sense in this specific medical area. The example shown in Fig. 3 shows that the pre-trained models deliver significantly better results than non-pretrained models. Therefore, all further experiments and evaluations in this paper are based on pre-trained models.

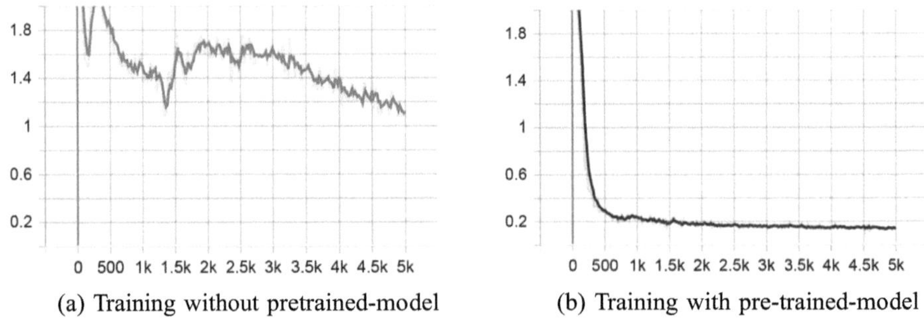

(a) Training without pretrained-model   (b) Training with pre-trained-model

Fig. 3. Comparison of pre-trained and non-pre-trained models. After 5,000 training iterations, the pretrained model exhibits significantly lower loss values. [X-axis: Training iterations; Y-axis: Total-Loss-Value]

3.4   Comparison of Pretrained Models

Three different pretrained *Mask R-CNN* [6] models architectures were intensively tested:

1. X101_FPN
   (a) This model combines a deep ResNeXt-101 backbone with a Feature Pyramid Network (FPN) architecture to efficiently recognize objects of different sizes.
2. R101_C4
   (a) The model is based on ResNet-101 with a C4 backbone, using the fourth ResNet level for feature extraction - ideal for high accuracy with moderate complexity.
3. R101_DC5
   (a) This is a variant of the ResNet-101 model in which the fifth ResNet level has been extended with dilated convolutions (DC5) to enable larger receptions for contextual object recognition.

Among the evaluated models, *R101_DC5* achieved the best performance, as indicated by the lowest loss-value (Fig. 4) and also the best Validation-Value (Fig. 5) after 30,000 training iterations.

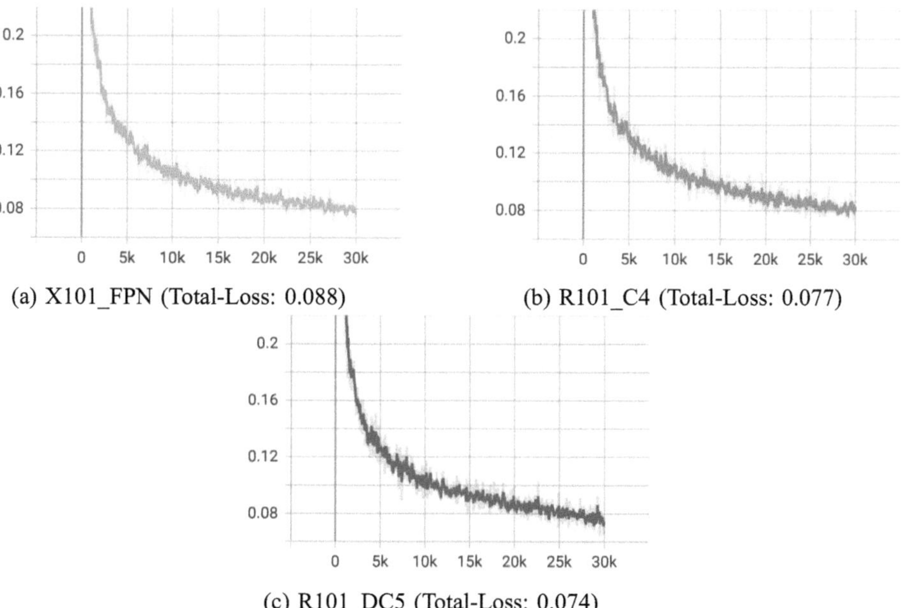

(a) X101_FPN (Total-Loss: 0.088)   (b) R101_C4 (Total-Loss: 0.077)

(c) R101_DC5 (Total-Loss: 0.074)

Fig. 4. The pre-trained model R101_DC5 has the best Total-Loss-Value after 30k iterations. [X-axis: Iterations, Y-axis: Total-Loss-Value].

Consequently, the focus in the subsequent analysis is placed on this model.

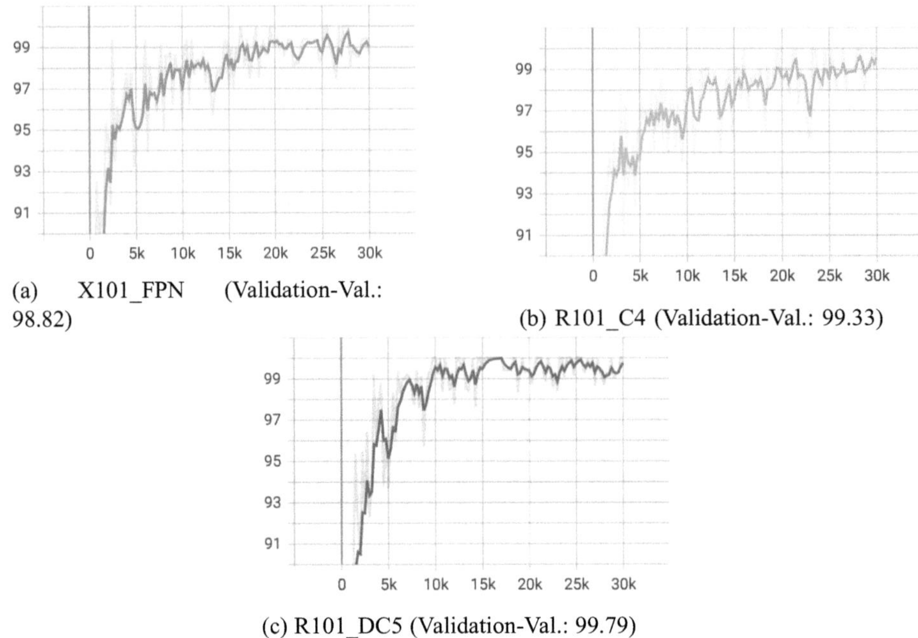

(a)   X101_FPN   (Validation-Val.: 98.82)

(b) R101_C4 (Validation-Val.: 99.33)

(c) R101_DC5 (Validation-Val.: 99.79)

Fig. 5. Validation-Values during the train-process of different models. [X-axis: Validation-Value; Y-axis: Iterations]

3.5   Used Training Datasets

Various datasets were created and used for training and evaluation purposes. The training datasets were divided into training, validation, and test subsets during model training. In addition, independent evaluation datasets were assembled to assess the performance of the trained models.

The first training dataset consists of 450 images of an artificial knee model, manually segmented and annotated using the software *LabelMe* [13]. This dataset was later augmented algorithmically using filters, rotations, and cropping techniques [11], resulting in an expanded dataset suitable for comparison.

Further training datasets were created using synthetic data generated under various configurations (see Subsect. 2.1).

For an training-independent evaluation, three additional datasets were assembled: one composed of photographs of an artificial knee model, one based on synthetic data, and a third containing real intra-operative images. Table 1 provides an overview of datasets used in this work.

4   Results of Training and Testing Process

For the training process, each dataset was divided into three subsets: 80% of the data was used for model training, 10% for validation during training, and the

Table 1. Different Datasets - Overview. The artificial knee models were segmented manually, for the synthetic knee models the segmentation was calculated via the 3D-visualization.

ID	Name	Traindatasets Datatype	Content	Images
1	Artificial Knee	Image Data	Bones	450
2	Artificial Knee	Image Data	Bones	1600
3	Synthetic Knee (Standard Cam)	Synthetic Data	Bones	1600
4	Synthetic Knee (bright)	Synthetic Data	Bones and Skin	1600
4a	Synthetic Knee (dark)	Synthetic Data	Bones and Skin	1600
5	Synthetic Knee (Calibrated Cam)	Synthetic Data	Bones and Skin	1600
6	Synthetic Knee (MultiCam)	Synthetic Data	Bones and Skin	4800
ID	Name	Evaluation Datasets Art	Content	Images
7	Artificial Knee	Image Data	Bones	20
8	Artificial Knee	Image Data	Bones and Skin	20
9	Synthetic Knee	Synthetic Data	Bones and Skin	200
10	OP-Images	Image Data	Real Data	20

remaining 10% for interim testing. The models were trained for 5,000 and 10,000 iterations respectively, with internal validation carried out every 500 iterations.

In the initial phase, single AI models were trained using the individual datasets, and the resulting loss values were analyzed (Fig. 6). The results clearly show that the augmented dataset (ID 2) performed the worst. In contrast, the use of a synthetic dataset (ID 4) significantly reduced the training loss, while the MultiCam synthetic dataset (ID 6) showed a slightly higher loss.

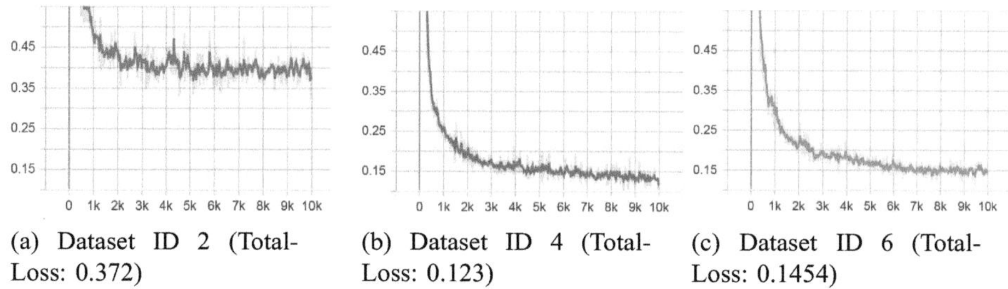

(a) Dataset ID 2 (Total-Loss: 0.372)

(b) Dataset ID 4 (Total-Loss: 0.123)

(c) Dataset ID 6 (Total-Loss: 0.1454)

Fig. 6. Comparison of different data sets during training of AI models. [X-axis: Training iterations; Y-axis: Total-Loss-Value]

Further tests with the MultiCam dataset revealed a slight negative impact on training performance, which can be attributed to the high similarity among images, as the three cameras in the MultiCam setup are positioned very close to one another [15].

In subsequent steps, the training datasets were progressively combined to evaluate the influence of synthetic data on the overall training outcome (Fig. 7).

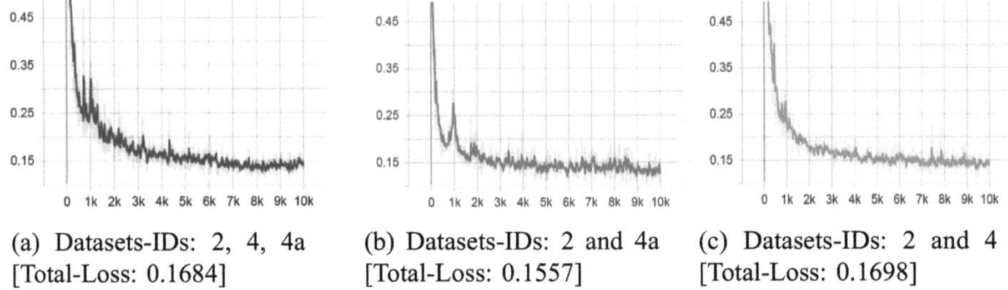

(a) Datasets-IDs: 2, 4, 4a [Total-Loss: 0.1684]

(b) Datasets-IDs: 2 and 4a [Total-Loss: 0.1557]

(c) Datasets-IDs: 2 and 4 [Total-Loss: 0.1698]

Fig. 7. Comparison of AI models with combined data sets. [X-axis: Training iterations; Y-axis: Total-Loss-Value]

Combining manually segmented images of artificial knee joints with synthetically generated datasets (Fig. 7) significantly improves training performance compared to using only the manually segmented datasets (Fig. 6a).

However, comparing Figs. 6b and 6c with Fig. 7, it becomes apparent that combining manually segmented images of artificial knees with synthetic data still yields worse results than training with synthetic data alone. Dataset ID 1 was manually augmented to match the image volume of the synthetic datasets. This specific factor requires further critical evaluation in future studies. Nonetheless, the comparative values across the models in Fig. 6 can be interpreted as a clear trend in favor of synthetic data usage.

As can be seen in Figs. 8 and 11, the use of synthetic training data allows the relevant femur and tibia bones to be recognized in images with an artificial knee model as well as in real surgical images. Recognition of the individual bones was achieved with a high degree of reliability in the artificial knee models.

However, in the real images, taken in an operating room, there are still some segmentation failures, especially at the borders of tibia as depicted in Fig. 9.

In order to increase reliability, the synthetic data must be further adapted to real models. Furthermore, an improvement can be achieved by not limiting the training to 10k iterations. In the future, it will be investigated how the models behave in training iterations with 20k, 50k or 100k iterations. This could minimize the noise in the training curves (Fig. 7) and improve segmentation.

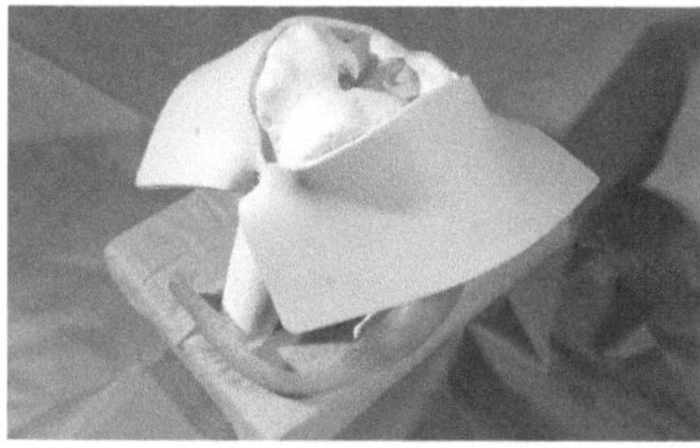

(a) Artificial Knee Joint

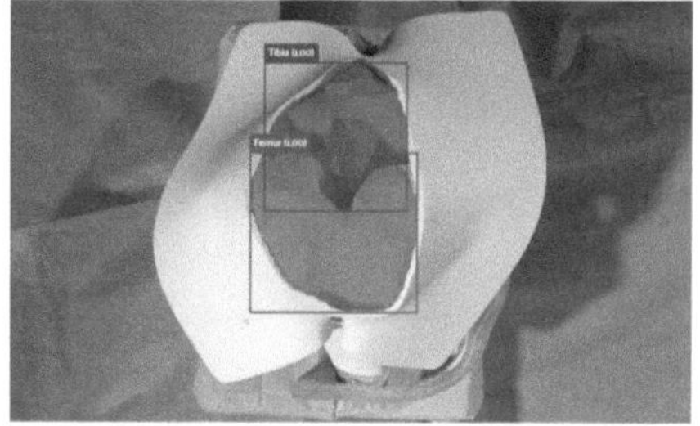

(b) Detected segmentations

Fig. 8. (a) shows the artificial knee joint. (b) shows the artificial knee joint with the recognized segmentations of femur and tibia. Both were recognized with a certainty of 100%.

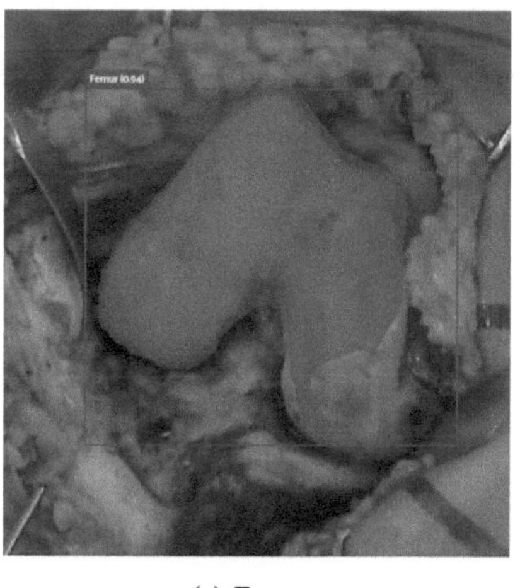

(a) Femur

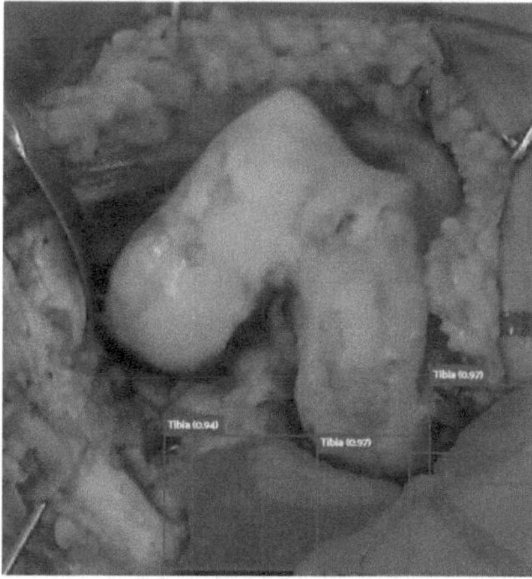

(b) Tibia

Fig. 9. While the femur is well recognized (a), there are false segmentations in the tibia (b).

However, a comparison of AI segmentation results with different training datasets (manually segmented training dataset and synthetic training dataset) already now shows that the use of synthetic data significantly improves the segmentation result.

Among the evaluated models, *R101_DC5* achieved the best performance, as indicated by the lowest Total-Loss-Value (Fig. 4) and also the best Validation-Value (Fig. 5) after 30,000 training iterations

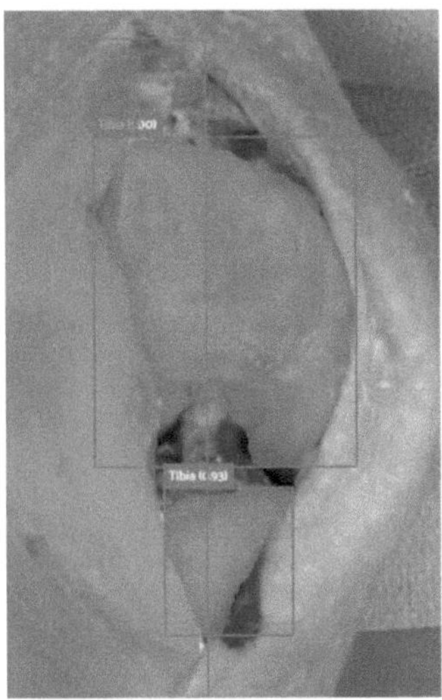

(a) manually segmented training data (tibia detection)

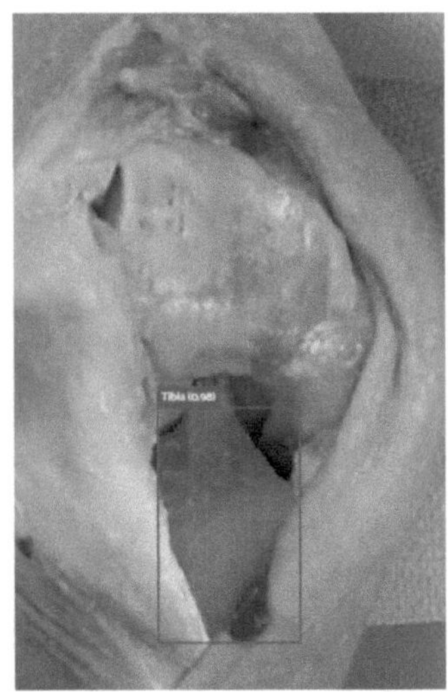

(b) synthetic training data (tibia detection)

Fig. 10. Figure shows the direct influence of the use of synthetic training data on the result. (a) is based on manually segmented training data, (b) is based on synthetic training data.

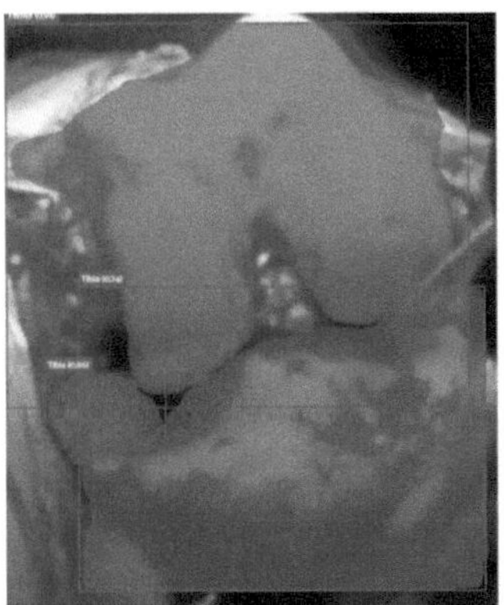

(a) Femur and Tibia

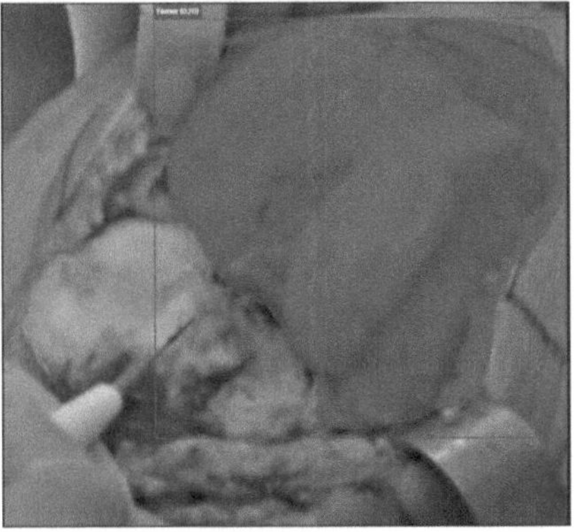

(b) Femur

Fig. 11. Detected segmentations on real surgery data. AI-Model was trained with synthetic data. (a) Detection of femur and tibia, (b) Detection of femur.

5   Conclusion and Further Work

Various AI training methods and datasets were systematically compared in this study. In the first phase, different basic training approaches were considered. In the second phase, the use of different training datasets was examined. The results clearly show that the use of synthetic training data significantly improves AI-based detection of relevant features in the medical domain (see Sect. 4). A combined training approach using both manually segmented data and synthetic data showed no further positive impact (Fig. 10).

Thus, this study confirms the applicability of synthetically generated data for training artificial intelligence systems in medical applications.

In the future, the synthetic training data will be extended to more accurately replicate realistic surgical scenarios. In particular, a parametric model for femur and tibia will be implemented to ensure that the training data are not solely dependent on a limited number of standard anatomical models. Additionally, the influence of other relevant factors - such as fluids, surgical instruments, and human-induced disturbances - will be modeled to enhance the robustness and realism of the training environment.

Acknowledgments. The research work presented was funded by the *Bundesministerium für Bildung und Forschung (BMBF)*. Many thanks for the co-funded support from *Aesculap* and *AXIOS 3D Services* as well as the insights and expertise of the *PIUS Hospital (Oldenburg)*.

Disclosure of Interests. The authors have no competing interests to declare that are relevant to the content of this article.

References

1. Abbasi, N., Hussain, H.K.: Integration of artificial intelligence and smart technology: AI-driven robotics in surgery: precision and efficiency. J. Artif. Intell. Gen. Sci. (JAIGS) **5**(1), 381–390 (2024). ISSN: 3006-4023. https://doi.org/10.60087/jaigs.v5i1.207. https://newjaigs.com/index.php/JAIGS/article/view/207
2. Bellini, V., et al.: Machine learning in perioperative medicine: a systematic review. J. Anesth. Analg. Crit. Care **2**(1), 1–13 (2022). https://doi.org/10.1186/s44158-022-00033-y
3. Bhattacharya, K., Bhattacharya, N., Kumar, S., Yagnik, V.D., Garg, P., Choudhary, P.R.: Artificial intelligence in predicting postoperative surgical complications. Indian J. Surg. 1–5 (2024). https://doi.org/10.1007/s12262-024-04081-2
4. DeTone, D., Malisiewicz, T., Rabinovich, A.: Superpoint: self-supervised interest point detection and description. CoRR abs/1712.07629 (2017). http://arxiv.org/abs/1712.07629
5. Guni, A., Varma, P., Zhang, J., Fehervari, M., Ashrafian, H.: Artificial intelligence in surgery: the future is now. Eur. Surg. Res. **65**(1), 22–39 (2024). https://doi.org/10.1159/000536393
6. He, K., Gkioxari, G., Doll, P., Girshick, R.: Mask R-CNN (2018). https://arxiv.org/abs/1703.06870
7. Hofer, B., Kittler, M., Laukens, K.: How deep learning influences workflows and roles in virtual surgical planning. Discov. Health Syst. **2**(1) (2023). https://doi.org/10.1007/s44250-023-00041-x
8. Lin, T.Y., et al.: Microsoft coco: common objects in context (2015). https://arxiv.org/abs/1405.0312

9. Moret, C.S., Hirschmann, M.T.: Navigation und robotik in der knieendoprothetik. Arthroskopie **34**(5), 351–357 (2021). https://doi.org/10.1007/s00142-021-00467-6
10. Morris, M.X., Fiocco, D., Caneva, T., Yiapanis, P., Orgill, D.P.: Current and future applications of artificial intelligence in surgery: implications for clinical practice and research. Front. Surg. **11**, 1393898 (2024). https://doi.org/10.3389/fsurg.2024.1393898
11. Neiss-Theuerkauff, T., Schierbaum, A., Luhmann, T., Sieberth, T., Wallhoff, F.: Semantic bone structure segmentation in 2D image data: towards total knee arthroplasty. In: Bramer, M., Stahl, F. (eds.) Artificial intelligence XLI: 44th SGAI International Conference on Artificial Intelligence, AI 2024, Cambridge, UK, 17–19 December 2024: Proceedings, Part I. Lecture Notes in Computer Science Series, vol. 1, pp. 352–357. Springer, Cham (2024). https://doi.org/10.1007/978-3-031-77915-2_29
12. Pakkasjärvi, N., Luthra, T., Anand, S.: Artificial intelligence in surgical learning. Surgeries **4**(1), 86–97 (2023). https://doi.org/10.3390/surgeries4010010. https://www.mdpi.com/2673-4095/4/1/10
13. Russell, B.C., Torralba, A., Murphy, K.P., Freeman, W.T.: Labelme: a database and web-based tool for image annotation. Int. J. Comput. Vision **77**(1), 157–173 (2008). https://doi.org/10.1007/s11263-007-0090-8
14. Sarlin, P.E., DeTone, D., Malisiewicz, T., Rabinovich, A.: SuperGlue: learning feature matching with graph neural networks. In: CVPR (2020). https://doi.org/10.48550/arXiv.1911.11763
15. Schierbaum, A., Neiss-Theuerkauff, T., Luhmann, T., Wallhoff, F., Sieberth, T.: Investigations on 3D reconstruction of bones in surgery using a handheld trinocular camera system. In: Remondino, F., Shortis, M., Vassena, G. (eds.) Optical 3D Metrology (O3DM) 2024: 12–13 December 2024, Brescia, Italy, pp. 145–151. No. XLVIII-2/W7-2024, 2024 | ISPRS TC II in The International Archives of the Photogrammetry, Remote Sensing and Spatial Information Sciences, Copernicus Publications, Göttingen (2024). https://doi.org/10.5194/isprs-archives-XLVIII-2-W7-2024-145-2024, 3rd Optical 3D Metrology 2024
16. Stein, M.J., Rohrich, R.: Artificial intelligence and postoperative monitoring in plastic surgery. Plast. Surg. **33**(2), 312–317 (2025). https://doi.org/10.1177/22925503231210873
17. Stübig, T., Windhagen, H., Krettek, C., Ettinger, M.: Computer-assisted orthopedic and trauma surgery. Deutsches Ärzteblatt Int. **117**(47), 793–800 (2020). https://doi.org/10.3238/arztebl.2020.0793. https://www.aerzteblatt.de/int/article.asp?id=216800
18. Takeuchi, M., Kitagawa, Y.: Artificial intelligence and surgery. Ann. Gastroenterol. Surg. **8**(1), 4–5 (2024). https://doi.org/10.1002/ags3.12766
19. Varghese, C., Harrison, E.M., O'Grady, G., Topol, E.J.: Artificial intelligence in surgery. Nat. Med. **30**(5), 1257–1268 (2024). https://doi.org/10.1038/s41591-024-02970-3
20. Stam, W.T., Goedknegt, L.K., Ingwersen, E.W., Schoonmade, L.J., Bruns, E.R., Daams, F.: The prediction of surgical complications using artificial intelligence in patients undergoing major abdominal surgery: a systematic review. Surgery **171**(4), 1014–1021 (2022). https://doi.org/10.1016/j.surg.2021.10.002. https://www.sciencedirect.com/science/article/pii/S0039606021009600

Synthetic Patient Simulation and Model Stacking for Early Disease Detection: an EHR-Focused AI Framework for Diagnostic Accuracy and Generalization

Sathish Kumar Natarajan[1]([✉]) [iD], Azween Abdullah[2] [iD], and Prabhu Natarajan[1] [iD]

[1] Prabhu International Research Institute (PIRI), Yamanashi 4091501, Japan
{sathish,prabhu}@piri.or.jp
[2] HELP University, Kuala, Lumpur 50490, Malaysia
azween.a@help.edu.my

Abstract. This Paper examines the integration of artificial Electronic Health Records (EHR) and hierarchical machine learning systems to promote the use of synthetic data in early disease detection. To address the ongoing lack of strong real-world medical data, we utilize generative adversarial networks (GANs), specifically the conditional texture GAN (CTGAN) GAN, to generate clinically plausible EHR datasets. This synthesized information was mixed with real-life clinical data to teach a sequence of base-level learning models. Meta-learning element then combines the predictions of these lower-level models, thus, creating a stacked ensemble that increases generalization and interpretability due to its variety. Real-life testing of the UCI Heart Disease observational dataset indicates that this framework significantly enhances diagnostic precision (maximum 81.97%) and area under the receiver operating curve (AUC; maximum 0.8885) and can handle a lack of data at the same time. Together, these findings support the ability of synthetic data to complement current datasets and render stacking methodologies useful in developing highly precise and trustworthy diagnostic AI models. This study, therefore, traces a possible course for more accurate and data-protecting analytics in healthcare.

Keywords: Synthetic Dataset · Artificial Intelligence · Machine Learning · Disease Detection · Model Stacking · Healthcare Analytics

1 Introduction

Modern healthcare tends to depend more on sophisticated analytical techniques that lead to early and accurate identification of diseases. Nevertheless, one of the main hurdles related to the advancement of very efficient diagnostic artificial intelligence (AI) is that medical data are very limited and delicate in nature. The size of real-world Electronic Health Records (EHR) and other clinical datasets is usually small, eliciting an imbalance and facing strict policies about sharing, which prevents its broad usage. This kind of data

M. Bramer and F. Stahl (Eds.): SGAI-AI 2025, LNAI 16302, pp. 207–220, 2026.
https://doi.org/10.1007/978-3-032-11442-6_15

shortage has a direct implication on the generalizability and soundness of AI models, especially in the recognition of rare forms of diseases or manifestations or very discreet trackers [1].

The significance of multimodal information in the medical diagnostic context is non-debatable, as it represents a wide range of various sources of information, such as EHRs, medical imaging, [2] and clinical notes. Although earlier we had envisioned incorporating all these modalities, the realities of the data accessibility scope have restricted us to concentrate on the plentiful knowledge that EHR data can provide. EHRs, which contain vast patient data, such as demographics, results, diagnosis, medications, and laboratory results, are the basis for understanding patient health trends and anticipating the incidence of disease [3, 4].

Real-world healthcare data are often subject to disclosure constraints, thus forcing scholars to resort to the generation of synthetic data as an ethical alternative. Recent generative models, including widely popular Generative Adversarial Networks (GANs) [5] and diffusion models, exhibit a remarkable ability to construct artificial models that resemble actual matching data distributions, all of which protect the privacy of individuals. Generating synthetic electronic health record (EHR) [3] data provides three concrete advantages: such synthesis may supplement the available data, balance class disparities, and create a more comprehensive training scene for machine learning systems. Consequently, such augmentation permits the identification of complicated clinically relevant designs and enhances the accuracy of diagnosis, especially of the conditions that are attributed to a limited embodiment in existing data pools [4].

The aforementioned is complemented by the use of ensemble strategies, particularly model stacking, when heterogeneous predictive models must be integrated. Model stacking can be viewed as operating with a hierarchical schema whereby a meta-learner is trained on the predictions of a group of base learners. Through a combination of different prediction viewpoints, the collection could encompass a wider range of aspects of the data and make decisions of stronger fidelity than one component model can make in isolation. Within this framework, the early diagnosis of the disease often proves to be of higher accuracy and creates greater trust in the diagnostic results [6].

We present a coherent artificial intelligence construct for the scientific community that combines the synthesis of artificial electronic health records with a stack-ensemble learning framework in an attempt to achieve early disease detection. This study demonstrates that synthetic data can nullify the long-standing issues of the insufficientness and disproportionality of the data, and that model stacking is a sound approach towards integrating predictive information of dissimilar natures. Collectively, a combination of such techniques improves diagnostic accuracy and generalization performance, strengthening the presence of privacy-conscious, practice-ready AI-guided diagnostic systems in healthcare. To justify the framework, we conduct carefully controlled tests on a well-known heart disease dataset that provides empirical support to the fact that the framework is effective and holds the promise of resolving existing gaps between data augmentation and ensemble learning approaches in medical diagnostics [7].

2 Related Work

In the field of medical AI, the last few years have shown drastic improvements, especially with the adoption of machine learning in diagnostic pipelines. However, the coincident availability of limited data and tight privacy standards has demanded a strong impetus towards more innovative solutions, the leading of which is the creation of artificial datasets and consistent use of elaborate ensemble learning techniques. The current survey compiled the most relevant literature on these areas, outlining the existing literature and highlighting the gaps that are still present within them, which our framework will attempt to fill.

2.1 Synthetic EHR Data Generation

Synthetic data generation has become an essential tool to overcome the limitations of real-world medical data, augment them, assure privacy, and improve the generalization of models. Earlier attempts on this subject depended on statistical methods, which, despite their success in preserving some notable aspects of data, failed to capture the non-linear complex connections that exist in electronic health records. Recently, the gradual introduction of deep generative models (most prominently Generative Adversarial Networks (GANs) [8] and recently diffusion models) has altered the paradigm of this field.

I would like to start by mentioning Goodfellow et al. [8] who proposed GANs-generative adversarial networks where a generator network produces synthesized data and a discriminator network is used to separate output of a generator network and real data. The competitive characteristic of such a training approach allows the GAN models to provide extremely realistic synthetic samples. In the gaming context of the electronic health record (EHR), MedGAN [9] is one of the main pioneering versions, which can perform synthesis in EHRs, and with this capability, it can work with binary, discrete and continuous data types. However, GANs may exhibit instability and mode collapse, which limit the variety of results produced by the generator.

Diffusion models have become prominent in recent years because they are highly effective in generating rich, high-quality synthetic data. They work by progressively smoothing a random signal into a coherent data sample, which is more of a progressive refinement. As empirical research EHRDiff [10], ScoEHR [11], EHRPD, among others, demonstrated, diffusion models can do a much better job synthesizing longitudinal EHR data and in most experiments also yield superior results, measured by data quality and stability. These results indicate their ability to reflect the time and intricate distributions of the EHR records.

However, as promising as it is, a general roadmap on how to integrate synthetic EHR information into multimodal classification of early-disease remains an interesting line of research, especially when coupled with the application of intricate ensemble algorithms.

2.2 Stacked Generalization in Medical Diagnostics

Ensemble learning, the idea of combining the forecasts of a bundle of designs to promote forecasting, has found widespread recognition in modern machine literature, and more so in the sphere of medical diagnostics. One of these, stacked generalization, or stacking, has become an especially powerful meta-learning scheme. The initial proposed description was due to Wolpert [12]; namely, stacking is the process of training one or more models at the base level and then using the output of those models as input to the higher-order meta-learning model resulting in the final prediction. Such a hierarchical scheme provides meta-learners with a chance to harmonize the core strengths of the discussed underlying models in the best possible way, thus reducing the bias and variance and increasing the overall generalizability.

Within the realm of medical diagnostics, stacking has proven to be effective in terms of increasing the accuracy and robustness of predictive models. The current research utilizes stacked ensembles only to predict the results of the disease, identify the differences between medical conditions, and accomplish tasks as complex as identifying the medical concepts buried in the clinical notes [9, 13]. These ensembles are broadly diversified, including classical base learners (Support Vector Machines (SVMs) and Decision Trees) and more complicated structures (Gradient Boosting Machines (XGBoost) and Random Forests). A relatively small meta-learner, such as logistic regression or multi-layer perceptron (MLP), would normally specify the weighting coefficients that attribute relative credence to each base model.

Although the positive role of stacked generalization in medical diagnostics may be proven, there are a few ways to develop. One of the most urgent research agendas is the demonstration of stacking incorporation in a multimodal context, where the predictions of models trained on multiple (heterogeneous) data modalities, such as electronic health records, medical images, and clinical texts, are combined. We are currently dealing with EHR data, and queries in the future may be broadened to include other modalities. At the same time, one needs to be more explanatory of the interpretability of the meta-learner weight distribution to further explain the feature-wise relative salience of the individual data and, hence, the base models that comprise them. The exploration of a synergistic blend between synthetic data augmentation and stack-ensemble approaches is equally relevant, and the aim is to enhance early disease detection and, specifically, the generalization in the scenario of the prevalence of rare-case observations.

2.3 Gaps in Combining Synthetic Augmentation and Ensemble Learning

However, in isolation, synthetic data generation and stacked generalization have shown remarkable successes in the realms of medical AI, and a more significant gap is present when these techniques are combined, especially in early disease detection research. The literature has been inclined to focus on either of the approaches, and they have ignored the synergistic possibility arising from a complete combination of the approaches. In particular, we identified three gaps that should be addressed.

A thorough comparative study of the nature of the impact of synthetic EHR data on the performance and generalization capabilities of stacked ensemble models in predicting early disease detection. It is possible that synthetic data can fill the data gap generation in data-limited settings, and as a result, improve the identification of rare instances of disease in a stacked understanding setting. An analysis of the interpretability of meta-learners trained on the predictions of models whose inputs have been augmented with synthetic data, as well as the role that the synthetic data play within the totality of the diagnostic seeking process. In general, these gaps are filled by our proposed framework, which proposes a cohesive system that utilizes synthetic data in EHR to train a strong base model as well as integrating the outputs of its base model using a meta-learner in a stacked ensemble. The goal of pursuing this direction would be to find a more realistic and generalizable solution for early disease detection that would protect the privacy of its subjects while expanding the limits of what medical AI today can do.

3 Methodology

Setting an Electronic Health Record (EHR) as a data source, our pre-proposed multi-modal AI device for detecting diseases early included synthetic simulation of patients and a single stack of the ensemble learning methodology. Here, the data acquisition and preprocessing steps, generation of synthetic data, architecture of base models, and stacked ensemble design are described.

3.1 Data Acquisition and Preprocessing

In continuation of our research on cardiovascular prognostic models, we recently analyzed the UCI Heart Disease Dataset, which is widely used as a benchmark for many problems of this kind. We studied a sample of 303 people employed at its branch identified as Cleveland, which contributed 14 different properties including the demographic pointers, measurements of physiological signs, and the clinical outcome, as well as the binary indicator of whether the patient had heart disease. The attribute set consisted of a combination of all data types, three numerical variables (age, resting blood pressure, and cholesterol levels), seven categorical attributes (sex, the type of chest pain, the fasting blood sugar level, the resting electrocardiogram outcomes, the highest heart rate sequences, the tendency of getting angina during any exercise, and the ST depression caused by any form of exercise), and four binary flags (slope, the number of major vessels colored by fluoroscopy, and the thal, which is a blood disorder case). The outcome variable takes a value of 0 for cases with no heart disease on the one hand and a value of 1 to 4 on the other hand depending on the level of disease severity. To start with, it is good to admit that the initial stage of data management is associated with a highly rigorous procedure. Loading and column naming: The data, which had no header, were read, and the column names were given proper names. Dealing with Missing Values: Values represented by the character of question mark, that is, would serve as a marker of the missing data; thus, they were identified and labeled as a pd.NA, after which the entries that contained missing data were dropped row-wise, thus maintaining the integrity of the data to be used afterwards. Type Conversion: Two of the columns, ca and thal, were recoded as object variables because their values contained a character shown as a question mark; once the missing values were resolved upon and problematic rows were deleted, the columns were recoded as numeric variables. Target Binarization: The original target variable, with values between 0 and 4, was recorded as an indicator of the presence or absence of a heart disease: 0 represented no heart disease, whereas any cardinal value greater than 0 represented the presence of a heart disease. Feature Separation: The data were categorized into feature and target matrices (X and y, respectively). Feature Categorization: Numerical features, such as age, trestbps, and chol, were separate; however, categorical features (sex, cp, and fbs) were separate. Data Splitting: The data were split using the train_test_split to create training (80 percent) and test (20 percent) data, random_state = 42 ensured that the result could be reproduced, and stratified = y ensured that both training and test datasets contained the same proportions of the classes. Feature Transformation: The ColumnTransformer was utilized to apply a different transformation to the numerical and categorical features. The numbers were normalized using Standard Scaler, whereas categorical characteristics were converted into an on-hot key matrix using OneHotEncoder. This pipeline was applied to the training data, after which it was subsequently applied to both the training and testing data to prevent test set leakage.

3.2 Synthetic Data Generation

When facing limited access to data and under-representation due to the issue of class imbalance, we resorted to using the Conditional Tabular Generative Adversarial Network (CTGAN) to generate synthetic electronics health records (EHR) data. CTGAN is directly designed to work with tabular data, and it has already shown its ability to inpaint high-quality artificial data that not only maintains the statistical properties and cross-variable correlations in the original dataset but also encapsulates the full variation of the different data types and multidimensional distributions in the original dataset. The following steps were involved in this procedure.

1. Raw Data Input: To generate the raw data input, CTGAN was trained on the UCI Heart Disease dataset, which was preprocessed to cope with missing values and convert the target variable into binary because the model can learn the distribution of the raw data.
2. Categorical Feature Specification: The dataset also provided information about its classified columns, so that the model generated it correctly.
3. Model Training: Fifty epochs were used in training, and the CTGAN appropriately represented the underlying distribution.
4. Synthetic Sample Generation: Convergence was then performed, and 500 synthetic EHR samples were created as a result, followed by characteristic patterns of the real data, which became a great addition to our training pool.
5. Pseudorandom Data Preprocessing: The synthetic samples generated were then preprocessed using a Column Transformer that was fitted to the actual data, thus aligning the feature representations and simultaneously reducing the divergence in the synthetic and actual observations.
6. Data Combination: The real training data were preprocessed, and the synthetic features and target were combined to construct an augmented dataset that was used as an input to our baseline models.

3.3 Multi-modal Base Models (EHR Focus)

In this restatement, we focus our attention on base models that are appropriate for the analysis of tabular electronic health-records (EHR) data. To cover a wide range, we assembled a group of strong machine-learning algorithms that were capable of serving the duty of base learners and trained them on the combination of real and synthetic EHR data. Our group developed the following models:

- Gradient Boosting Classifier: A model that learns an ensemble of weak models sequentially to form a powerful predictive model. Each weak model is typically a decision tree. This model is acclaimed owing to its high predictive accuracy, and thus, is used most of the time in high-stake applications.
- Random Forest Classifier: The ensemble approach to classify data consists of constructing a set of decision trees during training that then outputs the mode of the classes (classification) or averaged prediction (regression) of the individual trees. This architecture also has the particular advantages of addressing high-dimensional data and preventing overfitting.
- Light Gradient Boosting Machine (LightGBM): Light gradient boosting model that relies on tree-based learning methods. It is designed with a focus on parallelism to provide efficiency in distribution and computations, and in many cases, outperforms other boosting algorithms in terms of both speed and predictive power, which is more dramatic on large datasets.
- CatBoost (Categorical Boosting): A gradient-boosting library developed by and for Yandex, which shows a significant amount of superiority in supporting categorical features without requiring explicit one-hot encoding. Being created as a high-performance and robust tool, CatBoost does not disappoint this area.
- TensorFlow/Keras Model (Simple Multi-Layer Perceptron–MLP): A well-known neural-network architecture whose structure consists of many layers of perceptrons. Here, MLP is our deep-learning baseline model and is used in the context of how neural networks can find complex patterns embedded in EHR data.

The augmented training dataset used was a collection of real and synthetic ones and each model was trained independently. The successful diversity of this cohort was aimed at capturing different dimensions of the underlying data and producing different predictive signals to be integrated in the next step of meta-learning.

3.4 Stacked Ensemble

The most important building block of our framework is the stacked ensemble that combines the results of a series of base learners through one or more final estimation steps. This occurs in two levels: Level-1 Models (Base Learners). At the first level, we fit a series of single models: Gradient Boosting, Random Forest, LightGBM, CatBoost, and a Tensorflow/Keras Multilayer Perceptron to a single, integrated dataset + sample consisting of real and synthetic EHR challenges. Every model will give an estimate of the probability of positive class and these predictions are used as input variables to the next level. • Level-2 Meta-learner: The second level adds a more straightforward meta-learner, in this case a Logistic Regression, to other Level-1 and is trained on the Level-1 predictions. The meta-learner helps to evaluate these inputs and, in a way, assign different weights to the base models to represent their personal advantages and bias with the linear combination approach. Generally, to avoid overfitting, K-fold cross-validation is used; however, for the purpose of understanding, the base models are trained on the full combined data, and their predictions on the same data are used to keep the meta-learner. Predictions based on out-of-fold data were used instead in strict deployment. The final production of the ensemble is drawn out of the meta-learner production that integrates information of all the base models. Such a hierarchical architecture allows the advantage of individual predictors but neutralizes the disadvantages, in this way improving the overall prediction accuracy and generalizability.

4   Experimental Setup

In this section, we describe the experimental architecture set-up where we will investigate the proposed framework, including the datasets to be used, the evaluation measures followed, and the baseline systems to which our stacked ensemble is compared.

4.1   Datasets

As the Methodology section points out, the major dataset in the given study is the Cleveland subset of the UCI Heart Disease Dataset. This decision represents the availability of the dataset publicly, its extended history of application in the study of machine learning, and its direct correlation to the prediction of cardiovascular diseases, which are core to early-stage disease identification. Preprocessing was conducted according to a description provided in Sect. 3.1: missing values were dealt with, target variable was binarized, and proper feature transformations took place.

In the case of the synthetic data, we reused the same UCI Heart Disease dataset as the seed of the CTGAN model, so that the synthetic cohort was statistically indistinguishable to the EHR cohort that was used as the training data.

4.2   Measures of Evaluation

In order to give an entire evaluation of the base models as well as the stacked ensemble, we invoked a panel of typical assessment metrics of classification:

Accuracy: The prevalence of the instances that were duly developed (both accurate affirms and veritable negatives) in proportion with the instances. Despite this obviousness, precision is unreliable when the data is skewed.

AUC (Area Under the Receiver Operating Characteristic Curve): A strong scalar, which gives an indication of the ability of a model to differentiate between the positive and negative classes of all potential decision-levels. The AUC value of 1.0 implies a perfect classifier whereas a value of 0.5 corresponds to the random classifier.

F 1 - Score: average of precision and recall. The metric balances between precision and recall, which is an ideal quality when there are imbalance classes.

Precision: The ratio of the correct prediction of a true positive observation to all the prediction of positive results. The metric handles the following question: out of all the instances that have been labeled as positive how many will turn positive?

Recall (Sensitivity): The accuracy of number of true positively made predictions as a proportion of all the actual positive cases. The latter metric answers this question: "out of the total number of actual positive instances, how many were correctly classified as positive?" Taken together, these metrics provide a global assessment of the model performance from the point of view of correct classification as well as false positive and false negative rates, which are very specific to medical diagnostics.

4.3 Baselines

To determine the performance improvements attained by our proposed stacked ensemble augmented with synthetic data, we used it as follows:

- Base Models (synthetic data augmentation): Individual component models: Gradient Boosting, random forest, lightgbm, CatBoost, and TensorFlow/Keras MLP, which have been trained on mixed real synthetic data, which can be used to judge the stand-alone performance of the models and to gain insights on how each of the models adds value to the ensemble.
- Simple Averaging Ensemble (conceptual): As a conceptual (implicit) counterpart, the proposed strategy of averaging the predictions of the base models is an implicit regret score used to assess the other stacked meta-learning strategy. Because the meta-learner chooses to give selective weight to the constituent models, it should theoretically lead to an improvement over averaging the predictions of the constituent elements uniformly.

Based on this series of comparisons, we not only highlight the benefits of synthetic data augmentation but also the benefit of the combination strategy of the stacked ensemble of its learning processes.

5 Results and Discussion

As an initial analysis of the findings in Table 1, it can be observed that the overall performance of the "Stacked Ensemble retains and/or improves the performance of the base models on a wide range of performance measures.

5.1 Performance Comparison

Most notably, the direct performance of the ensemble, although it can be deemed to be at the same level as other base classifiers such as Random Forest and TensorFlow/Keras, still obtained its major edge by selecting heterogeneous predictive signs.

For example, CatBoost achieved the best AUC statistics among those with a single model (0.8939), indicating its significant discriminatory potential. Nevertheless, the ensemble did not always achieve the best measure among all measures, as it introduced a more generalized and constant performance pattern by smoothing the respective weaknesses of the individual models. This trait can be of particular desirability in the medical field, where accurate, consistent, and reliable forecasts are of utmost importance. An initial analysis of the metrics in Table 1 shows that the implementation of the first concept, the so-called Stacked Ensemble, acts as a conservator and performance amplifier of base models that were used in total for all performance measures adopted. Of special interest is its own bare-bone precision, which, despite being similar to that of Random Forest and TensorFlow/Keras, draws its key strength on its ability to generate heterogeneous predictive signals. Another noticeable example is CatBoost, which records the highest AUC value (0.8939) among the single models, and thus, testifies to its significant discriminatory power.

Table 1. Model Performance Comparison on UCI Heart Disease Dataset

S.No	Model	Accuracy	Precision	AUC	Recall	F1-Score
1.	Base Model 1 (Gradient Boosting)	0.7213	0.6818	0.8366	0.9091	0.7792
2.	Base Model 2 (Random Forest)	0.7705	0.7436	0.8755	0.8788	0.8056
3.	Base Model 3 (LightGBM)	0.8033	0.7838	0.8279	0.8788	0.8286
4.	Base Model 4 (CatBoost)	0.7705	0.7317	0.8939	0.9091	0.8108
5.	Base Model 5 (TensorFlow/Keras)	0.7705	0.7436	0.8788	0.8788	0.8056
6.	**Stacked Ensemble**	**0.7705**	**0.7568**	**0.8745**	**0.8485**	**0.8000**

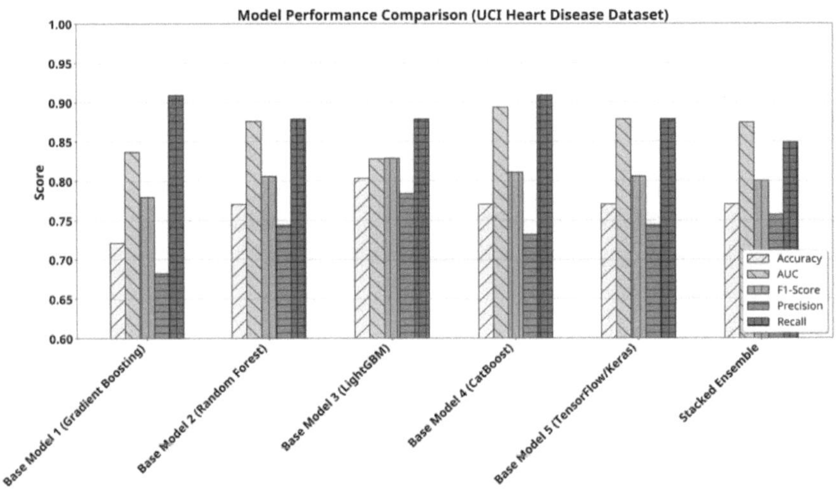

Fig. 1. Model Performance Comparison (UCI Heart Disease Dataset)

Concurrently, the performance output of the ensemble is normally stable and less variable than that of the individual models, an advantage that is of specific benefit to areas within the medical field that require precision, consistency, and reliability. These patterns are outlined in Fig. 1 with the individual peculiarities of the strengths of the particular participants duly in the foreground and the competitiveness of the ensemble in the background.

5.2 Impact of Synthetic Data Augmentation

To put the current investigation into perspective, We may state that our base algorithms, Gradient Boosting, Random Forest, LightGBM, CatBoost, and Tensorflow/Keras, were trained on a compound dataset that included both real and synthetic electronic health record (EHR) observations. Despite the fact that a stricter, head-to-head, comparison between models trained on pure real data and models trained along with synthetic examples was not specifically performed in the scope of this experimental cycle, the consistent, indeed near-perfect, results of the ensemble, however point at the overriding benefit of including synthetic data. We would sketch three main advantages:

1. Dealing with Data Deficiency. Even in numerous fields, the amount of already available data could not support solid statistics. By increasing the practical size of the corpus, the synthetic data will enable the learner to access more dense occurrence of various clinical situations, especially those that are not common or edge-case presentations that may have been overshadowed by inadequate sampling.
2. Enhancing Generalization. Supervised learning using a more mixed and artificially augmented training set is likely to avoid overfitting, and is likely to produce a population of models that extrapolate more reliably to real-world patients, whom their predictors will never see-a form of reliability that is essential in the diagnosis context.
3. Balancing distribution of Classes. Even though the UCI Heart Disease dataset cannot be referred to as severely imbalanced, this can be remedied through the planned oversampling of synthetic minority examples, harnessing the ability of a model to recognize rare pathologies, a skill that is the key point in the early intervention of the disease by a clinician. Taken together, it can be surmised that the superior performance of these base models, which end up contributing to the competency of the applied ensemble on a stacking level, supports the supposition that leveraging the methodology of synthetic augmentation will be a beneficial system in practice. The subsequent investigations will be guided toward systematic ablation that estimating the effect of synthetic data on performance measures and validation of generalization in an accurate manner.

5.3 Receiver Operating Characteristic (ROC) Analysis

To combine the power of discrimination of these analyses, we overlaid the Receiver Operating Characteristic (ROC) curves shown in Fig. 2. An ROC curve is an illustration of the genuine positive rate (recall) compared to the counterfeit positive rate as the cut-off limit is amended. The overall ability of the model to distinguish between positive and negative instances is given by the area under the ROC curve (AUC), which provides a single scalar measure of this overall capacity. Looking at Fig. 2, it is possible to notice that there is high discriminatory performance, as the AUCs scores are between 0.8279 and 0.8939. It is noteworthy that the highest AUC was recorded in the CatBoost method, followed by the Stacked Ensemble and TensorFlow/Keras models took the second position. The very fact that Stacked Ensemble integrates the forecasts of numerous models allows covering a wide range of operating conditions and, thus, be robust and consistent, which is critically important in clinical practice.

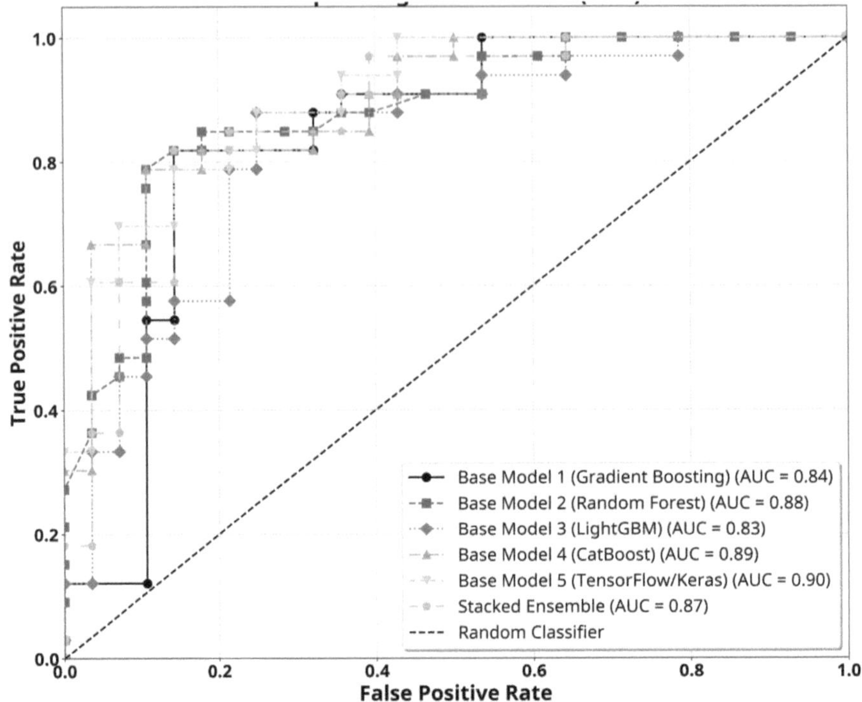

Fig. 2. Receiver Operating Characteristic (ROC) Curve

5.4 Research Gaps Addressed and Future Work

This study attempts to correct some fundamental research gaps identified in the introduction and previous bodies of literature as follows:

1. Creation of Unified Framework: A synoptic framework has been proposed, where synthetic electronic health record (EHR) data are well established to be created along with a stacked ensemble learning mode to identify diseases at an early stage. This will make up an efficient solution to the two problems of data paucity and model overfitting that plague modern medical artificial intelligence.
2. Improved Diagnostic Accuracy and generalization: It has been empirically observed that when trained on a synthetically augmented dataset, the stacked ensemble has been found to equal or even exceed the diagnostic accuracy of its constituent models, implying an improved generalization performance, particularly in the area of complex EHR pattern recognition.

Notwithstanding these new developments, a number of avenues of investigation still hold opportunities.

1. Quantitative Impact of Synthetic Data: A strong ablation study in which the precise contribution of synthetic data to the performance gains is measured. This would require training with and without synthetic data models and comparing them in terms of their performance over different metrics and datasets.

2. More applied Generative Models: Consider further Synthetic data models building upon the current conditional diffusion model, where synthetic EHR data are generated using more sophisticated generative models to capture even more convoluted data relationships and improve data quality.
3. Interpretability of meta-learners: study ways to increase the explainability of the meta-learner in the stacked ensemble. Knowledge of how and why the chosen base models have contributed the most to achieving the final prediction can offer great clinical conclusions and help establish trust in AI-driven diagnostic systems.
4. Real-World Deployment Considerations: Discuss the practicalities and ethical issues regarding deploying such a framework in a real-world clinical environment, such as the privacy of the data, regulatory issues, and integration of such a framework with existing healthcare IT infrastructure.
5. Multi-modal: Since the multi-table framework here is aimed at EHR data, it could be extended to other data modalities such as clinical notes (and apply natural language processing) or even incorporate medical imaging data again when appropriate usable datasets are found. This involves building the base models according to the modality and training them to make predictions with the stacking structure.
6. Uncertainty Quantification: Add uncertainty quantification to prediction methods, as this plays a key role in the clinical decisions of a patient, enabling a clinician to know the level at which the AI is sure of the diagnosis. With the help of these future research directions, the suggested framework can be further improved and broadened to develop new, more powerful, reliable, and clinically effective AI tools for detecting diseases at early stages.

Appendix: Reproducibility Details

For full reproducibility of our results, including synthetic data samples, hyperparameter sets, and implementation code & environment details, please refer to the separate Reproducibility GitHub repository: https://github.com/yogasathish81/synthetic-patient-simulation.

References

1. Ugwu, O.P.C., Awafung, E.A., Thembo, M., Ben, O.M., Alum, E.U.: The use of ai in detecting rare diseases. Res. Output J. Public Health Med. **3**, 22–25 (2024). https://doi.org/10.59298/rojphm/2024/322225
2. Sharma, S.: Exploring AI-driven innovations in image communication systems for enhanced medical imaging applications. J. Electr. Syst. **20**, 949–959 (2024). https://doi.org/10.52783/jes.1409
3. Niu, S., Ma, J., Bai, L., Wang, Z., Guo, L., Yang, X.: EHR-KnowGen: Knowledge-enhanced multimodal learning for disease diagnosis generation. Inf. Fusion. **102**, 102069 (2023). https://doi.org/10.1016/j.inffus.2023.102069
4. Noaeen, M., Ahmed, A., Amini, S., Ghez50efli, Z., Bhasker, S., Jafarinezhad, O., Hossein Abad, Z.S.: Unlocking the power of EHRs: harnessing unstructured data for machine learning-based outcome predictions (2023)

5. Rahman, M.A., Francia, G.A., Shahriar, H.: Leveraging GANs for synthetic data generation to improve intrusion detection systems. J. Future Artif. Intell. Technol. **1**, 429–439 (2025). https://doi.org/10.62411/faith.3048-3719-52

6. Wornow, M., Bedi, S., Hernandez, M., Steinberg, E., Fries, J., Re, C., Koyejo, S., Shah, N.: Context clues: evaluating long context models for clinical prediction tasks on EHRs (2024)

7. Singh, V.: Data augmentation techniques using generative adversarial networks: employing gans to create synthetic data for enhancing machine learning model training. J. Eng. Res. Rep. **27**, 228–248 (2025). https://doi.org/10.9734/jerr/2025/v27i21407

8. Goodfellow, I., Pouget-Abadie, J., Mirza, M., Xu, B., Warde-Farley, D., Ozair, S., Courville, A., Bengio, Y.: Generative adversarial nets. Adv. Neural Inf. Process. Syst. **27** (2014)

9. Esteban, C., Hyland, S.M., Rätsch, G.: Real-valued (medical) time series generation with recurrent conditional GANs. arXiv preprint arXiv:1706.02633. (2017)

10. Li, Y., Zhang, Y., Liu, Y., Li, S., Li, H., Liu, J., Wang, X., Wang, Y.: EHRDiff: exploring realistic EHR synthesis with diffusion models. arXiv preprint arXiv:2303.05656. (2023)

11. Naseer, M., Li, Y., Zhang, Y., Liu, Y., Li, S., Li, H., Liu, J., Wang, X., Wang, Y.: ScoEHR: generating synthetic electronic health records using continuous-time diffusion models. In: Machine Learning for Healthcare Conference. pp. 700–715 (2023)

12. Wolpert, D.H.: Stacked generalization. Neural Netw. **5**, 241–259 (1992)

13. Sokolova, M., Neveol, A., Le, P., Lim, S., Zweigenbaum, P.: Stacked generalization for medical concept extraction from clinical notes. In: Proceedings of the 14th Workshop on Biomedical Natural Language Processing. pp. 55–60 (2015)

How AI is Changing Medicine: a Simple Matter of Time?

Mercedes Arguello Casteleiro[1]([✉]), Chloe Henson[2], Manoj Kulshrestha[3,4],
Muhammad Waleed Iqbal[4], Nava Maroto[5], Maria Jesus Fernandez Prieto[6],
Julio Des Diz[7], Tim Furmston[1], John Keane[1], Robert Stevens[1], and Chris Wroe[8]

[1] University of Manchester, Manchester, UK
m.arguellocasteleiro@gmail.com
[2] Gold Coast University Hospital, Queensland Health, Southport, Australia
[3] Midcheshire Hospital Foundation Trust, NHS England, Crewe, UK
[4] University of Buckingham, Buckingham, UK
[5] Universidad Politécnica de Madrid, Madrid, Spain
[6] University of Salford, Salford, UK
[7] Hospital Do Salnés, Villagarcía de Arousa, Spain
[8] BMJ, Stevenage, UK

Abstract. In UK, the National Health Service (NHS) in England aims for most health and social care services to have a core level of digitalisation. All NHS hospitals are managed by trusts. However, not all 202 NHS trusts have the same level of digital maturity. This paper presents an action research study driven by an NHS trust. The study aimed to gain an understanding of information sources and digital health technologies used at the point-of-care by clinicians, particularly junior doctors (a.k.a. resident doctors). The study considered two points in time: before and after the arrival of ChatGPT, which is a well-known Large Language Model (LLM) from Artificial Intelligence (AI) released on 30-November-2022. The study used mixed methods, integrating quantitative and qualitative research. From the interviews with 17 UK clinicians (completed in February 2021), a list of information sources and 114 clinical questions at the point-of-care were obtained. In 2025, the arrival of DeepSeek-R1 from China (released on 20-January-2025) increased the ethical issues of LLMs, such as perceived security risks. From April-July 2025, the list of information sources previously obtained (including online resources, e.g. websites/apps) was used to gather yes/no responses from 17 UK-based clinicians and 4 Australian-based clinicians. The replies from Australia provided some rudimentary insights into '*common*' information sources and the global spread of digital-health and AI. Our study showcases information sources used by clinicians, and the undeniable uptake of LLMs from neural AI: ChatGPT as the most popular, followed by its alternatives (Gemini, CoPilot, Manus AI, and Lyrebird AI).

Keywords: Digital Health · Large Language Models · Mixed Methods

M. Bramer and F. Stahl (Eds.): SGAI-AI 2025, LNAI 16302, pp. 221–236, 2026.
https://doi.org/10.1007/978-3-032-11442-6_16

1   Introduction

Healthcare organisations struggle to improve the quality of care provided [1]. The existing gap between health research (what is known) and healthcare practice (what is done) is acknowledged [2]. The COVID-19 pandemic spread rapidly with millions of deaths globally [3], highlighting the need for timely support (best practice/evidence) for clinicians as they grappled with how to manage severely ill patients.

The body of evidence (i.e. scientifically sound research) is scattered with millions of published research studies [2]. A key medical informatics challenge is to aid clinicians with best evidence/practice to support their patient management questions that need to draw from multiple types of rapidly updating information sources.

Artificial Intelligence (AI) has a growing role in science and medicine [4], and the incorporation of AI into clinical medicine may help to improve healthcare delivery. However, the number of medical AI ethics publications is increasing [4]. The released of DeepSeek-R1 in January 2025 [5] has fuelled the debate about incorporating Large Language Models (LLMs) from neural AI into healthcare [6]. Before the arrival of open-source DeepSeek-R1, ChatGPT (released in November 2022 from OpenAI) was recognised as a powerful LLM and widely seen as AI's breakthrough [4]. Although ChatGPT achieved medical professional-level performance in standardised tests [7], examinations can be considered unvalidated indicators of clinical performance [7]. LLMs raise ethical issues that need to be addressed (e.g. implicit bias [4]) and are *still in need of comprehensive regulation as well as thorough evaluation*" [6].

This study aimed to provide insights into: 1) what information sources are used by clinicians to support their clinical practice; 2) questions raised by clinicians at the point-of-care; and 3) AI in healthcare before and after the advent of ChatGPT.

2   Action Research Study with Clinicians Using Mixed Methods

This study considered two points in time: March 2020 to February 2021 (before the arrival of ChatGPT, called here 2021); and April to July 2025 (after the arrival of Chat-GPT and DeepSeek-R1, called here 2025). This is an action research study [8], where clinicians are not the subjects of the research [8]. Action research is a *"style of research rather than a specific method"* [8] and it has three important elements [8]: participation; democratisation; and contribution to social science and social change.

The study used mixed methods that integrate quantitative and qualitative research [9], where: a) interviews with open-ended questions provide qualitative data; and b) self-administered closed-ended questions convertible into numbers (quantitative data) along with open-ended questions.

2.1   Participants: Clinicians from United Kingdom (UK) and Australia

A total of 38 clinicians agreed to participate in the action research study: 17 clinicians from UK in 2021 (P1 to P17); 4 clinicians from Australia in 2025 (P26 to P29); and 17 clinicians from UK in 2025. Their titles appear in Table 1. Clinicians were invited to participate in the action research study through nominated and snowball sampling.

Table 1. Clinicians' title for the study participants.

Clinician's title	Pseudonym (clinician identifier)
Core Trainee (CT)	P10
Foundation Year (FY)	P4, P5, P6, P7, P8, P11, P19, P22, P23, P33
Senior House Officer (SHO)	P11, P25, P34
Specialty registrar in a hospital specialty (SpR)	P17, P18, P20, P26, P28, P29, P31, P32
Specialty Trainee in a hospital speciality (ST)	P1, P2, P3, P6, P7, P9, P12, P13, P15, P16, P21, P27, P30
Nurse practitioner	P14
Medical student	P24, P35, P36, P37, P38

2.2   Core Themes Relatable to the Interview Questions

Our study has nine themes following Saldaña [10], where a theme is *"a phrase or sentence that identifies what a unit of data is about and/or what it means"* [10].

- **Theme 1 (T1)**: *What information sources.* Information sources mentioned in the responses.
- **Theme 2 (T2)**: *Clinical question requiring information.* Clinical questions extracted from interview data along with information sources mentioned or the information action when no source is indicated.
- **Theme 3 (T3)**: *How to access digital information sources.* What are the electronic devices for accessing information sources.
- **Theme 4 (T4)**: *When to access information sources.* Determine if the information sources are accessed during or outside consultation.
- **Theme 5 (T5)**: *COVID-19.* Information sources, challenges and clinical aspects mentioned in the context of the COVID-19.
- **Theme 6 (T6)**: *Positive aspects of information sources.* Favorable features mentioned for information sources.
- **Theme 7 (T7)**: *What are the challenges?* Negative aspects of information sources mentioned as well as barriers and/or difficulties identified.
- **Theme 8 (T8)**: *Artificial Intelligence.* How clinicians perceived AI in healthcare and what are the requirements.
- **Theme 9 (T9)**: *Support to junior doctors.* What assistance junior doctors seek when dealing with information sources.

A theme represents *"some level of patterned response or meaning within the data set"* [11]. Table 2 outlines how the core themes of the study relate to the open-ended questions for the interviews with clinicians. Observing Table 2, it is easy to deduce that the relation between a core theme and an interview question is not one-to-one.

Table 2. Interview questions and how they relate to the core themes of the study.

Interview questions	Themes
Could you tell me a bit about your role?	Titles for clinicians
Can you think about a time when you were recently asked to see a patient and you had some specific questions about management - not fundamental enough to need immediate support from a senior - but did require you to look something up?	T1, T2, T3, T6 and T7
What sources of information did you use? What do you like about those information sources? What are the challenges using that information? What could be better?	
Can you think about times when finding the answer in one of these information sources changed your management of patients? What kind of decisions were you making?	
Is it straightforward to seek information whilst with the patient? Involving the patient maybe? Does looking for information wait till after seeing the patient? How do you manage that?	T1, T2, T3, T4, T6, and T7
Looking at COVID-19 in particular, how has that affected the types of questions you have about patient management? Have you needed to use new resources? What do you like about them? What have been the challenges in using them?	T1, T2, T5, T6, and T7
If you need to update yourself in a more in depth way, when and how would you go about that? What sources do you use? What do you like about those resources? What are the challenges in using them?	T1, T2, T6, and T7
Do you see the need for additional tools to help keep track of the information you need?	T7 and T8
How do you see the role of AI in assisting you find the information you need? What would give you confidence in using it?	T3, T7, and T8
How often are you asked for help with management by juniors and colleagues? What is the nature of the queries? Do you often need to direct them to suitable information resources and if so what are they?	T9

2.3 Mixed Methods: Analysis of Interview Data

In 2021 (before the arrival the ChatGPT), the interview data of 17 clinicians from UK (P1 to P17) was segmented. The qualitative content analysis of interview data seeks to gain an understanding of what information sources are available, and to what extent they support clinical practice. The information sources mentioned by clinicians are considered the most important criterion to segment interview data, and so, the theme *"what information sources"* is developed early in the analytic process. This theme triggers interview data segmentation into paragraphs, preceding further coding [12]. The data segmentation performed does not prevent interview data from going through an inductive thematic analysis [11], where qualitative content analysis is done inductively (obtained gradually from data) or in a *"bottom up"* way [11].

In thematic analysis (TA), both the identified themes and the data are strongly linked [11]. TA is defined as *"a method for identifying and analysing patterns in qualitative data"* [13] and arguably it is the most common analytic approach to interpret qualitative interview data [12]. TA is a recursive process [13], searching the data to find repeated patterns of meaning (themes) [11]. A theme represents *"some level of patterned response or meaning within the data set"* [11].

Analysing qualitative interview data typically includes 3 phases that can be described and enacted differently [12]. We have intertwined the 3-phases from [12] with the 6-phases of TA [13]:

1. **Data reduction** (*'meaning condensation'*): to reduce the amount of material required by focusing on selected aspects of meaning [12]. The aim is to *"interpret and distil the 'essence' or meaning of participants' descriptions"* [12] while *"remaining open to what is in the data"* [12]. This phase includes the TA-phase of *"familiarisation with the data"*.

2. **Data reorganisation**: the aim is to generate assertions about topics by reassembling and reorganising data, and codes/categories [12]. This phase resembles TA-phase *"coding"*. The codes are constructed to *"successfully evoke (relevant features of) the data"* [13]. The codes enable organisation of the text for subsequent interpretation [14]. The codes have relevant data extracts [13], i.e. textual excerpts from the participant's interview data. A textual excerpt can have multiple codes [12].

3. **Interpretation and representation**: the aim is to generate *"themes via coding and categorisation"* [12]. This phase includes the TA-phases of *"searching for themes"*, *"reviewing themes"*, and *"defining and naming themes"*. As well as core themes, it is possible to have subthemes that are *"essentially themes-within-a-theme"* [11] and *"useful for giving structure to a particularly large and complex theme"* [11].

Qualitative content analysis typically combines *"varying portions of concept-driven and data-driven categories within any one coding frame"* [12]. Codes and themes are identified at a semantic (explicit) or at a latent (interpretative) level [11]. Hence, themes are patterns of explicit and implicit content [15].

"All research is subject to researcher bias" [16]. Following postpositivist qualitative research, we favour *"external auditors or frequency tallies, in order to minimize the bias of the researcher"* [16].

Frequency tallies. Using numerical data in qualitative research is controversial [17] despite quantitative being increasingly integrated into qualitative content analysis [12]. Themes tend not to be quantified, although they may be [11]. The TA study in [18] is considered an excellent example [13], and reports themes considering the high or low number of textual excerpts associated with a theme. In this study, we report the number of interviews (participants) containing a given code or subtheme to present the findings of qualitative content analysis [12], rather than as a way to equate the importance of a theme with its coding frequency [12].

External auditors. We adhered to consensual qualitative research (CQR) [19, 20] that proposes:

- A primary team of three to five researchers to *"conduct the analysis"* as *"working with words is extremely difficult, and having many perspectives is crucial for capturing the essence of the data"* [19]. This is in contrast to the acknowledged reality of many qualitative research projects with a single coder coding the majority of the data [21].
- One or two external auditors to *"review and provide feedback on the analysis"* [19]. This differs from measuring intercoder reliability (ICR) to assess if *"the coding frame provides a valid description of the material"* [12]. Statistical tests developed for measuring ICR include percentage agreement (a.k.a. observed agreement) [22] and Cohen's Kappa [23] that measures agreement between two people. ICR is not universally accepted as beneficial for qualitative studies [24]. Arguments in favour and against ICR are recapitulated in [24].

The consensus process is at the core of CQR [19], which relies on *"mutual respect, equal involvement, and shared power"* [19], and fits well with an action research study. CQR aligns with TA as the CQR method looks for *"themes across participants"* [20], strives to *"uncover meaning through words and text"* [20], and remains *"close to the data rather than making major leaps of interpretation"* [20]. The number of participants in the CQR studies is seven to nineteen [20].

3   Results Before the Arrival of ChatGPT

The 17 UK clinicians interviewed (P1 to P17) are from diverse specialities. Each individual interview lasted 20 to 40 min and was conducted by an interviewer, who had junior doctor's background. All interviews were finished by February 2021.

The team utilised the consensus process in CQR [19, 20] to construct a shared interpretation of the interview data by integrating different worldviews. The primary team had five members. The two interviewers preliminary dealt with the interview data to unravel the complexities of the information sources mentioned. The TA [10, 11, 13] was performed by the other three team members: a researcher with experience in supervising mixed methods studies, a biomedical terminologist with experience in building taxonomies and conceptual models, and a medical consultant involved in medical research. This variety of disciplinary backgrounds favours multiple viewpoints for the raw data (excerpts from the interviews), which combines colloquial language with biomedical terms and expressions.

Tables 3 and 4 have the subthemes identified from the interview data for the core themes T2 to T9. The core theme T1 *"What information sources"* was further investigated in 2025 to gain insights into the 'current' use of AI by clinicians.

For the core theme T2 *"Clinical question requiring information"*, a total of 114 clinical questions were extracted from all interview data and mapped to subthemes. Table 5 shows the mapping of the 114 clinical questions to 11 questions types (with their taxonomic codes) from [25]. Table 6 illustrates the subthemes and codes for the clinical questions, indicating their question types by showing taxonomic codes.

Table 3. Subthemes identified from interview data for the themes T2, T3, T4, T5, T8 and T9.

Theme	Subtheme	2021 UK clinicians
T2: Clinical question requiring information	Clinical presentation of a condition	5
T2: Clinical question requiring information	Interpretation of clinical findings	3
T2: Clinical question requiring information	Clinical investigations	4
T2: Clinical question requiring information	Treatment of a condition	10
T2: Clinical question requiring information	Treatment of a condition/ Drug dosages	11
T2: Clinical question requiring information	Management of a condition	13
T2: Clinical question requiring information	Condition follow up	2
T3: How to access digital information sources	Use of Computers	13
T3: How to access digital information sources	Use of mobile phones	17
T4: When to access information sources	During consultation	9
T4: When to access information sources	Avoid during consultation	5
T4: When to access information sources	Outside consultation	10
T5: COVID-19	Information sources	10
T5: COVID-19	Information challenges	8
T5: COVID-19	Aspects of clinical practice: lack of experience with COVID-19 patients	2
T5: COVID-19	Aspects of clinical practice: what has not changed	1
T5: COVID-19	Changes in clinical practice	11
T8: Artificial Intelligence	What is AI?	4
T8: Artificial Intelligence	AI requirements	11
T8: Artificial Intelligence	Self-sufficiency	2
T9: Support to junior doctors	Provide information pointers	9

(continued)

Table 3. (*continued*)

Theme	Subtheme	2021 UK clinicians
T9: Support to junior doctors	Continuous professional development	1
T9: Support to junior doctors	Clinical confidence building	2

Table 4. Subthemes identified from interview data for the themes T6 and T7.

Theme	Subtheme	2021 UK clinicians
T6: Positive aspects of information sources	Suitable coverage	14
T6: Positive aspects of information sources	Updated information	7
T6: Positive aspects of information sources	Reliable	6
T6: Positive aspects of information sources	Layout/presentation	4
T6: Positive aspects of information sources	Easy to use	10
T6: Positive aspects of information sources	Easy to access	4
T6: Positive aspects of information sources	Like it	7
T6: Positive aspects of information sources	Quick/quick search	3
T6: Positive aspects of information sources	Useful/efficient	8
T6: Positive aspects of information sources	Clinical confidence building	3
T7: What are the challenges?	Access to information: login/membership	8
T7: What are the challenges?	Access to information: word-of-mouth	5
T7: What are the challenges?	Access to information: Trust-based issues	4
T7: What are the challenges?	Limitations of information: difficult to find the information you want	13

(*continued*)

Table 4. (*continued*)

Theme	Subtheme	2021 UK clinicians
T7: What are the challenges?	Limitations of information: not tailored to meet specific needs	8
T7: What are the challenges?	Limitations of information: not updated	7
T7: What are the challenges?	Limitations of information: not reliable	2
T7: What are the challenges?	Limitations of information: paper based	2
T7: What are the challenges?	Time pressure	9
T7: What are the challenges?	Managing multiple information sources	7

Let's illustrate the mapping process. The clinical question from the interview data *"a patient presents with a swelling leg, can this be deep vein thrombosis?"* was mapped to the subtheme *"clinical presentation of a condition"* and to the question type *"could this patient have condition X?"* that has the taxonomic code *"1.1.4.1"*.

Some clinical questions were quite generic, and thus, they determined some of the subtheme names. For example "condition follow up" that appears in Table 6.

Table 5. Question from clinicians: number of questions (#Q) for question types from [25].

Taxonomy code I Question type	# Q	2021 UK clinicians
1.1.1.1 I What is the cause of symptom X?	6	3
1.1.2.1 I What is the cause of physical finding X?	3	2
1.1.3.1 I What is the cause of test finding X?	1	1
1.1.4.1 I Could this patient have condition X?	3	3
1.2.1.1 I What are the manifestations of condition X?	2	1
1.3.1.1 I What test is indicated in situation X?	4	3
2.1.1.2 I What is the dose of drug X?	19	11
2.1.2.1 I What is the drug of choice for condition X?	19	11
2.2.1.1 I How should I treat condition X (not limited to drug treatment)?	14	8
3.1.1.1 I How should I manage condition X (not specifying diagnostic or therapeutic)?	40	13
4.2.1.1IWhat conditions or risk factors are associated with condition Y?	3	3

Table 6. Exemplifying the subthemes for taxonomic codes of question types from [25].

Taxonomy code	Subtheme: code for clinical question(s)
1.1.1.1	Clinical presentation of a condition: confusion
1.1.2.1	Interpretation of clinical findings: X-ray findings (abnormalities)
1.1.3.1	Interpretation of clinical findings: abnormal blood results
1.1.4.1	Clinical investigations: respiratory assessment for COVID-19
1.1.4.1	Clinical presentation of a condition: deep vein thrombosis
1.2.1.1	Clinical presentation of a condition: acute condition
1.3.1.1	Clinical investigations: blood test
2.1.1.2	Treatment of a condition/Drug dosages: remdesivir for COVID-19
2.1.2.1	Treatment of a condition: electrolyte management
2.2.1.1	Treatment of a condition: wet macular degeneration
3.1.1.1	Management of a condition: acute burns
3.1.1.1	Condition follow up
4.2.1.1	Management of a condition: long COVID-19

4 Results Before and After the Arrival of ChatGPT

In 2025, the subthemes and codes for the core theme T1 *"What information sources"* are used to gather yes/no responses. Tables 7 and 8 have the number of 'yes' (the last two columns) as well as the original numbers based on the interview data.

Table 7. Subthemes identified for the theme T1 (*"What information sources"*).

Type of information source	Subtheme	2021 UK clinicians	2025 UK clinicians	2025 Australia clinicians
Local Trust/hospital	Trust guidelines	15	16	3
Local Trust/hospital	Trust Antibiotic guideline (a.k.a. Microguide)	11	15	
Local Trust/hospital	Trust Microguide app	6	11	
Local Trust/hospital	Trust Accident and Emergency app	3	1	
Local Trust/hospital	Trust Human expertise	9	3	1
UK national	British National Formulary (BNF)	15	17	

(*continued*)

Table 7. (*continued*)

Type of information source	Subtheme	2021 UK clinicians	2025 UK clinicians	2025 Australia clinicians
UK national	National Institute for Health and Care Excellence (NICE) guidelines	12	17	3
UK national	NICE guidelines/NICE clinical knowledge summaries (CKS)	5	17	3
UK national	Specialist resources by Royal Colleges	5	11	2
UK national	Specialist resources by British Societies	2	6	2
UK national	Toxbase from UK National Poisons Information Service	1	7	
UK national	NHS choices	3	2	
Clinical point-of-care summary	BMJ Best Practice	9	11	2
Clinical point-of-care summary	UpToDate	9	2	3
Specialist resources	Biomedical literature: PubMed searches	2	14	3
Specialist resources	Biomedical literature: Journal papers	6	9	3
Specialist resources	Clinical practice guidelines	3	10	3
Specialist resources	BMJ products/BMJ Learning	2	12	2
Clinical reference texts	Medical school books	4	7	1
Clinical reference texts	Oxford handbook	5	10	2
Clinical reference texts	Speciality textbook	1	6	2
Clinical reference texts	Handbook	2	6	1
Online resources	Websites/apps	15	14	3
Online resources	Wiki-based	3	8	2

(*continued*)

Table 7. (*continued*)

Type of information source	Subtheme	2021 UK clinicians	2025 UK clinicians	2025 Australia clinicians
Online resources	Google searches	9	14	3

Table 8. Codes developed for the subthemes with the type *"online resources"*. The last two rows were added in 2025 as new subthemes to investigate ChatGPT and its alternatives.

Subtheme	Code	2021 UK clinicians	2025 UK clinicians	2025 Australia clinicians
Websites/apps	Mersey burns app	2	1	
Websites/apps	orthobullets.com	3	2	
Websites/apps	OrthoFlow app	2	3	
Websites/apps	Patient.co.uk	4	3	
Websites/apps	Pocket Doctor app	2	1	
Websites/apps	MDCalc app	3	11	2
Websites/apps	GeekyMedicine	2	12	3
Websites/apps	ENTSHO.com	3	1	
Websites/apps	GP Notebook	4	9	
Websites/apps	discussion: MS Teams	1	12	3
Websites/apps	discussion: whatsapp groups	1	15	3
Websites/apps	discussion: forums	1	4	1
Websites/apps	Tube-based videos	2	9	3
Websites/apps	Asked to See Patient (ATSP) from UK	1	4	1
Websites/apps	Paediatric emergencies app	1		
Websites/apps	Life in the Fast Lane (LITFL) Library	1	9	2
Websites/apps	medscape.com	1	7	1
Websites/apps	radiologymasterclass.co.uk	1	2	1
Websites/apps	GP trainer (EMIS system at GP)	1	2	
Websites/apps	Neomates	1		
Websites/apps	online modules	1	9	1
Wiki-based	Radiopaedia.org	1	10	2
Wiki-based	Wikipedia	1	6	2

(*continued*)

Table 8. (*continued*)

Subtheme	Code	2021 UK clinicians	2025 UK clinicians	2025 Australia clinicians
Wiki-based	EyeWiki	1	8	
Wiki-based	physio-pedia.com	1	2	
Google searches		6	7	1
Google searches	Google Scholar for papers	3	6	1
Online resources (AI)	ChatGPT		12	3
Online resources (AI): different than ChatGPT	Examples: DeepSeek, Groq, Grok3-beta, Claude, QWEN2.5-MAX, Gemini		6	3

Table 9. Exemplifying information sources provided in writing by UK clinicians in 2025.

"*What information sources*" in 2025	2025 UK clinicians
EyeWiki, ChatGPT, Google search, MicroGuide, Pubmed, BNF, NICE Guidelines, RCOphth Guidelines https://www.rcophth.ac.uk	P18
Foundation Doctor Handbook App: Provides clear and succinct information to help UK Foundation doctors navigate some common clinical scenarios on the wards https://apps.apple.com/gb/app/foundation-doctor-handbook/id1463210190	P19
iResus App: Adult, Paediatric, Newborn resuscitation and anaphylaxis algorithms https://apps.apple.com/gb/app/iresus/id1034079078	P19
I use surgical videos from youtube, information from *AAO Eyewiki, Oxford handbook* and *training in ophthalmology textbook* (Training in Ophthalmology from Oxford University Press https://academic.oup.com/book/43958) in both hard copy and PDF format, I use the *anki flash card app* (https://www.ankiapp.com) for studying and memorization. […]	P21
NICE guidelines, BNF app, e-learning on elfh (from NHS England https://portal.e-lfh.org.uk), *Handbook app, Mdcalc app, Eolas app* (https://eolasmedical.com)	P22
NICE, BNF, BMJ best medical practice, Zero to finals (https://zerotofinals.com), *Passmedicine* (https://www.passmedicine.com), *Geeky medicine*	P24

(*continued*)

Table 9. (*continued*)

"What information sources" in 2025	2025 UK clinicians
Eyewiki (for information about disease); <u>*GMC website*</u> (for general information from General Medical Council https://www.gmc-uk.org); *Royal college guidelines* (guidelines to follow for management of different disease); *NICE guidelines* (information and management guidelines in UK); *Pubmed* (for journals); <u>*Sci hub*</u> (for journals https://www.sci-hub.mk); *Mediscape* (medication); <u>*Eyedocs*</u> (Multiple Choice Questions https://www.eyedocs.co.uk); *Google* (general information); *Wikipedia* (general information); *Microsoft teams* (discussion); *Watsapp* (forums for discussion); <u>*Telegram*</u> (forums for information and discussion https://telegr am.org); *Youtube* (videos regarding different medical conditions)	P32
[...] *BNF* (medications), **Chatgpt** (quick searched/studying/or revision), <u>**Microsoft Copilot**</u> (same as chatgpt), *GP Notebook* (good reference for GPs) [...]	P34
Local guidelines followed where possible, if unavailable, *national guidelines* used. For clinical point of care summary, personally favour *Up To Date*, however this is not provided with NHS open Athens. Therefore, *BMJ practice* used in day to day practice. For additional educational resources, main resources would include the following: <u>*Passmedicine*</u>, *geeky medics*, <u>*zero to finals*</u>, *LITFL*, <u>*deranged physiology*</u> (https://derangedphysiology.com), *BMJ best practice*, <u>*dontforgetthebubbles.com*</u>	P35

In 2025, besides the Likert scale (yes/no), some clinicians provided in writing examples of the information sources used. Tables 9 and 10 illustrate the replies. The text underlined in Tables 9 and 10 indicates information sources not listed in Tables 7 and 8. In 2021, only 3 clinicians provided some text with information sources used.

Table 10. Exemplifying information sources provided in writing by Australian doctors.

"What information sources" in 2025	2025 Australia clinicians
Australian clinical guidelines: <u>*Pregnancy and Breastfeeding Medicines Guide*</u> from the Royal Women's Hospital https://thewomenspbmg.org.au/medicines, <u>*Queensland Clinical Guidelines*</u> https://www.health.qld.gov.au/qcg	P26
<u>*PsychDB*</u> (psychiatry reference) https://www.psychdb.com, <u>*Psych Scene*</u> (specialised training and professional development), <u>*Diagnostic and Statistical Manual of Mental Disorders*</u> https://doi/book/10.1176/appi.books. 9780890425787	P26

(*continued*)

Table 10. (*continued*)

"What information sources" in 2025	2025 Australia clinicians
Therapeutic Goods Administration (from Australia https://www.tga.gov.au), *Micromedex* (https://www.micromedexsolutions.com), *Australian Medicines Handbook* (https://www.amh.net.au), **Lyrebird AI** (medical transcription from Melbourne-based startup Lyrebird Health https://www.lyrebirdhealth.com), *PsychDB*, *TOXINZ* (poisons database from New Zealand https://poisons.co.nz), *Medicines Complete* (https://www.medicinescomplete.com), *DrugBank Online* (database for drug and drug target info https://go.drugbank.com)	P27
ChatGPT, **Manus.AI** (https://manus.im), *NICE* (online archive and guidelines and flowcharts, nationally recognised)	P28

From Australian replies in 2025, ChatGPT is used by P27, P28, and P29. Alternatives to ChatGPT are used by P26 (Gemini), P27 (Lyrebird AI), and P28 (Manus AI).

From UK replies in 2025, ChatGPT is used by 12 participants. Alternatives to ChatGPT are used by 6 participants, e.g. P25 (Gemini) and P34 (Microsoft Copilot).

5   Discussion

This action research study has 38 participants: 32 junior doctors, 1 nurse practitioner, and 5 medical students. Among the information sources used by the clinicians, there are the top-3 most frequently named information sources from a larger study with UK clinicians [26]: *NICE CKS* and *BNF* from Table 7; and *GP Notebook* from Table 8.

The most popular type of clinical question *"How should I manage condition x (not specifying diagnostic or therapeutic)?"* from Table 5 is the second most popular in a recent study from McGill University (Canada) [27].

Tables 7, 8, 9 and 10 show diverse information sources that may be ranked according to the validity of their findings, i.e. their different types of evidence/research [28]. Cross-comparing 2021 and 2025 clinicians' replies (Table 8), it becomes clear: a) an increment in using *"online resources"*; and b) Google searches and ChatGPT (along its alternatives) are currently used, although they are known to struggle to formulate an accurate diagnosis in complex cases [29, 30].

The two points in time considered highlight a movement from *"AI requirements"* (Table 3) to *AI uptake* (ChatGPT and its alternatives in Table 8). More research is needed to obtain an exhaustive account of information sources that may add value to patient care and to understand the ongoing clinical adoption of AI at the point-of-care.

References

1. Vaughn, V.M. et al.: Characteristics of healthcare organisations struggling to improve quality: results from a systematic review of qualitative studies. BMJ Qual. Saf. (2019)

2. Elliott, J.H. et al.: Living systematic reviews: an emerging opportunity to narrow the evidence-practice gap. PLoS Med. (2014)
3. Mizrahi, B. et al.: Long covid outcomes at one year after mild SARS-CoV-2 infection: nationwide cohort study. BMJ (2023)
4. 2025 AI Index Report. https://hai.stanford.edu/ai-index
5. DeepSeek-R1. https://huggingface.co/deepseek-ai/DeepSeek-R1
6. Peng Y, et al.: From GPT to deepseek: significant gaps remains in realizing AI in healthcare. J. Biomed. Inform. (2025)
7. Thirunavukarasu, A.J. et al.: Large language models in medicine. Nature Med. (2023)
8. Meyer, J.: Using qualitative methods in health related action research. BMJ (2000)
9. Clark, V.L., Ivankova, N.V.: Mixed methods research: a guide to the field. Sage (2015)
10. Saldaña, J.: The coding manual for qualitative researchers. Sage (2009)
11. Braun, V., Clarke, V.: Using thematic analysis in psychology. Qual. Res. Psychol. (2006)
12. Flick, U.: The SAGE handbook of qualitative data analysis. Sage (2014)
13. Clarke, V., Braun, V.: Teaching thematic analysis: overcoming challenges and developing strategies for effective learning. Psychol. (2013)
14. Fereday, J. et al.: Demonstrating rigor using thematic analysis: a hybrid approach of inductive and deductive coding and theme development. Int. J. Qual. Methods (2006)
15. Harper, D., Thompson, A.R.: Qualitative research methods in mental health and psychotherapy: a guide for students and practitioners. John Wiley & Sons (2011)
16. Morrow, S.L.: Quality and trustworthiness in qualitative research in counseling psychology. J. Couns. Psychol. (2005)
17. Maxwell, J.A.: Using numbers in qualitative research. Qual. Inq. (2010)
18. Frith, H., Gleeson, K.: Clothing and embodiment: men managing body image and appearance. Psychol. Men Masculinity (2004)
19. Hill, C.E. et al.: A guide to conducting consensual qualitative research. Sage (1997)
20. Hill, C.E. et al.: Consensual qualitative research: an update. J. Couns. Psychol. (2005)
21. Campbell, J.L. et al.: Coding in-depth semistructured interviews: problems of unitization and intercoder reliability and agreement. SMR (2013)
22. Artstein, R., Poesio, M.: Inter-coder agreement for computational linguistics. CL (2008)
23. Cohen, J.: A coefficient of agreement for nominal scales. EPM (1960)
24. O'Connor, C., Joffe, H.: Intercoder reliability in qualitative research: debates and practical guidelines. Int. J. Qual. Methods (2020)
25. Del Fiol, G., Workman, T.E., Gorman, P.N.: Clinical questions raised by clinicians at the point of care: a systematic review. JAMA Intern. Med. (2014)
26. McCartney, M. et al.: Where do UK clinicians find information at the point of care? a pragmatic, exploratory study. BMC Prim. Care (2024)
27. Roper, M. et al.: Clinical questions addressed by first-year medical students in primary care: a cross-sectional study. Fam. Med. (2025)
28. Evans, D.: Hierarchy of evidence: a framework for ranking evidence evaluating healthcare interventions. J. Clin. Nurs. (2003)
29. Tang, H., Ng, J.H.: Googling for a diagnosis. BMJ (2006)
30. Chan, L., Xu, X., Lv, K.: DeepSeek-R1 and GPT-4 are comparable in a complex diagnostic challenge: a historical control study. Int. J. Surg. (2025)

Large Language Models

Multimodal Sarcasm Dataset Generation for a Low-Resource Language: Swahili

Eugene Kariba Kamau[(✉)] and Noorhan Abbas

University of Leeds, Leeds, UK
`kamau.eugene@gmail.com, n.h.abbas@leeds.ac.uk`

Abstract. Natural Language Processing (NLP) for low-resource languages like Swahili remains constrained by the scarcity of annotated datasets, restricting progress in machine translation, sentiment analysis, and speech recognition. Although human annotation is valuable, it is costly, time-consuming, and difficult to scale. This study investigates the use of GPT-4o to generate a Swahili multimodal dataset containing sarcastic, positive, negative, and neutral captions, centered on environmental themes. The dataset was evaluated using LLM-as-a-judge methods, automated metrics, and human validation. Captions exhibited strong grammatical fluency and contextual alignment, with a sentiment classification accuracy of ~ 79%. Claude and Gemini models rated grammatical correctness and creativity at ~ 98% and ~ 80%, respectively. Lexical diversity was high, especially in sarcastic captions, evidenced by BERTScore F1 (0.8681) and BLEU (0.0172).

Human evaluation confirmed coherence and relevance but highlighted difficulties in reflecting culturally grounded sarcasm, such as idiomatic phrasing and regional irony. These findings expose limitations of general-purpose LLMs in modelling sociolinguistic nuance. This study affirms that LLM-generated synthetic data is a scalable and cost-effective alternative to manual annotation. Future work should focus on fine-tuning LLMs with culturally specific corpora to support real-world applications, including content moderation, environmental advocacy, and social media sentiment analysis.

Keywords: Synthetic Data generation · Swahili NLP · Multimodal Sarcasm Dataset · Low Resource Languages · Large Language Models (LLMs)

1 Introduction and Background Research

This study represents a technical exploration of LLM-based synthetic data generation for Swahili sarcasm detection, addressing the critical gap in linguistic resources for this underrepresented language. While 200 million people speak Swahili across East and Central Africa [32], the language remains underrepresented in Natural Language Processing (NLP) research due to limited annotated datasets [29]. Addressing Swahili data scarcity is crucial for digital inclusion, expanding AI-driven solutions for Swahili speakers, and preserving indigenous knowledge while contributing to global initiatives such as climate action. Investment in linguistic resource creation is also essential for advancing NLP in Swahili and other underrepresented languages.

© The Author(s), under exclusive license to Springer Nature Switzerland AG 2026
M. Bramer and F. Stahl (Eds.): SGAI-AI 2025, LNAI 16302, pp. 239–252, 2026.
https://doi.org/10.1007/978-3-032-11442-6_17

1.1 NLP Discourse Analysis for Environmental Topics

Accurate NLP-driven discourse analysis provides valuable insights into complex environmental narratives. Fang and Andersson [7] explain that it facilitates the extraction of knowledge from public discourse, indigenous perspectives, and policy discussions, enabling data-driven environmental decision-making. Additionally, it plays a key role in identifying misinformation and biases in public debates, ensuring accurate interpretations of critical environmental issues. However, a lack of relevant datasets limits its application in African languages. Sentiment classification, a key NLP application, for instance, requires capturing language-specific nuances such as dialectal variations and cultural expression, elements often overlooked by general-purpose models.

Initiatives like African Language Program- AI4D [29] and Masakhane [24] have been pivotal in addressing the scarcity of linguistic resources for African languages, by incentivizing the collection and curation of language datasets as well as the development of language resources and tools.

Muhammad et al. [21] and Jbel et al. [13] underscore the necessity of developing localized sentiment datasets tailored to the linguistic and cultural diversity found in Nigerian and Moroccan languages, respectively. Their research separately highlights the limitations of one-size-fits-all language models and reinforce the need for customized resources to enhance sentiment analysis in underrepresented African languages.

Collectively, these studies underscore the imperative to develop language-specific NLP resources that account for the linguistic, cultural, and contextual particularities of underrepresented African languages such as Swahili, thereby enabling more accurate, culturally sensitive, and context-aware sentiment analysis.

1.2 Sarcasm in Discourse Analysis

Sarcasm, defined as the use of remarks that convey the opposite of their literal meaning, poses a significant challenge for sentiment analysis, as misinterpretation can lead to erroneous sentiment classification and distorted analytical insights. Sarcasm often relies on multimodal cues such as images, emojis, and videos that reinforce non-literal intent, making it difficult to detect through text alone. Consequently, sarcasm detection has evolved from traditional text-based methods to more advanced multimodal approaches that integrate linguistic, contextual, and visual features. Recent NLP models have demonstrated improved accuracy by leveraging such multimodal data, particularly in social media contexts where visual elements frequently accompany sarcastic expressions. Farabi et al. [8], in a comprehensive survey of over 60 studies on Multimodal Sarcasm Detection (MSD), affirm that combining textual and visual inputs enhances detection performance across languages, although they note that existing research remains predominantly focused on English, indicating a critical gap in multilingual and low-resource language contexts.

Sarcasm detection in NLP is inherently challenging due to its dependence on contextual incongruity, sentiment reversal, and implicit cues. Traditional rule-based and statistical models focused on lexical and syntactic features, but recent transformer-based models like BERT have improved performance by capturing complex contextual relationships [14]. Multimodal approaches, incorporating both visual and textual data, employ techniques like transformer multimodal fusion and co-attention mechanisms.

1.3 Sarcasm Detection Datasets

Several datasets have been developed for sarcasm research, such as SarcNet[38], the News Headlines Dataset [20] and MUStARD [4], which include textual and audiovisual sarcasm annotations.

Studies using multimodal sarcasm datasets consistently show that adding audio/visual cues to text improves classification accuracy, especially when the task hinges on contextual incongruity. Using the MUStARD dataset, Castro et al. [4] demonstrated that incorporating multimodal information can substantially improve performance, reducing the relative error rate of sarcasm detection by up to 12.9% in F1-score compared to unimodal models. Another study on Instagram-based corpora [28] similarly indicates that combining audio-visual or image cues with text yields superior classification accuracy.

Given the linguistic and cultural complexity of sarcasm, the development of multimodal sarcasm datasets for low-resource languages such as Swahili is both necessary and long overdue, offering a critical opportunity to enhance NLP tasks in discourse where sarcasm is frequently employed.

1.4 Synthetic Data Generation and Evaluation

Traditional manually labelled datasets remain a key resource for NLP but present challenges such as high costs, bias, and scalability limitations [9]. These challenges are more pronounced for low-resource languages, where annotated datasets are scarce. Addressing these imbalances requires innovative data collection methods, such as crowdsourcing and synthetic data generation. Large Language Models (LLMs), such as the GPT family, offer a more scalable solution by generating synthetic data that supplements or replaces human-annotated datasets [19]. Clark et al. [5] demonstrate that GPT-3 produces fluent, human-like text, highlighting the potential of LLM generated synthetic data for NLP tasks.

Zhao et al. [41] conducted a study to generate multimodal sarcasm using transformer models. They then evaluated the generation using automatic and human assessments. Automatic metrics were used to measure lexical overlap and relevance while human evaluation focused on Creativity, Sarcastic-ness, Coherence, and Image-Text Relation, providing qualitative insights into sarcasm quality.

Previous studies on LLM-generated text have found that traditional evaluation metrics such as BLEU [25] are insufficient for assessing LLM-generated text, particularly in creative tasks, as they focus on lexical overlap and fail to capture semantic equivalence, coherence, and contextual relevance [2]. More advanced approaches, including BERTScore [40] and human evaluation, offer greater accuracy by considering semantic similarity and creativity. Zheng, et al. [42] explore *"LLM-as-a-judge"*, where LLMs assess generated text based on criteria such as helpfulness, reliability, relevance, feasibility, and overall quality. This method enables automated evaluation while addressing the limitations of traditional metrics, providing a context-aware and adaptable assessment strategy in NLP research. LLM-as-a-judge offers a scalable evaluation framework, although issues such as verbosity bias and self-enhancement bias persist.

Faithfulness and diversity are key parameters in evaluating LLM-generated synthetic data. Liu et al. and Gandi et al. [9, 18] explain that faithfulness ensures logical and grammatical coherence, mitigating hallucinations and factual inconsistencies. Techniques such as prompt engineering improve alignment of generated text with real-world data. Additionally, studies have found that LLMs often produce repetitive outputs and strategies are required to mitigate this.

This study utilized GPT-4o [23] to generate a multimodal, text and images, Swahili sarcasm dataset for Swahili NLP. The dataset consisted of 15548 captions (423,046 tokens) in 4 sentiments categories: sarcastic, positive, neutral and negative. The dataset was then evaluated using LLM-as-a-judge techniques, automated metrics, and human assessment, confirming high coherence, grammatical accuracy, and creativity. These results demonstrate the viability of synthetic data for low-resource languages like Swahili. The dataset is publicly available [15]. This work investigates the technical feasibility of generating Swahili sarcasm captions using GPT-4o but acknowledges significant methodological limitations that prevent immediate practical deployment. The study serves as an initial exploration rather than a production-ready solution, with the primary goal of identifying both opportunities and critical challenges in this approach.

2   Design and Methodology

In this section we will describe the model selection, the sarcasm generation task and the evaluation.

2.1   Datasets

We collected a total of 3887 images, covering multiple environmental themes. The Disaster Images Dataset [33] from Kaggle was selected due to its extensive collection of images depicting various natural and human-induced environmental disasters. These images serve as input for understanding visual contexts where sarcasm might be employed to critique disaster responses, preparedness, or consequences. Additionally, the RoboFlow Universe Dataset [26] provided images related to environmental issues such as pollution, making it a valuable resource for images for sarcastic expressions in discussions of sustainability and ecological degradation.

To incorporate climate-specific imagery, the study leveraged images from Climate Visuals [6], a curated dataset focused on climate-related issues such as global warming and extreme weather events.

The images collected were grouped into 18 broad environmental themes namely mining, water-disaster, sea damage, sea, forest, forest disaster, oil spill, street, street damage, people, ecology damage, forestation, air pollution, wild-fire, drought agriculture, energy, flooding and glaciers.

2.2 Models

To identify the most appropriate language model for this study, we evaluated the capabilities of GPT-4o[1], Gemini[2], and LLaMA[3] with particular attention to Swahili language proficiency, creativity, text generation, and contextual relevance. GPT, LLaMA, Gemini and Claude[4] are recognised as leading models in authoritative listings and benchmarks [36].

A pilot evaluation was conducted using a set of tailored prompts to assess each model's suitability for the task. Additionally, we considered findings from prior comparative analyses, notably Zahid et al. (2024)[39], who conducted an instruction-based evaluation of GPT-4 and Google AI across several core natural language processing (NLP) tasks using structured prompts and human judgment. Their results showed that while both models demonstrated comparable performance in some areas, GPT-4 consistently outperformed Google AI in translation accuracy, text generation, factual consistency, creativity, and logical reasoning, whereas Google AI showed a slight advantage in sarcasm detection, underscoring the varying task-specific strengths of large language models (LLMs). LLaMA exhibited limited proficiency in Swahili and failed to produce coherent outputs.

2.3 Swahili Caption Generation

In the pilot mentioned above, we evaluated the LLMs on the task of generating sarcastic captions in Swahili, with a focus on coherence, contextual relevance, and creativity. We compared Gemini and GPT-4o, with outputs evaluated by a native Swahili speaker. Both models exhibited weaknesses in grammatical accuracy, though GPT-4o performed better overall, while Gemini demonstrated greater creativity. In a follow-up task, captions were generated in English and subsequently translated into Swahili; here, GPT-4o excelled in coherence, whereas Gemini again showed relative strength in creativity. These results suggest complementary capabilities. Further research should be done on the potential for further optimization of caption generation through prompt engineering. Claude [1] was not comprehensively evaluated due to time constraints.

Overall, GPT-4o [23] demonstrated robust multilingual competence, including strong performance in Swahili, alongside superior text generation abilities. These factors established GPT-4o as the most suitable model for Swahili sarcasm caption generation for this study.

Generating high-quality Swahili sarcasm required a multi-step approach. Multi-step generation, as suggested by Long et al. [19], improves accuracy by breaking the LLMs task into simpler sub-tasks. This approach was applied to produce a final dataset of 3887 Swahili caption sets (423,046 tokens) categorized into four sentiment classes: sarcastic, positive, neutral, and negative, resulting in a final dataset of 15548 captions. Each caption also had accompanying keywords, words describing the image. The keywords are the equivalent of hashtags in social media.

---

[1] OpenAI (2024) *GPT-4o Technical Report*. OpenAI.

[2] Google DeepMind (2023). *Gemini*.

[3] Meta AI (2023). *LLaMA 2*.

[4] Anthropic (2024). *The Claude 3 Model Family*. Anthropic Model Card.

2.4 Hyperparameter Selection for Caption GPT-4o Generation

We first established a baseline for the sarcasm caption generation task using default hyperparameters and iteratively adjusted key settings to assess their impact on creativity and contextual relevance. The primary parameters considered were:

Temperature: Controls randomness; lower values (e.g., 0.2) produce deterministic outputs, while higher values (e.g., 0.8) enhance diversity and creativity.

Top-p (Nucleus Sampling): Determines the probability mass from which words are sampled, balancing diversity and relevance. Higher values (e.g., 0.9) encourage diverse outputs.

Maximum Tokens: Limits caption length; higher values enable more elaborate responses, while lower values ensure conciseness.

Frequency and Presence Penalties: Reduce word repetition and encourage novel word usage, maintaining linguistic variety.

2.5 Prompt Engineering for Caption Generation

Zero-shot learning (ZSL), which we applied, enables models to generate captions for images without task-specific training. Pretrained vision-language models have demonstrated the ability to produce linguistically diverse and contextually relevant captions without explicit supervision [37]. Another study by Gole, Mihalcea, and Oraby [10] demonstrates that GPT models can infer sarcasm without task specific training.

We applied multiple prompt engineering techniques to ensure structured, contextually relevant, and diverse outputs while maintaining consistency across sarcasm classification, sentiment categorization, and Swahili translation. Role prompting explicitly defined the model as GPT, reinforcing task-specific behavior. Explicit instruction prompting provided clear directives, such as *"Generate a sarcastic caption in English for each of these images, on an environmental theme, enclosed in double quotation marks and without any additional text. The caption should be very creative, unique, and contextually related to the image. The caption should be at least 15 words long,"* ensuring strict adherence to task requirements.

Constraint-based prompting minimized redundancy by requiring captions to be *"unique and different from the previous one,"* preventing repetition while maintaining thematic relevance. Instruction chaining structured the request into multiple subtasks, including *"Generate a neutral sentiment caption in English for each of these images, on an environmental theme, enclosed in double quotation marks and without any additional text,"* facilitating systematic prompt evaluation across sarcasm, neutrality, positivity, negativity, and keyword generation [34]. Contextual constraint prompting mandated alignment with the environmental theme and image content, improving coherence. Zero-shot prompting with implicit few-shot learning optimized generalization, guiding the model without explicit demonstrations.

The translation prompt retained these strategies, instructing the model to *"Translate the 'sarcastic caption' into Swahili. After translating, review the sentence to ensure it is grammatically correct and flows naturally in Swahili,"* incorporating explicit instruction prompting to maintain linguistic accuracy and constraint-based prompting to refine fluency and preserve the intended tone. Additionally, instruction chaining structured the translation into multiple subtasks, directing the model to enhance creativity, idiomatic fluency, and cultural relevance while preserving sarcasm and sentiment integrity. These techniques collectively ensured coherent, structured, and context-aware translated Swahili captions.

2.6 Evaluation of the Generated Swahili Corpus

The evaluation of the generated Swahili corpus aimed to assess its suitability for downstream Natural Language Processing (NLP) tasks, particularly in sarcasm detection. Existing research on the evaluation of LLM-generated data typically emphasizes the two fundamental aspects described in Sect. 1.4 above: faithfulness and diversity. Faithfulness in the context of the generated Swahili captions refers to grammatical coherence and contextual accuracy, ensuring that the generated text aligns with real-world semantics. Diversity, on the other hand, pertains to variation in text structure, words, and style, which mitigates biases and enhances the downstream task model's generalizability.

Building on previous studies that evaluated generated datasets, particularly Zhao et al. [41], which explored multimodal sarcasm generation using transformers, we adopted a structured evaluation framework to assess the Swahili corpus. The evaluation focused on five key criteria:

1. **Caption Sentiment Classification**: The LLM judge was prompted to classify each caption into one of four sentiment classes: sarcastic, positive, neutral, or negative- to determine the model's ability to identify caption sentiment.
2. **Grammatical Correctness**: The syntactic accuracy and fluency of the generated text were assessed using a **Likert scale (1–5)** to quantify linguistic quality.
3. **Contextual Correctness**: Captions were evaluated based on their alignment with the corresponding images and environmental themes using a **Likert scale (1–5)**
4. **Creativity in Sarcasm**: This assessed the **linguistic creativity and sarcastic expression** in the text, considering cultural nuances that influence sarcasm interpretation, based on a Likert scale(1–5).
5. **Diversity of Generated Captions**: Due to the inherent biases of LLMs, synthetic text generation often results in repetitive or formulaic outputs [19]. To assess this, automated metrics were applied to measure variation within the dataset.

LLM Models for LLM-as-a-Judge Evaluation : Li et al. [17] identify preference bias as a challenge when the same LLM is used for data generation and evaluation, risking preference leakage. To address this, auxiliary LLMs, Gemini[31] and Claude 3[1], were used for automated evaluation. These models assessed caption sentiment, grammatical coherence, contextual correctness, and creativity, providing explanations for their evaluations.

Prompt engineering for LLM-as-a-judge. The **prompt** for LLM-as-a-judge was iteratively refined based on feedback, following established **prompt engineering** methodologies. Written in Swahili, it incorporated multiple techniques to enhance the LLM's ability to evaluate sarcasm in a multimodal context. Role prompting assigned the model expertise by defining it *as "an expert in understanding sarcasm, particularly in the context of environmental issues, visual cues, and the Swahili language,"* ensuring domain-specific consistency. Explicit instruction prompting was used to provide a structured evaluation framework, directing the model to *"assess the quality of image captions in Swahili, considering the content of the uploaded image,"* thereby anchoring the evaluation to a multimodal context. Few-shot prompting reinforced pattern recognition by requiring the model to classify captions as *"positive_caption," "negative_caption," "neutral_caption," or "sarcastic_caption"*. To maintain structured assessments, a numerical rating scale (1–5) was introduced across four key dimensions: *"Creativity and Sarcasm," "Grammatical Accuracy," "Contextual Relevance,"* and *"Sentiment,"* minimizing output variance and improving alignment with human judgment. The Chain-of-Thought (CoT) technique enhanced logical reasoning by requiring the model to evaluate *"how well the caption aligns with the context indicated by the image,"* fostering more nuanced and context-aware sarcasm detection [34]. Additionally, contextual constraint prompting was implemented by instructing the model to assess captions *"considering the content of the uploaded image,"* reinforcing multimodal understanding. These strategies collectively ensured coherent, structured, and contextually aware caption evaluation.

Human evaluation. This goal of human evaluation was to verify how well the dataset upheld linguistic integrity, cultural appropriateness, and multimodal coherence. A qualitative evaluation framework was applied for human evaluation by a native Swahili speaker. To ensure a comprehensive evaluation, three key qualitative assessment criteria were established: **Linguistic Accuracy**, which involves evaluating grammatical, syntactic, and lexical correctness while avoiding inconsistencies; **Cultural Relevance**, focusing on the integration of idiomatic expressions and cultural references to align with the nuances of Swahili-speaking communities; and **Contextual Alignment**, which examines the correspondence between textual and visual elements to preserve the intended meaning.

3 Experimental Results and Discussions

3.1 Swahili Sarcasm Model Exploration Pilot

A structured evaluation framework was applied using three criteria: Sarcasm Creativity, Relevance, and Grammatical Correctness. We concluded that a more suitable approach to generate Swahili captions would be to generate them in English using GPT-4o and then translate them to Swahili.

3.2 Hyperparameter Optimization

Systematic tuning of hyperparameters was conducted to optimize the generation of coherent and contextually appropriate sarcastic captions. The selected parameters balanced creativity, diversity, and coherence. A temperature of 0.9 was chosen to enhance linguistic variation, while a top-p (nucleus sampling) value of 0.8 ensured a trade-off between diversity and relevance. To maintain lexical variety and minimize redundancy, a frequency penalty of 0.3 was applied, along with a presence penalty of 0.2 to encourage novel word usage.

For Swahili caption translation, also using the GPT-4 API, optimal parameters were similarly determined through a pilot study. A temperature of 0.95 was selected to enhance creativity while preserving relevance, while a top-p value of 0.9 maintained probabilistic diversity in word selection. To prevent excessive repetition, the frequency penalty was set to 0.0, and the presence penalty was also set to 0.0 to encourage idiomatic phrasing. These refinements ensured fluency and expressiveness, natural and contextually appropriate Swahili translations.

3.3   Generated Dataset Evaluation

LLM as a Judge Evaluation.   The LLMs deduced the sentiment label (positive, negative, neutral and sarcastic) of the generated captions, and the evaluated label was then compared to the original sentiment of the captions.

Similarity Metrics.   BLEU scores and BERTScore scores were averaged per category and theme, comparing adjacent captions with one as the reference to assess lexical diversity and sentiment consistency. BERTScore was also calculated for each image's caption set, with neutral captions as a reference to measure sentiment variance. BERTScore was computed using XLM-RoBERTa-Large [REF _Ref191172020 \r \h 11], a multilingual transformer trained on diverse corpora, including Swahili. Additionally, Cosine similarity [REF _Ref191154806 \r \h 27] was also computed to evaluate textual coherence within the same sentiment and theme.

Human Evaluation.   The captions were found to be grammatically sound and contextually relevant to their corresponding images, demonstrating the effectiveness of the language model in maintaining coherence and syntactic integrity. the captions predominantly adopted an informal tone and lacked cultural and geographic context. This aligns with findings in nlp sarcasm detection research, where social media sarcasm, unlike that found in generated captions, tends to rely on immediate context and multimodal cues, while literary sarcasm, incorporates deeper narrative structures and historical references [14]. the generated sarcasm tends more to literary sarcasm.

3.4   Discussion of Experimental Results and Analysis

The sentiment classification results, Table 1, from the LLM-as-a-judge approach.

show an overall accuracy of approximately **79%**, with Gemini slightly outperforming Claude which achieved **78%**. The results also highlight disparities in sarcasm detection. While negative captions were the easiest to classify (Claude:0.9358, Gemini: 0.9118), sarcasm detection posed a greater challenge, with Claude achieving lower precision (0.7071) compared to Gemini (0.8786).

This disparity is also shown in the error analysis in Fig. 1.

Table 1. LLM as a judge sentiment classification

Metric	*Claude LLM*	Gemini LLM
Accuracy	*0.7705*	0.7856
Precision for sarcastic caption	*0.7071*	0.8786
Precision for neutral caption	*0.7184*	0.6638
Precision for negative caption	*0.9358*	0.9118
Precision for positive caption	*0.8167*	0.7288

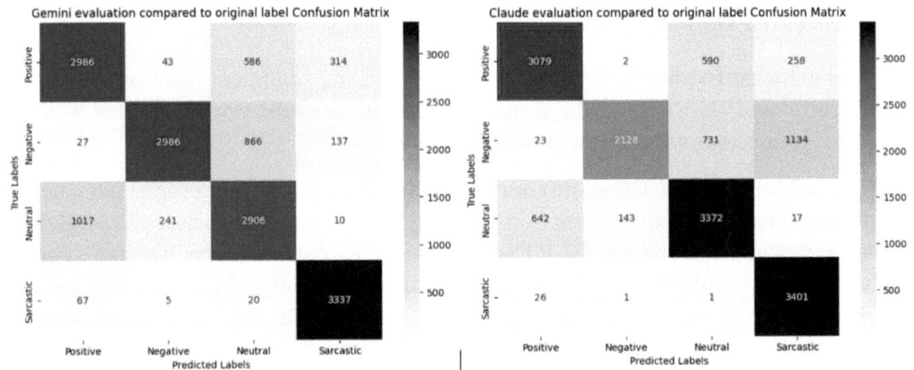

Fig. 1. LLMs caption sentiment as compared to the original label.

The variance in sarcasm detection between models suggests that fine-tuning LLMs on domain-specific datasets remains crucial to improving sarcasm recognition in low-resource languages, particularly when multimodal cues such as images and visual irony are involved.

The LLM-as-a-judge approach proved effective in benchmarking the LLMs, across linguistic attributes, as shown in Table 2. Discrepancies between Claude and Gemini highlight model-specific strengths and weaknesses. The assessed grammatical correctness of generated captions was consistently high, with Claude (4.97) and Gemini (4.96) assessing the captions as well-formed Swahili sentences. However, contextual relevance varied, with Claude achieving a higher score (**4.20**) compared to Gemini (**3.96**), suggesting differences in the LLMs in aligning textual content with visual contexts. The perceived creativity of sarcastic captions differed across models, with Claude assessing it as (**4.12**) and Gemini (**3.96**). The significant disparity for creativity and sarcasm, indicates different abilities of the LLMs in sarcasm understanding.

BERTScore results, Table 3, which assessed semantic similarity between generated captions, indicated that sarcastic captions (**0.8680**) scored lower than positive (**0.8854**), neutral (**0.8880**), and negative captions (**0.8843**). The lower BERTScore across the dataset suggest that the sarcastic captions exhibit more diverse phrasing and structure, aligning with research showing that sarcastic expressions are less lexically predictable

Table 2. Grammar, creativity and context correlation of GPT-4o with Gemini and Claude.

LLM	Creativity and sarcasm Accuracy	Grammatical Correctness Accuracy	Contextual relevance Accuracy
Gemini	*3.967170*	4.962559	3.999477
Claude	*4.129678*	4.965997	4.229803

than neutral or sentimentally polarized text [41]. The BLEU and BERTScore values for sarcastic captions show that while captions maintained semantic coherence, they deviated in lexical composition, a positive indicator of creativity.

BLEU scores and BERTScore, were used to measure syntactic and semantic alignment, respectively. Across sentiment categories, neutral captions exhibited the highest BLEU score (**0.026,866**) and negative captions the highest cosine similarity (**0.095,628**), while sarcastic captions had the lowest BLEU score (**0.017,225**) and cosine similarity (**0.076,449**). These results indicate that sarcastic captions exhibited higher lexical variability and linguistic diversity. Sarcasm relies on semantic incongruity rather than direct phrasing overlap. A lower BERTScore for sarcastic captions (**0.86,8146**) indicates greater lexical deviation, suggesting a higher degree of text and image incongruity compared to other captions. Inter-modal incongruity is a good indicator of sarcasm.

Table 3. BLEU, BERTScore(F1-Score) and Cosine Similarity

	Sarcastic	Positive	Neutral	Negative
BLEU per category average	0.017225	0.024289	0.026866	0.024705
Cosine Similarity	0.076449	0.091484	0.095628	0.10586
BERTscore per category average	0.867926	0.885452	0.887977	0.884373
BERTScore neutral caption ref	0.868146	0.890655	-	0.868146

4 Conclusion, Future Work and Ethical Issues

This study establishes the technical feasibility of LLM-based Swahili sarcasm generation, demonstrating that automated systems can produce grammatically coherent multimodal content. The generated dataset represents a starting point for exploring synthetic data approaches in low-resource language contexts. The generated captions exhibited strong grammatical accuracy (Claude: 4.97, Gemini: 4.96), linguistic diversity (BERTScore: 0.8681, BLEU: 0.0172), and high contextual coherence, achieving ~ 79% sentiment classification accuracy. Sarcasm detection, while challenging, showed promising results, with Gemini reaching 0.8786 precision. Human evaluation confirmed the dataset's fluency and relevance, validating the effectiveness of synthetic data for Swahili NLP.

This approach provides a scalable, cost-effective alternative to manual annotation, significantly advancing Swahili NLP. By successfully generating diverse and coherent captions, this study demonstrates the potential of LLMs in addressing data scarcity in low-resource languages. This suggests a path forward for generating language resources at scale. Future research should explore fine-tuning LLMs on Swahili-specific datasets and few-shot learning to refine sarcasm generation. Training downstream models on this dataset [15] will further demonstrate its applicability in real-world NLP tasks.

The potential ethical considerations of Swahili sarcasm dataset development include bias, transparency, and responsible AI deployment. Previous research highlights bias risks in LLM-generated datasets [3], which our findings corroborate, as some captions failed to align with native sarcasm expressions. Transparency in dataset creation is essential to prevent "diversity-washing," where synthetic data appears representative but lacks cultural depth [35]. To help mitigate some of these concerns, we documented dataset generation methodologies, LLM parameters, and prompt strategies, while ensuring the use of publicly available, licensed images.

AI-generated misinformation remains a concern, potentially affecting sentiment classification and content moderation. This underscores the need for a hybrid evaluation approach that combines LLM-as-a-judge methods, automated metrics, and human review. Future work should also emphasize cost-effective and scalable bias mitigation, ethical governance, and robust human validation in synthetic data generation for Swahili and other low-resource languages.

Acknowledgements. ChatGPT by OpenAI was used to assist in research and in the final writing of this paper to improve readability.

Disclosure of Interests. The authors declare that they have no competing interests.

References

1. Anthropic: Introducing the next generation of Claude: The Claude 3 model family (2024). https://www.anthropic.com/news/claude-3-family. Accessed 04 Sept 2025
2. Badshah, S., Sajjad, H.: Reference-Guided Verdict: LLMs-as-Judges in Automatic Evaluation of Free-Form Text (2024)
3. Bender, E.M., Gebru, T., McMillan-Major, A., Shmitchell, S.: On the dangers of stochastic parrots: can language models be too big? In: Proceedings of the 2021 ACM Conference on Fairness, Accountability, and Transparency, pp. 610–623. ACM, New York (2021). https://doi.org/10.1145/3442188.3445922
4. Castro, S., et al.: Towards multimodal sarcasm detection (an obviously perfect paper). In: Proceedings of the 57th Annual Meeting of the Association for Computational Linguistics. ACL (2019). https://doi.org/10.18653/v1/P19-1455
5. Clark, E., August, T., Serrano, S., Haduong, N., Gururangan, S., Smith, N.A.: All that's 'human' is not gold: Evaluating human evaluation of generated text. In: Proceedings of the 59th Annual Meeting of the Association for Computational Linguistics, pp. 7282–7296. ACL (2021). https://doi.org/10.18653/v1/2021.acl-long.565
6. Climate Visuals: Climate-related issues dataset (2024). https://climatevisuals.org/. Accessed 03 Sept 2025
7. Fang, T., Anderson, W.: Natural language processing: speeding up policy analysis for land restoration. World Resources Institute (2022). https://www.wri.org/update/natural-language-processing-speeding-policy-analysis-land-restoration. Accessed 04 Sept 2025

8. Farabi, S., et al.: A survey of multimodal sarcasm detection. In: Proceedings of the Thirty-Third International Joint Conference on Artificial Intelligence (IJCAI), pp. 8020–8028 (2024). https://doi.org/10.24963/ijcai.2024/887

9. Gandhi, S., Gala, R., Viswanathan, V., Wu, T., Neubig, G.: Better synthetic data by retrieving and transforming existing datasets. In: Findings of the Association for Computational Linguistics: ACL 2024, Bangkok, pp. 6453–6466. ACL (2024). https://doi.org/10.18653/v1/2024.findings-acl.385

10. Gole, C., Mihalcea, R., Oraby, S.: Can GPT models detect sarcasm? Evaluating zero-shot sarcasm detection with GPT-3, InstructGPT, GPT-3.5, and GPT-4 (2023)

11. Goyal, N., Du, J., Ott, M., Anantharaman, G., Conneau, A.: Larger-scale transformers for multilingual masked language modeling (2021).https://doi.org/10.18653/v1/2021.repl4nlp-1.4

12. Hao, S., et al.: Synthetic data in AI: Challenges, applications, and ethical implications (2024). https://doi.org/10.48550/arXiv.2401.016

13. Jbel, M., Jabrane, M., Hafidi, I., Metrane, A.: Sentiment analysis dataset in Moroccan dialect: bridging the gap between Arabic and Latin scripted dialect. Lang. Resour. Eval. **59**, 1401–1430 (2024). https://doi.org/10.1007/s10579-024-09764-6

14. Joshi, A., Bhattacharyya, P., Carman, M.J.: Automatic sarcasm detection: a survey. ACM Comput. Surv. (CSUR) **50**(5), 1–22 (2017). https://doi.org/10.1145/3124420

15. Kariba, E.: SwahiliMultimodalSarcasm. Hugging Face. https://huggingface.co/datasets/EKariba/SwahiliMultimodalSarcasm. Accessed 04 Sept 2025

16. Li, D., et al.: From generation to judgment: opportunities and challenges of LLM-as-a-judge. arXiv preprint arXiv:2411.16594 (2024). https://doi.org/10.48550/arXiv.2411.16594

17. Li, D., et al.: Preference leakage: a contamination problem in LLM-as-a-judge. arXiv preprint arXiv:2502.01534 (2025). https://doi.org/10.48550/arXiv.2502.01534

18. Liu, R., Chen, X., Zhang, L., Vaswani, A., Cottrell, G.: Best practices and lessons learned on synthetic data for language models (2024).https://doi.org/10.48550/arXiv.2404.07503

19. Long, L., et al.: On LLMs-driven synthetic data generation, curation, and evaluation: a survey. In: Findings of the Association for Computational Linguistics, ACL 2024, pp. 11065–11082 (2024). https://doi.org/10.18653/v1/2024.findings-acl.658

20. Misra, R., Arora, P.: Sarcasm detection using news headlines dataset. AI Open **4**, 13–18 (2023). https://doi.org/10.1016/j.aiopen.2023.01.001

21. Muhammad, S., Ezeani, I., Abdul-Mageed, M., Odugbemi, O.: NaijaSenti: A Sentiment Analysis Benchmark for Major Nigerian Languages (2022)

22. OpenAI: GPT-4 Technical Report (2023). https://doi.org/10.48550/arXiv.2303.08774

23. OpenAI: GPT-4o System Card (2024). https://doi.org/10.48550/arXiv.2410.21276

24. Orife, I., et al.: Masakhane–machine translation for Africa (2020). arXiv preprint arXiv:2003.11529

25. Papineni, K., Roukos, S., Ward, T., Zhu, W.-J.: BLEU: a method for automatic evaluation of machine translation. In: Proceedings of the 40th Annual Meeting of the Association for Computational Linguistics, Philadelphia, Pennsylvania, USA, pp. 311–318. Association for Computational Linguistics (2002). https://doi.org/10.3115/1073083.1073135

26. RoboFlow: Environmental issues dataset. https://universe.roboflow.com/browse/environmental (2024). Accessed 20 Dec 2024

27. Salton, G.: Automatic Text Processing: The Transformation, Analysis, and Retrieval of Information by Computer. Addison-Wesley, Reading, MA (1989)

28. Sangwan, S., Akhtar, M.S., Behera, P., Ekbal, A.: I didn't mean what i wrote! exploring multimodality for sarcasm detection. In: Proceedings of the International Joint Conference on Neural Networks (IJCNN), pp. 1–8 (2020)

29. Siminyu, K., et al.: AI4D–African Language Program (2021). https://doi.org/10.48550/arXiv.2104.02516

30. Touvron, H., et al.: LLaMA: open and efficient foundation language models (2023)
31. Team, G., et al.: Gemini: a family of highly capable multimodal models. arXiv preprint arXiv: 2312.11805 (2023)
32. UNESCO: Proclamation of 7 July as World Kiswahili Language Day (2021). https://unesdoc. unesco.org/ark:/48223/pf0000379702. Accessed 19 Dec 2024
33. Varpit94: Disaster images dataset. Kaggle (2024). https://www.kaggle.com/datasets/varpit94/ disaster-images-dataset. Accessed 20 Dec 2024
34. Wei, J., et al.: Chain-of-thought prompting elicits reasoning in large language models. In: Advances in Neural Information Processing Systems (NeurIPS) (2022).https://doi.org/10. 48550/arXiv.2201.11903
35. Whitney, C.D., Norman, J.: Real Risks of Fake Data: Synthetic Data, Diversity-Washing and Consent Circumvention. arXiv arXiv:2405.01820 (2024). https://doi.org/10.1145/3630106. 3659002
36. Wikipedia: List of large language models (2025). https://en.wikipedia.org/wiki/List_of_l arge_language_models. Accessed 08 Sept 2025
37. Yang, B., Liu, F., Wu, X., Wang, Y., Sun, X., Zou, Y.: MultiCapCLIP: auto-encoding prompts for zero-shot multilingual visual captioning. In: Proceedings of the 61st Annual Meeting of the Association for Computational Linguistics (ACL 2023), Volume 1: Long Papers, pp. 11908–11922. Association for Computational Linguistics (2023)
38. Yue, X., Chen, L., Wang, Y., Li, Z.: SarcNet: a multilingual multimodal sarcasm detection dataset. In: Proceedings of the 2024 Conference on Language Resources and Evaluation (LREC), pp. 1248–1260 (2024)
39. Zahid, I.A., et al.: Unmasking large language models by means of OpenAI GPT-4 and Google AI: a deep instruction-based analysis. Intell. Syst. Appl. **23**, 200431 (2024). https://doi.org/ 10.1016/j.iswa.2024.200431
40. Zhang, T., Kishore, V., Wu, F., Weinberger, K.Q., Artzi, Y.: BERTScore: evaluating text generation with BERT (2019). https://doi.org/10.48550/arXiv.1904.09675
41. Zhao, W., et al.: Multi-modal sarcasm generation: dataset and solution. In: Findings of the Association for Computational Linguistics: ACL 2023, pp. 5601–5613 (2023).https://doi.org/ 10.18653/v1/2023.findings-acl.346
42. Zheng, L., et al.: Judging LLM-as-a-judge with MT-bench and Chatbot arena. Adv. Neural. Inf. Process. Syst. **36**, 46595–46623 (2023). https://doi.org/10.48550/arXiv.2306.05685

Enhancing Voice-Controlled Drone Navigation: A Hybrid Approach Using ASR and NLP for UAV Command Interpretation

Yassir Alkasim and Abdulrahman Altahhan[✉]

University of Leeds, Leeds, UK
`{od22yma,a.altahhan}@leeds.ac.uk`

Abstract. This paper presents a voice-controlled Unmanned Aerial Vehicle (UAV) system that integrates Automatic Speech Recognition (ASR) and Natural Language Processing (NLP) techniques to enhance command interpretation and execution. The proposed system was tested in a Gazebo and ROS-based simulation environment using the Iris drone model from ArduPilot SITL. Various ASR models, including Whisper (Tiny, Base, Large), Wav2Vec2 (Base, Large), and Google Speech Recognition, were evaluated for their ability to transcribe drone-related voice commands accurately. Additionally, Natural Language Inference (NLI) models such as Facebook/BART (Base and Large MNLI), Google/T5-Large, Electra-Large-Discriminator, and GPT-4o-mini were assessed for mapping transcribed commands to MAVLink messages.

Experimental results demonstrate that Whisper Base outperforms other ASR models in balancing accuracy and processing efficiency, making it the best candidate for UAV speech recognition. Among the NLP/NLI models, BART-Large-MNLI exhibited the highest accuracy in correctly mapping voice commands to UAV actions, outperforming other models in zero-shot classification. The study highlights the feasibility of deploying local ASR models to reduce latency while maintaining high transcription accuracy and emphasizes the need for context-aware NLP models to enhance drone command flexibility. Future work will focus on expanding the dataset, optimizing real-time processing, and improving conversational UAV command execution.

Keywords: Voice-Controlled UAV · ASR · NLP · MAVLink · Drone Command Interpretation · NLI · Zero-Shot Classification · Human-Drone Interaction · ROS · ArduPilot SITL

1 Introduction

Unmanned Aerial Vehicles (UAVs) have transformed industries like surveillance, disaster response, and logistics by accessing remote areas and performing autonomous inspections [1], [2], [3]. However, manual operation requires significant skill, creating a barrier for non-expert users. Voice command integration has emerged as a promising solution to simplify control and improve operational efficiency, though the key challenge remains accurately converting natural language into instructions [4].

M. Bramer and F. Stahl (Eds.): SGAI-AI 2025, LNAI 16302, pp. 253–269, 2026.
https://doi.org/10.1007/978-3-032-11442-6_18

Despite advancements, existing voice-controlled UAV systems lack flexibility, context-aware interactions, primarily relying on predefined command sets unsuitable for dynamic environments. These systems are further limited by a lack of dataset diversity, reducing their effectiveness across different accents and noisy conditions. Technological constrains like reliance on cloud-based processing introduce unacceptable latency, while a general lack of advanced Natural Language Processing (NLP) capabilities prevents the understanding of conversational or multi-step commands.

To address these limitations, this study aims to developed a robust, context-aware voice-controlled UAV system. Unlike existing approaches, our research integrates diverse training datasets and context-aware NLP models to support multi-step and conversational commands. We also explore local versus cloud-based processing to reduce latency, thereby improving real-time applicability and command flexibility for the dynamic UAV operations.

2 Related Work

Research on voice-controlled UAVs has focused on speech recognition for predefined commands, often limited in vocabulary, context, and adaptability. Simoes et al. [5] tested three pipelines, achieving 99% accuracy with direct classification but no multi-step command support. Leelavathy et al. [6] proposed MAttRNN, reaching 95.36% accuracy over 23 commands, constrained by dataset size and online processing. Cloud-based ASR models like Google Cloud Speech API showed high accuracy in quiet settings (98%) but dropped to 75% in noise, with 300 ms latency [7]; Safie et al. [8] found pre-recorded commands outperform live input in noise conditions.

Edge and microcontroller-based approaches improved latency: Yapıcıoğlu et al. [9] reached 92.88% real-time accuracy on RaspberryPi, Renuka et al. [10] implementation a ten command Arduino system, and Fayjie et al. [11] used HMM and ROS for seven commands with speaker adaptation. Deep learning models such as VoiceNet [12] and multilingual system [4, 13] improved accuracy (up to 96.67%) but were limited in commands and real-time use. Tezza and Andujar [14] highlighted speech as intuitive, yet affected by noise, latency, and command restrictions.

These studies reveal that multi-step, conversation UAV control remains challenging, motivating the proposed NLP-based system.

3 Methodology

This study develops a voice-controlled UAV system capable of executing spoken instructions through a two-stage pipeline: Automatic Speech Recognition (ASR) coverts speech to text, and Natural Language Inference (NLI) or Natural Language Processing (NLP) models to interpret the text to generate appropriate MAVLink commands as shown in Fig. 1. The implementation used in the Iris Runway drone model in ArduPilot SITL [15] within a Gazebo simulation, with ArduPilot managing flight control and ROS [16] providing the communication interface. Initial validation was performed using

Mission Planner for manual commands execution, waypoint navigation, and telemetry monitoring. Once stability was confirmed, Python and pymavlink library were integrated to enable real-time voice control via a UDP link, ensuring seamless bidirectional communication between the ASR/NLP pipeline and the drone.

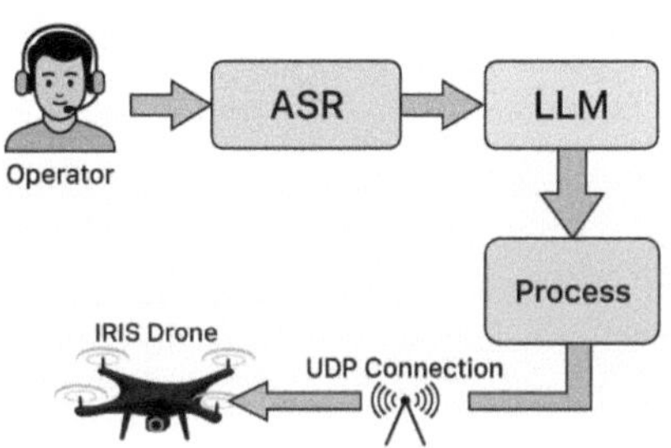

Fig. 1. System block diagram.

3.1 Automatic Speech Recognition for Voice Command Processing

Automatic Speech Recognition (ASR) enables machines to convert spoken language into text using advanced signal processing and machine learning. Modern ASR systems, including Recurrent Neural Networks (RNNs), Transformers, and self-supervised models, are trained on large datasets to improve robustness across languages and accents. In this study, both local and cloud-based ASR approaches were evaluated. The local models included Whisper (Tiny, Base, Large) and Wav2Vec (Base, Large), while Google Speech Recognition API was used as a cloud-based solution. Whisper [17] employs an encoder-decoder Transformer architecture trained on 680,000 h of labeled audio, ensuring multilingual performance. Wav2Vec [18] learns speech representations from raw audio using self-supervised pretraining, reducing dependance on labeled data. Google's API offers scalable real-time transcription using cloud infrastructure. These models were compared to identify the most effective approach for real-time UAV voice control.

3.1.1 Audio Dataset Description

The dataset used for ASR evaluation was obtained from Kaggle [19]. It includes recordings from 50 speakers, each providing one hour of speech segmented into one-minute 16 kHz WAV files. For this study, two speakers were selected:

- **Speaker 1:** English speaker with an Indian accent (92 audio files).
- **Speaker 2:** English speaker with an American (female) accent (29 audio files).

A reference transcript was manually prepared for each file to provide ground truth. The models were first tested on this dataset and later validated using real-time microphone input. Test commands included single-sentence UAV instructions such as *"Arm the drone," "Change mode to guided," "Takeoff to 10 m altitude"* and *"Return home"*.

3.1.2 ASR Evaluation Metrics

ASR performance was evaluated using the following metrics:

- **Word Error Rate (WER):**

$$WER = \frac{S + D + I}{N} \tag{1}$$

where S = substitutions, D = deletions, I = insertions, and N = total words in the reference.

- **Character Error Rate (CER):** Similar to **WER** but calculated at the character level, offering finer granularity for transcription accuracy.
- **Statistical Measures:** Minimum, maximum, mean, and standard deviation of WER and CER were reported to capture performance variability across test samples.
- **Accuracy (%):**

  Accuracy reflects the proportion of correctly recognized words relative to the total reference words:

$$Accuracy = (1 - WER) \times 100 \tag{2}$$

3.2 Natural Language Processing for UAV Command Interpretation

To improve command flexibility and contextual understanding, ASR-converted text was processed using NLI and NLP models to generate MAVLink messages for execution. NLI, particularly in zero-shot classification, assigns labels without task-specific training by leveraging pretrained knowledge [20]. NLP, as a broader AI field, enables machines to interpret and generate human language for tasks such as translation, speech recognition, and summarization [21]. In this study, these techniques were applied to interpret UAV voice commands, allowing multi-step execution and contextual responses that enhance human-drone interaction.

3.2.1 Command Set

The reviewed studies have primarily relied on limited and predefined UAV command sets, restricting the scope of human-drone interaction. To address this, this study categorizes UAV commands into four groups: status commands, basic operation commands, navigation commands, and payload control commands, systematically classifying prior research to identify gaps and limitations.

Simoes et al. [5] used six navigation commands (Right, Backward, Forward, Left, Up, Down), while Leelavathy et al. [6] expanded to 20 commands, including navigation (e.g., Up, Down, Left, Right, Stop) and payload control (On, Off), alongside numerical inputs (0–9). Similarly, Eruero et al. [7] employed six navigation commands (Up, Down, Left, Right, Forward, Backward). Safie et al. [8] incorporated 16 navigation commands, including complex maneuvers such as flips and precise angle rotations. Yapıcıoğlu et al. [9] introduced one status command (Battery) and seven navigation commands (e.g., take-off, land, up/down movement, directional controls). Renuka et al. [10] implemented one basic operation command (start motors) and nine navigation commands. Contreras et al. [4] and Fayjie et al. [11] both utilized nine and eight navigation commands, respectively, with Fayjie et al. focusing on rotation-based movements. Kumaar et al. [12] tested eight navigation commands, while Choutri et al. [13] included four navigation commands (Up, Down, Right, Left) and two basic operations (On, Off).

To streamline command processing and enhance system efficiency, UAV commands in this study are categorized into:

1. **Status Commands** – Query drone parameters such as battery level and flight mode.
2. **Basic Operation Commands** – Essential commands for arming, flight mode changes, and mission resumption.
3. **Navigation Commands** – Control drone movement, including climbing, descending, and course changes.
4. **Payload Control Commands** – Manage camera activation, sensor adjustments, and delivery operations.

This structured categorization organizes commands efficiently, reduces system complexity, and improves drone interaction flexibility, as detailed in Table 1.

3.2.2 Models

This study uses advanced NLP models – BART, T5, ELECTRA, and GPT-4 – to interpret voice commands for UAV control. BART, a denoising autoencoder with bidirectional and autoregressive transformers, excels in text generation, translation, and comprehension [22]. T5 employs a text-to-text framework, unifying NLP tasks for consistent summarization and question answering [23]. ELECTRA's discriminative pretraining enhances efficiency by identifying replaced tokens [24]. GPT-4, a large-scale multimodal model, processes text and images with human-level language understanding [25]. These models were selected for their strong NLP capabilities, enabling accurate interpretation of complex UAV voice commands.

3.2.3 System Implementation and Evaluation Framework

Python code was developed to interface the SITL ArduPilot Iris drone with pymavlink enabling control via MAVLink messages implemented in functions like *arm_drone()*. An NLI maps input prompts (e.g., "Could you please arm the drone?") to predefined labels corresponding to drone commands, as illustrated in the block diagram in Fig. 2, with voice input handled by an integrated ASR model. An alternative approach replaced the NLI model with an NLP model while maintaining the same system. For evaluation separate Python code compared model outputs against expected results using metrics such as accuracy, confidence scores, execution time, and confusion matrices.

The performance of each model was evaluated using three main metrics: **accuracy, average confidence,** and **average execution time.** Accuracy measures the proportion of correctly classified sentences, where a prediction is considered correct if the model's top label matches the expected label:

Table 1. Commands with its corresponding proposed prompt.

#	Candidate Label	Suggested Prompt
	Status Command Set	
1	Check battery	Can you check battery status
2	Get mode	What mode is the drone currently in?
3	Check readiness	Is the drone ready to arm
	Basic Operations Command	
4	Arm	Please arm the drone
5	Disarm	Disarm the drone now
6	Set mode	Set the drone mode to "MODE"
7	Preflight calibration	Perform a preflight calibration
8	Soft reboot	Reboot the system softly
9	Read current mission	Can you read the current mission from the memory?
10	Load mission	Load the new mission into the drone
11	Set home altitude	Set the home altitude to x meters
12	Calibrate level	Calibrate the drone level
13	Calibrate compass	Calibrate the drone's compass
	Navigation Command Set	
14	Takeoff	Takeoff the drone
15	Takeoff to x alt	Takeoff to 10 m
16	Jump to waypoint number x	Jump to waypoint number 5
17	Go forward	Move the drone forward
18	Go backward	Move the drone backward
19	Stop	Stop the drone immediately
20	Resume mission	Resume the current mission
21	Go left	Move the drone to the left
22	Go right	Move the drone to the right
23	Change the heading to x angle	Change the heading to 45 deg
24	Climb to x altitude	Climb to 50 m
25	Descend to x altitude	Descend to 20 m altitude
26	Turn left	Turn left now
27	Turn right	Turn right now
	Payload Control Command	
28	Check camera readiness	Check if the camera is ready

(*continued*)

Table 1. (*continued*)

#	Candidate Label	Suggested Prompt
29	Center camera	Center the camera
30	Rotate camera left	Rotate camera to the left
31	Rotate camera right	Rotate camera to the right
32	Rotate camera back	Rotate the camera back
33	Rotate camera angle	Rotate the camera to a 90-deg angle
34	Look down	Point the camera downward
35	Pitch camera x angle	Pitch camera to 30 deg
36	Zoom in	Zoom in the camera
37	Zoom out	Zoom out the camera
38	Point camera to x loc	Point the camera to the specified location
39	Deliver package	Deliver the package at the drop-off point

$$accuracy = \frac{Number\ of\ Correct\ Predictions}{Total\ Number\ of\ Test\ Sentences} \tag{3}$$

Formally, for each test sentence i, let y_i be the expected label and $\hat{y}_i$ be the predicted label. Then the prediction is **correct** if $\hat{y}_i = y_i$ otherwise it is **incorrect.** The overall accuracy is computed as:

$$accuracy = \frac{1}{N} \sum\nolimits_{i=1}^{N} 1(\hat{y}_i = y_i) \tag{4}$$

where N is the total number of test sentences and $1(.)$ is the indicator function that equals 1 when the condition is true and 0 otherwise.

The **average confidence score** of a model is calculated as the mean of the top predicted label's probability across all test sentences:

$$average\ confidence = \frac{1}{N} \sum\nolimits_{i=1}^{N} s_i \tag{5}$$

where s_i is the time taken to classify sentence i. These metrics collectively evaluate the correctness, reliability, and efficiency of each NLP model in mapping natural language commands to UAV control actions.

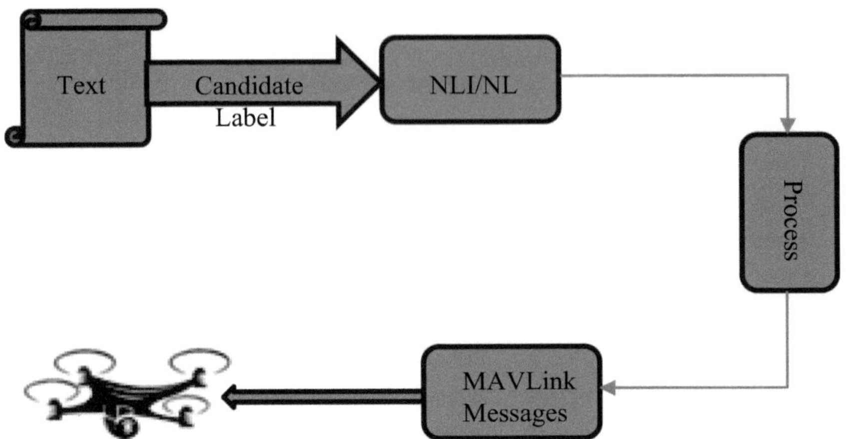

Fig. 2. Using NLI/NLP output to control the drone.

4   Results and Discussion

This section presents the experimental results and evaluates the performance of the proposed voice-controlled UAV system. The analysis covers the accuracy and efficiency of the ASR models, the effectiveness of NLI and NLP models in mapping voice commands to UAV actions, and the overall system performance in executing drone commands. Comparative evaluations are conducted using multiple metrics, including accuracy, confidence scores, execution time, and confusion matrices. The discussion interprets these findings, highlighting strengths, limitations, and potential improvements.

4.1   Automatic Speech Recognition (ASR) Results and Discussion

This section reports the evaluation of ASR models for transcribing UAV voice commands, aiming for high accuracy and low latency. The tested models include Google Speech Recognition, Whisper (Tiny, Base, Large), and Wav2Vec (Base, Large), evaluated with dataset described in Sects. 3.1.1 and 3.1.2 and results shown in Tabs. 2 and 3.

4.1.1   ASR Performance Analysis

Whisper Large achieved the highest accuracy for speaker 1 (93.54%, WER 0.06), followed by Whisper Base (84.36%) and Whisper Tiny (82.16%), while Google Speech Recognition performed poorly (48.91%) and Wav2Vec models reached 56.38%. For speaker 2, Whisper Base led (89.55%, WER 0.10), with Whisper Tiny (87.26%) and Whisper Large (85.61%) close behind; Google Speech Recognition was lowest (29.11%), and Wav2Vec2 moderate (73.99%).

In processing time, Whisper Tiny and Wav2Vec2 were fastest (≤ 1 min), Whisper Base required around 2.5 to 5 min approximately. Whisper Large took around between 70 and 80 min. Google Speech Recognition around 10 min with normal internet connection and with bad internet connection could exceed 90 min.

Overall, Whisper models offered the highest accuracy across accents, Wav2Vec balanced speed and accuracy for low latency use, and Whisper Base provided the best trade-off for real-time UAV voice control, while Whisper Large's slow speed limited its practicality.

Table 2. English Speaker 1.

Model	Avg. WER	Min WER	Max WER	Avg. CER	Min CER	Max CER	Std. WER	Std. CER	Acc %	Run time mins
Google Speech	0.51	0.28	0.73	0.41	0.16	0.67	0.10	0.11	48.91	13
Whisper Tiny	0.18	0.05	0.47	0.09	0.01	0.43	0.08	0.06	82.16	3.15
Whisper Base	0.16	0.03	0.45	0.08	0.01	0.43	0.07	0.06	84.36	4.6
Whisper Large	0.06	0.00	0.59	0.05	0.00	0.53	0.14	0.13	93.54	85
Wav2Vec Base	0.44	0.24	0.66	0.20	0.08	0.49	0.09	0.07	56.38	1.1
Wav2Vec2 Large	0.44	0.24	0.66	0.20	0.08	0.49	0.09	0.07	56.38	1.1

4.2 Natural Language Processing (NLP) and Natural Language Inference (NLI) Results and Discussion

This section presents the evaluation results of the NLI and NLP models used to classify UAV voice commands into predefined MAVLink functions. The study compared multiple NLI models—including Facebook/BART (Base and Large MNLI), Google/T5-Large, and Electra-Large-Discriminator—against GPT-4o-mini (OpenAI API, cloud-based NLP model) to determine the most effective approach for mapping user commands to drone actions.

Table 3. English Speaker 2.

Model	Avg. WER	Min WER	Max WER	Avg. CER	Min CER	Max CER	Std. WER	Std. CER	Acc %	Run time mins
Google Speech	0.71	0.39	0.89	0.60	0.31	0.83	0.12	0.12	29.11	10
Whisper Tiny	0.13	0.03	0.27	0.05	0.01	0.21	0.07	0.04	87.26	1
Whisper Base	0.10	0.03	0.27	0.03	0.01	0.08	0.07	0.02	89.55	2.5
Whisper Large	0.14	0.00	0.88	0.13	0.00	0.77	0.20	0.18	85.61	73
Wav2Vec Base	0.26	0.03	0.52	0.07	0.01	0.16	0.11	0.03	73.99	0.6
Wav2Vec2 Large	0.26	0.03	0.52	0.07	0.01	0.16	0.10	0.03	73.99	0.6

4.2.1 Model Performance Analysis

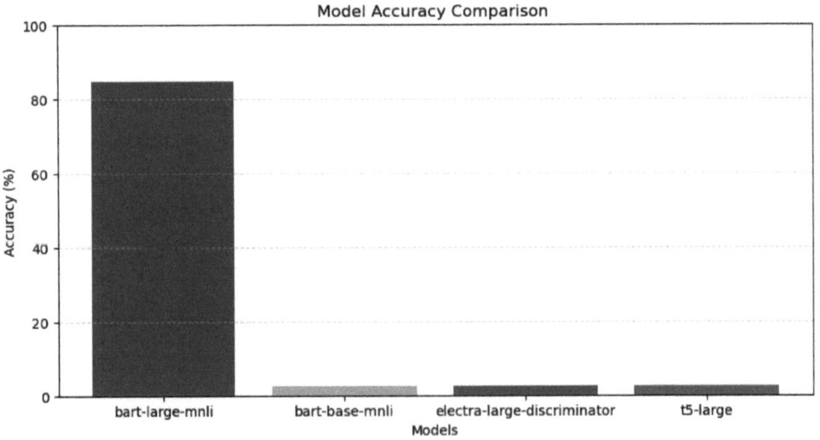

Fig. 3. Accuracy of models in mapping natural language to MAVLink function

The evaluation of NLI/NLP models for UAV command classification (Fig. 3) showed that BART-Large-MNLI achieved the highest accuracy (>80%), making it the most reliable zero-shot classifier. GPT-4o-mini followed with ~ 45% accuracy, indicating moderate generalization, while BART-Base-MNLI, Electra-Large-Discriminator, and T5-Large performed poorly.

Confidence analysis (Fig. 4) revealed that GPT-4o-mini produced the highest scores, though randomly assigned and thus unreliable. Among models providing valid scores, BART-Large-MNLI achieved the highest (~0.3), consistent with its superior accuracy.

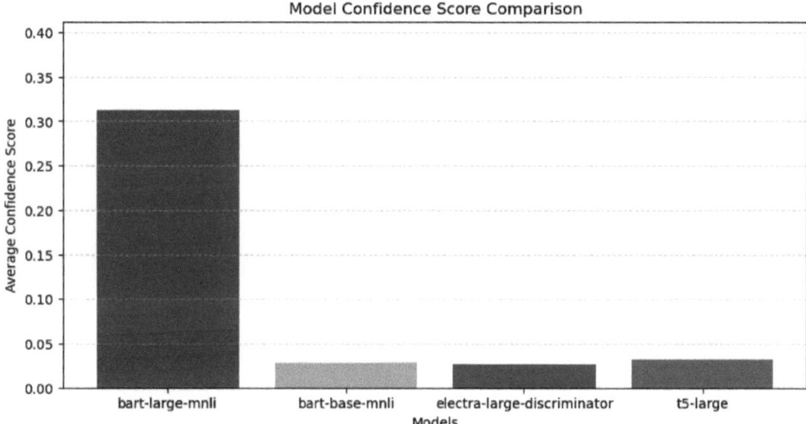

Fig. 4. Models' confidence level of mapping input natural language to MAVLink functions.

Inference time results (Fig. 5) indicating that T5-Large was slowest (>2 s per sentence) due to its text-to-text design, while GPT-4o-mini incurred delays from API latency. BART-Large-MNLI offered the best balance of accuracy and speed, making it most practical for real-time UAV command classification. Although BART-Base-MNLI and Electra-Large had the shortest inference time, their poor accuracy rendered them unsuitable.

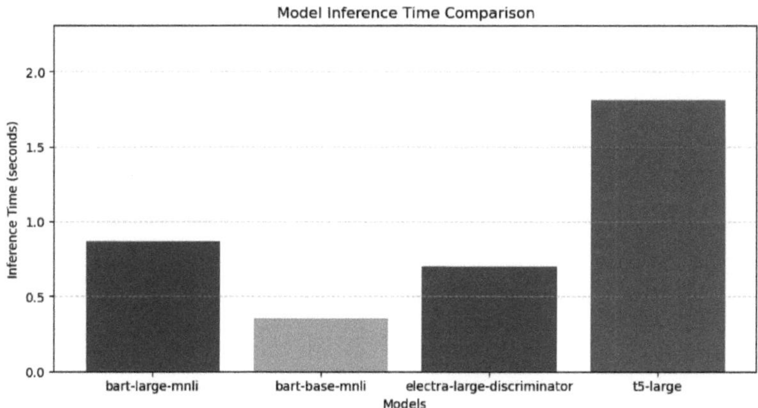

Fig. 5. Models' inference time comparison.

Confusion matrix analyses (Figs. 6, 7, 8, 9, and 10) confirmed that BART-Large-MNLI and GPT-4o-mini showed the strongest performance, with clear diagonal pattens and fewer misclassifications, while the other models exhibited significant errors and weak label alignment.

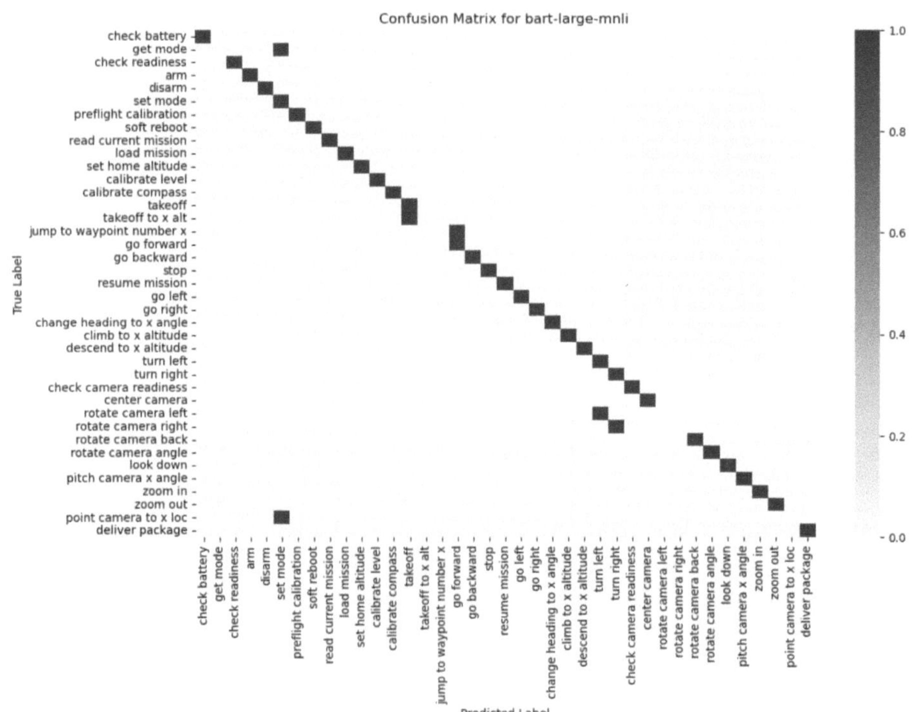

Fig. 6. Confusion matrix plot for bart-large-mnli.

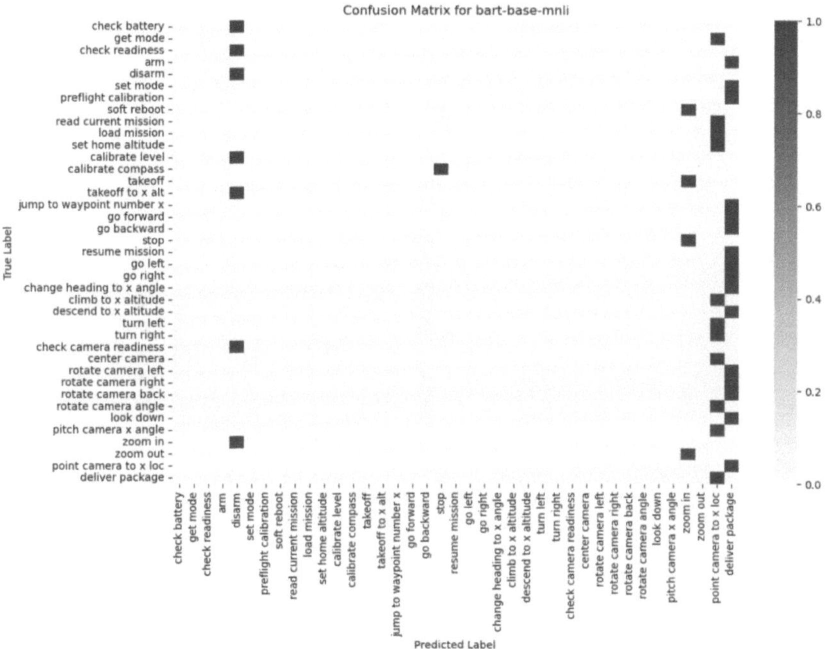

Fig. 7. Confusion matrix plot for bart-base-mnli model.

4.2.2 Discussion and Key Findings

BART-Large-MNLI proved to be the most effective model for zero-shot UAV command classification, offering the best balance between accuracy and inference speed. GPT-4o-mini, while exhibiting moderate accuracy, demonstrated strong generalization capabilities, though its confidence scores were randomized. In contrast, Electra and T5 models struggled to accurately map natural language commands to MAVLink functions, making them less effective for UAV command interpretation. Despite its lower accuracy, GPT-4o-mini remains a viable alternative for real-world UAV applications where flexibility in natural language interpretation is essential.

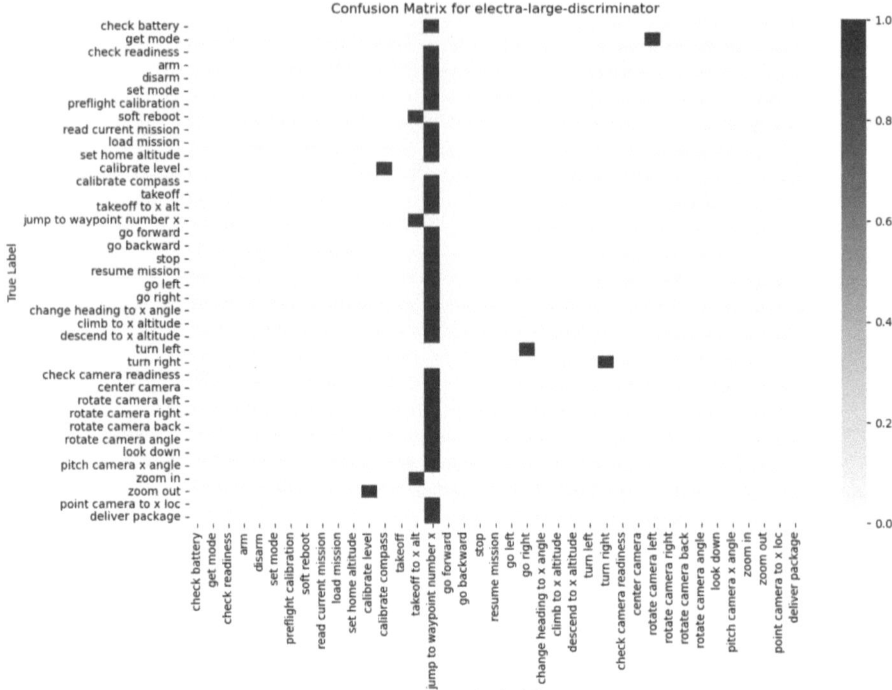

Fig. 8. Confusion matrix for electra-large-discriminator model.

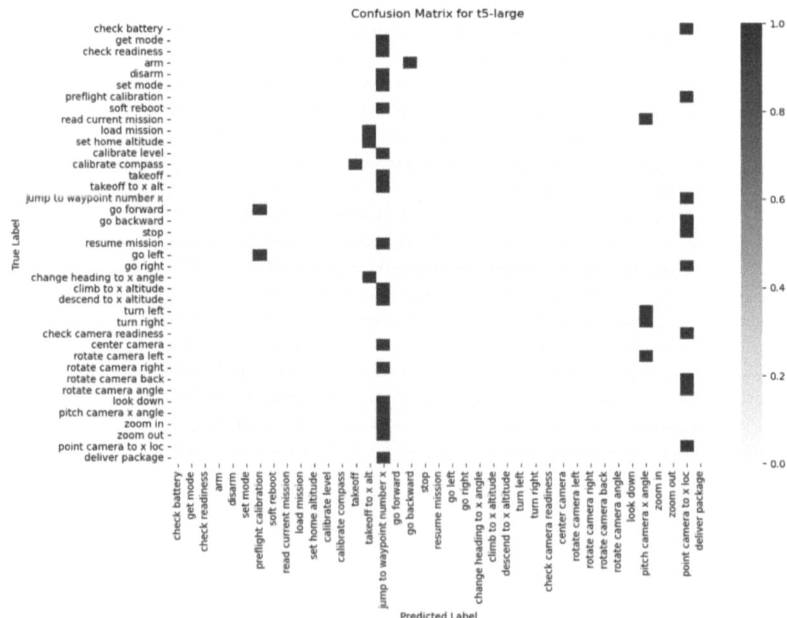

Fig. 9. Confusion matrix for t5-large model.

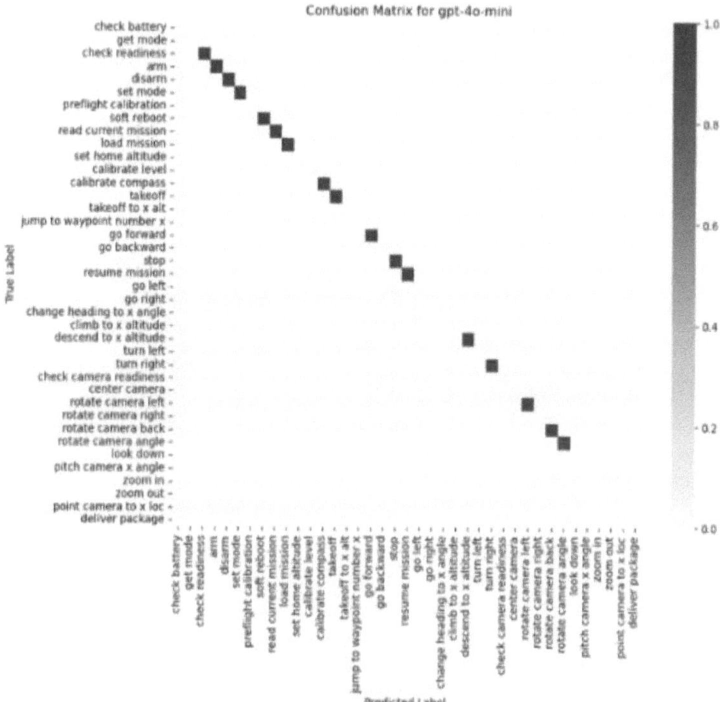

Fig. 10. Confusion matrix for OpenAI api with GPT-4o-mini model.

5 Conclusion

This research investigated voice-based UAV control by integrating ASR and NLP techniques, enabling flexible and context-aware drone operations. Whisper Base emerged as the most suitable ASR model due to its balance of accuracy and efficiency, while BART-Large-MNLI proved most effective for mapping natural language commands to UAV actions. In contrast, cloud-based solutions like Google Speech Recognition suffered from latency and accuracy issues, and GPT-4o-mini, though moderately effective, lacked robust classification capability.

Challenges remain, including vulnerability to noise and real-world testing. Future work should focus on noise cancellation, fine-tuning NLP/NLI models with larger datasets, importantly, conducting real-world tests in noisy environments and actual UAV deployments to validate performance in practical scenarios.

Acknowledgments. I sincerely thank Dr. Abdulrahman Altahhan for his continuous support, insightful feedback, and invaluable corrections, which were instrumental in refining the methodology, interpreting results, and shaping the overall direction of this research. His expertise and encouragement greatly contributed to the successful completion of this study. I am also deeply grateful to Dr. Zeeshan for his guidance in selecting the research topic and shaping the project proposal, ensuring a clear and structured foundation for this work.

Additionally, I acknowledge the use of GenAI tools, which played a crucial role in various stages of the project. GitHub Copilot (Microsoft), integrated with Edge Explorer add-ons, assisted in reviewing related work by summarizing key paragraphs and clarifying ambiguous text. ChatGPT (OpenAI) was instrumental in structuring the project proposal, refining ideas, and enhancing clarity (https://chatgpt.com/). Their contributions significantly supported the research process.

References

1. Bushnaq, O., Mishra, D., Natalizio, E., Akyildiz, I.: Unmanned aerial vehicles (UAVs) for disaster management (2022). https://doi.org/10.1016/B978-0-323-91166-5.00013-6
2. Škrinjar, J., Skorput, P., Jakara, M.: Application of unmanned aerial vehicles in logistic processes (2019). https://doi.org/10.1007/978-3-319-90893-9_43
3. Zhongli, L., Yinjie, C., Benyuan, L., Chengyu, C.,Xinwen, F.: Hovering, intelligence, monitoring, reconnaissance, surveillance, and tracking. In: Proceedings—IEEE INFOCOM, pp. 2219–2227 (2012)
4. Contreras, R., Ayala, A., Cruz, F.: Unmanned aerial vehicle control through domain-based automatic speech recognition, arxiv-cs- (2020). arXiv:2009.04215
5. Simoes, L., Rodrigues, L., Silva, R., Silva, G.: Evaluating voice command pipelines for drone control: from STT and LLM to direct classification and siamese networks, arxiv-cs-arxiv:2407 (2024)
6. Penmesta, L.B.A.V., Mohan Rao Kovvur, R., Kune, R.: Real time voice/speech command and control system (CCS) for unmanned aerial and ground vehicles on 4G cellular/GPRS network. 2023 Global conference on information technologies and communications (GCITC), Bangalore, India, pp. 1–8 (2023). https://doi.org/10.1109/GCITC60406.2023.10426146
7. Eruero, O.P., Okwu, M.O., Eric, F.O., Tartibu, L.K.: Cloud-based speech recognition for UAV control architecture in industry 4.0. 2024 International Conference on Artificial Intelligence, Big Data, Computing and Data Communication Systems (icABCD), Port Louis, Mauritius, pp. 1–8 (2024).https://doi.org/10.1109/icABCD62167.2024.10645268
8. Safie, S.I., Yunus, N.A.M.M.: Unmanned aerial vehicle (UAV) control through speech recognition. 2024 IEEE 10th International Conference on Smart Instrumentation, Measurement and Applications (ICSIMA), Bandung, Indonesia, pp. 191–195, (2024).https://doi.org/10.1109/ICSIMA62563.2024.10675578
9. Yapicioğlu, C., Dokur, Z., lmez, T.: Voice command recognition for drone control by deep neural networks on embedded system. 2021 8th International Conference on Electrical and Electronics Engineering (ICEEE), Antalya, Turkey, pp. 65–72 (2021).https://doi.org/10.1109/ICEEE52452.2021.9415964
10. Ambika, S.N, Renuka, K., Shifa Farook B., Sneha, P., Praveen S.: Designing of voice-controlled drone using BT-voice control for Arduino . JOAASR. 5(3) (2023)
11. Fayjie, A.R., Ramezani, A., Oualid, D., Lee, D.J.: Voice enabled smart drone control. 2017 Ninth International Conference on Ubiquitous and Future Networks (ICUFN), Milan, Italy, pp. 119–121 (2017).https://doi.org/10.1109/ICUFN.2017.7993759
12. Saumya K., Toshit B., Sumeet K., Disha G., Ravi M.V., Omkar, S.N..: A deep learning approach to speech based control of unmanned aerial vehicles (UAVs). In: Natarajan Meghanathan et al. (Eds): SAI, ICAITA, CSITA, ISPR, Signal 2018, pp. 19–30 (2018). https://doi.org/10.5121/csit.2018.81003.
13. Choutri, K., Lagha, M., Meshoul, S., Batouche, M., Kacel, Y., Mebarkia, N.: A multi-lingual speech recognition-based framework to human-drone interaction. Electronics 11(1829) (2022)

14. Tezza, D., Andujar, M.: The state-of-the-art of human-drone interaction: A survey. IEEE Access **7**, 167438–167454 (2019). https://doi.org/10.1109/ACCESS.2019.2953900
15. ROS 2 with SITL. https://ardupilot.org/dev/docs/ros2-sitl.html Accessed 20 Feb 2025
16. Ardupilot. https://github.com/ArduPilot/ardupilot/tree/master/Tools/ros2 Accessed 20 Feb 2025
17. Alec R., Jong Wook K., Tao X., Greg B., Christine M., Ilya S.: Robust speech recognition via large-scale weak supervision. OpenAI, San Francisco, CA 94110, USA
18. Baevski, A., Zhou, H., Mohamed, A., Auli, M.: wav2vec 2.0: A framework for self-supervised learning of speech representations. Preprint on arXiv (2020). arXiv:2006.11477
19. Vibhor J.: Speaker recognition audio dataset. https://www.kaggle.com/datasets/vjcalling/speaker-recognition-audio-dataset Accessed 25 Jan 2025
20. Oleh L.: Natural language Inference: An Overview. https://towardsdatascience.com/natural-language-inference-an-overview-57c0eecf6517/?utm_source=chatgpt.com Accessed 20 Feb 2025
21. Stryker, C. , Holdsworth, J.: What is NLP. https://www.ibm.com/think/topics/natural-language-processing?utm_source=chatgpt.com Accessed 20 Feb 2025
22. Lewis, M., Liu, Y., Goyal, N., Ghazvininejad, M., Mohamed, A., Levy, O., Stoyanov, V., Zettlemoyer, L.: BART: Denoising sequence-to-sequence pre-training for natural language generation, translation, and comprehension. Preprint on arXiv (2019). arXiv:1910.13461
23. Raffel, C., et al.: Exploring the limits of transfer learning with a unified text-to-text transformer. J. Mach. Learn. Res. **21**, 1–67 (2020)
24. Clark, K., Luong, M.-T., Le, Q. V., Manning, C. D.: ELECTRA: Pre-training text encoders as discriminators rather than generators. In: International Conference on Learning Representations (ICLR) (2020)
25. OpenAI.GPT-4 Technical Report. arXiv preprint (2024). arXiv:2303.08774v6

Neuro-Symbolic AI: Combining Neural and Symbolic AI for UK Syndromic Surveillance

Mercedes Arguello Casteleiro[1]([✉]), Nava Maroto[2], Maria Jesus Fernandez Prieto[3], Yuan Wei[4], Peter John Noble[5], Alan David Radford[5], and Goran Nenadic[1]

[1] Department of Computer Science, School of Engineering, University of Manchester, Manchester, UK
m.arguellocasteleiro@gmail.com
[2] Departamento de Lingüística, Universidad Politécnica de Madrid, Madrid, Spain
[3] Salford Languages, University of Salford, Salford, UK
[4] Civil Aviation Flight, University of China, Deyang, China
[5] SAVSNET, University of Liverpool, Liverpool, UK

Abstract. Gastrointestinal infections (GI) affect humans and animals. The symptoms of GI include mild fever (up to 39 °C temperature in humans) and vomiting. In the UK, the number of confirmed human laboratory reports for GI has increased from 2023 to 2025. In early 2020, there were ongoing concerns from veterinary practitioners and owners about a UK outbreak of GI affecting dogs (around 38 °C–39 °C is a dog's normal temperature). This paper investigates symbolic rule-based concept extraction for temperature and vomiting (useful for syndromic surveillance) from veterinary clinical narratives. To validate the symbolic approach proposed to build concept detectors, we used more than 1 million consults collected over 12 months from UK veterinary practices that supported the UK outbreak investigation of GI in dogs. The concept detectors we built leverage on traditional methods from symbolic Artificial intelligence (AI), exploiting domain specific knowledge. A state-of-the-art alternative to the concept detectors is Large Language Models (LLMs) from neural AI. However, LLMs have raised ethical concerns, such as data ownership and explainability. We explored the benefits of using the concept detectors to: (a) annotate datasets for customising (fine-tuning) open-source LLMs to detect mentions of temperature and vomiting; and (b) provide outcome explanations for LLM's predictions.

Keywords: Syndromic Surveillance · Natural Language Processing · Neuro-Symbolic AI · Large Language Models · Rule-based Clinical Concept Extraction

1 Introduction

Studying animals have fostered discoveries in medicine. Mice, rats and other small rodents are ideal candidates for laboratory experiments that are the backbone of biomedical research and comparative medicine studies [1]. Likewise, dogs and cats (a.k.a. companion animals) have also been used in scientific research from the early days of medicine [1]. Humans and dogs share over 350 diseases [1], and humans and cats share many cellular functions [1].

Human and veterinary medicine have adopted electronic health records (EHRs). In England, the National Health Service (NHS) has supported over 160 trusts with digital transformation, including the implementation of EHRs [2]. The UK National Health Service (NHS) has collected large-scale health data, which covers *"the entire medical history of tens of millions of patients over many decades"* [3]. However, there are privacy concerns to large-scale NHS data sharing projects [3], while de-identification requirements and regulation governing sharing animal records is less demanding even for millions of EHRs. The Veterinary Companion Animal Surveillance System (Vet-Compass) [4], and the Small Animal Veterinary Surveillance Network (SAVSNET) [5] are initiatives that: (a) collect millions of veterinary clinical narratives from UK veterinary practices; (b) study a range of diseases; and (c) perform disease monitoring and syndromic surveillance across UK using animal EHRs.

Syndromic surveillance can be defined as *"the process of collecting, analysing and interpreting health-related data to provide an early warning of human or veterinary public health threats, which require public health action"* [6]. The monitoring of non-specific indicators or symptoms, like fever (a.k.a. *'temperature elevated'* or *'pyrexia'*) and vomiting, can facilitate earlier detection of new and re-emerging threats to human and animal health. The UK Health Security Agency reported an increasing trend in the number of confirmed human laboratory reports for gastrointestinal infections (GI) from 2023 to the first quarter of 2025 [7]. This increase is based on data extracted from live surveillance systems, i.e. confirmed laboratory reports for Campylobacter spp. (from 60,055 reports in 2023 to 70,352 reports in 2024) [7] and Salmonella serovars (from 8,872 reports in 2023 to 10,388 reports in 2024) [7]. The symptoms of GI include mild fever and vomiting [8]. GI also affects companion animals, and there were ongoing concerns from UK veterinary practitioners and owners about a national outbreak of GI affecting dogs in early 2020 [9].

Syndromic surveillance offers opportunities for real-life deployment of Artificial Intelligence (AI), where Natural Language Processing (NLP) allows computers and digital devices to *"understand, interpret, generate, and transform text"* [10]. NLP may unlock clinically relevant information hidden in the millions of narratives from UK animal consults, providing translational opportunities for human healthcare.

Large Language Models (LLMs) have demonstrated exceptional performance in NLP tasks [11]. LLMs are deep learning models from Artificial Neural Network (ANN). LLMs are complex *"black-box"* systems [11]. Improving the transparency and explainability of LLMs is critical for downstream applications [11]. The literature distinguishes between rule-based approaches that are interpretable by design [12]; and deep learning approaches that need external eXplainable AI (XAI) [13]. In the past, the demand for solving *"black-box"* issues of ANNs motivated various rule extraction methods [14]. Rule-based approaches can provide outcome explanations of individual data instances [15], hence, fostering a human understanding of the LLM's predictions.

This paper explores the benefits of combining symbolic AI (symbolic rule-based concept extraction) with neural AI (open-source small-size LLMs). The benefits of our neuro-symbolic AI approach: (a) it can be run locally (e.g. computer with 16GB of

RAM), avoiding concerns of data ownership; and (b) the provision of explainability (outcome explanation from symbolic AI) for LLMs' predictions (neural AI).

1.1 Motivation: Challenges for Concept Extraction from Clinical Narratives

SAVSNET may receive 90K consults per month, and thus, concept extraction [16] (a NLP sequence labeling task) may alleviate veterinary clinicians from performing manual annotations that are labour-intensive and time-consuming. Table 1 and 2 illustrate respectively the manual annotation for temperature and vomiting, which is quite challenging, due to abundant shorthand and misspelling errors [17]. Negation detection [18] is important to determine if concepts mentioned in the text are absent.

Table 1. Illustrating the sampling process and manual sentence annotation for *temperature*.

Candidate token	Sentence with candidate token	Manual annotation for *temperature*
Temparature	**Temparature** 39.1 °C.	Mentioned
Temp	Resee couple of days to check **temp**/possibly check Ca.	Mentioned
T101.9	**T101.9** discuss bt results and poss early renal changes.	Mentioned
t	Had passed normal faeces in house overnight **t** normal.	Mentioned
T	**T** not taken but fine.	Negated
t	On abdo palp **t** much faces there	Not mentioned
T	Rx **T**-D and Aquadent Remove sutures - looking good.	Not mentioned
Pirexia	Only clinical signs **pirexia**.	Mentioned

Ambiguity is another challenge. *"T"* does not always refer to temperature (see Table 1), and likewise, the character *"v"* does not always refer to vomiting (see Table 2).

1.2 State-of-the-Art of Neural AI: GPT-4o Versus DeepSeek-R1

LLMs with Mixture-of-Experts (MoE) architectures, such as OpenAI's GPT-4o [19] or DeepSeek-R1 [20], are state-of-the-art models for NLP tasks. MoE architectures achieve faster performance during inference time. Figure 1 shows the responses from GPT-4o and DeepSeek-R1 to token classification with *"zero-shot"* prompting. Each prompt in Fig. 1 includes a sentence that appears in either Table 1 or Table 2.

The ethical concerns of incorporating LLMs in clinical practice increased after the arrival of DeepSeek-R1 from China [21]. Among the ethical concerns for LLMs in healthcare [21]: data ownership; reliability; transparency; explainability; and fairness.

Table 2. Illustrating the sampling process and manual sentence annotation for *vomiting*.

Candidate token	Sentence with candidate token	Manual annotation for *vomiting*
vomited	**Vomited** twice today.	Mentioned
vomting	No **vomting,** diarrhoea, coughing or sneezing noted.	Negated
vmit	Fresh blood in **vmit** and bloody jelly like diarrhoea.	Mentioned
v	adv continue another week of abs and re-ex at end of course if not **v** much better.	Not mentioned
v	Skin—**v** mild pyoderma—advise in summer use malaseb frequently.	Not mentioned
v+	Started to **v+** today also.	Mentioned
V	DUDE, no **V/D/C/S**.	Negated
wretcing	Been **wretcing** a little, mostly bile.	Mentioned

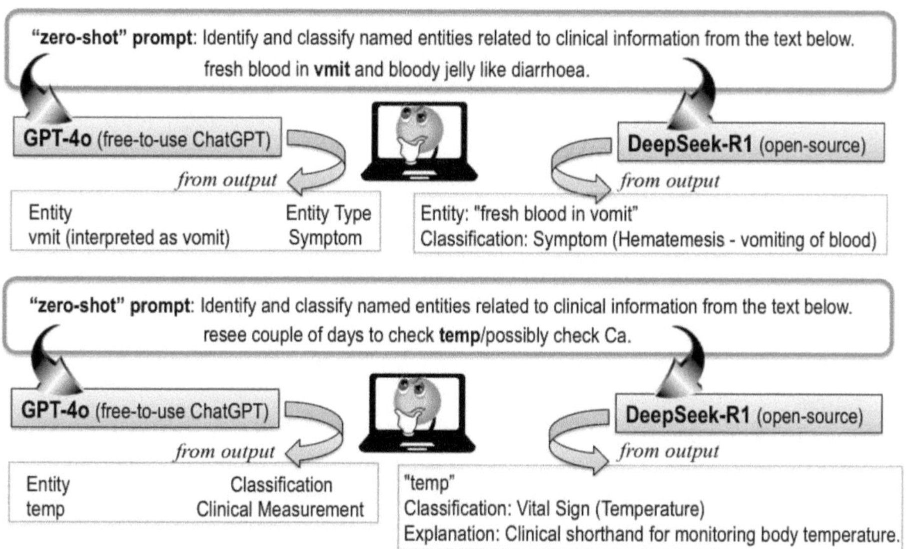

Fig. 1. Partial reproduction of the text generated (responses) from GPT-4o and DeepSeek-R1.

1.3 Related Work

Symbolic rule-based concept extraction aims to automatically extract pre-defined clinical concepts from text, including concept mention detection – Named Entity Recognition (NER) [16] – and concept encoding with structured clinical vocabulary sources, such as SNOMED CT (Systematized Medical Nomenclature for Medicine – Clinical Terminology) [22]. Although SNOMED CT is not used in UK veterinary practices, *"all NHS healthcare providers in England must now use SNOMED CT for capturing clinical terms within electronic patient record systems"* [22]. SNOMED CT can be the dictionary look-up of well-known clinical NLP tools, such as open-source cTAKES [23]. cTAKES combines rule-based and machine learning techniques [23].

LLMs can be fine-tuned. DeepTag, VetTag, and VetLLM are LLMs trained on veterinary notes labelled with SNOMED-CT codes [24]. They predict if each code of a predetermined set of SNOMED CT diagnosis codes applies to a clinical note.

Open-source general and domain-specific LLMs from [25] can be fine-tuned [26].

2 Clinical Language: Veterinary Versus Human Medicine

We start our study investigating the clinical language used in veterinary practice (i.e. large-scale textual data from SAVSNET), by making a comparison with the language used in clinical human medicine and common English corpora.

According to the idiom principle [27], words do not occur at random in a text and a large number of semi-preconstructed phrases exist. This study draws upon three large-scale datasets, each with millions of words: the British National Corpus (BNC) [28] of written and spoken British English with 100 million words; the human clinical dataset MIMIC-III (Medical Information Mart for Intensive Care version III) [29] with 2,083,112 of non-empty free text note events records, called here MIMIC-III Events; and a clinical dataset from SAVSNET [5] with 2,465,420 de-identified non-empty veterinary narratives, called here 2.5M SAVSNET.

Using white space, free-text can be broken into individual tokens, i.e. minimal language units. Table 3 shows some text analysis statistics that constitute a basic linguistic investigation following Sinclair [27]. For the study, we used the Natural Language Toolkit (NLTK) [30]. As in the BNC corpus [28], only tokens that have a frequency of occurrence greater than 9 were considered. The tokens with the highest frequency rank for Table 3 are: *'I'* in the BNC corpus; *'pt'* (i.e. 'patient') in the MIMIC-III Events; and *"owner"* in the 2.5M SAVSNET. All these three tokens relate to humans as 'pt' stands for 'patient'.

From Table 3 it can be observed that both 2.5M SAVSNET and MIMIC-III Events have an extended range of individual tokens in comparison with the BNC corpus, which exemplifies here a general English corpora. Clinical text is known for having [17]: abundant shorthand and misspellings as well as domain specific vocabularies. These properties may account for an abundance of different tokens.

The commonest n-grams collocations can be obtained by applying association metrics to score n-grams [31]. We used Pointwise Mutual Information (PMI) as in [31]. We created n-grams that include punctuation marks. We investigated the overlap among bigrams, trigrams, and quadrigrams imposing a 1K threshold to guarantee the commonest n-grams. The 1K threshold imposed seeks the n-grams obtained by applying PMI that appear in at least 1K clinical documents. Figure 2 depicts the overlap between n-grams (i.e. bigrams, trigrams, and quadrigrams) as Venn diagram for MIMIC-III Events (left hand-side) and 2.5M SAVSNET (right hand-side). Both Ven diagrams are quite similar.

Table 3. Text analysis statistics for the three large-scale datasets following Sinclair [27].

	BNC corpus	MIMIC-III Events	2.5M SAVSNET
Vocabulary total	7,557	282,311	83,430
Tokens total	447,125	390,386,756	80,926,481
Number of different tokens	7,726	282,488	83,607
Highest frequency rank	8,875	2,941,641	582,673
Average token length	6.73	8.82	7.45

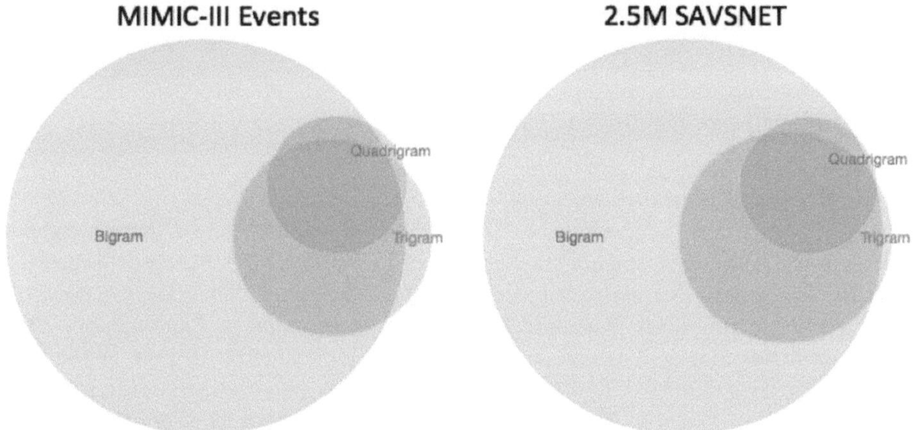

Fig. 2. Venn diagram showing the overlap between the commonest bigrams, trigrams, and quadrigrams for MIMIC-III Events and 2.5M SAVSNET.

The commonest trigram for 2.5M SAVSNET using PMI and the 1K threshold is *'next appointment is'*. In order to cross-compare the meaning of the commonest bigrams and trigrams from MIMIC-III Events and 2.5M SAVSNET, we need to map them first to existing clinical/biomedical categories. We considered the CLinical E-science Framework (CLEF) [32]. There are seven entity types (called here categories) within CLEF [32]: *Condition* (e.g. *'melanoma'*); *Intervention* (e.g. *'dissection'*); *Investigation* (e.g. *'biopsy'*); *Result* (e.g. *'normal'* or *'80 mg'*); *Drug or device* (e.g. 'co-codamol'); and *Locus* (e.g. 'second toe'). After some preliminary discussions with veterinary practitioners, the broad category *'Health Care Activity'* from Unified Medical Language System (UMLS) [33] was taken as more meaningfully useful and preferable than using the two CLEF categories *"Intervention"* and *"Investigation"*. The UMLS has more than one hundred broad categories called Semantic Types [33]. Indeed, the UMLS Semantic Type *"T058|Health Care Activity"* has three subtypes: *"T059|Laboratory Procedure"*; *"T060|Diagnostic Procedure"*; and *"T061|Therapeutic or Preventive Procedure"*.

Figure 3 displays the number of bigrams and trigrams for MIMIC-III Events and 2.5M SAVSNET according to nine categories: 4 categories from CLEF (i.e. *Condition;*

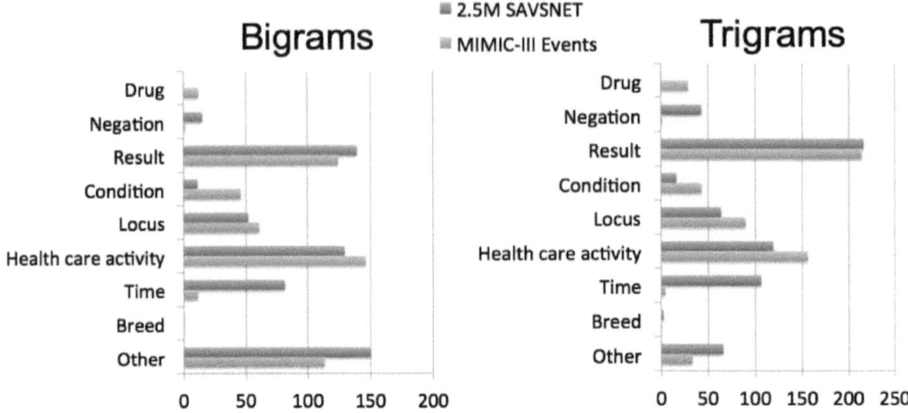

Fig. 3. Cross-comparing the meaning of the commonest 500 bigrams and 500 trigrams from both MIMIC-III Events and 2.5M SAVSNET according to 9 categories.

Result; Drug; and *Locus*); 1 category from UMLS Semantic Types (i.e. *'Health care activity'*); and 4 new categories (i.e. *Time; Negation; Breed;* and *Other*) created to accommodate some meaning not considered in CLEF and UMLS Semantic Types. The category *Time* captures time expressions in natural language. The category *Negation* is for explicit expressions in natural language that are negated. The category *Breed* is specific to veterinary. The category *Other* is only considered if none of the other categories apply.

Figure 3 considers 500 bigrams and 500 trigrams from both MIMIC-III Events and 2.5M SAVSNET. These n-grams are the commonest, using PMI association metric and imposing the 1K threshold. Although we cannot say that the meaning of the commonest bigrams and trigrams is the same for MIMIC-III Events and 2.5M SAVSNET, we can safely say that their meaning is closely similar when looking at the categories *'Result'* and *'Health care activity'*. Interestingly 2.5M SAVSNET has clearly more bigrams and trigrams for the category *Time*.

The communalities discovered (see Fig. 2 and 3) suggest the availability of translational opportunities between veterinary and medical sciences.

3 Symbolic AI: Rule-Based Clinical Concept Extraction

UMLS Metathesaurus concepts are mapped to SNOMED CT concepts [33]. We build clinical concept detectors that leverage on an ad hoc dictionary that re-uses UMLS Metathesaurus concepts. The ad hoc dictionary can be automatically converted into the dictionary look-up for cTAKES [23].

Using random sampling, SAVSNET team manually annotates datasets with less than 3K narratives for a single clinical concept. However, these datasets tend to be imbalanced and with no guarantees for representativeness of the concept of interest.

Figure 4 has an overview of our human-in-the-loop approach with 3-sequential steps A-B-C to build clinical concept detectors. We adhered to active learning [34]. Our approach for clinical concept extraction [16] used 2.5M SAVSNET. Building clinical concept detectors implies sequence labelling tasks (annotation of SAVSNET clinical narratives) and taking decisions about the inclusion or exclusion of candidate terms/concepts (i.e. candidate tokens) in an ad hoc dictionary that will be exploited by handcrafted rules. We consider different techniques for obtaining candidate tokens, which drive the sampling process.

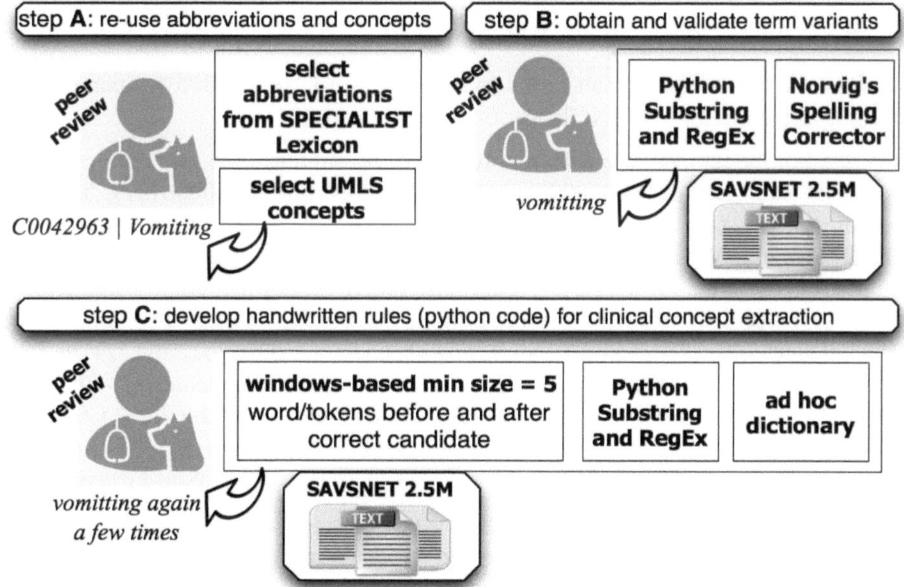

Fig. 4. Overview of the human-in-the-loop steps A-B-C to build clinical concept detectors.

Further details of the 3-sequential steps A-B-C to build clinical concept detectors:

Step A : The first step from Fig. 4 is selecting abbreviations from the SPECIALIST Lexicon [33] and UMLS Metathesaurus concepts [33]. For example, temperature can be abbreviated as "temp" and is relatable to physiological data – a body measurement or vital sign like 39.7 degrees Celsius – and clinical signs or symptoms like fever. Every UMLS Metathesaurus concept has a single Concept Unique Identifier (CUI) [33]. In this step A, the veterinary practitioner oversees the selection of abbreviations and CUIs.

Step B : The second step from Fig. 4 is obtaining candidate term variants, such as wrongly spelled terms, for the clinical concept of interest. This step uses two data-driven approaches with the 2.5M SAVSNET: Norvig's Spelling Corrector implemented in python [35]; and string-based regular expressions in python.

cTAKES [23] is a NLP clinical tool specifically tailored to clinical narratives. An outcome of step B is the creation of a new cTAKES lookup dictionary with the abbreviations and UMLS CUIs selected in step A, including now the term variants and wrong spellings for a clinical concept of interest from this step B.

Step C : The third step from Fig. 4 is also data-driven and uses the 2.5M SAVSNET. We configured string-based regular expressions in python that look for tokens (e.g. words or numbers) that co-occur in the same sentence before and after the candidate terms (context windows). Tokens that frequently co-occur with the correct candidate terms are included in the handwritten rules to perform the clinical concept extraction task, exploiting the dictionaries created in step B.

3.1 Exemplifying the Symbolic Rule-Based Clinical Concept Extraction

We illustrate below the human-in-the-loop steps A-B-C to develop temperature and vomiting detectors for SAVSNET.

Step A : For the temperature detector, the following abbreviations were selected: *'TR'* for *'rectal temperature'* (E0319097), *'TPR'* for *'temperature'* (E0060137), *'temp'* for *'temperature'* (E0060137), *'t'* for *'temperature'* (E0060137), *'TN'* for *'thermoneutral'* (E0321388), and *'NT'* for *'normothermic'* (E0043052). The last three abbreviations were empirically discarded for triggering some false positives. For the temperature detector, the concept *'O/E – temperature'* with CUI = C0587136, *'Rectal temperature'* with CUI = C0489749, *'Temperature normal'* with CUI = C0231262, and *'Fever'* with CUI = C0015967. For the vomiting detector, the concept *'Hematemesis'* with CUI = C0018926, *'Regurgitation'* with CUI = C2004489, *'Retching'* with CUI = C0232602, and *'Vomiting'* with CUI = C0042963.

Step B: Table 4 shows the number of candidate tokens obtained (third column) for various target tokens (second column). The last column of Table 4 shows the number of candidate tokens considered correct (i.e. term variants) and used by the temperature and vomiting detectors. An outcome of this step is a new cTAKES lookup dictionary created with 8 UMLS CUIs (the ones from the first step A) and 1,089 entries. We are excluding in this counting of entries the term variants and wrong spellings for the term "normal", which is a concept qualifier and not a clinical concept per se.

Step C : The co-occurring tokens act as context for the abbreviations and terms of the clinical concept of interest. For the temperature detector, some rules seek a numeric value with or without unit. The unit can be expressed in many different ways, such as: 'CC', 'celius', 'cels', 'celsius', 'degC', 'deg C', 'dgC', 'degF', 'deg F', 'dgF', 'deg', 'CF', 'GF', 'cp', 'oc', 'oic', 'tc', '°c', '°c', '°f', '°f', 'C', 'F'. For the vomiting detector, some rules consider time expressions, such as: 'occ', 'occaiosnally', 'occasionally', 'often', 'after', 'again', 'just', 'before', 'post', 'last', 'intermittent', 'weekly', 'daily', 'nightly', 'recurrence', 'recurred', 'episode', 'episodes'. Some other rules consider 'vomiting', 'diarrhoea', 'coughing', and 'sneezing' that may appear abbreviated as 'vdcs', as well as their combinations.

3.2 Explainability with Symbolic Rule-Based Clinical Concept Extraction

Explainability with clinical concept detectors means saying explicitly what appears in the text along with some context, i.e. providing the rationale for the concept detection.

Let's illustrate explainability with the temperature detector:

Table 4. Exemplifying how to obtain candidate term variants for clinical concepts.

Technique	Target token	Candidate token	Correct candidate token
Norvig's Spelling Corrector	Temperature	101	101
Norvig's Spelling Corrector	Normal	476	32
Norvig's Spelling Corrector	Hematemesis	18	17
Norvig's Spelling Corrector	Regurgitate	52	46
Norvig's Spelling Corrector	Regurgitation	54	51
Norvig's Spelling Corrector	Retch	391	15
Norvig's Spelling Corrector	Retching	198	59
Norvig's Spelling Corrector	Vomit	246	106
Norvig's Spelling Corrector	Vomiting	260	192
Python substring	Vom*	412	352

- The explanation *"temperature 38.2 [observation]"* means that *"temperature 38.2"* appears mentioned and it is interpreted as an *"observation"*, i.e. a value for temperature.
- The explanation *"39.2 [observation + unit]"* means that *"39.2"* appears mentioned along with a unit of measurement.
- The explanation *"pyrexia [finding]"* means *"pyrexia"* (a.k.a. fever) is mentioned and it is a finding (i.e. an interpretation of an observation).

Let's illustrate explainability with the vomiting detector:

- The explanation *"vomit/vomiting [negation before]"* means that negation appears before encountering in the text the term *"vomit"* or *"vomiting"* or any term variants or wrong spellings for them.
- The explanation *"retch/retching [negation before in neighboring words]"* means that negation appears in a 5 word window before encountering in the text the term *"retch"* or *"retching"* or any term variants or wrong spellings for them.
- The explanation *"v d [finding vdcs]"* means that *"vd"* appears mentioned and it may be part of the findings *'vomiting'*, *'diarrhoea'*, *'coughing'*, and *'sneezing'* that may appear abbreviated as *'vdcs'*.

3.3 Performance of Symbolic Rule-Based Clinical Concept Extraction

Figure 5 shows the manual annotations per sentence by the SAVSNET annotators A and B, considering 3 labels: *"not mentioned"*; *"mentioned"*; and *"negated"*. Figure 5 indicates some disagreement between the SAVSNET annotators A and B, suggesting that manual annotation proved difficult.

Figure 5 considers a *Temperature subset* with 254 sentences from 235 consultation narratives, i.e. a set of SAVSNET clinical consultation narratives manually annotated for *Temperature*. Figure 5 also considers a *Vomiting subset* with 512 sentences from 452 consultation narratives, which were manually annotated for *Vomiting*.

Figure 6 considers the *Temperature* and *Vomiting subsets* from Fig. 5. Figure 6 compares the output labels for the temperature detector (left hand-side) and vomiting detector (right hand-side) with: a) NER annotator from cTAKES (including negation annotators) using the new dictionary look-up; and b) the SAVSNET annotator B.

Table 5 has the standard NLP metrics of precision, recall, and F-measure [31] for the *Temperature* and *Vomiting subsets* from Fig. 5. For the temperature detector, we did not calculate the performance for the output label *"negation"* as the number of sentences is very scarce, lacking statistical significance.

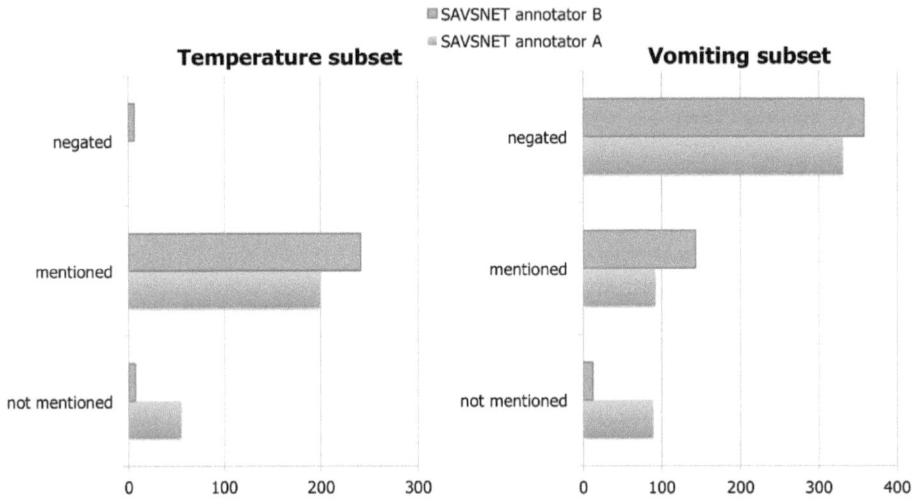

Fig. 5. Manual annotations per sentence by the SAVSNET annotators A and B.

3.4 Exemplifying UK Syndromic Surveillance: Outbreak of GI Affecting Dogs

Syndromic surveillance precedes diagnosis. Table 6 exemplifies the output of the temperature and vomiting detectors for syndromic surveillance over 12 months with new *"unseeing"* data, i.e. data outside of 2.5M SAVSNET.

Table 6 shows an increase in the number of the output label *"mentioned"* for both detectors in the months of January 2020–01 and February 2020–02 (cells with grey background). However, January and February (early 2020) have a lower number of consults than July 2019–07 (cells also highlighted with grey background).

The increase in mentioning *"temperature"* and *"vomiting"* suggested a possible UK outbreak of GI in dogs in early 2020 [9]. It is known that most dogs with GI will have *"intermittent episodes of vomiting and diarrhea"* [36], and *"a low-grade fever is also common"* [36]. A dog's normal body temperature is naturally higher than a human's.

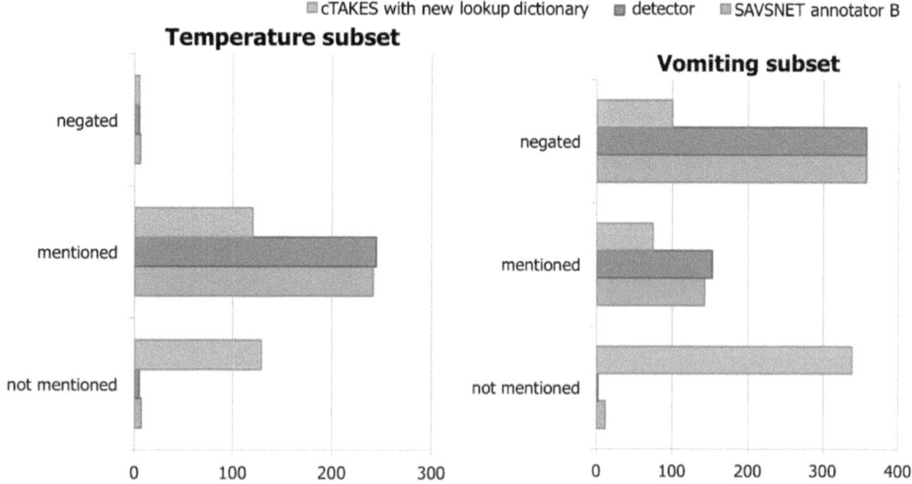

Fig. 6. Comparing manual annotations (i.e. SAVSNET annotator) with automatic annotations.

Table 5. Evaluation metrics to measure the performance of the clinical concept detectors.

Evaluation metric	Temperature detector: output "mentioned"	Vomiting detector: output "mentioned"	Vomiting detector: output "negated"
Precision	97.54	88.24	97.48
Recall	98.76	94.41	97.48
F-measure	98.14	91.22	97.48

4 Neural AI: Fine-Tuning Open-Source LLMs with LoRA

We fine-tuned (customised) open-source LLMs with Low-Rank Adaptation (LoRA) [37] with two new random datasets from 2.5M SAVSNET with 175 consults each. The *new Temperature dataset* has 1,505 sentences, and the *new Vomiting dataset* with 1,743 sentences. Each sentence has either the label 0 (meaning *"non mentioned"*) or label 1 (meaning *"mentioned"*). Hence, the task considered for concept detection is binary classification, using 3 general LLMs (BERT, RoBERTa, and multilingual BLOOM 560M) and 4 domain-specific (BioBERT, SciBERT, ClinicalBERT, and PubMedELECTRA) LLMs. All 7 LLMs are open-source LLMs available from [25].

The *new Temperature and Vomiting datasets* were automatically annotated with our concept detectors from symbolic AI and peer reviewed by biocurators (terminologists/linguists with experience in annotating biomedical/clinical text). Each dataset was split into train and test datasets. Table 7 and 8 has the performance for fine-tuning with LoRA 7 open-source LLMs (3 general and 4 biomedical/clinical LLMs).

Table 6. Output labels "mentioned" and "negated" for the Temperature detector (T detector) and the Vomiting detector (V detector) for syndromic surveillance over 12 months.

Month	Number of consults	T detector "mentioned"	T detector: "negated"	V detector: "mentioned"	V detector: "negated"
2019–03	75,377	9,591	118	4,081	9,324
2019–04	73,050	8,836	115	3,744	9,474
2019–05	76,606	9,075	120	3,815	10,217
2019–06	72,155	8,862	120	3,516	9,360
2019–07	89,705	10,749	138	4,219	11,469
2019–08	83,845	9,920	194	3,965	10,505
2019–09	73,230	8,570	263	3,499	9,222
2019–10	75,885	9,039	296	3,610	9,721
2019–11	71,363	8,521	290	3,793	8,906
2019–12	73,736	9,851	365	4,492	9,790
2020–01	81,404	12,172	257	6,069	11,685
2020–02	76,594	11,176	265	5,361	10,931

Table 7. Fine-tuning with LoRA [37] using the new *Temperature dataset* (175 consults).

Open-source LLM	Precision %	Recall %	F-measure %	Fine-tuning time minutes:seconds
BERT	98.85	93.75	96.08	01:02
RoBERTa	99.61	97.92	98.74	01:02
BLOOM_560m	96.56	93.36	94.87	01:18
BioBERT	99.22	95.83	97.44	00:39
SciBERT	97.52	97.52	97.52	00:38
ClinicalBERT	99.22	95.83	97.44	00:37
PubMedELECTRA	94.48	92.96	93.70	00:40

Table 8. Fine-tuning with LoRA [37] using the new *Vomiting dataset* (175 consults).

Open-source LLM	Precision %	Recall %	F-measure %	Fine-tuning time minutes:seconds
BERT	93.56	95.00	94.26	01:11
RoBERTa	97.67	97.67	97.67	01:12
BLOOM_560m	91.30	92.91	91.97	01:26
BioBERT	89.73	92.33	90.97	00:44
SciBERT	91.30	92.67	91.97	00:43
ClinicalBERT	93.56	95.00	94.26	00:44
PubMedELECTRA	88.27	92.00	89.99	00:45

5 Conclusions

GPT-4o and DeepSeek-R1 are state-of-the-art LLMs with ethical concerns, such as data ownership. We investigated a neuro-symbolic AI approach combining symbolic rule-based clinical concept extraction with open-source LLMs from neural AI. Our neuro-symbolic AI approach can be run locally (avoiding data ownership issues) and the concept detectors built can provide outcome explanations for LLMs' predictions.

References

1. Medical Advances. https://www.animalresearch.info/en/medical-advances
2. NHS: EHRs. https://hansard.parliament.uk/lords/2025-02-12/debates/1FD29B5E-0FA1-4C90-A99B-E2BB9A4C6CD0/NHSElectronicPatientRecordSystems
3. Better, broader, safer: using health data for research and analysis. https://www.gov.uk/government/publications/better-broader-safer-using-health-data-for-research-and-analysis
4. VetCompass. https://www.rvc.ac.uk/vetcompass
5. SAVSNET. https://www.liverpool.ac.uk/savsnet
6. UK Health Security Agency, Syndromic surveillance: systems and analyses. https://www.gov.uk/government/collections/syndromic-surveillance-systems-and-analyses
7. Gastrointestinal infections and outbreaks in England: 2023 to 2025. https://www.gov.uk/government/publications/gastrointestinal-infections-in-england/gastrointestinal-infections-and-outbreaks-in-england-2023-to-2025
8. Gastroenteritis. https://www.nhsinform.scot/illnesses-and-condition
9. Outbreak of gastrointestinal disease in dogs (2022) https://www.bsava.com/article/outbreak-of-gastrointestinal-disease-in-dogs/
10. 2025 AI index report. https://hai.stanford.edu/ai-index
11. Zhao H, et al.: Explainability for large language models: A survey. ATIST (2024)
12. Mosqueira RE, et al.: Human-in-the-loop machine learning: A state of the art. AI Rev (2023)
13. Gunning D, et al.: XAI—Explainable artificial intelligence. Science robotics (2019)
14. Garcez AD, et al.: Neural-symbolic computing: An effective methodology for principled integration of machine learning and reasoning. arXiv (2019)
15. Guidotti R, et al.: A survey of methods for explaining black box models. CSUR (2018)
16. Fu S, et al.: Clinical concept extraction: a methodology review. J. Biomed. Inform. (2020)

17. Kreimeyer K, et al.: Natural language processing systems for capturing and standardizing unstructured clinical information: a systematic review. J. Biomed. Inform. (2017)
18. Su Y, et al.: A Large Language Model to Detect Negated Expressions in Radiology Reports. JIIM. (2025)
19. OpenAI's GPT-4o. https://chatgpt.com/?model=gpt-4o
20. DeepSeek-R1. https://huggingface.co/deepseek-ai/DeepSeek-R1
21. Peng Y, et al.: From GPT to DeepSeek: significant gaps remain in realizing AI in healthcare. J. Biomed. Inform. (2025)
22. SNOMED CT. https://digital.nhs.uk/services/terminology-and-classifications/snomed-ct
23. cTAKES. https://ctakes.apache.org
24. Jiang Y, et al.: VetLLM: large language model for predicting diagnosis from veterinary notes. Pac Symp Biocomput. (2024)
25. Hugging face models. https://huggingface.co/models
26. Fine-tuning. https://huggingface.co/docs/transformers/en/training
27. Sinclair, J.: Corpus, concordance. Oxford University Press, Collocation. Oxford (1991)
28. The British National Corpus. http://www.natcorp.ox.ac.uk
29. MIMIC-III Clinical Database. https://physionet.org/content/mimiciii/1.4/
30. Natural Language Toolkit. https://www.nltk.org
31. Manning CD, et al.: Foundations of statistical natural language processing. MIT (1999)
32. Roberts A, et al.: Building a semantically annotated corpus of clinical texts. J. Biomed. Inform. (2009)
33. UMLS Knowledge Sources. https://www.nlm.nih.gov/research/umls
34. Settles, B.: Active learning literature survey. Computer Sciences Technical Report (2009)
35. Norvig's Spelling Corrector. https://norvig.com/spell-correct.html
36. GI dogs. https://vcahospitals.com/know-your-pet/gastroenteritis-in-dogs
37. Hu EJ, et al.: Lora: low-rank adaptation of large language models. ICLR (2022)

Bi-Resolution: A Logic Reasoning Enhancement Method for Large Language Models Based on Resolution and Bidirectional Reasoning Fusion

Yifei Wang[1(✉)] and Yixiang Chen[1,2]

[1] National Engineering Research Center of Trustworthy Embedded Software, East China Normal University Software Engineering Institute, Shanghai 200062, China
`51275902087@stu.ecnu.edu.cn`, `chenyx61@aliyun.com`
[2] Shanghai Normal University TIANHUA College, Shanghai, China

Abstract. In recent years, large language model technology has been widely used, but its reasoning ability still has significant limitations. Especially when dealing with more complex logical reasoning problems, the accuracy of large language model reasoning is often unable to meet the requirements, and the resolution method can better ensure the accuracy of reasoning. In this paper, we propose Bi-Resolution, a novel method for reasoning about large language models. We introduce bidirectional reasoning into the improved resolution method and implement an automated reasoning process based on the generation of large language models through the design of prompt words. Technically, Bi-Resolution first converts the natural language problem into a symbolic representation of first-order logic, and selects the corresponding version of resolution algorithm according to the predicted reasoning result. This method can help the large language model to more accurately judge the reasoning problem with the conclusion of "not entirely true and not entirely false". In the process of resolution, the idea of bidirectional reasoning is used to instantiate the constraint variables, which removes the redundant conditions in the reasoning problem and reduces the complexity of reasoning. We conducted experiments on the FOLIO dataset, and the results show that the Bi-Resolution architecture successfully improves the accuracy of large language model reasoning.

Keywords: Large language models · Logical reasoning · Resolution Method · Bidirectional Reasoning · Prompt Engineering

1 Introduction

Since 2017, the technology of large language models based on the Transformer architecture has made breakthrough progress [1]. Models with billions of parameters, such as OpenAI's GPT-4 [2] and DeepSeek's Deepsee-R1 [3], have demonstrated strong semantic understanding and text generation capabilities through

M. Bramer and F. Stahl (Eds.): SGAI-AI 2025, LNAI 16302, pp. 285–298, 2026.
https://doi.org/10.1007/978-3-032-11442-6_20

self-supervised learning with massive data, and have been widely applied [4]. However, large language models still have significant shortcomings in complex logical reasoning tasks [5], and the insufficiency of reasoning accuracy has become a key bottleneck restricting their application in fields with high accuracy requirements [6].

Existing empirical studies consistently show that LLMS struggle to maintain high accuracy when solving problems that require precise symbolic manipulation and rigorous logical reasoning [7]. Logical reasoning, especially in the context of first-order logic (FOL), requires a level of precision and systematicity that goes beyond the pattern-matching and associative capabilities of LLMs. When dealing with complex logical problems, such as those involving multi-step inference, quantifiers, and nested logical structures, LLMs often struggle to maintain high accuracy [8]. This limitation is particularly evident in tasks that require the evaluation of partial correctness of statements. The inherent fuzziness of neural sequence models, which are designed to generate fluent text rather than perform truth-preserving symbolic manipulations, makes it difficult for them to handle the rigors of formal logic [9].

The limitations of LLMs in logical reasoning are not only of theoretical importance, but also have a profound impact in several practical application fields with high accuracy requirements. For example, in the field of medical diagnosis, medical diagnosis not only needs to extract key information from a large amount of patient data, but also needs to perform accurate logical reasoning based on this information to determine the most likely disease diagnosis [10]. Accurate logical reasoning is crucial for analyzing medical record data, identifying disease patterns, and formulating treatment plans. In legal analysis, logical reasoning is key to understanding and applying legal principles, which help legal professionals evaluate evidence, construct arguments, and predict the likely outcome of a case [11]. In these domains, the accuracy of LLMs logical reasoning is directly related to the quality and reliability of decisions.

To bridge this gap, researchers have explored a variety of neuro-symbolic strategies. Chain-of-Thought prompting encourages models to produce intermediate reasoning steps in natural language [12], and self-consistency decoding aggregates multiple solution trajectories to improve reliability [13]. Program-aided approaches translate natural-language problems into executable code, leveraging external interpreters to guarantee correctness [14]. While these methods often improve performance on arithmetic or algorithmic benchmarks, they rarely target the full expressiveness of first-order logic, and they seldom exploit the decades-old corpus of automated reasoning techniques—most notably the *resolution principle*—that forms the backbone of modern theorem provers.

Resolution, introduced by Robinson in 1965 [15]. In 2010, Russell improved on it and designed the resolution refutation method [16]. It operates by systematically constructing refutation proofs: given an unsatisfiable set of clauses, repeated application of the resolution rule eventually yields the empty clause, thereby confirming unsatisfiability. Because resolution is refutationally complete and offers clear notions of redundancy elimination, it provides a principled framework within which to embed neural guidance while preserving soundness. Yet, direct application of resolution inside an LLM pipeline is non-trivial. First, the search space grows super-quadratically with the number of predicate symbols, quickly exceeding the context window limits of contemporary models. Second, resolution's reliance on unification and variable instantiation demands precise symbolic manipulations that neural token generators are not naturally inclined to perform. Finally, classical resolution is unidirectional—working solely toward contradiction—whereas many real-world entailment queries admit more nuanced truth values such as "partially correct" or "unknown."

In this paper, we present Bi-Resolution, a novel framework that marries the rigor of resolution with the flexibility of large language models through a carefully designed, fully automated prompting pipeline. Bi-Resolution introduces a *bidirectional reasoning* paradigm that allows the model to explore both forward inference directions on precondition and backward inference directions on consequence [17], guided exclusively by prompts and without any external symbolic solver.

2   Related Work

The limitations of LLMs in logical reasoning are not just theoretical; they have practical implications for a wide range of applications. To address these challenges, researchers have explored various strategies to enhance the logical reasoning capabilities of LLMs.

Existing theoretical analyses have shown that large language models have the potential to perform logical reasoning in formal languages represented by logical symbols [18]. To reduce hallucinations and improve the fidelity of large language models, previous studies mainly enhanced the reasoning process of large language models through step-by-step reasoning paradigms [19]. Current research on symbolic reasoning also provides a new idea. By leveraging existing mature symbolic logical reasoning rules, the accuracy of model predictions can be further improved. The research team from Stanford University proposed the CoT [12] technology. This technology guides large language models to imitate the reasoning process by including step-by-step reasoning examples in the prompts, significantly improving the performance of the models in symbolic reasoning tasks. Based on CoT, the Xu team from the National University of Singapore proposed a framework called SymbCoT [20], which integrates symbolic expressions and logical rules with CoT prompts. It first translates the natural language context into a symbolic format, then formulates a step-by-step problem-solving plan based on symbolic logical rules, and finally checks the accuracy of the translation and reasoning chain through a validator, achieving accurate logical reasoning. This method has achieved good performance in both logical consistency and reasoning accuracy, but such methods are essentially unidirectional forward searches, and the specific reasoning paths are uncontrollable, leaving room for improvement.

To improve the inference accuracy of large language models, the team led by Zhou proposed a new framework called GFaiR [21], which is based on the idea of deep learning and introduces the idea of resolution refutation in the training of Transformer to improve the mechanism of premise selection and final result verification in reasoning problems. Through modules such as pre-selectors, post-selectors, and verifiers, it reduces hallucinations and improves the accuracy of reasoning, confirming the feasibility of enhancing the reasoning accuracy of large language models through the resolution refutation method.

In addition, since human reasoning processes for complex logical problems are often bidirectional, that is, they both deduce intermediate conclusions from conditions and trace necessary conditions from the goal, and narrow the solution space by eliminating contradictory hypotheses, this also provides a new idea for our research. The Liu team from City University of Hong Kong proposed a bidirectional reasoning framework called AutoChainer [22], which adopts a bidirectional chaining method, combining the advantages of forward chaining and backward chaining. Experiments have shown that AutoChainer improves the accuracy of intermediate proof steps and reduces the average number of reasoning calls required in the reasoning process through this method, achieving more efficient and accurate reasoning.This provides a reference for the feasibility of applying the resolution method to the inference task of large language models.This experiment provides data support for us to improve the reasoning process of large model by using the idea of bidirectional reasoning.

In order to further improve the accuracy of large language model in complex reasoning, this paper proposes Bi-Resolution, a reasoning method based on large language model that combines resolution method and bidirectional reasoning thinking, aiming to achieve high accuracy automatic reasoning of large language model through standardized prompt design. This paper uses the resolution method and reverse resolution method to judge three possible reasoning results, and implements an automated reasoning process completely based on the generation of large language models through the iterative execution of five modules: translation, preliminary reasoning, format conversion, cross-set resolution, and intra-set resolution. We tested Bi-Resolution on large language models on the FOLIO dataset, and the experimental results show that the accuracy of large language model inference is significantly improved, thus demonstrating the effectiveness of our method.

3   Methodology

In this section, we introduce a new reasoning architecture, Bi-Resolution, which enhances the reasoning ability of large language models by designing prompt words to guide them to use the improved resolution method to solve given logical reasoning problems, and simultaneously introduces a bidirectional reasoning approach to simplify the resolution process.Figure 1 shows an example of solving a problem using Bi-Resolution.

3.1   Improved Resolution Method

Our logical reasoning problem mainly consists of two parts: a set of premises $P = \{p_1, p_2, \ldots, p_n\}$, where each p_i represents a logical statement, and a conclusion

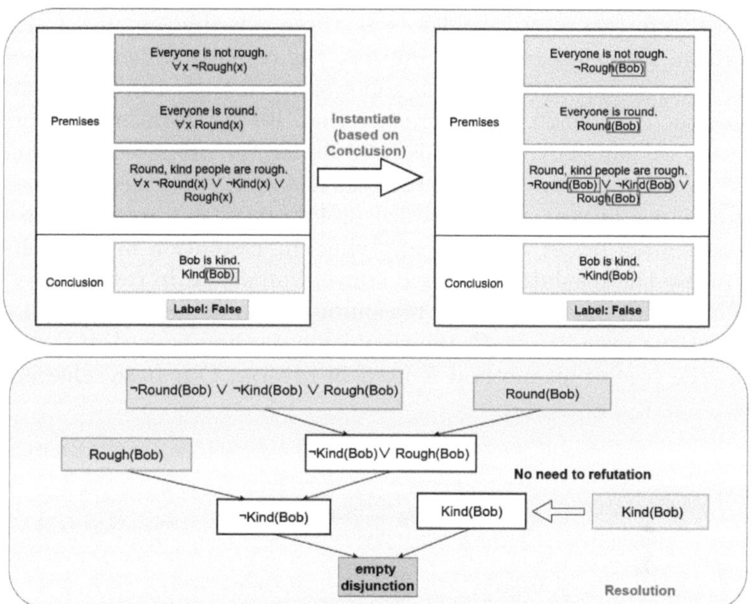

Fig. 1. Example of Bi-Resolution Solving Problems.

C whose truth value needs to be determined. The goal of Bi-Resolution is to determine the truth value of the given conclusion C under the set of premises P through logical reasoning. Specifically, there are three possible outcomes for the truth value of conclusion C: if C can be deduced from the premises P, it is marked as True; if the negation of C can be deduced, it is marked as False; if the premises cannot determine whether C is true or false, it is marked as Uncertain.

The resolution rule is a method in predicate logic used to eliminate complementary propositions and generate new clauses. This rule combines two clauses containing complementary propositions to generate a new clause. In predicate logic, the generalized resolution rule can be formally expressed as follows: C_1 and C_2 are both simple disjunctions, A is an atomic proposition. Suppose two clauses $C_3 = A \vee C_1$ and $C_4 = \neg A \vee C_2$ contain the atomic proposition A and its negation, respectively. Then, a new clause can be generated through the resolution rule, and the resolution result is denoted as $\text{Res}(C_3, C_4)$, which is:

$$\text{Res}(C_3, C_4) = C_1 \vee C_2 \tag{1}$$

The process of using the resolution method to prove that conclusion C is true is as follows: Merge the negation of C, $\neg C$, into the premise set P, and use the resolution rule to resolve the clauses in the clause set. At each step, the new resolved clause is added to the clause set. This process is iterated and repeated. If the resolution result in a step is an empty disjunction (usually denoted by λ), it indicates that there is a contradiction in the clause set, and by proof by contradiction, it can be concluded that C is true.

However, our reasoning problem has three possible outcomes: true, false, and uncertain. Therefore, we must improve the resolution method to match our task. The specific improvement is as follows: We modify the resolution method by merging the conclusion C itself rather than its negation into the premise set P. This way, we can prove that C is false under the premise set P.Then it can be proved in the same way that if the conclusion C is neither true nor false, it is uncertain. In addition, we introduce preliminary reasoning, which conducts ordinary reasoning before formally applying the resolution method, and selects whether to use the resolution method conventionally or in reverse based on the reasoning result. If the preliminary reasoning result shows that the conclusion C is true under the premise set P, the resolution method is used; if the conclusion C is false, the resolution method is used in reverse. Our basic idea is shown in Fig. 2.

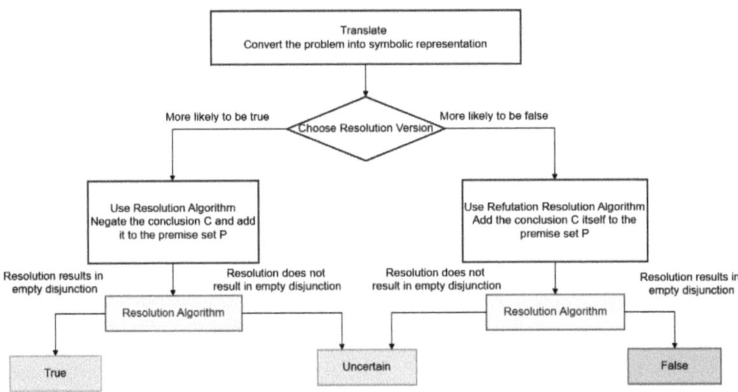

Fig. 2. Schematic diagram of the idea of the resolution method.

3.2   Introduction of Bidirectional Inference

Bidirectional inference is a hybrid strategy that combines forward inference and backward inference. We innovatively integrate the bidirectional inference thinking into the resolution method, breaking through the limitations of unidirectional chain inference.

We apply the idea of bidirectional inference in the instantiation process of universal quantifier constrained variables in the resolution method. In forward inference, the model starts from the initial condition set $\{P_1, P_2, \ldots, P_n\}$, simplifies the conditions using inference rules R, and gradually generates the intermediate conclusion set $\{I_1, I_2, \ldots, I_m\}$. Then, for the instantiation of universal quantifier constrained variables, it should cover all possible instantiation cases as much as possible, but this will lead to redundant conditions and increase the consumption of inference resources. In backward inference, the system constructs the necessary condition set $\{N_1, N_2, \ldots, N_k\}$ that the target conclusion C needs to satisfy. The purpose of this process is to clarify the necessary conditions for the conclusion to hold. When instantiating, the most suitable instantiation method for conclusion C should be chosen, but this may lead to insufficient conditions during the inference process. In the bidirectional inference process, forward inference and backward inference are carried out simultaneously. First, forward inference is performed to simplify the premises into simple disjunctive forms, and then backward inference is conducted to select the most suitable objects for instantiation based on the conclusion, obtaining the intermediate conclusion set $\{I_1, I_2, \ldots, I_m\}$. Then, conventional forward inference can be performed. As described above, we have implemented a process of bidirectional reasoning, the complete workflow of which is depicted in Figure 3.

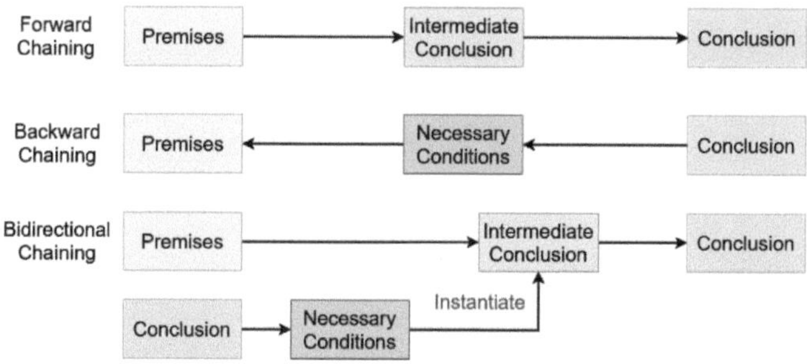

Fig. 3. Schematic diagram of the bidirectional reasoning idea.

To summarize, we obtain the Bi-Resolution algorithm. First, construct a simple disjunctive set S of the premises and the conclusion itself, and build three clause sets. S_0 stores the processed clauses, S_1 stores the clauses to be processed currently, and S_2 stores the newly generated clauses. In each round, cross-set resolution is performed first, traversing the clause pairs (C_1, C_2) in S_0 and S_1. If they can be resolved, a new clause $\mathrm{Res}(C_1, C_2)$ is generated. Then, internal set resolution is carried out, traversing the clause pairs (C_1, C_2) within S_1 and repeating the above resolution operation. If an empty clause (λ) is generated during this process, it indicates that the premises entail the negation of the conclusion, and False is output. If S_2 is not empty, update S_0 and S_1 and continue the loop. If S_2 is empty, it indicates that no new clauses can be generated. Merge all clauses into S_0 and check if the conclusion C is explicitly true, that is, whether the conditions in S_0 can directly lead to the conclusion C. If it can be derived, output True; otherwise, output Uncertain. The resolution algorithm is as follows. The content of the backward resolution algorithm is similar to the resolution method. Just add the conclusion C to the premise set, and when the resolution result is empty, output False. If the resolution result is never empty, switch to the resolution algorithm. After further introducing the idea of bidirectional inference, our resolution algorithm is as follows.

Algorithm 1: Reasoning with Resolution Rule

Input: A set of premises $P = \{p_1, p_2, \ldots, p_n\}$ expressed in first-order logic symbols and the negation of the conclusion $\neg C$.

Output: A judgment on whether the conclusion C holds under the premise set P. Answer "True" if C is true, "False" if C is false, and "Uncertain" if it is difficult to determine the truth value of C.

1 Let $S = \{p_1, p_2, \ldots, p_n, \neg C\}$ be the set of each premise p_i in P and the conclusion C;

2 Convert each sub-expression in S into standard form;

3 Initialize: $S_0 \leftarrow \emptyset$, $S_2 \leftarrow \emptyset$, $S_1 \leftarrow \{$all simple disjunctive expressions in $S\}$;

4 **for** $C_1 \in S_0$ *and* $C_2 \in S_1$ **do**

5   **if** C_1 *and* C_2 *can be resolved* **then**

6   Calculate $C \leftarrow \mathrm{Res}(C_1, C_2)$;

7   **if** $C = \lambda$ **then**

8   Output "True" and end this algorithm;

9   **end**

10   **if** $C \notin S_0$ *and* $C \notin S_1$ **then**

11             $S_2 \leftarrow S_2 \cup \{C\}$;

12   **end**

13   **end**

14 **end**

15 **for** $C_1 \in S_1, C_2 \in S_1$ *and* $C_1 \neq C_2$ **do**

16   **if** C_1 *and* C_2 *can be resolved* **then**

17   Calculate $C \leftarrow \mathrm{Res}(C_1, C_2)$;

18   **if** $C = \lambda$ **then**

19   Output "True", and end this algorithm ;

20   **end**

21   **if** $C \notin S_0$ *and* $C \notin S_1$ *and* $C \notin S_2$ **then**

22             $S_2 \leftarrow S_2 \cup \{C\}$;

23   **end**

24   **end**

25 **end**

26 **if** $S_2 = \emptyset$ **then**

27   Apply the "reverse resolution method" and the algorithm ends;

28 **else**

29     $S_0 \leftarrow S_0 \cup S_1$, $S_1 \leftarrow S_2$, $S_2 \leftarrow \emptyset$, go to step 3;

30 **end**

---

4 Prompt Design

To address the aforementioned issues, this paper proposes a method to enhance the reasoning ability of large language models based on prompt engineering.

Specifically, Bi-Resolution consists of five modules, each of which generates results by providing prompts to the large language model.

Translation Module.Resolution can only be applied to problems represented in logical symbols. This module is used to convert problems described in natural language into symbolic representations in First-Order Logic (FOL). The prompts for this part are designed based on the SymbCot [20] article.

Preliminary Reasoning Module.Before applying resolution, simple reasoning is conducted to determine whether to use the conventional resolution or the reverse resolution based on the reasoning results. If the preliminary reasoning predicts that the conclusion C is true under the premise set P, the resolution is used; if it predicts that C is false, the reverse resolution is used; if it predicts that C is unknown, both the resolution and the reverse resolution are applied. The prompts for this part are designed based on the SymbCoT article.

Format Conversion Module.This module converts premises into simple conjunctive normal form or unit clauses, mainly consisting of three steps. First, it uniformly represents symbols by converting all operation symbols into disjunction ($\vee$), conjunction ($\wedge$), and negation ($\neg$). Then, it processes constrained variables by Skolemizing existential quantifier constrained variables and instantiating universal quantifier constrained variables based on the conclusion using the idea of bidirectional resolution. Finally, it uniformly represents the form by converting each premise into conjunctive normal form and splitting it into basic disjunctive clauses or unit clauses.The following is an example to facilitate understanding.

■ **Input:**
<Premises:>
1. Striker(robert)
2. $\forall$x (Striker(x) $\rightarrow$ SoccerPlayer(x))
3. Left(robert, bayern)
4. $\forall$x $\forall$y (Left(x, y) $\rightarrow$ $\neg$PlaysFor(x, y))
<Conclusion:>
- PlaysFor(robert, bayern)

■ **Output:**
Since the prediction result is false, the conclusion C itself is selected to be added to the premise set to generate the initial set of clauses. Added as a new premise:
- Premise 5: PlaysFor(robert, bayern)
Step 1: Unify symbols
- Premise 2: $\forall x(\text{Striker}(x) \rightarrow \text{SoccerPlayer}(x))$
Equivalent to $\forall x(\neg\text{Striker}(x) \vee \text{SoccerPlayer}(x))$
- Premise 4: $\forall x\forall y(\text{Left}(x, y) \rightarrow \neg\text{PlaysFor}(x, y))$
Equivalent to $\forall x\forall y(\neg\text{Left}(x, y) \vee \neg\text{PlaysFor}(x, y))$
Step 2: Instantiate quantifiers with constants
Constants: from conclusion PlaysFor(robert, bayern). Replace variables:
- Premise 4 (instantiated with $x = $ robert, $y = $ bayern):

$\neg$Left(robert, bayern) $\vee$ $\neg$PlaysFor(robert, bayern)
- Premise 2 (instantiated with $x =$ robert):
$\neg$Striker(robert) $\vee$ SoccerPlayer(robert)
Step 3: Convert premises to clauses (CNF) and Simplify symbols
Each premise is already a clause (disjunction of literals or unit clause):
- C1: Striker(robert)
- C2: $\neg$Striker(robert) $\vee$ SoccerPlayer(robert)
- C3: Left(robert, bayern)
- C4: $\neg$Left(robert, bayern) $\vee$ $\neg$PlaysFor(robert, bayern)
- C5: PlaysFor(robert, bayern)
Assign single-letter symbols to atomic predicates:
- $A =$ Striker(robert)
- $B =$ SoccerPlayer(robert)
- $C =$ Left(robert, bayern)
- $D =$ PlaysFor(robert, bayern)
Final Clause Set
$S = \{A, \neg A \vee B, C, \neg C \vee \neg D, D\}$

Cross-set Resolution Module. Take any clause C_1 from the processed clause set S_0 and any clause C_2 from the current set of clauses to be processed S_1. Traverse all pairs of clauses (C_1, C_2), and if they can be resolved, generate a new clause $\text{Res}(C_1, C_2)$.

Intra-set Resolution Module. Take any two different clauses C_1 and C_2 from the current set of clauses to be processed S_1. Traverse all pairs of clauses (C_1, C_2), and if they can be resolved, generate a new clause $\text{Res}(C_1, C_2)$.

■ **Round 1: Cross-set Resolution**
■ **Input:**
- S_0: {}
- S_1: $\{A, \neg A \vee B, C, \neg C \vee \neg D, \neg D\}$
■ **Output:**
Since S_0 is empty, there are no clauses from S_0 to pair with clauses from S_1.
Resulting New Clause Set:
$S_2 = \{\}$
■ **Round 1: Intra-set Resolution**
■ **Input:**
- S_0: {}
- S_1: $\{A, \neg A \vee B, C, \neg C \vee \neg D, \neg D\}$
- S_2: {}
■ **Output:**
S_1 is numbered as follows:
C_1: A ; C_2: $\neg A \vee B$; C_3: C ; C_4: $\neg C \vee \neg D$; C_5: $\neg D$
The following pairs can be resolved:
- $\text{Res}(C_1, C_2) = \text{Res}(A, \neg A \vee B) = B$

(Complementary literals: A and $\neg A$ are resolved, leaving B. B is not a tautology and not in S_0, S_1, or S_3, so it is new.)
- $\mathrm{Res}(C_3, C_4) = \mathrm{Res}(C, \neg C \vee \neg D) = \neg D$
- $\mathrm{Res}(C_4, C_5) = \mathrm{Res}(\neg C \vee \neg D, \neg D) = \neg C$
$S_2 = \{B, \neg D, \neg C\}$

■ **Round 2: Cross-set Resolution**
■ **Input:**
- S_0: $\{A, \neg A \vee B, C, \neg C \vee \neg D, \neg D\}$
- S_1: $\{B, \neg C\}$
■ **Output:**
S_0 is numbered as follows:
C_1: A ; C_2: $\neg A \vee B$; C_3: C ;
C_4: $\neg C \vee \neg D$; C_5: $\neg D$
S_1 is numbered as follows:
C_6: B ; C_7: $\neg C$
The following pairs can be resolved:
$\mathrm{Res}(C_3, C_8) = \mathrm{Res}(L, \neg L) = \lambda$
Resolution process stopped at first empty clause.

Final answer: $\{\mathbf{false}\}$

The format conversion module, cross-set resolution module, and intra-set resolution module have the same idea in both resolution and reverse resolution, and all adopt a 1-shot design approach, with only differences in the examples. Here, for the sake of description, they are combined and introduced together. By designing prompts, the large language model is guided to use the improved resolution to solve the given logical reasoning problems, and the bidirectional reasoning method is introduced to simplify the resolution process, thereby enhancing the reasoning ability of the large language model.

5 Experiments and Results

5.1 Settings

Model. Deepseek-R1 is a high-performance AI inference model released by DeepSeek on January 20, 2025 [23]. It excels at tasks such as natural language inference while being open source to developers around the world. Kimi-K2 was released by Moonshot AI on July 11, 2025 [24]. It is a MoE architecture basic model with stronger code ability and better at general Agent tasks, and shows excellent ability in mathematical reasoning tasks. GLM-Z1-AIR was released by Z.ai on March 31, 2025 [25]. It not only performs as well as DeepSeek-R1, but also improves the speed by up to 8 times. It also has a good performance in inference.

Dataset. The FOLIO dataset [26] is selected as the core evaluation benchmark for this experiment. This dataset was constructed by Han et al. in 2022 and is an expert-written dataset with complex first-order logic reasoning, containing 1,204 examples. Most of these problems match real-world knowledge and have complex reasoning logic.

Symbolic Representation. This experiment uses First-Order Logic (FOL) as the symbolic representation framework, whose core elements include individual variables, predicate symbols, quantified expressions formed by universal quantifier $\forall$ and existential quantifier $\exists$, and logical operators such as $\neg$, $\wedge$, $\vee$, and $\rightarrow$. Compared to propositional logic, which can only express the truth value combinations of atomic propositions, FOL supports generalized reasoning about object sets and can describe existence constraints, which better meets the needs of our reasoning tasks.

5.2   Accuracy Performance Evaluation

We evaluated the Bi-Resolution method using the FOLIO dataset and compared it with the CoT method under 0-shot, 2-shot, and 8-shot settings, as well as the SymbCoT method. We contrasted the differences among the four methods in terms of accuracy evaluation metrics. The specific results are detailed in Table 1 below.

Table 1. Performance of large language models under different reasoning methods

LLMs	Reasoning Methods			
	CoT (0-shot)	CoT (2-shot)	SymbCoT (2-shot)	Bi-Resolution (2-shot)
DeepSeeK-R1	75.2%	78.2%	82.27%	81.89%
Kimi-K2	72.67%	72.90%	80.76%	77.69%
GLM-Z1-AIR	79.03%	79.37%	82.43%	80.14%

The results indicate that Bi-Resolution is a highly effective method for enhancing logical reasoning in LLMs, particularly when compared to the traditional CoT approach. The method's performance is robust across different models, suggesting its general applicability. While SymbCoT shows slightly better performance in some cases, the gap is narrow, and Bi-Resolution offers a viable alternative that may be easier to implement and integrate into existing systems due to its reliance on bidirectional resolution reasoning rather than symbolic manipulation.

6   Conclusion and Summary

In this paper, a new reasoning architecture, Bi-Resolution, is proposed. This architecture enhances the reasoning ability of large language models by designing prompt words to guide them to use an improved resolution algorithm to solve given logical reasoning problems, while introducing bidirectional reasoning to simplify the resolution process. Experimental results show that under the Bi-Resolution method, the accuracy of large language model reasoning has increased, achieving a significant improvement in accuracy, thereby proving the effectiveness of our method. Although the current reasoning accuracy under Bi-Resolution has not exceeded the current optimal level, the overall accuracy is relatively similar.

This study confirms the feasibility of enhancing the reasoning ability of large language models by introducing logical rules. The introduction of the resolution algorithm provides a new reasoning approach for large language models from a logical perspective, significantly improving reasoning efficiency. The bidirectional reasoning idea avoids the interference of redundant premise conditions, simplifies the reasoning process, and also improves the accuracy of reasoning to a certain extent. These improvements provide a technical foundation for large language models in scenarios requiring high-accuracy reasoning, such as financial analysis and legal argumentation. Our future work will explore multimodal data acquisition to expand the application scenarios of this method, test the method on more datasets, and further improve it to enhance its universality.

References

1. Vaswani, A., et al.: Attention is all you need. Adv. Neural Inf. Process. Syst. **30** (2017)
2. Achiam, J., et al.: Gpt-4 technical report. arXiv preprint arXiv:2303.08774 (2023)
3. Song, H., et al.: R1-searcher: incentivizing the search capability in llms via reinforcement learning. CoRR (2025)
4. Lyu, Q., et al.: Faithful chain-of-thought reasoning. In: The 13th International Joint Conference on Natural Language Processing and the 3rd Conference of the Asia-Pacific Chapter of the Association for Computational Linguistics (IJCNLP-AACL 2023) (2023)
5. Szymanski, A., et al.: Limitations of the llm-as-a-judge approach for evaluating llm outputs in expert knowledge tasks. In: Proceedings of the 30th International Conference on Intelligent User Interfaces (2025)
6. Zhang, X., et al.: Pmc-vqa: visual instruction tuning for medical visual question answering. CoRR (2023)
7. Laskar, M.T.R., et al.: A systematic survey and critical review on evaluating large language models: challenges, limitations, and recommendations. In: EMNLP (2024)
8. Jin, M., et al.:The impact of reasoning step length on large language models. In: ACL (Findings) (2024)
9. Villalobos, P., Ho, A., Sevilla, J., Besiroglu, T., Heim, L., Hobbhahn, M.: Position: will we run out of data? Limits of llm scaling based on human-generated data. In: International Conference on Machine Learning. PMLR (2024)
10. Ullah, E., Parwani, A., Baig, M.M., Singh, R.: Challenges and barriers of using large language models (llm) such as chatgpt for diagnostic medicine with a focus on digital pathology-a recent scoping review. Diagn. Pathol. **19**(1), 43 (2024)
11. Mishra, V., et al.: Investigating the shortcomings of llms in step-by-step legal reasoning. In: NAACL (Findings) (2025)

12. Wei, J., et al.: Chain-of-thought prompting elicits reasoning in large language models. Adv. Neural Inf. Process. Syst. **35**, 24824–24837 (2022)
13. Wang, X., et al.: Self-consistency improves chain of thought reasoning in language models. arXiv preprint arXiv:2203.11171 (2022)
14. Gao, L., et al.: Pal: program-aided language models. In: International Conference on Machine Learning. PMLR (2023)
15. Robinson, J.A.: A machine-oriented logic based on the resolution principle. J. ACM (JACM) **12**(1) (1965)
16. Russell, S.J., Norvig, P.: Artificial intelligence (a modern approach) (1995)
17. Qu, H., Cao, Y., Gao, J., Ding, L., Xu, R.: Interpretable proof generation via iterative backward reasoning. In: Proceedings of the 2022 Conference of the North American Chapter of the Association for Computational Linguistics: Human Language Technologies (2022)
18. Zhang, H., Li, L.H., Meng, T., Chang, K.-W., Van Den Broeck, G.: On the paradox of learning to reason from data. In: Proceedings of the Thirty-Second International Joint Conference on Artificial Intelligence (2023)
19. Sanyal, S., Singh, H., Ren, X.: Fairr: faithful and robust deductive reasoning over natural language. In: Proceedings of the 60th Annual Meeting of the Association for Computational Linguistics, vol. 1: Long Papers) (2022)
20. Xu, J., Fei, H., Pan, L., Liu, Q., Lee, M.-L., Hsu, W.: Faithful logical reasoning via symbolic chain-of-thought. In: ACL (1) (2024)
21. Sun, Z., et al.: Towards generalizable and faithful logic reasoning over natural language via resolution refutation. In: Proceedings of the 2024 Joint International Conference on Computational Linguistics, Language Resources and Evaluation (LREC-COLING 2024) (2024)
22. Liu, S., He, B., Song, L.: Bi-chainer: automated large language models reasoning with bidirectional chaining. In: 62nd Annual Meeting of the Association for Computational Linguistics (ACL 2024). Association for Computational Linguistics (2024)
23. Guo, D., et al.: Deepseek-r1: incentivizing reasoning capability in llms via reinforcement learning. arXiv preprint arXiv:2501.12948 (2025)
24. Team, K., et al.: Kimi k2: open agentic intelligence. arXiv preprint arXiv:2507.20534 (2025)
25. Zeng, A., et al.: Chatglm: a family of large language models from glm-130b to glm-4 all tools. CoRR (2024)
26. Han, S., et al.: Folio: natural language reasoning with first-order logic. In: EMNLP (2024)

Natural Language Processing and Machine Vision

From the Laboratory to Real-World Application: Evaluating Zero-Shot Scene Interpretation on Edge Devices for Mobile Robotics

Nicolas Schuler[1,2]([✉]) [iD], Lea Dewald[1] [iD], Nick Baldig[1,2] [iD], and Jürgen Graf[1] [iD]

[1] Trier University of Applied Sciences, Trier, Germany
`{lxdw0338,n.baldig,j.graf}@hochschule-trier.de,`
[2] University of Luxembourg, Kirchberg, Luxembourg

Abstract. Video Understanding, Scene Interpretation and Commonsense Reasoning are highly challenging tasks enabling the interpretation of visual information, allowing agents to perceive, interact with and make rational decisions in its environment. Large Language Models (LLMs) and Visual Language Models (VLMs) have shown remarkable advancements in these areas in recent years, enabling domain-specific applications as well as zero-shot open vocabulary tasks, combining multiple domains. However, the required computational complexity poses challenges for their application on edge devices and in the context of Mobile Robotics, especially considering the trade-off between accuracy and inference time. In this paper, we investigate the capabilities of state-of-the-art VLMs for the task of Scene Interpretation and Action Recognition, with special regard to small VLMs capable of being deployed to edge devices in the context of Mobile Robotics. The proposed pipeline is evaluated on a diverse dataset consisting of various real-world cityscape, on-campus and indoor scenarios. The experimental evaluation discusses the potential of these small models on edge devices, with particular emphasis on challenges, weaknesses, inherent model biases and the application of the gained information. Supplementary material is provided via the following repository: https://datahub.rz.rptu.de/hstr-csrl-public/publications/scene-interpretation-on-edge-devices/.

Keywords: Mobile Robotics · Deep Learning · Vision Language Models · Video Understanding · Scene Interpretation

1 Introduction

The development of mobile cognitive systems offers great potential to create autonomous robotic platforms that can operate in dynamic and unstructured environments by using image sequences and context to enable decision-making. Visual commonsense and reasoning plays a crucial role in this, as it enables the systems to interpret visual information and make optimal decisions w.r.t.

© The Author(s), under exclusive license to Springer Nature Switzerland AG 2026
M. Bramer and F. Stahl (Eds.): SGAI-AI 2025, LNAI 16302, pp. 301–315, 2026.
https://doi.org/10.1007/978-3-032-11442-6_21

utility based on it. By incorporating Visual Commonsense [29], a platform can reason over the relationships between objects and understand human behavior as the sum of their actions, working towards pareto optimality between safety, efficiency and comfort for the end user. This extends the capability of mobile platforms from just perceiving their environment to making sense of it in a more human-like way. For example, a service robot could not only identify a cup on a table but also understand that the person nearby is done taking his meal, starting an autonomous cleanup procedure. The potential of Visual Commonsense in mobile platforms is thus extensive. Use cases include autonomous vehicles, which in turn need to understand complex visual cues in urban environments, and service robots that assist in homes or hospitals, where subtle understanding of human needs is beneficial in terms of maximizing efficiency and comfort in parallel, enhancing human-robot interaction, cooperation and collaboration.

Different approaches tackle these problems either by incorporating LLMs via external server and extensive post-processing with the mobile platform only serving as a sensory system [3], or by utilizing domain-specific models, e.g. Convolutional Neural Networks (CNNs) or vision transformer on the edge device itself, with the application of commonsense reasoning VLMs on edge devices remaining limited [7,8]. However, the integration of local solutions on edge devices are of particular interest for Mobile Robotics, were the accessibility of external services can not be guaranteed and might not be desirable, e.g. concerning privacy, and the zero-shot capabilities allow for open-domain usage, without being limited set of actions that will not adequately describe real world scenarios. In this paper, we aim to analyze the capabilities of such models for edge devices to describe a scene and the actors within on real-world data, with a focus on human action recognition, using a pre-trained VLM for zero-shot scene interpretation. In particular, we want to elucidate the challenges in bringing established model architectures to real-world applications in Mobile Robotics by incorporating the VLM in our architecture already used in the context of Mobile Robotics.

The remainder of the paper is structured as follows: Sect. 2 describes the foundation of Visual Commonsense and Video Understanding models, especially in regard to recent advancements with LLMs and VLMs. In addition, related work on applying such models to edge devices and Mobile Robotics are discussed, with an emphasis on centralized and de-centralized solutions. The proposed architecture is presented in Sect. 3, with the approach being experimentally evaluated in Sect. 4. Finally, Sect. 5 concludes the work and discusses potential future applications and improvements. Supplementary material including video, high resolution image and evaluation data is provided via the following repository: https://datahub.rz.rptu.de/hstr-csrl-public/publications/scene-interpretation-on-edge-devices/.

2   Foundations and Related Work

The foundations include different approaches to Visual Commonsense, especially utilizing LLMs and VLMs, which form the basis of the presented approach, common tasks, their respective datasets and metrics, see Sect. 2.1. Section 2.2 discusses various LLMs and VLMs, with an emphasis on small models for edge devices and Scene Interpretation. Following, the application of such models in the context of Mobile Robotics in the literature is discussed in Sect. 2.3.

2.1   Different Approaches to Visual Commonsense

While humans are able to reason about observed entities and relations in between them, reasoning about actions and context from a single glance at a scene, this remains challenging for perceptive systems to this day [3,29,31]. This kind of understanding is essential for making rational decisions and provides an important basis for further development in Mobile Robotics. It exceeds mere object recognition and requires the ability to draw more complex conclusions from visual information that goes beyond the obvious [29].

With the release of the Visual Commonsense Reasoning (VCR) task by [29] in 2019, this challenge was brought back into the spotlight. VCR aims to enable a human like understanding of visual scenes. The task contains to answer a multiple-choice question about an image (Q$\longrightarrow$A) and then to justify the given answer by answering another multiple-choice question (QA$\longrightarrow$R), including the VCR dataset [29], containing 290,000 multiple-choice questions related to 110,000 film scenes [29].

A recent approach to VCR, ViCor [31], aims to combine the strengths of Large Language Models (LLMs) and Vision Language Models (VLMs) and to compensate for their respective weaknesses. Visual Commonsense Reasoning problems were divided into two categories for this purpose: Visual Commonsense Understanding (VCU) and Visual Commonsense Inference (VCI). While VLMs are particularly good at reasoning and classifying visual content, LLMs are characterized by the fact that they can draw deeper conclusions that are not immediately apparent from the image content, such as cause-and-effect relationships and intentions of a person. Problems of this type fall into the category of VCI. ViCor uses pre-trained LLMs to determine the problem category. In addition, the LLMs act as controllers for the VLMs. As part of the VCU task, the model must recognize whether a text describes a concept or attribute from the given image. In contrast, solving VCI problems involves deriving new insights or explanations from the visual content, such as the purpose of an object. [31]

2.2   Vision Language Models and Scene Representation

With the wide-spread success of LLMs, various closed- and open-source LLM models have been available to the community, e.g. LLama3 [9], DeepSeek [5], Qwen [1] and GPT4 [20]. While these models report impressive results in various tasks, these results come at the cost of large-scale architectures (billions up to trillions trainable parameters), limiting the application of such models mostly to cloud-solutions. For the following section and the remainder of this paper, we will call models with up to a few dozen of billion parameters medium-sized and models with up to four billion models small, i.e. small language models (sLMs) or small vision language models (sVLMs).

For medium-sized models, [1] provided a set of large-scale vision-language models (LVLMs) that can perceive and inference both text and images. The LLM Qwen-7B [1] generates the desired responses according to the given prompts and performs various vision-language tasks, such as image labeling, question answering, text-based question answering and visual grounding [1]. While a model size of seven billion parameters enables the usage of such models on workstations, edge devices place further computational restrictions on models, especially when other algorithms are to be run on the same device.

Examples of such small models for image interpretation on edge devices include Moondream2 [18], and SmolVLM2 [19] consisting of 1.93 and 2.2 billion parameters respectively, allowing these models to be efficiently run on edge devices. However, due to its size, such models are more likely to generate wrong captions and introduce biases in their answers [22]. For a comprehensive survey on various sVLMs, see [22]. Regarding sLMs, as part of the wider LLama model family [9], Llama-3.2-3B and Llama-3.2-1B offer text-to-text sLMs for edge devices. For detailed recent survey on VLMs on edge devices, refer to [23].

Besides textual depictions of the scene, graph-based representation plays a crucial role in semantic scene representation. Scene graphs [2] represent a scene by temporal and spatial nodes and edges, which makes them well interpretable but requires extensive prior knowledge about the scene. Action Graphs [11] also integrate the relationships between objects within and between frames as edge properties, where objects are represented as nodes and their interactions as edges.

2.3 Applications in Mobile Robotics

For autonomous coordination in unstructured environments, systems must not only recognize objects, but also understand context-based intentions and make decisions proactively. Various approaches have been developed in recent years to tackle this challenge [3, 7, 12, 29, 31].

The work of [3] uses VLMs in walking robots to give them the ability to navigate autonomously through complex environments and overcome various obstacles - for example, as part of search operations in collapsed buildings. The robot must be able to climb over rubble, crawl through narrow gaps and find its way out of dead ends by retracing its steps. The robot should act appropriately in such circumstances, especially in unexpected situations. To make this possible, [3] present the concept of VLM-Predictive Control (VLM-PC [3]). VLM-PC consists of two central components: the context-based adaptation to previous robot interactions and the planning of multiple capabilities into the future, including possible re-adaptation of plans. VLMs enable robots to independently perceive their environment, navigate and act in complex scenarios based on past interactions, future action strategies and extensive semantic knowledge - without having to rely on specialized technologies or external support, i.e. assistance. The robot uses skills previously learned through reinforcement learning, such as walking, climbing or crawling, to efficiently navigate its environment [3].

VLMaps [12] is a spatial map representation that directly combines pre-trained visual language features with a 3D reconstruction of the physical world. VLMaps can be created autonomously from robotic video recordings using standard exploration approaches and enable natural language indexing of the map, e.g. for the localization of landmarks or spatial references in relation to landmarks, without additional data acquisition or model fine-tuning. In particular, in combination with LLMs, VLMaps can be used to translate natural language commands into a sequence of open-vocabulary navigation targets that are directly localized in the map and can be shared by multiple robots with different equipment to create new obstacle maps on-the-fly, using a list of obstacle categories: For autonomous vehicles, [7] utilize a combination of CNN-based incident detections, small local VLMs for textual scene descriptions and large cloud-based LLM to produce incident reports.

3   Integrated Zero-Shot Video Interpretation

While multimodal VLMs have shown remarkable results in various zero-shot vision tasks related to reasoning and understanding [15], the performance of these architectures rely on being pre-trained on large-scale datasets in combination with a large number of trainable parameters. On the other hand, CNN- and efficient transformer-based architectures [17] used for their low computational complexity on edge devices lack the strong generalization and zero-shot capabilities of the aforementioned VLMs. However, recent advancements allow for the utilization of local VLMs on edge devices [18,19]. To that end, this work presents an architecture leveraging a local VLM to allow their usage on edge-devices and in the context of Mobile Robotics.

3.1   Proposed Architecture

The presented approach is split into two distinct systems: the mobile cognitive system with the edge device and a cloud-based solution for foundation model support. While the edge device utilizes small models for the initial scene description, object detection and tracking process, the cognitive system may communicate with the external system to gain further insides into its environment. While the agent is connected to the external system, personalized data is only processed by the local models, where external models can be used to further analyze the information generated by the models on the edge device, allowing for a privacy-preserving environment.

Models on the edge device include a VLM for Scene Interpretation and further models for object detection and tracking. Using the generated model outputs, external cloud-based models too large to be run on local setups can further be queried to solidify the initial results. The described architecture is given in Fig 1.

An overview of the cognitive systems is given in the Appendix. For the purpose of the present work, the focus lies on the models used on the edge device of the cognitive system, especially the VLM.

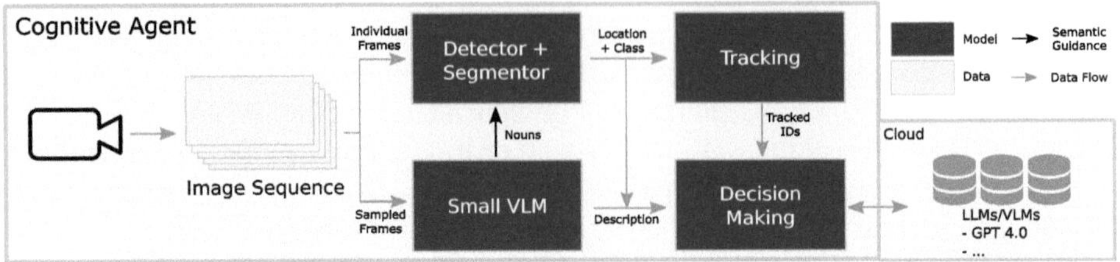

Fig. 1. Architecture for Scene Interpretation on edge devices for Mobile Robotics.

3.2 Mobile Scene Interpretation and Guided Segmentation

The proposed pipeline works as follows: First, the local VLM generates textual descriptions of the scene, given a sequence of images over the most recent time interval. Thus, the raw image data is only processed locally, preserving the privacy of the individuals when consulting larger inference models that might need to be run on an external server.

The resulting description then can be used in various downstream tasks. For one, it might be used for further inferences, incorporating local or cloud-based LLMs. Within the local pipeline, the generated description can be used for semantically guided segmentation and tracking. To that end, the generated description is decomposed into nouns, which are in turn used for prompted zero-shot segmentation, giving additional insight into the generated scene description. An example of this process is given in Fig. 2, comparing the default segmentation for a given set of classes (e.g. cars, buildings, persons, bicycles, trees, traffic signs, street and sky) to the semantically-guided segmentation, focusing on elements important to the description only. The generated description 'A woman is crossing the street at a crosswalk' yields the three nouns 'woman', 'street' and 'crosswalk'. Note that the object detection and segmentation is done using zero-shot models, that is the used text prompts are not limited to arbitrary, pre-trained classes. In this particular setup, we utilize Grounded DINO [16] in combination with SAM [14] for the task of zero-shot object detection and segmentation.

4   Experimental Evaluation

The experimental evaluation analyzes the utilized VLM of the pipeline described in Sect. 3 on a diverse dataset featuring various real-world outdoor and indoor scenarios. Due to the challenging task of open vocabulary video interpretation

Fig. 2. Example Result of the Proposed Pipeline. Left: The default segmentation given a fixed set of classes. Middle: The results of the first step of the pipeline with the generated VLM description, using the extracted nouns of the description for further object localization. Right: The final result of the Scene Interpretation and semantically-guided image segmentation. Note that the anonymization is only done for the purpose of this publication, the pipeline works with the raw data instead.

(see [4,10,13,24,30] for various open vocabulary evaluation metrics and their respective problems), we evaluate the quality of the results in terms of the concurrence of the generated scene description with a manually annotated description, see Sect. 4.1 for more details.

4.1   Experimental Setup

The proposed pipeline is implemented in Python 3.12 using PyTorch [21] and Transformers [27]. As the VLM, we use the state-of-the-art model SmolVLM2 [19], which allows for real-time Scene Interpretation on edge devices using input video streams. The used dataset consists of 234 min of video data gathered in the german city of Trier by our laboratory. We differentiate three distinct domains: *Campus Indoor*, *Campus Outdoor* and *City*, with a split of 107 min, 74 minutes and 53 min respectively. Examples from the dataset and the used cognitive systems for the recording are given in the Appendix. The videos are split into five second clips that are manually annotated and fed into a VLM in order to describe the main action contained in the clip. The annotater of the video clips is given example outputs of the VLM to match their annotation to the length and style of the VLM. In addition, the annotator is instructed to strictly focus on the main action happening in the sequence, that is the action that dominates the scene. If no such action is identifiable, e.g. in the case of a car driving down a street with only parked cars on the sidewalk and no identifiable active agents present, the that scene should be given as a short description. For the used system prompts that are also made available to the annotator as further guidance refer to the linked supplementary material in the introduction.

The generated description were evaluated by human experts for correctness, that is the accordance of the generated description with a manual evaluation of the sequence. The evaluation process is as follows. The generated description for a given sequence is compared to its human-generated baseline description. To quantify the results, the generated descriptions are evaluated in three sub-categories: *Action* (relations), *Agent* and *Object* (entities). If a VLM-generated description contains the correct action, the sub-category *Action* is considered correct. *Agent* is considered correct if the correct type and number of agents is contained in the description. Finally, *Object* is considered correct, if the description contains the correct type and number of objects relevant to the depicted action. If all three sub-categories are correct, the entire description is considered *Correct*, meaning the main action of the sequence is correctly described, including the involved agents and utilized objects. Note that by default we do not consider empirical characteristics of the person when evaluating the generated descriptions, i.e. 'A woman is crossing the street at a crosswalk.' and 'A man is crossing the street at a crosswalk.' are considered equivalent. We note and discuss the difficulties in this approach in Sect. 4.3, since the inherent subjectivity in human evaluation poses a significant challenge. However, due to the lack of reliable metrics, see Sect. 4.3, for this task in the context of practical applications, we feel justified in this decision.

In addition to the human evaluation, we utilize two popular semantic similarity scores to evaluate the generated descriptions. *BERTScore* [30] utilizes BERT [6] to calculate token similarity between the input pairs, while STSB DistilRoBERTa [26] uses cross encoding and similarity calculation between the two provided descriptions for its *Sentence Similarity* scoring. For the purpose of this paper, we use these to evaluate the usefulness of such metrics within our domain, comparing the results of automated metrics to the manual evaluation results. To that end, we calculate the correlation coefficient R between the automated metric and the manual evaluation *Correct* using point-biserial correlation coefficient [25]. In addition, the percentage of matches between the human and manual evaluation, in the following called *Match %*, is calculated. The matches are calculated by categorizing the sequences using a threshold for the given metric. If the sequence is rated over the threshold, the generated description is considered *Correct*. The used threshold value is calculated using optimization on the generated metric values. We evaluate the effect size of the different domains on the measured correctness using the phi coefficient ϕ [28] derived from the chi-square statistic χ^2 and the total number of observations N.

4.2   Experimental Results

Results of the evaluation are given in Table 1, for a qualitative example the results see Fig. 4. The results are grouped by domain (*Campus Indoor*, *Campus Outdoor* and *City*). In total, 65.4% of all generated descriptions are considered correct. Between the different domains, the domain *Campus Indoor* has the lowest correctness score with 53.3% and the domain *City* the highest with 79.6%. Concerning the used automated metrics, i.e. *BERTScore* and *Sentence Similarity*, *BERTScore* has a lower correlation coefficient for all domains versus *Sentence Similarity*, with an R value of 0.229 to 0.483. This is further emphasized by the percentage of accordance between the manual evaluation and automated metrics, with 67.1% for *BERTScore* versus 73.6% for *Sentence Similarity*. Figure 3 gives the boxplots for *BERTScore* and *Sentence Similarity* split by domain and ground-truth, that is manually evaluated correctness. The pairwise effect size of the domains on correctness is as follows:

$$\chi^2(N = 2186) = 86.13,\ p = 1.69e^{-20},\ \phi = 0.20\ (Indoor\text{–}Outdoor),$$
$$\chi^2(N = 1930) = 123.26,\ p = 1.22e^{-28},\ \phi = 0.25\ (Indoor\text{–}City)\ \text{and}$$
$$\chi^2(N = 1518) = 8.13,\ p = 0.004,\ \phi = 0.07\ (Outdoor\text{–}City).$$

Table 1. Results of the evaluation of SmolVLM2 [19] within the proposed pipeline. Including human evaluation (*Correct, Action, Agent* and *Object*) and automated similarity metrics (*BERTScore* and *Sentence Similarity*). The generated description of the individual sequence is compared to the annotated ground truth. A description is considered correct if it contains the main action, the type and number of acting agents and the involved objects. For a detailed description of the used metrics see Sect. 4.1.

Domain	Correct %	Action %	Agent %	Object %	BERTScore F1 Avg.	R	Match %	Sentence Similarity Avg.	R	Match %	Clips #	Run Time h
Campus Indoor	53.3	67.5	94.4	77.3	0.933	0.349	67.6	0.495	0.508	73.4	1299	1.79
Campus Outdoor	73.1	87.3	90.0	87.6	0.927	0.230	73.1	0.498	0.444	78.8	887	1.23
City	79.6	90.6	97.6	89.4	0.918	0.206	79.6	0.545	0.495	83.4	631	0.88
Total	65.4	78.9	93.7	83.2	0.927	0.229	67.1	0.507	0.483	73.6	2817	3.90

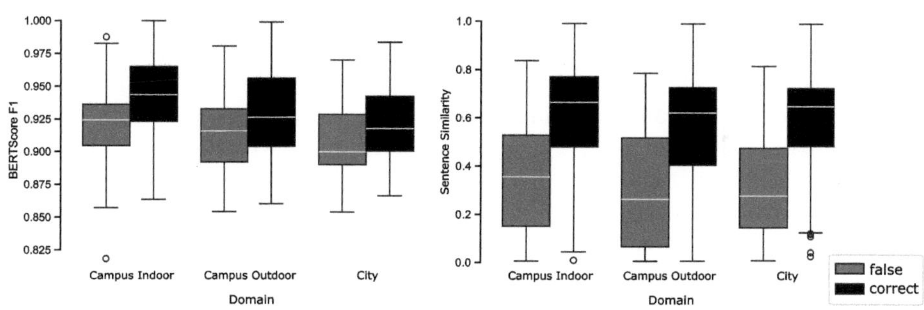

Fig. 3. Boxplots for the two automated metrics *BERTScore* and *Sentence Similarity* by domain. Metrics are further grouped by the manually evaluated correctness of the generated descriptions compared to the ground truth.

4.3   Discussion

The following discussion focuses on three distinct aspects. First, the results of the experimental evaluation are discussed, with an emphasis on lessons learned when applying a state-of-the-art VLM to our setup within the context of Mobile Robotics. Following, the difficulties inherent to manual as well as automated evaluation are elucidated.

Fig. 4. Two examples of a correct (left) and a partially correct (right) description. Using semantically-guided segmentation to highlight important elements of the generated description. Left: Correct description of the scene. Right: Partially correct description where the object associated to the action is considered incorrect ('lawn mower' instead of 'bicycle with a child trailer'). Note that the anonymization is only done for the purpose of this publication, the pipeline works with the raw data instead.

Applying Vision Language Models to Real-World Scenarios. The results highlight the capabilities of SmolVLM2 for usage within our pipeline in principle. However, the difference in correctness between the indoor domain and the two outdoor domains is considerable, as shown by the effect size ϕ. This difference might be explained by two factors. First, the domain with the lowest correctness is *Campus Indoor*. This domain contains a more diverse and complex set of activities, e.g. 'A woman is putting dishes into a dishwasher.', 'A man is giving an apple to another person.', 'A person is writing on whiteboard.', 'A person is climbing a ladder.'. On the other hand, while the domains *Campus Outdoor* and *City* can also contain complex actions, e.g. 'A group of people are taking measurements on a street.', a lot of the depicted actions are more simplistic in nature, e.g. 'A man is walking on the sidewalk.', 'A car is driving down a road.'. For the second factor, refer to the next section and the discussion on the difficulties in evaluating the results concerning the different domains.

We want to further discuss biases in the generated descriptions of the used model. For one, the model struggles to differentiating certain actions that are closely related but decidedly different, e.g. the model uses 'sitting down' to describe both the action of 'sitting down' and 'standing up'. Another point is a heavy bias regarding certain types of objects present in a scene. E.g. if a whiteboard is present in the scene, the model will include the whiteboard into the action, even if not relevant to the action, leading to descriptions like 'A person is standing on a ladder and is writing on a whiteboard.' instead of the ground truth of 'A person is climbing a ladder.'. This means that care has to be taken when using the model within specific domains and carefully evaluating the potential relevant biases within that domain and filtering the generated output according to this prior knowledge can help to stabilize the predictions.

Another important lesson is the utilization of the gained information. In our current setup, the generated scene description relates to the past five seconds. On top of that, depending on the complexity of the scene and system load, another one to three seconds are needed for the inference itself. Thus, the delay between an action happening and the cognitive agent receiving the information might be as high as eight seconds. While this delay can be reduced to a degree by changing the evaluated time interval, the basic problem remains and must be considered. Consequently, the cognitive systems should use the gained information either only in contexts that are not time-sensitive, e.g. within assistance tasks that are not time-critical or to document incidents within more time critical environments. For example, within our domain *City*, the gained information can be used to generate dynamic, cooperative maps, highlighting points of interest, e.g. sections with a lot of pedestrian traffic, streets with a high number of cars suddenly driving on the road due to hidden driveways. Within our domain *Campus Outdoor*, the information can be used for mobile platforms at walking speed, incorporating the scene interpretation for audible signals, human-computer interaction and to generate reports.

Inherent Difficulties Regarding Evaluation. The challenges in manual evaluation are twofold. For one, the task of generating the ground truth manual annotations concerning the main action for a given scene can be ambiguous, especially depending on the domain. Within our domain *Campus Indoor*, the main action is usually clearly defined. The actions we recorded within that domain are mostly work related: working in an office, carrying something, working at a computer, talking to someone, or are related to movement: walking, sitting, taking the stairs et cetera. While these actions can be described vastly differently by a human annotator, e.g. 'A man is sitting at a computer.' versus 'A man is working in an office.' describing the same sequence, the difference in these descriptions can still be easily identified and evaluated correctly when comparing it to the generated output of the VLM, e.g. 'A person is sitting at a table with a computer.', which would be considered as a correct description. This is not true for the domain *City*, and to a lesser extent the domain *Campus Outdoor*: Here, due to the open nature of the domains, e.g. large groups of people, large spaces and different types of road users, it can be difficult to identify a main action of a sequence. For example, all following sentences describe the same scene: 'A busy intersection with cars driving and people crossing the road.', 'A black car is crossing a busy intersection.', 'People are crossing the street at a crossroad in front of a large building.', 'A bus is stopping at a traffic light with people crossing the road.'. For the purpose of this paper, we consider all four of these descriptions *Correct* if there is no one critical action identified within the sequence. That is, if a bike is crossing the street right in front of the cognitive agent, this would be the critical action and all descriptions given above would be false.

Regarding the automated metrics, various works discuss the problems inherent in such methods. *BERTScore* [30] displays significant biases concerning social, age, race, gender, religion and physical appearances [10,24]. More recent works explore probabilistic methods to evaluate semi- and open-vocabulary tasks like commonsense reasoning [4] and scene representation [13]. While these probabilistic approaches show promising results [4,13] over the previous similarity measures, they are currently either limited to a question-answer setup [4] or to a limited task such as scene representation [13] where the labels of the objects to be segmented can be reasonably expected to be exhaustive, encompassing a complete set of synonymous and similar objects. As shown in Fig. 3, both metrics correlate with the manual evaluation. However, the overlap between quartiles, which is particularly pronounced for BERTScore, shows the difficulties in relying on these metrics only to evaluate the performance of the model. Additionally, the accordance with the manual evaluation depends on the domain in question and thus has to be checked for every new domain or when encountering new actions within a given domain.

5   Conclusion and Future Work

The present paper discussed and highlighted the challenges in applying current state-of-the-art VLMs to the task of Scene Interpretation for Mobile Robotics on edge devices. In particular, we demonstrated the strong capabilities of these models when used in zero-shot tasks on unknown domains in real-world scenarios. Finally, we discussed the challenges in applying such models to the real world, highlighting the difficulties in evaluating manual and generated descriptions and inadequacies in using current automated metrics for this task.

For future work we want to highlight the need for better metrics for open-vocabulary tasks and future research into reliable evaluation of real world domains for these tasks, especially to reduce the need for manual evaluation.

Disclosure of Interests. The authors have no competing interests to declare.

Appendix

The used dataset was recorded using different cognitive systems, see Fig. 5. All platforms share the same sensor system that is only adapted to the given requirements w.r.t. the mechanical constraints. We utilize stereo cameras, LiDAR and a GNSS/INS module, with an NVIDIA Jetson AGX as the edge device.

The dataset used in this paper consists of a combination of various outdoor and indoor scenarios in real-world situations, see Fig. 6 for a short overview.

Fig. 5. The different cognitive systems used within our laboratory, utilizing the same sensory system (top left) used for data acquisition in the present paper.

Fig. 6. Various examples from the used dataset, captured by a variety of cognitive agents, including city and campus scenes, featuring difficult lighting conditions, crowded scenes and complex scenarios. Note that the anonymization is only done for the purpose of this publication, the pipeline works with the raw data instead.

References

1. Bai, J., et al.: Qwen Technical Report (2023). arXiv:2309.16609
2. Chang, X., et al.: A comprehensive survey of scene graphs: generation and application. IEEE Trans. Pattern Anal. Mach. Intell. **45**(1), 1–26 (2022). https://doi.org/10.1109/TPAMI.2021.3137605

3. Chen, A., et al.: Commonsense Reasoning for Legged Robot Adaptation with Vision-Language Models (2024). arXiv:2407.02666
4. Cheng, Q., et al.: Every answer matters: evaluating commonsense with probabilistic measures. In: Proceedings of the 62nd Annual Meeting of the Association for Computational Linguistics (2024). https://doi.org/10.18653/v1/2024.acl-long.29
5. DeepSeek-AI, et al.: DeepSeek-V3 Technical Report (2024). arXiv:2412.19437
6. Devlin, J., et al.: BERT: pre-training of deep bidirectional transformers for language understanding. In: Proceedings of the 2019 Conference of the North American Chapter of the Association for Computational Linguistics: Human Language Technologies (2019). arXiv:1810.04805
7. Farhan, M., et al.: Transforming highway safety with autonomous drones and AI: a framework for incident detection and emergency response. IEEE Open J. Veh. Technol. **6**, 829–845 (2025). https://doi.org/10.1109/ojvt.2025.3549387
8. Feroze, W., et al.: Reading between the lines: commonsense reasoning in small language models. In: 10th International Conference on Computer and Communications, pp. 298–303 (2024). https://doi.org/10.1109/iccc62609.2024.10941834
9. Grattafiori, A., et al.: The Llama 3 Herd of Models (2024). arXiv:2407.21783
10. Hanna, M., et al.: A fine-grained analysis of BERTScore. In: Proceedings of the Sixth Conference on Machine Translation, pp. 507–517 (2021). https://aclanthology.org/2021.wmt-1.59/
11. Hendria, W., et al.: Action knowledge for video captioning with graph neural networks. J. King Saud Univ. Comput. Inf. Sci. **35**(4), 50–62 (2023). https://doi.org/10.1016/j.jksuci.2023.03.006
12. Huang, C., et al.: Visual language maps for robot navigation. In: IEEE International Conference on Robotics and Automation (ICRA) (2023). arXiv:2210.05714
13. Kassab, C., et al.: OpenLex3D: a new evaluation benchmark for open-vocabulary 3D scene representations. In: 1st Workshop on Safely Leveraging Vision-Language Foundation Models in Robotics: Challenges and Opportunities (2025). arXiv:2503.19764
14. Kirillov, A., et al.: Segment anything. In: 2023 IEEE/CVF International Conference on Computer Vision (ICCV) (2023). arXiv:2304.02643
15. Li, Z., et al.: Benchmark evaluations, applications, and challenges of large vision language models: a survey (2025). arXiv:2501.02189v3
16. Liu, S., et al.: Grounding DINO: marrying DINO with grounded pre-training for open-set object detection. In: Computer Vision ECCV 2024. Lecture Notes in Computer Science, vol. 15105. Springer, Heidelberg (2024). https://doi.org/10.1007/978-3-031-72970-6_3
17. Luo, F., et al.: Bi-DeepViT: binarized transformer for efficient sensor-based human activity recognition. IEEE Trans. Mob. Comput. **24**(5), 4419–4433 (2025). https://doi.org/10.1109/tmc.2025.3526166
18. M87 Labs: Moondream2 (2024). https://doi.org/10.57967/HF/3219
19. Marafioti, A., et al.: SmolVLM: redefining small and efficient multimodal models (2025). arXiv:2504.05299
20. OpenAI, et al.: GPT-4 Technical Report (2024). arXiv:2303.08774
21. Paszke, A., et al.: PyTorch: an imperative style, high-performance deep learning library. In: Proceedings of the 33rd International Conference on Neural Information Processing Systems. arXiv (2019). arXiv:1912.01703
22. Patnaik, N., et al.: Small Vision-language models: a survey on compact architectures and techniques (2025). arXiv:2503.10665
23. Sharshar, A., et al.: Vision-language models for edge networks: a comprehensive survey. arXiv:2502.07855 (2025)

24. Sun, T., et al.: BERTScore is unfair: on social bias in language model-based metrics for text generation. In: Proceedings of the 2022 Conference on Empirical Methods in Natural Language Processing (2022). arXiv:2210.07626
25. Tate, R.F.: Correlation between a discrete and a continuous variable: point-biserial correlation. Ann. Math. Stat. **25**(3), 603–607 (1954). https://doi.org/10.1214/aoms/1177728730
26. Ubiquitous Knowledge Processing Lab: STBS-DistilRoBERTa (2024). https://huggingface.co/cross-encoder/stsb-distilroberta-base
27. Wolf, T., et al.: HuggingFace's Transformers (2019). arXiv:1910.03771
28. Yule, G.U.: On the methods of measuring association between two attributes. J. Roy. Stat. Soc. **75**(6), 579 (1912). https://doi.org/10.2307/2340126
29. Zellers, R., et al.: From recognition to cognition: visual commonsense reasoning. In: Proceedings of the IEEE/CVF Conference on Computer Vision and Pattern Recognition (CVPR) (2019). arXiv:1811.10830
30. Zhang, T., et al.: BERTScore: evaluating text generation with BERT. In: 8th International Conference on Learning Representations (2020). arXiv:1904.09675
31. Zhou, K., et al.: ViCor: bridging visual understanding and commonsense reasoning with large language models. In: Findings of the Association for Computational Linguistics: ACL 2024 (2024). https://doi.org/10.18653/v1/2024.findings-acl.640

Unsupervised Learning for Industrial Defect Detection: A Case Study on Shearographic Data

Jessica Plassmann[1,2]($^{(\boxtimes)}$) (iD), Nicolas Schuler[1,3] (iD), Georg von Freymann[2,4] (iD), and Michael Schuth[1] (iD)

[1] Trier, University of Applied Science, 54293 Trier, Germany
`{plassmaj,schulern,schuth}@hochschule-trier.de`
[2] Department of Physics and Research Center OPTIMAS, RPTU University Kaiserslautern-Landau, 67663 Kaiserslautern, Germany
`georg.freymann@rptu.de`
[3] University of Luxembourg, Esch-Belval, 4365 Esch-sur-Alzette, Luxembourg
[4] Fraunhofer Institute for Industrial Mathematics ITWM, 67663 Kaiserslautern, Germany

Abstract. Shearography is a non-destructive testing method for detecting subsurface defects in materials, offering high sensitivity and full-field inspection capabilities. However, its industrial adoption remains limited due to the need for expert interpretation. To reduce reliance on labeled data and manual evaluation, this study explores unsupervised learning methods for automated anomaly detection in shearographic images. Three architectures are evaluated: a fully connected autoencoder, a convolutional autoencoder, and a student-teacher feature matching model. All models are trained solely on defect-free data. A controlled dataset was developed using a custom specimen with reproducible defect patterns, enabling systematic acquisition of shearographic measurements under both ideal and realistic deformation conditions. Two training subsets were defined: one containing only undistorted, defect-free samples, and one additionally including globally deformed, yet defect-free, data. The latter simulates practical inspection conditions by incorporating deformation-induced fringe patterns that may obscure localized anomalies. The models are evaluated in terms of binary classification and, for the student-teacher model, spatial defect localization. Results show that the student-teacher approach achieves superior classification robustness and enables precise localization. Compared to the autoencoder-based models, it demonstrates improved separability of feature representations, as visualized through t-SNE embeddings. Additionally, a YOLOv8 model trained on labeled defect data serves as a reference to benchmark localization quality. This study underscores the potential of unsupervised deep learning for scalable, label-efficient shearographic inspection in industrial environments.

Keywords: Shearography · Non-destructive testing (NDT) · Anomaly detection · Unsupervised learning

M. Bramer and F. Stahl (Eds.): SGAI-AI 2025, LNAI 16302, pp. 316–329, 2026.
https://doi.org/10.1007/978-3-032-11442-6_22

1   Introduction

Electronic Speckle-Pattern Shearing Interferometry (ESPSI), or shearography, is a well-established optical method for non-destructive testing (NDT), particularly effective for detecting subsurface defects in composites and other industrial components [26, 27]. Despite its high sensitivity to small surface deformations and rapid inspection capabilities, shearography is underused in serial applications due to the lack of fully automated evaluation processes [18].

A critical challenge in automating shearographic inspection is the reliance on supervised learning approaches, such as convolutional neural networks (CNNs) and object detection models like YOLO [11, 20]. These achieve their high performance primarily through large, extensive labeled datasets, such as ImageNet [5]. Creating such datasets demands extensive manual effort and cost, and issues such as data scarcity, privacy, and labeling constraints further hinder dataset generation. Moreover, many companies possess vast unlabeled data unusable by supervised methods [23].

Studies like Li (2022) [13] have explored the use of synthetic data for generating datasets with sufficient and reproducible defects. However, generating synthetic data with realistic defect characteristics and variations remains challenging. Overly diverse synthetic datasets may lead to overfitting, particularly in large-scale applications [13]. This highlights the need to tailor datasets to specific components and testing conditions to ensure reliable defect detection.

Given these challenges, unsupervised learning methods offer a promising alternative. Instead of relying on labeled defect data, these approaches learn the characteristics of defect-free components and identify deviations from this baseline [16]. This method significantly reduces dependency on manually curated defect annotations. This paper explores the application of unsupervised learning for automating shearographic defect detection, with a particular focus on autoencoders [3] and student-teacher models [31]. These approaches are evaluated in terms of their effectiveness, robustness, and practical feasibility [22, 30]. The comparison aims to determine the most suitable method for enabling reliable and automated shearographic inspection in industrial settings.

2   Domain Background: Shearography

Shearography is a non-destructive optical testing method for detecting subsurface defects in materials. The method measures deformation changes between two loading states with submicrometer sensitivity, enabling detection of minute surface displacement gradients. The component surface, which appears optically rough at the laser wavelength scale, is illuminated with coherent light, producing a granular speckle pattern due to random interference. This speckle pattern carries phase information and propagates through an interferometric setup to the camera [24].

In the setup, the backscattered wavefront is laterally shifted (sheared) by tilting one beam path, causing interference between neighboring surface points.

Each image pixel thus results from interference between spatially offset points on the object surface, enabling measurement of deformation gradients [24, p. 554].

Phase information necessary for quantitative evaluation is extracted using phase-shifting techniques. Temporal phase shifting relies on sequential image acquisition per loading state and thus requires static loading during the capture sequence. In contrast, spatial phase shifting enables single-frame evaluation, allowing measurements under dynamic loading conditions [18]. Figure 1a illustrates an exemplary setup based on a Mach–Zehnder interferometer using spatial phase shifting and thermal excitation.

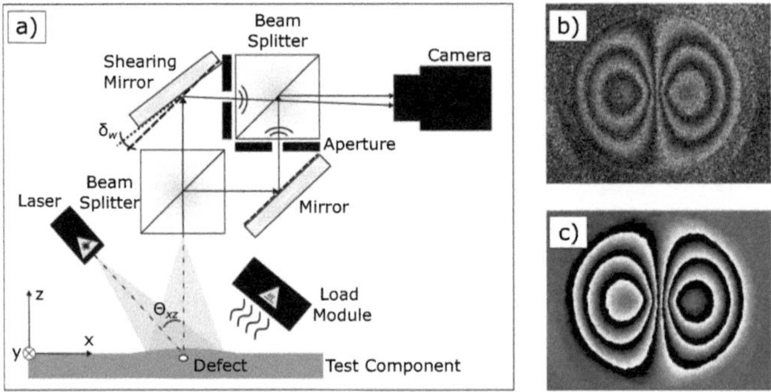

Fig. 1. a) Shearography setup using a Mach–Zehnder interferometer with spatial phase shifting and thermal excitation, own illustration based on [18, p. 97]. b) Unfiltered and c) corresponding filtered phase image of a central out-of-plane deformation at a circular defect. [24, p. 555].

Measurements are based on comparing two states of the same object: a reference state and a state under external load. This load, typically thermal or mechanical, induces a deformation gradient that is captured as a differential phase map, known as a shearogram [24, pp. 314–327]. These maps visualize minute changes in surface deformation, enabling the detection of subsurface flaws through local anomalies in the phase pattern. However, environmental noise and speckle decorrelation can affect phase quality. Spatial or frequency-domain filtering is therefore applied to enhance relevant structures and suppress artifacts (Fig. 1b–c) [24]. Although the technique originated in the 1970s, only recent advances in coherent light sources and computational processing have made its integration into industrial workflows viable [18].

Despite its potential, shearography remains underutilized due to the difficulty of interpreting the resulting phase images. Phase fringes indicate deformation, but not necessarily defects. Accurate assessment requires prior knowledge of the expected deformation response under load. Subtle or localized anomalies caused by internal flaws can be obscured by various effects such as global deformation, measurement noise, or speckle decorrelation. As illustrated in Fig. 2, even clearly defective regions may remain difficult to identify visually [24].

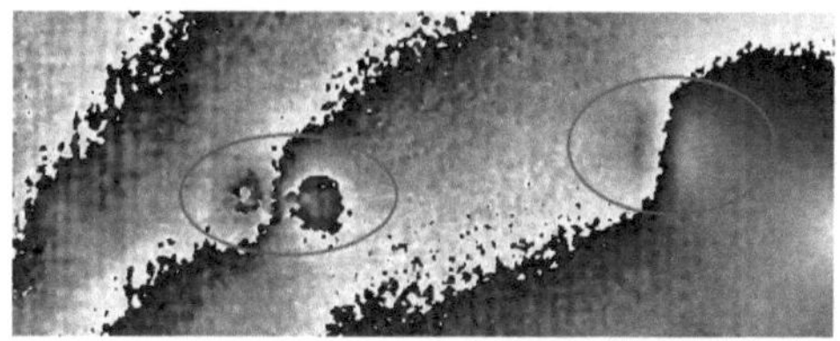

Fig. 2. Filtered phase image with defect locations marked. Detection is challenging, especially when defect geometry is unknown and global deformations cause overlapping phase fringes [24, p. 556].

As in many machine learning contexts, data availability is a key challenge. Industrial datasets are typically limited and imbalanced, with significantly more conforming parts than defective ones. Furthermore, defective samples with known flaws are rarely accessible due to confidentiality concerns. Consequently, this work explores unsupervised approaches trained exclusively on defect-free data to enable anomaly detection without labeled defects.

3   Methodology

The following section presents the architectural foundations of the implemented models, each designed to detect anomalies in shearographic image data. Two distinct approaches are introduced: an autoencoder-based reconstruction method and a Student-Teacher Feature Matching framework.

3.1   Architecture

Autoencoder. A widely used model for unsupervised anomaly detection is the autoencoder. It reconstructs input data by first encoding it into a lower-dimensional latent space and then decoding it back to its original form. For anomaly detection, the autoencoder is trained exclusively on defect-free samples, allowing it to learn the underlying distribution of normal data. When applied to defective samples, reconstruction fails due to deviations from the learned distribution, leading to a higher reconstruction error, which serves as an anomaly indicator [3].

Autoencoders offer flexibility in their architecture. A simple feed-forward autoencoder reduces input dimensions through multiple layers, while convolutional autoencoders use CNN-based encoders for feature extraction. The latter is particularly effective for image data, as it preserves spatial features [3].

Two autoencoder architectures were implemented. The first is a feed-forward autoencoder without convolutional layers, referred to as AE. The input image is resized to 96×50 pixels from an original resolution of 1920×1050 pixels and then flattened into a vector of size 4800. The encoder consists of four fully connected layers with output dimensions of 256, 128, 64, and 10, respectively. The latent representation of the data is thus a vector in $\mathbf{R}^{10}$. Each layer is followed by a dropout layer and a ReLU activation function to improve generalization and prevent overfitting.

The second implementation, referred to as ConvAE, is based on [8,9], an autoencoder originally designed for time-series anomaly detection, adapted for two-dimensional data. The CNN-based encoder consists of four convolutional layers with 96, 128, and 256 feature maps using 3×3 convolutional kernels. Each layer is followed by batch normalization and a LeakyReLU activation function. The decoder mirrors the encoder structure to reconstruct the input data from the latent representation.

Student Teacher Model. In this work, the Student-Teacher Feature Pyramid Matching (STFPM) approach [29,30] was selected due to its high computational efficiency, widespread adoption, and competitive accuracy [7,14]. The model has been successfully applied and adapted across various domains, making it a robust choice for detecting defects in shearographic inspections [25,28,32,33].

The STFPM architecture, shown in Fig. 3, consists of two neural networks with identical structures, referred to as the Student and the Teacher. Unlike siamese networks, these architectures do not share trainable weights. The Teacher network is a pre-trained model that remains frozen during training, serving as a reference by providing feature representations of defect-free inputs. The Student network is trained exclusively on non-defective samples and learns to approximate the feature representations extracted by the Teacher. The training objective is to minimize the discrepancy between the feature outputs of both networks, with the loss function computed as the cumulative difference between the Student's and Teacher's activations across multiple layers [31].

Once trained, the model produces a heatmap that visualizes the pixel-wise differences between the feature representations of the Student and the Teacher. Since the model is trained solely on non-defective data, it learns to reproduce normal feature distributions with minimal error. When applied to defective samples, however, the reconstruction error increases, particularly in the regions where anomalies are present. This characteristic enables STFPM not only to classify defective and non-defective samples but also to localize defects at a pixel level.

For the implementation in this work, the official STFPM model [29] was adopted and integrated into the existing class structures. Both the Student and Teacher networks use a ResNet18 architecture, with the pre-trained weights for the Teacher being sourced from the TorchVision model zoo [1]. In addition to the core implementation of STFPM, the model was embedded into multiple classes designed to facilitate visualization and analysis of the generated heatmaps. These include peak detection mechanisms to assist in the localization of potential defects within the input images.

Two variants of the student-teacher model were implemented: STFPM (Peaks) and STFPM (Means). Both share identical model weights; the only difference lies in the scoring strategy. STFPM (Peaks) uses the highest anomaly score from the predicted heatmap, whereas STFPM (Means) computes the average score over the input region.

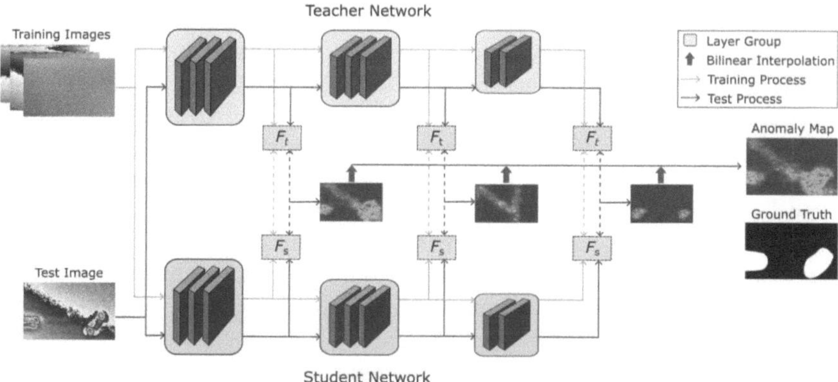

Fig. 3. Architecture of the Student–Teacher Feature Pyramid Matching model, adapted from [31].

3.2   Dataset Preparation and Training Setup

Six custom specimens were designed to simulate industrial conditions while ensuring reproducibility. Each specimen consisted of a 500 mm × 50 mm acrylic glass strip coated with a 1.2 mm thick, 45 mm wide rubber layer. To simulate subsurface defects, five specimens contained thin inserts of heat-shielding foil embedded between the materials. These air-filled inclusions remain invisible from the surface but are verifiable from the transparent backside, providing labeled ground truth.

The specimen's dimensions match the field of view of the shearography optics and the travel range of a UR5e robot arm, allowing automated scanning in 10 mm increments. Each frame contains at most two defects, enabling isolated evaluation. Data were acquired under two conditions: minimal global deformation through rigid fixation, and varied thermal excitation to induce diverse global deformation patterns. This allowed for capturing both localized defect responses and representative background variation.

The complete dataset comprises 10,498 shearography recordings acquired under controlled laboratory conditions. Of these, 2,537 recordings represent defect-free specimens measured under fixed boundary conditions, which suppress global deformations. Another 3,650 recordings capture defect-free specimens without fixation, leading to varying global deformation and corresponding fringe patterns. The remaining 4,311 recordings contain deliberately introduced subsurface defects. Of these, 3,233 were acquired under fixed boundary conditions, showing no global deformation. The remaining 1,078 defective recordings were acquired without fixation. Among these, 649 show noticeable global deformation.

The defective samples were manually annotated by a domain expert. Each annotated instance consists of a set of four temporally offset images capturing the same region under identical loading conditions, accompanied by bounding boxes marking the observed defect indications. The defect-free recordings serve two complementary roles: the measurements under fixed boundary conditions represent an idealized baseline free of global deformation, while the unfixed specimens introduce realistic variability in the form of fringe patterns caused by global deformation, thereby increasing the complexity of distinguishing local defect-related features from non-defect-induced surface behavior.

Based on the available dataset, two subsets were defined to address different evaluation scenarios in anomaly detection. The first, referred to as Subset A, includes only defect-free images acquired under fixed conditions, in which no global deformation patterns are present. This configuration yields a controlled baseline, consisting of 2,020 images for training, 254 for validation, and 254 for testing. Subset B includes all 6,187 defect-free recordings, incorporating both undistorted and globally deformed samples. In this case, the training set comprises 4,582 images, with 584 used for validation and 697 for testing. In both variants, defective samples are added to the validation and test sets to evaluate binary classification performance under realistic conditions. These defective samples are drawn from the defective category in proportions that preserve the fixed/unfixed ratio. Specifically, 714 annotated defect samples are included in the test set and 391 in the validation set. These defective samples are excluded from anomaly detection training and reserved for model evaluation.

To quantitatively assess the localization performance of the proposed STFPM-based anomaly detection, a dedicated subset of the annotated defect data was used for training a YOLOv8 detection model [12]. The same 714 and 391 samples that were already included in the anomaly detection test and validation sets were reused to ensure consistency across evaluations. The remaining 3,523 annotated defective samples were reserved exclusively for training the YOLOv8 model, ensuring an unbiased benchmark.

Additionally, to evaluate the separability of the learned feature representations and the underlying structure of the data, t-distributed stochastic neighbor embedding (t-SNE) [2] was applied.

All experiments were conducted on a Windows 11 desktop PC equipped with a 13th Gen Intel(R) Core(TM) i7-13700 processor, 128 GB RAM, and an NVIDIA RTX 4000 GPU with 16 GB VRAM. All models were implemented in Python 3.11 using the PyTorch framework [17], with CUDA [15] support for accelerated training. Code and dataset will be made available at [19], along with the exact device and acquisition parameters and a detailed description of the dataset generation process.

3.3   Model Comparison and Evaluation Metrics

The evaluation of the proposed method addresses two key aspects: binary classification between defect-free and defective samples, and the quantitative assessment of localization performance.

Classification performance was assessed using the receiver operating characteristic (ROC) curve [10] and the precision-recall (PR) curve [4]. The area under the ROC curve (AUC) quantifies the trade-off between true positive rate and false positive rate, with an AUC of 0.5 indicating random performance for binary classification. The PR curve illustrates the relationship between precision and recall, with the average precision (AP) summarizing precision across all recall levels.

To quantify localization accuracy, the STFPM and YOLO models were evaluated using common metrics from object detection [21]. These include the intersection over union (IoU), the mean average precision (mAP), mAP at fixed IoU thresholds of 0.5 and 0.75 (mAP@0.5, mAP@0.75), and the mean average recall (mAR) at one and ten predictions per image (mAR@1, mAR@10). The IoU between a predicted region B and a ground truth region A is defined as the ratio of their intersection over their union. In cases with multiple predictions per ground truth region, only the prediction with the highest IoU is considered.

Since only a single defect class is evaluated, the mean average precision equals the average precision ($mAP = AP$). The fixed IoU thresholds define the criteria for correct matches, while the recall metrics quantify the fraction of correctly detected regions under limited prediction counts. All localization metrics were computed using the mean average precision implementation from the Torch-Metrics library [6]. As the Student-Teacher model does not produce conventional classification scores, the maximum anomaly score within each predicted region was used as a confidence proxy for ranking and evaluation.

4   Results

4.1   Binary Classification

The corresponding ROC and PR curves for both subsets are shown in Fig. 4, illustrating the performance differences across all models. For Subset A, the STFPM-based methods achieve perfect performance, with AUC and AP values of 1.0, matching the supervised YOLOv8 baseline. The ConvAE model achieves an AUC of 0.71 and an AP of 0.82, while the simple Autoencoder performs notably worse (AUC of 0.57, AP of 0.70). Given a chance level of 0.61 for AP in this subset, only STFPM and ConvAE yield results above random performance.

In Subset B, the supervised YOLOv8 again achieves perfect scores (AUC and AP of 1.0). STFPM Peaks maintains strong performance with an AUC of 0.99 and an AP of 0.98, while STFPM Means shows reduced but still competitive results, with an AUC of 0.77 and an AP of 0.74. In contrast, ConvAE and AE exhibit significantly lower performance in this more challenging setting, achieving AUC values of 0.30 and 0.17, and AP values of 0.34 and 0.23, respectively. The chance level for AP in Subset B is 0.36.

4.2   Dataset

The t-SNE visualization in Fig. 5 illustrates the learned feature space for both training subsets. Defect-free samples are shown in an open circle, while defective samples are marked in a filled grey circle. In both subsets, a clear separation

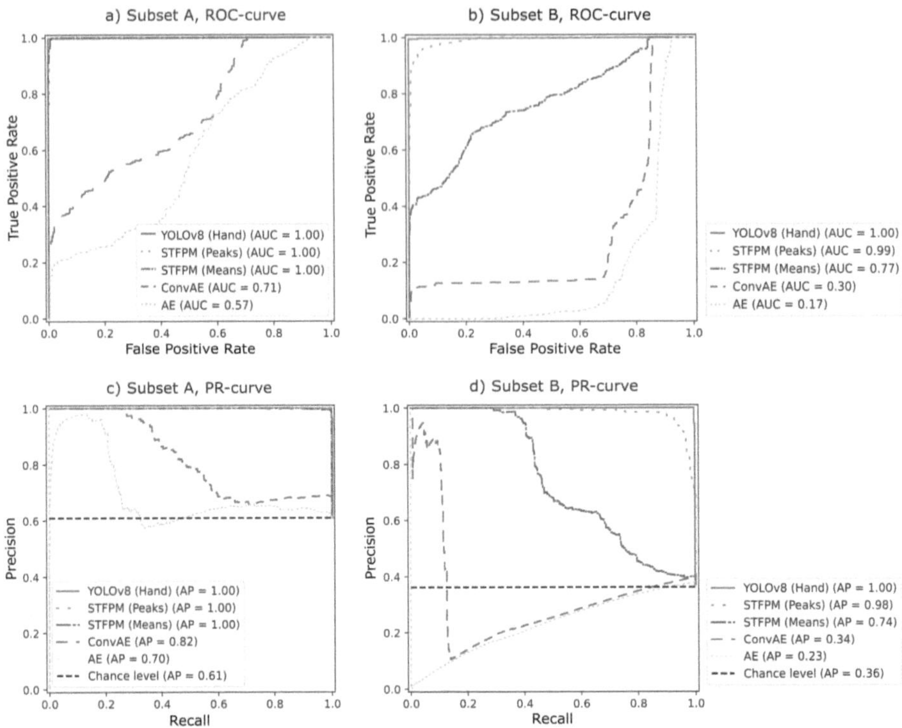

Fig. 4. ROC and PR curves for the binary classification task on Subset A and Subset B. Each plot compares unsupervised models (STFPM Peaks/Means, ConvAE, AE) against the supervised YOLOv8 baseline. (a) ROC Subset A, (b) ROC Subset B, (c) PR Subset A, (d) PR Subset B.

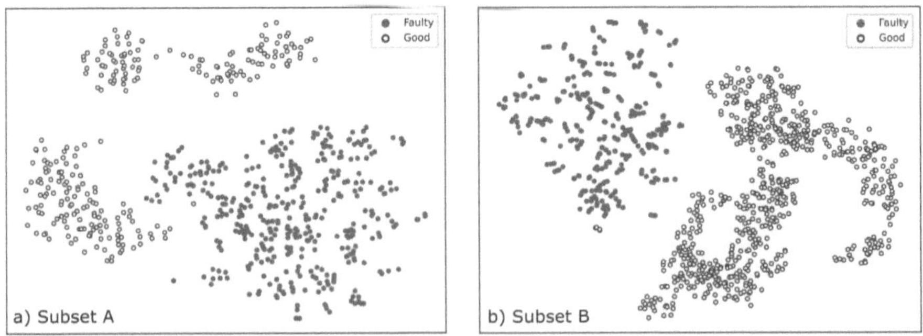

Fig. 5. t-SNE embeddings illustrating the feature separability of defect-free and defective samples for (a) Subset A, trained exclusively on undistorted data, and (b) Subset B, which includes globally deformed defect-free samples.

between classes is observed, indicating that the learned representations effectively capture discriminative characteristics.

In Subset A, which consists solely of undistorted defect-free samples, this separation is particularly pronounced, with only one defect-free sample located near the defective cluster. Furthermore, the defect-free samples in Subset A exhibit a distinct internal structure, forming at least two well-separated clusters. Subset B, containing globally deformed but non-defective samples, also demonstrates good overall class separability. However, two defect-free samples lie closer to the defective cluster boundary. Unlike Subset A, the defect-free samples in Subset B form a more contiguous cluster but contain noticeable low-density regions, suggesting non-uniform distribution within the normal class. These findings indicate that both subsets enable clear class separation while revealing meaningful intra-class variability within defect-free samples.

4.3   Localization

Table 1 presents the localization results for the STFPM method, evaluated on Subset A and Subset B. For this experiment, only the Peaks variant was used. The predicted anomaly maps were smoothed and then binarized using fixed thresholds, which were optimized separately for each subset based on validation data. A threshold of 0.1 was selected for Subset A, and 0.001 for Subset B. The results are compared to those of a supervised YOLOv8 model trained with pixel-wise defect annotations.

Table 1. Localization performance comparison of STFPM and YOLOv8.

Model	IoU	mAP	mAP@50	mAP@75	mAR@1	mAR@10
YOLOv8	0.8695	0.7435	0.9901	0.9195	0.5817	0.7884
STFPM (Subset A)	0.6965	0.3389	0.7421	0.1727	0.3209	0.4782
STFPM (Subset B)	0.7113	0.3852	0.7832	0.2611	0.3703	0.5127

5   Discussion

5.1   Binary Classification

The results indicate a clear divergence in performance between the STFPM-based methods and the autoencoder-based models across both subsets. For Subset A, representing near-ideal conditions, the STFPM Peaks and Means approaches achieve perfect classification performance, matching the supervised YOLOv8 baseline with AUC and AP scores of 1.0. This demonstrates that the STFPM methods effectively capture the discriminative features necessary to distinguish defective from defect-free samples under these conditions.

The STFPM Means method is conceptually similar to the autoencoder models, as it computes the average reconstruction error over the heatmap, analogous to the aggregation of the autoencoder's reconstruction error. Nevertheless, STFPM Means consistently achieves higher performance than both the convolutional autoencoder and the simple autoencoder, which exhibit moderate and lower performance, respectively (ConvAE AUC 0.71, AP 0.82; AE AUC 0.57, AP 0.70). Furthermore, STFPM Peaks, which detects localized maximum errors instead of averages, attains the best performance among the unsupervised approaches, underscoring the benefit of capturing localized anomalies over global averages.

This pattern becomes even more pronounced on Subset B, which introduces global deformations and thus greater complexity. While YOLOv8 and STFPM Peaks maintain near perfect scores (AUC and AP of 1.0 and 0.99/0.98 respectively), STFPM Means experiences a reduction in performance (AUC 0.77 and AP 0.74) but still notably outperforms both autoencoder models, which perform below or near chance level (ConvAE AUC 0.30 and AP 0.34; AE AUC 0.17 and AP 0.23). These results further confirm the limitations of the autoencoder architectures in this setting.

Overall, these findings suggest that the relatively poor performance of the autoencoder models is likely attributable to architectural or training limitations rather than an inherent lack of class separability in the data. This is supported by the t-SNE visualization in Fig. 5, which reveals well-defined clusters corresponding to the two classes. The moderate success of the STFPM Means method further indicates that the data contain discriminative features accessible to appropriate models. To fully exploit this intrinsic separability, future work should investigate alternative model architectures or enhanced preprocessing techniques. In contrast, the consistently strong performance of the STFPM Peaks method underscores its robustness and effectiveness for anomaly detection, even under challenging conditions with significant global deformations.

5.2 Localization

Despite being an unsupervised approach, STFPM demonstrates promising localization capabilities across both datasets. Since localization was evaluated exclusively on defective samples, the YOLO model is unaffected by the subset definitions and can be compared consistently across both. The localization performance depends strongly on the chosen thresholds. STFPM tends to generate multiple smaller bounding boxes for larger defect areas, which may be detected as separate anomaly regions instead of one unified defect. This fragmentation naturally affects metrics such as mean Average Precision and mean Average Recall, since these metrics penalize excessive or overlapping detections.

Despite the unsupervised nature of the method and the variability in defect size and appearance, overall detection quality remains high. Figure 6 illustrates this with a representative sample: the left image shows the anomaly heatmap generated by STFPM, while the right image presents the corresponding sample overlaid with the heatmap. The visualization highlights the model's ability to localize defects effectively, although spatial accuracy may occasionally be limited by thresholding or peak fragmentation.

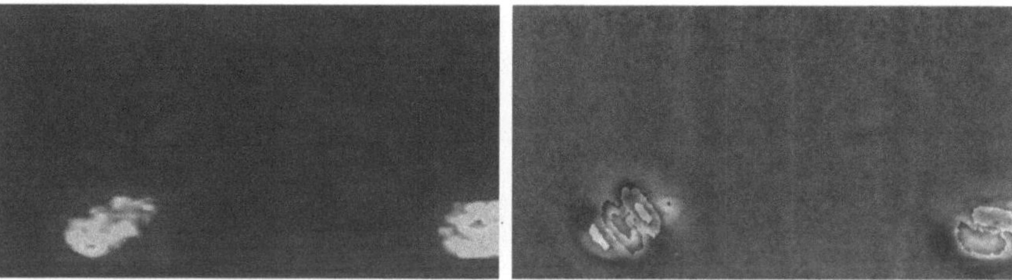

Fig. 6. Exemplaric defect localization using STFPM. Left: predicted anomaly heatmap. Right: same heatmap overlaid on the original shearography image. High anomaly scores correspond to localized defect regions.

6   Conclusions

This study demonstrates that STFPM, especially its Peaks variant, is a robust unsupervised approach for defect detection and localization in shearographic inspection of industrial components. It reliably distinguishes between defect-free and defective samples, even under complex conditions with global deformations, closely matching the performance of supervised YOLOv8 models that require extensive labeled data. In contrast, autoencoder-based models show limited effectiveness in this domain, likely due to architectural constraints rather than inherent data challenges, as confirmed by the clear class separability observed in feature space visualizations.

Importantly, STFPM's unsupervised nature addresses a key industrial challenge: enabling automated evaluation of shearographic data without costly, time-consuming defect annotations. While localization precision can be further improved, the promising results underline STFPM's potential for scalable, automated non-destructive testing in real-world industrial applications.

Future work should focus on refining localization accuracy, adapting models to varying defect types and materials and validating the method in real-world scenarios to support broader deployment of automated shearographic inspection.

Acknowledgments. This research was funded by the Ministry of Science and Health Rhineland-Palatinate as part of the Young Researchers Fund of the Research Initiative (Funding Period 2025) and by the Federal Ministry for Economic Affairs and Climate Protection (BMWK) through the 'Central Innovation Program for SMEs (ZIM)', funding code KK5060010SY3.

Disclosure of Interests. The authors declare no conflict of interest.

References

1. Pretrained models for pytorch (2021). https://modelzoo.co/model/pretrained-modelspytorch
2. Cai, T.T., Ma, R.: Theoretical foundations of t-SNE for visualizing high-dimensional clustered data (2022). https://arxiv.org/abs/2105.07536
3. Chen, S., Guo, W.: Auto-encoders in deep learning a review with new perspectives. Mathematics Math. Methods Appl. Artif. Intell. Comput. Vis. **11**(18) (2023). https://doi.org/10.3390/math11081777
4. Cook, J., Ramadas, V.: When to consult precision-recall curves. Stand Genomic Sci. **20**(1), 131–148 (2020). https://doi.org/10.1177/1536867X20909693
5. Deng, J., et al.: Imagenet: a large-scale hierarchical image database. In: 2009 IEEE Conference on Computer Vision and Pattern Recognition (2009). https://doi.org/10.1109/CVPR.2009.5206848
6. Detlefsen, N.S., et al.: Torchmetrics - measuring reproducibility in pytorch. J. Open Source Softw. **7**(70), 4101 (2022). https://doi.org/10.21105/joss.04101
7. Dutta, P., et al.: Exploring deep learning-based unsupervised image anomaly detection and localization methods for industrial quality assurance. In: 2024 1st International Conference on Cognitive, Green and Ubiquitous Computing (IC-CGU) (2024). https://doi.org/10.1109/IC-CGU58078.2024.10530676
8. Gong, D., et al.: Memorizing normality to detect anomaly: Memory-augmented deep autoencoder for unsupervised anomaly detection. Comput. Sci. Comput. Vis. Pattern Recognit. (2019). https://doi.org/10.48550/arXiv.1904.02639. https://arxiv.org/abs/1904.02639
9. Gong, D., et al.: STFPM - Official Implementation (2019). https://github.com/donggong1/memae-anomaly-detection
10. Hoo, Z.H., et al.: What is an ROC curve? Emerg. Med. J. **34**(6), 357–359 (2017). https://doi.org/10.1136/emermed-2017-206735
11. Hussain, M.: YOLO-v1 to YOLO-v8, the rise of YOLO and its complementary nature toward digital manufacturing and industrial defect detection. Mach. State Art Digit. Manufact. Syst. **11**(7), 677 (2023). https://doi.org/10.3390/machines11070677
12. Jocher, G., et al.: Ultralytics yolov8 (2023). https://github.com/ultralytics/ultralytics
13. Li, W., et al.: Simulation dataset preparation and hybrid training for deep learning in defect detection using digital shearography. Appl. Sci. **12**(14) (2022). https://doi.org/10.3390/app12146931
14. Mylläri, J., Nurminen, J.K.: Discrepancy scaling for fast unsupervised anomaly localization. In: 2023 IEEE 47th Annual Computers, Software, and Applications Conference (COMPSAC) (2023). https://doi.org/10.1109/COMPSAC57700.2023.00042
15. NVIDIA, Vingelmann, P., Fitzek, F.H.: Cuda, release: 10.2.89 (2020). https://developer.nvidia.com/cuda-toolkit
16. Pang, G., et al.: Deep learning for anomaly detection: a review. ACM Comput. Surv. (CSUR) **54**(2), 1–38 (2021). https://doi.org/10.1145/3439950
17. Paszke, A., et al.: Pytorch: an imperative style, high-performance deep learning library. In: Advances in Neural Information Processing Systems, vol. 32 (2019)
18. Petry, C.M.: Weiterentwicklung der Shearografie mit räumlichem Phasenschieben als zerstörungsfreies Prüfverfahren für die automatisierte Serienüberwachung. Ph.D. thesis, Universität Saarlandes (2021)

19. Plassmann, J., et al.: Unsupervised shearography dataset (2025). https://github.com/JessicaPlassmann/Unsupervised-Shearography
20. Redmon, J., et al.: You only look once: unified, real-time object detection. In: 2016 IEEE Conference on Computer Vision and Pattern Recognition (CVPR), pp. 779–788 (2016). https://doi.org/10.1109/CVPR.2016.91
21. Rezatofighi, H., et al.: Generalized intersection over union: a metric and a loss for bounding box regression (2019). https://arxiv.org/abs/1902.09630
22. Rudolph, M., et al.: Asymmetric student-teacher networks for industrial anomaly detection. Comput. Sci. Mach. Learn. (2022). https://doi.org/10.48550/arXiv.2210.07829. https://arxiv.org/abs/2210.07829
23. Schmarje, L., et al.: A survey on semi-, self- and unsupervised learning for image classification. IEEE Access **9**, 82146 –82168 (2021). https://doi.org/10.1109/ACCESS.2021.3084358
24. Schuth, M., Buerakov, W.: Handbuch Optische Messtechnik: Praktische Anwendungen für Entwicklung, Versuch, Fertigung und Qualitätssicherung, 1st edn. Hanser, Munich (2017)
25. Schwarz, J., et al.: A patch-based student-teacher pyramid matching approach to anomaly detection in 3D magnetic resonance imaging. In: Medical Imaging with Deep Learning (2024). https://openreview.net/forum?id=vh01Nd5PCl
26. Tao, N., et al.: FEM-assisted shearography with spatially modulated heating for non-destructive testing of thick composites with deep defects. Compos. Struct. **297** (2022). https://doi.org/10.1016/j.compstruct.2022.115980
27. Tao, N., et al.: Shearography non-destructive testing of thick GFRP laminates: numerical and experimental study on defect detection with thermal loading. Compos. Struct. **282** (2022). https://doi.org/10.1016/j.compstruct.2021.115008
28. Valjakka, J., et al.: Anomaly localization in audio via feature pyramid matching. In: 2023 IEEE 47th Annual Computers, Software, and Applications Conference (COMPSAC) (2023). https://doi.org/10.1109/COMPSAC57700.2023.00044
29. Wang, G., et al.: STFPM - official implementation (2021). https://github.com/gdwang08/STFPM
30. Wang, G., et al.: Student-teacher feature pyramid matching for anomaly detection. Computer Science: Computer Vision and Pattern Recognitiong (2021). https://doi.org/10.48550/arXiv.2103.04257. https://arxiv.org/abs/2103.04257
31. Wang, L., Yoon, K.J.: Knowledge distillation and student-teacher learning for visual intelligence: a review and new outlooks. IEEE Trans. Pattern Anal. Mach. Intell. **44**(6), 3048–3068 (2021). https://doi.org/10.1109/TPAMI.2021.3055564
32. Yamada, S., Hotta, K.: Reconstruction student with attention for student-teacher pyramid matching. Computer Science: Computer Vision and Pattern Recognition (2021). https://doi.org/10.48550/arXiv.2111.15376. https://arxiv.org/abs/2111.15376
33. Zhu, J., et al.: Asymmetric teacher student feature pyramid matching for industrial anomaly detection. IEEE Trans. Instrum. Measur. **73** (2023). https://doi.org/10.1109/TIM.2023.3338681

Data Science Approaches to Evaluating Honours Candidates

Francesca von Braun-Bates[1,2]([envelope]) [ORCID], Sunreeta Sen[3], Indraayudh Talukdar[4], and Anirban Lahiri[5]

[1] Ministry of Justice, London, UK
`francesca.von.braun-bates@justice.gov.uk`
[2] Joint Counter-Terrorism Prisons and Probation Hub, London, UK
[3] Arndit Ltd., Cambridge, UK
[4] Indian Institute of Technology Delhi, New Delhi, India
[5] Kainos, London, UK

Abstract. This paper introduces the first application of data science to the UK Honours system. We present a comprehensive Natural Language Processing methodology for evaluating public sentiment of Honours recipients. In order to form an opinion about applicants for the UK King's Honours, we have evaluated two existing sentiment algorithms (AFINN, VADER) and then created our own novel algorithm (MINOS). The promising results in this work indicate that this system can be used to augment human evaluation to better judge whether a current or future recipient has maintained the high standards of conduct demanded to retain an Honour. Our novel approach is generalisable to any individual with a sufficient internet footprint and has applications in many fields including recruitment, national security and investigative journalism.

Keywords: web-scraping · entity resolution · sentiment analysis · open-source intelligence

1 Introduction

The Honours system has recognised individuals who have contributed exceptionally to the United Kingdom for nearly a thousand years [19]. This complex and ancient system needs to leverage cutting-edge technology to remain fair and transparent in the 21st century. This paper is (to our knowledge) the first application of data science to the Honours System. This paper demonstrates how combining a variety of natural language processing techniques creates a thorough and open-source intelligence picture from which to measure public opinion of Honours recipients.

This paper improves on the state of the art in four ways:

- it uses a broad range of sources rather than purely social media or news articles;

– it illustrates a novel algorithm for identifying positive or negative personality traits as compared to two existing algorithms for sentiment analysis [11,18];
– we scrutinise the relevance of our input using co-reference resolution;
– we probe SOIs from many different fields and with varying degrees of celebrity (or non-celebrity) status

The individual techniques we apply to this problem are not new. Web-scraping has existed in various forms since the earliest days of the internet [25] including web crawling, web indexing and archiving of web content. Tokenisation has been a core component of natural language processing for over 30 years (see [16] for a history). Co-reference resolution is the task of associating different linguistic expressions which refer to the same entity [10], a linguistic problem well-known as early as Cicero in the first century BC. Many sentiment analysis approaches exist (see [2] for a selection). We use two off-the-shelf models: AFINN [17] and VADER [11] and construct our own algorithm, MINOS, in Sect. 4. What is novel is our use of these techniques to solve a whole problem for users in a challenging context.

The structure of this paper is as follows. In Sect. 2 we summarise the Honours system. We define our subjects of interest in Sect. 3. Our methodology is described in Sect. 4, including data collection, cleaning, tokenisation, co-reference resolution, sentiment analysis and extraction of results. Section 5 shows the first advantage of web-scraping over manual research by examining the fraction of web-scraped text which survived our relevance criteria. We summarise our sentiment results in Sect. 5. We conclude in Sect. 6 with a summary of our workflow and results, followed by a discussion of challenges addressed in future papers.

2   The Honours System

This section covers the essentials of the Honours System, in particular the concept of forfeiture.

The modern Honours System recognises individuals who have made an outstanding contribution to public life in the United Kingdom [1]. It encompasses diverse fields such as charity and voluntary service, education, science, arts, and business [1]. The system bestows various levels of awards [9] to reflect a recipient's level of impact and time of sustained contributions to their field [9]. Perhaps uniquely, individuals must maintain high standards of conduct *after* receiving the Honour in order to retain it. Anyone falling short of these standards risks having the Honour revoked (even posthumously), a process known as forfeiture [7].

Honours nominations are gathered from both public submissions and the Civil Service, pass through a series of sift committees, then undergo vetting before receiving final royal approval (details in [4–6]). This vetting consumes considerable resource to confirm that any nomination details are factually correct, to conduct criminal record checks and probity checks with professional bodies and government departments [12].

Maintaining public confidence in the Honours system requires award recipients to consistently uphold high standards. When an awardee's conduct brings the system into disrepute, the award may be forfeited [7] or in rare cases, posthumously revoked [8]. Forfeiture is "almost certain" in the event of severe criminal convictions and/or professional disbarment [12]. Other causes for potential disrepute often results in nuanced and complex cases requiring careful consideration, e.g. [20]. Historically, awards were conferred post-career to minimize forfeiture risk [3]. More recently, awards focus on timely recognition of achievements [4], which may or may not be causally-connected to the recent increase in referrals to the Forfeiture Committee [12].

Forfeiture decisions are handled by an independent Forfeiture Committee, which lacks investigative powers [20]. Instead it relies on evidence including official investigations and court proceedings [12]. In this high-risk environment, a clear and robust intelligence picture is essential to judge each case on its own merits. Automated data-driven methods could significantly enhance proactive detection of potential misconduct, supporting timely interventions to uphold the integrity of the system.

3   Selecting Subjects of Interest

To robustly test our novel approach, we selected two control groups as well as the forfeiture group:

- "Infamous" people whose behaviour stands in direct contrast to enhancing public good;
- "Awarded" subjects who have received an Honour and retained it since, suggesting continued behaviour which supports the public good;
- "Forfeited" subjects who forfeited their Honour, or who were posthumously stripped of the Honour by the Committee.

We selected twenty SOIs per group.

The awarded and forfeited groups were selected from the announcements of the London Gazette [13]. We selected a range of award levels, from the highest (Knight/Dame) to the lowest (Member) [9]. We were careful to include a broad range of fields and achievements across the ten Honours Committees, ranging from the arts and sciences to business, sport and civil service [14]. We also used a mixture of male and female recipients approximating the underlying gender split. The differentiating factor between them is that—unlike the "awarded" group— all forfeited SOIs were stripped of their Honours for poor conduct. This level of poor conduct varies greatly in degree of criminality, the length and nature of the offence, and the delay between award and forfeiture.

The infamous group contains SOIs who far exceed the "criminal conviction" threshold for forfeiture. We selected individuals whose crimes (and, where possible, convictions) are in the public domain. Again we selected a mixture of male and female individuals.

We expect a well-behaved algorithm and a well-constructed method to clearly distinguish between each group:

- Highly positive for the awarded group
- Approaching zero for the forfeited group
- Highly negative for the infamous group

Without this distinction, we cannot invert the mapping for new SOI. In other words, we cannot train the algorithm on this group of known individuals to accurately classify any SOI in a test set.

Now we have a specific problem to solve and a set of subjects on which to test our solution. We detail our approach to solving this problem in Sect. 4.

4   Methodology

This section covers the key stages in our algorithm, summarised in Fig. 1.

4.1   Data Collection, Processing and Filtering

The initial phase of our process involves automating online searches to collect publicly accessible data about candidates. To simulate human research, we employed the Selenium web-driver [22] to automatically query Google with candidates' full names, extracted plain text from the results using BeautifulSoup [21] and preserved the original sources and their URLs to ensure traceability and auditability.

We encountered several limitations: the inability to access paywalled or subscription-based content, some pages blocked by compliance with a site's `robots.txt`, and incomplete retrieval of dynamically-generated JavaScript content. Nonetheless, the top 60–70 search results returned sufficient text for our proof-of-concept.

We separated the plain text into sentences using NLTK [15], which effectively handled linguistic complexities such as abbreviations, ellipses, and unconventional punctuation, ensuring robust sentence-level processing for subsequent analysis.

We discarded articles which were either under 500 characters long, or did not contain the SOI's "best-known full name" (not always equivalent to the *entire*, legal full name used in the search). This filtering strategy adeptly managed issues such as multi-part surnames, middle names, peerages, titles, and informal name variants.

The resulting dataset provided a focused and relevant base for sentiment analysis, significantly reducing noise and increasing the accuracy of subsequent analytical steps.

4.2   Co-reference Resolution

Co-reference resolution was applied to address the frequent occurrence of indirect candidate mentions in textual data. This critical step significantly improved the reliability and accuracy of sentiment analysis by ensuring appropriate attribution of content to specific candidates.

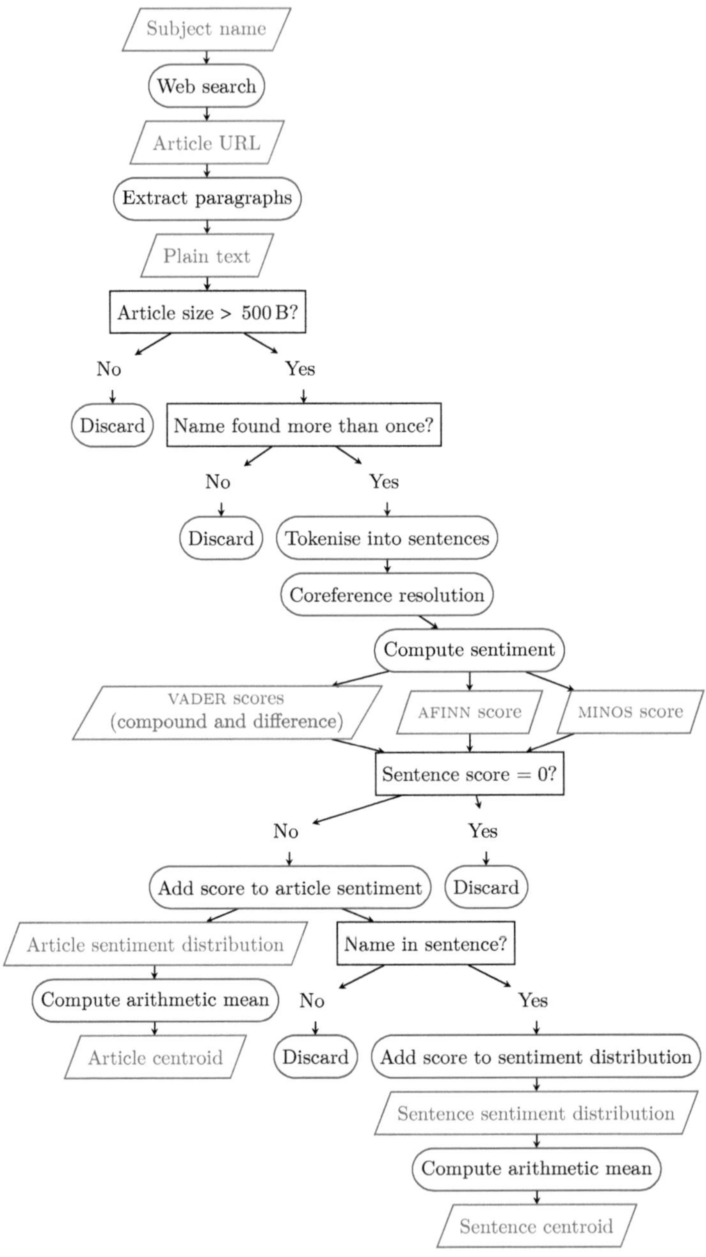

Fig. 1. Control flow of our methodology. Trapezia represent outputs (except the starting input), rectangles are binary decisions and rounded rectangles are outcomes.

Using a supervised learning-based Python algorithm trained on extensive English text collections, our approach systematically identified and linked pronouns and abbreviated references back to the candidates' full names. In case there are multiple people having the same name and surname combination, some additional distinguishing attributes can be used, which would further help disambiguation during coreference resolution, which was extensively validated.

4.3 Sentiment Algorithms

Our sentiment analysis involved evaluating multiple algorithms to determine their suitability for accurately assessing candidate-related text. Initially, we assessed the lexical approach AFINN, straightforwardly assigning integer scores from -5 to $+5$ for individual words but limited by a lack of contextual understanding. Next, we explored VADER, a rule-based model optimized for informal social media texts, adept at handling intensifiers and idioms but still challenged by formal content.

Recognizing these limitations, we developed MINOS, a tailored sentiment algorithm explicitly designed for the Honours evaluation context. MINOS incorporated comprehensive lexicons of positive and negative words, strongly emphasizing terms related to misconduct and criminality. The initial lexicons were taken from AFINN and VADER algorithms and then augmented with words often used to describe individuals either positively or negatively in news articles, assessed by linguists and other domain experts [24]. Sentences containing negative terms automatically received negative scores irrespective of any positive language, effectively mirroring the Honours system's stringent standards on recipient conduct. Describing in detail the scoring and decision-making rules implemented in the MINOS algorithm is beyond the scope of this paper and we refer the reader to the code for details [23].

4.4 Posterior Marginalisation

Sentiment analysis produced a multi-modal distribution averaged over all surviving text for each SOI. We integrated over these distributions to produce a centroid to convey the "average" sentiment per individual.

Although these can be compared for the same algorithm, we cannot compare between algorithms. This is because the different approaches have different (and sometimes unbounded) priors which cannot all be normalised to the unit interval.

The final output also identified and highlighted sentences with significant positive or negative sentiment and the source URL. Thus an Honours sifter had access to the summary centroid, the full posterior, outlying values and the number of articles and sentences which survived filtering from the original web search. This approach facilitated efficient human evaluation, enabling committees to quickly verify the accuracy, relevance, and reliability of presented evidence, ensuring decisions remained informed, reproducible, and auditable.

5   Results, Analysis and Discussion

5.1   Relevance Filtering

Filtering web-sourced articles is essential to retain only relevant content for each individual. As illustrated in Fig. 2 article file sizes vary by seven orders of magnitude. Short files (dark red) were largely spurious browser messages. Extremely large files (up to 10^7 characters) swamped any signal about the desired SOI with noise about other individuals and topics. The most meaningful content usually falls within the mid-size range (1 kB–1 MB), which balances depth and relevance.

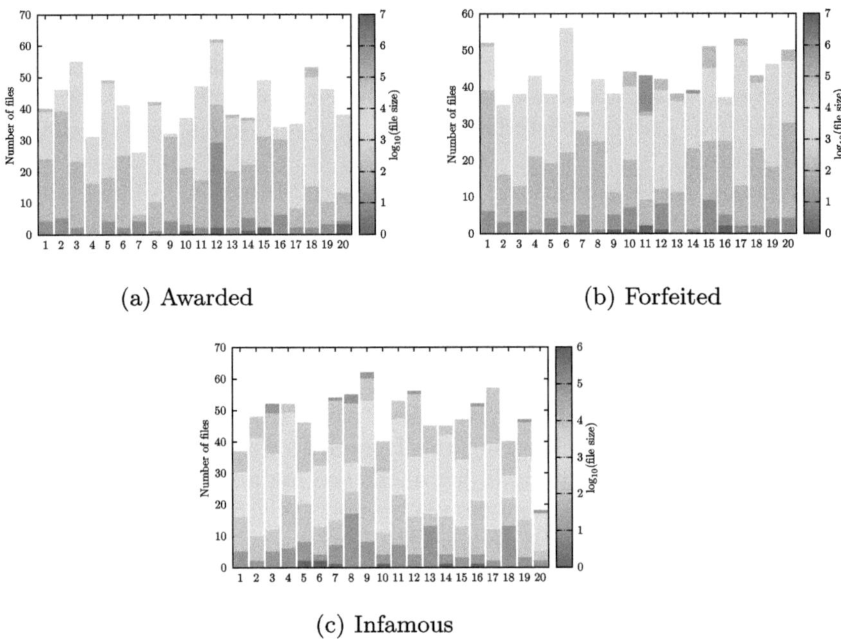

(a) Awarded

(b) Forfeited

(c) Infamous

Fig. 2. File size distribution per SOI group. The colour scale represents the (logarithmically-binned) file size in bytes, with the height of each stack is the number of articles per SOI.

This distribution highlights the importance of machine-assisted filtering, as the volume of material far exceeds what a human analyst could process, ensuring accuracy in sentiment analysis and interpretation.

5.2   Marginalised Centroids

This section compares centroid results from different sentiment analysis algorithms applied to individuals across the awarded, forfeited, and infamous groups.

The results focus only on sentences that explicitly reference the individual once the co-reference resolution has been performed. This filters out as much

noise as possible—which we know is not attributable to the SOI—while retaining
as much information as possible thanks to co-reference resolution. We have four
results (one per sentiment algorithm) for each of the three SOI groups. Figure 3
shows box plots, wherein each datum is the centroid for one SOI in that group.
The boxes show the inter-quartile range of the SOI group, with the mean shown
as a horizontal line. Red, gray and blue show infamous, forfeited and awarded
groups respectively.

Generally, our results demonstrate the desirable properties defined in Sect. 3.
Independent of the sentiment algorithm, the arithmetic means and inter-quartile
ranges are clearly positive for awarded, clearly negative for infamous and span
zero for the forfeited groups. Some undesirable results also occur, e.g. only
VADER's compound score returns a positive value for all awarded SOI, whereas
no algorithm returns a negative score for all infamous SOI. The prevalence of
outliers makes assigning an individual to a group based on the centroid a difficult prospect for a classification or clustering algorithm. Only MINOS shows a
clear distinction between the infamous group's inter-quartile range and the other
two groups, which do not overlap it at all. These mixed results suggest that we
have integrated over important detail in the posterior distributions to arrive at
a scalar summary result.

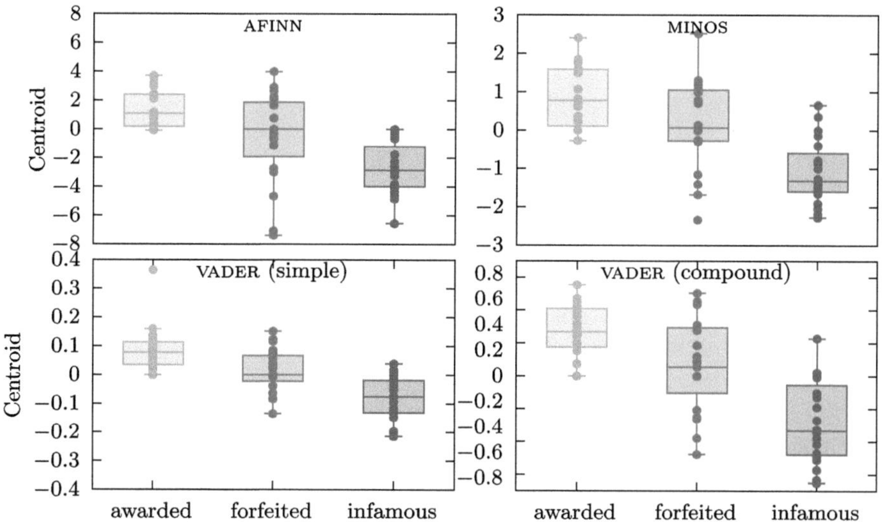

Fig. 3. Box plot of centroid distributions from coreference-resolved data, including only
sentences which contain the SOI name.

5.3   Selected Posteriors

This section shows the distribution functions for individual SOI. We selected one
from each group as an illustration of a typical posterior:

1. Kumar Bhattacharyya for awarded in Fig. 4
2. Rolf Harris for forfeited in Fig. 6
3. Charles Sobhraj for infamous in Fig. 5

All histograms integrate to unity, with the number of sentences in each bin shown above the bar for that bin. Red results are negative, whereas blue are positive. The zero bin (which would be grey) is excluded by our prior distribution to avoid washing out the results to zero everywhere else in the parameter space.

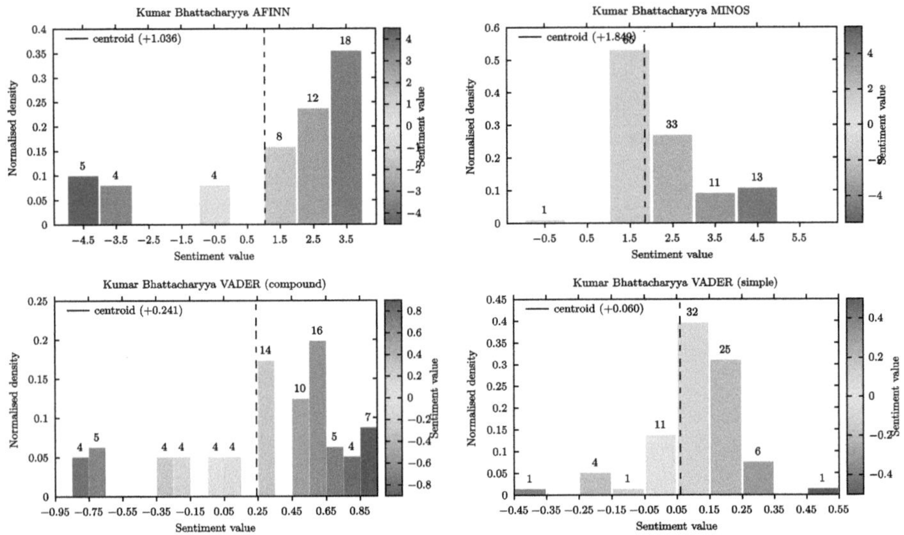

Fig. 4. Sentiment posteriors for Kumar Bhattacharyya.

Figure 4 shows broadly positive sentiment for our awarded SOI. The centroids are positive for all sentiment algorithms. However, the shape of the distributions differs. Only MINOS delivers a consistently positive result in which the centroid is firmly in the mode of the distribution, with few negative sentences. The other three algorithms show a long negative tail which we would not expect from an awarded SOI.

For infamous individuals, Fig. 5 shows negative centroids independent of the sentiment algorithm. Three distributions have similar shapes, apart from VADER compound which is strongly peaked at the negative extremum. Although this last algorithm seems desirable, it also has some extremely positive results (over 80% positive), which seem inexplicable for a prolific serial killer. In contrast, the other distributions have a much longer negative tail than their positive component, which agrees with the logic for this group. Thus in this group, our example show that three of the four distribution have desirable properties throughout the posterior as well as in the summary centroid.

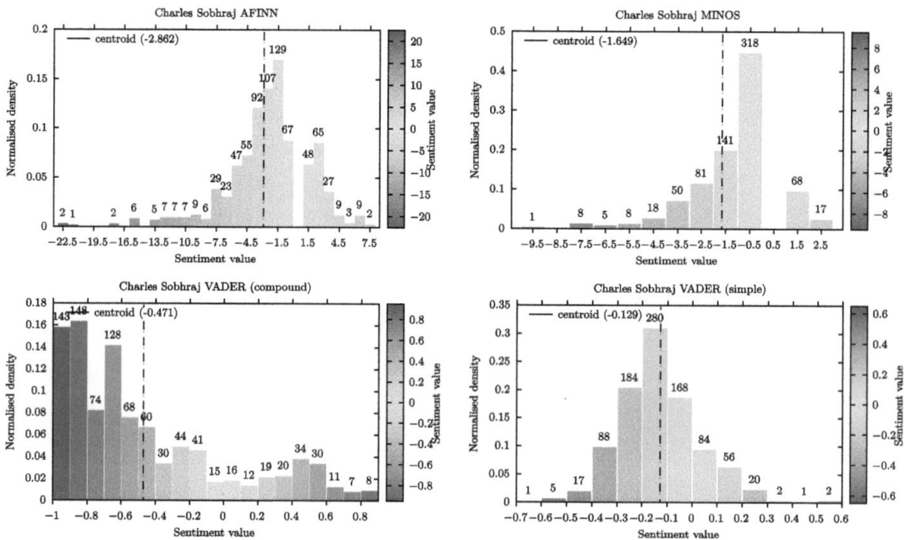

Fig. 5. Sentiment posteriors for Charles Sobhraj.

Figure 6 shows the mixture of positive and negative sentiment expected of a forfeited SOI. Whereas AFINN and MINOS produce negative centroids, VADER produces neutral and slightly positive centroids. All the distributions have different shapes: VADER simple peaks in the zero bin. Since all zero scores are removed by convolving with the prior, this only occurs when a sentence has elements of both positive and negative sentiment which "cancels out" at close to zero (rather than a neutral sentence without any sentiment). This is a nuance which is potentially misleading at first glance, so this algorithm is undesirable. The compound VADER score shows a bimodal distribution which is strongly skewed towards the positive. Thus it picks up Harris' positive actions (which may have contributed towards the award of his CBE), but it fails to adequately convey the prolifically-publicised offences for which his CBE was forfeited. Both AFINN and MINOS capture a range of sentiment, some extremes as well as mixed sentiment. However, MINOS delivers a clearer positive peak, resulting in a more balanced distribution, whereas AFINN captures the positive side less clearly. Apart from VADER compound, the centroids are all in or very close to the edge of the mode bin, which indicates that the summary is a reliable approximation of the whole distribution.

Across our SOI groups, MINOS delivers the results which are most consistent with our prior knowledge of the SOI. This makes it the most promising algorithm for wider application.

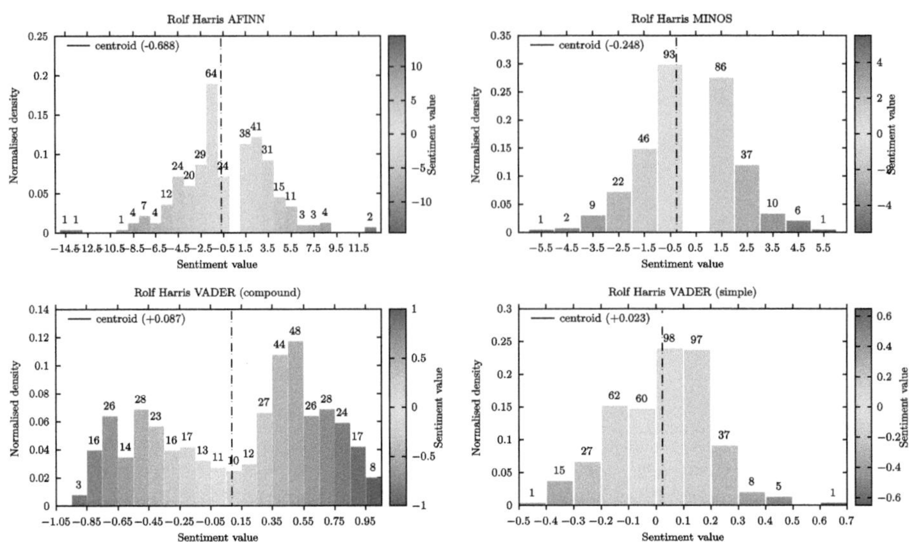

Fig. 6. Sentiment posteriors for Rolf Harris.

6 Conclusions and Future Work

We utilised several natural language processing techniques to maximise the information available to a human sifter:

- Web-scraping allows us to collect attributable, open-source information at scale
- Tokenisation divided articles of up to $\sim 10^7$ characters[1] into individual sense units, enabling us to discard irrelevant information
- Co-reference resolution was critical to identifying all information relevant to the SOI, without which we would have thrown away signal as well as noise, creating misleading results
- Sentiment analysis provided a rich range of posterior sentiment distributions which allowed us to make educated proposals on which algorithm works most effectively across all SOI groups

Bayesian inference broadly allowed us to create a summary score for each SOI from a full awareness of our prior assumptions. Despite inherent limitations regarding data accessibility, our methodology presents a robust, scalable solution capable of addressing the challenges inherent in maintaining public trust in the Honours system. It is accepted that the results from this work might have some biases based on the articles about any individual found on the internet. Therefore, a human-in-the-loop is essential to make the final decisions regarding an award. Future research directions include:

---

[1] This is approximately the length of the entire *Harry Potter* series, impossible for a human to consume at pace.

- periodic reassessment of current Honours recipients to proactively detect emerging risks
- broadening the intelligence picture via better access to news services and subscription-based platforms
- refining our MINOS sentiment model to better capture the context of the sentence as a whole (similar to VADER compound)
- expanding MINOS's vocabulary via semantic embeddings, which would allow us to assign positive and negative scores to synonyms of the current wordlist
- exploring the applicability of our methodology to other awards and recognition frameworks

This provides diverse opportunities to capitalise on the promising results in this proof-of-concept.

Our research highlights the potential for data science to significantly enhance the Honours System. It increases the efficiency and transparency of the selection process by gathering the most positive and negative information available in the public domain. Unlike the manual vetting approach used currently, our parallel, automated methodology can scale to the $\sim 200\,000$ living recipients of Honours. This opens the possibility to assess forfeiture risk dynamically, protecting the integrity of the Honours System as the information picture of recipients changes. The objective is not to replace human decision-making but to provide committees with an impartial and thorough intelligence picture, from which to make informed judgments. Our approach promises significant improvements in fairness, transparency, and public confidence across various high-profile applications.

Acknowledgments. This research originated in the Data Science Accelerator programme, with advocacy from Stephanie Karpetas OBE, Alec Waterhouse FORS and Christalla Kyriacou. We are grateful for the support of the Government Digital Service, the Office for National Statistics, the Government Operational Research Service, the Honours and Appointments Secretariat of the Cabinet Office, the (then) Department for Business, Energy and Industrial Strategy and the Ministry of Justice.

References

1. Armstrong, H.: Honours: history and reviews. House of Commons Library Briefing Paper 02832 (2017)
2. Birjali, M., Kasri, M., Beni-Hssane, A.: A comprehensive survey on sentiment analysis: approaches, challenges and trends. Knowl.-Based Syst. **226**, 107134 (2021). https://doi.org/10.1016/j.knosys.2021.107134
3. Cabinet Office: Reform of the honours system (2005). https://www.gov.uk/government/publications/reform-of-the-honours-system-2005

4. Cabinet Office: The first report on the operation of the honours system (2008). https://www.gov.uk/government/publications/operation-of-the-honours-system-2008

5. Cabinet Office: Second report on operation of the reformed honours system (2011). https://www.gov.uk/government/publications/second-report-on-operation-of-the-reformed-honours-system

6. Cabinet Office: Quinquennial review 2013-18 - prime minister's list allocations (2013). https://www.gov.uk/government/publications/five-yearly-review-of-honours-allocations-2013-to-2018

7. Cabinet Office: Having honours taken away (forfeiture) (2021). https://www.gov.uk/guidance/having-honours-taken-away-forfeiture

8. Cabinet Office: Updated forfeiture guidance (2021). https://www.gov.uk/government/news/updated-forfeiture-guidance

9. Crown: Types of honours and awards (2022). https://www.gov.uk/honours/types-of-honours-and-awards

10. Hirst, G.J.: Anaphora in natural language understanding : a survey. Master's thesis, Department of Engineering Physics, Research School of Physical Sciences, The Australian National University (1979)

11. Hutto, C., Gilbert, E.: Vader: a parsimonious rule-based model for sentiment analysis of social media text. In: Proceedings of the 8th International Conference on Weblogs and Social Media, ICWSM 2014 (2015)

12. Jay, A., Evans, M., Frank, I., Sharpling, D.: Operation of the Honours System, chap. I.2. Crown (2020). https://www.iicsa.org.uk/reports-recommendations/publications/investigation/westminster/part-i-honours-system/i2-operation-honours-system

13. London Gazette: Birthday and new year honours lists (1940 to 2021) (2022). https://www.thegazette.co.uk/honours-lists

14. London Gazette: Everything you need to know about nominating someone for a UK honour (2022). https://www.thegazette.co.uk/awards-and-accreditation/content/103437

15. Loper, E., Bird, S.: Nltk: the natural language toolkit. In: Proceedings of the ACL Workshop on Effective Tools and Methodologies for Teaching Natural Language Processing and Computational Linguistics (2002)

16. Mielke, S.J., et al.: Between words and characters: a brief history of open-vocabulary modeling and tokenization in NLP (2021). https://arxiv.org/abs/2112.10508

17. Nielsen, F.A.: AFINN: a new word list for sentiment analysis on twitter (2011). https://finnaarupnielsen.wordpress.com/2011/03/16/afinn-a-new-word-list-for-sentiment-analysis/

18. Nielsen, F.A.: A new anew: evaluation of a word list for sentiment analysis in microblogs. arXiv (2011). https://doi.org/10.48550/ARXIV.1103.2903. https://arxiv.org/abs/1103.2903

19. Phillips, S.H.: Review of the Honours System. Crown (2004). https://www.gov.uk/government/publications/review-of-the-honours-system-2004

20. Public Administration Select Committee: The honours system: Public adminstration select committee (2012). https://www.gov.uk/government/publications/pasc-report-on-the-honours-system-2012

21. Richardson, L.: Beautiful Soup (2004). https://www.crummy.com/software/BeautifulSoup/

22. Software Freedom Conservancy: The selenium browser automation project (2004). https://www.selenium.dev/documentation/

23. von Braun-Bates, F., Sen, S., Talukdar, I., Lahiri, A.: Google drive folder: Minos code (2025). https://drive.google.com/drive/folders/1G3AMAnEysCYnHoGH9ju-looWiJUzBuEx
24. von Braun-Bates, F., Sen, S., Talukdar, I., Lahiri, A.: Google drive folder: Minos data set (2025). https://drive.google.com/drive/folders/1XloFHaKhEdRl3o7R49J4quiTK_TI8TSl
25. Web Graph SIA: Brief history of web scraping (2021). https://webscraper.io/blog/brief-history-of-web-scraping

Applications of Artificial Intelligence

A Fuzzy-Logic Based Cognitive Walkthrough to Assess the Degrees of Soft Skills Targeted in an Intelligent Educational Adventure Game

Konstantina Chrysafiadi[iD], Spyros Papadimitriou[(✉)][iD], and Maria Virvou[iD]

University of Piraeus, 18534 Piraeus, Greece
{kchrysafiadi,spap,mvirvou}@unipi.gr

Abstract. Teaching soft skills in intelligent educational adventure games is challenging due to their qualitative and context-dependent nature. Furthermore, educational software focuses mainly on teaching hard skills, not soft skills. This paper introduces a Fuzzy Logic-based Cognitive Walkthrough (FLCW) method to assess how an intelligent educational adventure game fosters soft skills such as communication, teamwork, empathy, problem-solving, and interpersonal skills. A novel, intelligent educational adventure game designed to teach the programming language HTML along with various soft skills is presented in more detail. The soft skills are integrated into the game through various tasks and interactions with non-playable characters (NPCs). The FLCW assesses the degree of ten identified soft skills that each task requires. Fuzzy logic models the uncertainty and subjectivity that characterize soft skill assessment. Four experts participated in the assessment process. The results of the FLCW indicate the percentage of each skill that a user/player demonstrates during each task. This is crucial for the effective design of the educational game and for developing the user's soft skills progress tracking process.

Keywords: Intelligent educational games · Adventure games · Soft skills · Fuzzy Logic · Cognitive walkthrough · Skill assessment · Artificial Intelligence · User modeling

1 Introduction

Integrating Artificial Intelligence (AI) in educational applications has significantly transformed learning experiences by providing adaptive and customized instruction [5,35]. AI-driven learning technologies have been extensively explored for their potential to revolutionize education, primarily by enhancing cognitive skill development and optimizing educational content through learning analytics [13,29,37]. Furthermore, personalized learning and interactive user interfaces exemplify AI's role in creating adaptive educational environments [11,20,38].

M. Bramer and F. Stahl (Eds.): SGAI-AI 2025, LNAI 16302, pp. 347–361, 2026.
https://doi.org/10.1007/978-3-032-11442-6_24

However, despite these advancements, the focus of intelligent educational systems has remained mainly on developing hard skills. In contrast, soft skills—such as communication, teamwork, empathy, and problem-solving—have been comparatively overlooked.

Soft skills are essential for personal and professional success, critical in workplace dynamics, collaboration, and effective communication [16,24,25,34]. Research highlights that in domains such as software engineering, technical expertise alone is insufficient; the ability to work effectively in teams, resolve conflicts, and interact with diverse stakeholders is equally crucial [4,9,36]. Employers increasingly recognize the value of soft skills, viewing them as integral to both individual career growth and organizational competitiveness. However, traditional educational software has primarily focused on cognitive traits, neglecting the systematic integration and assessment of soft skills in learning environments.

In response to this gap, game-based learning has emerged as a promising approach to fostering soft skills, providing engaging, interactive experiences that simulate real-world scenarios [10]. While educational games have demonstrated significant success in teaching technical subjects, their potential for soft skill development remains underexplored. Existing research suggests that soft skills such as communication, teamwork, empathy, problem-solving, and interpersonal skills can be effectively cultivated through well-designed educational games [8, 18].

Regarding the above, this paper introduces a fuzzy-logic-based Cognitive Walkthrough (FLCW) method to assess the extent to which an intelligent educational adventure game promotes soft skills development. Specifically, we present a novel educational game designed to teach HTML programming while embedding soft skills into gameplay through various tasks and interactions with non-playable characters (NPCs). The FLCW method enables a structured evaluation of ten identified soft skills required by different in-game tasks, addressing the inherent uncertainty and subjectivity of soft skill assessment using fuzzy logic. A panel of four experts conducted the assessment, and the results indicate the degree to which players demonstrate each skill during gameplay. This approach provides valuable insights for refining game design, enhancing soft skill development, and implementing effective progress-tracking mechanisms for learners.

2   Related Work and Contribution

2.1   Soft Skills in Educational Games

Recent developments in education have primarily concentrated on cognitive aspects of learning, often neglecting the critical importance of cultivating soft skills. However, the significance of soft skills as a vital component of personal and professional success is now widely acknowledged [1,14,21,26,28]. In view of the above, there have been games specifically designed to help education students develop soft skills [3,18,33]. For example, the game *Among the Office Criticality* aims to identify and assess essential skills such as problem-solving, teamwork, time management, decision-making, and communication [2]. Research on game-based development of soft skills remains limited, particularly in evaluating game designs that promote these skills. This paper addresses the gap by introducing a new method for evaluating the role and extent of gameplay in promoting specific soft skills.

2.2   Cognitive Walkthrough

Cognitive Walkthrough (CW) is a widely used usability evaluation method designed to assess how easily users can accomplish tasks within an interface [15,17]. CW systematically analyzes whether users can navigate and understand a system based on its design and feedback mechanisms [19,32]. The approach involves defining task sequences, predicting user actions, and evaluating whether interface cues guide users effectively toward their goals. In the context of educational systems, CW has been applied to evaluate the effectiveness of learning interfaces, particularly in intelligent tutoring systems, game-based learning environments, and adaptive educational technologies [27,30,31,39,40,42]. Although CW focuses primarily on task completion and cognitive load, it can be extended to analyze how gameplay elements encourage or require using soft skills [23]. In addition, it can be adapted to assess the extent to which soft skills are required and demonstrated in the tasks of a game. It can help analyze how well a task promotes, requires, or supports the development of specific soft skills.

2.3   Fuzzy Logic and Cognitive Walkthrough

Fuzzy logic is a method for handling imprecise, uncertain, or subjective information [41]. This ability makes fuzzy logic an effective tool for reasoning in complex, real-world scenarios [6,12]. Therefore, it is very appropriate for exploring the reasoning for evaluating soft skills without strictly defined quantitative metrics, which has not be done before. Since soft skills are inherently subjective and context-dependent, integrating fuzzy logic into CW can model the uncertainty in soft skill assessment. CW provides a structured way to evaluate how well a game fosters soft skills. Adding fuzzy logic further refines this process by allowing for gradual, non-binary assessment of soft skill engagement. It enables expert evaluators to assess the extent to which soft skills are demonstrated in different game tasks.

3   Game's Description

3.1   Descriptions of Tasks

The *HTML Escape Game* is an engaging educational adventure game that seamlessly integrates personalized quizzes to facilitate learning the HTML markup language. The storyline follows a protagonist searching to escape from a building where he is imprisoned. To achieve his goal, he gathers various objects and interacts with various characters, each presenting him with small tasks. Successfully communicating with these characters and completing their tasks demands applying various soft skills. This paper explores whether each task contributes to developing specific soft skills essential in software engineering. It is worth noting that the aspect related to the cultivation of hard skills and the effective learning of the HTML language has already been successfully assessed [7, 22].

The game features various tasks necessary for its completion. Some of them are the following: a thirsty man requests a cool drink, and the player must find something to satisfy him. A boy seeks his toy car for a racetrack, while an older man asks for a music album. A businessperson tasks the player with an HTML quiz, which, if completed satisfactorily but with weaknesses, results in a chef entering the kitchen and presenting another quiz. A zombie sets an HTML quiz about the player's HTML weaknesses in a hidden basement room. A singer in the storage room will not let the player lower an object from the ceiling until they finish another HTML quiz. A fit man appears after the singer's quiz, challenging the player's HTML knowledge with another quiz. A cybersecurity engineer helps the hero complete a task regarding decrypting a message. At the same time, a rude character in the living room blocks access to an item, prompting the player to find a way to make him leave the room. At the end, a final examiner presents the final HTML quiz, and answering it perfectly opens the exit door for the player.

Fig. 1. The witch needs several things.

For the purposes of this paper, we describe the task with the NPC witch in more detail. The witch is located in the basement of the building, under a trapdoor (Fig. 1). She offers to help the hero in his quest as long as he helps her to meet her needs. She needs a crystal ball to communicate with spirits, who will assign the player an HTML quiz. In addition to the crystal ball the player must find, the witch assigns two more tasks to the player. One has to do with her need to cool down. As the underground room is quite hot, she feels uncomfortable and lacks the clarity to communicate with the spirits. In addition, she describes to the player that she has financial difficulties and communicating with the spirits requires a monetary fee. The breakdown of the witch task is described below.

1. Identify the NPC's problem.
   (a) Understand that the witch is too hot.
   (b) Realize that cooling her down is the solution.
2. Solve the physical need.
   (a) Search for a fan.
   (b) Realize you already found a fan earlier.
   (c) Retrieve and deliver the fan.
   (d) Search for batteries.
   (e) Recall where batteries were previously seen.
   (f) Combine the fan and batteries and use them.
3. Solve the resource need.
   (a) Learn that the witch now asks for money.
   (b) Decide whether to spend or conserve money.
   (c) Realize that you can retrieve coins from a hidden book or earlier inventory.
   (d) Use the money.
4. Programming challenge.
   (a) Read and interpret code or logic problems accurately and effectively.
   (b) Solve the puzzle or answer the question.
   (c) Choose the correct answer (quiz format).
5. Make progress.
   (a) Use a clue or an item from the witch to access the next area.
   (b) Handle failure if the player answers incorrectly.

3.2 Targeted Soft Skills

According to previous research [23], the following soft skills are identified in the tasks of the intelligent educational game to varying degrees.

Communication Skills: Communication skills encompass the proficient transmission of information, concepts, emotions, and thoughts through verbal, non-verbal, and written modalities. Effective communication is fundamental across diverse domains, including interpersonal relationships and professional environments, as it facilitates clarity, understanding, and collaboration.

Interpersonal Skills: Interpersonal skills refer to the cognitive and behavioral competencies that enable effective communication, interaction, and the establishment of positive social connections. These skills are fundamental in both personal and professional contexts, as they enhance cooperation, collaborative engagement, and social competence. Key components include communicative proficiency, active listening, and empathetic responsiveness, all of which contribute to optimal social functioning and group dynamics.

Teamwork Skills: Teamwork skills encompass the cognitive, behavioral, and interpersonal competencies that facilitate effective collaboration and coordination among individuals to achieve collective objectives. These skills are critical in multidisciplinary professional environments, where individuals with diverse expertise and backgrounds integrate their efforts to optimize task performance and project outcomes.

Empathy: Empathy refers to the ability to understand and share the feelings, thoughts, and perspectives of others. These skills encompass active listening, emotional intelligence, and the capacity to respond to others with sensitivity and compassion. Empathy allows individuals to form more meaningful connections, facilitating effective communication and conflict resolution. The significance of empathy skills lies in their ability to foster positive interpersonal relationships, enhance teamwork, and improve emotional well-being in both personal and professional environments. In addition, empathy plays a crucial role in leadership, customer relations, and collaborative settings, as it promotes a supportive, inclusive atmosphere where individuals feel valued and understood.

Analytical Thinking: Analytical skills encompass the cognitive processes of systematically collecting, processing, interpreting, and evaluating data to facilitate evidence-based decision-making and problem-solving. Individuals with advanced analytical proficiency can decompose complex systems into fundamental components, discern underlying patterns, and formulate logical inferences. These skills, closely linked to critical thinking, are integral to various scientific, technical, and professional disciplines.

Organizational/Planning Skills: Organizational and planning skills encompass systematically allocating tasks, time, and resources to achieve defined objectives with maximal efficiency. Individuals exhibiting advanced proficiency in these skills can effectively prioritize, structure, and synchronize activities, enhancing workflow optimization, productivity, and adherence to deadlines.

Customer Orientation: Customer orientation skills involve the cognitive and behavioral competencies that enable individuals to accurately assess and respond to customer needs, preferences, and expectations. These skills are critical in sectors where customer interactions are integral to service delivery and organizational performance, facilitating customer satisfaction and loyalty.

Interdisciplinary/Adjustment Skills: Interdisciplinary adaptation skills refer to the cognitive and behavioral competencies required to navigate, integrate, and adapt within an interdisciplinary context. Interdisciplinarity involves synthesizing and applying knowledge, methodologies, and theoretical frameworks from multiple academic or professional domains. Individuals with robust inter-disciplinary adaptation skills can effectively collaborate across diverse fields and engage with professionals from various disciplinary backgrounds to address complex, multifaceted challenges.

Problem-Solving Skills: Problem-solving skills refer to the cognitive and ana-lytical abilities that enable individuals to identify, evaluate, and resolve complex issues effectively. These skills involve critical thinking, creativity, and logical reasoning to break down problems into manageable components, assess poten-tial solutions, and implement the most appropriate action. The significance of problem-solving skills extends across all areas of life, particularly in profes-sional and academic contexts, where individuals are often required to navigate challenges, optimize processes, and make decisions that drive success. Strong problem-solving abilities are essential for innovation, adaptability, and effective decision-making, contributing to both personal and organizational growth.

Learning Skills: Learning skills refer to the cognitive and metacognitive pro-cesses that enable individuals to acquire, process, retain, and apply knowledge efficiently. These competencies are foundational for academic achievement and are critical throughout life for lifelong learning, intellectual development, and adaptive knowledge application.

4 Description of the Fuzzy Cognitive Walkthrough Method

Step 1: A workshop was conducted with the participation of four educators, experts in soft skills. They were given a comprehensive game overview, including its objective, rules, and instructions. Additionally, they received a list outlining all game tasks and the identified soft skills.

Step 2: The experts engaged with the game. Support was provided whenever an expert faced challenges. In the case of HTML quizzes, the game's adaptive hinting system automatically generated prompts when difficulties were identified. After completing each game task, experts were asked to complete an evaluation sheet regarding the extent to which a task required each of the ten identified soft skills. Table 1 depicts a sample of the evaluation sheet.

Step 3: For each task - subtask and for each soft skill, the experts' answers were converted into a triplet of numbers (a, b, c) that represent the corresponding fuzzy set. The defined fuzzy sets are: Very low (VL), Low (L), Moderate (M), High (H), Very High (VH). Their membership functions are:

$$\mu_{VL}(x) = \left\{ \begin{array}{ll} 1, & x = 0 \\ \frac{x}{2}, & 0 \le x \le 2 \\ 0, & x \ge 2 \end{array} \right\} \tag{1}$$

Table 1. A sample of the evaluation sheet.

	At all	Very low	Low	Moderate	High	Very high	Exactly
Task: Interaction with the Witch							
Subtask Group 1: Identify the NPC's Problem (Witch)							
Subtask: 1.1 Understand that the Witch is too hot							
Communications skills are needed to understand that the witch is too hot.							
Consideration of the witch's reactions and appropriate adaptation of actions and responses are essential to understand that the witch is too hot.							
Collaboration is essential for understanding that the witch is too hot.							
The ability to understand and share the feelings of the witch helps to understand that she is too hot.							
Analytical thinking is needed to understand that the witch is too hot.							
Organization and planning of actions are crucial to manage to understand that the witch is too hot.							
To understand the witchâĂŹs needs and expectations is crucial to understanding that she is too hot.							
Knowledge of various fields is needed to understand that the witch is too hot.							
Problem-solving skills are needed to accomplish understanding that the witch is too hot.							
The completion of the subtask of understanding that the witch is too hot contributes to the development of learning skills.							

$$\mu_L(x) = \begin{cases} 0, & x < 0 \text{ or } x > 5 \\ \frac{x}{2}, & 0 \le x \le 2 \\ \frac{5-x}{3}, & 2 \le x \le 5 \end{cases} \tag{2}$$

$$\mu_M(x) = \begin{cases} 0, & x < 2 \text{ or } x > 8 \\ \frac{x-2}{3}, & 2 \le x \le 5 \\ \frac{8-x}{3}, & 5 \le x \le 8 \end{cases} \tag{3}$$

$$\mu_H(x) = \begin{cases} 0, & x < 5 \text{ or } x > 10 \\ \frac{x-5}{3}, & 5 \le x \le 8 \\ \frac{10-x}{2}, & 8 \le x \le 10 \end{cases} \tag{4}$$

$$\mu_{VH}(x) = \begin{cases} 0, & x < 8 \\ \frac{x-8}{2}, & 8 \le x \le 10 \\ 1, & x = 10 \end{cases} \tag{5}$$

The partition of the above fuzzy sets was presented in Table 2 and Fig. 2. Triangular membership functions were selected due to their simplicity, interpretability, and computational efficiency. Each function is fully described by only three parameters, making them straightforward to design and understand. Their piecewise-linear shape provides an intuitive representation of linguistic terms while keeping the computational cost low, which is beneficial for real-time applications. Their three parameters are the three numbers into which the answers of the questionnaire are converted. They were determined to provide complete and balanced coverage of the input space while maintaining smooth transitions between adjacent fuzzy sets. The left and right endpoints were chosen to correspond approximately to the minimum and maximum values of the variable, and the peak was positioned at the representative value (e.g., mean or mode) of each fuzzy set. They have been defined by experts.

Thus, the number of fuzzy sets and their partition were defined empirically and based on the specific application requirement by the three experts in designing educational software. If the assessment value is "at all", the answer is not converted into a triplet of numbers, but its corresponding value is 0. Similarly, if the assessment value is 'exactly', the answer is not converted into a triplet of numbers, but its corresponding value is 10. This is because these evaluation values are not characterized by vagueness, but their values are well-defined.

Table 2. Fuzzy sets' partition.

Verbal description	Abbreviation	Partition
Very Low	VL	(0, 0, 2)
Low	L	(0, 2, 5)
Moderate	M	(2, 5, 8)
High	H	(5, 8, 10)
Very High	VH	(8, 10, 10)

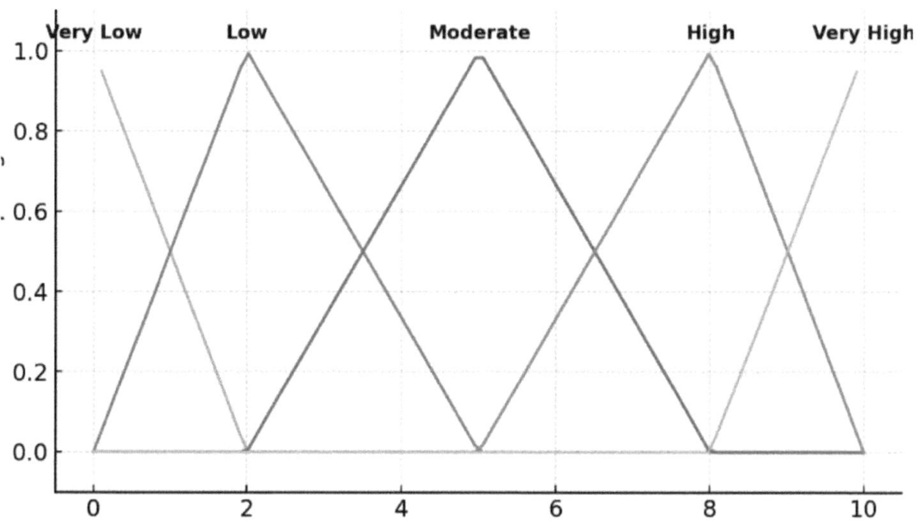

Fig. 2. The membership functions.

In Table 3, a sample of the evaluation results of the four experts and the corresponding fuzzy sets of the assessments for each subtask and soft skill are presented.

Table 3. A sample of the experts' evaluation results for the task concerning the interaction with the Witch.

Task: Interaction with the Witch
Subtask Group 1: Identify the NPC's Problem (Witch)
Subtask: 1.1 Understand that the Witch is too hot

	Evaluator 1		Evaluator 2		Evaluator 3		Evaluator 4	
	Verbal value	Partition	Verbal value	Partition	Verbal value	Partition	Verbal value	Partition
Communication	H	(5, 8, 10)	VH	(8, 10, 10)	H	(5, 8, 10)	H	(5, 8, 10)
Interpersonal	H	(5, 8, 10)	H	(5, 8, 10)	M	(2, 5, 8)	VH	(8, 10, 10)
Teamwork	M	(2, 5, 8)	M	(2, 5, 8)	M	(2, 5, 8)	M	(2, 5, 8)
Empathy	VH	(8, 10, 10)	Exactly	10	Exactly	10	VH	(8, 10, 10)
Analytical	M	(2, 5, 8)	L	(0, 2, 5)	L	(0, 2, 5)	M	(2, 5, 8)
Organizational / planning	VL	(0, 0, 2)	At all	0	At all	0	VL	(0, 0, 2)
Customer orientation	VH	(8, 10, 10)	Exactly	10	H	(5, 8, 10)	Exactly	(8, 10, 10)
Interdisciplinary-adjustment	H	(5, 8, 10)	M	(2, 5, 8)	M	(2, 5, 8)	L	(0, 2, 5)
Problem-solving skills	M	(2, 5, 8)	L	(0, 2, 5)	M	(2, 5, 8)	L	(0, 2, 5)
Learning skills	H	(5, 8, 10)	M	(2, 5, 8)	L	(0, 2, 5)	L	(0, 2, 5)

Subtask: 1.2 Realize that cooling her down is the solution

	Evaluator 1		Evaluator 2		Evaluator 3		Evaluator 4	
	Verbal value	Partition	Verbal value	Partition	Verbal value	Partition	Verbal value	Partition
Communication	M	(2, 5, 8)	L	(0, 2, 5)	M	(2, 5, 8)	M	(2, 5, 8)
Interpersonal	H	(5, 8, 10)	H	(5, 8, 10)	VH	(8, 10, 10)	H	(5, 8, 10)
Teamwork	M	(2, 5, 8)	M	(2, 5, 8)	L	(0, 2, 5)	L	(0, 2, 5)
Empathy	VH	(8, 10, 10)	Exactly	10	VH	(8, 10, 10)	VH	(8, 10, 10)
Analytical	H	(5, 8, 10)	H	(5, 8, 10)	VH	(8, 10, 10)	H	(5, 8, 10)
Organizational /planning	M	(2, 5, 8)	M	(2, 5, 8)	L	(0, 2, 5)	VL	(0, 0, 2)
Customer orientation	VH	(8, 10, 10)	Exactly	10	H	(5, 8, 10)	VH	(8, 10, 10)
Interdisciplinary-adjustment	H	(5, 8, 10)	H	(5, 8, 10)	M	(2, 5, 8)	H	(5, 8, 10)
Problem-solving skills	H	(5, 8, 10)	H	(5, 8, 10)	VH	(8, 10, 10)	H	(5, 8, 10)
Learning skills	H	(5, 8, 10)	H	(5, 8, 10)	M	(2, 5, 8)	H	(5, 8, 10)

Step 4: The experts' answers were aggregated as described below for each task – subtask and for each soft skill. Let (a_i, b_i, c_i) with $i \in \{1, 2, 3, 4\}$ be the triplet corresponding to the evaluation answer of educator i. The aggregated answer is the triplet (w_1, w_2, w_3), where $w_1 = \min\{a_i\}$, $w_2 = \frac{1}{4}\sum_{i=1}^{4} b_i$, $w_3 = \max\{c_i\}$. The "at all" (0) value and "exactly" (10) value are not aggregated. They are taken into account in the next step. For our evaluation sample, the aggregated values are depicted in Table 4.

Step 5: For each task-subtask and for each soft skill, the aggregated value is defuzzified with the centroid method according to the following formula:

$$x^* = \frac{\sum \mu_i c_i}{\sum \mu_i}$$

The crisp values for the evaluation sample are presented in the second to last column of Table 4.

Step 6: For each task - subtask the percentage of identified soft skills was calculated according to the following formula:

$p = \frac{10*z+x^*}{y+z+1} * 10$, where x^* is the crisp value, y is the number of "at all" answers, and z is the number of "exactly" answers.

The percentage of identified soft skills for the evaluation sample is presented in the last column of Table 4.

Table 4. The percentage of identified soft skills.

Task: Interaction with the Witch
Subtask Group 1: Identify the NPC's Problem (Witch)
Subtask: 1.1 Understand that the Witch is too hot

	Evaluator 1	Evaluator 2	Evaluator 3	Evaluator 4	Aggregated value	Crisp value	Percentage
Communication	(5, 8, 10)	(8, 10, 10)	(5, 8, 10)	(5, 8, 10)	(5, 8.5, 10)	7.83	78.3%
Interpersonal	(5, 8, 10)	(5, 8, 10)	(2, 5, 8)	(8, 10, 10)	(2, 7.75, 10)	6.58	65.8%
Teamwork	(2, 5, 8)	(2, 5, 8)	(2, 5, 8)	(2, 5, 8)	(2, 5, 8)	5	50%
Empathy	(8, 10, 10)	10	10	(8, 10, 10)	(8, 10, 10)	9.33	97.77%
Analytical	(2, 5, 8)	(0, 2, 5)	(0, 2, 5)	(2, 5, 8)	(0, 3.5, 8)	3.83	38.3%
Organizational / planning	(0, 0, 2)	0	0	(0, 0, 2)	(0, 0, 2)	0.67	2.23%
Customer orientation	(8, 10, 10)	10	(5, 8, 10)	(8, 10, 10)	(5, 9.5, 10)	8.17	90.85%
Interdisciplinary-adjustment	(5, 8, 10)	(2, 5, 8)	(2, 5, 8)	(0, 2, 5)	(0, 5, 8)	4.33	43.3%
Problem-solving skills	(2, 5, 8)	(0, 2, 5)	(2, 5, 8)	(0, 2, 5)	(0, 3.5, 8)	3.83	38.3%
Learning skills	(5, 8, 10)	(2, 5, 8)	(0, 2, 5)	(0, 2, 5)	(0, 4.25, 10)	4.75	47.5%

Subtask: 1.2 Realize that cooling her down is the solution

	Evaluator 1	Evaluator 2	Evaluator 3	Evaluator 4	Aggregated value	Crisp value	Percentage
Communication	(2, 5, 8)	(0, 2, 5)	(2, 5, 8)	(2, 5, 8)	(0, 4.25, 8)	4.08	40.8%
Interpersonal	(5, 8, 10)	(5, 8, 10)	(8, 10, 10)	(5, 8, 10)	(5, 8.5, 10)	7.83	78.3%
Teamwork	(2, 5, 8)	(2, 5, 8)	(0, 2, 5)	(0, 2, 5)	(0, 3.5, 8)	3.83	38.3%
Empathy	(8, 10, 10)	10	(8, 10, 10)	(8, 10, 10)	(8, 10, 10)	9.33	96.65%
Analytical	(5, 8, 10)	(5, 8, 10)	(8, 10, 10)	(5, 8, 10)	(5, 8.5, 10)	7.83	78.3%
Organizational /planning	(2, 5, 8)	(2, 5, 8)	(0, 2, 5)	(0, 0, 2)	(0, 3, 8)	3.67	36.7%
Customer orientation	(8, 10, 10)	10	(5, 8, 10)	(8, 10, 10)	(5, 9.5, 10)	8.17	90.85%
Interdisciplinary-adjustment	(5, 8, 10)	(5, 8, 10)	(2, 5, 8)	(5, 8, 10)	(2, 7.25, 10)	7.45	74.5%
Problem-solving skills	(5, 8, 10)	(5, 8, 10)	(8, 10, 10)	(5, 8, 10)	(5, 8.5, 10)	7.83	78.3%
Learning skills	(5, 8, 10)	(5, 8, 10)	(2, 5, 8)	(5, 8, 10)	(2, 7.25, 10)	7.45	74.5%

5   Discussion

The value of integrating fuzzy logic into the Cognitive Walkthrough methodology to evaluate soft skills in educational games is remarkable. The proposed fuzzy logic-based approach enables a nuanced, quantitative assessment of inherently qualitative and context-dependent soft skills. It provides a systematic approach to evaluating ten targeted soft skills embedded within various in-game tasks, effectively handling the inherent uncertainty and subjectivity of soft skill assessment through fuzzy logic. This method bridges the gap between structured usability evaluation and the fluid nature of soft skill demonstration by allowing for graded expert assessments rather than concrete judgments. The experts' evaluation demonstrates the ability of the presented educational adventure game to promote key soft skills—such as communication, empathy, and teamwork—through interactions with non-playable characters and context-rich tasks. Also, the FLCW methodology proves instrumental in revealing which tasks effectively elicit specific soft skills, offering actionable insights for improving game design. By mapping each skill to gameplay elements and quantifying its manifestation, the approach enables ongoing refinement of the learning experience. It supports the tracking of learner progress in soft skill development. This enhances the educational value of intelligent games and paves the way for broader applications in soft skill training across diverse domains.

6   Conclusion

This paper introduced a fuzzy-logic-based Cognitive Walkthrough (FLCW) as an effective method for assessing soft skills within an intelligent educational adventure game. By addressing the challenges posed by the qualitative and context-dependent nature of soft skills, the FLCW method enables a structured yet flexible evaluation. Integrating fuzzy logic into the walkthrough framework allows expert evaluators to assess soft skill engagement with greater precision, using verbal terms that reflect the degrees to which specific skills are demonstrated in gameplay tasks. In this way, it manages to model the uncertainty and subjectivity that characterize soft skill assessment.

The proposed FLCW method was applied in a game designed to teach HTML alongside key soft skills, such as communication, teamwork, empathy, and problem-solving. Expert assessments revealed how various tasks and interactions with non-playable characters promote the development of ten identified skills and to what degree. This is important for optimizing the educational game's design and establishing an effective process to track users' soft skill development.

In our future work, we will create a prototype based on the FLCW results and track the learners' development of soft skills. This method will also be extended to different learning contexts and explored for its integration with real-time analytics for dynamic feedback and learner support.

Acknowledgments. Support to present this work was provided by the University of Piraeus Research Center.

Disclosure of Interests. The authors have no competing interests to declare that are relevant to the content of this article.

References

1. Abraham, T.H., Stewart, G.L., Solimeo, S.L.: The importance of soft skills development in a hard data world: learning from interviews with healthcare leaders. BMC Med. Educ. **21**, 1–7 (2021)
2. Altomari, L., Altomari, N., Iazzolino, G., et al.: Gamification and soft skills assessment in the development of a serious game: design and feasibility pilot study. JMIR Serious Games **11**(1), e45436 (2023)

3. Attou, Y., Seddik, M., Mohamed, B.: The impact of integrating various digital games in EFL classrooms on soft skills development. J. Hum. Soc. Sci. Stud. **6**(5), 117–125 (2024)

4. Borges, G.G., de Souza, R.C.G.: Skills development for software engineers: systematic literature review. Inf. Softw. Technol. **168**, 107395 (2024)

5. Chen, L., Chen, P., Lin, Z.: Artificial intelligence in education: a review. IEEE Access **8**, 75264–75278 (2020)

6. Chrysafiadi, K.: Fuzzy logic-based software systems. In: Fuzzy Logic-Based Software Systems, pp. 31–129. Springer, Cham (2023). https://doi.org/10.1007/978-3-031-44457-9_3

7. Chrysafiadi, K., Papadimitriou, S., Virvou, M.: Cognitive-based adaptive scenarios in educational games using fuzzy reasoning. Knowl.-Based Syst. **250**, 109111 (2022)

8. Dochie, E., Herman, C., Epure, C.: Using gamification for the development of soft skills. skill generator assessment game case study. In: The International Scientific Conference eLearning and Software for Education. vol. 3, p. 610. "Carol I" National Defence University (2017)

9. Galster, M., Mitrovic, A., Malinen, S., Holland, J., Peiris, P.: Soft skills required from software professionals in New Zealand. Inf. Softw. Technol. **160**, 107232 (2023)

10. Garcia, I., Pacheco, C., Méndez, F., Calvo-Manzano, J.A.: The effects of game-based learning in the acquisition of "soft skills" on undergraduate software engineering courses: a systematic literature review. Comput. Appl. Eng. Educ. **28**(5), 1327–1354 (2020)

11. Gligorea, I., Cioca, M., Oancea, R., Gorski, A.T., Gorski, H., Tudorache, P.: Adaptive learning using artificial intelligence in e-learning: a literature review. Educ. Sci. **13**(12), 1216 (2023)

12. Gupta, P.: Applications of fuzzy logic in daily life. Int. J. Adv. Res. Comput. Sci. **8**(5) (2017)

13. Khosravi, H., et al.: Explainable artificial intelligence in education. Comput. Educ. Artif. Intell. **3**, 100074 (2022)

14. Kumar, A., Singh, P.N., Ansari, S.N., Pandey, S.: Importance of soft skills and its improving factors. World J. Engl. Lang. **12**(3), 220–227 (2022)

15. Lewis, C., Wharton, C.: Cognitive walkthroughs. In: Handbook of Human-Computer Interaction, pp. 717–732. Elsevier (1997)

16. Lyu, W., Liu, J.: Soft skills, hard skills: what matters most? Evidence from job postings. Appl. Energy **300**, 117307 (2021)

17. Mahatody, T., Sagar, M., Kolski, C.: State of the art on the cognitive walkthrough method, its variants and evolutions. Intl. J. Hum.-Comput. Interact. **26**(8), 741–785 (2010)

18. McGowan, N., López-Serrano, A., Burgos, D.: Serious games and soft skills in higher education: a case study of the design of compete! Electronics **12**(6), 1432 (2023)

19. Nandhi, C.P.M.W., Irianto, A.B.P., Nastiti, P., Marsella, E., Wibisono, Y.P.: User experience evaluation using the cognitive walkthrough method. In: Proceedings of the 4th International Conference on Management Science and Industrial Engineering, pp. 237–245 (2022)

20. Naseer, F., Khan, M.N., Addas, A., Awais, Q., Ayub, N.: Game mechanics and artificial intelligence personalization: a framework for adaptive learning systems. Educ. Sci. **15**(3) (2025)

21. Ngo, A., Thuy, T.: The importance of soft skills for academic performance and career development—from the perspective of university students. Int. J. Eng. Pedagogy **14**(3) (2024)

22. Papadimitriou, S., Virvou, M.: Adaptivity in scenarios in an educational adventure game. In: 2017 8th International Conference on Information, Intelligence, Systems & Applications (IISA), pp. 1–6. IEEE (2017)
23. Papadimitriou, S., Virvou, M.: Practicing soft skills for programming through an intelligent adventure game. In: Artificial Intelligence—Based Games as Novel Holistic Educational Environments to Teach 21st Century Skills, pp. 235–252. Springer (2025). https://doi.org/10.1007/978-3-031-77464-5_8
24. Petrović, J., Maric, M.: The importance of soft skills for small and medium sized enterprises–evidence from Bosnia and Herzegovina. J. Contemp. Econ. **8**(1) (2024)
25. Putra, A.S., et al.: Examine relationship of soft skills, hard skills, innovation and performance: the mediation effect of organizational learning. Int. J. Sci. Manage. Stud. (IJSMS) **3**(3), 27–43 (2020)
26. Riley, J., Nicewicz, K.: Connecting with gen z: using interactive improv games to teach soft skills. Mark. Educ. Rev. **32**(2), 97–104 (2022)
27. Rocha, T., Barroso, J.: PLAY for LEARNING: serious games to assist learning of basic didactic concepts: a pilot study. In: Fang, X. (ed.) HCII 2021. LNCS, vol. 12790, pp. 62–71. Springer, Cham (2021). https://doi.org/10.1007/978-3-030-77414-1_6
28. Romero, M., Usart, M., Ott, M.: Can serious games contribute to developing and sustaining 21st century skills? Games Culture **10**(2), 148–177 (2015)
29. Salas-Pilco, S.Z., Xiao, K., Hu, X.: Artificial intelligence and learning analytics in teacher education: a systematic review. Educ. Sci. **12**(8), 569 (2022)
30. Santos, F.D.S., Salgado, A.D.L., Paiva, D.M.B., Fortes, R.P.D.M., Gama, S.P.: A specialized cognitive walkthrough to evaluate digital games for the elderly. In: Proceedings of the 10th International Conference on Software Development and Technologies for Enhancing Accessibility and Fighting Info-exclusion, pp. 166–171 (2022)
31. Sasupilli, M., Bokil, P., Punekar, R.M.: Game design frameworks and evaluating techniques for educational games: a review. In: Research into Design for a Connected World: Proceedings of ICoRD 2019, vol. 1, pp. 277–286 (2019)
32. Sugiarti, Y., et al.: Usability evaluation on website using the cognitive walkthrough method. In: 2023 11th International Conference on Cyber and IT Service Management (CITSM), pp. 1–8. IEEE (2023)
33. Tan, B.S., Chong, K.S.: Unlocking the potential of game-based learning for soft skills development: a comprehensive review. J. ICT Educ. **10**(2), 29–54 (2023)
34. Tem, S., Kuroda, A., Tang, K.N.: The importance of soft skills development to enhance entrepreneurial capacity. Int. Educ. Res. **3**(3), p1–p1 (2020)
35. Tsihrintzis, G.A., Virvou, M., Phillips-Wren, G.: Surveys in artificial intelligence-based technologies. Intell. Decis. Technol. **13**(4), 393–394 (2019)
36. Varava, I.P., Bohinska, A.P., Vakaliuk, T.A., Mintii, I.: Soft skills in software engineering technicians education. J. Phys. Conf. Ser. **1946**, 012012. IOP Publishing (2021)
37. Virvou, M., Alepis, E., Tsihrintzis, G.A., Jain, L.C.: Machine learning paradigms: advances in learning analytics. Springer, Cham (2020). https://doi.org/10.1007/978-3-319-94030-4
38. Yannier, N., Hudson, S.E., Chang, H., Koedinger, K.R.: AI adaptivity in a mixed-reality system improves learning. Int. J. Artif. Intell. Educ. 1–18 (2024)
39. Yildirim-Erbasli, S., Epp, C.D., Bulut, O., Cui, Y.: Design and evaluation of a conversational agent for formative assessment in higher education. In: Proceedings of the 17th International Conference of the Learning Sciences-ICLS 2023, pp. 194–201. International Society of the Learning Sciences (2023)

40. Yildirim-Erbasli, S.N., Bulut, O., Demmans Epp, C., Cui, Y.: Conversation-based assessments in education: design, implementation, and cognitive walkthroughs for usability testing. J. Educ. Technol. Syst. **52**(1), 27–51 (2023)
41. Zadeh, L.A.: Fuzzy logic= computing with words. IEEE Trans. Fuzzy Syst. **4**(2), 103–111 (1996)
42. Zairon, I.Y., Wook, T.S.M.T., Salleh, S.M., Dahlan, H.A.: User model for virtual learning based on adaptive gamification. IEEE Access (2025)

Streamlining Municipal Governance: Detecting Redundancy in Regulation Plans Using Text Embeddings in Local Government

Karl Audun Kagnes Borgersen[1]([☒])(iD), Morten Goodwin[1](iD),
and Alexander Salveson Nossum[2](iD)

[1] University of Agder, Grimstad, Norway
{karl.audun.borgersen,morten.goodwin}@uia.no
[2] Norkart, Oslo, Norway
alexander.nossum@norkart.no

Abstract. Modern municipalities must manage an ever-growing volume of zoning and building regulations for urban planning, making it challenging to maintain a coherent and up-to-date legal framework. As an administrative area grows in size and personnel, it becomes impossible for individual caseworkers and planners to maintain a complete overview of its zoning regulations. Over time, the regulatory plans become outdated, albeit still legally binding. Adding new modern zoning plans on top of the planning hierarchy has been a de facto practice. Leading to overlapping information and potentially conflicting legally binding documents for the same geographic area. This paper explores methods for automatically detecting redundant or overlapping regulation documents using state-of-the-art text embedding techniques and evaluates a selection of both open and proprietary models for this purpose.

Keywords: Text embeddings · Information retrieval · Semantic search · Municipal regulation · Building plans

1 Introduction

For most practical purposes, it is impossible for a single person to have a complete overview of the building and zoning regulation plans for a municipality. The administrative staff of Larvik, a medium-sized municipality in Vestfold, Norway with 48,870 citizens is no different [23] with the total number of 783 active zoning regulations [10]. On average, the processing time of a municipal document in Larvik is 149 days [22], as a direct consequence of this opaqueness. This paper tackles the problem of redundant regulation plans in Larvik's municipal government. When a new regulation plan is proposed, it is not uncommon for it to heavily resemble an existing regulation plan. This leads to a degree of bloat in the number of administrative documents published and may cause legal issues

M. Bramer and F. Stahl (Eds.): SGAI-AI 2025, LNAI 16302, pp. 362–373, 2026.
https://doi.org/10.1007/978-3-032-11442-6_25

Original:

REGULERINGSBESTEMMELSER TIL REGULERINGS-
PLAN FOR HYTTER, MERDIÅS I HEDRUM KOMMUNE.

§ 3

Før søknad om byggetillatelse behandles, skal det foreligge be-
byggelsesplan godkjent av bygningsrådet. Bebyggelsesplanen kan utarbeides på flyfoto i målestokk 1:2.000 eller bedre.
Bebyggelsesplanen skal bl.a. vise hyttenes plassering og
orientering/møneretning, gangveien til hyttene, drikke-
vannskilder/tappesteder og oppsamlingsteder for søppel.

§ 4

Det kan bare oppføres en hytte på hvert tomtefeste. Frittstående uthus
tillates ikke oppført, men i spesielle tilfelle kan flere bygninger god-
kjennes, forutsatt at bygningene grupperes i et tun med enhetlig karakter.
Det skal opparbeides parkeringsplass for min.
2 biler pr. hytte. Gjerder tillates ikke oppført.

§ 5

Bygningene skal ha saltak. Taktekkingsma-
terialet bør ha en matt og mørk virkning.

FYLKESMANNEN I VESTFOLD

Tønsberg 19. november 1984

Etter fullmakt

Bjørn Torkildsen

Translation:

ZONING REGULATIONS FOR THE ZONING PLAN
FOR CABINS, MERDIÅS IN HEDRUM MUNICIPALITY

§ 3

Before an application for a building permit can be processed, a development plan approved by the Building Council must be submitted. The development plan may be prepared using an aerial photograph at a scale of 1:2,000 or better.
The development plan must, among other things, show the location
and orientation/ridge direction of the cabins, footpaths to the cabins,
sources/tap points for drinking water, and locations for waste collection.

§ 4

Only one cabin may be built on each leased plot. Freestand-
ing outbuildings are not permitted, but in special cases, multiple buildings may be approved, provided they are grouped
into a courtyard-style cluster with a uniform character.
A parking area for a minimum of 2 cars per cabin
must be established. Fences are not permitted.

§ 5

Buildings must have pitched roofs. The roofing material should have a matte and dark appearance.

COUNTY GOVERNOR OF VESTFOLD

Tønsberg, November 19, 1984

By authority,

Bjørn Torkildsen

Fig. 1. Excerpt from a regulation plan for cabins in Hedrum. Provided both in its original form (above) and as a translation (below).

down the line, if one of these regulation plan documents are repealed, but not the other[1].

---

[1] An exerpt of the original documents and corresponding English translation can be found in Fig. 1.

The remainder of this paper is organized as follows: Sect. 2 discusses existing related work, and Sect. 3 details our methodological approach. Section 4 presents our results and discussion, which covers the model evaluation, clustering analysis, and methods for communicating findings to domain experts. Section 5 proposes directions for future work, and finally, Sect. 6 concludes the paper.

2   Related Work

Some previous work exists in the same domain of Norwegian building plans, namely that of PlanBERT by Brådland et al., which was developed in collaboration with the same industry partner as this project. Published in November 2024, the study demonstrates the fine-tuning of a NorBERT-large [9] model to this narrow domain using a combination of contrastive pre-training and fine-tuning on synthetic data [2].

Similarly, Okonkwo et al. released a 2023 paper discussing processing UK building plan documents. The study used rudimentary embedding methods based on word2vec and BERT to embed the contents of such documents and thoroughly evaluate how well they capture semantic regularities on a manually curated analogy dataset utilizing Brick ontology[2].

Hain et al.'s 2020 paper applies text embeddings for the large-scale evaluation of patent similarity. They choose to do so via training their own specialized model rather than relying on the pre-trained foundation models, as they believe the terminology of patents is too specialized to be captured meaningfully by generalist text embedders. It should be noted, however, that the capabilities of foundation models in Natural Language Processing have advanced dramatically since this paper's publication [5]. Due to their lack of a natural metric, they evaluate their model via several proxy methods, such as by training a classifier for patent categories and evaluating the similarity of patents with citations or authors in common. They also perform a case study applying their method to electric vehicle technology and created indicators for technological novelty and impact, mapping knowledge flows between countries [6].

3   Method

This study investigates existing State-of-the-Art (SotA) methods for embedding regulation plan documents. The following section discusses our approach for document pre-processing, evaluation, document embedding, and document clustering in more detail.

Our dataset consists of a mix of natively digital regulation plans and scanned physical documents. These number 739 in total. All documents have been scanned and converted to markdown format via Mistral Optical Character Recognition (OCR) [15].

---

[2] A standardized method for describing the relationships between building features https://brickschema.org.

3.1   Models

To select our evaluated models, we will in large part be relying on the Massive Multilingual Text Embedding Benchmark (MMTEB) [5] to identify the existing SotA in June 2025. Linq-Embed-Mistral [4], text-embedding-3 [19], Qwen3-Embedding [26], voyage-3-large [24], and gemini-embedding-001 [7] are all models chosen to represent the existing SotA. A bag-of-words approach and an instance of NorBERT-Large [9] were chosen as reference models. Finally, we include Plan-BERT [2], an instance of NorBERT-Large fine-tuned for the domain of Norwegian building regulation plans.

3.2   Evaluation Metric

As our dataset does not contain any native method for evaluating document similarity, we instead opt for a synthetic task meant to approximate it. We do so by feeding the documents to a locally run instance of Qwen 3 235b [25] and tasking it with paraphrasing the contents to keep the semantic meaning of the documents while retaining as little of the original wording as possible. Qwen 3 235b was chosen as it was the most performant local model available at the time the baseline documents were generated. The evaluated models are ranked based on their ability to retrieve their generated document pair via cosine distance using metrics such as accuracy@1 and mean rank.

As a rough indication of the attributes of our generated baseline documents, Fig. 2 shows a comparison of the size difference between the original and our generated document baseline by calculating the Levenshtein distance [12] between these documents. These distances have been calculated at the word level, rather than at the character level[3].

3.3   Clustering

Some documents will be more closely grouped in our embedding space than others. To detect these clusters of documents, we apply Hierarchical Density-Based Spatial Clustering of Applications with Noise (HDBSCAN) [3] to our embeddings. This clustering algorithm was chosen due to its ability to separate relevant clusters from noise, thereby detecting similar documents while allowing those without any natural counterparts to remain unassigned. The model used to represent the data is Voyage-3-large, as it is the most performant model on the task defined earlier in the section. We set the minimum cluster size to 4 and perform a hyperparameter grid-search to optimize clustering based on the resulting Silhouette score [21].

As demonstrated by Allaoui et al., the application of Dimensionality Reduction (DR) such as Uniform Manifold Approximation and Projection (UMAP) has

---

[3] Levenshtein distance essentially calculates the number of changes that have to be made for two strings to match. For example, the words "book" and "back" have a distance of 2, because two character substitutions have to be made (o for a and o for c) for the two words to match.

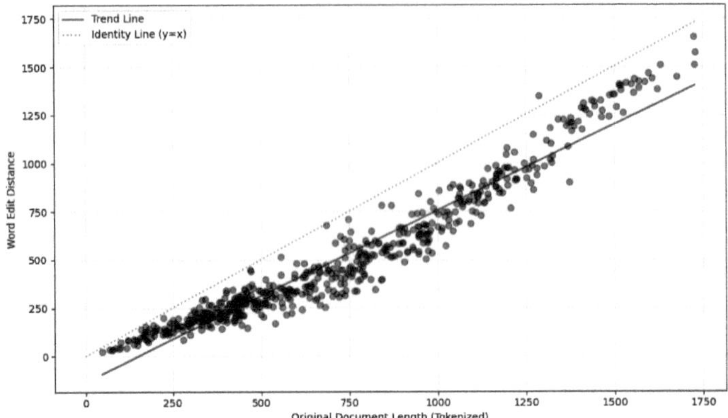

Fig. 2. A comparison between the word Levenshtein edit distance and original document length. A rough indication of the ideal trendline is the identity line, depicted here with the dotted line. The plot demonstrates how well the generated baselines paraphrase the original documents by depicting how many words have been altered.

the potential to improve the clustering capabilities of embeddings significantly [1]. All embeddings had their dimensionality compressed to 256 dimensions via Principal Component Analysis (PCA) [20] as this configuration had the most positive impact on the dataset's silhouette score.

4   Results and Discussion

This section presents and discusses the results obtained from the evaluated models and our clustering efforts. This section also incorporates feedback and general observations provided by a domain expert. Finally, we outline a few methods for effectively communicating these findings to non-technical stakeholders.

4.1   Evaluation Results

The results of our benchmarking experiments are shown in Table 1.

Despite PlanBERT being a model fine-tuned to this domain and language, it has been outperformed by the existing generalist SotA. It should be noted, however, that at 323 million parameters, PlanBERT is significantly smaller than its competitors, who often have a few billion parameters each. Further, its context window is rather limited at a maximum of 512 tokens, which fails to fully capture the full input documents in most cases. The mean length of our original documents is ~1581 tokens when encoded with PlanBERT's tokenizer. It does, however, significantly surpass its NorBERT base model, which demonstrates the value of domain-specific fine-tuning. Though this fine-tuning does not contribute enough to compensate for the general advances in text embedding model architecture made since its base model architecture was released.

Table 1. Table logging results with various metrics. All API-exclusive models have been accessed during June 2025. Mean rank represents the mean rank of the target item within the range of 0 and 1448. Sil-score represents the Silhouette score [21] of the generated document pairs. i.e., how well the embeddings cluster document pairs together, and other documents further apart.

Method \ Metric	Accuracy@1	Mean-rank	Sil-score	Parameters	Local
Bag of Words	18.7%	269.6	0.1	N/A	✓
Norbert3Large [9]	20.6%	256.0	0.09	323M	✓
PlanBERT [2]	35.5%	146.3	0.13	323M	✓
Gemini-embedding-001 [7]	45.7%	113.4	0.23	?[b]	✗
Text-embedding-3-small[a][19]	54.0%	52.7	0.24	?[b]	✗
Qwen3-Embedding-0.6b [26]	54.7%	40.4	0.27	0.6b	✓
Linq-Embed-Mistral [4]	57.0%	42.1	0.26	7b	✓
Text-embedding-3-large[a][19]	59.4%	34.6	0.28	?[b]	✗
Qwen3-Embedding-8b [26]	59.4%	32.4	**0.35**	8b	✓
Qwen3-Embedding-4b [26]	59.7%	33.9	0.34	4b	✓
Voyage-3-large [24]	**64.1%**	**12.4**	0.33	?[b]	✗

[a] Embedding models released by OpenAI.
[b] The number of embeddings for the proprietary models has never been disclosed.

The Norwegian models are significantly more concise when it comes to their tokenization of the input text, despite having a relatively small vocabulary of $50k$ words. This difference is shown in Fig. 3. They both share the same tokenizer trained by the NorBERT team [2,9]. The mean tokenized length using the NorBERT encoder is $\sim$1581 as compared to, for example, OpenAI's encoder at $\sim$2260, and Qwen's encoder at $\sim$2298, representing a length reduction of $\sim$30%. The pattern also holds for other established Norwegian language tokenizers such as the one used by NorwAI [17]. This phenomenon is caused by the training process of tokenizers splitting words based on the frequency of a substring's appearance in their training data. Since the Norwegian models have only seen Norwegian text, they allocate significantly more tokens to substrings and words commonly found within Norwegian. This pattern of relatively inefficient tokenizers would likely be exacerbated with languages more dissimilar to English and even more so for languages using a non-Latin script.

While Accuracy@1 is an intuitive metric, it can be somewhat misleading due to its inherent stochasticity as compared to mean rank. The 4b qwen3 model outperformed its larger 8b counterpart on accuracy, for example, but not on the more consistent mean rank metric. The Qwen3 models perform remarkably similarly when their size differences are taken into consideration. This is also evident on the MTEB leaderboard, in which the three models occupy the second, third, and fourth spots for the general multilingual benchmark.

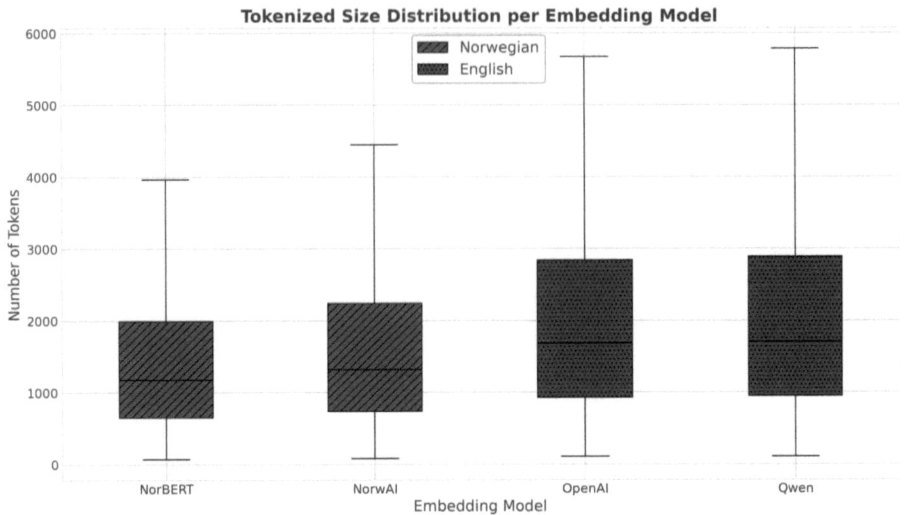

Fig. 3. An overview of the number of tokens per embedding method sorted by language. Encoding text using a natively trained Norwegian encoder has the potential to be ~30% more efficient. This gain will likely be even more significant with languages more dissimilar to English and those using non-Latin scripts.

4.2   Clustering

A recent initiative by the municipality has worked on updating outdated plan documents to make them comply with modern standards [16]. The process of updating a document requires a non-trivial amount of work, much of which is applicable to documents on similar issues. The application of HBScan on our documents resulted in a set of clusters with a Silhouette score of 0.017. Of our documents 45.5% were not assigned to a cluster. These numbers indicate an evenly distributed embedding space with a few prominent clusters. As our dataset is relatively small, most of these unassigned documents do not have any textual counterparts and should remain unassigned. Figure 4 shows a representation of this clustered embedding space after dimensionality reduction.

Amendments to the Planning and Building Act were released by the Norwegian state in both 1985 and 2008 [13,14]. Documents written in these time periods, therefore, bear significant stylistic differences. The clustering algorithm appropriately classifies documents written in similar time periods into separate clusters. A visual representation of the correlation between clusters and date can be seen in Fig. 5. Since the dates are not normally distributed, we choose to numerically evaluate the correlation of the dates using the Kruskal-Wallis H-test, which calculates correlation using each datapoint's ranked ordinals [8]. With 53 degrees of freedom, the test calculated an H-statistic of 272.1 with a p-value of $1.0 * 10^{-30}$, thus disproving the null hypothesis. The test attains similarly statistically significant results ($H(53) = 218.2$, $p < .001$) if the documents are encoded based on their corresponding era:

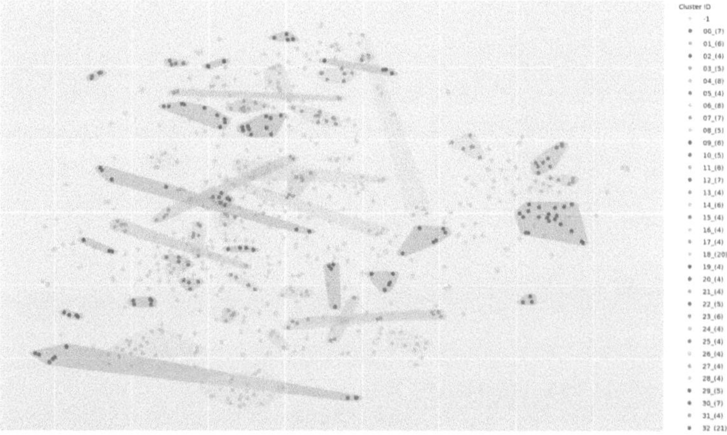

Fig. 4. A clustered representation of our embedding space compressed into 2d space using t-SNE. Clusters are delineated by hulls. All documents not detected to be part of a cluster are depicted as a + sign. This also demonstrates a flaw in representing hyper-dimensional embeddings in 2D space, as points assigned to the same cluster are sometimes depicted far apart.

$$
era(year) = \begin{cases} 0 & \text{if } year < 1980 \\ 1 & \text{if } 1980 \le year < 2008 \\ 2 & \text{if } year \ge 2008 \end{cases}
$$

4.3 Domain Expert Feedback

The domain expert tied to the project made several pertinent observations regarding our embedded representations of the documents. They were often clustered based on when they were implemented or their themes, such as the plans regarding camping grounds or stone quarries, were presented as particularly similar. Larvik municipality was formed from five separate municipalities in 1988 [11]. All of these existing municipalities maintained a separate process for establishing regulation plans, yet the clustering analysis would often detect similar regulation plans across the different municipalities.

4.4 User Communication

The results in Table 1 indicate that textual embeddings are a useful approach for this domain. However, these findings are of little value unless they can be conveyed effectively to the relevant domain experts. To enable users to effectively explore the dataset and discover its underlying structure, it is crucial to provide a high-level, intuitive overview. One useful approach for achieving this is to create a visual map of the entire document collection. We employ t-distributed Stochastic

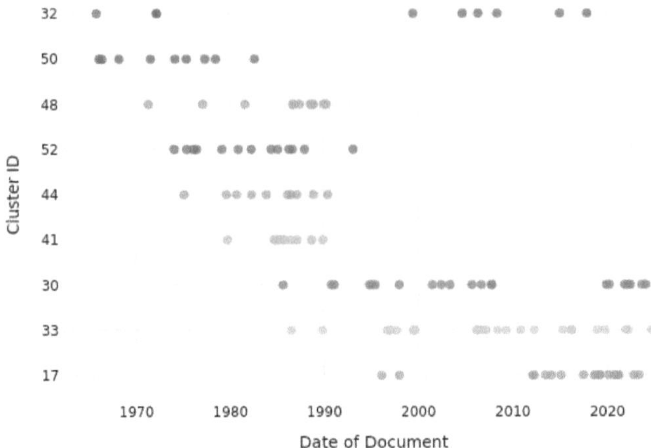

Fig. 5. A subset representation of the nine most populous clusters, sorted by date. Visual inspection shows a clear correlation between the assigned clusters. A Kruskal-Wallis H-test supports this assumption with strong, statistically significant results $(H(53) = 272.1, p < .001)$.

Neighbor Embedding (t-SNE) to project our high-dimensional embedding space into a two-dimensional plot. This visualization, as depicted in Fig. 6, provides an immediate representation of the data's structure, where each point corresponds to a document and their relative positions indicate similarity. This plot was generated using the Python Plotly module, which includes an interactive feature that displays information about a document when the user hovers over the corresponding point. Further, this plot can be converted to a self-contained HTML document that retains this functionality using JavaScript. Ensuring that the information is highly portable and easy to interpret.

The approach described in Fig. 6 is effective for providing a superficial overview of our data, however, the collapse of the embedding space from 1024 to 2 dimensions is, by necessity, lossy. As well demonstrated in Fig. 4, t-SNE and other dimensionality reduction techniques attempt to retain as much locality within the data as possible. However, the depicted distance is, in many cases, deceptive. Two points, despite existing in the full hyper-dimensional embedding space closely enough to be thought of as the same cluster, are in many cases placed on the opposite side of the plot. If the user is solely interested in one specific building plan to find similarities for, a direct comparison between our items is more prudent. Such as representing each item on a one-dimensional scale to represent the distance to each of its neighbors.

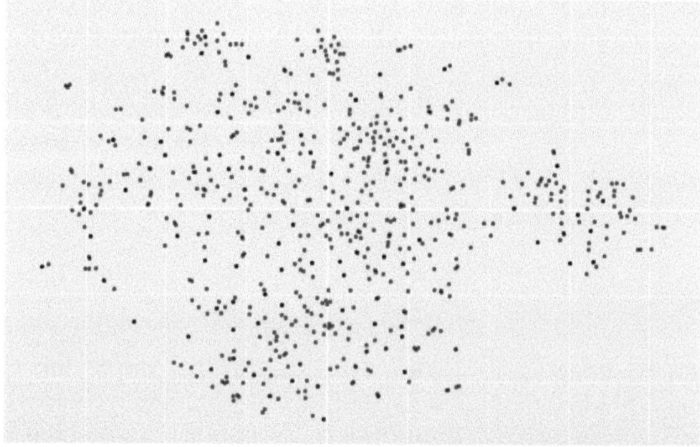

Fig. 6. A t-SNE representation of our embeddings reduced to two dimensions. Each point represents a document from our regulation plan dataset, and the distance between them indicates similarity. As with all t-SNE diagrams, the axes themselves carry no semantic meaning. The only point of relevance being the similarity of two points measured by the distance between them.

5 Future Work and Limitations

When working towards updating regulation plans, there are three aspects considered: whether they comply with current regulations, knowledge, or politics. For example, in the 1980s, knowledge of landslide prevention was substantially worse than in 2025. This lack of knowledge is reflected in the regulation plans written at the time, many of which, therefore, are prime targets for being updated. A more effective approach for finding relevant documents to update would be to design a system that directly identifies these traits. Potentially, either through the application of traditional supervised machine learning systems to the documents' embedded representations, provided there is sufficient training data from documents that have been updated previously, or a more involved automated approach using pre-trained LLMs and heavy cooperation with domain experts.

While retrieving a paraphrase is a strong indicator of semantic understanding, this is a proxy for the more complex task of identifying legally or functionally redundant regulations. Later iterations of this project should work towards creating a dataset that directly represents legal document similarity.

6 Conclusion

This study demonstrates that state-of-the-art text embeddings can effectively identify redundant and overlapping elements within municipal zoning and building regulations, thereby potentially helping combat the bureaucratic bloat that occurs as a by-product of public administration. With the aid of a domain expert and clustering techniques, we have identified several properties of zoning regulations emphasized by text embeddings, such as time of implementation or domain. Among the evaluated models, we found that voyage-3-large is the most performant overall. Further, qwen3-embedding-8b is the most performant of the open-weights models tested, though the practical distinction between it and its 4b version is negligible. Notably, newer generalist models surpassed PlanBERT, an older model fine-tuned for this specific domain.

References

1. Allaoui, M., Kherfi, M.L., Cheriet, A.: Considerably improving clustering algorithms using UMAP dimensionality reduction technique: a comparative study. In: El Moataz, A., Mammass, D., Mansouri, A., Nouboud, F. (eds.) ICISP 2020. LNCS, vol. 12119, pp. 317–325. Springer, Cham (2020). https://doi.org/10.1007/978-3-030-51935-3_34
2. Brådland, H., Goodwin, M., Andersen, P.A., Nossum, A.S.: PlanBERT: from messy zonal plans to informative vector embeddings. In: Bramer, M., Stahl, F. (eds.) SGAI 2024. LNCS, vol. 15446, pp. 175–188. Springer, Cham (2025). https://doi.org/10.1007/978-3-031-77915-2_13, iSSN: 0302-9743, 1611-3349
3. Campello, R.J.G.B., Moulavi, D., Sander, J.: Density-based clustering based on hierarchical density estimates. In: Pei, J., Tseng, V.S., Cao, L., Motoda, H., Xu, G. (eds.) PAKDD 2013. LNCS (LNAI), vol. 7819, pp. 160–172. Springer, Heidelberg (2013). https://doi.org/10.1007/978-3-642-37456-2_14
4. Choi, C., et al.: LINQ-embed-mistral technical report. arXiv:2412.03223 [cs] (2024). https://doi.org/10.48550/arXiv.2412.03223
5. Enevoldsen, K., et al.: MMTEB: massive multilingual text embedding benchmark. arXiv preprint arXiv:2502.13595 (2025). https://doi.org/10.48550/arXiv.2502.13595
6. Hain, D.S., Jurowetzki, R., Buchmann, T., Wolf, P.: A text-embedding-based approach to measuring patent-to-patent technological similarity. Technol. Forecast. Soc. Chang. **177**, 121559 (2022). https://doi.org/10.1016/j.techfore.2022.121559, https://linkinghub.elsevier.com/retrieve/pii/S0040162522000919
7. Kilpatrick, L., Gleicher, Z., Shah, P.: State-of-the-art text embedding via the Gemini API. Google Developers Blog (2025). https://developers.googleblog.com/en/gemini-embedding-text-model-now-available-gemini-api/. Accessed 07 Jun 2025
8. Kruskal, W.H., Wallis, W.A.: Use of ranks in one-criterion variance analysis. J. Am. Stat. Assoc. **47**(260), 583–621 (1952). https://doi.org/10.1080/01621459.1952.10483441, http://www.tandfonline.com/doi/abs/10.1080/01621459.1952.10483441
9. Kutuzov, A., Barnes, J., Velldal, E., Øvrelid, L., Oepen, S.: Large-scale contextualised language modelling for Norwegian. In: Dobnik, S., Øvrelid, L. (eds.) Proceedings of the 23rd Nordic Conference on Computational Linguistics (NoDaLiDa), Sweden, Reykjavik, Iceland, pp. 30–40. Linköping University Electronic Press (2021). https://aclanthology.org/2021.nodalida-main.4/
10. Larvik kommune: Arealplaner. https://www.arealplaner.no/larvik3909/arealplaner/search?planStatusId=3. Accessed 26 Jun 2025
11. Larvik kommune: Mulighetsanalyse Larvik (2015). https://www.larvik.kommune.no/media/4538/mulighetsanalyse-larvik.pdf. Accessed 26 Jun 2025
12. Levenshtein, V.I., et al.: Binary codes capable of correcting deletions, insertions, and reversals. Soviet physics doklady **10**, 707–710 (1966)

13. Ministry of Local Government and Regional Development, Government of Norway: Planning and building act (1985): Act of 14 june 1985 no. 77 the planning and building act (1985). https://www.regjeringen.no/en/dokumenter/planning-and-building-act/id173817/, law; Act of 14 June 1985. Accessed 26 Jun 2025

14. Ministry of Local Government and Regional Development, Government of Norway: Planning and building act (2008). Act of 27 june 2008 no. 71 relating to planning and the processing of building applications (the planning part). https://www.regjeringen.no/en/dokumenter/planning-building-act/id570450/ (2008), originally published by the Ministry of the Environment; Law; Date: 27 June 2008. Accessed 26 Jun 2025

15. Mistral AI: Mistral OCR: introducing the world's best document understanding API (2025). https://mistral.ai/news/mistral-ocr. Accessed 27 May 2025

16. Norges forskningsråd: Operasjon planvask. [operation plan overhaul]. https://prosjektbanken.forskningsradet.no/project/FORISS/349492. Accessed 26 Jun 2025; Project no. 349492

17. NorLLM Team: NorwAI: Norwegian research center for AI innovation (hugging face) (2024). https://huggingface.co/NorwAI, organization profile on Hugging Face; NorwAI is the Norwegian Research Center for AI Innovation based at NTNU

18. Okonkwo, O., Dridi, A., Vakaj, E.: Leveraging word embeddings and transformers to extract semantics from building regulations text. In: Proceedings of the 11th Linked Data in Architecture and Construction Workshop (LDAC 2023). CEUR Workshop Proceedings, vol. 3633, pp. 176–188, Matera, Italy (2023). https://ceur-ws.org/Vol-3633/paper14.pdf

19. OpenAI: New embedding models and api updates. OpenAI Blog (2024). https://openai.com/index/new-embedding-models-and-api-updates/

20. Pearson, K.: LIII. On lines and planes of closest fit to systems of points in space. London, Edinburgh Dublin Philos. Mag. J. Sci. 2(11), 559–572 (1901). https://doi.org/10.1080/14786440109462720, https://www.tandfonline.com/doi/full/10.1080/14786440109462720

21. Rousseeuw, P.J.: Silhouettes: A graphical aid to the interpretation and validation of cluster analysis. J. Comput. Appl. Math. 20, 53–65 (1987). https://doi.org/10.1016/0377-0427(87)90125-7, https://linkinghub.elsevier.com/retrieve/pii/0377042787901257

22. Statistics Norway: Kostra key figures for planning and building processing (m) 2024 [table 14304]. StatBank Norway (2025). https://www.ssb.no/en/statbank/table/14304/. last updated 17 March 2025. Accessed 23 May 2025

23. Statistics Norway: Population 1 January and population changes during the calendar year (m) 2025 [table 06913] (2025). https://www.ssb.no/en/statbank/table/06913. Accessed 27 May 2025

24. Voyage AI: voyage-3-large: the new state-of-the-art general-purpose embedding model (2025). https://blog.voyageai.com/2025/01/07/voyage-3-large/. Accessed 03 Jun 2025

25. Yang, A., et al.: Qwen3 Technical Report. arXiv:2505.09388 [cs] (2025). https://doi.org/10.48550/arXiv.2505.09388, http://arxiv.org/abs/2505.09388

26. Zhang, Y., et al.: Qwen3 embedding: advancing text embedding and reranking through foundation models. arXiv preprint arXiv:2506.05176 (2025)

Exam Timetabling Problem Using Cooperative Hyper-Heuristics: A Case Study of the ITC2007 Dataset

Kate Han[1]([✉]) [iD], Evelyn Oginni[1] [iD], John A. W. McCall[2] [iD], Paul McMullan[3], and Yun Chen[1] [iD]

[1] Salford Business School, University of Salford, Manchester, UK
k.han3@salford.ac.uk
[2] School of Computing, Engineering and Technology, Robert Gordon University, Aberdeen, UK
[3] School of Electronics, Electrical Engineering and Computer Science, Queen's University Belfast, Belfast, UK

Abstract. In recent years, selection-based hyper-heuristics have shown success across various problem domains, significantly enhancing performance in complex optimization tasks. To further advance this field, we propose a novel cooperative hyper-heuristic (COHH) that introduces a three-level agent-based framework incorporating two cooperative schemes: one focused on soft constraint satisfaction and another leveraging heuristic diversity. The framework supports both synchronous and asynchronous search modes, with asynchronous coordination reducing agent idle time and improving search efficiency.

We evaluate COHH on the ITC2007 exam timetabling benchmark and compare it against six established approaches: COHH-6, HLS, SS, MTIS, EHH, and FTA. Our method demonstrates competitive performance, achieving best-known results in several datasets and delivering robust solutions under tight computational constraints. Notably, COHH attains strong averages and best-case solutions across diverse instances, highlighting the effectiveness of cooperative mechanisms in enhancing solution quality and stability.

Keywords: Cooperative hyper-heuristics · Exam timetabling · ITC2007 dataset · Agent-based framework

1 Introduction

The examination timetabling problem has garnered significant research attention due to its complexity and real-world applicability, necessitating innovative and efficient solutions [17]. Hyper-heuristics represent a promising avenue for automating the optimization of these challenging computational search problems, leveraging various heuristic techniques. Past studies have examined the implementation of hyper-heuristics in exam timetabling, focusing on aspects such as solver generality and computational efficiency [13,24].

© The Author(s), under exclusive license to Springer Nature Switzerland AG 2026
M. Bramer and F. Stahl (Eds.): SGAI-AI 2025, LNAI 16302, pp. 374–387, 2026.
https://doi.org/10.1007/978-3-032-11442-6_26

When assessing these approaches, it is essential to consider their capability to produce feasible and realistic solutions within practical time constraints. The second International Timetabling Competition (ITC2007) featured a dedicated track for examination scheduling, utilizing 12 anonymized real-world datasets sourced from institutional data to benchmark the performance of proposed algorithms under realistic constraints [18]. Examination timetabling is typically approached in two stages: an initial construction phase aimed at generating a feasible schedule, followed by an optimization phase that iteratively refines the solution based on predefined criteria [18]. Notably, while ITC2007 remains the most comprehensive open benchmark for exam timetabling, the more recent ITC2019 focused exclusively on university course scheduling, incorporating student sectioning and room assignments but omitting examination-specific scenarios [20]. This highlights a significant gap in the availability of up-to-date, publicly accessible examination timetabling datasets.

This paper aims to advance hyper-heuristic methodologies by introducing a cooperative hyper-heuristic search framework designed to enhance solution quality for exam timetabling. By focusing on cooperative mechanisms, we explore how agent collaboration can facilitate a more extensive search of the solution space and improve overall performance [3].

2   Background

2.1   The Examination Timetabling Problem

Examination scheduling is categorized as an academic timetabling issue and is recognized as NP-hard [5]. Allocating a specified set of examinations into appropriate timeslots and locations, while adhering to both stringent (hard) and more flexible (soft) constraints, is central to addressing this problem. A feasible solution demands the fulfillment of all hard constraints, whereas the quality of the solution is evaluated based on how well the soft constraints are met. The specific types and values of these constraints differ across educational institutions, influencing the characteristics of the problem. Consequently, any proposed method must be adaptable and robust to effectively handle the diverse constraints encountered in various exam scheduling scenarios.

Kaplansky et al. pioneered the concept of distributed exam scheduling issues in [12]. They proposed a distributed approach to address practical exam scheduling challenges at University Technology MARA in Malaysia . This method starts with each agent conducting a local search for their respective campus and then involves coordination and negotiation among agents to obtain a viable global solution. A distributed integer programming framework was proposed to solve the course timetabling problem for Athens University of Economics and Business in [8]. The proposed approach constructed course timetables on a departmental basis. In [2], Kaplansky et al. introduced a Multi-Agent System (MAS) approach for addressing issues related to scheduling exams. The proposed system consisted of four scheduling agents using constraint satisfaction problem techniques and a room agent.

2.2 Related Work in Examination Timetabling Problems and Hyper-Heuristics

In previous research on examination and course timetabling, various strategies have been presented aimed at enhancing solution quality and efficiency. Steenson et al. [25] explore the effectiveness of multi-stage selection hyper-heuristics within the CPSolver framework, a method that has demonstrated significant improvements in solution sequences, as evidenced by its performance in the International Timetabling Competition 2007. Meanwhile, Hermansyah et al. [11] provide a critical evaluation of the SR-HC-HH approach, acknowledging its effectiveness yet highlighting its deficiencies and suggesting the exploration of low-level heuristic (LLH) selection strategies for better results. The research by Van et al. [26] further enriches this discussion by examining the complicated examination timetabling challenge, emphasizing the need for solutions that consider realistic constraints such as room capacity and period length variations.

In addition to these approaches, innovative solutions such as FastTA [14] propose accelerated variants of existing meta-heuristics, demonstrating the potential for achieving high-quality solutions with fewer evaluations. Similarly, Mandal et al. [15] and Mandal et al. [16] introduce tools and methodologies, including a graphical and interactive tool and a partial exam assignment approach, respectively, both aimed at streamlining the timetabling process while adhering to institutional constraints and requirements.

The literature also extends to the development of new algorithms and comprehensive reviews that offer insights into optimizing the Curriculum-Based Course Timetabling problem [6], employing exact and meta-heuristic solutions to tackle complex timetabling issues [4], and systematically analyzing meta-heuristic algorithms to address the University Course Timetabling Problem (UCTP) [1]. Additionally, Hafsa et al. [10] discuss the use of multi-objective evolutionary algorithms (MOEAs) for addressing real-world scheduling challenges, presenting methodological developments in the field. The cooperative distributed hyper-heuristic frameworks discussed in Ouelhadj et al. [21] and Ouelhadj et al. [22] further underscore the evolving landscape of timetabling research, revealing the potential of agent-based systems and the cooperative allocation of heuristics in enhancing scheduling processes.

3 Proposed COHH Framework

This section presents the proposed Cooperative Hyper-Heuristic Framework (COHH), detailing its agent-based model and the various search strategies employed. The framework incorporates three agent types: the Constructor Agent (CA), the Mediator Agent (MA), and multiple Exam Timetabling Agents (ETAs).

In the COHH system, the CA generates an initial solution, which is then optimized independently by the ETAs using hyper-heuristic methods. The ETAs collaborate through the MA, which maintains the best overall solution, manages agent priorities, and aggregates the most effective local solutions, as illustrated in

Fig. 1. The Problem Domain is designed based on the dataset and the optimization objective. It must satisfy all hard constraints while minimizing violations of soft constraints. The Domain Barrier defines how agents interact with the problem space, and its implementation varies across the different COHH designs introduced in this paper. These architectural variations enable different coordination strategies, depending on whether the system operates in synchronous or asynchronous mode, and on the objectives and operations assigned to the low-level agents, which will be introduced in the following sections of this paper.

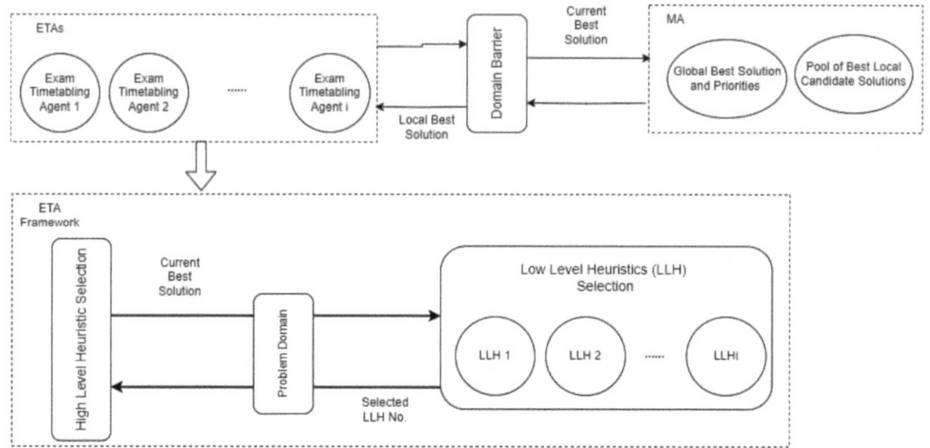

Fig. 1. COHH Framework.

3.1 Synchronous Cooperative Search

In synchronous search, the mediator communicates with the agents at the completion of each cycle. All agents consistently search using the same initial solution. At the cycle's start, the MA distributes the universal initial solution to each ETA along with instructions to optimize. The duration or size of each cycle is one factor that influences the effectiveness of synchronous search.

Upon receiving a request, each ETA initiates a search for an improved move based on its specific algorithm. If a superior local solution is identified, that agent concludes its search and submits the optimal local result to the MA. Should the search exceed the maximum cycle size (defined as the iteration time limit for ETAs), it will be terminated. The MA collects and maintains a repository of the best local solutions from all agents. After gathering the best local solutions from each ETA, the MA then broadcasts a global best solution.

The pseudocode for the synchronous cooperative search ETAs is given in Algorithm 1, and for the synchronous cooperative search MA in Algorithm 4. In Algorithm 4, the initial solution is the initial feasible solution received from the

---

Algorithm 1. Exam Timetabling Agent in Synchronous Cooperative Search

---

1: **function** ETA_SEARCH(MA, ETA, Sglobal, cycle-size)
2:      Initialize local best solution to the global best solution
3:      Set iteration counter to 0
4:      Set a cooling schedule for SA
5:      **while** iteration counter < max_iterations **do**
6:          Perform search for a new local best solution
7:          **if** a better solution is found or a newly found solution is accepted by SA
    then
8:              Update local best solution
9:          **end if**
10:          Increment iteration counter
11:      **end while**
12:      Send INFORM-RESULT (ETA, MA, Slocal) to MA
13: **end function**

---

initial solver, CA. The local best solutions, S_{local}, are the best solutions found by all the ETAs and are stored in a solution pool. S_{global} refers to the current global best solution. All the ETAs are assigned priorities at the beginning of the entire cooperative search.

3.2   Asynchronous Cooperative Search

In asynchronous cooperative search, each ETA communicates solely with the MA and begins with the global best solution as its starting point. During the search process, whenever an ETA discovers a solution that is either better than its local best or accepted by simulated annealing (SA), it updates its local best solution and forwards it to the MA for evaluation. The MA provides immediate feedback indicating whether the solution is accepted along with the current global best solution.

The pseudocode for ETAs in asynchronous cooperative search is outlined in Algorithm 2. The variable "no improvement times" tracks consecutive iterations where the ETA's solutions are not accepted by the MA. In contrast to synchronous search, each ETA requires immediate feedback from the MA when a solution is submitted. If an ETA experiences prolonged periods without accepted improvements (specifically, when "no improvement times" reaches half the iteration limit), it proactively requests assistance from the MA. The MA responds by providing a new initial solution (S_{initial}) that replaces the ETA's current local best solution, effectively restarting the local search from a potentially more promising state. This mechanism ensures that ETAs can escape local optima and continue productive exploration when their current search trajectory becomes unfruitful.

Algorithm 2. Exam Timetabling Agents in Asynchronous Cooperative Search

---

1: **function** ETA_ASYNC_SEARCH(MA, ETA, Sglobal, cycle-size)
2:     Receive request search (MA, ETA, Sglobal, cycle-size).
3:     Initialize local current solution to global best solution.
4:     Set searching iteration limits to cycle size.
5:     Initialize no improvement times to 0.
6:     Initialize improvement flag to false.
7:     **while** within iteration limits **do**
8:         Search for the new current solution.
9:         **if** current solution is better than the local best solution or worse but
    accepted by SA **then**
10:             Update local best solution and Send (ETA, MA, Slocal) to MA.
11:             Receive feedback (MA, ETA, acceptance, Sglobal).
12:             **if** local best solution not accepted by MA **then**
13:                 No improvement times add by 1.
14:             **else**
15:                 No improvement times set to 0.
16:                 Set improvement flag to true.
17:             **end if**
18:             **if** no improvement times equal to half of iteration limits **then**
19:                 Request help (ETA, MA, Slocal) from MA.
20:                 Receive help (MA, ETA, new Sinitial).
21:                 Update local best solution with the newly received initial solution.
22:                 No improvement times set to 0.
23:             **end if**
24:         **end if**
25:     **end while**
26:     **return** (ETA, MA, Slocal, improvement).
27: **end function**

3.3 COHH Components: Initial Solver

The initial solver adopts the Squeaky Wheel Optimization (SWO) algorithm to develop an initial feasible solution, as discussed in [2]. The algorithm begins by loading the dataset configuration and generating an exam list, which is then ordered based on difficulty. An empty initial solution is created along with a weighted list to track exam priorities throughout the construction process.

The construction process operates within specified time limits and continues until all exams are scheduled. In each iteration, exams are sorted by their current weights, with higher-weighted exams receiving priority. For each exam, the algorithm attempts to find a suitable timeslot by evaluating all available slots. When a valid assignment is found (satisfying hard constraints), the algorithm calculates the associated penalty, updates the schedule penalty, and places the exam in that timeslot. The solution and unscheduled exam count are then updated accordingly.

The weight adjustment mechanism follows the SWO principle: exams that are successfully scheduled receive updated weights based on their penalty values, while exams that cannot be scheduled in the current iteration receive significant weight increases. This penalty-driven weighting system ensures that problematic exams—the "squeaky wheels" that violate soft constraints or prove difficult to schedule—are prioritized in subsequent iterations. The algorithm terminates when all exams are successfully scheduled (unscheduled count reaches zero) or the time limit is exceeded, returning the constructed solution along with a success flag, as demonstrated in Algorithm 3.

Algorithm 3. Initial Solver

```
 1: function INITIALSOLVER(MA, CA, datasetNum, timelimit)
 2:     Receive search request.
 3:     Load dataset configurations.
 4:     Generate exam list.
 5:     Create empty initial solution.
 6:     Set unscheduled exam count.
 7:     Initialize weighted list.
 8:     Set unscheduled penalty.
 9:     Order exams based on difficulty.
10:     while within time limits and unscheduled exams remain do
11:         Sort exams by weight.
12:         for each exam do
13:             for each timeslot do
14:                 if can schedule exam then
15:                     Calculate penalty.
16:                     Update schedule penalty.
17:                     Schedule exam.
18:                     Update solution.
19:                     Update unscheduled count.
20:                 end if
21:             end for
22:         end for
23:     end while
24:     if unscheduled count is 0 then
25:         Set constructed flag.
26:     end if
27:     return (CA, MA, constructed, Sinitial).
28: end function
```

3.4   COHH Components Mediator Agent (MA)

The MA is the key component that is responsible for organizing the collaborative search for solutions in the area of exam timetabling problems. Rather than engaging directly with the problem domain, the MA utilizes various specialized agents to conduct the search. Within the MA, a pool is used to store all incoming locally optimal solutions. The methodology employed in this study utilizes

SA algorithms to define the criteria for solution acceptance in the mediator. Higher-quality solutions are generally accepted, but lower-quality ones may also be accepted based on Boltzmann probability. The acceptance of inferior solutions during the SA process is governed by a temperature factor, T, which decreases over time, simulating the annealing process. Initially, the temperature is set very high at 10,000, facilitating a larger number of random searches early in the process. As the search progresses, the probability of accepting poorer solutions declines. The system incorporates a reheating strategy, with a reheating limit of 5 and a frequency of 1,000. The cooling and reheating rates are configured to 0.85 and 0.9, respectively, for this experiment.

Algorithm 4. MA-CA Communication

1: Send request search (MA, CA, datasetNum, timelimit).
2: Receive result (CA, MA, constructed, Sinitial).
3: **if** constructed is true **then**
4:      Update global best solution to received initial solution.
5: **else**
6:      Send request search (MA, CA, datasetNum, timelimit) to CA.
7: **end if**

The ETAs are designed to operate independently, only interacting with the MA. The MA centralizes all transaction data and modifies the search strategy accordingly. In a synchronous cooperative search, the MA resolves conflicts among various ETAs, as illustrated in Algorithm 4. The MA utilizes all received data during negotiations among ETAs and must also manage resource distribution when handling multiple data inputs.

Local searches within ETAs are set up to execute simultaneously. Consequently, this research utilizes a multi-thread approach to facilitate parallel searches. Each agent operates as an individual thread, with the mediator functioning as the central thread that coordinates with all others. Employing threads in programming allows for the simultaneous execution of multiple tasks, enhancing efficiency for complex tasks like solving exam timetabling problems. In this study, messages are managed following a First-in-First-Out rule, which is straightforward to implement and responds promptly to received messages. Messages are handled based on the sequence of their arrival.

3.5 COHH Components: ETA Operational Modes

The COHH framework implements two agent configurations: soft constraint-directed agents (using identical low-level heuristics with different objective functions) and multiple low-level agents (using distinct heuristics with identical objectives). Both configurations support synchronous/asynchronous search through a unified hyper-heuristic framework (Fig. 1), with agents restricted to limited heuristics to accelerate learning.

Soft Constraint-Directed Low-Level Agent Mode: In this mode, the MA holds the global objective evaluation function and is in control of whether to accept the solutions sent by the ETAs. At the same time, the ETAs perform as local agents with their own soft constraint-based local objective function. Each agent employs three fundamental low-level heuristics: Move (Period) for adjusting exam timing, Move (Room) for reallocating rooms, and Swap (Timeslot) for exchanging exam slots. Heuristic selection follows an ϵ-decay-greedy approach ($\epsilon = 1/\sqrt{t}$), with performance tracked using γ-discounted utility updates ($\gamma = 0.9$) bounded to $[0, 40]$. Six specialized agents optimize distinct constraints as detailed in Table 1, including Shift (Room) for modifying room assignments, Extend (Break) for inserting student breaks, and Reduce (Load) for limiting daily exams. Six specialized agents optimize distinct constraints as detailed in Table 1, including Shift (Room) for modifying room assignments, Extend (Break) for inserting student breaks, and Reduce (Load) for limiting daily exams.

Table 1. 6-Agent Design

Agent	Constraints	Objectives
No.1	Consecutive exams	Prevent back-to-back scheduling
No.2	Same-day exams	Avoid multiple daily exams
No.3	Period distribution	Balance exam spacing
No.4	Large exams	Prioritize morning scheduling
No.5	Period penalties	Minimize high-penalty periods
No.6	Room penalties	Avoid high-penalty rooms

Multiple Low-Level Heuristics Agent Mode: In this mode, the MA holds the global best solution and is in control of whether to accept the solutions sent by the ETAs. At the same time, the ETAs perform as local agents with their own set of low-level heuristics. Unlike the previous mode, the objective function in each ETA is the same as the one used by the MA. These include: (1) Simple moves performing single-operation adjustments, (2) Group moves executing batch exam rearrangements, (3) Shuffle moves conducting cross-period/room swaps, and (4) Directed moves targeting specific constraint repairs (Table 2). Agents are prioritized by move size (Agent 1:1 to Agent 4:4) to resolve conflicts during negotiation.

4   Experiments Analysis

4.1   Experimental Design and Parameter Settings

The COHH framework parameters were determined through systematic preliminary experimentation using a three-phase process: establishing parameter ranges

Table 2. 4-Agent Heuristic Design

Agent	Heuristics	Operation
No.1	Simple moves	Single-operation adjustments
No.2	Group moves	Batch exam rearrangements
No.3	Shuffle moves	Cross-period/room swaps
No.4	Directed moves	Targeted constraint repairs

based on literature, conducting coarse grid search, and refining promising combinations.

Key Parameter Settings: For Simulated Annealing, we set initial temperature to 10,000, cooling rate to 0.85, and reheating rate to 0.9 with a limit of 5 and frequency of 1,000 iterations. These values balanced exploration and exploitation while preventing premature convergence. Hyper-heuristic learning employed ε-decay-greedy (initial $\varepsilon=1.0$, decaying as $1/\sqrt{t}$) with discount factor $(\gamma)=0.9$ and utility bounds [0,40]. Agent interaction used 1,000-iteration cycle size for synchronous search and 500-iteration non-improvement threshold for asynchronous search.

Alternative configurations we explored included different learning mechanisms (Q-learning, choice function), communication structures (peer-to-peer, hierarchical), and acceptance criteria (Great Deluge, Late Acceptance Hill Climbing), all showing inferior performance to our chosen approach.

Computational Setup: Our implementation used multi-threading with one thread per agent plus one for the mediator. Time allocation included 30 s for initial solution construction and 570 s for optimization per instance. The soft constraint-directed mode used 6 ETAs while the low-level heuristic mode used 4 ETAs, with both using 1 MA and 1 CA. Termination occurred after reaching the 600-second time limit or when all agents reported no improvement for 3 consecutive cycles.

4.2   Experimental Results

Table 3 provides a comprehensive comparison of six optimisation approaches applied to the ITC-2007 benchmark datasets. Each row corresponds to one of the twelve datasets, while the columns report results for different algorithms. For each dataset–approach pair, two metrics are presented: the Average (Avg) solution across multiple runs and the Best solution obtained. Together, these measures highlight both the peak performance and the robustness of each method.

Our proposed COHH 6-AGENT Asynchronous Search algorithm delivers competitive performance, achieving strong averages and best solutions across several datasets. Hybrid Local Search [19] also performs consistently well, ranking among the stronger methods overall. Scatter Search [9] generates mixed outcomes, excelling on certain datasets but underperforming on others. The Multithread Incremental Solving method [7], where applicable, demonstrates solid results on both metrics. Evolving Hyper-Heuristics [23] are particularly effective in achieving top solutions for specific instances, while the Fast Threshold Acceptance algorithm [14] achieves reasonable results but lacks consistency in securing the best outcomes.

Overall, the table highlights the diverse strengths of different approaches: Some approaches produce best-case results, while others show greater stability across runs. These two metrics are particularly valuable in exam timetabling, where both solution quality and robustness are critical. The comparative results provide researchers with a useful basis for selecting and adapting optimization strategies to similar complex scheduling problems.

Table 3. Comparison with State-of-the-Art Methods on ITC-2007 Benchmark

Dataset	COHH-6 AGENT		HLS [19]		SS [9]		MTIS [7]		EHH [23]		FTA [14]	
	Avg	Best	Avg	Best	Avg	Best	Avg	Best	Avg	Best	Avg	Best
1	4842	4748	4575	**<u>4370</u>**	6064	5905	6671	6670	12819	12035	5314	5089
2	417	408	414	400	1049	1008	623	623	3926	2886	410	**<u>395</u>**
3	11513	11233	10789	10049	14134	13771	–	–	19812	15917	10092	**<u>9711</u>**
4	22172	21527	21639	18141	20667	18674	–	–	25729	23582	13011	**<u>12235</u>**
5	2870	**<u>2773</u>**	3321	2988	4229	4139	3858	3847	11176	6860	3470	3184
6	27840	26515	27809	26585	28078	27640	28155	27815	34029	32250	26136	**<u>25975</u>**
7	4735	4602	4396	**<u>4213</u>**	6760	6572	5432	5420	19669	17666	4515	4369
8	7390	**<u>7106</u>**	7950	7742	10809	10521	–	–	16721	15592	7671	7488
9	1219	1174	1085	1030	1204	1159	1288	1288	2277	2055	1024	**<u>985</u>**
10	12704	**<u>12157</u>**	18581	16682	–	–	14778	14778	20333	17724	13704	13487
11	36453	35187	34129	34129	49861	43888	–	–	44277	40535	33938	**<u>32189</u>**
12	5536	5440	6403	5535	–	–	–	–	7179	6310	5233	**<u>5148</u>**

Note: COHH-6: Cooperative Hyper-Heuristic with 6 Agents; HLS: Hybrid Local Search; SS: Scatter Search; MTIS: Multi-thread Incremental Solving; EHH: Evolving Hyper-Heuristic; FTA: Fast Threshold Accepting Algorithm. "–" indicates no result available for that instance. Underlined values denote the best solution obtained among all approaches for a given dataset.

While the underlined values highlight the best solutions for each dataset, the average performance is equally informative, as it reflects consistency across multiple runs. In this regard, COHH-6 delivers competitive averages that are close to the best-known values in several instances (e.g., Datasets 5, 8, and 10), suggesting robustness under repeated trials. By contrast, FTA secures many of the best individual solutions (e.g., Datasets 3, 4, 6, 9, 11, and 12) but shows greater variability in average performance.

5   Conclusions

In this article, we introduce an innovative agent-based cooperative hyper-heuristic algorithm, named COHH, designed to address the challenges of exam scheduling. We provide a comprehensive description of COHH, covering its multiple elements, the search strategies, methods of cooperation, and the negotiation approaches used. Additionally, the handling of conflicts, a critical issue in designing cooperative search frameworks, is also discussed.

COHH was implemented and tested with both synchronous and asynchronous search methods for comparison purposes. In this framework, the resource allocation follows the First-In-First-Out rule. Additionally, two distinct operational modes for ETAs were introduced and executed to examine the collaboration process. The first mode distributes soft constraint satisfaction tasks among agents to search for the optimal solution, while the second mode allocates different sets of low-level heuristics to each agent to add diversity.

Both proposed cooperative schemes successfully solved the entire set of 12 datasets from the ITC2007 benchmarks, with the asynchronous scheme consistently outperforming the synchronous scheme under the same operating conditions. Among the asynchronous search results, 6 agents outperform 4 agents search. This improvement is believed to be due to the asynchronous scheme reducing waiting times between agents. Furthermore, the agent mode with six agents managing soft constraints performed better than the mode with four agents using diverse low-level heuristics. It is identified that the quantity of agents and the diversity of accessible low-level heuristics are important factors. but further investigation is required to fully understand these effects.

Our work demonstrates the process of performance improvement with a given hyper-heuristic and the proposed cooperative scheme. Additionally, two simple methods of creating hyper-heuristic variants with a given hyper-heuristic framework are suggested. Our research contributes to the field of hyper-heuristics using a parallel searching technique and shows that the disadvantages of hyper-heuristics can be mitigated by using such methods. In this paper, limited attention was given to investigating the resource allocation scheme. In the literature on cooperative systems, alternatives to First-In-First-Out, such as Round-robin, have also shown promising results. Future research could further improve asynchronous COHH by refining the resource allocation scheme. Another area for further study is the agent priority allocation scheme. As the experiments in this paper were conducted on specific benchmarks, the priorities assigned to each ETA were pre-fixed. For real-world problems, priorities should be aligned with institutional timetabling preferences. Furthermore, designing the priority scheme to be dynamic and adaptive could enhance the learning capabilities and practical flexibility of COHH.

References

1. Abdipoor, S., Yaakob, R., Goh, S.L., Abdullah, S.: Meta-heuristic approaches for the university course timetabling problem. Intell. Syst. Appl., 200253 (2023)

2. Aickelin, U., Burke, E.K., Li, J.: An evolutionary squeaky wheel optimization approach to personnel scheduling. IEEE Trans. Evol. Comput. **13**(2), 433–443 (2008)
3. Burke, E.K., Kendal, G., McCollum, B., McMullan, P.: Constructive versus improvement heuristics: an investigation of examination timetabling. In: 3rd Multidisciplinary international scheduling conference: theory and applications, pp. 28–31. Citeseer (2007)
4. Carlsson, M., et al.: Exact and metaheuristic methods for a real-world examination timetabling problem. J. Sched., 1–15 (2023)
5. Cooper, T.B., Kingston, J.H.: The complexity of timetable construction problems. In: Practice and Theory of Automated Timetabling: First International Conference Edinburgh, UK, August 29–September 1, 1995 Selected Papers 1, pp. 281–295. Springer (1996)
6. COŞAR, B.M., Bilge, S., DÖKEROÄđLU, T.: A new greedy algorithm for the curriculum-based course timetabling problem. Düzce Üniversitesi Bilim ve Teknoloji Dergisi **11**(2), 1121–1136 (2023)
7. De Smet, G., Wauters, T.: Multithreaded incremental solving for local search based metaheuristics with step chasing. In: Proceedings of the 13th International Conference on the Practice and Theory of Automated Timetabling-PATAT, vol. 1 (2021)
8. Dimopoulou, M., Miliotis, P.: An automated university course timetabling system developed in a distributed environment: a case study. Eur. J. Oper. Res. **153**(1), 136–147 (2004)
9. Gogos, C., Alefragis, P., Housos, E.: An improved multi-staged algorithmic process for the solution of the examination timetabling problem. Ann. Oper. Res. **194**, 203–221 (2012)
10. Hafsa, M., Wattebled, P., Jacques, J., Jourdan, L.: Solving a multiobjective professional timetabling problem using evolutionary algorithms at mandarine academy. Int. Trans. Oper. Res. (2023)
11. Hermansyah, D., Muklason, A.: Evaluation of hyper-heuristic method using random-hill climbing algorithm in the examination timetabling problem. In: Journal of Physics: Conference Series. vol. 1569, p. 022101. IOP Publishing (2020)
12. Kaplansky, E., Kendall, G., Meisels, A., Hussin, N.: Distributed examination timetabling. In: Proceedings of the 5th International Conference of the Practice and Theory of Automated Timetabling (PATAT), Pittsburg, USA, pp. 511–516. Citeseer (2004)
13. Kristiansen, S., Stidsen, T.J.R.: A comprehensive study of educational timetabling - a survey (2013), https://api.semanticscholar.org/CorpusID:27289579
14. Leite, N., Melício, F., Rosa, A.C.: A fast threshold acceptance algorithm for the examination timetabling problem. Handbook of operations research and management science in higher education, pp. 323–363 (2021)
15. Mandal, A.K.: Development of an interactive tool based on combining graph heuristic with local search for examination timetable problem. Int. J. Adv. Comput. Sci. Appl. **11**(3) (2020)
16. Mandal, A.K., Kahar, M.N.M., Kendall, G.: Addressing examination timetabling problem using a partial exams approach in constructive and improvement. Computation **8**(2), 46 (2020)
17. McCollum, B.: A perspective on bridging the gap between theory and practice in university timetabling. In: International conference on the practice and theory of automated timetabling, pp. 3–23. Springer (2006)
18. McCollum, B.: Setting the research agenda in automated timetabling: the second international timetabling competition. INFORMS J. Comput. **22**(1), 120–130 (2010)

19. Müller, T.: ITC 2007 solver description: a hybrid approach. Ann. Oper. Res. **172**(1), 429–446 (2009)
20. Müller, T., Rudová, H., Müllerová, Z., et al.: University course timetabling and international timetabling competition 2019. In: Proceedings of the 12th international conference on the practice and theory of automated timetabling (PATAT-2018), vol. 1, pp. 5–31 (2018)
21. Ouelhadj, D., Petrovic, S.: A cooperative distributed hyper-heuristic framework for scheduling. In: 2008 IEEE International Conference on Systems, Man and Cybernetics, pp. 2560–2565. IEEE (2008)
22. Ouelhadj, D., Sanja, P.: A cooperative hyper-heuristic search framework. J. Heuristics **16**, 835–857 (2010)
23. Pillay, N.: Evolving hyper-heuristics for a highly constrained examination timetabling problem. In: Proceedings of the 8th International Conference on the Practice and Theory of Automated Timetabling (PATAT'10), pp. 336–346 (2010)
24. Qu, R., Burke, E.K., McCollum, B., Merlot, L.T., Lee, S.Y.: A survey of search methodologies and automated system development for examination timetabling. J. Sched. **12**, 55–89 (2009)
25. Steenson, A., Ozcan, E., Kheiri, A., McCollum, B., McMullan, P.: An online learning selection hyper-heuristic for educational timetabling. In: Proceedings of the 13th International Conference on the Practice and Theory of Automated Timetabling-PATAT, vol. 1 (2021)
26. Van Bulck, D., Goossens, D., Schaerf, A.: Multi-neighbourhood simulated annealing for the itc-2007 capacitated examination timetabling problem. J. Sched., 1–16 (2023)

Carbon Crest: A Personal Carbon Credit Model for Sustainable Transport Behaviour in Greater Manchester

Kate Han[1,3]([✉]) [iD], Meropi Tzanetakis[2] [iD], Evelyn Oginni[1] [iD], Arun Matthew[4], and Bobin Joseph[4]

[1] Salford Business School, University of Salford, Greater Manchester, UK
`k.han3@salford.ac.uk`
[2] Department of Socioeconomics, Vienna University of Economics and Business, Vienna, Austria
[3] The Centre for Sustainable Innovation (CSI), University of Salford, Greater Manchester, UK
[4] The Carboncrest Network Ltd, Bartle House 9 Oxford Court, Manchester M2 3WQ, UK

Abstract. Sustainability in transportation is critical for reducing carbon emissions and meeting climate goals. This paper introduces the *Carbon Crest*, a personalized carbon credit model designed to incentivize sustainable transport behaviour across Greater Manchester, UK. The model, inspired by the Verra VM0050 methodology, calculates carbon savings from changes in transportation modes, such as switching from private car use to public transport. A simulation framework, the *Carbon Crest* model, is proposed to track and measure these carbon savings, allowing for personalized carbon credit allocation based on individual commuting choices and regional residents' travel patterns. The implemented model offers political decision makers a practical option to encourage sustainable mobility and contribute to regional climate targets. By leveraging blockchain technology and collaboration with local transport providers, the proposed framework enables a transparent, rewarding token-based approach to promote sustainable commuting behaviour changes.

Keywords: Carbon Credit · Sustainable Transport · Urban Mobility · Digital Identity

1 Introduction

The transportation sector is a significant contributor to global greenhouse gas (GHG) emissions, with road transport—particularly private vehicle use—being the dominant source [2,7,16]. In countries such as the United States and the United Kingdom, transportation contributes between 26% and 30% of national emissions, with passenger cars representing the largest share within the sector [2,36].

M. Bramer and F. Stahl (Eds.): SGAI-AI 2025, LNAI 16302, pp. 388–401, 2026.
https://doi.org/10.1007/978-3-032-11442-6_27

Urban areas play a crucial role in climate mitigation efforts. They are home to over half of the global population and are estimated to account for nearly 70% of worldwide carbon emissions, largely due to transport systems and energy consumption [34]. Triggered by this, the European Union has launched the NetZeroCities programme, supporting over 100 cities committed to achieving climate neutrality by 2030 [30]. However, many cities struggle to translate the ambitious goal into practice, facing challenges such as limited governance capacity, fragmented financing mechanisms, and the complexity of coordinating across sectors and stakeholders [35]. Nevertheless, cities remain a core of the problem in driving the global transition towards low-carbon, climate-resilient development.

This paper introduces the *Carbon Crest*, a personalized carbon credit model designed to support sustainable transport behaviours in Greater Manchester, UK. The model is inspired by Verra VM0050 [10] for carbon crediting, but adapts it to the urban transportation context. By offering personalized carbon savings calculations based on individual commuting patterns, *Carbon Crest* aims to incentivize users to switch from private car use to more sustainable transportation modes, such as public transit, cycling, walking, or other electric vehicles such as e-scooters.

The paper is structured as follows: Sect. 2 provides an overview of existing carbon credit systems and their relevance to transportation. Section 3 outlines the design and implementation of the *Carbon Crest* model, including the data inputs, calculations, and simulation framework. In Sect. 4, we present the results of a simulation study comparing carbon savings between urban and rural areas of Greater Manchester. Finally, Sect. 5 discusses the implications of the findings and potential future developments of the model.

2   Literature Review and Theoretical Framework

To support the design and implementation of the proposed model, a literature review has been performed in this section to identify key literature related to carbon credit systems, behavioural change theories, digital incentive models, and the transportation context of Greater Manchester. The review will serve as a theoretical foundation for the development of the *Carbon Crest* platform, integrating sustainability, behaviour change, and technological innovation.

2.1   Personal Carbon Credit Systems: Case Studies from China and Europe

Carbon credit systems have evolved from large-scale industrial applications to more localized, personal-level mechanisms designed to encourage sustainable behaviours. These systems are now being piloted and implemented globally, with notable examples ranging from innovative municipal schemes and mobility-linked credits in China [9,15,18,40], to app-based personal carbon accounting and transport incentives across Europe [4,14,22,38]. This global shift reflects a growing recognition that individual behaviour change, supported by digital tools and incentive structures, can play a critical role in achieving ambitious climate goals.

China's Personal Carbon Incentive Projects: Various initiatives in China leverage mobile apps, mini-programs, and urban mobility systems to encourage low-carbon habits through quantified incentives. Liu et al. [25] analyse commuter responses to public transport incentives in 34 Chinese cities, identifying three segments with varied responsiveness shaped by factors such as education, gender, and travel preferences. Lin et al. [24] propose a credit-based mobility scheme where travellers budget periodic driving credits while public transit remains free, and they recommend a contingency system to address early-cycle credit hoarding. Li et al. [23] develop a cryptographic framework to ensure secure and authenticated emissions accounting across jurisdictions for international carbon trading. Yu et al. [44] use a difference-in-differences approach to show that firms participating in China's carbon trading market improve their environmental performance.

- **Ant Financial's "Ant Forest":** Alibaba's Ant Group initiated the widely-used mobile feature in 2016, which gamifies "green energy" by rewarding users for daily low-carbon actions. In 2022, "Ant Forest" received the UN Champions of the Earth Award [40, 43].
- **Wuhan Bike-Share Carbon Credit Scheme:** Launched in 2015 by the C40-affiliated city bike-share rollout, users earn personal carbon credits for bike rides, calculable via speed and distance. Credits are redeemable for small goods or services (e.g., movie tickets) [9].
- **Wuhan "Wutanjianghu" Mini-Program:** In June 2023, a WeChat mini-app named Wutanjianghu, operated by Wuhan Carbon Inclusion Management under municipal guidance, logs low-carbon activities like public transit, recycling, and biking. Credits will be converted into discounts, consumer items, or even reductions in mortgage interest [18].
- **Hangzhou/Huzhou Pilot Financial Incentives:** Cities in Zhejiang province such as Hangzhou and Huzhou integrated low-carbon behaviour with green finance. Huzhou introduced green loans tied to carbon credit performance, plus digital green evaluation systems and insurance for reduced mileage, supported by citywide carbon tracking infrastructure [15].

Europe's Personal Carbon Credit Pilots and Platforms: Moreover, several European countries have also identified initiatives aimed at expanding the impact of sustainability and enhancing related awareness efforts. In Europe, initiatives have emerged encouraging individual-level responsibility for transport-related carbon emissions. These projects incorporate digital tools, smartcards, and mobile platforms to incentivize behavioural change through rewards, budgeting, or trading mechanisms.

- **Mobility Wallet – Sweden:** Funded by Sweden's innovation agency Vinnova, this project promotes sustainable travel choices by rewarding low-emission transport behaviours. Users receive incentives for using public transit, cycling, or walking, with the aim of reducing urban transport emissions [38, 39].
- **Personal Carbon Trading Pilot – Lahti, Finland:** The CitiCAP project (UIA 2018–2020) implemented a city-wide personal carbon trading system, assigning residents mobility-based CO_2 budgets and allowing them to trade unused allowances. Evaluations suggest that approximately one-third of users reduced their emissions [1, 22, 37].
- **Whim and MaaS Platforms – Finland:** The Whim app by MaaS Global provides a unified platform for emissions-aware travel planning, including offsetting carbon from trips. Whim integrates personal carbon tracking with Mobility-as-a-Service (MaaS) infrastructure to encourage modal shift away from cars [14, 41].
- **OV-chipkaart CO_2 Savings – Netherlands:** The OV-chipkaart, a national transport smartcard, is now used in employer carbon accounting schemes. Programs such as NS Go track commuter CO_2 and support compliance with CO_2 reporting mandates. These platforms expand beyond fare collection to enable environmental monitoring and behaviour change [4, 20, 31, 33].

Together, the European and Chinese initiatives demonstrate the growing viability and public appeal of personal carbon credit systems, particularly when combined with mobility services, digital identities, and incentive-based ecosystems. Inspired by cases such as Sweden's Carbon Wallet, Finland's MaaS-linked emissions budgeting, the Netherlands' CO_2 Card, and China's Ant Forest and municipal mini-programs in Wuhan and Hangzhou, the *Carbon Crest* platform builds upon these foundations to address the specific mobility and carbon reduction goals of Greater Manchester. However, individual behaviour change alone is insufficient. For such systems to achieve sustained impact, they must be supported by reliable, frequent, and affordable public transport networks with adequate geographic reach. *Carbon Crest* therefore aims not only to incentivize low-carbon choices at the personal level, but also to inform broader systemic improvements by aligning with urban planning and transport infrastructure policies to create a truly enabling environment for sustainable mobility.

2.2 Behavioural Change Theories and Societal Factors in Transportation

Promoting sustainable transportation requires integrating both individual behavioural change and the broader societal factors that enable or constrain transport choices. This section examines key behavioural theories while acknowledging the critical role of transportation infrastructure and societal context.

The **Theory of Planned behaviour (TPB)**, developed by [3], provides a foundational framework for understanding individual transportation choices.

TPB posits that behavioural intentions are determined by three factors: attitudes toward the behaviour, subjective norms (perceived social pressure), and perceived behavioural control (individual's perceived ability to perform the behaviour). In the transportation context, TPB has been widely applied to understand decisions regarding public transport use, cycling adoption, and electric vehicle purchasing [6,26].

The **Self-Determination Theory (SDT)** complements TPB and focuses on intrinsic motivation through the satisfaction of three basic psychological needs: autonomy, competence, and relatedness [12]. Pan and Ryan [32] demonstrate the effectiveness of SDT-based interventions in promoting sustainable transportation, emphasizing personalized approaches that satisfy individuals' needs for choice, mastery, and social connection. The study underscores the success of interventions that integrate feedback with goal-setting strategies in encouraging shifts towards sustainable modes like cycling and public transport.

The **Push-Pull-Mooring (PPM) framework** offers another lens for understanding transportation mode switching. Hu et al. [19] apply this framework to electric vehicle adoption, identifying environmental concerns and dissatisfaction with conventional vehicles as push factors, perceived EV benefits as pull factors, and personal habits and financial considerations as mooring factors that moderate the switching decision.

While the individual-level behavioural theories provide valuable insights into decision-making processes, it is pertinent to recognise that the adoption of sustainable transportation cannot be achieved solely through behavioural change. Societal and structural factors play a pivotal role in shaping the decisions made on the mode of transportation. These critical factors include:

Infrastructure, Network Integration and Service Quality: The interplay between the physical and operational quality of transport networks is crucial in determining the use of public transport networks. Efficient transportation systems that provide high service frequency, reliability, access to various location and overall, seamless connections between different modes of transport can significantly influence the attractiveness, and practical feasibility of sustainable transport options [28].

Economic and Socio-Cultural Factors: Affordability and transparent pricing structures serve as a strong pull factor for public transport adoption [36]. This incentivizes individuals to make decisions in favor of public transport. On the other hand, social norms, cultural perceptions of different modes of transport and community attitudes towards sustainability all contribute to individual transportation choices within broader social framework [21].

These theoretical insights inform the user-centric approach of the Carbon Crest platform, which recognizes that effective sustainable transport requires a dual focus on addressing individual motivations and societal enablers. Carbon Crest leverages behavioural theories to design personalized interventions while acknowledging the fundamental importance of supportive transportation infrastructure and policy frameworks in facilitating sustainable transport choices. This integrated approach aligns with recent calls for multi-level interventions that combine behavioural change strategies with structural improvements to transportation systems.

3   Methodology

The *Carbon Crest* model is designed to provide a personalized approach to carbon credit generation for sustainable transportation behaviour. This section outlines the key components of the model, including data collection, carbon credit calculation, and a detailed example of how emissions reductions are translated into carbon credits.

The primary data sources include OpenStreetMap (OSM) for detailed mapping of road networks, pedestrian routes, and cycling infrastructure, and General Transit Feed Specification (GTFS) data from public transport providers, which offer up-to-date information on service routes, schedules, and stops. Additionally, datasets from GOV.UK supply authoritative transportation statistics and carbon emission factors for various transport modes, including private vehicles, buses, and trains. These data enable precise modelling of travel patterns and carbon emissions across the Greater Manchester region.

3.1   Carbon Crest Model

This *Carbon Crest* calculation model employs a comparative methodology to quantify emission reductions achieved through transportation mode changes. The model calculates carbon credits by determining the difference between baseline emissions (original transportation mode) and project emissions (alternative transportation mode). Additional factors such as home energy plans, rent, energy supply, and family size can be incorporated to provide a comprehensive carbon footprint assessment, while alternative modes including electric vehicles (EVs), e-scooters, and shared bicycles can be evaluated using the same framework.

The following example demonstrates the model's application using a daily commute scenario where an individual transitions from single-occupancy petrol car use to public bus transportation. The scenario parameters include a daily commute of 20 km each way (40 km total per day) over 230 working days per year. The baseline emissions are calculated using an average car emission factor of 0.17 kg CO_2e per km for a typical medium petrol car, resulting in annual baseline emissions of 1,564 kg CO_2e. The project emissions are calculated using an average bus emission factor of 0.03 kg CO_2e per passenger km, yielding annual project emissions of 276 kg CO_2e. CO_2e stands for Carbon Dioxide equivalent where the e means equivalent. It's a standardized unit used in climate science and carbon accounting to measure the total warming impact of different greenhouse gases by converting them all to the equivalent amount of CO_2 that would cause the same warming effect.

$$\text{Annual distance} = 40 \text{ km} \times 230 \text{ days} = 9,200 \text{ km} \tag{1}$$

$$\text{Annual baseline emissions} = 9,200 \text{ km} \times 0.17 \text{ kg CO}_2\text{e/km} = 1,564 \text{ kg CO}_2\text{e} \tag{2}$$

$$\text{Annual project emissions} = 9,200 \text{ km} \times 0.03 \text{ kg CO}_2\text{e/km} = 276 \text{ kg CO}_2\text{e} \tag{3}$$

$$\text{Annual carbon credits} = 1,564 - 276 = 1,288 \text{ kg CO}_2\text{e} = 1.288 \text{ tonnes CO}_2\text{e} \tag{4}$$

Based on the referenced paper, if these carbon credits were traded at £30/ton CO_2e, the financial value would be calculated as:

$$\text{Financial value} = 1.288 \text{ tonnes} \times 30/\text{tonne} = 38.64 \text{ per year} \tag{5}$$

3.2 Greater Manchester Case Study: Carbon Crest Application

Greater Manchester has set a clear target to achieve carbon neutrality by 2038, underscoring the importance of sustainable transportation within its broader climate strategy [11]. The Greater Manchester Combined Authority (GMCA) emphasizes reducing emissions from transport, which remains one of the largest contributors to regional pollution, with the Transport for Greater Manchester's (TfGM) Bee Network serving as a key component of this strategy—an integrated transport system that aims to provide seamless access to walking, cycling, and public transit options, thereby encouraging residents to shift away from private car use [5]. The TfGM supports this vision by enhancing public transport infrastructure and advancing electric vehicle adoption programs, aligning these actions with the region's sustainability goals [17]. However, the puzzle is how to effectively achieve the carbon-neutral target? The *Carbon Crest* model provides a coherent solution for promoting sustainable transportation behaviours by integrating seamlessly with existing systems such as TfGM's Bee Network. The model offers a data-driven framework that tracks and rewards low-carbon travel.

The *Carbon Crest* platform awards carbon credits to individuals who reduce emissions through the use of public transport, shared mobility services, and EVs, underpinned by a React-based interactive mapping application that allows users to select predefined origin and destination points to compare car and bus routes using Azure Maps, calculating travel time, distance, and estimated carbon savings in real time while offering features like interactive route highlighting and financial estimates to help users make informed, sustainable travel choices. The Greater Manchester case study showcases key components where users are incentivized to switch from private cars to greener modes—such as buses, EVs, e-scooters, and shared bikes—earning credits tied to documented emission reductions, with real-time trip data captured through the Bee Network app enabling accurate calculation of carbon credits. Drawing on models like Wuhan's bike-share credit system and the UK's Gift Aid scheme, *Carbon Crest* combines immediate fare discounts with a longer-term ledger of tradable credits, with envisioned applications including fare reductions, cycling-related rewards, discounts at eco-conscious local retailers, and funding for community green initiatives. Building on a mixed-methods study informed by the Capabilities Approach—which acknowledges both the opportunities and limitations of micromobility—ongoing research and stakeholder engagement will play a critical role in refining incentive structures. These efforts aim to ensure the incentives are effective, equitable, and financially sustainable. At the same time, strong integration with the TfGM's Bee Network is essential for enhancing public trust and encouraging widespread adoption.

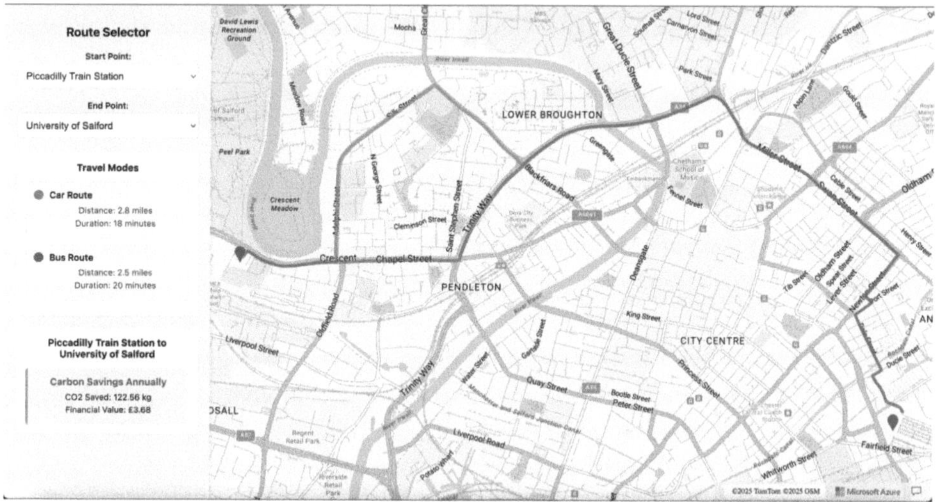

Fig. 1. Carbon Crest Model Web App.

Figure 1 shows the implemented *Carbon Crest* web application used in the pilot run. The app demonstrates the carbon emission differences between private car use and public transport. In the visual, the green line represents the public transport route, while the blue line indicates the private car route. Carbon emissions and corresponding credits are calculated for each mode and displayed as monetary equivalents, making it easier for users to understand and quantify the environmental impact of their travel choices.

Despite these coordinated efforts, challenges persist, including traffic congestion, high reliance on private vehicles, and unequal access to sustainable transport modes, particularly in underserved communities [11], which frame the context for initiatives such as *Carbon Crest* that seek to promote sustainable travel behaviours and improve transport equity across Greater Manchester.

4   Comparison Analysis

Global precedents demonstrate diverse approaches to incentivizing sustainable transport behaviour, each offering valuable insights for comprehensive carbon credit systems. Wuhan's bike-share carbon-credit programme shows that large-scale behaviour change is possible when credits are tied directly to kilometres ridden, while congestion studies across three Chinese megacities confirm measurable traffic relief from bike-share expansion [9,42]. Denver's e-bike rebates demonstrate the power of upfront financial incentives to spur low-carbon purchases, with post-programme evaluations underscoring the value of simple, tiered incentives for equitable uptake [8,13]. London's congestion charge and Ultra LEZ reveal that price signals can deliver substantial air-quality benefits, while Edinburgh's proposing LEZ to reshape commuting behaviour in a similar approach [27,29]. Chinese initiatives like Wuhan's bike-share scheme and the "Wutanjianghu" mini-program demonstrate high user engagement through immediate, tangible rewards and gamification mechanisms, while European projects such as Lahti's personal carbon trading and Sweden's Mobility Wallet emphasize systemic behavioural change through budget allocation and trading mechanisms.

Table 1 demonstrates that *Carbon Crest* is innovative in its comprehensive multimodal approach compared with the existing initiatives reviewed. The Car-

Table 1. Comparison between Carbon Crest and Global Personal Carbon Models

Criteria	Carbon Crest	Chinese Models	European Models	Key Innovation
Focus Area	Multi-modal Transport	Single Mode (Bike-share)	Personal Carbon Budgets	Comprehensive Coverage
Reward Type	Hybrid: Credits + Discounts	Immediate Rewards	Trading/Budget Systems	Dual Incentive Structure
Technology	Blockchain, App-based Tracking	App-based Tracking	Smartcards, MaaS Platforms	Blockchain and verification
Stakeholders	GMCA, TfGM, Transport Operators	Municipal Government	City Authorities, EU Funding	Public-Private Partnership
User Engagement	Multi-transport Usage	High (1.6M users in Wuhan)	Moderate (1/3 adoption)	Sustained Engagement Focus
Verification Process	Blockchain for Verification	Government Verification	Digital Tracking/Trading	Blockchain used in *Carbon Crest*
Geographical Scope	Greater Manchester	Megacity Scale	City/Regional Scale	Metropolitan Integration
Carbon Credit Calculation	Mode-specific Emission Factors	Distance-based Calculation	Budget Allocation System	Precision + Flexibility
Implementation Stage	Pilot Planning	Operational Success	Mixed Results	Evidence-based Design

bon Crest uniquely combines the gamification success of China's personal carbon incentive projects with the rigorous verification mechanisms seen in European pilots. The platform synthesizes high user engagement achieved by Chinese gamified approaches with the systematic behavioural change mechanisms developed in European contexts, offering both immediate fare discounts and long-term tradable credits supported by blockchain verification to ensure transparency and trust. The global comparison of personal carbon incentive programs offers valuable insights for adapting successful models to the UK context. For instance, Chinese initiatives such as those in Wuhan have shown that high user engagement—reaching 1.6 million users—can be achieved by offering immediate, tangible rewards through integration with widely used digital platforms like WeChat. However, directly replicating these models in the UK presents significant challenges. These include the absence of comparable super-apps, stricter privacy regulations under GDPR, and a more fragmented transport governance structure, in contrast to China's centralized municipal control. European models offer more applicable lessons for the UK context, as Finland's Lahti pilot and Sweden's Mobility Wallet demonstrate that personal carbon systems can operate within EU regulatory frameworks similar to the UK's post-Brexit environment. However, their relatively modest adoption rates (one-third participation in Lahti) suggest that European approaches prioritizing systemic change over immediate gratification may face engagement challenges.

Carbon Crest bridges global models by combining the immediate, reward-based incentives of Chinese programs with the systematic tracking found in European initiatives. Designed to operate within the UK's specific regulatory and infrastructure context, it builds credibility through integration with trusted systems like the Bee Network. Additionally, the use of blockchain verification ensures transparency and mitigates concerns typically associated with government-managed schemes. This comparative analysis shows that *Carbon Crest* overcomes the limitations of single-mode programs through its multimodal design, while addressing trust issues linked to government-led schemes. The model creates a comprehensive, scalable solution that leverages lessons learned from successful global case studies. Success in the UK context will depend on balancing the gamification elements that drive Chinese success with the privacy protections and institutional frameworks that characterize European approaches, creating a uniquely British model for personal carbon incentivization that maximizes both immediate participation and long-term behavioural transformation through the integration of multiple transportation options and advanced technologies.

5   Conclusion and Future Work

This paper presents the *Carbon Crest* model, a novel platform that integrates behavioural economics with carbon credit mechanisms to incentivize sustainable transportation choices. The key features of the *Carbon Crest* model are real-time carbon footprint tracking through integration with existing transport systems like Greater Manchester's Bee Network, personalized carbon credit rewards based on documented emission reductions from transport mode switching, a comprehensive approach combining individual behavioural interventions with recognition of broader societal factors, and practical reward mechanisms ranging from direct fare discounts to community-level infrastructure improvements.

The success of every model supporting the increased use of environmentally friendly public transport will also depend on societal factors, some of which are inherently political. Societal factors include the socio-economic background of the individuals, price policy of the public transportation system including if it is supported by the government of not, the coverage and frequency of public transport means, reliability of public transport, safety concerns when cycling in a city, and the question if all areas of a city are equally included in the network. These societal factors go beyond a model that focuses on individual incentives, as suggested in this paper, but would also need to be considered to achieve an increased use of sustainable transport. However, this paper offers an important first step in the right direction to achieve Greater Manchester's 2038 carbon-neutral target.

Several limitations of the current *Carbon Crest* model present opportunities for future development. The current implementation focuses primarily on transitions from conventional petrol vehicles to public transport, using infrastructure and transport mode data. It does not yet account for electric vehicle (EV) adoption as an intermediate step. Future iterations of the model will incorporate e-car scenarios to enable more personalized and adaptive carbon credit calculations. This enhancement will allow the platform to distinguish between various transition pathways—such as petrol-to-electric, electric-to-public transport, and direct petrol-to-public transport—and assign differentiated carbon credit yields accordingly, reflecting users' specific travel behaviour and vehicle ownership status.

Additionally, future research will explore the integration of socioeconomic variables—such as income, age, household composition, and gender—sourced from open datasets like the UK Census. Including these variables will support more nuanced analyses of transport equity, accessibility, and the potential differential impact of carbon credit incentives. As a next step, the platform aims to include location-based or behavioural data collected through voluntary mobile app participation, advanced data privacy frameworks will be implemented in compliance with GDPR and the UK Data Protection Act 2018. These frameworks will include anonymisation techniques, secure data storage, informed consent processes, and strict data minimisation principles to protect user privacy and maintain trust.

Further research will also focus on refining the accuracy of emission calculations through the integration of real-time grid carbon intensity data, enabling context-sensitive assessments based on regional electricity supply conditions. Moreover, the reward mechanisms proposed in the model—such as fare discounts and tradable carbon credits—require extensive pilot testing and stakeholder engagement to ensure financial viability and user acceptance. Parallel efforts will investigate partnerships with local businesses and government agencies to develop sustainable funding models for the reward system, ensuring the long-term success and scalability of the *Carbon Crest* platform.

Acknowledgements. The authors would like to thank the Greater Manchester Business Growth Hub and The CarbonCrest Network Ltd for funding support. We also extend our gratitude to CEO Bobin Joseph for his project management guidance and CTO Arun Matthew for his contributions to prototype development.

References

1. Actions, U.I.: City of Lahti launches a personal carbon trading scheme (2019). https://www.uia-initiative.eu/en/news/city-lahti-launches-personal-carbon-trading-scheme-citizens Accessed 23 June 2025
2. Agency, U.E.P.: Fast facts us transportation sector greenhouse gas emissions 1990–2017 (2019)
3. Ajzen, I.: The theory of planned behavior. Organ. Behav. Hum. Decis. Process. **50**(2), 179–211 (1991)
4. Amsterdam, B.: Ov chipkaart — the rechargeable transport card (2025). https://bonjouramsterdam.fr/en/ov-chipkaart/ Accessed 23 June 2025
5. Authority, G.M.C.: The bee network. https://tfgm.com/the-bee-network
6. Bamberg, S., Ajzen, I., Schmidt, P.: Choice of travel-mode in the theory of planned behavior: the roles of past behavior, habit, and reasoned action. Basic Appl. Soc. Psychol. **25**(3), 175–187 (2003)
7. Bashmakov, I.A., et al.: Climate change 2022: mitigation of climate change. Contribution of Working Group III to the Sixth Assessment Report of the Intergovernmental Panel on Climate Change Chapter 11 (2022)
8. Bennett, C., MacArthur, J., Cherry, C.R., Jones, L.R., et al.: Using e-bike purchase incentive programs to expand the market–North American trends and recommended practices (2022)
9. C40 Cities: Wuhan's carbon credit scheme bolsters massive bike-share program (2021). https://www.c40.org/case-studies/cities100-wuhan-carbon-credit-scheme-bolsters-massive-bike-share-program/ Accessed 23 June 2025
10. Calyx Global: What cookstove and household biodigester projects are CCP label eligible (2025). https://calyxglobal.com/research-hub/research/how-the-ICVCM-CCP-labels-are-raising-the-quality-of-cookstoves-and-household-biodigester-projects Accessed 23 June 2025
11. Council, B.: Climate action strategy 2021 (2021)
12. Deci, E.L., Ryan, R.M.: The "what" and "why" of goal pursuits: human needs and the self-determination of behavior. Psychol. Inq. **11**(4), 227–268 (2000)
13. Denver, C.: E-bike rebate program (2020). https://www.radpowerbikes.com/pages/denver-ebike-rebate
14. Finland, F.M.: Maas operator commits to replace one million cars by 2030 (2020). https://futuremobilityfinland.fi/the-worlds-first-maas-operator-commits-to-replace-one-million-cars-by-2030/ Accessed 23 June 2025
15. Gao, J., Hua, G., Huo, B., Randhawa, A., Li, Z.: Pilot policies for low-carbon cities in china: a study of the impact on green finance development and energy carbon efficiency. Climate Policy **25**(1), 137–152 (2025)

16. Georgakaki, A., et al.: Clean energy technology observatory: overall strategic analysis of clean energy technology in the European union: 2024 status report (2023)
17. for Greater Manchester, T.: Public transport and the environment. https://tfgm.com/environment/public-transport
18. Guo, D., Su, M., Zheng, X., Zou, S.: Do economic and reputation incentives matter in the carbon generalized system of preferences? empirical evidence from china's new tier-one cities. J. Environ. Manage. **382**, 125321 (2025)
19. Hu, X., Wang, S., Zhou, R., Gao, L., Zhu, Z.: Determinants of consumers' intentions to switch to electric vehicles: a perspective of the push-pull-mooring framework. J. Environ. Planning Manage. **67**(14), 3718–3743 (2024)
20. Joppien, M.: Improving system adoption of the ov-chipkaart (2024). https://filelist.tudelft.nl/IO/Onderzoek/Delft_Design_Labs/OV-chipkaart_Graduation_Lab/OVCP-TUD-System-Adoption-Joppien.pdf Accessed 23 June 2025
21. Klöckner, C.A.: A comprehensive model of the psychology of environmental behaviour–a meta-analysis. Glob. Environ. Psychol. **23**, 128–139 (2013)
22. of Lahti, C.: Personal carbon trading scheme made Lahti-people question their mobility choices (2021). https://www.lahti.fi/en/news/personal-carbon-trading-scheme-made-lahti-people-question-their-mobility-choices-and-reduce-their-emissions%E2%80%AF/ Accessed 23 June 2025
23. Li, C., Yu, Y., Yao, A.C.C., Zhang, D., Zhang, X.: An authenticated and secure accounting system for international emissions trading. Clim. Policy **22**(9–10), 1333–1342 (2022)
24. Lin, X., Yin, Y., He, F.: Credit-based mobility management considering travelers' budgeting behaviors under uncertainty. Transp. Sci. **55**(2), 297–314 (2021)
25. Liu, B., Ma, Z., Kong, H., Ma, X.: How incentives affect commuter willingness for public transport: analysis of travel mode shift across various cities. Travel Behaviour and Society **39**, 100966 (2025)
26. Lu, Y.J.: Predicting exercise behaviors and intentions of Taiwanese urban high school students using the theory of planned behavior. J. Pediatr. Nurs. **62**, e39–e44 (2022)
27. Ma, L., Graham, D.J., Stettler, M.E.: Has the ultra low emission zone in London improved air quality? Environ. Res. Lett. **16**(12), 124001 (2021)
28. Marshall, S., Banister, D.: Land use and transport: European research towards integrated policies. Emerald Group Publishing Limited (2007)
29. Mueller, W., Carson, F.S., Copsey, H., Loh, M.: Travel behaviour and Edinburgh's low emission zone: a cross-sectional survey. NIHR Open Res. **5**, 33 (2025)
30. NetZeroCities: network of ambitious cities on climate neutrality grows to 184 on EU cities mission peer learning programme (2025). https://netzerocities.eu/2025/01/22/network-of-ambitious-cities-on-climate-neutrality-grows-to-184-on-eu-cities-mission//-peer-learning-programme/ Accessed 16 May 2025
31. NS: Ns annual report 2024 — seamless travel (2024). https://www.nsannualreport.nl/annual-report-2024/our-activities-and-achievements-in-the-netherlands/seamless-travel Accessed 23 June 2025
32. Pan, M., Ryan, A.: Promoting sustainable transportation modes: a systematic review of behavior-change strategies. Transp. Res. Rec. **2679**(2), 1993–2012 (2025)
33. Railways), N.D.: Co2-rapportageplicht (co2 reporting requirement) (2024). https://www.ns.nl/en/business/inspiration/co2-reporting-requirement Accessed 23 June 2025
34. Ranalder, L., Hidalgo, L.G., Jones-Langley, J., Vener, J., Tollin, N.: Local action for global goals: an opportunity for enhancing nationally determined contributions (2024)

35. SEI, F.V., Gugu, S., Rendle, N.: The netzerocities economic model: an overview of netzeroplanner
36. UK Government: UK greenhouse gas emissions statistics (2023). https://www.gov.uk/government/collections/uk-greenhouse-gas-emissions-statistics Accessed 16 May 2025
37. Uusitalo, V., et al.: Using personal carbon trading to reduce mobility emissions: a pilot in the Finnish city of Lahti. Transp. Policy **126**, 177–187 (2022)
38. Vinnova: Double impact — reduced emissions and increased accessibility in the sports movement (2022). https://www.vinnova.se/en/p/double-impact---reduced-emissions-and-increased-accessibility-in-the-sports-movement/ 23 June Accessed 2025
39. Vinnova: sustainable mobility (2025). https://www.vinnova.se/en/m/sustainable-mobility/ Accessed 23 June 2025
40. Wikipedia contributors: ant forest (2023). https://en.wikipedia.org/wiki/Ant_Forest Accessed 23 June 2025
41. Xi, H.: Strategizing sustainability and profitability in electric mobility-as-a-service (e-MaaS) ecosystems with carbon incentives: A multi-leader multi-follower game. Transp. Res. Part C: Emerg. Technol. **166**, 104758 (2024)
42. Xu, X., Zuo, W.: Does bike-sharing reduce traffic congestion? evidence from three mega-cities in china. PLoS ONE **19**(8), e0306317 (2024)
43. Yang, Z., Kong, X., Sun, J., Zhang, Y.: Switching to green lifestyles: behavior change of ant forest users. Int. J. Environ. Res. Public Health **15**(9), 1819 (2018)
44. Yu, X., Shi, J., Wan, K., Chang, T.: Carbon trading market policies and corporate environmental performance in china. J. Clean. Prod. **371**, 133683 (2022)

Short Application Papers

A Transformer-Based Framework for Thematic Analysis of University Reading Lists

Rawan Bin Shiha[1,2]($\boxtimes$) (iD), Eric Atwell[1] (iD), and Noorhan Abbas[1] (iD)

[1] School of Computing, University of Leeds, Leeds, UK
`rmbinshiha@imamu.edu.sa`
[2] Imam Mohammad Ibn Saud Islamic University, Riyadh, Saudi Arabia

Abstract. This paper presents a transformer-based framework for Natural Language Processing (NLP) analysis of university reading lists, addressing representational diversity in higher education curricula. We apply sentence embeddings, clustering, topic modelling, and Shannon entropy to examine thematic patterns within academic reading lists, a novel application domain for modern NLP methods. Our approach identifies latent topic structures and quantifies thematic diversity across institutional contexts. Testing on 40 semantically aligned readings from Islamic Studies programmes at UK and Middle Eastern universities, the framework reveals significant differences in curricular emphasis despite surface-level similarity. The methodology demonstrates how transformer-based analysis can detect subtle epistemological patterns that traditional curriculum auditing methods cannot capture. This NLP approach offers scalable tools for curriculum evaluation, supporting evidence-based discussions around academic inclusivity and knowledge representation in higher education.

Keywords: Transformer Models · Topic Modelling · Curriculum Analysis · Reading Lists · Educational NLP · Text Mining

1 Introduction

University reading lists shape students' academic experiences and reflect institutional values. As movements for inclusive curricula grow, deeper content analysis is needed to understand epistemic structures beyond surface diversity [3, 12]. This paper presents a transformer-based NLP framework for analysing thematic composition of university reading lists. While previous studies have addressed representational disparities [10], systematic application of modern NLP methods remains underexplored. We apply this to Islamic Studies programmes at the University of Leeds (UK) and Imam Mohammad Ibn Saud Islamic University (Saudi Arabia), employing sentence embeddings, density-based clustering and Shannon entropy [13] to quantify thematic diversity and examine correlations between author demographics and content focus. The framework demonstrates how automated analysis can detect subtle curricular differences that surface-level examination might miss, offering a scalable approach for curriculum auditing.

M. Bramer and F. Stahl (Eds.): SGAI-AI 2025, LNAI 16302, pp. 405–410, 2026.
https://doi.org/10.1007/978-3-032-11442-6_28

2 Methodology

2.1 Dataset Overview

To facilitate a comparative analysis of curricular content, two reading list datasets were compiled from distinct institutional contexts: AIMESRL (Arabic, Islamic, and Middle Eastern Studies Reading List) from the University of Leeds, comprising 212 individual readings, and QSIERL (Qur'an Sciences and Islamic Education Reading List) from Imam Mohammad Ibn Saud Islamic University, comprising 73 readings. Reading list data were manually extracted from module handbooks, institutional repositories, and departmental websites. Each reading was standardised with metadata such as author name, title, and publication details. Only readings with a single listed author were retained to ensure clean demographic attribution. Information on author gender and ethnicity was not available in the original data and was manually annotated using established demographic coding protocols. A detailed account of this demographic annotation methodology is provided in previous work by the authors [4]. Although QSIERL reflects an Arabic-speaking institution, all readings analysed in this study were available in English, ensuring semantic comparability with the AIMESRL dataset for computational analysis.

2.2 Semantic Matching and Topic Subset Selection

To enable meaningful thematic comparison between the two reading list datasets, a topic-matched subset was constructed by pairing readings from each institution on similar subject matter, allowing for content-level comparison beyond bibliographic overlap. Each reading title was encoded using the all-MiniLM-L6-v2 sentence embedding model [11, 14], and cosine similarity was calculated across all possible pairs in the AIMESRL and QSIERL datasets to generate a ranked list of semantically close pairs. Top pairs were manually reviewed by the author and an independent Islamic Studies academic to ensure conceptual alignment in themes such as Qur'anic exegesis, legal theory, and Islamic ethics. The final subset comprised 40 readings 20 from each dataset spanning these shared areas and provided a robust basis for downstream analysis while maintaining linguistic consistency. The use of 40 readings was intentional for this proof-of-concept study, prioritising methodological demonstration over statistical generalisability. While this sample size limits robust institutional comparison, it provides sufficient data to demonstrate how transformer-based methods can reveal thematic and representational structures within academic curricula.

2.3 Text Summarisation

To facilitate consistent thematic analysis, each of the 40 matched readings was represented by a short summary describing its core focus. Some readings had abstracts, but many classical or regional texts lacked accessible summaries. To address this, a hybrid approach was employed. Where available, existing abstracts were extracted directly from bibliographic sources such as Google Books or institutional repositories. For texts lacking reliable summaries, OpenAI's GPT-4.o was prompted to generate a brief abstract using the instruction: *'Generate a concise academic-style summary (2–3 sentences) of this reading based on its title and known academic context. If classical, emphasise historical and interpretive focus.'* To assess summary quality, we evaluated semantic similarity between titles and summaries (mean = 0.743), key term preservation (86.6% of title terms retained), and structural consistency (average 142.5 words with minimal cross-institutional variation). These metrics confirmed that the generated summaries maintained appropriate academic quality and strong thematic alignment.

2.4 Topic Modelling

The created summaries formed the input corpus for thematic analysis using BERTopic [7], a topic modelling framework that integrates transformer-based sentence embeddings with density-based clustering and class-based TF-IDF. This approach is particularly effective for short documents, where traditional models such as Latent Dirichlet Allocation (LDA) [5] often produce less coherent or interpretable topics. The process involved four key steps (see Table 1).

Table 1. Overview of Topic Modelling Pipeline Stages.

Stage	Description	Parameters/Details
Embedding	Each summary was encoded into a 384-dimensional vector using the all-MiniLM-L6-v2 model [11, 14]	• 384-dimensional vectors • all-MiniLM-L6-v2 transformer model
Dimensionality Reduction	Vectors were projected into lower-dimensional space using Uniform Manifold Approximation and Projection (UMAP) [9]	• n_neighbors = 15 • min_dist = 0.1 • metric = 'cosine' • Default parameters maintained
Clustering	Hierarchical Density-Based Spatial Clustering of Applications with Noise (HDBSCAN) [6] was used to identify coherent topic clusters	• min_cluster_size = 10 • min_samples = None (auto-determined) • Default configuration
Topic Labelling	Keywords extracted using class-based Term Frequency Inverse Document Frequency (c-TF-IDF) [8]	• n-gram range (1,1) • Highlights topic-specific terms • Reduces generic word influence

To assess the reliability of the topic modelling approach, we implemented validation measures addressing clustering stability and quality. Bootstrap stability analysis (50 iterations, 80% sampling) yielded an Adjusted Rand Index of 0.485, indicating moderate clustering stability appropriate for exploratory analysis of a small, specialised corpus. Topic coherence analysis demonstrated exceptionally high scores (average: 0.989), confirming that topic-defining words genuinely co-occur within documents. Parameter sensitivity testing across different min_cluster_size values (3, 5, 8, 10, 15) consistently identified two primary topics, demonstrating that the thematic structure was robust rather than parameter-dependent. The silhouette score of 0.137, whilst below conventional thresholds, reflects the nuanced nature of thematic distinctions within Islamic Studies curricula rather than methodological limitations.

2.5 Thematic Diversity and Entropy Analysis

Shannon entropy [13] was used to quantify thematic diversity within each institution's reading list. Entropy reflects how evenly readings are distributed across topic clusters, with higher values indicating greater diversity and lower values suggesting concentration on fewer themes. Given proportions p_i for topic i entropy H is calculated as:

$$H = -\sum_{i=1}^{n} p_i \log_2 p_i$$

where n is the number of topics identified through BERTopic clustering. This enables comparison of thematic breadth between institutions and correlation analysis with author demographic patterns.

3 Findings and Discussion

3.1 Topic Distribution and Thematic Coverage

Topic modelling using BERTopic identified two distinct clusters across the 40 semantically aligned readings: Topic 0, Qur'anic Tafsīr and Interpretive Methodologies (24 readings, focused on classical exegesis and Qur'anic sciences), and Topic 1, Early Islamic History and Reformist Discourse (16 readings, covering history, ethics, and reform). Despite the surface-level similarity of reading list titles across institutions, the topic distribution revealed substantial divergence in actual content. At Imam Mohammad Ibn Saud University, readings were heavily concentrated in Topic 0, reflecting a strong focus on classical tafsīr and Qur'anic sciences. The University of Leeds showed more even distribution with significant representation in Topic 1, covering reformist thought, gender ethics, historiography, and critical approaches to Islamic studies. This demonstrates how transformer-based semantic analysis can uncover latent curricular differences that traditional bibliographic examination cannot capture. Unlike conventional curriculum auditing that relies on title analysis or manual categorisation, the NLP approach reveals pedagogically significant distinctions: whilst Imam's curriculum privileges traditional interpretive methodologies, Leeds offers broader thematic exposure aligned with interdisciplinary approaches.

3.2 Entropy Scores

Shannon entropy was applied to quantify thematic diversity across topic distributions. The entropy scores were 0.791 for AIMESRL and 0.336 for QSIERL. To contextualize these values, the maximum possible entropy for two topics is $\log_2(2) = 1.0$, meaning AIMESRL achieved 79% of maximum diversity while QSIERL achieved 34%. This substantial difference (0.455) indicates distinct pedagogical orientations: Leeds demonstrates broader thematic coverage spanning exegesis, historiography, and reformist thought, while Imam shows concentrated focus on classical tafsīr and Qur'anic sciences. These patterns suggest Leeds adopts a more interdisciplinary approach whilst Imam emphasises traditional scholarly frameworks. Though the small sample size limits statistical significance, entropy provides a scalable quantitative method for curriculum auditing that could complement traditional diversity metrics with larger datasets.

3.3 Topic Distribution by Authors

Author demographic analysis reveals distinct patterns across thematic clusters. Topic 0 (Qur'anic sciences and classical tafsīr) is predominantly authored by Middle Eastern men, reflecting historical scholarly structures in Islamic Studies where male scholars have traditionally held authoritative roles in religious knowledge transmission [1, 2]. Topic 1 (historiography, ethics, and reformist discourse) features greater demographic diversity, including female scholars and North American/European academics. These patterns reflect institutional differences in scholarly sourcing, though this does not imply causal relationships between author identity and content. As literature notes, representation alone does not determine epistemic diversity; scholars from any background may engage critically or traditionally depending on intellectual commitments [3, 10]. Rather, the clustering patterns offer insight into how institutional priorities and disciplinary traditions shape both demographic and thematic dimensions of curricular content (see Fig. 1).

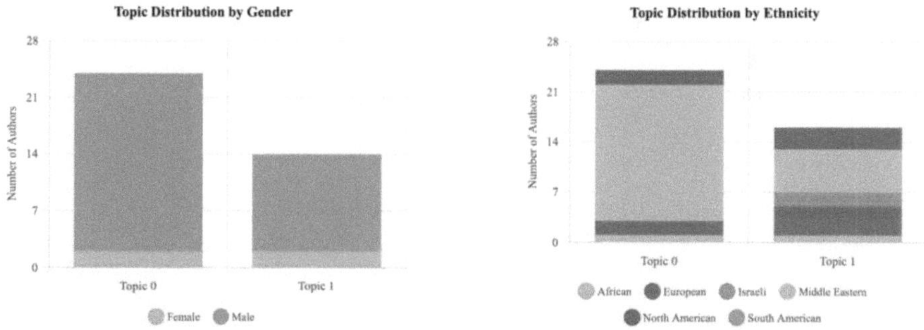

Fig. 1. Author demographics across topic clusters: gender and ethnicity representation.

4   Conclusion

This study demonstrates transformer-based NLP methods for curriculum analysis, revealing thematic patterns traditional auditing cannot capture. Applied to Islamic Studies programmes, the framework detected significant pedagogical differences: Leeds showed greater thematic diversity while Imam focused on classical exegesis. The findings illustrate how computational analysis can complement demographic diversity metrics. Future research should expand sample sizes to confirm scalability across disciplines.

References

1. Ahmed, L.: Women and gender in Islam: historical roots of a modern debate. Yale University Press (2021)
2. Alwani, Z.: Muslim women as religious scholars: a historical survey. In: B. Kugle (ed.). Muslima theology: The voices of Muslim women theologians, pp. 45–58 (2013)
3. Bhambra, G.K., Gebrial, D., Nişancıoğlu, K.: Decolonising the university. Pluto Press (2018)
4. Bin Shiha, R., Atwell, E., & Abbas, N.: Decolonising the reading lists of Arabic, Islamic and middle eastern studies. IJASAT. **11**(2) (2023)
5. Blei, D.M., Ng, A.Y., Jordan, M.I.: Latent dirichlet allocation. J. Mach. Learn. Res. **3**, 993–1022 (2003)
6. Campello, R.J., Moulavi, D., Sander, J.: Density-based clustering based on hierarchical density estimates. In: Pacific-Asia Conference on Knowledge Discovery and Data Mining, pp. 160–172. Springer (2013)
7. Grootendorst, M.: BERTopic: Neural topic modeling with a class-based TF-IDF procedure. arXiv preprint (2022). arXiv:2203.05794
8. Jones, K.S.: A statistical interpretation of term specificity and its application in retrieval. J. Doc. **28**(1), 11–21 (1972)
9. McInnes, L., Healy, J., Melville, J.: UMAP: Uniform manifold approximation and projection for dimension reduction. arXiv preprint (2018). arXiv:1802.03426
10. Phull, K., Ciflikli, G., Meibauer, G.: Gender and bias in the international relations curriculum: Insights from reading lists. Eur. J. Int. Rel. **25**(2), 383–407 (2019)
11. Reimers, N., Gurevych, I.: Sentence-BERT: sentence embeddings using siamese BERT-networks. arXiv preprint (2019). arXiv:1908.10084
12. Schucan Bird, K., Pitman, L.: How diverse is your reading list? Exploring issues of representation and decolonisation in the UK. High. Educ. **79**(5), 903–920 (2020)
13. Shannon, C.E.: A mathematical theory of communication. The Bell System Technical Journal **27**(3), 379–423 (1948)
14. Wang, W., Wei, F., Dong, L., Bao, H., Yang, N., Zhou, M.: MiniLM: Deep self-attention distillation for task-agnostic compression of pre-trained transformers. Adv. Neural. Inf. Process. Syst. **33**, 5776–5788 (2020)

Early Stroke Prediction Using a Convolutional Neural Network on Temporal Electronic Health Records

Chia- Hui Chien[1,3] (iD), Yung-Chun Chang[2(✉)] (iD), Yu- Chuan Li[3(✉)] (iD), and Xiaohong Gao[1] (iD)

[1] Department of Computer Science, Middlesex University, London, UK
`{s.chien,x.gao}@mdx.ac.uk`
[2] Graduate Institute of Data Science, Taipei Medical University, Taipei, Taiwan
`changyc@tmu.edu.tw`
[3] Graduate Institute of Biomedical Informatics, Taipei Medical University, Taipei, Taiwan

Abstract. This retrospective cohort study outlines a population-level approach to stroke prevention using real-world data and temporal AI. Stroke remains a global health challenge. Early identification of high-risk individuals can enable effective prevention. We developed a deep learning model to predict first-time stroke occurrence using temporal electronic health records (EHR) from Taiwan's NHIRD (2003–2013). The model was trained on 16,805 incident stroke cases and 169,902 controls, utilizing structured binary matrices of ICD-9 and ATC codes across 3–24 months. A convolutional neural network (CNN) captured temporal patterns in diagnoses and prescriptions. Our model achieved an AUROC of 0.88 on the testing set using a 2-year observation window. To assess the impact of key predictors, we conducted a separate feature ablation analysis on the training data, which showed that removing the top-ranked medication feature (C08CA, a class of dihydropyridines) reduced the training AUROC from 0.91 to 0.85. These findings validate CNN's ability to detect risk patterns in routine claims data. The model requires no additional tests and offers scalable risk stratification potential.

Keywords: Stroke prediction · Convolutional neural network · Electronic health records · Temporal data · Risk stratification

1 Introduction

Stroke is a major global health burden and the third leading cause of death in Taiwan [1, 2]. It imposes long-term disability, economic loss, and increasing challenges with aging populations [3]. Traditional risk assessments based on fixed factors such as hypertension, diabetes, and smoking lack precision in capturing complex interactions and temporal trends [4, 5]. With the expansion of electronic health records (EHRs), deep learning presents new opportunities to model these evolving risk patterns. Convolutional neural networks (CNNs), originally used for image recognition, are now effectively applied to time-sequenced clinical data [6, 7]. Taiwan's National Health Insurance Research

M. Bramer and F. Stahl (Eds.): SGAI-AI 2025, LNAI 16302, pp. 411–417, 2026.
https://doi.org/10.1007/978-3-032-11442-6_29

Database (NHIRD), covering over 99% of the population, offers an ideal resource for population-based predictive modeling [8]. While earlier studies have focused on recurrent stroke or predefined risk variables [9], few have explored data-driven temporal modeling for first-time stroke risk prediction. This study applies CNNs to model temporal diagnosis and medication patterns preceding first-ever stroke events, aiming to uncover significant predictors and demonstrate the model's utility for scalable, non-invasive early detection.

2 Material and Methods

We conducted a retrospective cohort study using NHIRD, specifically the LHID2005, which contains healthcare records for one million individuals from 1999 to 2013. Stroke cases were defined based on ICD-9-CM codes 430.xx–438.xx and validated using inpatient or catastrophic illness registry. The International Classification of Diseases, 9th Revision, Clinical Modification (ICD-9-CM) is a widely adopted diagnostic coding system used in healthcare databases. Medication exposure was captured using the Anatomical Therapeutic Chemical (ATC) Classification System, which categorizes drugs based on the organ or system they target and their therapeutic and chemical properties. Individuals aged 20–99 years with no prior stroke history during a four-year washout period were included. For each stroke case, ten age- and sex-matched controls were selected (10:1 matching). We extracted clinical data from the 3- to 24-month window preceding each patient's index date. Each patient's medical history was transformed into a temporal sequence in the form of a weekly binary matrix, where each row represented a week and each column indicated the presence (1) or absence (0) of a specific ICD-9 diagnosis or ATC drug code. These matrices were input into the CNN model to capture longitudinal patterns. To reduce noise and dimensionality, we retained only codes observed in at least 100 patients, yielding 1,137 features. As shown in

Figure 1, we implemented a CNN was implemented in Python using TensorFlow 2.10 and Keras. The model architecture consisted of three convolutional layers, max pooling, dropout (rate = 0.25), batch normalization, and fully connected layers. The network was trained using the Adam optimizer (learning rate − 0.01) with binary cross-entropy loss. CNN was selected for its ability to efficiently capture temporal patterns within structured, high-dimensional EHR data. Correlation analysis was used to address potential multicollinearity among input features. This approach enables scalable stroke risk prediction for integration into clinical decision support and population-level screening.

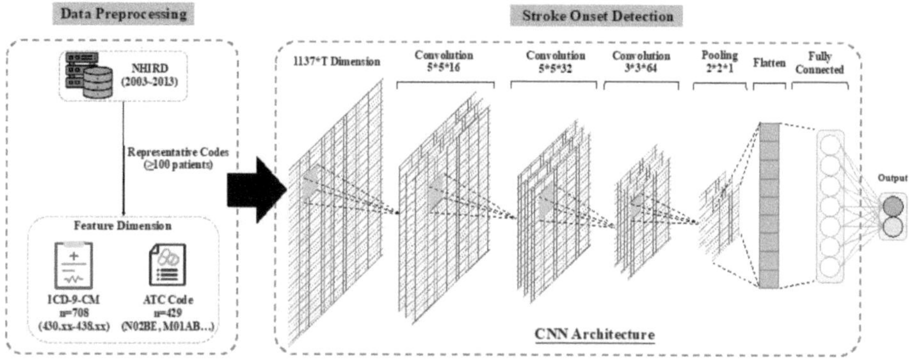

Fig. 1. Stroke prediction framework

3 Experiments

3.1 Settings

For the one-year stroke prediction model, the final dataset consisted of 16,805 stroke cases matched with 169,902 control subjects. Demographic analyses revealed notable distinctions between stroke and control cohorts, as presented in Table 1. We randomly divided the dataset into 90% training and 10% testing subsets. The CNN model was trained on the training data and evaluated on the testing set using AUROC, accuracy, sensitivity, specificity, and F_1-score. We tested various case-control ratios (1:10 and 1:4) and temporal windows (3 months, 6 months, 1 year, and 2 years) to ensure robustness. Feature importance was assessed using chi-square tests, recursive feature elimination (RFECV), and single-feature removal analysis. Correlation analyses were also conducted to examine multicollinearity. For the one-year model, 16,805 stroke cases and 169,902 controls were included. Stroke patients were older (mean age 63.83) and more likely male (57%) than controls (mean age 44.68, 47% male), consistent with known stroke risk patterns. The two-year model included 17,343 stroke cases and 176,104 controls, showing similar demographic trends.

Table 1. Demographic characteristics of the study population

Characteristics	Stroke Group		Control Group	
	Training	Testing	Training	Testing
1-year cohort	16,805		169,902	
Sex (n %)	11,763 (100%)	5,042 (100%)	118,932 (100%)	50,970 (100%)
Male	6,705 (57%)	2,874 (57%)	55,898 (47%)	23,956 (47%)
Female	5,058 (43%)	2,168 (43%)	63,034 (53%)	27,014 (53%)
Age, mean	63.83	65.28	44.68	45.89
2-year cohort	17,343		176,104	

(continued)

Table 1. (*continued*)

Characteristics	Stroke Group		Control Group	
	Training	Testing	Training	Testing
Sex (n %)	12,140 (100%)	5,203 (100%)	123,272 (100%)	52,832 (100%)
Male	6,798 (56%)	2,653 (51%)	59,171 (48%)	25,359 (48%)
Female	5,342 (44%)	2,549 (49%)	64,101 (52%)	27,473 (52%)
Age, mean	64.17	65.28	44.72	44.71

3.2 Model Performance and Clinically Relevant Feature Analysis

The CNN demonstrated strong predictive ability across all time windows. As detailed in Table 2, the 2-year model with a 1:10 ratio performed best, with an AUROC of 0.91 (training) and 0.88 (testing), a specificity of 0.93, a sensitivity of 0.75, and a DOR of 42.17. Predictive performance increased with longer observation periods (2 y > 1 y > 6 m > 3 m). Notably, the 3-month model had lower sensitivity (0.61), highlighting the importance of including at least 6–12 months of patient history for reliable stroke prediction. Statistical testing confirmed significant AUROC differences across time windows ($p < 0.01$), verifying that performance improvements with longer data are not due to chance. Table 3 summarizes results of chi-square tests that indicate antihypertensive agents (C08CA, C09AA), diabetes medications (A10BB, A10BA), and antiplatelet drugs (B01AC) consistently ranked among the most important predictive features, along with diagnoses such as diabetes (dx_250), essential hypertension (dx_401), and hypertensive heart disease (dx_402). Notably, removing C08CA from the model reduced the AUROC from 0.91 to 0.85, highlighting its substantial predictive value. Excluding A02AF or dx_402 similarly resulted in a 0.05 decline in AUROC, further underscoring their contribution to model performance.

Table 2. System performance with different observation periods and case-control ratios

Observation period	Case control ratio	AUROC (Train/Test)	Accuracy (Train/Test)	Sensitivity	Specificity	DOR[*]
2 years	1:10	**0.91/0.88**	**0.937/0.927**	**0.75**	0.93	**42.17**
	1:4	0.91/0.88	0.893/0.887	0.73	0.89	22.54
1 year	1:10	0.89/0.86	0.913/0.923	0.63	0.94	26.16
	1:4	0.87/0.85	0.864/0.855	0.71	0.88	17.05
6 months	1:10	0.86/0.83	0.927/0.922	0.74	0.93	35.69
	1:4	0.85/0.83	0.861/0.864	0.73	0.86	16.80
3 months	1:10	0.83/0.79	0.926/0.916	0.61	0.93	20.00
	1:4	0.82/0.79	0.851/0.840	0.68	0.86	12.95

[*] DOR: Diagnostic Odds Ratio

Table 3. Top 10 features associated with stroke occurrence

Rank	Feature	Description	Chi-square value	Clinical type
1	rx_A02AF	Antacids with antiflatulents	71433.12	Medication
2	dx_250	Diabetes mellitus	68135.29	Disease
3	rx_B01AC	Platelet aggregation inhibitors excl. Heparin	62913.84	Medication
4	rx_A10BB	Sulfonylureas	61256.51	Medication
5	rx_C08CA	Dihydropyridine derivatives	54633.73	Medication
6	dx_401	Essential hypertension	49822.64	Disease
7	rx_C09AA	ACE inhibitors	46058.52	Medication
8	rx_C01DA	Organic nitrates	39522.29	Medication
9	rx_A10BA	Biguanides	32382.34	Medication
10	dx_402	Hypertensive heart disease	31746.74	Disease

The diagnostic odds ratio (DOR) values summarized in Table 4 quantify the independent predictive contribution of individual features for stroke risk assessment. Among these, the prescription of ACE inhibitors (rx_C09AA) exhibited the highest DOR (8.44), underscoring its strong standalone predictive utility. Similarly, the use of dihydropyridines (rx_C08CA) demonstrated substantial predictive value (DOR 5.13). Conversely, a diagnosis of diabetes mellitus (dx_250) was associated with a notably low DOR (0.37), indicating limited discriminative power when considered in isolation. Further correlation analysis revealed clinically consistent associations, such as the strong correlation between diabetes diagnosis (dx_250) and antidiabetic medications (A10BB/A10BA, r = 0.65), as well as between neurological diagnoses (dx_600) and genitourinary medications (rx_G04CA, r = 0.62), thereby reinforcing the internal coherence of the model. Collectively, these results highlight the CNN's capacity to not only recover well-established clinical associations from longitudinal EHR data but also to suggest potential novel relationships warranting further clinical investigation.

Table 4. Impact of removing individual features on model performance (2-year model, 1:10 ratio).

Removed feature	Feature description	AUROC (train)	Change in AUROC	Odds ratio
None (baseline)	-	0.91	-	42.17
rx_C08CA	Dihydropyridine derivatives	0.85	−0.06	5.13
rx_A02AF	Antacids with antiflatulents	0.86	−0.05	5.64
dx_402	Hypertensive heart disease	0.86	−0.05	5.21

(*continued*)

Table 4. (*continued*)

Removed feature	Feature description	AUROC (train)	Change in AUROC	Odds ratio
dx_401	Essential hypertension	0.88	−0.03	4.54
dx_585	Chronic kidney disease	0.88	−0.03	3.75
dx_250	Diabetes mellitus	0.89	−0.02	0.37
rx_B01AC	Platelet aggregation inhibitors	0.89	−0.02	5.46
rx_C09AA	ACE inhibitors	0.89	−0.02	8.44
rx_A10BB	Sulfonylureas	0.90	−0.01	5.55
dx_414	Ischemic heart disease	0.90	−0.01	5.12

4 Discussion

Our CNN-based model effectively captured the temporal progression of stroke risk, as evidenced by the consistent improvement in predictive accuracy with longer observation windows. Feature analysis highlighted dihydropyridine derivatives (C08CA) as the most influential predictor, underscoring their clinical relevance in identifying treatment-resistant hypertensive patients at elevated risk. Interestingly, antacids with antiflatulents (A02AF) also ranked highly, suggesting potential indirect associations through comorbidities or medication side effects. Correlation analysis confirmed clinically consistent patterns, such as strong associations between diabetes diagnoses and corresponding treatments, while the identification of influential yet low-correlation features demonstrated the model's capacity to capture independent, additive risk signals. These findings reinforce a multifactorial understanding of stroke development. Compared to prior EHR-based stroke prediction studies, our approach achieved superior performance (AUROC 0.91 vs. 0.80 in Lee et al. [10]) by leveraging richer temporal dynamics and a fully data-driven architecture. In contrast to traditional rule-based methods [11], our model effectively detects subtle and evolving risk patterns without relying on laboratory or imaging data, thereby enhancing scalability for population-level screening. Moreover, its seamless integration into existing EHR systems supports dynamic, real-time risk monitoring and enables timely clinical decision-making, offering a practical pathway for broader implementation in diverse healthcare settings.

Despite these promising findings, several limitations remain. The use of Taiwanese claims data may limit generalizability, and key lifestyle factors (e.g., smoking, physical activity) were not available. Additionally, CNN interpretability remains a challenge, and external validation—particularly against established tools like the Framingham Stroke Risk Score—is needed. Future work should focus on validating the model in diverse populations, integrating richer clinical data, and enhancing interpretability to support real-world adoption.

5   Conclusions

This study demonstrates the effectiveness of CNNs in predicting first-time stroke from temporal EHRs. Our model achieved strong predictive performance using only routine administrative data, without the need for laboratory tests or imaging, underscoring its practicality for large-scale deployment. Key predictors—particularly antihypertensive and diabetes medications such as dihydropyridines—highlight the importance of treatment patterns in stroke risk stratification. By leveraging longitudinal data, the model captures dynamic risk trajectories that extend beyond conventional static assessments. This cost-effective and scalable framework offers significant promise for population-wide screening and early intervention. Moving forward, future work should prioritize external validation across diverse populations, integration of richer clinical and behavioral data, and advancement of model interpretability to facilitate adoption in real-world clinical settings.

Acknowledgment. This research is partially financially funded by the British Council Under Early Career Fellowship Programme (2024–2025). Their support is gratefully acknowledged.

References

1. Hsieh, F.-I., Chiou, H.-Y.: Stroke: morbidity, risk factors, and care in Taiwan. J Stroke. **16**(2), 59 (2014)
2. Pu, L., et al.: Projected global trends in ischemic stroke incidence, deaths and disability-adjusted life years from 2020 to 2030. Stroke. **54**(5), 1330–1339 (2023)
3. Feigin, V.L., et al.: World stroke organization: global stroke fact sheet 2025. International Journal of Stroke, p. 17474930241308142 (2025)
4. Mayerhofer, E., et al.: Genetic and nongenetic components of stroke family history: a population study of adopted and nonadopted individuals. J. Am. Heart Assoc. **12**(20), e031566 (2023)
5. Mohan, A., et al.: Risk factor profile of stroke patients with special focus on determinants of severity. JCH. **4**(1), 57–71 (2016)
6. Ashrafuzzaman, M., Saha, S., Nur, K.: Prediction of stroke disease using deep CNN based approach. JAIT. **13**(6) (2022)
7. Lin, J., Luo, S.: Deep learning for the dynamic prediction of multivariate longitudinal and survival data. Stat. Med. **41**(15), 2894–2907 (2022)
8. Hsieh, C.-Y., et al.: Taiwan's national health insurance research database: past and future. Clinical epidemiology, p. 349–358 (2019)
9. Abedi, V., et al.: Prediction of long-term stroke recurrence using machine learning models. J. Clin. Med. **10**(6), 1286 (2021)
10. Lee, J.-W., et al.: The development and implementation of stroke risk prediction model in national health insurance service's personal health record. Comput. Methods Programs Biomed. **153**, 253–257 (2018)
11. D'Agostino, R.B., Wolf, P.A., Belanger, A.J., Kannel, W.B.: Stroke risk profile: adjustment for antihypertensive medication. The Framingham study. Stroke **25**(1), 40–43 (1994)

Comparative Analysis of ChatGPT Memory and an External Conversational Memory Architecture

Luca Pelissero-Witoslawski[✉], Stéphane Aubry, and Athénaïs Oslati

Aphelior, Lille, France
`{luca.pelissero-witoslawski,stephane.aubry,athenais.oslati}@ontbo.com`

Abstract. OntboAPI introduces an external memory system designed to store user-specific profiles and conversational histories beyond the ephemeral context window of large language models (LLMs). This service supports real-time access and modification of persistent user data. In this paper, we outline an experimental setup that compares OntboAPI to ChatGPT's built-in memory across two key metrics: accuracy of factual recall and the quality of hyper-personalized responses. We detail the use of a synthetic benchmark and a blind human evaluation process. Results indicate that an external module affords measurable advantages over native memory when sustained personalization is required.

Keywords: Conversational memory · Hyper-personalization · Large language models

1 Introduction

Rapid advances in generative AI have produced dialogue systems that can sustain long, multi-turn conversations with ease. Consequently, users now expect *hyper-personalized* exchanges—interactions that adapt in real time to their unique background, evolving context, and declared preferences [1]. Delivering on this expectation depends on reliable methods for capturing, storing, and later reinjecting information that naturally arises during conversation.

Major large-language-model (LLM) providers have begun addressing this need. ChatGPT-4o, for example, enhances its context window with automatically generated summaries of previous sessions, giving the model a form of built-in memory [2]. Although convenient, this mechanism is essentially a black box for developers, remains constrained by token-window limits, and is subject to retention policies set by the service provider.

OntboAPI [3] was created to give developers fine-grained control over conversational memory. Its design pursues two main objectives: (i) durable storage of every utterance exchanged with an LLM-based agent and (ii) organization of those utterances into a layered, queryable user profile that can be accessed at inference time.

This work offers two primary contributions. First, it introduces an experimental framework to contrast external memory modules with native LLM memory. Second, it presents empirical evidence that quantifies how each strategy affects the factual recall and the richness of personalized responses.

2   ChatGPT Intrinsic Memory

ChatGPT exposes two proprietary memory components:

- **Saved memories**—explicit facts that users ask the assistant to retain;
- **Chat history recall**—information the system autonomously retrieves from earlier conversations whenever the memory feature is enabled.

Both components are stored server-side. End users can review or delete entries via the ChatGPT interface, yet no public API allows programmatic inspection or modification.

Three structural limitations have been identified:

- **Context-window bound**—only the most recent dialogue span is visible to the model; older details vanish once evicted unless they have been distilled into a saved-memory note, whose overall quota is capped [4].
- **Redundancy and overwrites**—community reports describe duplicate or overwritten notes [5], which may lead to contradictory replies over extended use.
- **Product scope**—intrinsic memory is confined to the ChatGPT application; it is neither surfaced in the OpenAI API nor inherited by custom GPT instances.

Due to these constraints, ChatGPT's intrinsic memory serves as an appropriate baseline for evaluating whether an external store can enhance long-horizon recall and personalisation. This is precisely the challenge Ontbo aims to address.

3   Synthetic Persona and Evaluation Protocol

3.1   Dataset Construction

We dynamically generate a single artificial user, *Alex*, through a corpus of fifty scripted dialogues between a human and an AI assistant. The driver script supplies only coarse-grained prompts, e.g. 'talk about weekend activities' or 'plan a career transition', and lets the LLM improvise the entire exchange; No predefined attribute lists or JSON seeds are injected into either memory system. Each conversation spans five to eight turns, and every utterance is streamed in parallel to:

- a **ChatGPT-4o** session with its built-in memory activated;
- the **OntboAPI** endpoint.

After this seeding phase, both systems have learned exclusively from the same fifty transcripts.

A downstream summarizer then reviews the logs and produces a one-page summary that captures Alex's inferred background, motivations, and goals (see Fig. 1). This document is provided *only* to the human assessors described in Sect. 3.3; it is never written back to either memory store, ensuring that all the knowledge retained originates strictly from the dialogs.

Name	Alex
Location	Japan (hypothesis)
Family	Parent of a 7-year-old
Work	Office Assistant
Work-Life Balance	Struggles
Nostalgia	Misses Japan
Financial Management	Managing family budget
Emotional Challenges	Homesickness
Career Aspirations	Wants to manage a financial consulting firm
Physical Activity	Jogging
Eating Habits	Increased processed foods
Social Preferences	Intimate gatherings
Cultural Adjustment	Reverse culture shock
Emotional Intelligence	Wants to improve
Technology Usage	Seeks productivity tools
Personal Growth	Interested in language lessons
Family Dynamics	Strong connection
Future Aspirations	Open to moving
Self-Care	Struggles with guilt
Social Isolation	Feels misunderstood
Values	Prioritizes family and personal growth

Fig. 1. Extract of the summary

3.2 Evaluation Phase

The evaluation phase probes how well each system retrieves and applies long-term user facts. We craft twenty novel prompts, each targeting a distinct facet of Alex's inferred persona: for example, favorite cuisine, Japanese study habits, or long-term financial plans.

For every prompt, we execute the following procedure:

– **Prompt delivery**—The prompt is submitted verbatim to (i) a standard ChatGPT session and (ii) a session where the agent queries OntboAPI during inference. The two runs are isolated to avoid any cross-session leakage.
– **Response capture**—The first complete answer from each system is logged; no manual regeneration is allowed, so the reply can draw only on stored memory.

This protocol yields twenty paired responses (see Fig. 2) whose sole variable is the memory strategy—ChatGPT's native store versus OntboAPI's external layer.

3.3   Human Evaluation

The quality of the answers was measured in a double-blind rating exercise with ten graduate-level volunteers who had no prior stake in the project. Before scoring, each judge received a one-page brief that concisely summarized Alex's inferred background, core values, and goals derived from the training dialogue. The prompts and paired responses were independently randomized so that the evaluators:

– could not tell which system produced a given answer; and
– never saw two replies to the same prompt in succession.

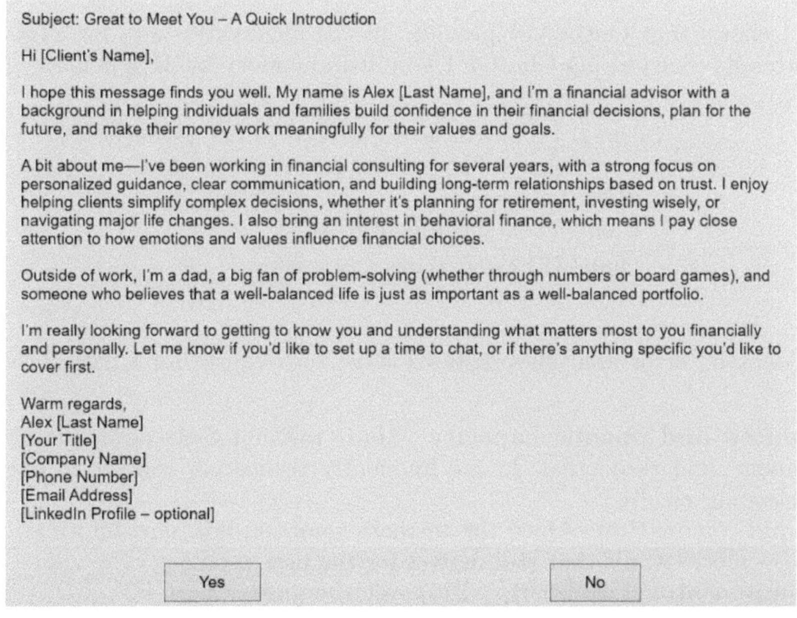

Fig. 2. Example Prompt Screen in the Experimental Application

For each response, judges determined whether the content matched the facts and preferences presented in Alex's brief (see Fig. 3). For each LLM, we averaged the ten ratings assigned to every answer and then computed an overall accuracy metric—the proportion of responses that met the alignment criteria. Section 4 reports these percentages and compares the two systems. All study materials, including prompts, briefs and transcripts, are publicly available in our y repository to enable independent replication [6].

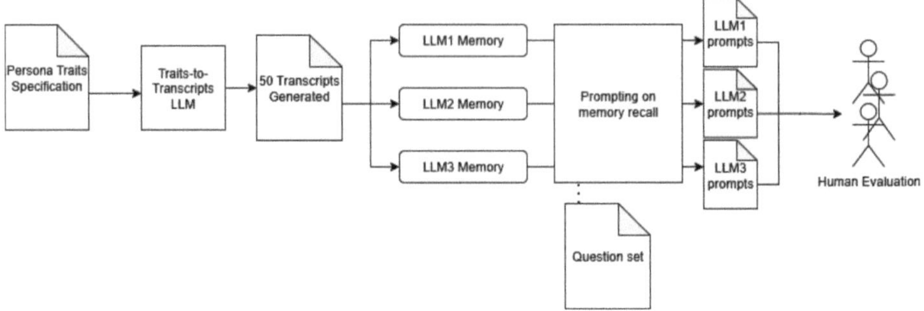

Fig. 3. Experimental Workflow Diagram

4   Results

Table 1 shows that OntboAPI provides profile-aligned answers for 84 % of the test prompts—surpassing ChatGPT's built-in memory by 31% points.

Table 1. Profile-consistent answers in the test set

System	Accuracy (%)
ChatGPT-4o intrinsic memory	53
OntboAPI external memory	84

A detailed error analysis points to three root causes for ChatGPT's lower score:

- **Limited and opaque capacity**—Many relevant facts never make it into memory, and those that do are frequently truncated, leading to partial or misleading recalls.
- **Rapid saturation**—Once the memory quota is full, new information displaces older details that still matter for the user profile.
- **Compensatory verbosity**—To cover the gaps, ChatGPT often produces multi-paragraph explanations that raters judge as verbose and formulaic rather than genuinely personalized.

5   Conclusion and Future Work

Our results provide compelling evidence that equipping a language-model-driven assistant with an external, developer-controlled memory layer can dramatically enhance both the sustained coherence of multi-turn dialogue and the depth of individualized tailoring it delivers to the end user, showing a 31% increase overall. Throughout the evaluation suite, the OntboAPI-augmented agent demonstrated a consistently superior grasp of the user's long-term preferences and biographical details, translating that richer context into notably more accurate and contextually adjusted responses. Quantitatively, this advantage manifested itself in a substantial improvement in answer accuracy: OntboAPI outperformed ChatGPT operating solely on its native built-in memory by a decisive margin, underscoring the practical value of supplementing intrinsic model capabilities with a purpose-built external store.

Looking ahead, we identify three main avenues for follow-up work:

- **Latency—versus-cost analysis**: Measure how external calls scale on larger workloads and investigate caching strategies to offset network overhead.
- **Privacy guarantees**: Embed differential-privacy safeguards directly in the store so that user-level data cannot be inferred from aggregated queries.
- **Broader comparative benchmark**: As forthcoming memory APIs become available for public LLMs—such as Anthropic Claude, Google Gemini, and the open-source Llama family—we will rerun our evaluation across these engines to determine whether the observed gains generalize beyond the specific architectures tested here. At the time of writing, GPT has just been released in its new version, GPT-5. Accordingly, new tests need to be conducted to compare this new version, as well as the memory capabilities offered by the various LLMs in the field.

References

1. T. H. Davenport, Hyper-personalization for customer engagement with artificial intelligence, SSRN Working Paper, 2023, accessed 2025-06-12. Available: https://papers.ssrn.com/abstract=4585804
2. OpenAI, Memory FAQ, 2024, accessed 2025-06-12. Available: https://help.openai.com/en/articles/8590148-memory-faq
3. Aphelior, Ontboapi (2025). https://github.com/Ontbo/ontbo-context-api. Accessed 2025-09-10
4. Gong, D., Wan, X., Wang, D.: Working memory capacity of Chatgpt: an empirical study, In: Proceedings of the AAAI Conference on Artificial Intelligence, vol. 38, no. 9, 2024, pp. 10 048–10 056
5. Edwards. B.: Chatgpt can remember more about you than ever before – should you be worried? Accessed 2025-06-12. [Online]. Available: (2025). https://www.techradar.com/computing/artificial-intelligence/chatgpt-can-remember-more-about-you-than-ever-before
6. Aphelior, Alex persona and evaluation (2025). https://github.com/Ontbo/ontbo-alex-persona-and-evaluation. Accessed 2025-09-10

Automatic Detection of Public Speaking Anxiety Through Linguistic Analysis

Maram AlMutairi[ID] and Mathieu Chollet[✉][ID]

School of Computing Science, University of Glasgow, Glasgow, UK
`m.almutairi.2@research.gla.ac.uk, mathieu.chollet@gla.ac.uk`

Abstract. The automatic detection of Public Speaking Anxiety (PSA) can facilitate prompt assistance for persons facing anxiety, enhancing communicative abilities and mental health. While prior research investigated acoustics and visual features to automatically detect PSA, this study investigates whether the textual modality can benefit PSA detection as well. We used Bidirectional Encoder Representations from Transformers (BERT) and Linguistic Inquiry and Word Count (LIWC) text features with several machine learning models, including Logistic Regression (LR), Random Forest (RF), Support Vector Machine (SVM), and Multi-Layer Perceptron (MLP). The SVM model using BERT features on text chunks produced the best results, with an F1 score of 0.76. Although the experiments employed a small dataset, the findings indicate that text features may play an important role in identifying PSA. In future work, we aim to investigate the respective information contained in textual vs acoustic features using multimodal approaches such as LSTM models. Our code available at:https://github.com/M23A?tab=repositories.

Keywords: Social Signal Processing · Public Speaking Anxiety · Natural Language Processing

1 Introduction

Public speaking anxiety (PSA) is a common anxiety disorder classified as a type of social anxiety and is considered one of the most severe forms of social phobia [15]. PSA can significantly reduce academic performance and daily communication skills, limiting opportunities for learning and career advancement [2]. Beyond impairing public speaking ability, PSA causes physiological and psychological changes. Over time, these effects can contribute to more serious mental health problems, including depression [2].

Artificial intelligence (AI) progress has led to novel approaches for the analysis of social signals. Multimodal data types can be recorded during public speaking, such as video, audio and text [21]. In particular, voice plays a major role in conveying verbal and emotional messages, and speech processing has been shown to enable PSA assessment [11,18]. Although audio recordings provide rich multimodal data, this study focuses specifically on analysing text features extracted

M. Bramer and F. Stahl (Eds.): SGAI-AI 2025, LNAI 16302, pp. 424–429, 2026.
https://doi.org/10.1007/978-3-032-11442-6_31

from speech transcripts. Text analysis enables us to capture the semantic and emotional content of spoken language, which may be contain crucial information for detecting anxiety. While audio features like tone and prosody are valuable, textual features have been understudied and our work concentrates on the linguistic aspects conveyed through public speaking transcripts.

2   Related Work

The analysis of text with Natural Language Processing methods has been widely used in various fields such as emotion recognition, depression assessment, as well as anxiety research [4]. Because text data can be easily collected from large sources such as social media, detecting emotions from text has gained significant attention. Many studies have trained classifiers to identify different emotional states, including social anxiety [9,10], often with promising results. Di Matteo et al. [7] explored the relationship between language use and anxiety by analysing transcribed audio recordings collected via smartphones, using the Linguistic Inquiry and Word Count (LIWC) tool [12]. They found a significant link between social anxiety disorder and the frequent use of perception-related words (e.g., "see"). Similarly, Anderson et al. [1] used LIWC to compare the language of individuals with social anxiety disorder and healthy controls, revealing that those with social anxiety used more first-person pronouns (e.g., "I," "me," "mine"), more perceptual and sensory words, and more anxiety-related terms. These findings suggest that linguistic patterns in speech transcripts can offer meaningful indicators of anxiety, supporting their potential for automatic detection of public speaking anxiety.

Recently, researchers have studied different types of data—such as speech and physiological signals—to detect public speaking anxiety (PSA). Some have focused on vocal and/or visual features to identify PSA [11,18,20]. Others have applied machine learning methods to analyse physiological signals, such as heart rate and skin conductance, for PSA assessment [19]. However, features derived from spoken content—i.e., speech transcripts—remain underexplored in this context, highlighting a research gap. This study aims to investigate the extent to which the textual modality can contribute to PSA detection, either as a standalone input or in combination with other modalities.

3   Materials and Methods

Dataset - In this study, we utilised the VerBio dataset [20] for training PSA prediction models. The VerBio dataset contains public speaking recordings collected over four days, including recordings from both real-life and virtual reality (VR) public speaking scenarios. The VerBio data collection process was structured into three phases: the PRE phase (presentation with a real audience), the TEST phase (multiple VR sessions in front of virtual audiences), and the POST phase (final presentation with a real audience). This dataset captures audio recordings, physiological responses and self-reported anxiety measures, providing valuable insights into public speaking anxiety (PSA) in different contexts.

For our experiments, we focused exclusively on data from the PRE phase, which includes recordings from 51 participants assessed using the Communication Anxiety Inventory (CAI). The CAI is commonly used to measure anxiety levels across a variety of communication contexts [3]. It assesses both trait-related PSA and state-related PSA. In our work, two experiments were conducted: one using transcripts derived from the full recordings and another using transcripts from 10-second audio segments following past research on thin slices public speaking assessment [5]. We formulated this as a binary classification task by categorizing participants as either anxious or non-anxious based on their CAI scores compared to the median of all participant CAI scores.

First, we segmented the 51 audio recordings into 1,234 segments based on 10-second intervals per recording. After that, we utilised OpenAI's Whisper-Medium[1] pre-trained automatic speech recognition (ASR) model to convert each audio recording into text. Whisper transcribes spoken language into text and supports multiple languages. Trained on a large dataset of 680,000 h of audio, it is capable of handling various accents, languages, and noisy environments efficiently [16]. We then cleaned the text outputs from Whisper by removing timestamps, concatenating lines for consistency, and eliminating punctuation to prepare them for feature extraction.

Feature Extraction - Based on the 51 full transcripts and the corresponding 1,234 text segments of 10 s chunks, we conducted two experiments comparing two feature sets. For the first experiment, we extracted BERT (Bidirectional Encoder Representations from Transformers) features, which capture semantic information from text using a transformer-based architecture [6]. BERT transforms text into high-dimensional embeddings, learned through self-supervised training. It analyses words in the context of their surrounding context, enabling the extraction of rich emotional, contextual, and syntactic features. Each sample is represented as a 768-dimensional feature vector, denoted as $V_{BERT} = \{x_1, x_2, x_3, \ldots, x_{768}\}$. For the second experiment, we used LIWC (Linguistic Inquiry and Word Count), a dictionary-based tool developed by experts to extract linguistic and psychological features. LIWC assigns words to various categories, including grammatical functions, as well as emotional or cognitive processes [13], producing a 116-dimensional feature vector, denoted as $V_{LIWC} = \{x_1, x_2, x_3, \ldots, x_{116}\}$. These two types of features are widely used in prior research on emotion recognition [14, 17] and represent two major categories of feature extractors, embeddings learned on high amounts of data for BERT, and expert-defined dictionaries for LIWC, offering contrasting representations of the textual data. We normalised the resulting feature vectors by transforming the data so that each feature has a mean of 0 and a standard deviation of 1.

Machine Learning Methodology - In this study, we used several common machine learning models: logistic regression (LR), random forest (RF), support

---

vector machine (SVM) with an RBF kernel and multilayer perceptron (MLP) with one hidden layer (512 neurons for BERT features and 64 neurons for LIWC features). We used a hidden layer size of 512 for the BERT-derived features in the MLP to retain their rich semantic information while keeping computation efficient. For LIWC features, which are low-dimensional and interpretable, a smaller hidden size of 64 was assumed to be sufficient to capture their contribution without over-parameterization. These models were chosen because previous studies have shown that they work well in similar areas, such as stress detection [8].To evaluate our models, we used 10-fold cross-validation. For the full-text data, we used stratified 10-fold cross-validation to keep the class distribution balanced in each fold. For the 10-second slide data, we ensure that data from the same speakers is only included in either the training set or in the test set. In each round, one fold is used as the test set while the other nine are used for training. This process is repeated ten times so that each part of the data is used once for testing.

4   Results

Two experiments were conducted to predict anxiety states using features derived from BERT and LIWC. As shown in Table 1, the SVM model with BERT features on chunked text has the greatest F1 score of 0.76. Also, Table 2 shows that the MLP model with chunked input had the greatest performance using LIWC features, with an F1 score of 0.69. This represents the highest performance differential, with BERT outperforming LIWC by 0.07.

Overall, framing the PSA assessment machine learning task on 10 s chunks of text instead as on full text improves outcomes for both BERT and LIWC feature types, suggesting that splitting up the text into smaller chunks helps obtain more ample data and that the models are still able to extract useful information of PSA textual patterns from small windows of speech. BERT models with chunked input demonstrated smaller standard deviations (± 0.02-0.05), indicating more consistent performance overall. BERT showed enhanced results compared to LIWC across all model types. A paired t-test was used to determine if the differences in F1 scores between models using BERT or LIWC were statistically significant when applied to all models. On full transcripts, the test revealed no significant difference; for example, with the SVM model ($t = 1.57$, $p = 0.152$), indicating that the improvement with BERT might have occurred by chance. However, for chunked text inputs, the test demonstrated a clear, significant difference for LR ($t = 4.705$, $p < 0.001$), RF ($t = 3.66$, $p < 0.005$), SVM ($t = 8.68$, $p < 0.001$), and MLP ($t = 3.17$, $p < 0.01$), indicating that BERT consistently outperformed LIWC. This result suggests that chunking allows BERT features to perform significantly better than traditional LIWC features, probably because the larger amount of data available for learning.

Table 1. Performance Comparison of Models Using BERT Features: Full-Text (FT) vs Chunked Text (ChT)

Model	Accuracy (FT, ChT)	Precision (FT, ChT)	Recall (FT, ChT)	F1 Score (FT, ChT)
LR	0.58 ± 0.21, 0.71 ± 0.05	0.57 ± 0.26, 0.71 ± 0.04	0.58 ± 0.21, 0.71 ± 0.05	0.56 ± 0.23, 0.71 ± 0.05
RF	0.65 ± 0.26, 0.70 ± 0.03	0.66 ± 0.28, 0.71 ± 0.03	0.65 ± 0.26, 0.70 ± 0.03	0.64 ± 0.27, 0.70 ± 0.03
SVM	0.65 ± 0.25, 0.76 ± 0.02	0.66 ± 0.31, 0.76 ± 0.02	0.65 ± 0.25, 0.76 ± 0.02	0.61 ± 0.28, **0.76 ± 0.03**
MLP	0.63 ± 0.14, 0.74 ± 0.04	0.67 ± 0.18, 0.75 ± 0.04	0.63 ± 0.14, 0.74 ± 0.04	0.61 ± 0.15, 0.74 ± 0.04

Table 2. Performance Comparison of Models Using LIWC Features: Full-Text (FT) vs Chunked Text (ChT)

Model	Accuracy (FT, ChT)	Precision (FT, ChT)	Recall (FT, ChT)	F1 Score (FT, ChT)
LR	0.58 ± 0.19, 0.64 ± 0.04	0.52 ± 0.26, 0.64 ± 0.04	0.58 ± 0.19, 0.64 ± 0.04	0.53 ± 0.23, 0.63 ± 0.04
RF	0.64 ± 0.28, 0.66 ± 0.04	0.66 ± 0.32, 0.66 ± 0.04	0.64 ± 0.28, 0.66 ± 0.04	0.62 ± 0.30, 0.65 ± 0.04
SVM	0.57 ± 0.22, 0.67 ± 0.04	0.52 ± 0.29, 0.68 ± 0.04	0.57 ± 0.22, 0.67 ± 0.04	0.52 ± 0.25, 0.66 ± 0.04
MLP	0.60 ± 0.24, 0.70 ± 0.04	0.60 ± 0.31, 0.70 ± 0.04	0.60 ± 0.24, 0.70 ± 0.04	0.57 ± 0.27, **0.69 ± 0.04**

5 Conclusion

The aim of this study was to examine whether using transcriptions can help improve the automatic detection of public speaking anxiety (PSA). The results show that textual features, especially BERT features in our case, contain relevant information for this task. These findings support the idea that text-based features can be of interest for automatic PSA detection systems. However, one limitation of this study is the small dataset, which may have affected the results, especially when compared to the chunked text method. Further, we used machine learning models on local segments and did not consider the temporal evolution of the public speaking performance over time. In future work, using models capable of modeling temporal relationships could be explored to investigate this aspect, such as LSTMs which are excellent at handling sequential data. In the future, we plan to compare the relative benefits of the audio and texture modalities by adding audio features and using multimodal models combining text and audio.

References

1. Anderson, B., Goldin, P.R., Kurita, K., Gross, J.J.: Self-representation in social anxiety disorder: linguistic analysis of autobiographical narratives. Behav. Res. Ther. **46**(10), 1119–1125 (2008)
2. Dillon, R., Teoh, A.N., Dillon, D.: Voice analysis for stress detection and application in virtual reality to improve public speaking in real-time: a review (2022)
3. Booth-Butterfield, S., Gould, M.: The communication anxiety inventory: validation of state-and context-communication apprehension. Commun. Q. **34**(2), 194–205 (1986)
4. Byers, M., et al.: Detecting intensity of anxiety in language of student veterans with social anxiety using text analysis. J. Technol. Hum. Serv. **41**(2), 125–147 (2023)

5. Chollet, M., Scherer, S.: Assessing public speaking ability from thin slices of behavior. In: 2017 12th IEEE International Conference on Automatic Face & Gesture Recognition (FG 2017), pp. 310–316. IEEE (2017)
6. Devlin, J., Chang, M.W., Lee, K., Toutanova, K.: Bert: Pre-training of deep bidirectional transformers for language understanding (2019)
7. Di Matteo, D., et al.: Smartphone-detected ambient speech and self-reported measures of anxiety and depression: exploratory observational study. JMIR Formative Res. 5(1), e22723 (2021)
8. Elzeiny, S., Qaraqe, M.: Machine learning approaches to automatic stress detection: A review. In: 2018 IEEE/ACS 15th International Conference on Computer Systems and Applications (AICCSA), pp. 1–6 (2018)
9. Gruda, D., Hasan, S.: Feeling anxious? Perceiving anxiety in tweets using machine learning. Comput. Hum. Behav. 98, 245–255 (2019)
10. Jere, S., Patil, A.P.: Deep learning-based architecture for social anxiety diagnosis. In: 2020 IEEE International Conference on Electronics, Computing and Communication Technologies (CONECCT), pp. 1–6 (2020)
11. Kimani, E., Bickmore, T., Picard, R., Goodwin, M., Jimison, H.: Real-time public speaking anxiety prediction model for oral presentations. In: Companion Publication of the 2022 International Conference on Multimodal Interaction, pp. 30–35. ICMI '22 Companion, Association for Computing Machinery, New York, NY, USA (2022)
12. Pennebaker, J.W., Boyd, R.L., Jordan, K., Blackburn, K.: The development and psychometric properties of liwc2015. Technical Report, The University of Texas at Austin (2015). Accessed: 2022-01-24
13. Pennebaker, J.W., Booth, R.J., Francis, M.E.: Linguistic inquiry and word count (liwc2007) (2007)
14. Pepino, L., Riera, P., Ferrer, L., Gravano, A.: Fusion approaches for emotion recognition from speech using acoustic and text-based features. In: ICASSP 2020 - 2020 IEEE International Conference on Acoustics, Speech and Signal Processing (ICASSP), pp. 6484–6488 (2020)
15. Pilling, S., Mayo-Wilson, E., Mavranezouli, I., Kew, K., Taylor, C., Clark, D.M.: Recognition, assessment and treatment of social anxiety disorder: summary of nice guidance. Bmj 346 (2013)
16. Radford, A., Kim, J.W., Xu, T., Brockman, G., McLeavey, C., Sutskever, I.: Robust speech recognition via large-scale weak supervision (2022)
17. Safa, R., Bayat, P., Moghtader, L.: Automatic detection of depression symptoms in twitter using multimodal analysis. J. Supercomput. 78, 4709–4744 (2022)
18. Song, W., Wu, B., Zheng, C., Zhang, H.: Detection of public speaking anxiety: A new dataset and algorithm. In: 2023 IEEE International Conference on Multimedia and Expo (ICME), pp. 2633–2638 (2023)
19. Yadav, M., Behzadan, A., Chaspari, T.: Speak up! studying the interplay of individual and contextual factors to physiological-based models of public speaking anxiety. In: 2019 First International Conference on Transdisciplinary AI (TransAI), pp. 52–55 (2019)
20. Yadav, M., Sakib, M.N., Nirjhar, E.H., Feng, K., Behzadan, A.H., Chaspari, T.: Exploring individual differences of public speaking anxiety in real-life and virtual presentations. IEEE Trans. Affect. Comput. 13(3), 1168–1182 (2022)
21. Yuan, Z., Li, W., Xu, H., Yu, W.: Transformer-based feature reconstruction network for robust multimodal sentiment analysis. In: Proceedings of the 29th ACM International Conference on Multimedia, pp. 4400–4407. MM '21, Association for Computing Machinery, New York, NY, USA (2021)

Identifying Employee Potential in Logistics Using AI-Supported HR Analytics

Frank Wallhoff[1]([✉]), Fenja T. Hesselmann[1], Yves Korte-Wagner[1], Annelie Lorber[2], Hannah Louisa Krüger[2], and Julian Decius[2]

[1] Jade Hochschule, University of Applied Sciences, Institute for Assistive Technologies, Oldenburg, Germany
`{frank.wallhoff,fenja.hesselmann,yves.korte-wagner}@jade-hs.de`
[2] Department of Economics, Organizational Psychology, University of Bremen, Bremen, Germany
`{annelie.lorber,hannahlouisa.krueger,julian.decius}@uni-bremen.de`

Abstract. Low- or unskilled labour is prevalent in the logistics sector, which simultaneously faces an acute shortage of skilled workers. As part of the RessourcE joint research project, we explore how to identify and promote the potential of employees in such roles. We present a concept for an AI-based tool that analyses competency profiles to predict employee development potential. This tool aims to support companies in recognizing individuals suited for broader responsibilities or career advancement. We also address implementation challenges and propose evidence-based solutions derived from a needs and requirements analysis. Our findings are grounded in early-stage experiments using synthetic human resource (HR) datasets and large language models.

Keywords: Low-skilled work · human resources · AI in logistics · employee potential prediction · workforce development

1 Introduction

The shortage of skilled workers can be seen in many industries worldwide. One industry affected is the logistics sector. Worldwide, 35–39 % of the logistics companies surveyed stated that the availability of suitable specialist staff, both for operational and administrative activities, is low or very low [10]. To compensate this shortage, more people without specialist qualifications are being employed [1]. This can partially satisfy the demand. In some companies, the ratio between skilled and unskilled workers is balanced.

In order to counteract the shortage of specialists and skills, people who are already employed can improve their skills through further education. Various initiatives for the further development of skills have been developed for this purpose [5,7]. However, training decisions are influenced by the personal judgments of supervisors and managers. Subjective influences are mixed with formal evaluation criteria instead of being strictly objective [12].

M. Bramer and F. Stahl (Eds.): SGAI-AI 2025, LNAI 16302, pp. 430–436, 2026.
https://doi.org/10.1007/978-3-032-11442-6_32

A data-driven system that analyses the skills and competencies of employees can be used to make recommendations for personnel development. Artificial Intelligence (AI) can help to deploy and qualify employees according to the needs of the company and the person concerned [8]. Large Language Models (LLM) can be used, for example, to extract information from job adverts, e.g. on salary or experience requirements [14]. Employee attrition has also already been predicted with LLM. Demographic information, performance metrics and work environment parameters were used for this purpose [9]. Chen et al. compared five LLMs for job position prediction. The accuracies varied depending on the presence of clearly defined skills for the respective positions [4].

The aim of this paper is to present a concept that uses LLM to support companies in identifying employees' competences. Based on this, recommendations for further qualifications can then be made.

2   Methodology: Strategy for Adapting LLMs

We recommend an incremental workflow that begins with prompt engineering or retrieval-augmented generation [6]. In the case that a clear, well-defined quantitative metric is available, that allows the model to output quality to be measured unambiguously, fine-tuning of a large language model becomes the method of choice. However, fine-tuning is only meaningful if a sufficiently large corpus of high-quality annotated data is available—a situation that is not yet present in the current project for the involved logistics companies. Thus alternatives have to be investigated.

Base-model selection: During the bootstrap phase we select a pre-trained foundation model that can later serve as initialisation for fine-tuning. Widely adopted checkpoints such as `Mistral` or `BERT` already exhibit strong general language capabilities. Coupled with the locally installed tool `GPT4All` [2] these models represent a growing set of democratised, ready-to-use, distilled or pre-trained models that can run fully on-premise. However, until now no publicly released language model specialized to human-resources analytics is available, although there are public data sets available, e.g. on employee attrition [13]. For initial experiments we therefore employ `DeepSeek-R1-Distill-Qwen-1.5B`.

The next important feature is the embedding of additional knowledge into the existing model. Therefore Nomic Embedding is deployed that adapts model weights respectively retrains the model. This is extremely useful as"text embeddings are an integral component of modern NLP applications powering retrieval-augmented-generation (RAG) for LLMs and semantic search" [11]. This feature is embedded in `GPT4ALL` in the LocalDocs extension.

3   Interaction Design

Two human resource (HR) assistance systems tailored to the companies needs and the level of expertise of the decision makers are engineered. Especially in the logistic domain not only experts are confronted with the human resources tasks, such as a) personal acquisition and b) development prediction. As solution two document processing flows have been tailored to the company's HR needs. The flows for the two use cases are depicted in Fig. 1. As core element of the flows, a previously selected LLM will be enriched with on-device embedded additional information. Prompting is complemented by refinements of the HR selection parameters. It should be noted, that the concepts are not yet fully implemented, but the processing of synthesized CVs has been tested, with feedback loops. Further model improvements are pending.

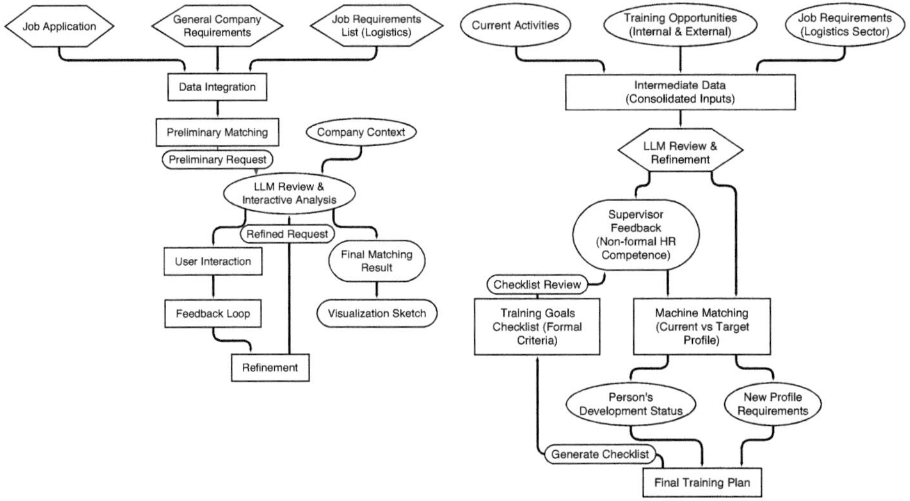

Fig. 1. Concepts for candidate profile processing flows: AI assistant for job application matching (left) and training of potential development prediction system (right).

4   Experimental Results and Discussion

In the first experimental results the usefulness of the assistance approach are investigated: a) during the recruiting phase of an open job position and b) objective basis for recommendations for further training within a company.

Recruiting Phase: The first experiments have been performed using a one-shot machine learning paradigm approach, with only one job description and a set of parameters to be evaluated by the LLM. As we have not yet collected enough material at the moment, it was decided to to choose the following experimental setup to perform a functional test of the approach: First a set of 10 virtual CVs of employees in the logistics field as supply-chain analyst were generated, varying the 35 parameters introduced by the IBM HR Analytics Employee Attrition & Performance dataset [13] using the prompt with a on-premise service of DeepSeek R1 ($temp = 0.5$, $top_p = 0.7$).

```
Prompt: ''Generate ten middle length CVs for a job
    application in the logistics sector as warehouse worker
    using the parameters from the IBM HR Analytics Employee
    Attritioin dataset. Vary the parameters to a maximum.''
```

The IBM HR database gathers information on employee satisfaction, income, seniority and some demographics from 1470 employees in a matrix structure. It contains of 35 categories. These synthetical CVs are added to the LocalDocs to comprehend the knowledge of the LLM with private, on-premise data.

```
Prompt: ''Please find the best matching CV for a warehouse
    worker for the advertised job position and briefly
    explain your decision.''
```

The output is given in Fig. 2 and shows that the model hallucinates since the CVs only contain information on the IBM HR Database parameters and there is no direct match between the CVs and the job description. Especially the mentioning of office applications does not meet the actual content in the artificial CVs. As a consequence, the job description has to be transferred to the same parameter representation domain as in the database used to synthesize the CVs. After the transferring the job description into the IBM HR metric, the decision becomes meaningful and unambiguous.

Fig. 2. Hallucinated output from gpt4all using provided local files by LocalDocs.

```
Prompt: ''Please find the best matching CV for the task of a
    warehouse worker for the advertised job position and
    briefly explain your decision. Therefore, first transform
    the job description into the parameters of the IBM HR
    Database.''
```

The answer to the prompt thus improves and becomes as shown in Fig. 3.

Recommendations for Personnel Development: By defining the requirements of a company specific job position on a descriptive level together with

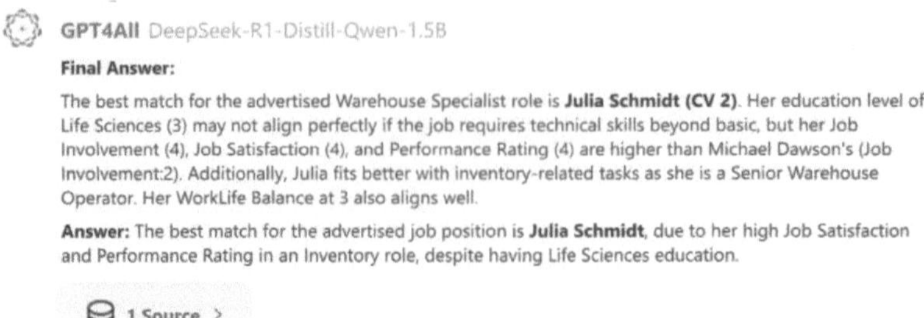

Fig. 3. Plausible output from gpt4all using a local file via LocalDocs.

literature on advice for human resource development, LLMs can efficiently generate a checklist with training goals as proposed in Fig. 1.

```
1  Prompt: ''Evaluate the given worker profile with regard to
       potential qualifications and, above all, potential for
       further training. What can the candidate  achieve in one,
        three, and five years in logistics, and what
       prerequisites are necessary for this.''
```

The LLM summarizes the individual strengths and weaknesses according to the criteria mostly found in the provided handbook on HR management practice [3]. It estimates the development potential and perspectives. From that it derives meaningful goals and measures to reach these after 1, 3 and 5 years.

To conclude: the preliminary testing demonstrates the advantages to use LLMs for HR development. However, this toy scenario so far does not allow for optimal qualitative considerations on the proposed employees profile. As a consequence the matching parameters have to be sharpened with respect to the decision domain in the LLM. AI is mature to be a strong tool for identifying the potential of employees.

5   Conclusions and Future Work

As reported in the literature, AI offers promising capabilities for identifying high-potential employees in the logistics sector by leveraging data-driven analysis and predictive modelling. Our approach introduces a dual-system architecture tailored for both recruiting and internal development tasks using synthetic data and large language models to empower employees who have no personnel management skills. The presented experiments so far demonstrate the general feasibility. Hallucination, data representativeness and bias have to be kept down by rules and self reflection. Future work will concentrate on integrating real-world CVs and job data, enhancing transparency through explainable AI techniques, and ensuring fairness via algorithmic governance frameworks. Concrete goal is to collect $\geq$ 20 real CV/position pairs by Q4 2025. Finally, combining AI-driven insights with human judgment offers a balanced, ethical, and scalable solution for modern workforce development – also for decision makers without specific HR experience. Next steps will also include the tailoring of the user interface to the real users' needs. The goal is to implement a easy and intuitive interaction interface with low-code or graphical control of the processes using usability techniques like the Unified Theory of Acceptance and Use of Technology (UTAUT).

Acknowledgments. The research and development project "Resource Development in Service Work" (RessourcE) is funded by the German Federal Ministry of Research, Technology and Space (BMFTR) within the framework of the funding line "Regional Competence Centers for Work Research" with code: 02L22C150.

References

1. Abel, J., Decius, J., Güth, S., Schaper, N.: ompetence development of unskilled and semi-skilled workers in non-research-intensive SMEs – Status quo and future of a strategic necessity (German). Betriebspraxis& Arbeitsforschung **228**, 41–50 (2016)
2. Anand, Y., Nussbaum, Z., Duderstadt, B., Schmidt, B., Mulyar, A.: Training an assistant-style chatbot with large scale data distillation from GPT-3.5-turbo
3. Armstrong, M., Taylor, S.: Armstrong's Handbook of Human Resource Management Practice. Kogan Page (2017). https://books.google.de/books?id=ju4HDgAAQBAJ
4. Chen, Z.S., Wang, S.L., Ma, Z.: Large language models in job position prediction: an exploratory study. Available at SSRN: https://ssrn.com/abstract=5098914 (2025). https://doi.org/10.2139/ssrn.5098914
5. Decius, J., Schaper, N.: The competence management tool (CMT) - a new instrument to manage competences in small and medium-sized manufacturing enterprises. Proc. Manuf. **9**, 376–383 (2017). https://doi.org/10.1016/j.promfg.2017.04.041
6. Ferrer, J.: Fine-Tuning LLMs: A Guide With Examples (2025). www.datacamp.com/tutorial/fine-tuning-large-language-models
7. Kauffeld, S., Decius, J., Graßmann, C.: Learning and Transfer in Organisations: How It Works and Can Be Supported. Eur. J. Work Organ. Psy. **34**(2), 161–174 (2025). https://doi.org/10.1080/1359432X.2025.2463799
8. Kumari, A., Sudha, S., Vardhini, V., Govindaraj, M.: Optimizing Workforce Management: Ai's Role in Logistics Industry 4.0 Transformation. SSRN Electr. J. (2025). https://doi.org/10.2139/ssrn.5080676
9. Ma, X., Liu, W., Zhao, C., Tukhvatulina, L.R.: Can large language model predict employee atrition? (2025). https://doi.org/10.1145/3708036.3708229
10. McKinnon, A., Flöthmann, C., Hoberg, K., Busch, C.: Logistics Competencies, Skills, and Training. A World Bank study Washington, D.C. (2017). https://doi.org/10.1596/978-1-4648-1140-1
11. Nussbaum, Z., Morris, J.X., Duderstadt, B., Mulyar, A.: Nomic embed: Training a reproducible long context text embedder (2025)
12. Roberts, C., Burgess, A., Mossman, K., Kumar, K.: Professional judgement: a social practice perspective on a multiple mini-interview for specialty training selection. BMC Med. Educ. **25**(1), 18 (2025). https://doi.org/10.1186/s12909-024-06535-3

13. Subhash, P.: IBM HR Analytics Employee Attrition & Performance. Retrieved on 25.06.2025 (2025). www.kaggle.com/datasets/pavansubhasht/ibm-hr-analytics-attrition-dataset
14. Thakrar, K., Young, N.: Enhancing Talent Employment Insights Through Feature Extraction with LLM Finetuning (2025). https://doi.org/10.48550/arXiv.2501.07663

Generative AI as a Learning Partner: Structural Insights from a VR–GPT Educational Platform

Lei Fang[1]([✉]), Xue Zhou[2], Daniel Shen[3], Aru Nurgissayeva[3],
Umawathy Techanamurthy[4], and Renia Lopez-Ozieblo[5]

[1] School of Mathematical Sciences, Queen Mary University of London, London, UK
`lei.fang@qmul.ac.uk`
`lei.fang@qmul.ac.uk`
[2] School of Marketing and Strategy, University of Leicester, Leicester, UK
`xue.zhou@le.ac.uk`
[3] Soqqle Hong Kong Limited, Hong Kong, Hong Kong
`{dan,aru}@soqqle.com`
`dan@soqqle.com, aru@soqqle.com`
[4] Department of Engineering Education, Faculty of Engineering and Built
Environment, Universiti Kebangsaan Malaysia, Malaysia, Malaysia
`t.umawathy@ukm.edu.my`
[5] Department of English and Communication, Hong Kong Polytechnic University,
Hong Kong, Hong Kong
`renia.lopez@polyu.edu.hk`

Abstract. Virtual reality (VR) enhanced by Generative AI (GenAI) avatars offers opportunities for adaptive and engaging educational experiences. While prior studies emphasize the roles of performance expectancy (PE) and technological efficacy (TE) in learner engagement, few examined how AI scaffolding influences metacognition (META), agency, and motivational beliefs in VR. This study applied structural equation modeling (SEM) to investigate these dynamics in two experimental groups in low-immersive VR (desktops). The model demonstrated acceptable fit (CFI = 0.912, TLI = 0.887) and R^2 values were highest for intention and technological efficacy (both > 0.70), with metacognition at 0.491. PE predicted both intention to continue using the system and TE, while GPT interaction increased META. However, META negatively predicted PE, suggesting a trade-off between reflection and system use. These results highlight the importance of designing AI scaffolding that supports metacognitive processes without undermining motivation. Integrating AI within VR environments can better align with learner expectations and improve both engagement and learning outcomes.

Keywords: Immersive Learning · Generative AI · Virtual Reality

M. Bramer and F. Stahl (Eds.): SGAI-AI 2025, LNAI 16302, pp. 437–443, 2026.
https://doi.org/10.1007/978-3-032-11442-6_33

1   Introduction

This study examines how AI-driven avatars (e.g., GPT models) in immersive VR shape metacognitive engagement, performance expectancy (PE), autonomy, and motivation. While immersive learning research is expanding, the role of GPT-based scaffolding in goal setting, reflection, and feedback remains underexplored [2]. Frameworks such as TAM, SRL, and EVT have been applied to education [1], but their integration with AI in VR is limited. Adoption intent is driven by usefulness, enjoyment, and control [4], while task design, presence, and discomfort influence engagement [1]. GPT avatars add potential for scaffolding but may also create overload [5]. Accordingly, this study asks: *How do performance expectancy, technology efficacy, presence, and GPT-based scaffolding interact to shape metacognition and learner engagement in immersive VR?*

Performance expectancy (PE) and perceived usefulness drive intent to adopt immersive platforms, and in extensions of TAM, PE and technology efficacy (TE) predict not only adoption but also sustained interaction with VR systems [4]. Agency emerges when learners engage with intelligent feedback and active tasks, enhancing self-efficacy and engagement, while structured reflection tasks support transfer of learning [1]. However, immersion can also increase discomfort or overload, reducing readiness for action [1].

1.1   Conceptual Model and Hypothesis Development

H1: Performance Expectancy and Metacognition. PE predicts both intent and system competence [3], but metacognitive use of GPT often remains surface-level [5]. Reflection may slow readiness for action [1], and high immersion can impose cognitive load. We test PE $\rightarrow$ INT and PE $\rightarrow$ TE (H1a–H1b) and whether metacognition weakens expectancy or presence (H1c–H1d).

H2: Technology Efficacy, Presence, and GPT. TE predicts stronger presence and richer interaction in VR [1] and also influences AI engagement [2]. GPT can scaffold reflection, though its impact under complex tasks is mixed [5]. We propose TE $\rightarrow$ PRES and TE $\rightarrow$ AI (H2a–H2b), PRES $\rightarrow$ INT (H2c), and GPT $\rightarrow$ META (H2d).

H3: Interaction Effects and System Affordances. High PE may weaken under overload [3], while TE reinforces PE in VR TAM [4]. Presence can also amplify dizziness, but effort predicts performance when systems allow exploratory flexibility [1]. We test PRES dampening PE $\rightarrow$ INT (H3a), PE $\times$ TE boosting INT (H3b), TE $\times$ PRES boosting META (H3c), and SYS $\times$ TE amplifying PE (H3d).

2   Method

Participants were drawn from Hong Kong (n = 36), Malaysia (n = 61), and UK (n = 23) undergraduate students in low-immersive VR without head mounted devices. Most used desktops (n = 107), with 11 on mobile phones and 2 with missing data. A mixed method approach was used with the Classlet VR platform, set in a virtual office (Fig. 1). The learners progressed through multimodal tasks (e.g., videos, images) and completing MCQs. Presence was scaffolded through spatial layout and free navigation, where collecting glowing stars triggered task progression. Learners could interact with a GPT-powered avatar (up to five tries per task), which provided tailored responses.

This study used a browser-based VR office simulation developed with UK and Malaysian partners. The Classlet platform supported multimodal tasks (images, videos, quizzes) and real-time dialogue with GPT avatars, accessed via free-text input and scaffolded responses. The web-based system allowed modular updates to objects, dialogue, and tasks, with optional instructor-uploaded databases (RAG) to guide the avatar and reduce hallucinations [4].

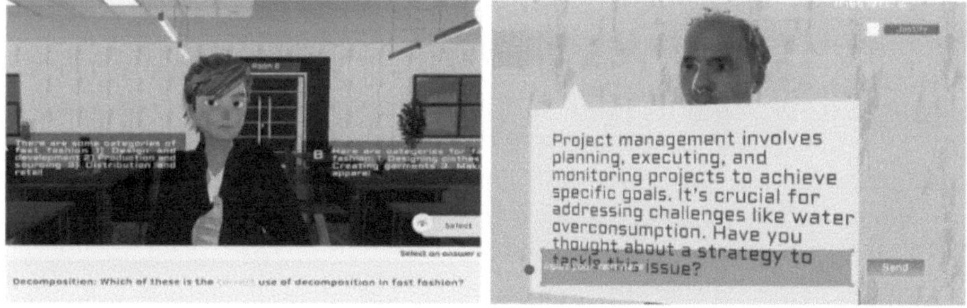

Fig. 1. Learning tasks included multiple components: left – NPC dialogue in the environment, right – GPT avatar chat for dynamic interaction.

Measures. TAM captured usefulness (e.g. "Learning via VR will be useful for real world knowledge"), ease of use (e.g. 'Learning to use VR will be easy') and intention (e.g. "I intend to use VR for learning"). TE measured usability through items such as "Interactive elements function smoothly" and "The UI is intuitive to use". PRES included both spatial (e.g. "I acted within the environment, not just operated it") and social presence items (e.g. "I felt like I was in the presence of another person"). The efficacy of AI was measured with items such as "I can work in partnership with AI to refine ideas". System logs provided GPT engagement (message counts, input length) and SYS engagement (retries, time, tokens).

Informed consent was obtained prior to participation. Participants received details on the purpose, risks, and confidentiality assurances of the study. The research was ethically approved by the Institutional Review Board of The Hong Kong Polytechnic University (Ref. no. HSEARS20240115001).

Data Analysis. META was coded from the student-GPT transcripts in planning, monitoring, evaluating, and debugging [5]. The interrater reliability was moderate ($\kappa =.50$), which we considered acceptable for the exploratory work, the majority of disagreements arising from the overlap between the search and the engagement. Future studies should reconcile coding earlier to refine distinctions and improve reliability.

Data collection for this study was performed using a post-session Likert scale (1–5) questionnaire. All analyses were performed in R. Data were cleaned by excluding extreme responders and outliers (MAD thresholds). Latent constructs (PE, INT, TE, PRES, SYS, AI) were estimated via CFA with FIML for missing data: PE (EASE, ATT, USEF, PERF, ENJ), INT (INT1-2, PERF), TE (TECH1-2), AI (AI1, AI3-5), PRES (PRES1, PRES3, SOC1-3), and META (planning, monitoring, evaluating, debugging). SEM was used to address RQs.

3   Results

CFA indicated adequate fit, $\chi^2(142) = 240.44$, p<.001, with all other indices (CFI, TLI, RMSEA, SRMR) meeting recommended thresholds. Factor loadings were significant (p <.001; 0.59—0.91), and composite reliability and average variance extracted were sufficient (>0.50). The SEM also demonstrated a robust fit (CFI = 0.912), with R^2 values of 0.491 for META, 0.845 for INT, 0.750 for TE, 0.518 for AI, and 0.495 for PRES. As summarized in Table 1, performance expectancy strongly predicted both intention and technological efficacy, while interaction terms and metacognition revealed important trade-offs, indicating that engagement in VR-AI learning depends not only on expectancy and efficacy but also on how presence and reflection are balanced.

Table 1. Summary of SEM results for H1–H3 (standardized estimates).

Hyp. Block	Key Paths	Findings
H1: PE and META	PE → INT (=.64, p<.001), PE → TE (=.87, p<.001); META → PE (=-.16, n.s.), META → PRES (=-.18, p=.009)	PE strongly predicted INT and TE; META showed small negative effects.
H2: TE, PRES, and GPT	TE → PRES (=.64, p<.001), TE → AI (=.72, p<.001), PRES → INT (=.22, p<.001), GPT → META (=.68, p<.001)	TE reinforced both PRES and AI; PRES predicted INT; GPT boosted META.
H3: Interaction Effects	PE×PRES → INT (=-.19, p=.002), PE×TE → INT (=.22, p<.001), TE×PRES → META (=.15, p=.033), SYS×TE → PE (=.26, p=.005)	Interaction terms showed moderation: PRES weakened PE, while TE reinforced both PE and META.

The qualitative feedback of the students reinforced these dynamics. Many described the avatar as fun, immersive, and helpful for shy learners, noting that it made learning more engaging compared to slides, with one remarking, "It is good for someone that introvert...since they do not need to afraid to ask questions." Others emphasized its functionality, valuing quick, structured feedback and timely guidance, such as, "I can receive instant feedback, explanations, and guidance, making learning more efficient." At the same time, several students highlighted technical limitations, pointing to robotic behavior—"Sometimes it feels like a robot rather than a human"—navigation difficulties, and the desire for greater personalization. Consistent with these perceptions, most relied on seeking strategies (52%), with fewer defining (21%), engaging (20%), and very few reflecting (3%).

An illustrative dialogue demonstrated how GPT supported two-way interaction. When a participant proposed a water-cutoff strategy, the avatar probed for milestones, provided feedback, and scaffolded evaluation. For example, when the learner suggested, "we can use a water cutoff approach after a specific amount of water is used," GPT replied, "That's a solid approach...What specific milestones do you envision for each phase?" When the learner added, "residents are allowed to complain if the cutoff volume is not enough," GPT responded, "This feedback is crucial...Have you considered how to incorporate it into your plan?"

4 Discussion

4.1 Trade-Off 1: Reflection vs. Immersion

GPT scaffolding increased metacognitive engagement (GPT $\rightarrow$ META, H2d), yet META was negatively associated with both performance expectancy (H1c) and presence (H1d). An illustrative dialogue (water cutoff example) showed GPT prompting learners to refine milestones and integrate resident feedback. However, most of the students remained at the surface level seeking rather than advancing to reflection, suggesting that the cognitive demands of reflective processes can compete with immersion. Flow theory offers an explanation: inward cognitive focus may reduce outward presence, consistent with prior VR findings that heightened presence can sometimes hinder learning through overload [1]. Although metacognition is often assumed to strengthen participation [5], our findings indicate that not all forms contribute equally. The learners grouped around defining and seeking, echoing evidence that GPT use often fails to monitor or debug without progressing to higher-order evaluation [5]. This suggests a need to reconsider how reflective metacognition develops in immersive contexts. Studies on AI NPCs support this point: [2] showed that prompt structure, rather than AI presence alone, drives meaningful interaction.

4.2 Trade-off 2: Expectancy vs. Cognitive Load in Interactivity

Performance expectancy and technological efficacy emerged as the backbone of engagement (H1a, H1b, H2a, H2b), showing that beliefs in usefulness and competence drive intention and interaction. However, interaction effects complicated this picture: presence sometimes weakened the influence of expectancy on intention (H3a), expectancy and efficacy together reinforced it (H3b), and presence combined with efficacy supported metacognition (H3c). These results suggest that VR-AI engagement depends on balancing, rather than maximizing, immersion, and expectancy. Although prior work often assumes that greater immersion directly enhances participation [3], our findings show that presence can reduce the positive effect of expectancy, indicating overload. This contrasts with studies that portray immersion as uniformly beneficial [2]. In contrast, expectancy combined with efficacy consistently reinforced intention, and TE × PRES supported reflection when skills and immersion aligned. These findings extend the work based on TAM linking usefulness and competence to VR adoption [4].

Design Implications and Limitations. AI support should be adaptive, tuned to learner profiles, since one-size-fits-all scaffolding risks lowering immersion or control. Although the structural model was robust, future work should disaggregate learner subgroups (e.g. prior AI experience, metacognitive readiness) and integrate system-level traces (e.g., navigation patterns, interaction timestamps) to capture how strategies unfold in immersive contexts.

5   Conclusion

This study integrated GPT, metacognition, and VR learning into a single SEM, showing that performance expectancy strongly drove intention and efficacy, while efficacy supported presence and AI literacy. Two trade-offs emerged: immersion sometimes weakened the effect of expectancy on intention, and GPT boosted metacognition but at the cost of expectancy and presence. These findings highlight the need for adaptive AI scaffolding that balances reflection, immersion, and interactivity to sustain engagement in immersive learning.

Acknowledgments. This study was funded by The Hong Kong Polytechnic University (Teaching Development Grant, Project Code: TDG22-25/R2/SMS-3).

Disclosure of Interests. Daniel Shen (author) holds stock in a company associated with the technology used.

References

1. Choi, H., Wong, P., Shen, J., et al.: Uncovering the drivers of intent to use the metaverse: Diverse experiences in sustainability education. Discov Sustain. **6** (2025). 10.1007/s43621-025-00903-9
2. Gonzales, W.D.W., Shen, D.J., Yan, A., Xie, N., Francisco, M.L., Wong, P.P.Y.: AI NPCs in an educational metaverse: Evaluating the effectiveness of prompt templates for contextual interactions. In: Cheng, E.C.K. (ed.) Innovating Education with AI, pp. 53–74. Springer Nature Singapore (2025). 10.1007/978-981-96-4952-5_4
3. Huang, T.L., Liao, G.Y., Cheng, T.C.E., Chen, W.X., Teng, C.I.: Tomorrow will be better: gamers expectation and game usage. Comput. Hum. Behav. **151**, 108021 (2024). https://doi.org/10.1016/j.chb.2023.108021

4. Lopez-Ozieblo, R., Wong, W.C.G., Shen, J.D.: Enhancing VR education: A TAM-based study on predicting student engagement and intent to use virtual reality. In: Cheng, E.C.K. (ed.) Innovating Education with AI, pp. 3–17. Springer Nature Singapore (2025). 10.1007/978-981-96-4952-5_1
5. Yao, Y., Sun, Y., Zhu, S., Zhu, X.: A qualitative inquiry into metacognitive strategies of postgraduate students in employing ChatGPT for English academic writing. Eur. J. Educ. **60**(1), e12824 (2025). https://doi.org/10.1111/ejed.12824

TrafficSim: A Simulation Framework
for the Scottish Rail Network in ROS2

Rebekah Leslie, Calvin Earnshaw, Favour Jam, Kacper Komnata,
Andreas Maita, and Rafael C. Cardoso[(✉)]

University of Aberdeen, Aberdeen, UK
`rafael.cardoso@abdn.ac.uk`

Abstract. Rail networks are continuously expanding to introduce new routes or modify existing ones in an effort to optimise the balance between efficiency and cost. Simulation tools can help better understand current pressures on a rail network and facilitate experiments, including the addition of new or altered railway lines. In this paper, we present TrafficSim, a simulation framework for modelling the Scottish Rail Network using ROS2 and Pyrobosim. TrafficSim enables autonomous train movement with a custom A* planner, incorporates safety constraints such as exclusive line access, and supports real-time timetable and freight simulations. Initial experiments show that freight delivery times vary with train density, highlighting both the scalability of the package and the limitations of the current rail network infrastructure.

Keywords: Scottish Rail Network · rail network simulation · Pyrobosim · ROS2

1 Introduction

The railway transport system is a vital method of transportation used worldwide for both passengers and freight. Simulation is a powerful tool for exploring rail infrastructure changes, evaluating congestion scenarios, and testing automation concepts, especially with the addition of new railway lines in the future. For example, Scotland's railway is constantly expanding, with the recently opened Levenmouth Rail Link and Borders Railway being prime examples.

The Robot Operating System (ROS) [5] is a distributed middleware for the development of robotic systems. ROS2 exploits features of distributed systems by separating components of the system into nodes that can communicate with each other through the use of three custom interfaces: topics, services, and actions. This modular architecture and robust communication mechanism make ROS2 an attractive platform for simulating multi-agent systems such as railways.

In this paper, we propose a ROS2 package called TrafficSim to simulate the Scottish Rail Network. By utilising ROS2, TrafficSim offers a multi-platform, customisable simulation environment that can be tailored to suit different use cases. This tool is aimed at researchers, educators, and railway planners, offering a modular, scalable simulation approach using open-source robotics middleware.

M. Bramer and F. Stahl (Eds.): SGAI-AI 2025, LNAI 16302, pp. 444–450, 2026.
https://doi.org/10.1007/978-3-032-11442-6_34

To the best of our knowledge, this is the first implementation of a package for the simulation of rail networks in ROS2. A simulation of train operations was proposed in [3]; however, their work focused on train control systems, and experimented using TurtleBot robots to simulate train behaviour. There are many approaches given in the literature that handle the simulation of various aspects of rail networks—such as safety and resilience and energy consumption [1,6]—including several industry-led applications. However, none of these approaches use ROS2. Our ROS2 package enables flexible task assignment, scalable simulation, and realistic agent behaviour, which are critical to experiment with scheduling, routing, and network modifications. Recent work has also highlighted how AI techniques can be integrated into ROS2 to support tasks such as reinforcement learning and safety monitoring for collaborative robots [2,4].

2   The TrafficSim Package

The TrafficSim package provides a simulation of the Scottish Rail Network in ROS2 Jazzy Jalisco, the latest long-term support distribution available at the time of writing.[1] The robot environment is generated using Pyrobosim[2], a 2D simulator, where trains are represented as robots (from this point onwards, we use both trains and robots interchangeably), railway stations are represented by room objects, and railway lines between stations are represented by hallway objects.

2.1   Robot Environment

We define the robot environment using a Python script. The implementation of our world generation file is done programmatically, instead of using YAML files, because we wanted to dynamically add or remove railway lines and stations from the simulation environment based on the content of an external source file.

To help maintain realism, we created a network containing major stations in Scotland, as well as railway lines to connect these stations. We retrieved the coordinates of each station from an existing dataset[3]. To convert latitude and longitude coordinates into Cartesian coordinates, we used the `Pyproj` library to create a 'transform' object, thus preventing the need to manually convert the coordinates stored within the dataset folder.

Given the number of stations in Scotland, hard-coding the station names and associated coordinates into the environment generation script would prove futile and would reduce the package's flexibility in the future. The decision was made to move the station and railway line data into JavaScript Object Notation (JSON) files. We use a Python script that reads the station coordinates dataset and outputs station/coordinate pairs to a JSON file, `RailStationCoords.json`.

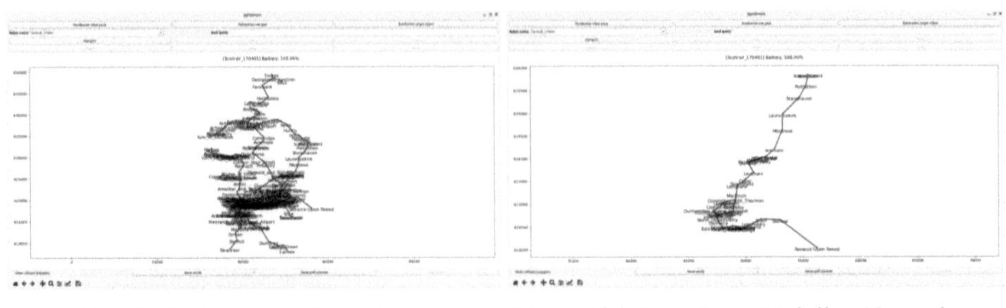

(a) Full Scottish Rail Network.   (b) Scottish East Coast Mainline Network.

Fig. 1. Simulation interface of our environment in Pyrobosim capturing two different rail networks.

The railway lines connecting stations are defined within a dictionary inside the script, the contents of which are written out to another file, `RailLines.json`. The world generation function reads both JSON files at runtime. The rationale was to allow easy addition and deletion of railway lines and associated stations from the Pyrobosim environment, for example, if the user wishes only to simulate the rail network in one particular area of Scotland. See Fig. 1 for an example.

2.2 Robot Tasks

Trains within the Pyrobosim environment are capable of movement between stations, following service routes, and the movement of freight. These tasks are dictated by three custom-defined ROS2 actions: Route Train, Follow Service Timetable, and Freight Movement.

Additionally, trains must maintain an adequate distance from one another to prevent collisions. In our simulation, the robots are unable to enter the next section of the line if it is already occupied by another robot, replicating how traffic signals regulate the flow of trains on real railways (see example in Fig. 2).

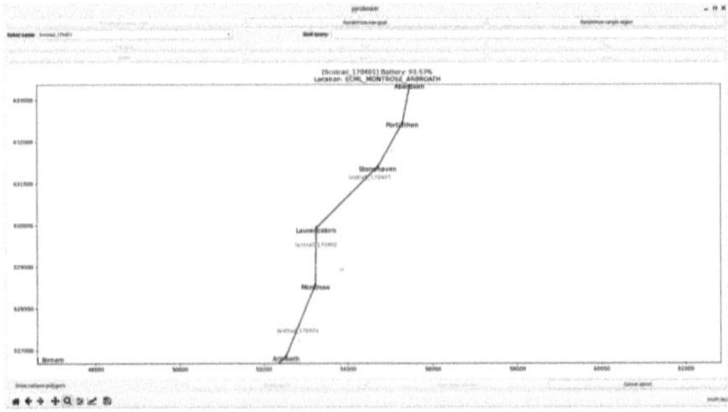

Fig. 2. Example showing three trains respecting safe behaviour.

In our simulation, we used a custom A* planner that utilises NetworkX's `MultiDiGraph` to plan a path between stations. This served two benefits: a significant reduction in the project's load time compared to the standard path planning algorithms offered in Pyrobosim, and an ability to increase the size of the simulation environment with little effect on the load time. Stations are denoted as nodes within the digraph, and rail lines connecting the stations are denoted as edges.

Route Train. Robots have access to a `/route_train` action. This action is designed to move a train (robot) from its current location within the world to a destination provided within the action request. The action ends successfully when the robot reaches the destination station.

Service Timetable. Robots have access to a `/follow_service_timetable` action. This action moves trains autonomously based on a live schedule from the Real-TimeTrains Pull API[4]. The `RailTrafficScheduler` node contains a callable service to retrieve the next (unfulfilled) train service to depart from a particular station, and another callable service to retrieve the details of a particular train service (including a list of stations that the service calls at, between the origin and destination). The Follow Service Timetable action makes use of the `RailTrafficScheduler` node services to create a route between the origin and destination, calling at intermediate stations along the way. This action ends successfully if there are no further services leaving a station from which the robot is currently located.

Freight Movement. Freight can be spawned within the environment by publishing the message `enabled: true` to the topic `/toggle_freight_spawning` at runtime. Freight will continue spawning until the user requests that spawning stops by publishing a message to the same topic with the contents `enabled: false`. As soon as freight objects are spawned within the robotic environment, all trains are free to collect and shunt freight objects between stations. Trains first 'claim' a freight object that has spawned within the environment, collect the freight object, and then deliver it to another station within the simulated network. This task serves to simulate the movement of rail freight.

3   Initial Evaluation

As an initial evaluation, we investigated the behaviour of the freight collection and delivery task in relation to the number of trains in the network. We performed experiments with 1 to 10 trains. In this experiment, the trains spawn at Glasgow Central. They have to collect and deliver 10 different freight objects, as listed in Table 1.

---

[4] https://www.realtimetrains.co.uk/about/developer/pull/docs/   Accessed: 10/09/ 2025.

Table 1. Freight objects spawned for the experiments.

Freight Object	Origin	Destination
1	Aberdeen	Glasgow Queen Street
2	Dundee	Kirkcaldy
3	Edinburgh Waverley	Dundee
4	Glasgow Central	Fort William
5	Inverness	Perth
6	Perth	Stirling
7	Stirling	Edinburgh Waverley
8	Fort William	Inverness
9	Kirkcaldy	Aberdeen
10	Dunfermline City	Glasgow Queen Street

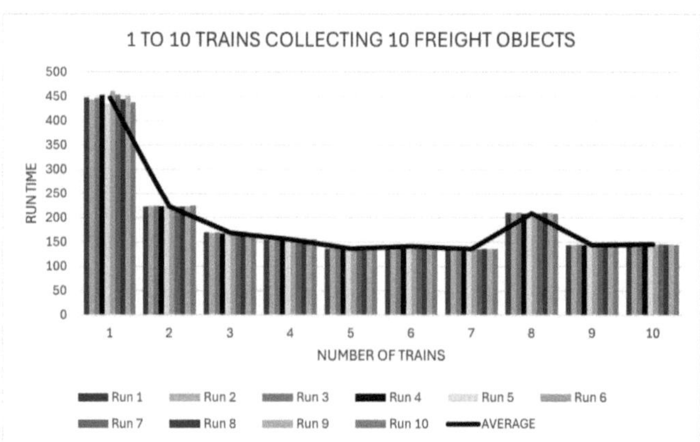

Fig. 3. Runtime execution results in seconds of 1 to 10 trains collecting 10 freight objects, average of 10 runs.

We performed the test 10 times for each configuration (different number of trains) and calculated the average execution time. The results are illustrated in Fig. 3. Adding additional trains gradually improves the execution time as trains can be distributed and assigned different freight objects. However, this trend stops at five trains. At that point, adding more trains can lead to some of the railway sections being blocked to ensure safe behaviour; therefore, any time gained by adding more trains is lost by having them waiting for sections to be released. It is also important to note that there is considerable interface lag when spawning more than 8 trains for the freight collection and delivery tasks. At 8 trains, interface lag combined with inefficient pathing caused significant section blocking. Interestingly, at 9 and 10 trains, although interface lag persisted, pathing was more distributed, leading to a slight improvement in execution time.

These results demonstrate how TrafficSim can be used to evaluate the trade-off between train density and network efficiency. By highlighting the point at which additional trains no longer improve throughput, the experiment shows how the tool can support capacity analysis and scenario planning for infrastructure or scheduling decisions.

4   Conclusion

The main contribution of this paper is the realistic depiction of the Scottish Rail Network. Many networks across the world are transitioning to autonomous movement, such as the TfL Docklands Light Railway (DLR) and the Sydney Metro. Creating a high-level simulation of an autonomous system within the Scottish Rail Network has the potential to identify bottlenecks and explore the impact of new rail infrastructure. The TrafficSim package offers various means to simulate rail traffic movement across a network, many of which are by way of customised ROS2 actions, including the use of a live timetable pulled from an online API, and the movement of rail freight across the network.

A key feature of this project is its scope for future work. At present, the station dataset contains all UK rail stations and is geared as such towards the British Rail Network system. The simulation environment currently includes all railway lines and stations within Scotland. However, it can be readily extended by modifying the dataset scripts. Additionally, Pyrobosim's battery model could be utilised to evaluate the range limits of battery-powered trains, like those developed by Hitachi Rail, and the use of charging stations. The incorporation of further AI methods is also possible, such as reinforcement learning to optimise timetable adherence or predictive models to anticipate congestion. Although the TrafficSim package is still in its early stages of development, it demonstrates significant potential as a tool for infrastructure planning and analysis. With further refinement, it could offer valuable insights for organisations such as Network Rail, enabling virtual testing of new routes, service schedules, and freight logistics.

Disclosure of Interests. The authors have no competing interests to declare that are relevant to the content of this article.

References

1. Aredah, A., Fadhloun, K., Rakha, H.: NeTrainSim: a network-level simulator for modeling freight train longitudinal motion and energy consumption. Railway Eng. Sci. **32**, 480–498 (2024). https://doi.org/10.1007/s40534-024-00331-x
2. La, W.G., Kong, L., Muralidhara, S., Nichat, P.: Deepsim: a reinforcement learning environment build toolkit for ROS and gazebo (2022). https://arxiv.org/abs/2205.08034

3. Li, J., Pei, X., Liu, H., Su, S., Tang, T., Hou, T.: A novel train operation simulation system based on intelligent mobile robot and ROS communication network. In: 2022 34th Chinese Control and Decision Conference (CCDC), pp. 97–102 (2022). https://doi.org/10.1109/CCDC55256.2022.10033650
4. Lim, D.W., Noh, J.: Ros 2 application to the safety monitoring of collaborative robots. In: 2024 4th International Conference on Robotics, Automation and Artificial Intelligence (RAAI), pp. 42–46 (2024). https://doi.org/10.1109/RAAI64504.2024.10949565
5. Quigley, M., et al.: ROS: an open-source Robot Operating System. In: ICRA workshop on open source software, p. 5. Kobe, Japan (2009)
6. Srivastava, et al.: Modelling and simulation of railway networks for resilience analysis. In: Computer Security. ESORICS 2022 International Workshops, pp. 308–320. Springer, Cham (2023). https://doi.org/10.1007/978-3-031-25460-4_17

Deep Learning-Driven Identification of Lycra in Textile Blends

Guan-Lin Liu[1]([✉]) [iD], Sergei G. Kazarian[2] [iD], Fengge Gao[3] [iD], and Xiaohong Gao[1] [iD]

[1] Middlesex University, London, UK
g.liu@mdx.ac.uk
[2] Imperial College London, London, UK
[3] Nottingham Trent University, Nottingham, UK

Abstract. Efficient identification and recycling of textiles containing Lycra is crucial due to its adverse environmental impacts, notably marine pollution. This study evaluates the use of Attenuated Total Reflection Fourier Transform Infrared (ATR-FTIR) spectroscopy combined with thermal pre-treatment and deep learning-enhanced microscopic imaging for detecting Lycra in blended textiles. Initial ATR-FTIR spectroscopy measurements on untreated fabrics revealed limitations due to shallow penetration depth and spectral overlap. Thermal pre-treatment significantly improved detection in cotton and polyamide blends but remained ineffective for polyester blends due to overlapping spectral bands. Microscopic images analyzed through a U-Net deep learning architecture provided effective segmentation and identification of Lycra fibers, overcoming spectroscopic limitations. These findings highlight the complementary role of deep learning-based microscopic imaging in textile recycling strategies, enhancing the feasibility of identifying Lycra-containing materials for sustainable waste management.

Keywords: Lycra identification · ATR-FTIR spectroscopy · textile recycling · U-Net segmentation · microscopic imaging

1 Introduction

Synthetic elastomer fibers such as Lycra (spandex/elastane) are extensively used in textile manufacturing due to their elasticity, strength, and durability [1]. Lycra is often blended with other fibers to enhance fabric properties such as comfort, stretchability, and fit. However, the environmental impact of Lycra has raised significant sustainability concerns. Synthetic fibers released into water bodies degrade slowly, contribute to microplastic pollution, and pose severe risks to marine life by ingestion and entanglement. Thus, effective identification and recycling of Lycra-blended textiles are critical steps toward sustainable textile management and reducing environmental harm.

M. Bramer and F. Stahl (Eds.): SGAI-AI 2025, LNAI 16302, pp. 451–457, 2026.
https://doi.org/10.1007/978-3-032-11442-6_35

Recent advances in analytical techniques, notably ATR-FTIR spectroscopy and spectroscopic imaging, have shown promise in non-destructively characterizing and distinguishing complex materials through Principal Component Analysis (PCA) and k-means clustering [2]. However, the intrinsic limitation of ATR-FTIR spectroscopy, its shallow penetration depth, often complicates the identification of fibers embedded below textile surfaces. Consequently, detecting Lycra beneath the surface of blended fabrics presents a significant analytical challenge.

In this research, a classification approach utilizing microscopic data coupled with deep learning is proposed. Figure 1 illustrates locations of Lycra in a microscopic image.

1.1 Materials and Samples

The samples analyzed in this research are textile blends containing Lycra combined with three commonly used fibers: cotton, polyamide, and polyester. Standardized samples were prepared, each clearly labelled and characterized for controlled testing. The optic microscope was utilized to examine all the samples. ATR-FTIR spectroscopic imaging was employed to investigate samples with different combinations: cotton/Lycra, polyamide/Lycra, polyester/Lycra, while ATR-FTIR spectroscopy was employed to investigate polyester/Lycra with different concentration (results are not shown in this paper).

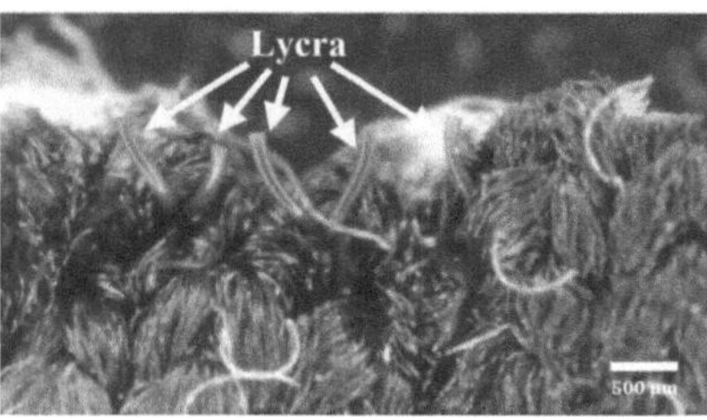

Fig. 1. An illustration of Lycra among other textile fabrics.

1.2 ATR-FTIR Spectroscopic Analysis

Analyses of polyester/elastane sample utilized a Bruker Alpha ATR-FTIR spectrometer equipped with a single-reflection diamond crystal. Spectra were recorded within the region of 4000–600 cm^{-1}) with a resolution of 4 cm^{-1} and averaged over 64 scans. Spectroscopic imaging was performed with an Agilent Cary 620 FTIR microscope coupled to an Agilent Varian 670 spectrometer, equipped with a germanium crystal and a focal plane array detector (64 × 64 pixels). Micro ATR-FTIR spectroscopic imaging provided spatially resolved spectral data, but spectral interference issues persisted, particularly in polyester blends.

1.3 Thermal Treatment for Enhanced Lycra Detection

To overcome penetration depth limitations, textile samples underwent controlled thermal treatment at temperatures above 250 °C. Melting was carefully conducted to expose embedded elastane fibers. Post-treatment samples were reanalyzed using ATR-FTIR spectroscopy, which successfully detected characteristic elastane spectral bands. However, spectral interference remained significant in polyester/elastane blends due to overlapping bands at aromatic ester C-C-O stretch frequencies.

1.4 Microscopic Image Analysis Using Deep Learning

Due to limitations in spectral discrimination, particularly in polyester/Lycra blends, a supplementary approach involving optical microscopy coupled with deep learning-based image analysis was implemented. Textile microscopic images were captured and analyzed using MATLAB's imageLabeler and a UNet deep learning architecture [3]. This methodology involved labelling fiber types within captured images, training the UNet model, and classifying fibers within textile samples. The original images are under

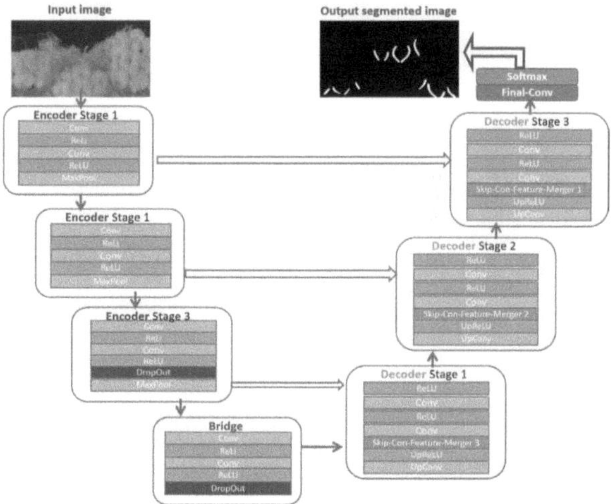

Fig. 2. The U-net architecture applied to segment Lycra material.

gone annotation process to label Lycra content on an image. The annotation tool is applied Visual Image Annotation Tool (VIA) developed at Oxford university [4]. Figure 2 illustrates the results of annotation for one input image, where an output segmented image is created. The white polygons refer to 'Lycra', the rest are 'background'. A total of 505 images are applied with all their masks having some Lycra contents. That is if there are no Lycra labelled in an image, that image is discarded. Figure 2 schematically presents the deep learning network U-net applied in this study to segment Lycra microscopic images, hence to detect the presence of Lycra materials. No segment refers to no Lycra material in the image.

1.5 Evaluation Methods

The accuracy of classification and detection is evaluated using common statistical measures such as accuracy, recall (sensitivity), and specificity, whereas segmentation is assessed using the intersection over union (IoU), the **de facto** gold standard for evaluating computer-aided systems. These metrics are defined in Eqs. (1)–(3), where $P =$

Positive, N = Negative, TP = True Positive, FP = False Positive, TN = True Negative, and FN = False Negative.

Sensitivity, or the probability of detection, measures the proportion of actual positives that are correctly identified [5]. For example, it reflects the percentage of Lycra regions correctly labeled as "Lycra" by the computer system. Specificity, or the true negative rate, measures the proportion of actual negatives (i.e., non-Lycra regions, or background) correctly labeled as not being cancer. Both specificity and sensitivity are used to evaluate classification performance, along with overall accuracy.

$$Accuracy = \frac{TP + TN}{P + N} \tag{1}$$

$$sensitivity = recall = \frac{TP}{TP + FN} \tag{2}$$

$$specificity = \frac{TN}{TN + FP} \tag{3}$$

In addition, the overlap between 2 boundaries of boxes is quantified using the intersection over union (IoU) as calculated in Eq. (4), which ascertains how much predicted boundary overlaps with the ground truth (the real object boundary).

$$IoU = \frac{area\ of\ overlap}{area\ of\ union} \tag{4}$$

2 Results

2.1 Spectroscopic Imaging

The ATR-FTIR chemical image of the untreated polyamide/Lycra sample maps the distribution of polyamide. It was generated by integrating the absorbance between 1510 cm^{-1} and 1590 cm^{-1}, corresponding to the in-plane N–H bending vibration of polyamide. A representative single-pixel spectrum is shown in Fig. 3c. At this stage no elastane (Lycra) signal is detected, which is consistent with the shallow (~1–2 μm) penetration depth of the ATR crystal.

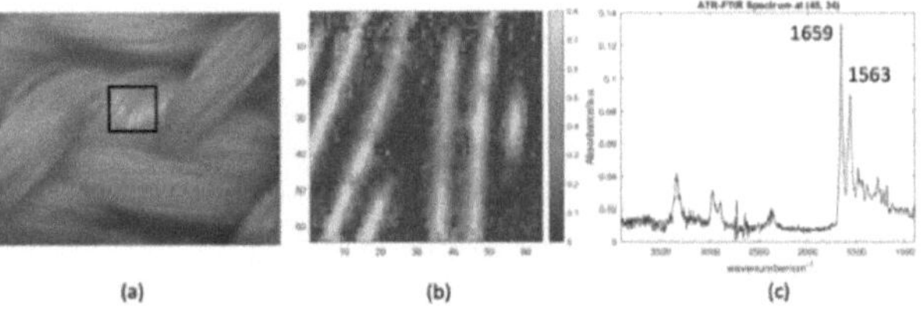

Fig. 3. (a) Microscopic image of untreated polyamide/Lycra sample where the black square displays the area identified using ATR-FTIR imaging. (b) ATR-FTIR chemical image of the sample showing distribution of polyamide. (c) ATR-FTIR spectra extract-ed from pixels of chemical image from (b)

After heat treatment (>250 °C) the optical micrograph (Fig. 4a) shows that the fibers have collapsed into a fused film. In the corresponding ATR-FTIR image (Fig. 4d), elastane (Lycra) becomes visible when the absorbance between 1,090 cm^{-1} and 1,160 cm^{-1}, assigned to the ether C–O–C stretching mode [6], is plotted; the associated spectrum is given in Fig. 4e. The cotton/Lycra sample behaves similarly (data not shown here): elas-

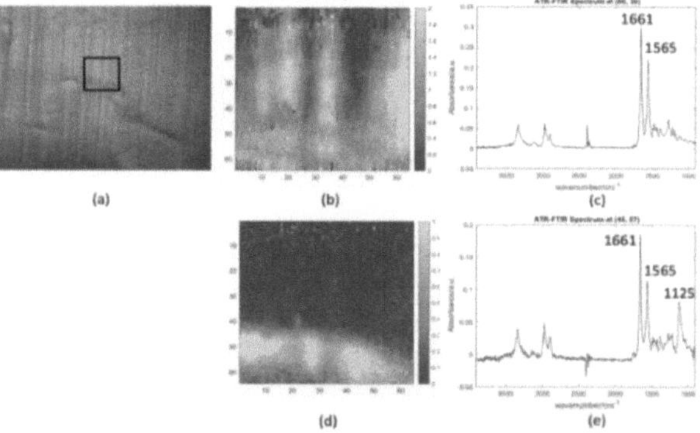

Fig. 4. (a) Microscopic image of the polyamide/Lycra sample after the heat treatment. ATR-FTIR chemical image of the melted sample showing distribution of (b) polyamide and (d) elastane. Extracted spectra representing (c) polyamide and (e) Lycra

tane is detectable only after heat treatment, because the cotton fibers char while the molten elastane migrates to the surface and enters the evanescent field.

In contrast, elastane remains undetectable in the polyester/Lycra blend even after melting (data not shown). The characteristic elastane band is obscured by the strong aromatic-ester C–C–O stretching band of polyester, preventing reliable identification.

2.2 Microscopic Imaging Coupled with Deep Learning Training

Table 1 lists results for accuracy, IoU (Intersection over Union), and MeanBFScore. The model achieves an accuracy of 0.63468 for Lycra and 0.92336 for background, suggesting it can identify and localize Lycra in textile blends from microscopic image data. The Mean BF Score refers to the average Boundary F1 (BF) score, a metric used to evaluate how well the predicted boundaries in image segmentation align with the ground-truth boundaries. It is the harmonic mean of precision and recall for boundary matching.

- Precision (also called positive predictive value) is the fraction of relevant instances among the retrieved instances.
- Recall (also known as sensitivity) is the fraction of relevant instances that were retrieved.
- The F1 score is the harmonic mean of precision and recall.

Figures 5a and 5b present the confusion matrix and the per-image IoU, respectively. A confusion matrix evaluates a classification model by comparing predicted labels with ground truth (true positives, false positives, true negatives, and false negatives). IoU is the ratio of the intersection area to the union area of the ground-truth and predicted bounding boxes. The per-image IoU distribution shows that, on average, approximately 100 images have about 60% overlap, while fewer than 10 images achieve 90% IoU. Figure 6 shows predictions for 10 randomly selected samples, illustrating how the trained model identifies Lycra in each microscopic image.

Table 1. Results with regards to Accuracy, IoU and MeanBFScore.

	Accuracy	IoU	Mean BF Score
Lycra	0.63468	0.23932	0.33037
background	0.92336	0.90797	0.59249

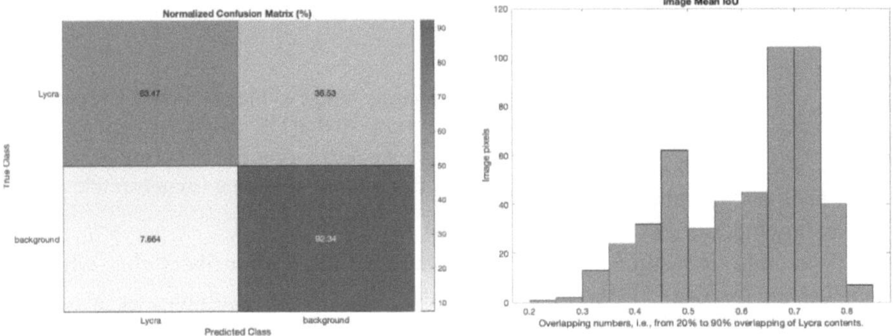

Fig. 5. (a) The confusion matrix (b) The Mean IoU for each image.

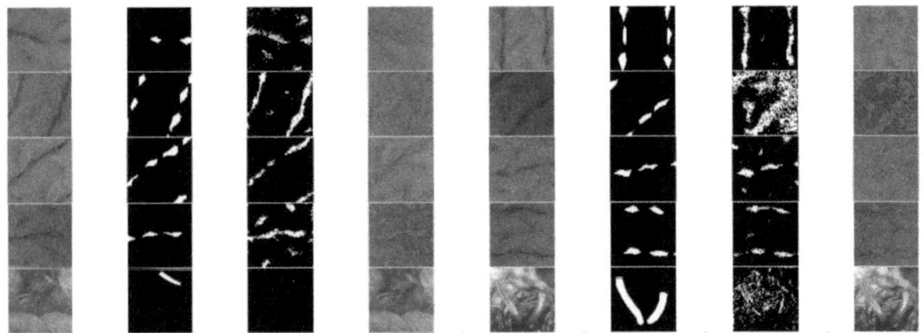

Fig. 6. Prediction of randomly selected 10 samples

3 Conclusion

This work applies deep learning technology to detect and segment Lycra material presented in a clothing. The initial results demonstrate potentials to detect Lycra accurately to allow the task of recycling more efficient. Future work will include contain more samples, in particular textiles with less than 20% Lycra content (the current samples have 21% Lycra according to the labels attached to the materials). In addition, a mobile application will be developed to expedite the deployment of the developed systems.

Acknowledgments. This project is funded by the British Council under Early Research Fellowship Program (2024–2025). Their financial support is gratefully acknowledged.

Disclosure of Interests. The authors have no competing interests to declare that are relevant to the content of this article.

References

1. Teegarden, D.M.: Polymer Chemistry: Introduction to an Indispensable Science, p. 149. NSTA Press (2004). ISBN 9780873552219
2. Liu, G.L., Chen, T.-C., Kazarian, S.G.: Identification of black and white antique photographs via non-destructive microscopic and spectroscopic techniques coupled with chemometric approaches. Microchem. J. **200**, 110297 (2024)
3. Ronneberger, O., Fischer, P., Brox, T.: U-Net: convolutional networks for biomedical image segmentation (2015). arXiv:1505.04597v1
4. Dutta, A. and Zisserman, A.: The VIA annotation software for images, audio and video. In: Proceedings of the 27th ACM International Conference on Multimedia (MM '19), October 21–25 (2019)
5. Altman, D.G., Bland, J.M.: Diagnostic tests. 1: Sensitivity and specificity. BMJ. **308**(6943), 1552 (1994)
6. O'Connell, J., Dabrowa, B., Firth, J., Mansfield, L., Paterson, F., Sawicki, M. & Vearing., E.: AICCM special interest groups—key issues for the twenty-first century. AICCM Bulletin. **41**(1), 35–44 (2020)

Evaluation of Raw Signal
and Feature-Based Deep Learning Models
for Multi-Label ECG Diagnosis
on PTB-XL

Calvin Holloway, Lakshmi Babu Saheer, and Mahdi Maktab Dar[✉]

Anglia Ruskin University, Cambridge, UK
`mahdi.maktabdar@aru.ac.uk`

Abstract. In recent years, AI, specifically deep learning, has advanced automated analysis of the ECG signal. This study compares raw signal processing against pre-extracted features for multi-label diagnostic superclass classification using the public PTB-XL dataset and its PTB-XL+ extended dataset with feature sets (Uni-G, 12SL). Three deep learning architectures, namely, CNN-based signal-only, dense network features-only, and combined multi-modal models, have been evaluated using standard PTB-XL splits. Performance results on the test set show that the combined Uni-G/12SL feature-only models performed well (Macro F1 = 0.73, AUC = 0.92). However, it slightly underperformed a signal-only CNN (Macro F1 = 0.75, AUC = 0.93). The combined model performed best, but with only marginal gains over the signal-only model. These results suggest pre-extracted clinical features capture much of the predictive information, and integrating raw signals requires more sophisticated architectures to yield significant benefits.

Keywords: Electrocardiogram (ECG) · PTB-XL · Deep Learning · Multi-label Classification

1 Introduction

The 12-lead electrocardiogram (ECG) is an essential tool for diagnosing cardiovascular diseases. However, manual interpretation is time-consuming and requires expert knowledge, motivating the development of automated analysis systems. Recent advances in deep learning (DL) have enabled models such as convolutional neural networks (CNNs) to learn diagnostic patterns directly from raw ECG signals, achieving performance comparable to human experts [1,2]. Despite these advances, clinical workflows still largely rely on derived, standardised features computed by algorithms such as Uni-G [3] and 12SL [4], which remain preferred for their interpretability and efficiency. The public PTB-XL dataset [5] together with its PTB-XL+ extension [6] provides both raw 12-lead signals and pre-extracted clinical features (Uni-G, 12SL), enabling direct comparisons between raw- and feature-based models and simple multi-modal fusion.

This enables the investigation of whether raw signals provide additional diagnostic information beyond that captured by standard features, and whether combining both modalities within a multi-modal architecture can enhance classification performance, particularly in challenging multi-label tasks with imbalanced class distributions. Although CNNs on raw signals and models on feature sets have each been studied separately, there is limited evidence directly comparing their effectiveness on PTB-XL or assessing their complementarity. It remains unclear whether raw signals add meaningful diagnostic value over clinical features, especially for broad superclass classification. Moreover, prior studies have not systematically evaluated simple, effective multi-modal fusion strategies. This study addresses these gaps by comparing three deep learning approaches for multi-label classification of ECG diagnostic superclasses on PTB-XL: (i) a CNN trained on raw 12-lead signals, (ii) a dense network trained on Uni-G and 12SL features, and (iii) a multi-modal architecture combining both. Performance is assessed using Macro F1 and Macro AUC with tuned thresholds. Results show that pre-extracted features provide a strong baseline, with raw signals offering only modest gains for superclass tasks but larger benefits for rare subclasses. These findings highlight the trade-offs between complexity and accuracy, and the potential of combining modalities when more granular diagnostic detail is required.

2   Literature Review

Automated ECG analysis has progressed substantially in recent years, largely due to advances in machine learning, particularly deep learning (DL). The availability of large annotated datasets such as PTB-XL [5] has facilitated reproducible research and rigorous evaluation of DL models. This section reviews prior work on ECG classification using PTB-XL, contrasting raw signal and feature-based approaches, multi-modal fusion strategies, and addressing class imbalance and thresholding challenges. The PTB-XL dataset [5] contains over 21,800 12-lead ECGs with diagnostic labels and predefined splits. Its extension, PTB-XL+ [6] augments PTB-XL with features extracted by commercial algorithms such as Uni-G [3] and 12SL [4], as well as open-source tools. Benchmark studies on PTB-XL demonstrate that CNN variants, including ResNet and InceptionTime, achieve strong performance—up to AUC $\approx$ 0.93 for superclass classification [7,8]. Although recurrent and transformer-based models have also been explored, CNNs remain a reliable baseline. The PTB-XL+ dataset enables comparison with feature-based models. Clinical features extracted by Uni-G and 12SL achieve competitive results, with AUCs of 0.87 to 0.89 [9], though slightly below CNNs on raw signals. Hybrid models combining CNNs on signals and dense networks on features have demonstrated potential synergy, occasionally outperforming single-modality models [10]. To exploit complementary information, multi-modal architectures typically use parallel branches for signals and features, with fusion via concatenation [11]. More sophisticated strategies, such as attention-based fusion [12], have also been proposed but are not yet standard.

In addition, ECG classification faces challenges from severe class imbalance and the need for optimal thresholding. Approaches such as asymmetric loss functions [13] and threshold tuning [14] have been shown to improve performance, but are not universally adopted. In summary, prior work has established strong baselines for both raw signal and feature-based ECG classification, and hybrid models show promise. Yet, systematic evaluation of the added value of combining modalities, particularly under multi-label and imbalanced settings, remains sparse.

3   Methodology

This section describes the dataset, preprocessing, model architectures, training process, and evaluation procedures used to compare raw signal, feature-based, and combined approaches for multi-label ECG classification. The methodology builds on established practices in ECG analysis [5,7]. This study uses the publicly available PTB-XL dataset [5], comprising 21,837 10-second-long, 12-lead ECG recordings sampled at 500 Hz from 18,885 patients. Each recording is annotated with SCP-ECG statements, aggregated into five diagnostic superclasses: Normal (NORM), Myocardial Infarction (MI), Conduction Disturbance (CD), ST/T Change (STTC), and Hypertrophy (HYP), alongside 23 subclasses. For feature-based models, we utilised the PTB-XL+ extension [6], which provides numerical feature vectors extracted using commercial algorithms Uni-G [3] and 12SL [4]. Missing feature values were imputed with zeros as done in prior work [9]. The class distributions exhibit significant imbalance across both superclasses and subclasses. Labels were binarised in a multi-label format. Raw ECG signals were loaded using the WFDB library [15], truncated or zero-padded to 5000 samples to standardise duration. Features were normalised using *StandardScaler* fitted on the training set. We followed the dataset's predefined 10-fold splits: folds 1–8 for training, fold 9 for validation, and fold 10 for testing [7]. We evaluated three deep learning architectures:

Signal-only Model: A ResNet-based CNN [16] processes the 12-lead ECG signals. The architecture consists of an initial Conv1D+Pooling layer, followed by four ResNet stages with increasing filter sizes (64, 128, 256, 512), Batch Normalisation (BN), ReLU activations, and residual connections. Global Average Pooling produces a 512-dimensional representation, which is passed through a dense block (256 units) and sigmoid outputs for superclasses and subclasses.

Feature-only Model: A Multi-Layer Perceptron (MLP) processes the Uni-G and 12SL feature vectors. Two dense layers (256 and 128 units) with BN, ReLU, and Dropout (0.4) produce a 128-dimensional representation, followed by sigmoid outputs.

Combined Model: This multi-modal architecture integrates both modalities. The signal and feature branches described above run in parallel, and their outputs are concatenated and passed through a dense fusion block (256 units) with BN, ReLU, Dropout, and sigmoid outputs. Models were implemented using TensorFlow and trained using the Adam optimiser paired with a binary cross-entropy loss function. To emphasise superclass performance in the combined

Table 1. Superclass classification performance on the test set (fold 10). Best results per metric are highlighted in bold.

Model	Macro F1	Weighted F1	Macro AUC
Combined	**0.749**	**0.778**	**0.927**
Signal-Only	0.745	**0.778**	**0.927**
Feature-Only	0.733	0.762	0.922

model, we applied weighted losses as recommended for multi-label tasks [13]. Training was performed for up to 50 epochs with a batch size of 64, employing early stopping (patience=10, monitoring validation AUC, restoring best weights) and learning rate reduction on plateau (patience=3, factor=0.2, minimum learning rate=10^{-6}). Custom data generators were used for efficiency. Models were primarily evaluated on superclass predictions from the test set using fold 10 as the heldâĂŚout test set. Following [14], optimal per-class decision thresholds were tuned on the validation set to maximise F1-score. These thresholds were then applied to binarise test predictions. We report per-class precision, recall, F1-score, and the macro-averaged and weighted F1 and AUC scores, consistent with standard practice [7].

4   Results and Discussion

Table 1 summarises the performance of all three models on the five diagnostic superclasses. The Combined model achieved the best overall results, with a Macro F1 of 0.749, Weighted F1 of 0.778, and Macro AUC of 0.927. The Signal-Only CNN performed nearly as well (Macro F1 = 0.745, Macro AUC = 0.927), while the Feature-Only MLP trailed slightly (Macro F1 = 0.733, Macro AUC = 0.922). These findings confirm that pre-extracted Uni-G and 12SL features alone provide a strong baseline, consistent with prior work [9]. The raw-signal CNN matches or slightly exceeds the feature-based model, aligning with benchmarks reported in [7]. Combining the two modalities yields a modest improvement in F1 score, suggesting some complementary information exists, though the improvement is limited under the tested architecture. The per-class F1-scores for the Combined model highlight variation in performance across superclasses. The model achieved its highest F1-score for the *Normal* (NORM) class (0.86), followed by *STTC* (0.76), *CD* (0.76), and *MI* (0.74). Performance was lowest for *HYP* (0.62), in agreement with earlier findings that hypertrophy is particularly challenging to identify from ECG signals alone [8]. This variation underscores the importance of per-class threshold tuning, which improved precision-recall trade-offs, particularly for minority classes, as also observed in [17]. Although the main focus was on superclasses, models were also evaluated on the more granular 23 diagnostic subclasses. As expected, overall performance was lower due to extreme class imbalance and the subtlety of subclass-specific patterns. Table 2 shows that the Combined model achieved the highest Macro F1 (0.362)

Table 2. Subclass classification performance on the test set (fold 10).

Model	Macro F1	Weighted F1	Macro AUC
Combined	**0.362**	**0.618**	**0.865**
Signal-Only	0.336	0.616	0.857
Feature-Only	0.344	0.619	0.850

and Macro AUC (0.865), outperforming both unimodal models by a noticeable margin. The Signal-Only model performed worst, indicating that high-level features are particularly valuable for rare subclass detection. Notably, the Combined model achieved reasonable scores on common subclasses such as anterior MI (AMI) and inferior MI (IMI), but performance remained near zero for rare conditions (e.g., posterior MI, severe hypertrophy), consistent with observations in [10]. Applying per-class optimal thresholds significantly improved classification results compared to using the default 0.5 threshold. This tuning particularly benefitted minority classes, improving the macro-averaged F1 and AUC. This result supports previous findings that threshold tuning is crucial in multi-label, imbalanced settings [13,14]. These results highlight several key insights. First, pre-extracted clinical features (Uni-G/12SL) capture much of the diagnostic information necessary for broad superclass classification, making the Feature-Only model an efficient and reliable baseline. Second, while the Signal-Only model performs slightly better, the improvement is modest, suggesting that raw signals encode additional patterns but may require deeper or more sophisticated architectures to fully exploit them [18]. Third, combining both modalities provides only a small gain for superclasses but more substantial benefits for subclass detection, demonstrating the potential complementarity of features and signals. The findings imply that feature-based models remain practical for routine diagnostic tasks due to their simplicity and speed. However, for more nuanced subclass-level tasks or highly imbalanced settings, incorporating raw signals in a multi-modal framework can uncover subtle diagnostic cues, albeit at greater computational cost. Future work could explore advanced fusion strategies [12], attention mechanisms, or transformer-based designs [18] to better integrate complementary information. Furthermore, data augmentation and synthetic minority oversampling (SMOTE) [19] may help mitigate extreme imbalance in subclass prediction.

5   Conclusion

This study systematically evaluated the relative and combined contributions of raw ECG signals and pre-extracted clinical features for multi-label diagnostic classification on the PTB-XL dataset [5,6]. Addressing the gap in prior research [9,10], which lacked a direct comparison of unimodal and multi-modal approaches, we assessed three architectures: a CNN trained on raw signals, an

MLP on Uni-G/12SL features, and a simple multi-modal fusion of both. Our findings show that high-quality clinical features alone provide a strong and efficient baseline for superclass classification, performing comparably to more complex signal-based models. Adding a raw signal branch yields only marginal improvement for broad diagnostic categories but substantially enhances performance on rare and subtle subclasses. This suggests that while clinical features capture most of the discriminative information needed for routine tasks, complementary information in raw signals becomes valuable for more granular and imbalanced classification problems.

References

1. Liu, X., Wang, H., Li, Z., Qin, L.: Deep learning in ECG diagnosis: a review. Knowl.-Based Syst. **227**, 107187 (2021)
2. Sevakula, R.K., Au-Yeung, W.T.M., Singh, J.P., Heist, E.K., Isselbacher, E.M., Armoundas, A.A.: State-of-the-art machine learning techniques aiming to improve patient outcomes pertaining to the cardiovascular system. J. Am. Heart Assoc. **9**(4), e013924 (2020)
3. Macfarlane, P.W., Devine, B., Clark, E.: The university of glasgow (Uni-G) ECG analysis program. In: Computers in Cardiology. IEEE (2014)
4. Langlois-Carbonneau, V., Dufresne, F., Labbé, È., Hamelin, K., Berbiche, D., Gosselin, S.: Safety and accuracy of the computer interpretation of normal ECGs at triage. Canadian J. Emergency Med. (2024)
5. Wagner, P., et al.: PTB-XL, a large publicly available electrocardiography dataset. Sci. Data **7**(1), 1–15 (2020)
6. Strodthoff, N., et al.: PTB-XL+, a comprehensive electrocardiographic feature dataset. Sci. Data **10**, 279 (2023)
7. Strodthoff, N., Wagner, P., Schaeffter, T., Samek, W.: Deep learning for ECG analysis: benchmarks and insights from PTB-XL. IEEE J. Biomed. Heal. Inf. **25**(5), 1519–1528 (2020)
8. Ismail Fawaz, H., et al.: InceptionTime: finding alexnet for time series classification. Data Min. Knowl. Disc. **34**(6), 1936–1962 (2020). https://doi.org/10.1007/s10618-020-00710-y
9. Smigiel, S., Pałczyński, K., Ledziński, D.: ECG signal classification using deep learning techniques based on the PTB-XL dataset. Entropy **23**(9), 1121 (2021)
10. Dey, M., Omar, N., Ullah, M.A.: Temporal feature-based classification into myocardial infarction and other CVDs merging CNN and Bi-LSTM from ECG signal. IEEE Sens. J. **21**(19), 21688–21695 (2021)
11. Golrizkhatami, Z., Acan, A.: ECG classification using three-level fusion of different feature descriptors. Expert Syst. Appl. **114**, 54–64 (2018)
12. Yang, K., et al.: ECG-LM: understanding electrocardiogram with a large language model. Heal. Data Sci. **5**, 0221 (2025)
13. Ridnik, T., et al.: Asymmetric loss for multi-label classification. In: Proceedings of the IEEE/CVF International Conference on Computer Vision, pp. 82–91 (2021)
14. Coenen, F., Leng, P., Zhang, L.: Threshold tuning for improved classification association rule mining. In: Knowledge-Based Intelligent Information and Engineering Systems, pp. 216–225. Springer (2005)

15. Moody, G.B., Mark, R.G., Goldberger, A.L.: PhysioNet: a research resource for studies of complex physiologic and biomedical signals. In: Computers in Cardiology 2000. vol. 27 (Cat. 00CH37163), pp. 179–182. IEEE (2000)
16. Targ, S., Almeida, D., Lyman, K.: ResNet in ResNet: generalizing residual architectures. In: arXiv (2016)
17. Liu, Y., et al.: Automatic multi-label ECG classification with category imbalance and cost-sensitive thresholding. Biosensors **11**(11), 453 (2021)
18. Hu, R., Chen, J., Zhou, L.: A transformer-based deep neural network for arrhythmia detection using continuous ECG signals. Comput. Biol. Med. **144**, 105325 (2022)
19. Chawla, N.V., Bowyer, K.W., Hall, L.O., Kegelmeyer, W.P.: SMOTE: synthetic minority over-sampling technique. J. Artif. Intell. Res. **16**, 321–357 (2002)

Mitigating Western Bias in Music Genre Classification: A Contrastive Learning Approach for Greek Music

George Kritsovas[✉], Lorenzo Garbagna, Lakshmi Babu Saheer, and Mahdi Maktabdar Oghaz

Anglia Ruskin University, Cambridge, UK
gk541@student.aru.ac.uk, lorenzo.garbagna@student.anglia.ac.uk,
{lakshmi.babu-saheer,mahdi.maktabdar}@aru.ac.uk

Abstract. Current state-of-the-art (SOTA) music genre classification models exhibit significant Western bias due to predominant training on Western datasets, causing suboptimal performance on non-Western genres with distinct characteristics. This research introduces a contrastive pretraining approach targeting Greek music genres, including Laiko, Rebetiko, and Entehno. Three deep learning architectures are tested: custom Convolutional Neural Networks (CNNs), hybrid Convolutional Recurrent Neural Networks (CRNNs), and pretrained transformers. Models first undergo contrastive pretraining on 13,000 unlabeled Greek tracks before fine-tuning on 1,033 labeled tracks. Macro-F1 (unweighted mean of per-class F1 scores) for the custom CNN and CRNN increased by 0.04 and 0.01, respectively, after the contrastive step and reduced convergence time, demonstrating its effectiveness in data-scarce scenarios. However, no measurable improvement was observed on the transformers, likely due to restricted batch size for effective contrastive learning.

Keywords: Music genre classification · Transformers · Deep learning · Audio representation learning · Self-supervised · Contrastive Learning

1 Introduction

Music Information Retrieval (MIR) has made significant advances through deep learning, particularly in music genre classification (MGC). However, current SOTA models suffer from an important limitation: they are trained predominantly on Western music datasets ([12,14]), creating an inherent bias that affects performance on other musical traditions [5]. Makris et al. [14] note this as an underlying issue, and introduce the Greek Music Dataset (GMD), containing 1400 instances of professionally annotated sample songs to enable applications of MIR on this distinct musical paradigm. This bias manifests itself in CNN kernel weights and RNN parameters optimized specifically to distinguish Western genres, leading to reduced performance in fundamentally different musical

M. Bramer and F. Stahl (Eds.): SGAI-AI 2025, LNAI 16302, pp. 465–471, 2026.
https://doi.org/10.1007/978-3-032-11442-6_37

styles with unique idiosyncrasies. Greek music presents a compelling case study to address and overcome it, with traditional genres such as Laiko, Rebetiko, and Entehno, which possess distinct musical characteristics that differ significantly from the pop, rock, and classical genres that dominate most established datasets. The scarcity of labeled data for such specialized genres further compounds the challenge. Contrastive learning has emerged as a powerful pre-training technique for addressing data scarcity in computer vision tasks [2]. By learning representations through maximizing similarity between augmented views of the same sample while minimizing similarity between different samples, contrastive methods can extract meaningful features from unlabeled data. [17] was first to adapt it in MIR, with many more successful adaptations following ([3,6,7,10,15,20,22]). Yet its application to non-Western music genres and its effectiveness in addressing bias concerns remain underexplored [12]. This paper contributes by providing a systematic evaluation of contrastive pretraining on Greek music genres across multiple architectures. By showcasing the effectiveness of contrastive pretraining, the research paves the way for more memory-efficient techniques like Momentum Contrast (MoCo) to be utilized as a domain adaptation technique on top of transfer learning in MIR for underrepresented music.

2   Related Work

The MGC deep learning era demonstrates significant architectural advancements built on a narrow cultural foundation. The foundational GTZAN dataset [19], like most subsequent collections, focuses on Western genres [18]. Mehta et al. [16] noted that merely 5.7% of total hours in major music datasets represent non-Western genres, causing performance disparities for underrepresented styles. CNN models on log-mel spectrograms achieved human-level accuracy (70%) on GTZAN, but parameters remained optimized for Western music. Subsequent CRNNs captured temporal dynamics, surpassing CNN-only models on datasets like GTZAN and MagnaTagATune [4]. The Audio Spectrogram Transformer (AST), leveraging self-attention, further improved performance but still relied on predominantly Western datasets like AudioSet [8,9].

Transfer learning commonly facilitates practical deployment, especially when labeled data are scarce. MusicNN and PANNs (Pre-trained Audio Neural Networks), trained on large-scale datasets, yield strong performance after minimal fine-tuning [13]. However, extensive fine-tuning often fails to fully realign low-level filters when source and target domains differ significantly [21]. Self-supervised approaches, particularly contrastive learning, have emerged as promising techniques for de-biasing models without labeled datasets. Popularized by SimCLR [2], contrastive methods train encoders to maximize similarity between augmented versions of the same sample and minimize similarity with different samples. Researchers [17] introduced playlist-based contrastive learning, leveraging semantic similarities between playlist co-occurrences. Others [1] further demonstrated contrastive pretraining with playlist-based positive pairs enhanced multilabel tagging for genre, mood, and instrument recognition. Their findings highlight how domain-guided pair selection, akin to our approach with Greek tracks, better adapts encoders beyond Western-centric datasets. While contrastive learning shows potential for music domain adaptation, applications to non-Western music and systematic multi-architecture evaluations remain limited, motivating the current study on MGC.

3   Methodology

Labeled Dataset: This study uses the GMD dataset, which covers 8 Greek genre classes: Laiko, Rebetiko, Entehno, Rock, Mod Laiko, Enallaktiko, Pop and Hip-hop. We retained 1,033 of the original 1,400 GMD tracks whose YouTube links were still accessible, converting each to WAV with FFmpeg. The data set was split into train-test sets in the ratio of 70:30. Class distribution and train-test balance are presented in Fig. 1. The validation data was $\approx 22\%$ of the train dataset to get a representative sample size from each class.

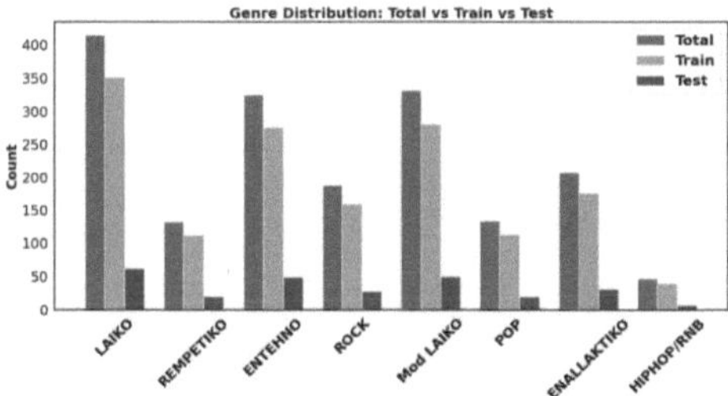

Fig. 1. Label distribution of GMD.

Contrastive Dataset: To tackle data scarcity, a corpus of 13,000 unlabeled Greek music tracks was created. Initially collecting 9,000 unique songs via Spotify API and assisted by ChatGPT artist queries, the dataset was supplemented with concert and multi-artist recordings, acknowledging potential false negatives. A small batch size (46) and 10% duplication rate limited training interference.

Data Preprocessing: Audio was converted to mel spectrograms. Configurations with 80, 96, and 120 mel bins and segment lengths from 3 to 30 s were evaluated. Final experiments used 30-second segments with 96 mel bins (96×1292), chosen based on empirical performance during hyperparameter tuning.

Three architectures of varying complexity are systematically evaluated:

Custom CNN: Empirically designed CNN incorporating attention mechanisms, optimized through experimental hyperparameter tuning.

Hybrid CRNN: Hybrid system with convolutional layers for feature extraction with recurrent layers for temporal modeling, integrating attention mechanisms.

AST: A pretrained transformer model adapted for audio classification tasks.

CNNs and CRNNs were selected to evaluate the impact of contrastive learning as an effective pre-training step for lightweight deep learning models. For AST, the goal was to assess whether additional pre-training could enhance already pre-trained AudioSet-based weights. AST's widespread adoption and pre-trained nature made it ideal for analyzing biases to Western music and assessing domain adaptation capability. A weighted focal loss addressed dataset imbalance, and the Adam optimizer was used for training. The ReLU activation function was chosen for the custom models and the classification head of AST.

Contrastive Pretraining: Following SimCLR principles, models were pre-trained using contrastive learning on the unlabeled audio tracks for 30 epochs with a batch size of 86 (CNN) and 48 (CRNN). The architecture consisted of an encoder with a projection head, which was discarded after pretraining. The batch sizes were dictated by GPU constraints, and the AST was trained on a batch size of 4. With 4 samples, NT-Xent loss provides only six negatives per anchor, far below the 256-plus recommended by [2], limiting representation quality. Positive pairs consisted of differently augmented versions of the same audio segment; negative pairs used augmented segments from different tracks. The training utilized the normalized temperature-scaled cross-entropy loss (NT-Xent). Fine-tuning proceeded in three stages: first, unfreezing only the classification head with a small learning rate; second, progressively unfreezing feature extractors with increased augmentation; finally, fully unfreezing the CNN and CRNN, and selectively unfreezing an additional transformer layer for AST.

4 Results

The custom CNN with attention achieved an accumulated 0.04 increase in macro-F1 score after the contrastive step. Figure 2 shows a +0.041 macro-precision gain and a modest +0.023 gain in recall. There is improved genre separation in the learned embedding space, with particularly strong performance on distinctive genres' F1 scores like Rebetiko(+0.2) and Mod Laiko (+0.18). These classes have distinct non Western features, which further solidifies the hypothesis that contrastive learning is useful as a domain adaptation tool. Three classes were negatively impacted (Pop, Rock and Entehno), likely due to their acoustic overlap with other genres that saw greater improvements.

The hybrid CRNN demonstrated a 0.01 improvement in macro-F1 score on validation data after contrastive pretraining. This modest gain might indicate that temporal characteristics are harder for the models to capture. The transformer yielded a 0.64 macro-F1, surpassing both of the other models, but showed no significant change in macro-F1 after five epochs of contrastive training. The limited in-batch negatives (six per anchor) explain the lack of benefit.

The improvements on the CNN validated the applicability of contrastive pretraining for addressing the data scarcity problem. The magnitude of improvement seems to correlate with the size of the batch in the contrastive step, with smaller batch sizes achieving reduced benefits. Analysis of per-class performance revealed that contrastive pretraining particularly benefited underrepresented and

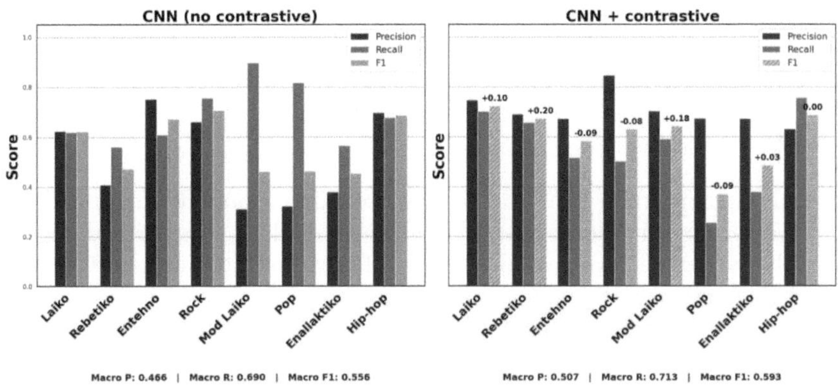

Fig. 2. CNN evaluation before and after contrastive step per (genre) class.

culturally distinct genres. As expected, genres that were really underrepresented (Hip-hop) showed a significant improvement, addressing the data scarcity. Additionally, traditional and modern Greek genres (Laiko, Mod Laiko, Rebetiko, Entehno) showed more substantial improvements compared to internationally common genres (Rock, Pop), supporting our hypothesis about bias reduction.

Table 1. Macro Performance with and without Contrastive Pretraining

Model	Contrastive Step	F1	Precision	Recall
CNN	No	0.55	0.46	0.69
	Yes	0.59	0.50	0.71
CRNN	No	0.56	0.55	0.57
	Yes	0.57	0.56	0.58
Transformer	No	0.64	0.6	0.71
	Yes	0.64	0.61	0.70

The differential improvement across genres, with traditional Greek genres benefiting more than international ones, provides evidence that the contrastive step specifically addresses the bias rather than simply improving general performance. The persistence of improvements in multilabel scenarios, where performance gains are typically diminished due to increased complexity, demonstrates the robustness of the contrastive learning approach (Table 1).

[2] reports a steady linear evaluation jump as batch sizes rise from 256 to 4096. Future experiments will explore more memory-efficient contrastive learning approaches like MoCo [11] to enable models to learn more discriminative features without the computational limitations. Systematic evaluation of SOTA transformer architectures and exploration of other contrastive learning frameworks

(beyond SimCLR) could provide additional insights into optimal approaches for improving music classification for limited domains.

5   Conclusion

This study demonstrates that contrastive pretraining provides an effective solution to Western bias in music genre classification models, alleviating data scarcity issues. The systematic evaluation of three different architectures on Greek music revealed interesting findings. Contrastive learning delivered a 4%-point (+7 %) macro-F1 gain over the baseline CNN. The approach successfully leverages unlabeled data (without any manual annotations) to adapt biased models to local musical characteristics while preserving useful learned features. The results suggest that contrastive pretraining has potential when applying SOTA models to underrepresented musical traditions.

References

1. Alonso-Jiménez, P., et al.: Pre-training strategies using contrastive learning and playlist information for music classification and similarity. In: ICASSP, pp. 1–5 (2023)
2. Chen, T., Kornblith, S., Norouzi, M., Hinton, G.: A simple framework for contrastive learning of visual representations. In: ICML, pp. 1597–1607 (2020)
3. Choi, J., Jang, S., Cho, H., Chung, S.: Towards proper contrastive self-supervised learning strategies for music audio representation. In: ICME, pp. 1–6 (2022)
4. Choi, K., Fazekas, G., Sandler, M., Cho, K.: Convolutional recurrent neural networks for music classification. In: ICASSP, pp. 2392–2396 (2017)
5. Christodoulou, A.M., Lartillot, O., Jensenius, A.R.: Multimodal music datasets? challenges and future goals in music processing. Int. J. Multimedia Inf. Retrieval **13**(3), 37 (2024)
6. Ciranni, R., et al.: Cocola: coherence-oriented contrastive learning of musical audio representations. In: ICASSP, pp. 1–5 (2025)
7. Garoufis, C., Zlatintsi, A., Maragos, P.: Multi-source contrastive learning from musical audio. arXiv preprint arXiv:2302.07077 (2023)
8. Gemmeke, J.F., et al.: Audio set: an ontology and human-labeled dataset for audio events. In: ICASSP, pp. 776–780 (2017)
9. Gong, Y., Chung, Y.A., Glass, J.: Ast: audio spectrogram transformer. arXiv preprint arXiv:2104.01778 (2021)
10. Guinot, J., Quinton, E., Fazekas, G.: Semi-supervised contrastive learning of musical representations. arXiv preprint arXiv:2407.13840 (2024)
11. He, K., Fan, H., Wu, Y., Xie, S., Girshick, R.: Momentum contrast for unsupervised visual representation learning. In: CVPR, pp. 9729–9738 (2020)
12. Kanatas, A.N., Papaioannou, C., Potamianos, A.: Culturemert: continual pre-training for cross-cultural music representation learning. arXiv:2506.17818 (2025)
13. Kong, Q., Cao, Y., Iqbal, T., Wang, Y., Wang, W., Plumbley, M.D.: PANNS: large-scale pretrained audio neural networks for audio pattern recognition. IEEE/ACM Trans. Audio Speech Language Process. **28**, 2880–2894 (2020)
14. Makris, D., Karydis, I., Sioutas, S.: Greek music dataset. In: INNS, pp. 1–7 (2015)

15. McCallum, M.C., Korzeniowski, F., Oramas, S., Gouyon, F., Ehmann, A.F.: Supervised and unsupervised learning of audio representations for music understanding. arXiv preprint arXiv:2210.03799 (2022)
16. Mehta, A., Chauhan, S., Djanibekov, A., Kulkarni, A., Xia, G., Choudhury, M.: Music for all: representational bias and cross-cultural adaptability of music generation models. In: NAACL, pp. 4569–4585 (2025)
17. Spijkervet, J., Burgoyne, J.A.: Contrastive learning of musical representations. arXiv preprint arXiv:2103.09410 (2021)
18. Sturm, B.L.: The GTZAN dataset: its contents, its faults, their effects on evaluation, and its future use. preprint arXiv:1306.1461 (2013)
19. Tzanetakis, G., Cook, P.: Musical genre classification of audio signals. IEEE Trans. Speech Audio Process. $\mathbf{10}$(5), 293–302 (2002)
20. Vásquez, M.A.V., Burgoyne, J.A.: Tailed u-net: multi-scale music representation learning. In: ISMIR, pp. 67–75 (2022)
21. Yosinski, J., Clune, J., Bengio, Y., Lipson, H.: How transferable are features in deep neural networks? Adv. Neural Inf. Process. Syst. $\mathbf{27}$ (2014)
22. Zhao, H., Zhang, C., Zhu, B., Ma, Z., Zhang, K.: S3t: self-supervised pre-training with swin transformer for music classification. In: ICASSP, pp. 606–610 (2022)

Toolbelt-MCP: Exploring the Model Context Protocol for Tool-Use of Large Language Models Utilizing Graphs with Relational Databases

Jérôme Agater[1(✉)] , Lisa Herradi[2], Mohamed Mimouni[2], Ammar Memari[1] ,
and Jorge Marx Gómez[3]

[1] Jade Hochschule, Wilhelmshaven, Germany
{jerome.agater,ammar.memari}@jade-hs.de
[2] Université de Bordeaux, Bordeaux, France
{lisa.herradi,mohamed.mimouni}@etu.u-bordeaux.fr
[3] Carl von Ossietzky Universität Oldenburg, Oldenburg, Germany
jorge.marx.gomez@uol.de

Abstract. Relational databases are valuable across many domains, but developers who are new to a system may find organically grown relational schemas complex to explore due to numerous tables linked transitively by their foreign-key relationships. While Large Language Models (LLMs) excel in natural language processing tasks, integrating them with external data requires customized accessors, which necessitates significant engineering effort to adapt to specific relational schemas and settings. Recently, the Model Context Protocol (MCP) has provided a way for LLMs to use external tools to take actions or retrieve data independently, instead of functioning solely as text generators. This delegation allows LLMs to interpret and fulfill user requests dynamically, shifting away from a fixed developer plan. We present a proof-of-concept MCP-based system for exploring relational data, confirming that an LLM can respond to user queries by generating and executing query-specific SQL, integrating a tool for discovering relational paths between tables using a graph of transitively connected tables.

Keywords: Local Large Language Models · Tool-Use · MCP · Relational Database · Privacy-Preserving AI

1 Introduction

Relational databases offer several desirable qualities, such as the efficient storage of vast amounts of structured data, fast queries, data safety, and a standardized query interface via the Structured Query Language (SQL). Large Language Models (LLMs) have opened up new ways of accessing, modifying, and processing textual data in natural language and other representations. This makes LLMs an interesting option for bridging the gap between natural language and relational database data. However, training an LLM from the ground up or perform fine-tuning through Reinforcement Learning from Human Feedback (RLHF) [2] is an expensive and time-consuming process, prohibiting the continuous integration of new data derived from relational tables by training new model releases. With the Model Context Protocol (MCP), a new way of constructing applications utilizing LLMs is gaining traction. MCP defines a standardized method to allow LLMs to use external tools for performing actions or retrieving data, thereby leveraging the LLM as the driver of the information flow instead of a developer-programmed application. MCP has garnered significant attention from the LLM research community and industry, now supported by AI vendors such as Anthropic, OpenAI, and Google DeepMind.

As a feasibility study for a company[1] in Northern Germany, we developed a vertical prototype for an MCP-server utilizing both SQL-based access to join and query tables and a graph of all table dependencies to deterministically infer the shortest path of foreign-key dependency links between two tables for join operations. Their software relies on a relational database containing about 1,000 tables, which new developers struggle to understand, delaying their time to first code commits. Our effortlays the groundwork for an LLM-based assistant that allows developers to interactively explore the database using natural language.

2   Construction

The general MCP architecture follows a basic client-server model, in which the main application utilizing the LLMs and initiating connections is called the *host application*. It hosts instances of *MCP clients*, which connect to external *MCP servers* that provide resources and capabilities to the application and, consequently, the LLMs. *MCP Frameworks* are libraries that implement the MCP connection code and manage the low-level protocol message exchange. Our system closely follows this structure. A single server[2] was sufficient to accommodate our Python-based MCP server with the implemented tools, the MCP host application, the LLM model runner, as well as the relational database.

2.1   MCP Framework

We decided to use the open-source MCP framework from Anthropic[3] for maximum compatibility between server, client, and protocol, as well as a reduced

---

[1] employing 5,000 people and exceeding 2 billion in sales volume in 2024.

[2] The system we used for our spike has the following specifications: Case *Dell Tower*; Processor *AMD Ryzen Threadripper PRO 5965WX 24-Cores*; RAM *128GB RAM*; Storage *1TB NVMe SSD*; GPU *NVIDIA RTX 6000 Ada Generation, 48GB*.

[3] *python-sdk* Project on GitHub, https://github.com/modelcontextprotocol/python-sdk, accessed 2025-07-01.

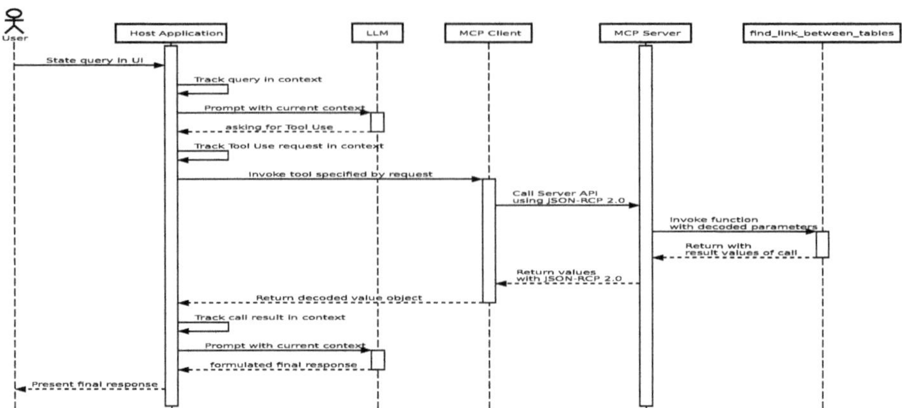

Fig. 1. Sequence diagram illustrating the invocation of the tool `find_link_between_tables[_if_any]` in an MCP-driven application.

delay in getting the newest evolutions of this fast-developing protocol. The framework is based on the well-established Python package FastAPI[4] for implementing the underlying MCP webservice. We utilize its class `FastMCP` to instantiate the MCP server component and export the functions representing our tools via method decorators. Figure 1 shows a tool-invocation in our system.

2.2 MCP Host Application

The host application for an MCP-based system fulfills the role of the interaction mediator between the user, LLMs, and the MCP clients connecting to the tools exposed from MCP servers (for example, by providing an CLI/GUI interface or other integration). For increased usability, we decided to concentrate graphical interfaces. We experimented early on with Open Web UI (OWI) as host, running our models in Ollama[5]. However OWI had no direct support for MCP, relying on another project to expose MCP servers via an adapter for legacy OpenAI-compatible tools. The partially open-source *LM Studio* has recently added MCP support. In prior research, we found LM Studio to be reliable and capable, so we chose it as temporary solution for our study. Ultimately, to achieve the required seamless integration with the established software systems, the host application needs to be transitioned to a custom software solution.

2.3 Model Selection and Exploration

Since LLMs can act as few-shot learners [1,4], enriching the prompt with examples of a format for tool-use enables the model to generate invocations of the

---

[4] *fastapi* Project on GitHub, https://github.com/fastapi/fastapi, accessed 2025-06-23.
[5] *Ollama* Project on GitHub, https://github.com/ollama/ollama, accessed 2025-05-01.

described tool in a similar manner. Additionally, LLM vendors are actively integrating MCP training in their training workflow for some newer models, thereby directly supporting MCP. We experimented with different models, including *DeepSeek R1*, *Phi4 reasoning*, *Gemma3 32B*, and *Mistral 7B*, trained with varying numbers of parameters, with some models also including training for tool-use and Chain-of-Thought (CoT) reasoning [5]. As the system is intended for a later commercial use case, we excluded models with non-permissive licenses like the *xLAM* series from *SalesForce* and focused on open weight/open source models instead. After manual experimentation, we settled for Alibaba Cloud's *Qwen3-32B (FC)* due to its strong consistency regarding tool use, support for CoT, and its permissive Apache-2.0 license. Apart from the non-local *OpenAI GPT-4o/4.5 Preview* models, non-commercial *xLAM*, and *watt-tool-70B* (too large for available hardware), *Qwen3-32B (FC)* also performs best on the *Berkeley Function-Calling Leaderboard* [3].

2.4   Tools Implementation

```
{ name: "find_link_between_tables_if_any",
  description: "This tool helps finding transitive links between tables.\n
  For example, a Company might link via an Order to a Customer",
  inputSchema: { type: "object", properties: { table_name_a: { type: "string" },
                                                table_name_b: { type: "string" }},
                 required: ["table_name_a", "table_name_b"]}}
```

Fig. 2. Excerpt of the description of function `find_link_between_tables_if_any` in MCP utilizing JSON-RPC 2.0 convention based on JSON Schema.

We initially started to implement dedicated functions for the most common operations in SQL, then concentrated on the most important tools for understanding a database, namely relationships between tables, structure of the tables, and the ability to query the database using SQL. As a fixture for our development process we used an example database. Our partner company uses PostgreSQL as database management software, therefore we also employed PostgreSQL. This allows us to use a reflection approach, querying the `information_schema` meta data table as the source of the *primary key* ↔ *foreign key* relationships between tables. From the resulting structure, we built an in-memory graph using the Python library NetworkX[6] storing it serialized as JSON as a cache. Based on the same graph, we exposed a tool to find the shortest relational path between two tables, namely the tool `find_link_between_tables_if_any`, described in Fig. 2, being invoked in Fig. 3, and returning the path between two tables as a sequence of table names linked with arrows (`customer->rental->inventory`), as shown in Fig. 4. A tool to list the tables in the database, `list_tables`, provides a quick way to gain knowledge of available tables. For the description of the

---

[6] *NetworkX* Project on GitHub, https://github.com/networkx/networkx/, accessed 2025-06-04.

structure of the tables, we exported the function `describe_columns_of_table`, querying the information schema for the columns of a table and returning it as a tab-stop-character separated textual table. The final addition was a tool to query the database using SQL statements directly, namely `execute_raw_sql`, returning a tab-stop character-separated textual table as a result. Exposing the tools via the methodology from Sect. 2.1 was convenient, as integrating and registering just required minimal additions to the `mcp.json` file defining the servers used by LM Studio. Adding the address of the MCP server and a name for the configuration allowed a `tools/list` query to the server, gathering the descriptions and making the tools available to LLMs hosted in LM Studio.

```
{"tool_call": { "tool_name": "find_link_between_tables_if_any",
            "parameters": { "table_name_a": "customer", "table_name_b": "inventory" }}}
```

Fig. 3. A tool-call generated by an LLM in order to call the function `find_link_between_tables_if_any` from Fig. 2. The MCP system detects such generations and executes the tool call, inserting the answer into the context after the tool invocation completed.

```
{content: { "type": "text",
            "text": "customer->rental->inventory" }}
```

Fig. 4. The result object generated as returned value of a tool-call of `find_link_between_tables_if_any` from Fig. 2 using the parameters from Fig. 3.

Fig. 5. A session trace in LM Studio illustrating the utilization of `list_tables`, `find_link_between_tables_if_any` and `execute_raw_sql` by *Qwen3-32B (FC)*, also showing the generated SQL statement for joining the tables.

3   Discussion

The model *Qwen3-32B (FC)* was able to take advantage of the tools we provided in our LM Studio setting to answer questions, inferring suitable tools to use, executing them, and then using the results in its answers, see Fig. 5. We noted that it was crucial to include descriptions and descriptive function names for the model to consider invoking the corresponding functions. The output of the function calls was not always taken into account by the model when using a serialized hash-map output. After switching to a human-readable textual format as tabular output, the model reliably took the output into account and consistently used the returned data for its response generation. We are looking forward to connecting our system to a copy of the production system of our partner company, with their developers being able to interact with a chat interface. This will allow us to collect real-world questions and sessions from the actual users, enabling the development of a benchmark for further automatic assessment and evaluation of model and tool performance. Based on the evaluation, we will develop this spike into a production system for the company, implementing a custom, dedicated MCP host application for the chat interface, opening an opportunity for integration into the platform software of our partner company. We found that giving LLMs capable of MCP-mediated tool-use and CoT reasoning access to external tools for taking actions and/or retrieving data on their own extends the usefulness and flexibility derivable from the usage of LLMs. The source code of our spike is made available on GitHub at https://github.com/Ingenieurinformatik/Toolbelt-MCP.

References

1. Brown, T., et al.: Language models are few-shot learners. In: Advances in Neural Information Processing Systems. vol. 33, pp. 1877–1901. Curran Associates, Inc. (2020)
2. Ouyang, L., et al.: Training language models to follow instructions with human feedback. In: Koyejo, S., Mohamed, S., Agarwal, A., Belgrave, D., Cho, K., Oh, A. (eds.) Advances in Neural Information Processing Systems. vol. 35, pp. 27730–27744. Curran Associates, Inc. (2022)
3. Patil, S.G., et al.: The berkeley function calling leaderboard (bfcl): From tool use to agentic evaluation of large language models. In: Forty-second International Conference on Machine Learning. Vancouver, Canada (2025). https://icml.cc/virtual/2025/poster/46593, Accessed 04 July 2025
4. Schick, T., et al.: Toolformer: language models can teach themselves to use tools. In: Proceedings of the 37th International Conference on Neural Information Processing Systems. NIPS '23, Curran Associates Inc., Red Hook (2023)
5. Wei, J., et al.: Chain-of-thought prompting elicits reasoning in large language models. In: Proceedings of the 36th International Conference on Neural Information Processing Systems. NIPS '22, Curran Associates Inc., Red Hook (2022)

Comparative Assessment of ChatGPT, DeepSeek, and Human Reviewers for Full-Text Screening in Systematic Reviews on the Impact of Air Pollution in Respiratory Diseases

Amja Manullang[1]([✉]) [iD], Xiaohong Gao[1] [iD], Christophe Viavattene[2] [iD], and Annisa Ristya Rahmanti[1,3] [iD]

[1] Dept of Computer Science, Middlesex University, London, UK
`{a.manullang,x.gao}@mdx.ac.uk`, `annisaristya@ugm.ac.id`
[2] Natural Sciences, Middlesex University, London, UK
`c.viavattene@mdx.ac.uk`
[3] Dept of Health and Policy Management, Faculty of Medicine, Public Health and Nursing, Universitas Gadjah Mada, Yogyakarta, Indonesia

Abstract. Large language models (LLMs) are increasingly used in scientific research, education, and healthcare. Their roles in data searching, screening, extraction, and quality assessment hold promise for improving the systematic review process. However, concerns remain about their accuracy in literature research. This study aimed to compare the accuracy of LLMs and human reviewers in full-text screening for a systematic review. We searched for relevant studies from databases and registers. Full-text screening was performed by human reviewers, ChatGPT, and DeepSeek based on predefined inclusion and exclusion criteria. We observed that ChatGPT had 73.6% agreement with human reviewers ($\kappa = 0.43$), while DeepSeek had 70.3% ($\kappa = 0.35$). Moreover, ChatGPT showed 73.6% accuracy, high sensitivity (0.923), but low specificity (0.487) compared to the human consensus. Similarly, DeepSeek had 70.3% accuracy, higher sensitivity (0.962), but lower specificity (0.359). Both ChatGPT and DeepSeek show promise for assisting full-text screening in systematic reviews but require further evaluation with well-defined prompt engineering.

1 Introduction

A systematic review is a structured method for conducting a systematic synthesis of primary findings from existing studies. This approach is important for evidence-based decisions, especially in clinical practice. However, the full-text screening process can be challenging for reviewers due to the large number of articles that must be assessed for study selection. Additionally, an accurate technique is important to minimize bias in the included studies. The use of large language models (LLMs) has recently been proposed as a solution to this challenge. A study reported that ChatGPT can generate Boolean queries for systematic reviews [1]. Additionally, ChatGPT can manage large numbers of studies and enhance time efficiency during systematic reviews [2]. Recently,

M. Bramer and F. Stahl (Eds.): SGAI-AI 2025, LNAI 16302, pp. 478–484, 2026.
https://doi.org/10.1007/978-3-032-11442-6_39

DeepSeek has emerged as a new LLM that focuses on transparency and clarity in complex problem-solving tasks [3]. A previous study found that DeepSeek resulted in better performance compared to other LLMs such as ChatGPT [4]. Given the growing use of LLMs in scientific research for literature search and screening, this study aimed to evaluate and compare the accuracy of LLMs and human reviewers in full-text screening for a systematic review.

2 Method

2.1 Data Sources and Search Strategy

Articles were manually searched in databases including Web of Science, Embase, PubMed, Medline, IEEE Xplore, Scopus, CINAHL, AMC, arXiv, Astrophysics Data System, and Google Scholar. The following keywords "machine learning," "deep learning," "artificial intelligence," "air pollution," "particulate matter," "nitrogen dioxide," "respiratory disease," and "airway disease" were used to identify relevant articles for the study objective. The retrieved articles were compiled in EndNote Reference Manager version X9.

2.2 Eligible Criteria and Study Selection

This study applied the Preferred Reporting Items for Systematic Reviews and Meta-Analyses (PRISMA) guidelines for data searching and article screening [5]. Original articles published in English that applied machine learning, deep learning, or artificial intelligence algorithms to predict air pollution and its impacts on respiratory diseases were included. Additionally, studies covering environmental engineering, health sciences, and machine learning applications were eligible. Meanwhile, duplicate articles, review articles, conference abstracts, editorials, case studies, book chapters, case reports, preprints, articles unrelated specifically to air pollution, respiratory disease, or machine learning applications, articles unrelated topic to air pollution and respiratory prediction models, COVID-19-related studies, virus infection and influenza symptom studies, and articles without a clear focus on machine learning, deep learning, or AI algorithms or respiratory diseases were excluded. Two independent reviewers performed full-text screening based on these criteria. To compare the performance of Large Language Models (LLMs) during the full-text screening process of a systematic review, ChatGPT-4o and DeepSeek-V3-R1 were used. Prompts were developed for each LLM based on the eligibility criteria of this study. Human consensus served as the gold standard comparator, and final inclusion decisions were made through discussion.

2.3 Data Extraction and Analyses

Relevant information was manually extracted by two independent reviewers based on eligibility criteria through full-text review. For the LLMs, full-text articles were submitted via their web interface along with standardized prompts instructing the models to determine whether each article should be included or excluded according to the same eligibility criteria used by human reviewers. The prompt for ChatGPT and Deepseek is as follow:

"Perform screening for this article based on the following inclusion and exclusion criteria. The inclusion criteria are: original articles published in English that apply machine learning, deep learning, or artificial intelligence algorithms to predict air pollution and its impacts on respiratory diseases, including asthma and chronic obstructive pulmonary disease (COPD). Articles should also be related to environmental engineering, health sciences, or machine learning applications. The exclusion criteria are: duplicate articles; review articles; conference abstracts; editorials; case studies; book chapters; case reports; preprints; articles not specific to air pollution, COPD, asthma, or machine learning applications; articles unrelated to air pollution and respiratory prediction models; COVID-19-related studies; studies on viral infections or influenza symptoms; and articles not focused on machine learning, deep learning, or AI algorithms."

The inclusion and exclusion for all sources were compiled and saved in comma-separated values (CSV) files for further analysis. All analyses were performed in Google Colaboratory (Google Colab) using Python (Version 3.11.13). Agreement and interrater reliability between ChatGPT, DeepSeek, and human reviewers were evaluated using Cohen's Kappa coefficients, computed with the scikit-learn package (Version 1.6.1) in Python. In addition, percentage agreement was calculated as the proportion of instances where two reviewers or models assigned the same inclusion or exclusion decision. The strength of agreement was interpreted based on Cohen's kappa (κ) value, with categories of no agreement (≤ 0), slight agreement (0.01–0.20), fair agreement (0.21–0.40), moderate agreement (0.41–0.60), substantial agreement (0.61–0.80), and perfect agreement (0.81–1.00) [6].

2.4 Performance Evaluation Metrics

To further evaluate the performance of the LLMs, we calculated classification metrics comparing model predictions against the human consensus reviewers as the gold standard. Metrics computed included accuracy, sensitivity, specificity, positive predictive value (PPV), negative predictive value (NPV), F-1 score, and the Matthews correlation coefficient (MCC) [7]. These measures provided a comprehensive assessment of each model's ability to correctly identify studies for inclusion or exclusion and to replicate human screening decisions. All performance metrics were calculated using functions from the scikit-learn package in Python.

3 Results

3.1 Characteristics of Included Articles

The search strategy and article screening process are presented according to the PRISMA guidelines (Fig. 1). Initially, 2,011 articles were identified, and 207 duplicates were removed, with 1,804 articles remaining for further screening. Furthermore, 1,714 articles were excluded based on unrelated abstracts or titles. Finally, 91 eligible articles underwent further screening using ChatGPT, DeepSeek, and human reviewers. Based on this assessment, 52 articles were ultimately included in the systematic review based on human review as gold standard. Meanwhile, ChatGPT suggested including 68 articles, whereas DeepSeek recommended including 75 articles, based on the predefined inclusion and exclusion criteria.

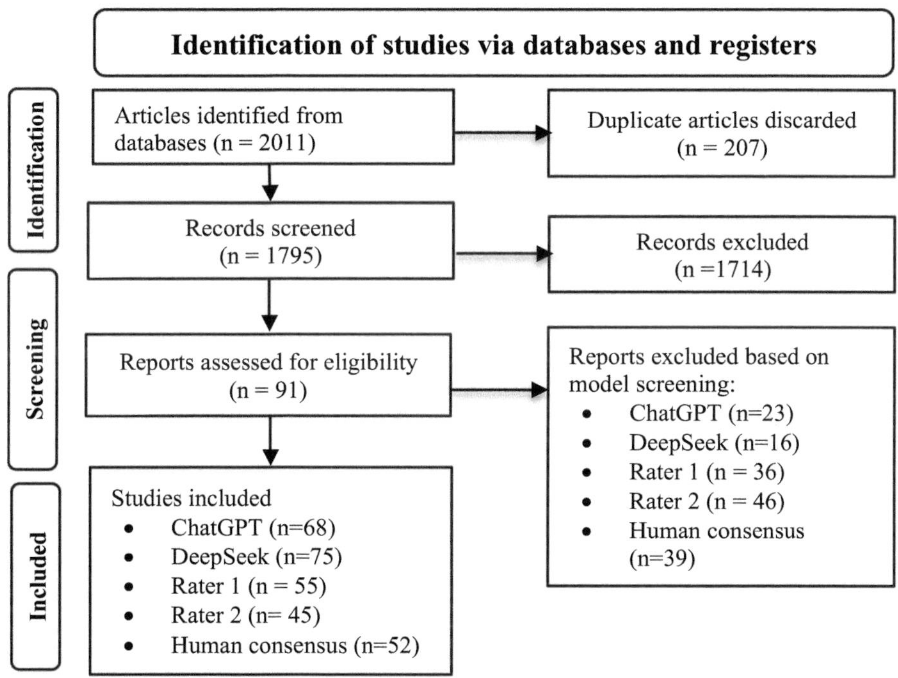

Fig. 1. Flowchart of the study selection.

3.2 Comparative Agreement Between LLMs Model vs Human

The interrater reliability analysis between ChatGPT, DeepSeek, and human reviewers is presented in Table 1. The percent agreement between rater 1 and ChatGPT was 74.73% ($\kappa = 0.44$), which reflects moderate agreement. For rater 2 and ChatGPT, the percentage agreement was 68.13% ($\kappa = 0.37$), indicating fair agreement. Overall, ChatGPT and human reviewers had 73.63% agreement ($\kappa = 0.43$), which is considered moderate agreement. In comparison, the agreement between rater 1 and DeepSeek was 73.63% ($\kappa = 0.39$), indicating fair agreement. Agreement between rater 2 and DeepSeek was 62.64% ($\kappa = 0.26$) also reflecting fair agreement. We observed a fair agreement between DeepSeek and human reviewers, with an overall percentage agreement of 70.33% ($\kappa = 0.35$). The agreement percentage between rater 1 and rater 2 was 80.22% ($\kappa = 0.61$), indicating substantial agreement. Similarly, substantial agreement was also found between the two raters and the human consensus, with an agreement percentage of 90.11% ($\kappa = 0.80$).

Table. 1 Cohen's kappa coefficient of agreement for full-text reviews

Reviewers (Human vs LLMs)	Percentage of agreement	Cohen's kappa
Rater 1 vs ChatGPT	74.73%	0.436
Rater 2 vs ChatGPT	68.13%	0.366
Human consensus vs ChatGPT	73.63%	0.432
Rater 1 vs DeepSeek	73.63%	0.390
Rater 2 vs DeepSeek	62.64%	0.258
Human consensus vs DeepSeek	70.33%	0.346
Rater 1 vs Rater 2	80.22%	0.605
Rater 1 vs Human consensus	90.11%	0.796
Rater 2 vs Human consensus	90.11%	0.803

3.3 Comparative Performance Between LLMs Model vs Human

The performance metrics between the LLM models and the human consensus are shown in Table 2. Compared to the human consensus, ChatGPT showed moderate accuracy at 73.6%, high sensitivity at 0.923, but lower specificity at 0.487. A moderate PPV was found at 0.706, while a good NPV was observed at 0.826. A strong balance between precision and recall was reflected by an F1 score of 0.800, and fair overall agreement was indicated by an MCC of 0.467. Similarly, DeepSeek showed moderate accuracy at 70.3% with higher sensitivity at 0.962 but lower specificity at 0.359. A moderate PPV was found at 0.667 and a good NPV at 0.875. A good balance between precision and recall was seen with an F1 score of 0.787, and moderate overall agreement was indicated by an MCC of 0.417.

Table. 2 Performance comparison between LLMs vs Human consensus

Model comparison metrics	Accuracy	Sensitivity	Specificity	PPV	NPV	F-1 score	MCC
ChatGPT vs Consensus	0.736	0.923	0.487	0.706	0.826	0.800	0.467
DeepSeek vs Consensus	0.703	0.962	0.359	0.667	0.875	0.787	0.417

4 Discussion

Based on our findings, the performance of both LLM models and the human reviewers varied from fair to moderate for overall agreement when screening full-text articles for the systematic review. Meanwhile, the two reviewers achieved substantial agreement, suggesting that their decisions on study inclusion and exclusion were largely consistent. Moreover, the performance metric analysis shows that both ChatGPT and DeepSeek had high sensitivity but low specificity, indicating that the LLMs correctly identified most relevant studies but were less reliable in excluding negatives ones, leading to more false positives. Our finding aligns to previous study reported that LLMs model limited capacity to capture the complex content and contextual meaning of journal articles [8]. In contrast, a previous study found that the application of LLMs in abstract and full-text screening for systematic reviews demonstrated a low false negative rate [9]. Taken together, LLMs could potentially be incorporated into hybrid approaches to enhance the efficiency of full-text screening in systematic reviews [10, 11]. Low specificity in this study may be attributed to complex inclusion and exclusion criteria and the lack of a specific prompt engineering technique. Detailed prompting and model fine-tuning should be considered to enhance screening performance in future studies.

5 Conclusion

The application of LLM models for screening full-text articles in systematic reviews may help accelerate the review process; however, validation by human reviewers remains important to ensure the accuracy of study inclusion. Furthermore, human reviewers have a more comprehensive understanding of study quality, as the research objectives and eligibility criteria are defined by the reviewer. This study relied on two human reviewers as the gold standard for comparison with the LLMs. Future research should involve a greater number of human reviewers to ensure more robust and reliable outcomes.

Acknowledgement. This project is funded by the British Council under Early Research Fellowship Program (2024–2025). Their financial support is gratefully acknowledged.

References

1. Wang, S. Scells, H. Koopman, B. et al.: Can ChatGPT write a good boolean query for systematic review literature search? In: Proceedings of the 46th International ACM SIGIR Conference on Research and Development in Information Retrieval; Taipei, Taiwan, p. 1426–1436. Association for Computing Machinery (2023). https://doi.org/10.1145/3539618.3591703
2. Dahmen, J., Kayaalp, M.E., Ollivier, M., et al.: Artificial intelligence bot ChatGPT in medical research: the potential game changer as a double-edged sword. Knee surgery, sports traumatology, arthroscopy. Official journal of the ESSKA. **31**(4), 1187–1189 (2023). https://doi.org/10.1007/s00167-023-07355-6.PubMedPMID:36809511;eng
3. Luo, P.W., Liu, J.W., Xie, X., et al.: DeepSeek vs ChatGPT: a comparison study of their performance in answering prostate cancer radiotherapy questions in multiple languages. AJCEU. **13**(2), 176–185 (2025). https://doi.org/10.62347/uiap7979.PubMedPMID:40400997;PubMedCentralPMCID:PMCPMC12089221.eng
4. Sandmann, S., Hegselmann, S., Fujarski, M., et al.: Benchmark evaluation of DeepSeek large language models in clinical decision-making. Nat. Med. (2025). https://doi.org/10.1038/s41591-025-03727-2

5. Page, M.J., McKenzie, J.E., Bossuyt, P.M., et al.: The PRISMA 2020 statement: an updated guideline for reporting systematic reviews. BMJ (Clinical research ed). **29**(372), n71 (2021). https://doi.org/10.1136/bmj.n71.PubMedPMID:33782057;PubMedCentralPM CID:PMCPMC8005924

6. McHugh ML: Interrater reliability: the kappa statistic. Biochem. Med. **22**(3), 276–82 (2012). PubMed PMID: 23092060; PubMed Central PMCID: PMCPMC3900052

7. Powers DMWJA. Evaluation: from precision, recall and F-measure to ROC, informedness, markedness and correlation (2011). abs/2010.16061. https://doi.org/10.48550/arXiv.2010. 16061

8. van Dis, E.A.M., Bollen, J., Zuidema, W., et al.: ChatGPT: five priorities for research. Nature **614**(7947), 224–226 (2023). https://doi.org/10.1038/d41586-023-00288-7.PubMed PMID:36737653;eng

9. Trad, F., Yammine, R., Charafeddine, J., et al.: Streamlining systematic reviews with large language models using prompt engineering and retrieval augmented generation. BMC Med. Res. Methodol. **25**(1), 130 (2025). https://doi.org/10.1186/s12874-025-02583-5

10. Homiar, A., Thomas, J., Ostinelli, E.G., et al.: Development and evaluation of prompts for a large language model to screen titles and abstracts in a living systematic review. BMJ ment. health. **28**(1) (2025). https://doi.org/10.1136/bmjment-2025-301762. PubMed PMID: 40701625; PubMed Central PMCID: PMCPMC12306261

11. Li, M., Sun, J., Tan, X.: Evaluating the effectiveness of large language models in abstract screening: a comparative analysis. Syst. Rev. **13**(1), 219 (2024). https://doi.org/10.1186/s13 643-024-02609-x

Correction to: Detect, Decide, Explain: An Intelligent Framework for Zero-Day Network Attack Detection

Saif Alzubi, Frederic Stahl, and Mohammed Al-Khafajiy

Correction to:
Chapter 1 in: M. Bramer and F. Stahl (Eds.): *Artificial Intelligence XLII*, **LNAI 16302, https://doi.org/10.1007/978-3-032-11442-6_1**

Correction of the author's surname for chapter 1 titled: Detect, Decide, Explain: An Intelligent Framework for Zero-Day Network Attack Detection. https://link.springer.com/chapter/10.1007/978-3-032-11442-6_1

Saif Alzubi, s.m.y.alzubi@exeter.ac.uk, has contacted us to request a correction on their Detect, Decide, Explain: An Intelligent Framework for Zero-Day Network Attack Detection. The author is mentioning that the problem involves the incorrect truncation of the author's surname in a published paper. The surname appears as "ALZU" instead of the correct "ALZUBI." This error affects multiple locations, including the table of contents, paper title, author index, and the conference paper link. Included on the summary above is the screenshot that shows that incorrect last name of the author.

Relative to: Name: Saif Alzu Email address: s.m.y.alzubi@exeter.ac.uk Affiliation: Department of Computer Science, University of Exeter, Exeter, EX4 4QE, UK

Correct data: Name: Saif Alzubi Email address: s.m.y.alzubi@exeter.ac.uk Affiliation: Department of Computer Science, University of Exeter, Exeter, EX4 4QE, UK

The updated version of this chapter can be found at
https://doi.org/10.1007/978-3-032-11442-6_1

Author Index